CONSUMER GUIDE

COMPLETE GUIDE TO

USED CARS

1999 EDITION

CONTENTS

CONTENTS

CONTENTS

CONTENTS

CONTENTS

CONTENTS

CONTENTS

How to Use This Book

Complete Guide to Used Cars, is packed with information to help you select a suitable vehicle and buy it for the right price. Inside you'll find over 186 different vehicles—from tiny subcompacts to full-size pickups. Inside each vehicle report is a wealth of information that, if you take a little time to read this introduction, is in easy-to-understand plain English.

Best Buys But, before you even read one report you need to know one thing: Not all used vehicles are created equal—some are much better buys than others. Don't worry though, we've done the homework for you. Throughout the body of this book and in the Table of Contents you will see the ☑ᴮᴱˢᵀ ᴮᵁʸ symbol. This indicates that we feel that that particular vehicle is a solid used car buy and one of the best values in its class. This is not to say that cars without the Best Buy symbol are bad choices, just that the Best Buys are better overall values. We base our Best Buy choices first and foremost on the vehicle itself and how well it does its job. Second, we consider factors like, reliability, cost, and overall utility.

The Buying Guide The main Buying Guide section consists of 186 reports that cover used cars, minivans, pickup trucks, and sport-utility vehicles from 1990 to the present. Vehicles are listed alphabetically according to make (Buick, Ford, etc.), then by model (Accord, Cavalier, etc.), and finally listed in ascending year order. The years are grouped so that the entire generation of a vehicle is listed in one report. For example, the Dodge Caravan was redesigned in 1991 and then again in 1996. Hence, we get the Dodge Caravan 1991-95 report that you will find on page xxx.

At the top of each listing is a picture that shows what one example of that vehicle looks like. Though the picture may be of a 4-door body style, for instance, the report covers all models listed for those years. Keep in mind that some cars look completely different as 2- or 4-door models.

Following the picture, you will find a summary of the vehicle's "Pros" and "Cons." These are not necessarily the only good or bad points of that particular vehicle; just the most pronounced. One important thing to remember is that the vehicles have been compared to like models. That is, if a Honda Civic lists passenger/cargo space as a "Good" point, it has exceptional room

HOW TO USE THIS BOOK

inside for a subcompact. If compared to a Cadillac DeVille, for example, that Honda naturally has vastly smaller interior dimensions.

After the "Pros" and "Cons" comes an "Evaluation" that provides performance, fuel economy, and passenger/cargo space information. Our auto editors discuss how the car accelerates, rides, and handles, and may warn of major service problems. In short, the "Evaluation" section lets you know what that vehicle would be like to live with on a daily basis.

After the "Evaluation," some reports may have a "Crash Test" table compiled from annual National Highway Traffic Safety Administration (NHTSA) tests. NHTSA tests a vehicle's crashworthiness in front and side collisions. Their ratings suggest the chance of serious injury: ☆☆☆☆☆—10% or less; ☆☆☆☆—10-20% or less; ☆☆☆—20-35% or less; ☆☆—35-45% or less; ☆—More than 45%. While we don't suggest choosing a vehicle solely based on its crash test score, we do think that it should be one of the factors that helps you make you decision.

The "Specifications" chart lists body styles and basic exterior measurements of each model, plus cargo capacity and fuel tank size. Dimensions often change slightly from year to year and vary among sub-models, so an individual car may differ from figures shown. The "Engines" chart lists all engines available in that particular vehicle: It lists the Type (number of cylinders); Displacement (size) in liters and cubic inches; Horsepower (single figure or range for the period covered); and MPG (miles per gallon). Our fuel economy estimates based on actual driving follow in the Consumer Guide Observed section. The following key might help you understand the engine charts a little better.

ohv = overhead valve; ohc = overhead camshaft; dohc = dual overhead camshafts; I = inline cylinders; V = cylinders in V configuration; flat = horizontally opposed cylinders; OD = overdrive transmission; NA = information not available.

Immediately following the engine charts are the "Price" charts. These charts detail a range of average prices in year-by-year listings, for vehicles in three condition levels: **Good**—a clean, low-mileage, solid-running vehicle that needs little or no repair. **Average**—a car with normal miles on the odometer, perhaps a few scrapes or dings; engine might need a minor repair or two, but runs acceptably well. **Poor**—might have potentially dangerous problems with the engine and/or body, or abnormally high mileage; definitely in need of mechanical attention. Valuations reflect wholesale prices paid by dealers at auction, and retail prices on used-car lots. Each range covers all trim levels and engine types for a vehicle with a typical amount of equipment— usually an automatic transmission, air conditioning, stereo, etc. Fully-loaded vehicles may cost more. Keep in mind that these are guidelines only. Actual selling prices vary widely.

The "Replacement Costs" table lists the costs of likely repairs—things like air conditioning, brakes, and transmission repairs. The dollar amount listed includes the cost of the part(s) and labor for the average repair. Like the pricing information replacement costs can vary widely depending on region. Expect charges at a new-car dealership to be slightly higher.

No vehicle is perfect, so in our "Trouble Spots" section we list the most common problems for each vehicle. We also list the solutions that the manufacturer has come up with for these problems. In the "Trouble Spots" section you'll likely find things like engine noises, transmission problems, or bad brakes. This section will help you determine if that noise coming from the engine is a costly repair or not.

Finally, you get an abbreviated listing of major recalls for each vehicle in our "Recall History" table. Not all recalls issued by NHTSA may be listed. Since manufacturers are not required to fix recall defects free of charge after an eight-year period. Minor defects, or problems that would be apparent immediately, have been omitted. To obtain a complete list of recalls for the vehicle you intend to buy, call NHTSA at (800) 424-9393.

Thank you for choosing Consumer Guide as your automotive information source. We welcome your criticism. If you have a comment feel free to write:

The Used Car Book
Consumer Guide
7373 N. Cicero Avenue
Lincolnwood, IL 60646

1990-93 ACURA INTEGRA

1993 Acura Integra GS 3-door

FOR   Fuel economy • Acceleration (5-speed) • Handling/road-holding • Anti-lock brakes (GS, GS-R) • Reliability

AGAINST   Acceleration (automatic transmission) • Rear-seat room (3-door) • Lack of air bag

EVALUATION   Well-known for reliability and solid construction, these competent front-drivers are toned down somewhat from their predecessors, but still offer plenty of refinement. All models offer a firm but comfortable ride—reasonably supple and pleasing.

Handling and roadholding are fine, if not quite as agile as the prior models. Integras hang on nicely around tight turns, suffering minimal body roll. Stopping power is especially impressive with the anti-lock braking that's standard on the top-line GS and higher-performance GS-R, and not bad at all on other models. Every Integra uses 4-wheel disc brakes.

This car's personality varies according to its transmission. Acceleration from the basic twin-cam 4-cylinder engine is brisk and zesty with the 5-speed gearbox, but not nearly so lively with 4-speed automatic. That's true even when using the transmission's Sport mode. A basic Integra with manual shift accelerated to 60 mph in a snappy 9.0 seconds, but an automatic-transmission sedan took a leisurely 11.5 seconds to perform that feat—and refused to downshift for passing without a long, hard stab at the gas pedal.

The high-performance GS-R model demonstrated that it was subjectively faster than other Integras. But that smaller engine stays very busy, thanks to short gearing that keeps it spinning on the high side of 3000 rpm—even in gentle cruising. GS-R's 1.7-liter four also is deficient in low-speed torque, so plan on lots of shifting in change-of-pace traffic.

On the plus side, both transmissions deliver attractive fuel mileage: 23-25 mpg around town and past 30 mpg on the highway. Even a GS-R managed 22.4 mpg in rigorous city/suburban driving. Abundant engine/road noise and vibration, on the other hand, remind occupants that Integras are not quite in the same refinement league as the larger Legends.

Visibility is fine; controls are sensible and fall easily to hand. Analog gauges are well marked and unobscured. A low driving position emphasizes the Integra's sporty nature. Seats are firm and supportive. The 4-door's longer wheelbase shows up in additional rear leg room, though shoulder space could be better back there. Sedans seat four adults without cramping, but the 3-door's rear seat is best for kids and cargo—it's basically a 2+2 coupe. Cargo space is better in the coupe, because of its fold-down rear seat, but liftover is high on both body styles.

SPECIFICATIONS

	2-door hatchback	4-door sedan
Wheelbase, in.	100.4	102.4
Overall length, in.	172.9	176.5
Overall width, in.	67.4	67.4
Overall height, in.	52.2	52.8
Curb weight, lbs.	2560	2605
Cargo volume, cu. ft.	16.2	11.2
Fuel capacity, gals.	13.2	13.2
Seating capacity	4	5
Front head room, in.	38.5	38.7
Max. front leg room, in.	41.8	41.6
Rear head room, in.	34.7	36.8
Min. rear leg room, in.	28.6	31.7

Powertrain layout: transverse front-engine/front-wheel drive

ENGINES

	dohc I-4	dohc I-4
Size, liters/cu. in.	1.7/102	1.8/112
Horsepower	160	130-140
Torque (lbs./ft.)	117	121-126
EPA city/highway mpg		
5-speed OD manual	24/29	25/31
4-speed OD automatic		23/29
Consumer Guide™ observed MPG		
5-speed OD manual	22.4	25.7

Built in Japan.

RETAIL PRICES

	GOOD	AVERAGE	POOR
1990 Integra	$2,500-4,200	$1,900-3,500	$900-1,800

ACURA

	GOOD	AVERAGE	POOR
1991 Integra	3,800-5,900	3,100-5,200	1,200-3,000
1992 Integra	5,000-7,200	4,200-6,400	2,200-4,000
1992 Integra GS-R	7,000-8,200	6,200-7,400	4,000-5,000
1993 Integra	6,300-8,800	5,500-8,000	3,400-5,500
1993 Integra GS-R	8,500-9,800	7,500-8,800	5,000-6,000

AVERAGE REPLACEMENT COSTS

A/C Compressor $600
Alternator 420
Radiator 380
Timing Chain or Belt 255
Automatic Transmission or
   Transaxle.........................895

Constant Velocity Joints.....720
Brakes.................................195
Shocks and/or Struts 620
Exhaust System.................505

TROUBLE SPOTS

• **Oil leak** Oil may appear behind the power steering bracket caused by a leaking camshaft seal. To replace the seal, the timing belt will have to be removed. Chances are the timing belt is also contaminated by the oil and should be replaced.

• **Brakes** The anti-lock brake modulator solenoid was prone to leaks, which sets an ABS trouble code number 1. When this happens the solenoid should be flushed or replaced if flushing will not clean it.

• **Alarm system** The security system controller picks up stray interference, which can make it malfunction so that the car will not start. The ROM (read only memory) chip in the controller must be replaced. This may be covered by a "good-will fix" upon the district service manager's approval if out of warranty.

• **Clutch** Cars with manual transmissions may suffer from short clutch life. Acura issued a revised clutch disc and pressure plate that wear longer. (They must be replaced as a set.)

• **Transmission slippage** Cars with automatic transmissions my not upshift, shift erratically, or suffer from no kickdown. The problem is debris in the modulator valve that sticks open flooding the shift solenoids. The fix is to replace the modulator and possibly the solenoid. This may be covered by a "good-will fix" upon the district service manager's approval if out of warranty.

• **Vehicle noise** Squeaking noises may come from the rear of the car when going over bumps or speed bumps. The fix involves placing shims between the two rubber halves of the trailing arm bushings.

• **Hard starting** The fuel pressure regulator may fail causing hard starting. The only fix is to replace the regulator.

RECALL HISTORY

1990-91 Front seatbelt release button can break and pieces can fall inside, causing improper operation.

1994-98 ACURA INTEGRA

✓ **BEST BUY**

1995 Acura Integra GS-R 4-door

FOR Air bags • Fuel economy • Acceleration (5-speed models) • Steering/handling • Roadholding • Anti-lock brakes (LS, GS-R)

AGAINST Acceleration (automatic transmission) • Rear seat room • No anti-lock brakes (RS) • Tire noise

EVALUATION Integra engines rev like crazy, but lack enough low-end torque to perform with much zest with the automatic transmission. All Integras are swift with the 5-speed. A GS-R accelerated to 60 mph in a quick 7.6 seconds, and a stick-shift LS took less than a second longer. That's commendable, and even frisky, but not quite as breathtaking as the figures might suggest. Despite the notchy feel of the stick shift, it's not always easy to tell which gear you're in. The clutch pedal is slightly heavy to push, but has outstanding feel and engages gradually.

Fuel economy is great—better than ever, in fact, and especially commendable with the 5-speed. Our test LS averaged nearly 25 mpg in city/freeway driving, and a GS-R yielded even more frugal results: an impressive 28.3 mpg. Around town, a manual-shift GS-R yielded close to 20 mpg. Automatic-transmission models are less frugal and slower. The automatic also shifts harshly in hard acceleration.

Both engines generate lots of noise at higher speeds, but cruise quietly. Tire hum is evident on all but mirror-smooth surfaces.

Each Integra corners adeptly, with a bit less body lean than

ACURA

before and almost no front-drive "plowing," helped by sharp steering. The ride is slightly smoother than before, and the car's overall "feel" stouter. However, hatchbacks in particular still tend to bounce and jiggle on freeways, due in part to their shorter wheelbase.

If you're fortunate enough to get your hands on a 1997 or '98 "Type-R" Integra, you'll be in for the ride of your life. This limited-production model comes equipped with a highly modified 195-horsepower version of the 1.8-liter GS-R engine, sport-tuned suspension, and meaty 195/55VR/15 tires. Expect brisk acceleration in the mid-6s. Built for performance, the Type-R omits some creature comforts (A/C for instance) and sound insulation to loose weight. Consequently, expect a noisier and bouncier ride than you get in other Integra models.

Passenger space in the hatchback models isn't as good as in the new Honda Civic hatchback. Medium-size people will fit fine up front, but only pre-teens are welcome in back. Because of its longer wheelbase, the sedan is roomier and more practical for buyers who often carry more than one passenger. Cargo room in the coupe is unexceptional. The glovebox offers scant space for anything other than the owner's manual. You can expect fine interior ergonomics and gauges in a typical Honda/Acura dashboard.

Any Integra should be reliable, but high resale value means they're not cheap secondhand. Great to look at and fun to drive, the sporty GS-R coupe, in particular, commands some extra dollars. A Honda Civic actually offers many of the Integra's features, at a considerably lower price.

NHTSA CRASH TEST RESULTS
1997 Acura Integra
4-DOOR SEDAN

Driver	☆☆☆☆
Passenger	☆☆☆

(The National Highway Traffic Safety Administration tests a vehicle's crashworthiness in front and side collisions. Their ratings suggest the chance of serious injury: ☆☆☆☆☆—10% or less; ☆☆☆☆—10-20% or less; ☆☆☆—20-30% or less; ☆☆—35-45% or less; ☆—More than 45%.)

SPECIFICATIONS

	2-door hatchback	4-door sedan
Wheelbase, in.	101.2	103.1
Overall length, in.	172.4	178.1
Overall width, in.	67.3	67.3
Overall height, in.	52.6	53.9
Curb weight, lbs.	2529	2628
Cargo volume, cu. ft.	13.0	11.0
Fuel capacity, gals.	13.2	13.2

	2-door hatchback	4-door sedan
Seating capacity	4	5
Front head room, in.	38.6	38.9
Max. front leg room, in.	42.7	42.2
Rear head room, in.	35.0	36.0
Min. rear leg room, in.	28.1	32.7

Powertrain layout: transverse front-engine/front-wheel drive

ENGINES

	dohc I-4	dohc I-4	dohc I-4¹
Size, liters/cu. in.	1.8/112	1.8/109	1.8/110
Horsepower	142	170	195
Torque (lbs./ft.)	127	128	130

EPA city/highway mpg

5-speed OD manual	25/31	25/31	25/31
4-speed OD automatic	24/31		

Consumer Guide™ observed MPG

5-speed OD manual	25.0	28.3	25.7

1. This highly modified Integra engine is only available on limited-production Type-R models, and comes mated to a 5-speed manual transmission.

Built in Japan.

RETAIL PRICES	GOOD	AVERAGE	POOR
1994 Integra	$7,600-9,200	$6,800-8,400	$4,500-5,800
1994 Integra GS-R	10,000-11,000	9,000-10,000	6,500-7,300
1995 Integra	9,500-12,500	8,500-11,500	6,000-8,500
1995 Integra GS-R	12,000-13,200	11,000-12,000	8,000-9,000
1996 Integra	11,000-14,200	10,000-13,000	7,200-9,800
1996 Integra GS-R	13,800-15,000	12,500-13,700	9,000-10,000
1997 Integra	12,500-15,500	11,300-14,000	8,300-10,800
1997 Integra GS-R	15,500-16,800	14,000-15,300	10,500-11,500
1998 Integra	14,500-18,000	13,000-16,500	9,800-12,800
1998 Integra GS-R	17,500-19,000	16,000-17,500	12,500-13,500

AVERAGE REPLACEMENT COSTS

A/C Compressor $530	Clutch, Pressure Plate, Bearing 580
Alternator 420	Constant Velocity Joints.....480
Radiator 380	Brakes.................................195
Timing Chain or Belt 255	Shocks and/or Struts 620
Automatic Transmission or Transaxle.........................895	Exhaust System.................505

TROUBLE SPOTS

• **Air conditioner** The air conditioner may stop working because the drive belt has come off the pulley. If the car is driven over a parking

ACURA

curb, the splash shield under the engine can snag the belt and pull it off when the car is backed up. It can be fixed by grinding off the five reinforcing ribs on the splash shield.

• **Trunk latch** The rear hatch may be hard to close on 1994-95 models because the rubber stops are too tall. If they are the non-adjustable type, they should be replaced with 24mm stops. If they are adjustable, they should be shortened. There is a field fix kit available with several other parts to correct the problem.

RECALL HISTORY

1994 Retaining clip at automatic transmission can come off, so position of lever does not match actual transmission gear range.

1991-95 ACURA LEGEND

1993 Acura Legend GS 4-door

FOR Air bags (later models) • Anti-lock brakes • Acceleration • Steering/handling • Instruments/controls • Passenger and cargo room

AGAINST Fuel economy • Rear-seat room (coupe) • Automatic transmission performance • Driver seating

EVALUATION The higher-powered V-6 engine in these Legends yielded quicker acceleration, but gas mileage is no bonus. Our tests ranged from 16-18 mpg in urban driving to the low 20s on the highway. Higher engine compression (9.6:1) demands premium fuel, too, though new dual knock sensors helped prevent damage from low-octane fuel. A Legend holds its own in acceleration against the costlier V-8 Lexus LS 400 and Infiniti Q45. Our early automatic-transmission sedan ran 0-60 mph in just 7.6 seconds. Still, the V-6 engine cannot match the V-8 in a top Lexus or Infiniti.

Despite the momentary ignition-retard setup, midrange downshifts in earlier models still border on harsh and can get rough under hard acceleration. Performance also slips quite a bit with automatic.

Ride quality is smoother and more absorbent than before. The taut ride is never harsh, but falls short of the suppleness displayed by some European rivals. Though stable, it can get harsh and abrupt over rough surfaces. Handling earns high marks, nearly like that of a sports car. Quick turns bring some body leans, but grip, balance, and control are laudable. Standard anti-lock makes the brakes feel strong and secure.

Though roomier in back than before, this is still essentially a spacious 4-seater (but with seatbelts for a third person in back). Front-seat occupants might lack head room with the sunroof, or find that the early non-tilting, telescoping steering wheel crowds one's thighs. Leg room in the coupe's back seat is scant, and long doors hamper access. Trunks are hardly huge, but have a flat floor and handy bumper-height opening. Instruments and controls are logical, with a feather-touch feel. In sum, sporty manners, copious luxury (on LS), worthy workmanship, and stout construction help the Legend rival some more costly premium automobiles.

NHTSA CRASH TEST RESULTS
1994 Acura Legend LS sedan   4-DOOR SEDAN

Driver ☆☆☆
Passenger ☆☆☆☆

(The National Highway Traffic Safety Administration tests a vehicle's crashworthiness in front and side collisions. Their ratings suggest the chance of serious injury: ☆☆☆☆☆—10% or less; ☆☆☆☆—10-20% or less; ☆☆☆—20-30% or less; ☆☆—35-45% or less; ☆—More than 45%.)

SPECIFICATIONS

	2-door coupe	4-door sedan
Wheelbase, in.	111.4	114.6
Overall length, in.	192.5	194.9
Overall width, in.	71.3	71.3
Overall height, in.	53.5	55.1
Curb weight, lbs.	3516	3516
Cargo volume, cu. ft.	14.1	14.8
Fuel capacity, gals.	18.0	18.0
Seating capacity	5	5
Front head room, in.	37.3	38.5
Max. front leg room, in.	42.9	42.7
Rear head room, in.	35.9	36.5
Min. rear leg room, in.	28.7	33.5

Powertrain layout: transverse front-engine/front-wheel drive

ACURA

ENGINES

	ohc V-6	ohc V-6
Size, liters/cu. in.	3.2/196	3.2/196
Horsepower	200	230
Torque (lbs./ft.)	210	206

EPA city/highway mpg

5-speed OD manual..	18/25	
6-speed OD manual..		18/26
4-speed OD automatic	19/24	18/23

Consumer Guide™ observed MPG

4-speed OD automatic	19.2	20.2

Built in Japan.

RETAIL PRICES	GOOD	AVERAGE	POOR
1991 Legend	$7,500-10,500	$6,500-9,500	$4,300-7,000
1992 Legend	9,000-13,000	8,000-11,800	5,500-8,700
1993 Legend	11,500-15,500	10,000-14,000	7,200-10,500
1994 Legend	14,500-18,000	13,000-16,500	9,800-13,000
1995 Legend	17,500-21,500	16,000-20,000	12,500-16,000

AVERAGE REPLACEMENT COSTS

A/C Compressor $715	Clutch, Pressure Plate,	
Alternator 360	Bearing 965	
Radiator 530	Constant Velocity Joints.....555	
Timing Chain or Belt 300	Brakes.................................200	
Automatic Transmission or	Shocks and/or Struts 895	
Transaxle.....................1,005	Exhaust System 810	

TROUBLE SPOTS

• **Cruise control** The cruise control may not engage on 1994 models due to a faulty actuator. If the technician jars it when removing to test, it may check out OK. If it is reinstalled, it may fail again, but not be suspected as the problem the second time. If the actuator is bad, the replacement may be covered by a "good-will fix" upon the district service manager's approval if out of warranty.

• **Security alarm** The security alarm may not deactivate with the key in the driver's door, which sets off the alarm. Turning the key again may disarm it. The only fix is to replace the driver's door lock.

• **Steering noise** Telescopic steering columns may groan when the wheel is turned because there is not enough lubrication on the column. To apply more grease to the column, the air bag must first be removed. This job may be covered by a "good-will fix" upon the district service manager's approval if out of warranty.

• **Steering problems** Steering may be difficult during parking maneuvers due to a problem with the vehicle speed sensor in the power steering unit on 1991-94 models. There is a kit available to fix the problem so that the entire unit need not be replaced.

• **Engine noise** Carbon buildup on the piston rings may cause piston slap. The fix is to clean the carbon using GM Top Engine Cleaner sucked in by way of a vacuum port on the throttle body. If this doesn't do the trick, the piston rings will have to be replaced.

RECALL HISTORY

1991 sedan Transmission shift cable bracket can be damaged and shift lever may then not correctly indicate gear position. **1992** Passenger-side air bag assembly in small number of cars was produced without igniter material, which would cause non-deployment or slow deployment in case of collision.

1996-98 ACURA TL

1996 Acura 2.5TL

FOR Air bags, dual • Anti-lock brakes • Acceleration (3.2TL) • Steering/handling • Instruments/controls • Visibility

AGAINST Automatic transmission performance • Road noise (3.2TL) • Engine noise (2.5TL) • Rear seat room

EVALUATION Sporty moves mark these upscale sedans, which deliver competent handling and good grip but performance that fails to beat the previous Vigor by all that much. All told, the 3.2TL is livelier, and its V-6 engine quieter. On the down side, the 3.2TL's more aggressive tires generate more road noise.

Superior in road behavior, both cars handle well and inspire confidence, helped by precise, neatly-assisted steering with ample feedback, plus fine high-speed braking. Front-drive cornering is predictable, with modest body lean and good grip. With less weight up front, the 2.5TL tends to corner with a crisper feel and slightly less understeer. Each model rides well, the fully independent suspension delivering solid comfort and taut control while smoothing out the rough spots with ease.

The automatic transmission is slow to kick down for passing. Also, its "Grade Logic" feature sometimes drops down a gear or two, whether you want it to or not. Also, it tends to hang onto each gear a little too long. The transmission often downshifts harshly or abruptly, too, even producing a lurch during hard acceleration. On the plus side, the gated gearshift lever looks handsome and is easy to manipulate.

Though generally smooth, the 5-cylinder engine gets noisy when worked hard, emitting a coarse, throaty growl during acceleration, which is out of character for a vehicle of this sort. Though not a slouch, it delivers only adequate pickup. Acceleration off-the-line is a bit lethargic, but the 2.5TL passes and merges quite quickly. Somewhat lumpy at idle, it's not as smooth as the silky, quiet V-6 in the 3.2TL.

Gas mileage is close to average for this league, depending on the type of usage the car sees. In a mix of city, suburban, and highway driving, we managed 19.2 mpg with a 2.5TL and 18.3 mpg from the 3.2TL. A long trip in a 2.5TL, on the other hand, involving mainly highway driving, yielded an impressive 25.7 miles per gallon—slightly above the EPA estimate. Both engines demand premium gasoline, however.

Interior space overall ranks as adequate rather than generous—unexceptional for the car's size, partly as a result of the typical Acura low profile.

Head room is just adequate for 6-footers. The same is true of rear leg space, though it's five inches larger than in the prior Vigor. Not every driver and passenger might be delighted with seat comfort—especially the occupant of the center rear position, who must endure a hard seat and straddle a tall tunnel.

Despite the low-slung styling, a glassy greenhouse with thin pillars produces easy viewing all around. Entry/exit is easy and the driving position is accommodating. Simple, intuitive instruments and controls are handy to see and reach. Panel fit and paint finish are top-notch, devoid of squeaks and rattles.

Although these TL sedans are well-constructed, pleasant, and better than the Vigor in every way, they still fail to overshadow the competition in the mid-luxury league. Neither version does any single thing well enough to stand out in this highly competitive market segment. Give the TL a look, but several worthy alternatives are on the market, so shop around before buying.

NHTSA CRASH TEST RESULTS
1996 Acura TL

4-DOOR HATCHBACK

Driver	☆☆☆☆
Passenger	☆☆☆☆

(The National Highway Traffic Safety Administration tests a vehicle's crashworthiness in front and side collisions. Their ratings suggest the chance of serious injury: ☆☆☆☆☆—10% or less; ☆☆☆☆—10-20% or less; ☆☆☆—20-30% or less; ☆☆—35-45% or less; ☆—More than 45%.)

SPECIFICATIONS

	4-door sedan
Wheelbase, in.	111.8
Overall length, in.	191.5
Overall width, in.	70.3
Overall height, in.	55.3
Curb weight, lbs.	3252
Cargo volume, cu. ft.	14.1
Fuel capacity, gals.	17.2
Seating capacity	5
Front head room, in.	39.1
Max. front leg room, in.	43.7
Rear head room, in.	36.9
Min. rear leg room, in.	35.2

Powertrain layout: longitudinal front-engine/front-wheel drive

ENGINES

	ohc I-5	ohc V-6
Size, liters/cu. in.	2.5/152	3.2/196
Horsepower	176	200
Torque (lbs./ft.)	170	210

EPA city/highway mpg

4-speed OD automatic	20/25	19/24

Consumer Guide™ observed MPG

4-speed OD automatic	19.2	18.3

Built in Japan.

RETAIL PRICES	GOOD	AVERAGE	POOR
1996 2.5TL	$18,000-20,000	$16,500-18,500	$13,000-15,000
1996 3.2TL	20,500-23,000	19,000-21,500	15,500-18,000
1997 2.5TL	22,000-24,000	20,500-22,500	16,500-18,500
1997 3.2TL	24,500-26,500	23,000-25,500	19,000-21,000
1998 2.5TL	26,000-28,000	24,000-26,000	20,000-22,000
1998 3.2TL	28,000-31,000	26,500-29,000	22,500-24,500

AVERAGE REPLACEMENT COSTS

A/C Compressor $725	Clutch, Pressure Plate,
Alternator 395	Bearing.....................1,010
Radiator 445	Constant Velocity Joints.....810
Timing Chain or Belt 230	Brakes................................215
Automatic Transmission or	Shocks and/or Struts 995
Transaxle....................1,270	Exhaust System.................610

TROUBLE SPOTS

• **Steering problems** Power steering pump leaks because the pump shaft was not machined properly causing the seal to wear. (1996)

• **Radio** Radio interference is caused by the ignition coils. (1996-97)

• **Radio** The grille cloth pulls loose from the tweeter (speaker). (1995-96)

• **Vehicle noise** Wind noise from the moonroof. (1996)

RECALL HISTORY

None to date.

1993-98 AUDI 90/CABRIOLET

1993 Audi 90 S 4-door

FOR Air bags, dual (later models) • Anti-lock brakes • Steering/ handling • Wet weather traction (Quattro) • Fuel economy

AGAINST Acceleration • Road noise • Rear seat room • Automatic transmission performance

EVALUATION Though a smooth runner, and a lot zippier than its predecessor when equipped with 5-speed manual shift, the V-6 Audi lags in off-the-line acceleration with 4-speed automatic. Without a doubt, the engine runs smoothly and quietly, and power delivery is very linear. However, that automatic transmission drains the engine's ability to deliver quick bursts of speed in around-town driving. The automatic also shifts rather abruptly and tends to hold each gear too long. Audi's 5-speed gearbox, on the other hand, is smooth and precise. So is the car's clutch. The V-6 engine demands premium fuel.

Expect plenty of tire and suspension noise on any imperfect surfaces, plus a ride that's a bit too firm on harsh urban pavements. Tar strips and small bumps do not go unnoticed, though bigger obstacles are taken in stride. Stable handling from the taut suspension imparts a secure feeling at highway speeds, with good grip in hard corners.

The dashboard layout is businesslike, with clear audio and climate controls, plus a large round speedometer and tachometer. Interiors look a bit austere in the 90 S, but CS versions with their wood accents appear somewhat dressier. Either way, the materials that are used impart an impression of quality.

Most drivers are likely to feel comfortable behind the wheel. Seats are firm and supportive, with height adjustments for the shoulder belt and lower cushion. Despite the longer wheelbase, interior dimensions are virtually identical to the previous model, but trunk space grew from 10.2 to 14.0 cubic feet, increasing its utility. Front-seat space is ample, but the rear lacks leg room, giving the interior a rather cramped ambience.

Cabriolets look great but suffer from excessive body shake and flex on bumpy roads—out of character for the car's hefty price when new (and used, too). Performance is acceptable in day-to-day driving, but the lack of low-speed power and imperfect shift action makes it feel lethargic. Front seat space is adequate for average-size adults, and head room beats most convertibles. The rear seat is useful only for children, and not for long. Controls are well positioned, but the radio has too many small, poorly marked controls. Several competitors offer a glass rear window with electric defogger, in contrast to the Cabriolet's plastic pane.

When these cars were new, dealers offered big discounts to spur sales, so expect to find lower-than-average used-car prices for all except convertibles and high-performance models. Recent models have been well assembled. The "Audi Advantage" plan covered most routine maintenance for three years or 50,000 miles.

Audi's 90 had some attractive features, including a sporty manner (at least with the 5-speed), available 4-wheel drive, and solid feel. Nevertheless, it did not sell strongly in the "near-luxury" market, which was dominated by such Japanese-brand models as the Acura Vigor, Infiniti J30, Lexus ES 300, and Nissan Maxima SE.

SPECIFICATIONS

	4-door sedan	2-door conv.
eelbase, in.	102.8	100.6
erall length, in.	180.3	176.0
erall width, in.	66.7	67.6
erall height, in.	54.3	54.3
rb weight, lbs.	3197	3494
rgo volume, cu. ft.	14.0	6.6
el capacity, gals.	17.4	17.4
eating capacity	5	4
ont head room, in.	37.8	38.3
ax. front leg room, in.	42.2	40.7
ear head room, in.	37.2	36.4
lin. rear leg room, in.	32.5	26.5

Powertrain layout: longitudinal front-engine/front- or all-wheel drive

ENGINES

	ohc V-6
Size, liters/cu. in.	2.8/169
Horsepower	172
Torque (lbs./ft.)	184

EPA city/highway mpg

5-speed OD manual	20/26
4-speed OD automatic	18/26

Consumer Guide™ observed MPG

4-speed OD automatic	18.7

Built in Germany.

AVERAGE REPLACEMENT COSTS

A/C Compressor	$1,040	Clutch, Pressure Plate, Bearing	975
Alternator	640	Constant Velocity Joints	680
Exhaust System	550	Brakes	300
Timing Chain or Belt	240	Shocks and/or Struts	1,410
Automatic Transmission or Transaxle	1,220	Exhaust System	450

RETAIL PRICES	GOOD	AVERAGE	POOR
1993 90 sedan	$8,000-11,500	$7,000-10,000	$4,800-7,500
1994 90 sedan	10,500-14,500	9,300-13,000	6,700-9,800
1994 Cabriolet	16,000-18,000	14,500-16,500	11,000-13,000
1995 90 sedan	12,500-16,000	11,500-14,500	8,000-11,000
1995 Cabriolet	19,000-21,000	17,000-19,000	13,000-15,000
1996 Cabriolet	22,500-25,000	20,500-23,000	16,500-18,500

	GOOD	AVERAGE	POOR
1997 Cabriolet	26,000-29,000	24,000-27,000	20,000-22,500
1998 Cabriolet	29,500-33,000	27,500-31,000	23,000-26,500

TROUBLE SPOTS

• **Windshield wipers** The wiper blades skip or jerk across the windshield which may damage the blades or even scratch the windshield. (1991-96)

• **Steering noise** If there is a clunk from the front when the steering wheel is turned, when going over bumps or when changing from drive to reverse, the heat shield on the left motor mount may be striking the bracket. (1993-94)

• **Climate control** If the heater or A/C does not work or works intermittently, the blue/black wire on the control center has been known to come loose. (1993-94)

• **Oil leak** On any model with the V-6 engine, the rear main seal may leak, and/or there may be an oil leak from the intake valley which appears to be a rear main leak. (1993-94)

• **Cruise control** The cruise control may not maintain speed due to a defective vacuum servo unit. (1995)

RECALL HISTORY

1993 Some air bag sensors do not comply with Audi's durability standards. **1994-96** Defective ignition switch can cause some accessories (turn signals, lamps, wipers) to malfunction when engine is started. **1995-97** Discharge of static electricity in low humidity conditions can activate driver's air bag when driver enters or exits car.

1992-98 BMW 318i

FOR Dual air bags (later models) • Ride • Steering/handling • Anti-lock brakes

AGAINST Wet-weather traction • Rear seat room

EVALUATION Four-cylinder BMWs target driving enthusiasts, who generally prefer manual shift. Because these engines come alive only at high rpm, they function better with manual shift than with automatic, which robs some of the engine's zest. Around town, though, you can expect to shift the 5-speed frequently.

Installation of the larger engine in 1996 did not boost performance appreciably. Fuel mileage has averaged more than 25 mpg with the manual shift.

Regardless of engine, all 3-Series BMWs shine brightest in

BMW

1993 BMW 318i 4-door

their sporty handling characteristics. They devour twisting roads with ease, helped by sharply precise yet fluid steering. Quick turns produce more body lean than expected, but the cars feel lithe and sure-footed. Though the suspension is firm, ride quality beats many cars with softer suspensions, absorbing plenty of road flaws. Brakes are potent, too.

In wet or snowy weather, however, these rear-drivers can get difficult to handle, as the tail slips easily sideways. Traction control in not all that effective.

Despite the increased size in this generation, interior space is not much larger than in previous BMWs. Rear space is acceptable only for two small adults, and rear head room is tight in the coupe due to its slightly lower roofline. Cabins are rather austere, with a lot of hard plastic surfaces that seem inappropriate for the car's price. Lack of a tilt feature means the steering wheel sits a bit high, but analog gauges are unobstructed and radio and climate controls are close at hand. Skimpy rear door openings hinder back seat entry into sedans. The trunk floor is flat, and its opening is large.

Despite high secondhand prices, 4-cylinder BMWs appeal to those who like spirited, high-revving driving enjoyment. For that purpose, they're hard to beat.

NHTSA CRASH TEST RESULTS
1997 BMW 318i   4-DOOR SEDAN

Driver	☆☆☆☆
Passenger	☆☆☆☆

(The National Highway Traffic Safety Administration tests a vehicle's crashworthiness in front and side collisions. Their ratings suggest the chance of serious injury: ☆☆☆☆☆—10%

or less; ☆☆☆☆—10-20% or less; ☆☆☆—20-30% or less; ☆☆—35-45% or less; ☆—More than 45%.)

SPECIFICATIONS	2-door coupe	2-door conv.	4-door sedan
Wheelbase, in.	106.3	106.3	106.3
Overall length, in.	174.5	174.5	174.5
Overall width, in.	67.3	67.3	66.8
Overall height, in.	53.8	53.1	54.8
Curb weight, lbs.	2866	3352	2866
Cargo volume, cu. ft.	14.3	9.0	15.4
Fuel capacity, gals.	17.2	17.2	17.2
Seating capacity	5	4	5
Front head room, in.	36.7	38.1	37.8
Max. front leg room, in.	41.2	41.2	40.9
Rear head room, in.	35.9	36.3	37.3
Min. rear leg room, in.	32.7	28.1	34.1

Powertrain layout: longitudinal front-engine/rear-wheel drive

ENGINES	dohc I-4[1]	dohc I-4	dohc I-4
Size, liters/cu. in.	1.8/110	1.8/110	1.9/116
Horsepower	134	138	138
Torque (lbs./ft.)	127	129	133
EPA city/highway mpg			
5-speed OD manual	NA	22/32	23/31
4-speed OD automatic	NA	21/29	22/31
Consumer Guide™ observed MPG			
5-speed OD manual		25.5	
4-speed OD automatic			20.2

1. Used in carryover-styled 1992 convertibles only.

Built in USA and Germany.

RETAIL PRICES	GOOD	AVERAGE	POOR
1992 318i/is	$8,500-10,000	$7,500-9,000	$5,000-6,200
1992 Convertible	10,800-12,000	9,500-10,500	6,500-7,500
1993 318i/is	10,500-12,000	9,200-10,500	6,200-7,400
1994 318i/is	12,500-14,000	11,000-12,500	8,000-9,500
1994 Convertible	16,500-18,000	15,000-16,500	11,500-13,000
1995 318i/is	15,000-17,000	13,500-15,500	10,000-12,000
1995 Convertible	19,500-21,500	17,000-19,000	13,500-15,000
1996 318i/is	18,000-20,500	16,200-18,500	12,500-14,500
1996 Convertible	22,500-24,500	20,500-22,500	16,500-18,000
1997 318i/is	21,000-23,500	19,000-21,500	15,000-17,500
1997 Convertible	26,000-28,000	24,000-26,000	19,500-21,500
1998 318i	24,000-27,000	22,000-25,000	18,000-21,000

AVERAGE REPLACEMENT COSTS

A/C Compressor	$1,200	Clutch, Pressure Plate, Bearing	570
Alternator	420	Brakes	260
Radiator	655	Shocks and/or Struts	1,225
Timing Chain or Belt	820	Exhaust System	1,450
Automatic Transmission or Transaxle	1,150		

TROUBLE SPOTS

• **Dashboard lights** The hazard flashers may begin flashing by themselves, the turn signals may flash at twice the normal speed or the turn signals may not flash at all due to condensation shorting out the circuit board for the hazard flasher relay. (1992-94)

• **Air conditioner** There was a silent service campaign to fix air conditioners that were not cooling well enough. The fix was to remove some of the R-12 (Freon®) since the system was overcharged. (1991-93)

• **Starter** The starter (or several starters) may fail because they keep running after the engine starts and eventually burn out. Additional problems may include a dead battery and window and sunroof that do not work because of unloader relay operation. The root cause is a sticking ignition switch. The whole lock and switch must be replaced. (1992-94)

• **Automatic transmission** The automatic transmission may suffer from delayed engagement after sitting overnight because the fluid drains out of the torque converter. The fix involves replacing the torque converter and installing a bleed-down kit. (1992-95)

• **Climate control** Small flakes ("snow") may come from the vents or a foul odor may be present when the A/C is operated. A redesigned evaporator is available to fix the problem. (1992-93)

• **Doors** If the central locking system unlocks itself after being locked or locks itself after being unlocked or if one or more doors malfunction, the actuators could be defective (most likely cause) or the trunk lock may need to be adjusted. (1992-93)

RECALL HISTORY

1992 Air bag contact ring locking tab can break without warning, eventually causing broken wiring; airbag would then not deploy in collision, and indicator would illuminate. **1992-93** Fuel hoses can harden and "set" over time, allowing seepage that could result in fire. **1992-97** Plastic bushing for cruise-control and throttle cables could break, causing throttle valve to remain partially open; car then might not decelerate as expected.

1992-98 BMW 325i/328i/323i

1992 BMW 325is 2-door

FOR   Dual air bags (later models) • Acceleration • Ride • Steering/handling • Standard anti-lock brakes and traction control (later models)

AGAINST   Wet-weather traction • Rear seat room • Fuel economy • Control layout

EVALUATION   Acceleration is swift and smooth at higher engine speeds, but early models suffered a shortage in low-end power, feeling somewhat lethargic until they revved past 3000 rpm or more. Performance in general is adequate with automatic, but these cars are best enjoyed with the highly-inviting 5-speed manual gearbox. In town, though, that 5-speed needs to be shifted often. Fuel economy averaged 20.4 mpg in a test of a 1992 model with manual shift.

Swift turns with the base suspension bring more body roll than expected, but the 3-Series feels tight, lithe, and sure-footed. Anti-lock brakes deliver commendable stopping power and excellent sensitivity. Steering is sharp and precise, road manners nicely balanced. A firm, yet absorbent suspension soaks up road flaws while keeping the body stable.

Beware in wet weather, as rear-drivers can get twitchy in rain or snow. Even with the traction control, snow tires are a must in northern climates.

Space up front is adequate, but the rear is sufficient only for two, on a narrow seat. Rear head room in coupes is tight, due to their slightly lower roofline, and the center rear occupant must straddle the driveline tunnel. Skimpy door openings on sedans hinder back-seat entry. The trunk floor is flat, with a large opening. Interiors are austere, with hard plastic surfaces. Radio and climate controls are close

BMW

at hand but feature a confusing array of buttons.

BMWs are far from cheap secondhand, but their many fans are willing to lay out the extra bucks for top-notch roadholding and high-quality materials.

NHTSA CRASH TEST RESULTS
1995 BMW 325i

4-DOOR SEDAN

Driver	☆☆☆☆
Passenger	☆☆☆☆

(The National Highway Traffic Safety Administration tests a vehicle's crashworthiness in front and side collisions. Their ratings suggest the chance of serious injury: ☆☆☆☆☆—10% or less; ☆☆☆☆—10-20% or less; ☆☆☆—20-30% or less; ☆☆—35-45% or less; ☆—More than 45%.)

SPECIFICATIONS

	2-door coupe	2-door conv.	2-door conv.	4-door sedan
Wheelbase, in.	106.3	101.2	106.3	106.3
Overall length, in.	174.5	175.2	174.5	174.5
Overall width, in.	67.3	64.8	67.3	66.8
Overall height, in.	53.8	53.9	53.1	54.8
Curb weight, lbs.	2866	2990	3352	2866
Cargo volume, cu. ft.	14.3	11.0	9.0	15.4
Fuel capacity, gals.	17.2	16.4	17.2	17.2
Seating capacity	5	4	4	5
Front head room, in.	36.7	NA	38.1	37.8
Max. front leg room, in.	41.2	NA	41.2	40.9
Rear head room, in.	35.9	NA	36.3	37.3
Min. rear leg room, in.	32.7	NA	28.1	34.1

Powertrain layout: longitudinal front-engine/rear-wheel drive

ENGINES

	ohc I-6[1]	dohc I-6	dohc I-6	dohc I-6
Size, liters/cu. in.	2.5/152	2.5/152	2.8/170	3.0/182
Horsepower	168	168-189	190	240
Torque (lbs./ft.)	164	181	206	225
EPA city/highway mpg				
5-speed OD manual	17/24	19/28	20/29	19/27
4-speed OD automatic		20/28	19/26	
Consumer Guide™ observed MPG				
5-speed OD manual		20.4		
4-speed OD automatic		17.6	19.8	19/28

1. *Used in carryover-styled 1992-93 convertibles only.*

Built in USA and Germany.

RETAIL PRICES

	GOOD	AVERAGE	POOR
1992 325i/is	$11,500-12,800	$10,500-11,500	$8,000-9,000
1992 Convertible	13,500-15,000	12,000-13,500	9,000-10,500
1993 325i/is	13,700-15,400	12,500-14,000	9,500-11,000

	GOOD	AVERAGE	POOR
1993 Convertible	16,000-18,000	14,500-16,500	11,500-13,200
1994 325i/is	16,000-18,000	14,500-16,500	11,500-13,300
1994 Convertible	20,500-23,000	19,200-21,000	16,000-17,800
1995 325i/is	19,000-21,000	17,200-19,000	14,200-15,800
1995 Convertible	24,500-27,500	22,500-25,500	19,000-21,500
1996 328i/is	22,000-25,000	20,000-23,000	16,500-19,000
1996 Convertible	29,000-32,000	27,000-29,500	23,000-25,000
1997 328i/is	25,500-29,000	23,500-27,000	19,500-22,000
1997 Convertible	32,500-36,000	30,500-33,000	26,000-28,000
1998 328i/is	29,500-33,500	27,500-31,000	23,000-26,000
1998 Convertible	36,500-40,000	34,000-37,000	29,000-32,000

AVERAGE REPLACEMENT COSTS

A/C Compressor $970
Alternator 590
Exhaust System 670
Timing Chain or Belt 1,265
Automatic Transmission or
  Transaxle.....................1,190

Clutch, Pressure Plate,
  Bearing 645
Brakes................................260
Shocks and/or Struts 980
Exhaust System.................790

TROUBLE SPOTS

• **Air conditioner** There was a silent service campaign to fix air conditioners that were not cooling well enough. The fix was to remove some of the R-12 (Freon®) since the system was overcharged. (1991-93)

• **Dashboard lights** The hazard flashers may begin flashing by themselves, the turn signals may flash at twice the normal speed, or the turn signals may not flash at all due to condensation shorting out the circuit board for the hazard flasher relay. (1992-94)

• **Starter** The starter (or several starters) may fail because they keep running after the engine starts and eventually burn out. Additional problems may include a dead battery and window and sunroof that do not work because of unloader relay operation. The root cause is a sticking ignition switch. The whole lock and switch must be replaced. (1992-94)

• **Climate control** Small flakes ("snow") may come from the vents, or a foul odor may be present, when the A/C is operated. A redesigned evaporator is available to fix the problem. (1992-93)

• **Doors** If the central locking system unlocks itself after being locked or locks itself after being unlocked or if one or more doors malfunction, the actuators could be defective (most likely cause) or the trunk lock may need to be adjusted. (1992-93)

• **Automatic transmission** The automatic transmission may suffer from delayed engagement after sitting overnight because the fluid drains out of the torque converter. The fix involves replacing the torque converter, and installing a bleed-down kit. (1992-95)

RECALL HISTORY

1992 Air bag contact ring locking tab can break without warning, eventually causing broken wiring; airbag would then not deploy in collision, and indicator would illuminate. **1992** Failed to meet safety standard for driver chest injury in crash test. **1992-93** Fuel hoses can harden and "set" over time. **1992-94 325i/iS** Brake lights may fail to operate, or be on continuously. **1992-95 325i** Plastic bushing for cruise-control and throttle cables could break, causing throttle valve to remain partially open; car then might not decelerate as expected. **1993-94 325i/iS** Replace front transmission crossmember support. **1994 325iC** Brake lights may fail to operate, or be on continuously. **1995 M3** Brake lights may fail to operate, or be on continuously. **1995-97 M3** Plastic bushing for cruise-control and throttle cables could break, causing throttle valve to remain partially open; car then might not decelerate as expected.

1990-96 BUICK CENTURY

1995 Buick Century Special Edition 4-door

FOR Driver-side air bag (later models) • Passenger and cargo room • Anti-lock brakes (later models) • Acceleration (V-6) • Quietness • Visibility

AGAINST Acceleration (4-cylinder) • Ride • Handling (base suspension)

EVALUATION The rough 2.5-liter 4-cylinder engine is barely adequate for sedans, and weaker yet in the heavier station wagon. A smooth, responsive 3.3-liter V-6 delivers ample power at low speeds and a surprisingly strong kick under heavy throttle, for brisk highway passing. That engine also is fairly quiet, unlike the noisy standard four. Also, the 2.5-liter four did not prove to be trouble-free, and fuel mileage wasn't much better than the V-6. We averaged nearly 20 mpg with a 3.3-liter V-6 in mixed city/suburban driving. A four gets only about two mpg more. The 2.2-liter four that replaced the 2.5-liter in 1993 isn't much improvement, lacking the power to move a car this size with any authority. Adding 10 horsepower to the four for '94 didn't make it a tempting choice, either. The 3.1-liter V-6 installed in more recent models delivers ample power for passing and spirited takeoffs.

Century's Dynaride suspension delivers a soft and reasonably good ride, but handling won't win any awards. The base suspension and narrow standard tires are fine for gentle commuting, but spirited cornering causes the narrow tires to lose their grip. That suspension absorbs most bumps easily, but the front end bounces over wavy surfaces for a floaty, poorly controlled ride. An optional Gran Touring Suspension, with fatter tires, improves cornering ability but results in a harsh ride.

Six adults will fit inside, but four will be far more comfortable. Head and leg room are adequate all around, but three cannot fit across without squeezing. Luggage space is ample, with a deep, wide trunk that has a flat floor. Wagons had an optional rear-facing third seat, for 8-passenger capacity.

Front brakes tend to wear out quickly. Many early problems, including trouble with the rack-and-pinion power steering system, were eventually corrected on the later models. Forget the 4-cylinder models and look for a livelier, quieter V-6. That shouldn't be difficult, as most late Centurys were sold with the V-6 engine.

NHTSA CRASH TEST RESULTS
1995 Buick Century   <small>4-DOOR SEDAN</small>

Driver	☆☆☆☆
Passenger	☆☆☆☆

(The National Highway Traffic Safety Administration tests a vehicle's crashworthiness in front and side collisions. Their ratings suggest the chance of serious injury: ☆☆☆☆☆—10% or less; ☆☆☆☆—10-20% or less; ☆☆☆—20-30% or less; ☆☆—35-45% or less; ☆—More than 45%.)

SPECIFICATIONS	2-door coupe	4-door sedan	4-door wagon
Wheelbase, in.	104.9	104.9	104.9
Overall length, in.	189.1	189.1	190.9
Overall width, in.	69.4	69.4	69.4

BUICK

	2-door coupe	4-door sedan	4-door wagon
Overall height, in.	53.7	54.2	54.2
Curb weight, lbs.	2903	2950	3118
Cargo volume, cu. ft.	16.2	16.2	74.4
Fuel capacity, gals.	16.4	16.5	16.5
Seating capacity	6	6	8
Front head room, in.	38.6	38.6	38.6
Max. front leg room, in.	42.1	42.1	42.1
Rear head room, in.	38.3	38.3	38.9
Min. rear leg room, in.	35.9	35.9	34.8

Powertrain layout: transverse front-engine/front-wheel drive

ENGINES

	ohv I-4	ohv I-4	ohv V-6	ohv V-6
Size, liters/cu. in.	2.2/133	2.5/151	3.1/191	3.3/204
Horsepower	110-120	110	160	160
Torque (lbs./ft.)	130	135	185	185

EPA city/highway mpg

3-speed automatic	24/31	22/31		19/26
4-speed OD automatic			20/29	19/30

Consumer Guide™ observed MPG

4-speed OD automatic			22.3	19.8

Built in USA.

RETAIL PRICES

	GOOD	AVERAGE	POOR
1990 Century	$2,300-3,500	$1,700-2,800	$800-1,400
1991 Century	2,800-4,200	2,100-3,500	1,200-1,800
1992 Century	3,500-4,800	2,800-4,000	1,700-2,200
1993 Century	4,200-5,500	3,500-4,800	2,200-2,800
1994 Century	5,200-6,300	4,400-5,500	2,700-3,400
1995 Century	6,500-8,000	5,700-7,200	3,700-4,800
1996 Century	7,800-9,500	7,000-8,600	4,700-6,000

AVERAGE REPLACEMENT COSTS

A/C Compressor $555	Constant Velocity Joints.....535
Alternator 195	Brakes..................................210
Radiator 430	Shocks and/or Struts 825
Timing Chain or Belt 350	Exhaust System.................450
Automatic Transmission or Transaxle.....................1,095	

TROUBLE SPOTS

• **Engine noise** A tick or rattle when the engine is started cold may be due to too much wrist pin-to-piston clearance. New piston and pin sets will be replaced under warranty if the customer complains of the noise. (1994-95)

- **Engine noise** Bearing knock was common on many 3300 and 3800 (3.3L and 3.8L) engines due to too much clearance on the number one main bearing, requiring it to be replaced with a 0.001 inch undersize bearing. (1992-93)

- **Transaxle leak** The right front axle seal at the automatic transaxle is prone to leak and GM issued a revised seal to correct the problem. It is supposed to be installed whenever a car is in for transmission or axle shaft service of any sort. (1992-94)

- **Oil leak** The plastic valve covers on 3.1L engines were prone to leaks and should be replaced with redesigned aluminum valve covers. GM no longer sells the plastic ones. (1994-95)

- **Engine misfire** Cars with the 3.1L engine may stall, idle roughly, or suffer from tip-in hesitation after extended idling. Additionally, the defroster may not clear the windshield when the temperature is around 40-50 degrees F. The fix is to get a new PROM and a vacuum hose elbow for the PCV system. (1994-95)

- **Steering noise** The upper bearing mount in the steering column can get loose and cause a snapping or clicking that can be both heard and felt, requiring a new bearing spring and turn signal cancel cam, which the manufacturer will warranty. (1994-96)

- **Transmission slippage** The 4T60E transmission may drop out of drive (neutral condition) while cruising, shift erratically, have no third or fourth gear, or no second and third gear because of a bad ground connection for the shift solenoids. Poor grounds also allow wrong gear starts. Many transmissions have been mistakenly rebuilt, which does not correct the problem. (1994)

- **Transmission slippage** Any car with a model TH-125 or 440-T4 automatic transmission may shift late or not upshift at all. The problem is a stuck throttle valve inside the transmission. It may be overlooked during rebuilding since the valve appears fine because it is hydraulic pressure, not a physical binding, that makes it stick. The problem is fixed by enlarging the hydraulic fluid balance hole by 0.010 inch. (1990-94)

- **Engine noise** What sounds like a rattling noise from the engine that lasts less than a minute when the car is started after sitting overnight is often caused by automatic transmission pump starvation or cavitation, or a sticking pressure regulator valve. According to GM, no damage occurs and it does not have a fix for the problem. (1994-95)

RECALL HISTORY

1990-91 with six-way power seats or power recliner Short circuit could set seats on fire. **1990-96** Rear outboard seatbelt anchors may

BUICK

not withstand required load; in a collision, metal may tear and allow anchor to separate from body. **1993** Right front brake hose on some cars is improperly manufactured and can cause reduced brake effectiveness **1994** Water can cause short circuit in power door lock assembly. **1994** Improperly tightened spindle nut can cause premature wheel bearing failure.

1992-98 BUICK LeSABRE

1994 Buick LeSabre Limited

FOR Air bags (later models) • Anti-lock brakes • Acceleration • Automatic transmission performance • Passenger and cargo room

AGAINST Steering feel • Fuel economy • Radio and climate controls (early models)

See the 1992-98 Oldsmobile Eighty Eight report for an evaluation of the 1992-1998 Buick LeSabre.

NHTSA CRASH TEST RESULTS
1997 Buick LeSabre   4-DOOR SEDAN

Driver	☆☆☆☆
Passenger	☆☆☆☆

(The National Highway Traffic Safety Administration tests a vehicle's crashworthiness in front and side collisions. Their ratings suggest the chance of serious injury: ☆☆☆☆☆—10% or less; ☆☆☆☆—10-20% or less; ☆☆☆—20-30% or less; ☆☆—35-45% or less; ☆—More than 45%.)

SPECIFICATIONS

	4-door sedan
Wheelbase, in.	110.8
Overall length, in.	205.9
Overall width, in.	74.1
Overall height, in.	55.1

	4-door sedan
Curb weight, lbs.	3536
Cargo volume, cu. ft.	20.3
Fuel capacity, gals.	18.0
Seating capacity	6
Front head room, in.	38.9
Max. front leg room, in.	42.7
Rear head room, in.	37.9
Min. rear leg room, in.	40.7

Powertrain layout: transverse front-engine/front-wheel drive

ENGINES

	ohv V-6	ohv V-6
Size, liters/cu. in.	3.8/231	3.8/231
Horsepower	170	205
Torque (lbs./ft.)	225	230

EPA city/highway mpg

4-speed OD automatic	18/28	19/30

Consumer Guide™ observed MPG

4-speed OD automatic	22.0	19.3

Built in USA.

RETAIL PRICES	GOOD	AVERAGE	POOR
1992 LeSabre	$5,300-6,700	$4,600-5,900	$2,800-3,800
1993 LeSabre	6,500-8,000	5,700-7,200	3,700-5,000
1994 LeSabre	8,000-9,800	7,200-9,000	5,000-6,500
1995 LeSabre	10,000-12,000	9,000-11,000	6,500-8,000
1996 LeSabre	12,000-14,000	11,000-13,000	8,000-9,500
1997 LeSabre	14,000-16,500	12,500-15,000	9,500-11,000
1998 LeSabre	17,000-20,500	15,500-19,000	12,000-14,500

AVERAGE REPLACEMENT COSTS

A/C Compressor	$500	Constant Velocity Joints	760
Alternator	195	Brakes	130
Radiator	360	Shocks and/or Struts	840
Timing Chain or Belt	265	Exhaust System	470
Automatic Transmission or Transaxle	1,045		

TROUBLE SPOTS

• **Engine knock and oil leak** Models with the 3800 (3.8L) engine are prone to excessive oil consumption often accompanied by spark knock (pinging) during normal driving conditions due to failure of the valve stem seals. (1993-95)

BUICK

• **Engine knock** Bearing knock was common on many engines due to too much clearance on the number one main bearing, requiring it to be replaced with a 0.001 inch undersize bearing. (1992-94)

• **Transmission slippage** The 4T60E transmission may drop out of drive (neutral condition) while cruising, shift erratically, have no third or fourth gear, or no second and third gear because of a bad ground connection for the shift solenoids. Poor grounds also allow wrong gear starts. Many transmissions have been mistakenly rebuilt, which does not correct the problem. (1992-94)

• **Transmission leak** The right front axle seal at the automatic transaxle is prone to leak; GM issued a revised seal to correct the problem, which is supposed to be installed whenever a car is in for transmission or axle shaft service of any sort. (1992-94)

• **Engine noise** What sounds like a rattling noise from the engine that lasts less than a minute when the car is started after sitting overnight is often caused by automatic transmission pump starvation or cavitation, or a sticking pressure regulator valve. According to GM, no damage occurs and it does not have a fix for the problem. (1992-95)

• **Cruise control** If the cruise control doesn't stay engaged, or drops out of cruise, the brake switch can usually be adjusted, but if it cannot, it will be replaced under normal warranty. (1992-95)

• **Transmission slippage** Any car with a model 440-T4 automatic transmission may shift late or not upshift at all. The problem is a stuck throttle valve inside the transmission. It may be overlooked during rebuilding since the valve appears fine because it is hydraulic pressure, not a physical binding, that makes it stick. The problem is fixed by enlarging the hydraulic fluid balance hole by 0.010 inch. (All years)

• **Steering noise** The upper bearing mount in the steering column can get loose and cause a snapping or clicking that can be both heard and felt, requiring a new bearing spring and turn signal cancel cam, which the manufacturer will warranty. (1994-95)

RECALL HISTORY

1992 Parking brake lever assembly may release one or more teeth when applied, so parking brake might not hold the car. **1992-93** Transmission cooler line in cars with certain powertrains sold in specified states can separate at low temperature. **1995** Driver-side headlamp lens has incorrect aim pad number. **1996** "Key in the Ignition" warning chime, driver seatbelt-unbuckled warning, and other functions may fail to operate properly. **1996-97** Backfire can break upper intake manifold, resulting in no-start condition and possible fire. **1997** Seatbelt might not latch properly.

1991-96 BUICK PARK AVENUE

1991 Buick Park Avenue

FOR Air bags (later models) • Anti-lock brakes • Acceleration • Transmission performance • Passenger and cargo room

AGAINST Fuel economy • Steering/handling (base suspension) • Climate controls (early models)

EVALUATION Although the initial engine in this heavyweight sounds harsh at full throttle, the sedan is fairly brisk and smooth, as the V-6 responds quickly. Engine flaws are more noticeable because the transmission shifts so beautifully—and doesn't slip repeatedly into and out of overdrive like so many 4-speed automatics. The Ultra edition's supercharger does its job well, with a noticeable increase in passing ability. Step on the gas and you get a spirited, satisfying response—but in an understated manner with no hint of raucousness. Adding 35 horsepower to the base engine in 1994 gave it ample power for most situations. Neither engine is particularly economical, but they could be worse. A base Park Avenue registered an average of 21.4 mpg in a long trial. Mileage around town, however, was in the 15-18 mpg neighborhood. An Ultra averaged 19.7 mpg, and the supercharged engine demands premium fuel.

The Park Avenue's ride is comfortable, even cushy, with a soft feel from the base suspension. The car gets bouncy and floaty over wavy surfaces, and leans heavily in turns, which yield plenty of tire howling. The automatic ride control introduced in '93 reduces the floating sensation. Expect some firmness with the Gran Touring option, which got wide tires for better grip and handling, with only slight sacrifice in ride comfort. Steering in both the base and Ultra editions is too light, and doesn't center well after turns.

BUICK

Four adults sit comfortably in pillowy seats, with generous head and leg room all around. Even six can ride without undue squeezing, helped by space under front seats for rear occupants' feet. Wide doors permit easy entry/exit. Automatic climate controls in the Ultra (optional on base model) are arranged in two rows of seven small buttons, mounted low and away on the dashboard, thus hard to reach. That situation improved in 1994. Park Avenue has sold well and is certainly worth a look. LeSabres offer many of the same features at a lower cost.

SPECIFICATIONS

	4-door sedan
Wheelbase, in.	110.8
Overall length, in.	205.9
Overall width, in.	74.1
Overall height, in.	55.1
Curb weight, lbs.	3536
Cargo volume, cu. ft.	20.3
Fuel capacity, gals.	18.0
Seating capacity	6
Front head room, in.	38.9
Max. front leg room, in.	42.7
Rear head room, in.	37.9
Min. rear leg room, in.	40.7

Powertrain layout: transverse front-engine/front-wheel drive

ENGINES	ohv V-6	ohv V-6	Supercharged ohv V-6
Size, liters/cu. in.	3.8/231	3.8/231	3.8/231
Horsepower	170	205	205-240
Torque (lbs./ft.)	200-225	230	260-280
EPA city/highway mpg			
4-speed OD automatic	18/27	19/29	18/27
Consumer Guide™ observed MPG			
4-speed OD automatic	21.4		19.7

Built in USA.

RETAIL PRICES	GOOD	AVERAGE	POOR
1991 Park Avenue	$5,500-6,300	$4,800-5,500	$2,800-3,400
1991 Park Avenue Ultra	6,500-7,500	5,800-6,700	3,700-4,500
1992 Park Avenue	6,800-7,600	6,000-6,800	3,800-4,500
1992 Park Auenue Ultra	8,000-9,000	7,000-8,000	4,500-5,200
1993 Park Avenue	8,400-9,400	7,500-8,500	5,000-5,800
1993 Park Avenue Ultra	9,800-11,000	8,800-10,000	6,000-7,000
1994 Park Avenue	10,500-11,500	9,500-10,500	6,500-7,500
1994 Park Avenue Ultra	12,000-13,200	10,800-12,000	7,500-8,500

	GOOD	AVERAGE	POOR
1995 Park Avenue	12,800-14,000	11,500-12,500	8,200-9,200
1995 Park Avenue Ultra	14,500-16,000	13,000-14,500	9,000-10,200
1996 Park Avenue	15,500-16,800	14,000-15,300	10,000-11,000
1996 Park Avenue Ultra	17,500-19,000	16,000-17,500	11,500-12,500

AVERAGE REPLACEMENT COSTS

A/C Compressor $725
Alternator 395
Radiator 445
Timing Chain or Belt 230
Automatic Transmission or
   Transaxle......................1,270

Clutch, Pressure Plate,
   Bearing.........................1,010
Constant Velocity Joints.....810
Brakes.................................215
Shocks and/or Struts 955
Exhaust System.................610

TROUBLE SPOTS

• **Oil consumption and engine knock** Models with the 3800 (3.8L) engine are prone to excessive oil consumption often accompanied by spark knock (pinging) during normal driving conditions due to failure of the valve stem seals. (1993-95)

• **Engine knock** Bearing knock was common on many 3800 (3.8L) engines due to too much clearance on the number one main bearing, requiring it to be replaced with a 0.001-inch undersize bearing. (1992-94)

• **Cruise control** If the cruise control doesn't stay engaged or drops out of cruise, the brake switch can usually be adjusted, but if it cannot, it will be replaced under normal warranty. (1991-95)

• **Steering noise** The upper bearing mount in the steering column can get loose and cause a snapping or clicking that can be both heard and felt requiring, a new bearing spring and turn signal cancel cam, which the manufacturer will warranty. (1994-96)

• **Transaxle leak** The right front axle seal at the automatic transaxle is prone to leak and GM issued a revised seal to correct the problem. It is supposed to be installed whenever a car is in for transmission or axle shaft service of any sort. (1992-94)

• **Engine noise** What sounds like a rattling noise from the engine that lasts less than a minute when the car is started after sitting overnight is often caused by automatic transmission pump starvation or cavitation, or a sticking pressure regulator valve. According to GM, no damage occurs and it does not have a fix for the problem. (1991-95)

• **Cruise control** Cruise control doesn't stay engaged, or drops out of cruise. (1991-95)

• **Transmission slippage** The 4T60E transmission may drop out of

BUICK

drive (neutral condition) while cruising, shift erratically, have no third or fourth gear, or no second and third gear because of a bad ground connection for the shift solenoids. Poor grounds also allow wrong gear starts. Many transmissions have been mistakenly rebuilt, which does not correct the problem. (1991-94)

RECALL HISTORY

1991 Parking brake lever assembly may release one or more teeth when applied, reducing cable load to rear brakes; parking brake might not hold the vehicle, allowing it to roll. **1992-93** Transmission cooler line in cars with certain powertrains sold in specified states can separate at low temperature. **1995** Driver-side headlamp lens has incorrect aim pad number; if headlamps are re-aimed using those numbers, result would be out of specified range. **1996** Cars were assembled with one or more incorrect safety belt and/or buckle ends, so belt may not latch properly. **1996** "Key in the Ignition" warning chime, driver seatbelt-unbuckled warning, and other functions may not operate properly. **1996** Backfire can break upper intake manifold, resulting in possible fire.

1990-96 BUICK REGAL

1990 Buick Regal Gran Sport 2-door

FOR Air bags (1994-96) • Acceleration (3.8-liter V-6) • Passenger and cargo room • Anti-lock brakes (optional until '94) • Ride

AGAINST Fuel economy (3.8-liter V-6) • Seat comfort • Steering feel • Engine noise (early models) • Instruments/controls (early models) • Performance (early models)

EVALUATION Front seat room is generous, and the rear is adequate for 6-footers. Both body styles are roomy, but leg and head room are better in the sedan, though the lower cushion feels puny for long-distance comfort. Front shoulder belts in the sedan were anchored to door pillars, so belts could ride on the neck of shorter passengers. Wide front pillars compromise visibility.

The initial Regal's lack of power was remedied by the arrival of the 3.8-liter engine in 1992. It gives the car sufficient oomph to accelerate smartly away from stoplights and pass safely. The early 3.1-liter, in contrast, sounds strained when a brisk getaway is called for, generating more noise than power. With the electronically-controlled automatic installed in 1993, shifts grew swifter and smoother. Gas mileage is better with the 3.1-liter. We've averaged better than 20 mpg. The 3.8-liter yielded no more than 17-18 mpg.

Analog instrumentation in early Regals is not the greatest and some instruments are blocked by the steering wheel. The optional electronic cluster has poorly designed graphics, and has to squeeze into the same tight space. Climate controls also are far to the right, but have big buttons. The new interior for 1995 cured many of these complaints.

Ride/handling aren't bad, even with the base suspension. It seems to strike a sensible compromise between soft ride and capable handling, though slanting toward the former. Steering is on the light side, and the car leans heavily in turns. The firmer Gran Sport suspension provides taut handling and a well-controlled ride, but gets a bit harsh when rolling through pavement irregularities. Anti-lock braking works well, but takes high pedal pressure for a quick stop.

A Regal might not be much to get excited about, but it's not a bad choice when prices are tempting. About three-fourths of Regals got the 3.8-liter V-6, and that's the one that approaches Ford Taurus in appeal.

NHTSA CRASH TEST RESULTS
1994 Buick Regal   4-DOOR SEDAN

Driver   ☆☆☆☆
Passenger   ☆

(The National Highway Traffic Safety Administration tests a vehicle's crashworthiness in front and side collisions. Their ratings suggest the chance of serious injury: ☆☆☆☆☆—10% or less; ☆☆☆☆—10-20% or less; ☆☆☆—20-30% or less; ☆☆—35-45% or less; ☆—More than 45%.)

SPECIFICATIONS	2-door coupe	4-door sedan
Wheelbase, in.	107.5	107.5
Overall length, in.	193.9	193.7
Overall width, in.	72.5	72.5
Overall height, in.	53.0	54.5

BUICK

	2-door coupe	4-door sedan
Curb weight, lbs.	3232	3335
Cargo volume, cu. ft.	15.6	15.9
Fuel capacity, gals.	16.5	16.5
Seating capacity	6	6
Front head room, in.	37.6	38.6
Max. front leg room, in.	42.3	42.4
Rear head room, in.	37.0	37.8
Min. rear leg room, in.	34.8	36.2

Powertrain layout: transverse front-engine/front-wheel drive

ENGINES

	ohv V-6	ohv V-6
Size, liters/cu. in.	3.1/191	3.8/231
Horsepower	135-160	170-205
Torque (lbs./ft.)	180-185	220-230

EPA city/highway mpg
4-speed OD automatic 20/29   19/30

Consumer Guide™ observed MPG
4-speed OD automatic 20.5   17.3

Built in Canada.

RETAIL PRICES

	GOOD	AVERAGE	POOR
1990 Regal	$3,200-3,900	$2,500-3,200	$1,400-2,000
1991 Regal	3,800-4,600	3,100-3,900	1,800-2,500
1992 Regal	4,500-5,800	3,700-5,000	2,300-3,400
1993 Regal	5,500-7,200	4,700-6,300	3,000-4,300
1994 Regal	6,900-8,600	6,100-7,700	4,200-5,500
1995 Regal	8,500-10,500	7,600-9,500	5,500-7,000
1996 Regal	9,800-11,800	8,800-10,800	6,400-8,200

AVERAGE REPLACEMENT COSTS

A/C Compressor $555	Constant Velocity Joints.....470
Alternator 215	Brakes...................................200
Radiator 340	Shocks and/or Struts 1,856
Timing Chain or Belt 170	Exhaust System.................470
Automatic Transmission or Transaxle......................1,075	

TROUBLE SPOTS

• **Oil consumption** Models with the 3800 (3.8L) engine are prone to excessive oil consumption often accompanied by spark knock (pinging) during normal driving conditions due to failure of the valve stem seals. (1993-95)

• **Engine noise** Bearing knock was common on many 3800 (3.8L) engines due to too much clearance on the number one main bearing, requiring it to be replaced with a 0.001-inch undersize bearing. (1992-94)

• **Engine noise** A tick or rattle when the engine is started cold may be due to too much wrist pin-to-piston clearance. New piston and pin sets will be replaced under warranty if the customer complains of the noise. (1994-95)

• **Engine noise** What sounds like a rattling noise from the engine that lasts less than a minute when the car is started after sitting overnight is often caused by automatic transmission pump starvation or cavitation, or a sticking pressure regulator valve. According to GM, no damage occurs and it does not have a fix for the problem. (1991-95)

• **Transaxle leak** The right front axle seal at the automatic transaxle is prone to leak and GM issued a revised seal to correct the problem. It is supposed to be installed whenever a car is in for transmission or axle shaft service of any sort. (1992-94)

• **Valve cover leaks** The plastic valve covers on the 3.1L engine were prone to leaks and should be replaced with redesigned aluminum valve covers. (GM no longer stocks the plastic ones.) (1994-95)

• **Steering noise** The upper bearing mount in the steering column can get loose and cause a snapping or clicking that can be both heard and felt. It requires a new bearing spring and turn signal cancel cam, which the manufacturer will warranty. (1994-96)

• **Transmission slippage** The 4T60E transmission may drop out of drive (neutral condition) while cruising, shift erratically, have no third or fourth gear, or no second and third gear because of a bad ground connection for the shift solenoids. Poor grounds also allow wrong gear starts. Many transmissions have been mistakenly rebuilt, which does not correct the problem. (1991-94)

• **Poor transmission shift** Any car with a model 440-T4 automatic transmission may shift late or not upshift at all. The problem is a stuck throttle valve inside the transmission. It may be overlooked during rebuilding since the valve appears fine because it is hydraulic pressure, not a physical binding, that makes it stick. The problem is fixed by enlarging the hydraulic fluid balance hole by 0.010 inch. (1990-92)

RECALL HISTORY

1990 Front shoulder belt may not properly restrain passenger in an accident. **1990** Brake lights may not illuminate, or will not stay lit all the time when brakes are applied, due to faulty switch. **1990 with Kelsey-Hayes steel wheels** Cracks may develop in wheel mounting surface; if severe, wheel could separate from car. **1990-91** Steering shaft could separate from steering gear. **1991** Front door shoulder belt guide loops may be cracked. **1992** Reverse servo apply pin of 4-speed automatic transmission may bind, which could cause loss or slipping of reverse, poor performance, or transmission to remain in reverse while indicator shows neutral. **1993** Manual recliner mechanisms on some front seats will not latch under certain conditions, causing seatback to recline without prior warning. **1993-95** Replace clear front side marker bulbs with amber. **1994-95** Strained wire can cause intermittent or nonexistent wiper/washer operation. **1994-95** Rear brake hoses can contact suspension components and wear through, resulting in loss of brake fluid. **1995** Seatbelt anchor can fracture during crash. **1995** On a few cars, steering-column support bolts could vibrate, loosen, or fall out. **1996** Left front brake line can contact transaxle mounting bracket or bolt, causing line to wear through, resulting in loss of fluid and eventual loss of half the brake system. **1996 with 3.8-liter V-6** Backfire can break upper intake manifold, resulting in possible fire.

1995-98 BUICK RIVIERA

1995 Buick Riviera

FOR   Air bags, dual • Anti-lock brakes • Acceleration • Ride • Steering/handling

AGAINST   Instruments/controls • Rear visibility • Entry/exit • Fuel economy (supercharged)

EVALUATION   Acceleration, handling, and ride quality are vastly better than in the old Riviera. In performance as well as refinement, this rendition rivals premium coupes that cost much more. Even at highway speeds, noise, vibration, and harshness of any sort are nearly absent.

We clocked a supercharged '95 model at a brisk 7.9 seconds to 60 mph. That kind of action sends the Riviera into the same league as some V-8 competitors. As for economy, we averaged 17.7 mpg in a supercharged Riviera, commuting through urban areas about two thirds of the time. The normally-aspirated engine offers acceleration that is more than adequate, though less lively.

Despite its rather abundant size, this Riviera feels balanced and nimble in turns, exhibiting body lean and good grip onto the pavement. Buick's suspension teams with the long wheelbase to provide a comfortable ride, even over bumps and broken pavement.

Though a front bench is standard, Riviera works best as a 4-seater. An occasional passenger might occupy the middle rear seat. Leg room is sufficient for four 6-footers to stretch out. Head room is generous in front but only adequate in back. Long, heavy doors are cumbersome in tight parking spaces.

One big weak spot is the dashboard, which lags in practical considerations. Not only are the speedometer and tachometer too far apart, but the steering wheel blocks the headlamp and cruise control switches. Visibility is generally good, but a high rear parcel shelf and thick rear roof pillars interfere with the driver's view aft and over the shoulders.

Buick aims the Riviera against such 2-door contenders as the Acura Legend Coupe, Cadillac Eldorado, Lincoln Mark VIII, and Mercedes E320. If the styling appeals, it's worth a serious test drive. If not, you might prefer to shop elsewhere.

SPECIFICATIONS

	2-door coupe
Wheelbase, in.	113.8
Overall length, in.	207.2
Overall width, in.	75.0
Overall height, in.	55.2
Curb weight, lbs.	3690
Cargo volume, cu. ft.	17.4
Fuel capacity, gals.	20.0
Seating capacity	5/6
Front head room, in.	38.2
Max. front leg room, in.	42.6
Rear head room, in.	36.2
Min. rear leg room, in.	37.3

Powertrain layout: transverse front-engine/front-wheel drive

ENGINES

	ohv V-6	Supercharged ohv V-6
Size, liters/cu. in.	3.8/231	3.8/231

	ohv V-6	Supercharged ohv V-6
Horsepower	205	225-240
Torque (lbs./ft.)	230	275-280
EPA city/highway mpg		
4-speed OD automatic	19/28	18/27
Consumer Guide™ observed MPG		
4-speed OD automatic		17.7

Built in USA.

RETAIL PRICES

	GOOD	AVERAGE	POOR
1995 Riviera	$13,000-14,200	$11,800-13,000	$9,000-10,000
1995 Supercharged	13,800-15,200	12,500-13,800	9,800-11,000
1996 Riviera	15,500-17,000	14,000-15,500	11,200-12,500
1996 Supercharged	16,500-18,000	15,000-16,500	12,000-13,500
1997 Riviera	18,500-20,500	16,800-18,500	13,500-14,500
1997 Supercharged	19,500-21,500	17,500-19,500	14,000-15,500
1998 Riviera	24,000-26,500	22,000-24,500	18,500-21,000

AVERAGE REPLACEMENT COSTS

A/C Compressor $685
Alternator 340
Radiator 480
Timing Chain or Belt 360
Automatic Transmission or

Transaxle 970
Brakes................................265
Shocks and/or Struts 795
Exhaust System.................235

TROUBLE SPOTS

• **Doors** The power door locks may not operate (although the doors can be locked manually) due to a rubber bumper falling off of the actuator arm. (1995-96) Also, the locks may malfunction, and the door locks fuse may blow due to a short inside the door. (1995)

• **Starter** The starter may keep running after the engine starts or the key is turned off due to a short in the wiring. (1995)

• **Suspension noise** A thumping or clunking sound from the rear is likely unless the original shock mounts are replaced with redesigned ones. (1995-96)

• **Traction control indicator light** The ABS or traction control system could quit working due to voltage surges from the electric radiator fan blowing out the ABS control module. (1995)

• **Climate control** The heater output on the driver's side may be inadequate because the sound insulation material may be protruding into the heater duct. (1995-96)

• **Engine misfire** The idle may be rough when restarting a warm engine (3088 supercharged only) and is fixed by replacing the fuel pressure regulator and computer MEM-CAL. (1995)

RECALL HISTORY

1996 "Key in the Ignition" chime, driver seatbelt-unbuckled warning and other functions may fail to operate properly. **1996** Backfire during engine startup can cause breakage of upper intake manifold, resulting in non-start condition and possible fire.

1990-93 CADILLAC DeVILLE/ FLEETWOOD

1992 Cadillac Coupe DeVille 2-door

FOR Acceleration • Quietness • Air bags • Anti-lock brakes • Passenger and cargo room • Drivability • Ride • Traction control

AGAINST Fuel economy • Instruments/controls (early models) • Rear visibility

EVALUATION Cadillac's 4.5-liter V-8 is impressive, moving these luxury heavyweights with authority. You get ample power for brisk takeoffs from stoplights, as well as for safe highway passing. Cadillac estimated a 0-60 mph acceleration time of 9.5 seconds—not bad at all for a big sedan. The 4-speed automatic transmission stays out of overdrive until the car reaches a cruising speed past 40 mph, and downshifts rapidly for passing/merging.

The 4.9-liter V-8 installed in '91 models turned these cars into some of the most powerful front-drive sedans around. Even if slightly rough at idle, the 4.9 is a fine V-8, delivering ample power for quick takeoffs and easy passing. A slicker automatic now complemented the engine with prompt, smooth gear changes. No economy improvement occurred, so expect 25 mpg on the highway but no more than 15 mpg or so around town. We got only 11.3 mpg in the city. Premium fuel is required.

Computer Command Ride improves both ride and handling. At speeds past 60 mph, CCR-equipped cars offer a stable, smooth ride with almost none of the bounding and floating of previous models. But CCR feels too soft between 40 and 60 mph, so you get a lot of bobbing up and down over wavy surfaces. With the regular suspension, in particular, handling and roadholding favor conservative driving. Those Cadillacs bounce and float too much at intermediate speeds.

Interior space is bountiful, cargo room ample. Even back-seat occupants can stretch out, and the spacious trunk has a flat, uncluttered floor. Occupants enjoy easy-chair softness. Doors are tall and wide, so there's easy entry to the huge cabin. Chunky styling and non-flush glass contribute to noticeable wind noise around roof pillars; otherwise, you cruise in near silence. Thick rear pillars and a narrow back window limit visibility.

If you're looking for a strong, refined engine plus appealing comfort and a host of convenience features in a full-size front-drive automobile, Cadillac might have just what you seek.

SPECIFICATIONS

	2-door coupe	4-door sedan
Wheelbase, in.	110.8	113.7
Overall length, in.	203.3	206.3
Overall width, in.	73.4	73.4
Overall height, in.	54.8	55.1
Curb weight, lbs.	3519	3605
Cargo volume, cu. ft.	18.1	18.4
Fuel capacity, gals.	18.0	18.0
Seating capacity	6	6
Front head room, in.	39.2	39.3
Max. front leg room, in.	42.0	42.0
Rear head room, in.	37.9	38.1
Min. rear leg room, in.	40.3	43.6

Powertrain layout: transverse front-engine/front-wheel drive

ENGINES

	ohv V-8	ohv V-8
Size, liters/cu. in.	4.5/273	4.9/300
Horsepower	180	200
Torque (lbs./ft.)	245	275

EPA city/highway mpg

4-speed OD automatic	16/25	16/25

Consumer Guide™ observed MPG

4-speed OD automatic	16.1	

Built in USA.

RETAIL PRICES	GOOD	AVERAGE	POOR
1990 DeVille	$4,800-5,800	$4,000-5,000	$2,400-3,200
1990 Fleetwood	5,400-6,400	4,600-5,400	2,800-3,400
1991 DeVille	6,000-7,300	5,000-6,300	3,200-4,200
1991 Fleetwood	6,700-8,200	5,700-7,200	3,900-5,000
1992 DeVille	7,200-8,700	6,200-7,700	4,200-5,500
1992 Fleetwood	8,200-10,200	7,200-9,200	5,000-6,400
1993 DeVille	9,000-11,000	8,000-10,000	5,500-7,000

AVERAGE REPLACEMENT COSTS

A/C Compressor $470
Alternator 270
Radiator 417
Timing Chain or Belt 250
Automatic Transmission or
    Transaxle......................1,010

Constant Velocity Joints.....875
Brakes.................................200
Shocks and/or Struts 745
Exhaust System.................429

TROUBLE SPOTS

• **Transmission slippage** The 4T60E transmission may drop out of drive (neutral condition) while cruising, shift erratically, have no third or fourth gear, or no second and third gear because of a bad ground connection for the shift solenoids. Poor grounds also allow wrong gear starts. Many transmissions have been mistakenly rebuilt, which does not correct the problem. (1991-94)

• **Transaxle leak** The right front axle seal at the automatic transaxle is prone to leak and GM issued a revised seal to correct the problem. It is supposed to be installed whenever a car is in for transmission or axle shaft service of any sort. (1992-94)

• **Engine noise** What sounds like a rattling noise from the engine that lasts less than a minute when the car is started after sitting overnight is often caused by automatic transmission pump starvation or cavitation, or a sticking pressure regulator valve. According to GM, no damage occurs and it does not have a fix for the problem. (1991-93)

• **Transmission slippage** Any car with a model 440-T4 automatic transmission may shift late or not upshift at all. The problem is a stuck throttle valve inside the transmission. It may be overlooked during rebuilding since the valve appears fine because it is hydraulic pressure, not a physical binding, that makes it stick. The problem is fixed by enlarging the hydraulic fluid balance hole by 0.010 inch. (1990-92)

• **Engine noise** The exhaust valves on the 5.7L engine may not get enough lubrication causing a variety of noises that sound like lifter tick, rod knock or a "whoop-whoop" noise like a helicopter. Usually, the same engine consumes excess oil because the valve guide seals on the exhaust valves are bad. (1994-96)

RECALL HISTORY

1991-93 Transaxle oil cooler hose can pull out of coupling, causing oil leak that could result in fire.

1994-98 CADILLAC DEVILLE/ CONCOURS

1994 Cadillac Sedan DeVille Concours

FOR Air bags • Anti-lock brakes • Acceleration • Passenger and cargo room • Interior noise levels • Traction control • Standard side air bags (1997 models)

AGAINST Fuel economy • Radio controls • Climate control • Rear visibility

EVALUATION Concours is the performance prince, but even a base DeVille boasts impressive acceleration, with brisk passing response. Power is plentiful with the 4.9-liter base engine—and even better with the later Northstar. With any of the Northstar V-8s under the hood, you can expect surprisingly sizzling action, which belies the car's heft. A Concours, with the most potent V-8 ready and waiting, actually rivals some sports sedans when pushing the pedal to the floor. Even better, Cadillac's 4-speed overdrive automatic transmission shifts with buttery smoothness.

Fuel economy is poor. Only on the highway did we average better than 20 mpg. Overall, a Concours averaged just 15.8 mpg in a long-term trial. Worse yet, all engines demand premium gasoline.

Because of a stiffer structure and better engine mounts, these two ride much more quietly than in previous years, with less noise and vibration. Both suspensions do a good job of isolating the cabin and keeping bouncing to a minimum. The Road Sensing Suspension does a commendable job of maintaining a stable, comfortable ride and minimizing body lean in turns. Agile may not be an appropriate word to describe either DeVille, but these sizable sedans handle reasonably well for cars in their category. Road and wind noise are minimal, though not necessarily nonexistent. Brakes are strong and fade-free. Steering is firm and responsive, but lacks true road feel and precision.

Inside, you get ample six-passenger seating in a spacious cabin, plus dual air bags. Basic dashboard design is borrowed from the Seville, so climate controls are just to the right of the steering wheel, where they're hard to see and reach. The trunk opens at bumper level and has a wide, flat floor that can hold loads of luggage.

Don't judge the latest DeVille and Concours just by their conservative styling, which continues to appeal mainly to older drivers. Both Cadillacs offer tempting performance and roomy accommodations, and represent good value for the money.

NHTSA CRASH TEST RESULTS
1996 Cadillac DeVille   4-DOOR SEDAN

Driver	☆☆☆
Passenger	☆

(The National Highway Traffic Safety Administration tests a vehicle's crashworthiness in front and side collisions. Their ratings suggest the chance of serious injury: ☆☆☆☆☆—10% or less; ☆☆☆☆—10-20% or less; ☆☆☆—20-30% or less; ☆☆—35-45% or less; ☆—More than 45%.)

SPECIFICATIONS

	4-door sedan
Wheelbase, in.	113.8
Overall length, in.	209.7
Overall width, in.	76.6
Overall height, in.	56.3
Curb weight, lbs.	3959
Cargo volume, cu. ft.	20.0
Fuel capacity, gals.	20.0
Seating capacity	6
Front head room, in.	38.5
Max. front leg room, in.	42.6
Rear head room, in.	38.4
Min. rear leg room, in.	43.3

BUICK

Powertrain layout: transverse front-engine/front-wheel drive

ENGINES

	dohc V-8	dohc V-8	ohv V-8
Size, liters/cu. in.	4.6/279	4.6/279	4.9/300
Horsepower	270-275	300	200
Torque (lbs./ft.)	300	295	275
EPA city/highway mpg			
4-speed OD automatic	17/26	17/26	16/26
Consumer Guide™ observed MPG			
4-speed OD automatic	15.8	17.2	

Built in USA.

RETAIL PRICES

	GOOD	AVERAGE	POOR
1994 DeVille	$13,000-14,500	$11,500-12,500	$8,500-9,500
1994 Concours	14,500-16,000	13,000-14,500	9,500-10,800
1995 DeVille	16,000-17,500	14,500-16,000	11,000-12,500
1995 Concours	17,800-19,500	16,000-17,500	12,000-13,500
1996 DeVille	19,000-21,000	17,000-19,000	13,000-15,000
1996 Concours	21,000-23,000	19,000-21,000	14,500-16,500
1997 DeVille	22,500-25,000	20,500-22,500	16,000-18,000
1997 Concours	25,000-27,500	22,500-25,000	17,500-19,500
1998 DeVille	26,500-30,000	24,000-27,500	20,000-23,000
1998 Concours	30,000-33,000	27,000-30,000	22,500-25,000

AVERAGE REPLACEMENT COSTS

A/C Compressor	$475	Transaxle	1,160
Alternator	350	Constant Velocity Joints	700
Radiator	490	Brakes	210
Timing Chain or Belt	720	Exhaust System	1,000
Automatic Transmission or			

TROUBLE SPOTS

• **Steering noise** The upper bearing mount in the steering column can get loose and cause a snapping or clicking that can be both heard and felt, requiring a new bearing spring and turn signal cancel cam, which the manufacturer will warranty. (1994-96)

• **Engine noise** What sounds like a rattling noise from the engine that lasts less than a minute when the car is started after sitting overnight is often caused by automatic transmission pump starvation or cavitation, or a sticking pressure regulator valve. According to GM, no damage occurs and it does not have a fix for the problem. (1994-95)

RECALL HISTORY

1996 Secondary hood latch may be improperly adjusted; if primary latch also is not engaged, hood could open unexpectedly. **1997** Brake/traction control module can cause anti-lock brake system to cycle in non-ABS braking; could increase stopping distance. **1998** Hood hinge pivot bolts can break; could cause either the corner of the hood near the windshield to rise, or one side of hood to be unstable when opened. **1998** Misrouted canister purge evaporative emissions harness could interfere with cruise control and throttle linkage, preventing return to close throttle position.

1992-98 CADILLAC ELDORADO

✓ BEST BUY

1993 Cadillac Eldorado Sport Coupe

FOR Standard side air bags (1997 models) • Acceleration • Steering/handling • Standard anti-lock brakes • Traction control (later models)

AGAINST Fuel economy • Rear visibility • Climate controls (early models)

EVALUATION Despite the car's weight, Eldo acceleration is brisk with the original 4.9-liter engine. Dropping in one of the Northstar engines turns performance from brisk to nearly blistering—especially in Touring Coupe form. Cadillac claimed that both Northstar engines yielded 0-60 mph acceleration of 7.5 seconds, or nearly two seconds quicker than the base V-8. No engine is economical. We averaged 16 mpg in a Touring Coupe and 18 mpg in a Northstar-engined base coupe.

Computer Command Ride, which adjusts according to speed, delivers a secure road feel. Unlike prior Eldorados, this one does not bob or wallow over dips and around corners. Steering is precise, and the car is stable at speed and in curves. A solid structure completes this excellent package, giving the sizable coupe a unified feel, worthy of its price and status. With a firmer suspension and new touring tires, the Touring Coupe is quieter and more supple than before.

Rear space is okay—generous for a coupe—but the rear seatback is too reclined for total comfort. Huge rear pillars impair the over-the-shoulder view. The large trunk has a usable shape. Buttons for heat and air conditioning are hidden behind the steering wheel. That flaw was corrected on 1996 Touring Coupes, but base coupes kept the former layout. Front bucket seats lack some lumbar bolstering, but are otherwise supportive.

In any guise, these are Cadillac's best premium coupes in a long while—excellent, expertly assembled, domestically built rivals to such imports as the Lexus SC 300/400, and competitive with Lincoln's Mark VIII.

SPECIFICATIONS

	2-door coupe
Wheelbase, in.	108.0
Overall length, in.	200.2
Overall width, in.	75.5
Overall height, in.	54.0
Curb weight, lbs.	3774
Cargo volume, cu. ft.	15.3
Fuel capacity, gals.	20.0
Seating capacity	5
Front head room, in.	37.4
Max. front leg room, in.	42.6
Rear head room, in.	38.3
Min. rear leg room, in.	36.0

Powertrain layout: transverse front-engine/front-wheel drive

ENGINES

	dohc V-8	dohc V-8	ohv V-8
Size, liters/cu. in.	4.6/279	4.6/279	4.9/300
Horsepower	270-275	295-300	200
Torque (lbs./ft.)	300	290-295	275
EPA city/highway mpg			
4-speed OD automatic	17/26	17/26	16/25
Consumer Guide™ observed MPG			
4-speed OD automatic	18.0	16.0	

Built in USA.

RETAIL PRICES

	GOOD	AVERAGE	POOR
1992 Eldorado	$9,000-10,000	$7,700-8,700	$5,200-6,200
1992 Touring Coupe	9,500-10,500	8,200-9,200	5,600-6,500
1993 Eldorado	11,500-12,700	10,000-11,200	7,500-8,500

	GOOD	AVERAGE	POOR
1993 Touring Coupe	12,000-13,200	10,500-12,700	8,000-9,000
1994 Eldorado	14,400-15,500	12,900-14,000	10,000-11,000
1994 Touring Coupe	15,000-16,200	13,500-14,500	10,500-11,500
1995 Eldorado	17,500-19,000	16,000-17,500	13,000-14,000
1995 Touring Coupe	18,500-20,000	17,000-18,000	13,500-14,500
1996 Eldorado	21,500-23,000	20,000-21,500	16,500-18,000
1996 Touring Coupe	22,700-24,500	21,000-22,500	17,500-19,000
1997 Eldorado	26,000-27,500	23,500-25,000	19,500-21,000
1997 Touring Coupe	27,500-29,500	25,000-26,500	21,000-22,500
1998 Eldorado	30,500-32,500	27,500-29,500	22,500-24,500
1998 Touring Coupe	32,500-34,500	29,500-31,500	24,500-26,500

AVERAGE REPLACEMENT COSTS

A/C Compressor $500
Alternator 350
Timing Chain or Belt 820
Automatic Transmission or
   Transaxle......................1,160

Constant Velocity Joints.....800
Brakes.................................210
Shocks and/or Struts 1,225
Exhaust System..............1,135

TROUBLE SPOTS

• **Steering noise** The upper bearing mount in the steering column can get loose and cause a snapping or clicking that can be both heard and felt requiring a new bearing spring and turn signal cancel cam, which the manufacturer will warranty. (1994-96)

• **Transmission slippage** The 4T60E transmission may drop out of drive (neutral condition) while cruising, shift erratically, have no third or fourth gear, or no second and third gear because of a bad ground connection for the shift solenoids. Poor grounds also allow wrong gear starts. Many transmissions have been mistakenly rebuilt, which does not correct the problem. (1992-93)

• **Transaxle leak** The right front axle seal at the automatic transaxle is prone to leak and GM issued a revised seal to correct the problem. It is supposed to be installed whenever a car is in for transmission or axle shaft service of any sort. (1992-93)

• **Transmission slippage** Any car with a model 440-T4 automatic transmission may shift late or not upshift at all. The problem is a stuck throttle valve inside the transmission. It may be overlooked during rebuilding since the valve appears fine because it is hydraulic pressure, not a physical binding, that makes it stick. The problem is fixed by enlarging the hydraulic fluid balance hole by 0.010 inch. (1992)

• **Engine noise** What sounds like a rattling noise from the engine that lasts less than a minute when the car is started after sitting overnight is often caused by automatic transmission pump starvation or cavitation, or

CADILLAC

a sticking pressure regulator valve. According to GM, no damage occurs and it does not have a fix for the problem. (1992-93)

RECALL HISTORY

1992 Intermediate shaft to steering rack lower-coupling pinch bolt may be missing on some cars; disengagement produces loss of steering control. **1993 with 4.6-liter engine** Fuel feed and return lines to fuel injection system could work loose, causing fuel leakage in engine compartment that could result in fire. **1993-94 with 4.6-liter V-8** If air conditioner compressor clutch assembly contacts auxiliary engine oil cooler hose, that hose may wear through, allowing leakage that could result in fire. **1994** Throttle cable can disengage and interfere with cam mechanism. **1996** Analog instrument cluster on some cars could have internal short circuit disrupting Pass-Key system, causing failure of gauges and most tell-tale indicators, and possible no-start condition; panel could go black while driving. **1997** Brake/traction control module can cause anti-lock system to cycle in non-ABS braking; could increase stopping distance. **1998** Misrouted canister purge evaporative emissions harness could interfere with cruise control and throttle linkage, preventing return to closed throttle position.

1993-96 CADILLAC FLEETWOOD

1993 Cadillac Fleetwood

FOR Air bags • Anti-lock brakes • Acceleration • Passenger and cargo room • Trailer towing capability • Interior noise levels

AGAINST Fuel economy • Size and weight • Rear visibility

EVALUATION "Fleet" is definitely the word for the 1994-96 Fleetwood, with its Corvette-derived engine. With that power-plant on tap, you get swift takeoffs, as well as vigorous passing—which takes only a little more pressure on the gas pedal. Cadillac claimed that 0-60 mph acceleration took just 8.5 seconds—two seconds faster than the 1993 model. Fuel economy is no bargain; we averaged only 14.8 mpg.

Fleetwood suspensions are firmer than those in a Caprice or Roadmaster, so you don't get the pillowy-soft ride that characterized big Cadillacs of the more distant past. Sure, it filters out fewer bumps, but the massive sedan also wallows less and has better control in turns than its GM siblings. Even so, body lean is excessive and the undeniably soft suspension allows lots of bouncing on wavy roads. Steering is firmer, too, for improved road feel. Traction control is a definite "plus." When actuated, it pushes back gently on the gas pedal, and an indicator light illuminates.

Inside, three can sit across, front or rear, but those in the middle won't have much leg room. Adults can stretch their legs at outboard positions. Front seats are "split-frame" design, in which the lower cushion adjusts independently of the backrest. Base-model seat cushions seem firmer and no less comfortable than the multi-adjustable seats in the costlier Brougham. Back seats are nothing short of cavernous, but the cushion lacks thigh support. Drivers face an uncluttered dashboard layout. A huge trunk holds several suitcases.

If you tow a trailer and travel cross-country, a Fleetwood just might be your best practical choice.

SPECIFICATIONS

	4-door sedan
Wheelbase, in.	121.5
Overall length, in.	225.0
Overall width, in.	78.0
Overall height, in.	57.1
Curb weight, lbs.	4477
Cargo volume, cu. ft.	21.1
Fuel capacity, gals.	23.0
Seating capacity	6
Front head room, in.	38.7
Max. front leg room, in.	42.5
Rear head room, in.	39.1
Min. rear leg room, in.	43.9

Powertrain layout: longitudinal front-engine/rear-wheel drive

ENGINES

	ohv V-8	ohv V-8
Size, liters/cu. in.	5.7/350	5.7/350
Horsepower	185	260
Torque (lbs./ft.)	300	330-335

CADILLAC

EPA city/highway mpg
4-speed OD automatic..................................... 16/25   17/26

Consumer Guide™ observed MPG
4-speed OD automatic..   14.8

Built in USA.

RETAIL PRICES	GOOD	AVERAGE	POOR
1993 Fleetwood	$10,000-11,500	$9,000-10,200	$6,000-7,200
1994 Fleetwood	12,500-14,000	11,300-12,500	8,000-9,000
1995 Fleetwood	16,000-17,500	14,500-16,000	11,000-12,500
1996 Fleetwood	20,500-22,700	18,500-20,500	14,500-16,000

AVERAGE REPLACEMENT COSTS

A/C Compressor $485
Alternator 225
Radiator 409
Timing Chain or Belt 220
Automatic Transmission or

Transaxle 780
Universal Joints 270
Brakes................................235
Shocks and/or Struts 430
Exhaust System.................420

TROUBLE SPOTS

• **Steering noise** The upper bearing mount in the steering column can get loose and cause a snapping or clicking that can be both heard and felt requiring a new bearing spring and turn signal cancel cam, which the manufacturer will warranty. (1994-96)

• **Transmission slippage** Any car with a model 700-R4 automatic transmission may shift late or not upshift at all. The problem is a stuck throttle valve inside the transmission. It may be overlooked during rebuilding since the valve appears fine because it is hydraulic pressure, not a physical binding, that makes it stick. The problem is fixed by enlarging the hydraulic fluid balance hole by 0.010 inch. (1993)

RECALL HISTORY

1993 Passenger-side air bag in a few cars could experience an inflator ignition delay in an accident; delayed deployment could increase risk of injury. **1994** Oil cooler inlet hose may be too close to steering gear, causing chafing; could result in leakage and fire. **1994** On small number of cars, paint between wheel and brake rotor/drum can cause lug nut to loosen. **1994** Fuel tank strap fasteners can detach, eventually allowing tank to sag. **1994-95** At low temperatures, throttle return spring could fail. **1994-95** Lower ball joint on a few cars sent to Guam and Puerto Rico can separate. **1995** Improperly adjusted transmission linkage may permit shifting from "park" position with ignition key removed. **1995-96** Wheel lug nuts were not tightened to the proper specification. This could result in wheel loss.

1992-97 CADILLAC SEVILLE

✓ BEST BUY

1992 Cadillac Seville

FOR Air bags (later models) • Acceleration • Steering/handling • Passenger and cargo room • Standard anti-lock brakes and traction control (later models)

AGAINST Fuel economy • Rear visibility • Climate controls (early models) • Ride (STS)

EVALUATION More than prior Sevilles, the 1992-96 edition displays fine road manners and a rock-solid feel, thanks to a stiffened chassis. Road noise was reduced, and improved engine-mounting better isolated the V-8 from the passenger compartment. Despite the extra bulk, acceleration is brisk with the initial 4.9-liter engine, never lacking for strength whether in the city or on the highway. Shifts are almost imperceptible. The Northstar V-8 added for 1993 is smoother and faster yet, but limits its most impressive acceleration to engine speeds above 3500 rpm. That gives the STS terrific performance on the open road.

Speed-dependent Computer Command Ride adds to the secure feel of early Sevilles. Sure, the base-model ride is a bit soft at lower speeds (under 45 mph or so), but the bounce is nearly gone at highway velocities, and the sedan cruises with commendable stability and comfort. At low speeds, the 1993-up STS's Road Sensing Suspension floats less than the base setup. It's also more absorbent at higher speeds, and handles better on bumpy pavement. Steering is firm and precise, and the sedan remains stable through corners. Stiff tires give the later STS impressive handling, but a harsh, even jittery ride. Softer tires on the base (SLS) sedan transmit less impact and generate less noise. The '96 STS adopted softer tires, reducing the contrast between models.

CADILLAC

Head room is ample, front and rear. Adult knees aren't likely to press into the front seatback. Wide rear doors make entry/exit a snap, but thick roof pillars hamper over-the-shoulder visibility. Dashboards are well laid out, but climate-control buttons are hidden to the right of the steering wheel. That flaw was corrected in the 1996 STS, but the SLS kept the prior layout. The roomy trunk has a flat floor that's wide and stretches well forward. Its lid opens nearly from bumper height for easy loading.

Especially in STS trim, the Seville is Cadillac's best premium sedan in ages, scoring strongly against such imported rivals as the BMW 740iL, Lexus LS 400, and Infiniti Q45.

SPECIFICATIONS

	4-door sedan
Wheelbase, in.	111.0
Overall length, in.	204.1
Overall width, in.	74.2
Overall height, in.	54.5
Curb weight, lbs.	3832
Cargo volume, cu. ft.	14.4
Fuel capacity, gals.	20.0
Seating capacity	5
Front head room, in.	38.0
Max. front leg room, in.	43.0
Rear head room, in.	38.3
Min. rear leg room, in.	39.1

Powertrain layout: transverse front-engine/front-wheel drive

ENGINES

	dohc V-8	dohc V-8	ohv V-8
Size, liters/cu. in.	4.6/279	4.6/279	4.9/300
Horsepower	270-275	295-300	200
Torque (lbs./ft.)	300	290-295	275
EPA city/highway mpg			
4-speed OD automatic	17/26	17/26	16/25
Consumer Guide™ observed MPG			
4-speed OD automatic	15.9	16.8	

Built in USA.

RETAIL PRICES

	GOOD	AVERAGE	POOR
1992 Seville	$9,500-10,500	$8,500-9,300	$6,000-6,800
1992 Seville STS	10,500-11,500	9,500-10,500	6,800-7,700
1993 Seville	11,500-12,500	10,200-11,200	7,400-8,300
1993 Seville STS	12,500-13,500	11,200-12,200	8,200-9,200
1994 Seville SLS	14,500-15,700	13,000-14,200	9,500-10,500
1994 Seville STS	15,700-17,000	14,200-15,500	10,500-11,500

	GOOD	AVERAGE	POOR
1995 Seville SLS	18,500-20,200	17,000-18,500	13,500-15,000
1995 Seville STS	19,800-21,500	18,000-19,500	14,500-15,500
1996 Seville SLS	23,000-24,800	21,000-22,500	17,000-18,500
1996 Seville STS	24,500-26,500	22,500-24,500	18,200-20,000
1997 Seville SLS	27,500-29,500	25,000-27,000	21,000-22,500
1997 Seville STS	29,500-31,500	27,000-29,000	22,500-24,500

AVERAGE REPLACEMENT COSTS

A/C Compressor $465
Alternator 295
Radiator 375
Timing Chain or Belt 265
Automatic Transmission or

Transaxle 1,085
Constant Velocity Joints.....810
Brakes..................................210
Shocks and/or Struts 1,360
Exhaust System.................998

TROUBLE SPOTS

• **Steering noise** The upper bearing mount in the steering column can get loose and cause a snapping or clicking that can be both heard and felt, requiring a new bearing spring and turn signal cancel cam that the manufacturer will warranty. (1994-96)

• **Transmission slippage** The 4T60E transmission may drop out of drive (neutral condition) while cruising, shift erratically, have no third or fourth gear, or no second and third gear because of a bad ground connection for the shift solenoids. Poor grounds also allow wrong gear starts. Many transmissions have been mistakenly rebuilt, which does not correct the problem. (1991-93)

• **Transaxle leak** The right front axle seal at the automatic transaxle is prone to leak and GM issued a revised seal to correct the problem. It is supposed to be installed whenever a car is in for transmission or axle shaft service of any sort. (1992-93)

• **Engine noise** What sounds like a rattling noise from the engine that lasts less than a minute when the car is started after sitting overnight is often caused by automatic transmission pump starvation or cavitation, or a sticking pressure regulator valve. According to GM, no damage occurs and it does not have a fix for the problem. (1992-93)

• **Transaxle leak** Any car with a model 440-T4 automatic transmission may shift late or not upshift at all. The problem is a stuck throttle valve inside the transmission. It may be overlooked during rebuilding since the valve appears fine because it is hydraulic pressure, not a physical binding, that makes it stick. The problem is fixed by enlarging the hydraulic fluid balance hole by 0.010 inch. (1992)

RECALL HISTORY

1992 Intermediate shaft to steering rack lower-coupling pinch bolt may be missing on some cars; disengagement of shaft produces loss of steering control. **1993 with 4.6-liter V-8** Fuel feed and return lines to fuel injection system could work loose, causing fuel leakage in engine compartment. **1993-94 with 4.6-liter V-8** If air conditioner compressor clutch assembly contacts auxiliary engine oil cooler outlet hose, that hose may wear through. **1994** Throttle cable can disengage and interfere with cam mechanism; car could accelerate unexpectedly. **1996** Analog instrument cluster on some cars could have internal short circuit disrupting Pass-Key system, causing failure of gauges and most tell-tale indicators, and possible no-start condition; panel could go black while driving. **1997** Brake/traction control module can cause anti-lock system to cycle in non-ABS braking; could increase stopping distance.

1990-98 CHEVROLET ASTRO

1991 Chevrolet Astro Ext. AWD

FOR Driver-side air bag (later models) • Anti-lock brakes • Optional AWD traction • Passenger and cargo room • Trailer towing capability

AGAINST Fuel economy • Entry/exit • Ride

EVALUATION Spacious inside, Astro vans can be fitted to tow up to three tons and seat up to eight. Like the now-extinct Ford Aerostar, the Astro and its GMC Safari cousin are truck-based vehicles, better suited to heavy-duty work than are front-drive minivans.

The penalty that must be paid for this brawn is a rough, bouncy ride—definitely less carlike than front-drive minivans, which serve as replacements from the family station wagon. Clumsy handling also ranks as subpar. Even the least-potent V-6 engine has plenty of torque for hauling heavy loads and towing, but that muscle does not translate into brisk acceleration. As for economy, we averaged just 14.5 mpg in an early AWD, regular-length Astro. Expect around 15 mpg in urban driving, and not a whole lot more on the highway. Servicing isn't so easy.

Entry/exit to the front seats is hampered by doorways that are narrow at the bottom. There's also a tall step-up, to get inside. Interiors offer loads of passenger and cargo room, though front-seat riders must deal with uncomfortably narrow footwells. The dashboard revised for 1996 has a convenient layout, with plenty of built-in storage space. With eight seats, a regular-length Astro has little rear cargo room.

All-wheel drive offers better rain/snow traction, but with even more thirst for gas. It also makes the Astro an inch higher, adding to step-in height.

NHTSA CRASH TEST RESULTS
1996 Chevrolet Astro

3-DOOR VAN

Driver	☆☆☆
Passenger	☆☆☆

(The National Highway Traffic Safety Administration tests a vehicle's crashworthiness in front and side collisions. Their ratings suggest the chance of serious injury: ☆☆☆☆☆—10% or less; ☆☆☆☆—10-20% or less; ☆☆☆—20-30% or less; ☆☆—35-45% or less; ☆—More than 45%.)

SPECIFICATIONS

	3-door van	3-door van	3-door van
Wheelbase, in.	111.0	111.0	111.0
Overall length, in.	176.8	186.8	189.8
Overall width, in.	77.5	77.5	77.5
Overall height, in.	76.2	76.2	76.2
Curb weight, lbs.	3897	3987	3998
Cargo volume, cu. ft.	151.8	170.4	170.4
Fuel capacity, gals.	27.0	27.0	27.0
Seating capacity	8	8	8
Front head room, in.	39.2	39.2	39.2
Max. front leg room, in.	41.6	41.6	41.6
Rear head room, in.	37.9	37.9	37.9
Min. rear leg room, in.	36.5	36.5	36.5

Powertrain layout: longitudinal front-engine/rear- or all-wheel drive

ENGINES

	ohv V-6	ohv V-6
Size, liters/cu. in.	4.3/262	4.3/262
Horsepower	150-165	175-200
Torque (lbs./ft.)	230-235	250-260
EPA city/highway mpg		
4-speed OD automatic	16/21	16/20

CHEVROLET

Consumer Guide™ observed MPG
4-speed OD automatic 14.5

Built in USA.

RETAIL PRICES	GOOD	AVERAGE	POOR
1990 Astro	$3,200-4,800	$2,500-4,000	$1,200-2,200
1991 Astro	4,000-6,500	3,200-5,500	1,600-3,500
1992 Astro	4,800-7,300	4,000-6,300	2,300-4,300
1993 Astro	5,800-8,500	4,900-7,500	3,000-5,400
1994 Astro	7,000-9,800	6,000-8,800	4,000-6,700
1995 Astro	9,000-11,500	7,700-10,000	5,500-7,500
1996 Astro	11,000-14,000	9,500-12,500	7,200-9,700
1997 Astro	13,500-16,500	12,000-14,700	9,000-11,500
1998 Astro	16,500-19,000	14,500-17,000	11,500-13,500

AVERAGE REPLACEMENT COSTS

A/C Compressor $515	Clutch, Pressure Plate,
Alternator 245	Bearing 555
Radiator 420	Universal Joints 153
Timing Chain or Belt 255	Brakes.................................225
Automatic Transmission or	Shocks and/or Struts 247
Transaxle.........................770	Exhaust System.................320

TROUBLE SPOTS

• **Engine noise** There may be a whooping noise (similar to a helicopter) coming from the engine caused by the exhaust valves sticking in their guides and new valve guide seals should correct the problem if the guides are not worn. (1996)

• **Engine misfire** New valve guide seals should eliminate the blue smoke from the tailpipe during cold starting. (1990-93)

• **Engine misfire** The fuel injector wires tend to get pinched when the air filter is reinstalled. (1990-93)

• **Doors** The sliding door is hard to open or close, or does not glide smoothly because various parts are out of adjustment. (1990-93)

• **Engine knock** A knocking sound from deep in the engine after sitting overnight may be due to three possible causes and may be fixed with either an oil filter having a built-in check valve, a revised PROM or replacement of the main bearings. (1990-95)

• **Transmission leak** The rear seal on the transmission may leak on vans with a one-piece drive shaft. (1990-94)

• **Transmission leak** Fluid may leak from the pump body on 4L60-E transmissions due to the pump bushing walking out of the valve body. (1995-96)

RECALL HISTORY

1990-91 Bucket seat's knob-type recliner mechanism with foam or vinyl "soft joint" may loosen and cause bolt failure, allowing seatback to recline suddenly; could produce loss of control. **1995 w/L35 engine** Fuel lines at tank were improperly tightened and could loosen, allowing leakage and possible fire. **1995** On a few vans, left lower control arm bolt could loosen, fatigue and break. **1996-97** Outboard seatbelt webbing on right rear bucket seat can separate during crash.

1992-98 CHEVROLET BLAZER/TAHOE

1995 Chevrolet Tahoe C1500 4-door

FOR Driver-side and dual air bags (later models) • Acceleration (5.7-liter) • Passenger and cargo room • Ride • Trailer towing capability

AGAINST Fuel economy • Maneuverability • Ride (2-door) • Entry/exit (2-door and 4WD)

EVALUATION Blazers and their Tahoe successors are brawny but civilized, both on-road and off. Acceleration with Blazer/Tahoe gasoline V-8s ranks as robust, and these models can pull a heavy trailer with ease. As for economy, an early 2-door Tahoe averaged 12.5 mpg in mostly city driving. Vortec engines of 1996-97 might be a bit more frugal. A 4-door 4WD returned 14.3 mpg.

Road behavior has improved, though body lean is still noticeable—but not as much. When loaded, at least, the big Blazer handles rough pavement with less bouncing and pitching than before. Unladen, the tail still tends to judder sideways over closely spaced bumps. Steering is a bit overassisted, but precise, and this version is quieter on the road than its predecessors.

Step-up into the interior isn't as high as before, and you get plenty of space for three abreast, with bountiful head and leg room. Dashboards have easy-to-read gauges and handy controls. Rear doors of the 4-door create unprecedented access to the back seat, but door openings are narrow at the bottom, and step-in height is tall. Cargo room in the 4-door benefits from the under-chassis location of the spare tire. Three-door models carry their spares inside.

Sure, a compact sport-utility is more sensible and economical for everyday driving. But if you require real muscle, especially for towing, try the 4-door Tahoe and also Ford's Expedition.

NHTSA CRASH TEST RESULTS
1997 Chevrolet Tahoe
4-DOOR WAGON

Driver	☆☆☆☆
Passenger	☆☆☆☆

(The National Highway Traffic Safety Administration tests a vehicle's crashworthiness in front and side collisions. Their ratings suggest the chance of serious injury: ☆☆☆☆☆—10% or less; ☆☆☆☆—10-20% or less; ☆☆☆—20-30% or less; ☆☆—35-45% or less; ☆—More than 45%.)

SPECIFICATIONS

	2-door wagon	4-door wagon
Wheelbase, in.	111.5	117.5
Overall length, in.	188.5	199.1
Overall width, in.	77.1	76.4
Overall height, in.	72.4	70.2
Curb weight, lbs.	4731	5134
Cargo volume, cu. ft.	99.4	122.9
Fuel capacity, gals.	30.0	30.5
Seating capacity	6	6
Front head room, in.	39.9	39.9
Max. front leg room, in.	41.9	41.7
Rear head room, in.	37.8	38.9
Min. rear leg room, in.	36.4	36.7

Powertrain layout: longitudinal front-engine/rear- or 4-wheel drive

ENGINES

	ohv V-8	ohv V-8	Turbodiesel ohv V-8
Size, liters/cu. in.	5.7/350	5.7/350	6.5/400
Horsepower	210	250-255	180
Torque (lbs./ft.)	300-310	330-335	360

EPA city/highway mpg

5-speed OD manual	12/16		
4-speed OD automatic	12/15	13/17	15/18

Consumer Guide™ observed MPG

4-speed OD automatic	12.5	14.3

Built in USA and Mexico.

RETAIL PRICES	GOOD	AVERAGE	POOR
1992 Blazer 4WD	$9,500-11,500	$8,500-10,500	$6,000-7,500
1993 Blazer 4WD	11,000-13,000	10,000-12,000	7,300-9,000
1994 Blazer 4WD	13,000-15,000	11,800-13,500	9,000-10,500
1995 Tahoe 2WD	14,000-16,000	12,600-14,500	9,500-11,000
1995 Tahoe 4WD	15,500-20,000	14,000-18,500	10,800-15,000
1996 Tahoe 2WD	16,800-20,500	15,300-19,000	12,000-15,200
1996 Tahoe 4WD	18,500-23,500	17,000-22,000	13,500-18,000
1997 Tahoe 2WD	19,000-24,000	17,700-22,500	14,500-18,500
1997 Tahoe 4WD	21,500-26,500	19,500-24,500	15,800-20,300
1998 Tahoe 2WD	22,000-26,500	20,500-25,000	17,000-21,000
1998 Tahoe 4WD	24,500-28,500	22,500-26,500	19,000-22,000

AVERAGE REPLACEMENT COSTS

A/C Compressor $555
Alternator 220
Radiator 650
Timing Chain or Belt 415
Automatic Transmission or
  Transaxle........................750
Clutch, Pressure Plate,
  Bearing 730
Universal Joints 225
Brakes..................................260
Shocks and/or Struts 340
Exhaust System.................380

TROUBLE SPOTS

• **Dashboard lights** The oil pressure gauge may read high, move erratically or not work because the oil pressure sensor is defective. (1990-93)

• **Transmission slippage** Automatic transmissions may suffer harsh or shuddering shifts between first and second or may buzz or vibrate in park or neutral. (1992)

• **Climate control** The temperature control lever may slide from hot to cold, usually when the blower is on high speed. (1992-94)

• **Transmission leak** Fluid may leak from the pump body on 4L60-E transmissions due to the pump bushing walking out of the valve body. (1995-96)

RECALL HISTORY

1995 w/M30/MT1 automatic transmission When shift lever is placed in "Park" position, its indicator light may not illuminate. **1995-96 w/gasoline engine** Throttle cable may contact dash mat and bind; engine speed might then not return to idle. **1998** On some vehicles, one or both front brake rotor/hubs may have out-of-spec gray iron that can fail during life of vehicle.

1995-98 CHEVROLET BLAZER

1995 Chevrolet Blazer 4-door

FOR Air bag, driver • Anti-lock brakes • Acceleration • Passenger and cargo room • Ride • 4WD traction

AGAINST Rear seat comfort • Fuel economy • No passenger-side air bag (early models)

EVALUATION Acceleration is above average for a sport-utility, livelier than an Explorer from a standstill, with stronger passing power. Unfortunately, the automatic transmission pauses a moment before downshifting. Naturally, too, the Blazer's V-6 cannot hope to match an Explorer's V-8 when hitting the gas pedal hard. Fuel economy wins no prizes. A long-term test of a 4-door 4WD Blazer averaged 15.2 mpg.

A variety of suspension choices have been offered, tailoring the ride from off-road firm to suburban-street soft. Of all the suspension packages available, we prefer the "premium ride" version, which absorbs most bumps easily and produces a comfortable, stable highway ride. In fact, that Blazer rides more like a car than a truck.

Blazers actually steer and handle much like a compact car. Body lean is moderate in tight corners. Steering feels more precise than on the old S10 Blazer. Stopping power is adequate, though our test vehicle suffered a mushy brake-pedal feel, as well as substantial nose-dive in quick stops. Things improved with the 4-wheel disc brakes on the '98 model.

Passenger space is about the same as before. That translates to good room for four adults in both body styles. In a pinch, five or even six can fit into the bigger 4-door. However, the rear seat has a short, hard backrest—bolt upright and uncomfortable. Cargo room is ample, improved in the 4-door by mounting the spare tire beneath the rear end. Visibility is fine on the 4-door, but obstructed by the 3-door's sloped roof pillars as well as the spare tire.

The modern-looking dashboard has clear gauges and easy-to-use controls. Power window and lock buttons are large and helpfully backlit. The climate system uses rotary switches for selecting mode and temperature.

Some engine roar remains in hard acceleration, but road and wind noise now are well muffled, ranking as moderate.

Blazers are competitive with the Explorer and Jeep Grand Cherokee in most areas, and beat them on price when new. Good buys also can be found in the secondhand market.

NHTSA CRASH TEST RESULTS
1995 Chevrolet Blazer

4-DOOR WAGON

Driver	☆☆☆
Passenger	☆

(The National Highway Traffic Safety Administration tests a vehicle's crashworthiness in front and side collisions. Their ratings suggest the chance of serious injury: ☆☆☆☆☆—10% or less; ☆☆☆☆—10-20% or less; ☆☆☆—20-30% or less; ☆☆—35-45% or less; ☆—More than 45%.)

SPECIFICATIONS

	2-door wagon	4-door wagon
Wheelbase, in.	100.5	107.0
Overall length, in.	174.7	181.2
Overall width, in.	67.8	67.8
Overall height, in.	66.9	67.0
Curb weight, lbs.	3867	4071
Cargo volume, cu. ft.	66.9	74.1
Fuel capacity, gals.	20.0	19.0
Seating capacity	4	6
Front head room, in.	39.6	39.6
Max. front leg room, in.	42.5	42.5
Rear head room, in.	38.2	38.2
Min. rear leg room, in.	36.3	36.2

Powertrain layout: longitudinal front-engine/rear- or 4-wheel drive

ENGINES

ohv V-6

Size, liters/cu. in.	4.3/262
Horsepower	190-195
Torque (lbs./ft.)	250-260

EPA city/highway mpg

5-speed OD manual	17/22
4-speed OD automatic	16/21
4-speed OD automatic	15.2

Built in USA.

RETAIL PRICES

	GOOD	AVERAGE	POOR
1995 Blazer 2WD	$10,200-12,000	$9,200-11,000	$6,800-8,500
1995 Blazer 4WD	12,000-14,000	10,800-12,700	8,200-10,000
1996 Blazer 2WD	12,600-14,500	11,500-13,100	8,600-10,200
1996 Blazer 4WD	14,500-16,500	13,200-15,000	10,200-12,000
1997 Blazer 2WD	15,000-17,000	13,700-15,500	10,500-12,200
1997 Blazer 4WD	17,000-19,000	15,500-17,500	12,000-13,500
1998 Blazer 2WD	17,500-19,500	16,000-18,000	12,500-14,000
1998 Blazer 4WD	19,500-22,000	18,000-20,000	14,000-15,500

AVERAGE REPLACEMENT COSTS

A/C Compressor $520
Alternator 225
Radiator 450
Timing Chain or Belt 230
Automatic Transmission or
   Transaxle.........................850

Clutch, Pressure Plate,
   Bearing 800
Universal Joints 270
Brakes..................................220
Shocks and/or Struts 410
Exhaust System.................485

TROUBLE SPOTS

• **Engine noise** The exhaust valves may not get enough lubrication causing a variety of noises that sound like lifter tick, rod knock or a whoop-whoop noise like a helicopter. Usually, the same engine consumes excess oil because the valve guide seals on the exhaust valves are bad and have to be replaced. (1996)

• **Engine noise** Engine knock when the engine is first started is usually eliminated by using an oil filter with a check valve (such as Fram PH3980), but if this does not fix it, GM has revised PROMs for the computers and may even replace the main bearings if no other solution is found. (1995)

• **Engine misfire** A problem with the powertrain control module may cause a lack of power (especially when carrying heavy loads or under heavy acceleration), early upshifts, late shifting in the 4WD-Low range and otherwise erratic performance. (1996-96)

• **Transmission leak** Fluid may leak from the pump body on 4L60-E transmissions due to the pump bushing walking out of the valve body. (1995-96)

RECALL HISTORY

1995 Brake pedal bolt on some vehicles might disengage, causing loss of braking. **1995 w/4WD** A few upper ball joint nuts were undertorqued; stud can loosen and fracture, resulting in loss of steering control. **1995 w/air conditioning** Fan blade rivets can break and allow blade to separate from hub. **1995-96 w/AWD/4WD** During development testing, prop shaft contacted inboard side of fuel tank, rupturing the tank; fuel leakage was beyond permissible level. **1998** Fatigue fracture of rear-axle brake pipe can occur, causing slow fluid leak and resulting in soft brake pedal; if pipe breaks, driver would face sudden loss of rear-brake performance. **1998 w/4WD or AWD** On a few vehicles, one or both attaching nut for lower control arm could separate from frame, resulting in loss of control.

1990-98 CHEVROLET C/K PICKUP

1995 Chevrolet C1500 Work Truck

FOR   Air bag, driver (later models) • Anti-lock brakes • Acceleration (V-8) • Cargo room • Visibility • Cargo and towing ability • Interior room

AGAINST   Fuel economy • Control layout • Ride quality

EVALUATION   The V-6 feels adequate with manual shift, but a 5.0- or 5.7-liter V-8 would be wiser for any significant work, especially with automatic transmission. Short-bed Sportsides have a more sporty appearance and, with a larger V-8, move impressively. A K2500 4x4 with 5.7-liter V-8 and automatic averaged 13.3 mpg, and yielded strong low-end pulling power as well as good passing response. Braking can be a problem with rear anti-locking, when the bed is unladen. Four-wheel ABS on later models is a better bet. Acceleration in a 454 SS is actually neck-snapping, and its wide tires and sports suspension make it the best-handling full-size pickup you're likely to find.

Visibility is good from a wide, spacious cab that has ample room for even the largest occupants. Gauges are unobstructed but can be hard to read in sunlight, and electronic heat/vent controls are complicated. Gloveboxes are tiny. Ride quality is better than in prior pickups, but higher-capacity models don't take bumps so well when the box is unloaded. Only the short wheelbase 4x4 with off-road suspension rides really harshly.

Engine improvements for '96 are impressive. The V-6 still isn't ideal for heavy work, but the 5.0-liter V-8 is now a smooth, capable choice (except for serious towing or hauling). The 5.7 V-8 feels much livelier, furnishing robust acceleration and fine pulling power. It's still our top choice.

RNHTSA CRASH TEST RESULTS
1995 Chevrolet C1500

REG. CAB LONG BED

Driver	☆☆☆☆☆
Passenger	☆☆☆☆☆

(The National Highway Traffic Safety Administration tests a vehicle's crashworthiness in front and side collisions. Their ratings suggest the chance of serious injury: ☆☆☆☆☆—10% or less; ☆☆☆☆—10-20% or less; ☆☆☆—20-30% or less; ☆☆—35-45% or less; ☆—More than 45%.)

SPECIFICATIONS	reg. cab short bed	reg. cab long bed	ext. cab short bed	ext. cab long bed
Wheelbase, in.	117.5	131.5	141.5	155.5
Overall length, in.	194.5	213.4	217.9	236.6
Overall width, in.	76.8	76.8	76.8	76.8
Overall height, in.	70.4	70.4	70.6	73.8
Curb weight, lbs.	3849	4001	4140	4387
Max. payload, lbs.	2412	5385	5261	5042
Fuel capacity, gals.	25.0	34.0	34.0	34.0
Seating capacity	3	3	6	6
Front head room, in.	39.9	39.9	39.9	39.9
Max. front leg room, in.	41.7	41.7	41.7	41.7
Rear head room, in.	NA	NA	37.5	37.5
Min. rear leg room, in.	NA	NA	34.8	34.8

Powertrain layout: longitudinal front-engine/rear- or 4-wheel drive

ENGINES	ohv V-6	ohv V-6	ohv V-8	ohv V-8
Size, liters/cu. in.	4.3/262	4.3/262	5.0/305	5.7/350
Horsepower	160-165	200	175-230	200-255
Torque (lbs./ft.)	235	255	270-285	300-335
EPA city/highway mpg				
4-speed manual	18/20			
5-speed OD manual		17/22	15/20	14/19
3-speed automatic	17/19		15/17	14/19
4-speed OD automatic		16/21	15/19	15/19
Consumer Guide™ observed MPG				
4-speed OD automatic			14.5	13.0

ENGINES

	Diesel ohv V-8	Diesel ohv V-8[1]	ohv V-8
Size, liters/cu. in.	6.2/379	6.5/400	7.4/454
Horsepower	140-143	155-180	230-290
Torque (lbs./ft.)	255	360	385-410

EPA city/highway mpg

4-speed manual.................................	19/21		
5-speed OD manual		NA	
4-speed OD automatic	18/24	15/18	10/12

1. Naturally aspirated (155 horsepower); turbodiesel (180 horsepower).

Built in USA and Canada.

RETAIL PRICES	GOOD	AVERAGE	POOR
1990 C/K 1500	$2,800-6,500	$2,200-5,700	$1,000-3,800
1990 C/K 2500	4,400-7,000	3,700-6,200	1,700-4,000
1991 C/K 1500	3,700-8,500	3,000-7,700	1,400-5,200
1991 C/K 2500	5,500-8,700	4,600-7,800	2,500-5,300
1992 C/K 1500	4,500-10,500	3,700-9,500	1,700-6,600
1992 C/K 2500	6,600-10,500	5,800-9,500	3,500-6,600
1993 C/K 1500	5,300-11,500	4,500-10,500	2,400-7,500
1993 C/K 2500	8,200-12,000	7,300-11,000	4,800-7,700
1994 C/K 1500	6,200-14,000	5,400-13,000	3,200-9,800
1994 C/K 2500	9,900-14,200	8,900-13,200	6,000-10,000
1995 C/K 1500	7,400-15,500	6,600-14,500	3,700-11,300
1995 C/K 2500	11,400-16,000	10,500-15,000	7,500-11,500
1996 C/K 1500	9,200-18,000	8,000-16,500	5,000-12,800
1996 C/K 2500	13,300-18,500	11,800-17,000	8,500-13,200
1997 C/K 1500	11,000-20,000	9,500-18,500	6,300-14,500
1997 C/K 2500	15,300-21,000	13,800-19,500	10,000-15,500
1998 C/K 1500	13,000-22,000	11,500-20,500	8,000-16,300
1998 C/K 2500	16,500-23,000	15,000-21,000	11,500-16,500

AVERAGE REPLACEMENT COSTS

A/C Compressor $560
Alternator 378
Radiator 350
Timing Chain or Belt 210
Automatic Transmission or
   Transaxle.........................725

Clutch, Pressure Plate,
   Bearing............................595
Brakes..................................230
Shocks and/or Struts 335
Exhaust System.................420

TROUBLE SPOTS

• **Clutch** A grinding or ticking noise when the clutch pedal is depressed and difficulty shifting into first or reverse is caused by a clutch master cylinder pushrod that is too long. Chevy will replace it free. (1992-93)

• **Transmission slippage** Trucks with the 6.5L engine may have a transmission shudder when the torque converter clutch applies and releases. Chevy will replace it with the converter used with 7.4L engines. (1991-94)

• **Engine knock** Engine knock when the engine (4.3L, 5.7L, or 7.4L) is started is usually eliminated by using an oil filter with a check valve (such as Fram PH3980), but if this does not fix it, GM has revised PROMs for the computers and will even replace the main bearings if all else fails. (1990-95)

• **Engine noise** The exhaust valves on the 4.3L, 5.0L, or 5.7L engine may not get enough lubrication causing a variety of noises that sound like lifter tick, rod knock, or a "whoop-whoop" noise like a helicopter. Usually, the same engine consumes excess oil because the valve guide seals on the exhaust valves are bad and have to be replaced. (1996)

• **Cruise control** If the cruise control cuts out and won't reset unless the key is turned off then back on, GM will replace the cruise control module. The original one is too sensitive to vibrations at the brake pedal that causes switch contact bounce. (1994-95)

• **Transmission slippage** Any truck with a model 700-R4 automatic transmission may shift late or not upshift at all. The problem is a stuck throttle valve inside the transmission. It may be overlooked during rebuilding since the valve appears fine because it is hydraulic pressure, not a physical binding, that makes it stick. The problem is fixed by enlarging the hydraulic fluid balance hole by 0.010 inch. (1990-92)

RECALL HISTORY

1990 diesel Fuel lines can contact automatic transmission linkage shaft and/or propshaft. **1990, '92** Brake-pedal pivot bolt could disengage. **1994** Some driver's seats could loosen. **1994** Brake pedal retainer may be missing, mispositioned, or poorly seated. **1994-95 extended-cab C10/15 with gas engine or 6.5-liter H.O. turbodiesel** If lap- and shoulder-belt energy-management loops on front seatbelt assemblies release at or near the same time, acceleration forces can cause release mechanism to activate and allow buckle to separate from latch. Also, a few trucks lack those loops. **1994-95 extended-cab C10/15 with high-back front bucket seats or 60/40 split bench seat** Recliner-to-frame bolts could loosen, fatigue, and fracture, allowing seatback to recline suddenly. **1995** Steering-column shaft nut could loosen and detach. **1995-96 with gasoline engine** Throttle cable may contact dash mat, which could bind the throttle; engine speed might then not return to idle. **1996 C10/15 with 7.4-liter engine** Fuel rail assemblies may have improperly crimped end retainer clip that results in leak. **1996** Four U-bolts on either side of rear axle were under-torqued and could loosen and eventually fall off; could result in sudden loss of control. **1997 C10/20** On some trucks, one or two front seat mounting bolts were not installed. **1998 C10 extended-cab and 4-door utility** Steering gear bolt can loosen and fall out, resulting in separation of shaft from gear. **1998** On some trucks, one or both front brake rotor/hubs may have out-of-spec gray iron that can fail during life of vehicle.

1993-98 CHEVROLET CAMARO

✓ BEST BUY

1993 Chevrolet Camaro Z-28 2-door

FOR Air bags • Anti-lock brakes • Acceleration (Z28) • Handling • Control layout

AGAINST Fuel economy (Z28) • Ride (Z28) • Tire noise (Z28) • Wet-weather traction • Visibility • Noise • Rear seat comfort

EVALUATION This latest Camaro generation beats its predecessor in two notable ways: ride quality and dashboard layout. Both the base model and the Z28 have softer suspensions, which reduces the harsh impacts commonly endured in prior models. Z28s are still quite harsh over rough pavement, but more easygoing than before, though optional high-performance tires generate too much noise at highway speeds. Both models retain their well-known handling prowess. Gauges are easily visible through the steering wheel. Radio and climate controls are high-mounted, easy to reach and see.

Climbing inside can be a chore because of low seats. Wide rear roof pillars still obscure the view to sides and rear quarters.

CHEVROLET

A hump in the right-front floorboard intrudes into passenger leg room. Rear head room is a tad better than before, but the cushion is narrow and knee space extremely limited. A deep cargo well doesn't hold much luggage. The low seating position hinders visibility.

Though somewhat gruff and noisy under acceleration, the 3.4-liter V-6 performs nicely—especially with 5-speed manual shift. Acceleration in a Z28 is strong with either transmission, but the V-8 demands premium fuel. We averaged only 13.2 mpg in mostly urban driving. Adding the 3.8-liter V-6 narrowed the performance gap between the two modes. The 200-horsepower engine matches the 4.6-liter V-8 in Ford Mustangs when the gas pedal hits the floor. Poor wet-weather traction remains a problem. Traction control wasn't optional until 1995.

This generation Camaro is the best ever, but we feel that it forces too many compromises to be a daily driver for anyone but the performance enthusiast.

NHTSA CRASH TEST RESULTS
1996 Chevrolet Camaro
2-DOOR HATCHBACK

Driver	☆☆☆☆☆
Passenger	☆☆☆☆☆

(The National Highway Traffic Safety Administration tests a vehicle's crashworthiness in front and side collisions. Their ratings suggest the chance of serious injury: ☆☆☆☆☆—10% or less; ☆☆☆☆—10-20% or less; ☆☆☆—20-30% or less; ☆☆—35-45% or less; ☆—More than 45%.)

SPECIFICATIONS

	2-door hatchback	2-door conv.
Wheelbase, in.	101.1	101.1
Overall length, in.	193.2	193.2
Overall width, in.	74.1	74.1
Overall height, in.	51.3	52.0
Curb weight, lbs.	3306	3440
Cargo volume, cu. ft.	33.7	7.6
Fuel capacity, gals.	15.5	15.5
Seating capacity	4	4
Front head room, in.	37.2	38.0
Max. front leg room, in.	43.0	43.0
Rear head room, in.	35.3	39.0
Min. rear leg room, in.	26.8	26.8

Powertrain layout: longitudinal front-engine/rear-wheel drive

ENGINES

	ohv V-6	ohv V-6	ohv V-8	ohv V-8
Size, liters/cu. in.	3.4/207	3.8/231	5.7/350	5.7/346
Horsepower	160	200	275-305	305-320
Torque (lbs./ft.)	200	225	325	335-345

EPA city/highway mpg	ohv V-6	ohv V-6	ohv V-8	ohv V-8
6-speed OD manual			16/27	17/25
4-speed OD automatic.....	19/28	19/29	17/25	18/27
5-speed OD automatic.....	19/28	19/30		

Consumer Guide™ observed MPG

6-speed OD manual			13.2	
4-speed OD automatic.....		18.6	17.4	15.1

Built in Canada.

RETAIL PRICES

		GOOD	AVERAGE	POOR
1993	Camaro Coupe	$6,000-7,000	$5,200-6,200	$3,200-4,000
1993	Z28 Coupe	7,600-8,500	6,700-7,600	4,500-5,300
1994	Camaro Coupe	7,000-8,000	6,200-7,200	4,000-5,000
1994	Convertible	9,500-10,800	8,500-9,500	6,000-7,000
1994	Z28 Coupe	9,100-10,500	8,100-9,200	5,600-6,500
1994	Z28 Convertible	11,400-12,800	10,200-11,500	7,400-8,500
1995	Camaro Coupe	8,500-9,700	7,600-8,800	5,200-6,100
1995	Convertible	11,000-12,500	9,800-11,000	7,200-8,200
1995	Z28 Coupe	11,000-12,200	9,500-10,700	6,800-7,700
1995	Z28 Convertible	13,500-14,800	12,000-13,300	9,000-10,200
1996	Camaro Coupe	10,300-11,500	9,300-10,500	6,700-7,700
1996	Convertible	13,100-14,800	11,800-13,300	9,000-10,200
1996	Z28 Coupe	13,000-14,000	11,500-12,500	8,500-9,500
1996	Z28 Convertible	16,000-17,500	14,500-16,000	11,000-12,500
1997	Camaro Coupe	12,300-13,800	11,000-12,500	8,000-9,300
1997	Convertible	15,000-17,500	13,500-16,000	10,500-12,500
1997	Z28 Coupe	15,000-16,500	13,500-15,000	10,500-11,500
1997	Z28 Convertible	18,500-20,000	17,000-18,500	13,500-15,000
1998	Camaro Coupe	14,500-16,000	13,000-14,500	10,000-11,500
1998	Convertible	17,500-19,000	16,000-17,500	13,000-14,500
1998	Z28 Coupe	17,000-19,000	15,500-17,500	12,500-14,500
1998	Z28 Convertible	21,000-23,500	19,200-21,500	16,000-18,000

AVERAGE REPLACEMENT COSTS

A/C Compressor $535		Clutch, Pressure Plate,	
Alternator 290		Bearing 775	
Radiator 410		Universal Joints 200	
Timing Chain or Belt 330		Brakes.................................255	
Automatic Transmission or		Shocks and/or Struts 527	
Transaxle.........................775		Exhaust System.................470	

TROUBLE SPOTS

• **Rear axle noise** GM had some problems with rear axles making noise or breaking. Under warranty the company will replace the

CHEVROLET

entire rear axle (excluding brake rotors on cars with rear disc brakes) on a complete exchange basis. (1995)

• **Steering noise** The upper bearing mount in the steering column can get loose and cause a snapping or clicking that can be both heard and felt requiring a new bearing spring and turn signal cancel cam, which the manufacturer will warranty. (1994-96)

• **Transmission slippage** Any car with a model TH-200 or 700-R4 automatic transmission may shift late or not upshift at all. The problem is a stuck throttle valve inside the transmission. It may be overlooked during rebuilding since the valve appears fine because it is hydraulic pressure, not a physical binding, that makes it stick. The problem is fixed by enlarging the hydraulic fluid balance hole by 0.010 inch. (1993)

• **Cruise control** If the cruise control cuts out and won't reset unless the key is turned off then back on, GM will replace the cruise control module. The original one is too sensitive to vibrations at the brake pedal that causes switch contact bounce. (1993-95)

• **Heater core** The seal on the heater core case gets loose and cold air enters, which reduces the heater performance. A new seal and a homemade strip to hold it in place will fix it. (1993-94)

RECALL HISTORY

1994 Misrouted V-8 fuel line may contact "air" check valve; heat could damage line, which could leak fuel into engine compartment. **1995** Lower coupling of steering intermediate shaft could loosen and rotate, resulting in loss of control. **1997** Seatbelt retractors on some cars can lock-up on slopes.

1991-96 CHEVROLET CAPRICE/IMPALA SS

FOR Air bags (later models) • Acceleration • Passenger and cargo room • Trailer towing capability • Anti-lock brakes

AGAINST Fuel economy • Steering feel (Caprice) • Ride/handling/roadholding (Caprice w/base suspension) • Wind noise

EVALUATION Despite the new look, not much changed in this full-size sedan and wagon. Caprice's traditional soft ride is distressingly bouncy and floaty with the base suspension. Qualifying as virtually aquatic, the car leans way over in turns and wallows over wavy roads. Loose, vague steering impairs quick maneuvers. An optional F41 Ride/Handling suspension offers a slightly more assured feel, without much comfort loss.

1994 Chevrolet Caprice Classic 4-door

The sporty LTZ sedan option drew praise, and its stiffer suspension tightens handling considerably. The entertaining Impala SS of 1994-96 offers quite a secure feel on the road, leaning little in curves, its big tires grasping the pavement tenaciously. Wagon suspensions are firmer than those in sedans.

The 5.0-liter V-8 is understressed and quiet, with good low-end torque for easy merging/passing as well as brisk getaways. Still, it doesn't respond quickly to sharp jabs at the gas pedal. Gas mileage is nothing to boast about, either: We averaged only 16 mpg in a '91 sedan. A 5.7-liter V-8 is quicker without guzzling much more fuel. The Corvette-based V-8 introduced in 1994 is swifter yet, and none of the V-8s demand premium gasoline.

Mechanical noise while cruising is low, but wind roars constantly around the thick side pillars, detracting from the quiet ride. A Caprice is roomy, soft and plush, though the bulky transmission tunnel robs leg room from center passengers, front and rear. The trunk is sizable. Controls are logical. Anti-lock braking is a welcome addition, but the nose dives too much in hard stops.

GM's front-drive full-size sedans (Buick LeSabre, Olds Eighty Eight, Pontiac Bonneville) handle better and consume less fuel, but can't match Caprice's towing ability.

NHTSA CRASH TEST RESULTS
1996 Chevrolet Caprice   4-DOOR SEDAN

Driver	☆☆☆☆
Passenger	☆☆

(The National Highway Traffic Safety Administration tests a vehicle's crashworthiness in front and side collisions. Their ratings suggest the chance of serious injury: ☆☆☆☆☆—10% or less; ☆☆☆☆—10-20% or less; ☆☆☆—20-30% or less; ☆☆—35-45% or less; ☆—More than 45%.)

SPECIFICATIONS

	4-door sedan	4-door wagon
Wheelbase, in.	115.9	115.9

CHEVROLET

	4-door sedan	4-door wagon
Overall length, in.	214.1	217.3
Overall width, in.	77.5	79.6
Overall height, in.	55.7	60.9
Curb weight, lbs.	4061	4473
Cargo volume, cu. ft.	20.4	92.7
Fuel capacity, gals.	23.1	21.0
Seating capacity	6	8
Front head room, in.	39.2	39.6
Max. front leg room, in.	42.2	42.2
Rear head room, in.	37.4	39.4
Min. rear leg room, in.	39.5	38.0

Powertrain layout: longitudinal front-engine/rear-wheel drive

ENGINES

	ohv V-8	ohv V-8	ohv V-8	ohv V-8
Size, liters/cu. in.	4.3/265	5.0/305	5.7/350	5.7/350
Horsepower	200	170	180	260
Torque (lbs./ft.)	235-245	255	300	330
EPA city/highway mpg				
4-speed OD automatic	18/26	17/26	16/25	17/26
Consumer Guide™ observed MPG				
4-speed OD automatic		16.0		17.0

Built in USA.

AVERAGE REPLACEMENT COSTS

A/C Compressor	$465	Universal Joints	260
Alternator	280	Brakes	220
Radiator	480	Shocks and/or Struts	250
Timing Chain or Belt	305	Exhaust System	460
Automatic Transmission or Transaxle	780		

RETAIL PRICES

		GOOD	AVERAGE	POOR
1991	Caprice	$3,400-5,400	$2,700-4,600	$1,200-2,500
1992	Caprice	4,500-6,500	3,800-5,700	1,900-3,400
1993	Caprice	6,000-8,000	5,200-7,000	3,000-4,500
1994	Caprice	8,000-10,000	7,000-9,000	4,200-5,800
1994	Impala SS	14,000-15,500	12,500-14,000	9,500-11,000
1995	Caprice	10,700-13,000	9,500-11,500	6,500-8,000
1995	Impala SS	16,000-18,000	14,500-16,500	11,000-12,500
1996	Caprice	13,500-16,000	12,000-14,000	9,000-10,500
1996	Impala SS	18,500-20,500	17,000-19,000	13,500-15,000

TROUBLE SPOTS

• **Transmission slippage** Any car with a model TH 700-R4 automatic transmission may shift late or not upshift at all. The problem is a stuck throttle valve inside the transmission. It may be overlooked during rebuilding since the valve appears fine because it is hydraulic pressure, not a physical binding, that makes it stick. The problem is fixed by enlarging the hydraulic fluid balance hole by 0.010 inch. (1991-93)

• **Engine noise** The exhaust valves on the 4.3L or 5.7L engine may not get enough lubrication causing a variety of noises that sound like lifter tick, rod knock, or a "whoop whoop" noise like a helicopter. Usually, the same engine consumes excess oil because the valve guide seals on the exhaust valves are bad and have to be replaced. (1994-96)

RECALL HISTORY

1991 Shoulder belt guide loop plastic covering may crack and expose the steel sub-plate; in a crash, seatbelt webbing can be cut. **1991-92** Secondary hood latch assembly can corrode. **1991-96 police/taxi** Rear lower control arm can crack. **1992** Anti-lock brake system modulator can corrode and leak fluid; may reduce brake effectiveness and increase stopping distance. **1992 with special-order 4.3-liter engine** Engine-mounted fuel feed and return pipes on some cars may fracture. **1994** Oil cooler inlet hose may be too close to steering gear, causing chafing that could result in leakage and fire. **1994** On small number of cars, paint between wheel and brake rotor/drum can cause lug nut to loosen. **1994** Fuel tank strap fasteners can detach, eventually allowing tank to sag. **1994-95** At low temperatures, throttle return spring could fail due to excess friction. **1994-95** Lower ball joint on a few cars sent to Guam and Puerto Rico can separate (also applies to 1995-96 police/taxi/limo). **1995** Improperly-adjusted transmission linkage may permit shifting from "park" position with ignition key removed. **1995-96 station wagon** Air bag caution label and roof-rack caution label were incorrectly installed on same side of sunvisor. **1995-96** Wheel lug nuts were not tightened to the proper specification. This could result in wheel loss.

1990-94 CHEVROLET CAVALIER

FOR Acceleration (V-6) • Fuel economy (4-cylinder) • Handling/roadholding (Z24) • Price • Anti-lock brakes

AGAINST Acceleration (4-cylinder) • Rear-seat comfort • Engine noise (4-cylinder)

CHEVROLET

1994 Chevrolet Cavalier 4-door

EVALUATION   Early 4-cylinder engines give only adequate performance, and decent mileage. However, the automatic transmission eats sharply into acceleration figures. Later fours, with extra horsepower, perform a bit better. The 3-speed automatic also trails 4-speed units, used by some Cavalier competitors, in fuel economy and quiet running. The Z24 with V-6 power ranks as a mini-muscle car, exhibiting brisk performance as well as styling flair. The 3.1-liter V-6 also is a sensible choice for a station wagon. Gas mileage is great with the 4-cylinder, but those engines sound harsh and crude during hard acceleration. A 5-speed VL averaged 23.1 mpg in rush-hour commuting, hitting 33.8 mpg on the highway.

Cavaliers ride reasonably comfortably. Capable handling/roadholding grows more athletic with an optional sport suspension. For truly spirited cornering, search for a Z24 coupe or convertible.

Updating of the dashboard for 1991 made controls easier to see and reach, though the turn-signal lever is still too short. Lack of an air bag is a drawback, especially since many rivals had one sometime in this period.

Coupes and sedans offer adequate space up front, but rear compartments are cramped. Convertibles offer decent rear space for two, as well as a convenient power top. But, they also cost far more than their solid-topped mates.

Neither as roomy nor as technically sophisticated as Japanese subcompacts of the same period, Cavaliers always offered good value.

NHTSA CRASH TEST RESULTS
1994 Chevrolet Cavalier

4-DOOR SEDAN

Driver	☆☆☆☆
Passenger	☆☆☆☆☆

(The National Highway Traffic Safety Administration tests a vehicle's crashworthiness in front and side collisions. Their ratings suggest the chance of serious injury: ☆☆☆☆☆—10% or less; ☆☆☆☆—10-20% or less; ☆☆☆—20-30% or less; ☆☆—35-45% or less; ☆—More than 45%.)

SPECIFICATIONS

	2-door coupe	2-door conv.	4-door sedan	4-door wagon
Wheelbase, in.	101.3	101.3	101.3	101.3
Overall length, in.	182.3	182.3	182.3	181.1
Overall width, in.	66.3	66.3	66.3	66.3
Overall height, in.	52.0	52.0	53.6	52.8
Curb weight, lbs.	2509	2678	2520	2623
Cargo volume, cu. ft.	13.2	10.7	13.0	64.4
Fuel capacity, gals.	15.2	15.2	15.2	15.2
Seating capacity	5	4	5	5
Front head room, in.	37.8	37.8	39.1	38.9
Max. front leg room, in. ...	42.6	42.2	42.1	42.1
Rear head room, in.	36.1	37.3	37.4	38.5
Min. rear leg room, in.	31.2	32.0	32.0	32.5

Powertrain layout: transverse front-engine/front-wheel drive

ENGINES

	ohv I-4	ohv V-6
Size, liters/cu. in.	2.2/133	3.1/191
Horsepower	95-120	135-140
Torque (lbs./ft.)	120-130	180-185

EPA city/highway mpg

5-speed OD manual...	25/36	19/28
3-speed automatic	23/33	20/28

Consumer Guide™ observed MPG

5-speed OD manual...	23.1
3-speed automatic	25.3

Built in USA.

RETAIL PRICES

	GOOD	AVERAGE	POOR
1990 Cavalier	$1,500-2,500	$1,000-1,900	$400-900
1990 Cavalier Z24	2,800-3,500	2,100-2,800	1,000-1,400
1991 Cavalier	1,900-3,200	1,300-2,600	600-1,200
1991 Cavalier Z24	3,500-4,300	2,800-3,600	1,400-1,900
1991 Convertible	3,300-4,200	2,600-3,500	1,300-1,900
1992 Cavalier	2,400-3,800	1,700-3,100	900-1,600
1992 Cavalier Z24	4,200-5,100	3,500-4,300	1,800-2,400
1992 Convertible	4,300-5,400	3,500-4,600	1,800-2,400
1992 Z24 Convertible	5,700-6,700	4,900-5,900	2,800-3,700
1993 Cavalier	3,100-4,600	2,400-3,800	1,200-2,100
1993 Cavalier Z24	5,200-6,200	4,400-5,400	2,500-3,200
1993 Convertible	5,300-6,400	4,500-5,600	2,600-3,300
1993 Z24 Convertible	6,800-7,900	6,000-7,000	3,800-4,600

CHEVROLET

	GOOD	AVERAGE	POOR
1994 Cavalier	3,800-5,500	3,100-4,700	1,600-2,700
1994 Cavalier Z24	6,300-7,300	5,500-6,500	3,400-4,100
1994 Convertible	6,400-7,500	5,600-6,700	3,500-4,300
1994 Z24 Convertible	8,200-9,500	7,300-8,500	5,000-5,800

AVERAGE REPLACEMENT COSTS

A/C Compressor	$540	Clutch, Pressure Plate, Bearing	620
Alternator	190	Constant Velocity Joints	545
Radiator	240	Brakes	210
Timing Chain or Belt	255	Shocks and/or Struts	315
Automatic Transmission or Transaxle	865	Exhaust System	350

TROUBLE SPOTS

• **Transmission slippage** Any car with a model TH-125 automatic transmission may shift late or not upshift at all. The problem is a stuck throttle valve inside the transmission. It may be overlooked during rebuilding since the valve appears fine because it is hydraulic pressure, not a physical binding, that makes it stick. The problem is fixed by enlarging the hydraulic fluid balance hole by 0.010 inch. (1990-94)

• **Brake wear** The front brakes wear out prematurely because of the friction compound. GM, and several aftermarket companies, have brakes with lining that will last longer. The GM part number is 12510050. This is not considered a warranty item. (1992-94)

• **Transaxle leak** The right front axle seal at the automatic transaxle is prone to leak and GM issued a revised seal to correct the problem and it is supposed to be installed whenever a car is in for transmission or axle shaft service of any sort. (1992-94)

• **Ignition switch** The ignition switch may not return from the start to the run position and the accessories such as the radio, wipers, cruise control, power windows, rear defroster or heater may not work because the screws that hold the switch in place were overtightened. (1991-94)

RECALL HISTORY

1991 Front door interlock striker may fail, causing door frame collapse and insufficient strength for shoulder belt anchorage. **1991** Front door shoulder belt guide loops may be cracked; occupant faces increased risk of injury in sudden stop or accident. **1992** Secondary hood latch spring in some cars is improperly installed or missing. **1993** Rear brake hoses on some cars are improperly manufactured and can cause reduced brake effectiveness. **1994** On small number of cars, drive axle spindle nuts may be overtorqued; can result in separation of steering knuckle tire-wheel assembly from axle.

1995-98 CHEVROLET CAVALIER

1995 Chevrolet Cavalier LS 4-door

FOR Air bags • Standard anti-lock brakes • Instruments/controls • Fuel economy • Acceleration (Twin Cam engine) • Visibility

AGAINST Rear head room • Seat comfort • Entry/exit (2-door models)

EVALUATION An improved suspension, lengthened wheelbase, and stiffer structure combine to furnish a comfortable ride that absorbs most bumps easily, without floating or wallowing on wavy surfaces. Base and LS models lean considerably in turns, however, and respond lazily to quick steering changes. For tight control, look into the Z24, which also rides quite well on most pavement surfaces.

Base-engine acceleration is adequate with either transmission, but the engine feels coarse under hard throttle. Fortunately, that engine noise settles down to a peaceful level at cruising speed. Wind and road noise are moderate. As for economy, we averaged 23.8 mpg with a base Cavalier sedan with the automatic transmission. We'd expect more than 30 mpg on the highway. The 2.4-liter Twin Cam unit is a better match to the automatic transmission than are some rival dual-cam engines. Because it produces slightly more torque over a broader range of engine speeds.

Gauges are clear and controls easy to reach and use, in a well-designed dashboard. Visibility is good to all angles. Six-footers have adequate room in front, though seats lack lower-back support. Rear leg room is okay, but head room suffices only for shorter folks. Getting in and out of the rear on 2-doors is tough. Trunk

CHEVROLET

space is ample, but a small opening makes it difficult to load bulky items. A one-piece folding rear seatback is standard.

Compared to its most natural rivals, the sportier-natured Dodge/Plymouth Neon, the refined Cavalier puts comfort and utility ahead of performance and style. All told, however, they don't match the refinement of the Toyota Corolla. For a reasonable sum, however, you get a car with dual air bags and anti-lock braking, even if it isn't quite as much fun to drive as a Neon.

NHTSA CRASH TEST RESULTS
1995 Cavalier sedan

2-DOOR CONVERTIBLE

Driver	☆☆☆
Passenger	☆☆☆

(The National Highway Traffic Safety Administration tests a vehicle's crashworthiness in front and side collisions. Their ratings suggest the chance of serious injury: ☆☆☆☆☆—10% or less; ☆☆☆☆—10-20% or less; ☆☆☆—20-30% or less; ☆☆—35-45% or less; ☆—More than 45%.)

SPECIFICATIONS

	2-door coupe	2-door conv.	4-door sedan
Wheelbase, in.	104.1	104.1	104.1
Overall length, in.	180.3	180.3	180.3
Overall width, in.	67.4	67.4	67.4
Overall height, in.	53.2	53.2	54.8
Curb weight, lbs.	2617	2838	2676
Cargo volume, cu. ft.	13.2	13.2	13.2
Fuel capacity, gals.	15.2	15.2	15.2
Seating capacity	5	4	5
Front head room, in.	37.6	38.8	39.0
Max. front leg room, in.	42.3	42.4	42.3
Rear head room, in.	36.6	38.5	37.2
Min. rear leg room, in.	33.2	32.8	34.6

Powertrain layout: transverse front-engine/front-wheel drive

ENGINES

	ohv I-4	dohc I-4	dohc I-4
Size, liters/cu. in.	2.2/132	2.3/138	2.4/146
Horsepower	115-120	150	150
Torque (lbs./ft.)	130	145	150
EPA city/highway mpg			
5-speed OD manual	25/37	22/32	23/33
3-speed automatic	24/31	21/31	
4-speed OD automatic			22/32
Consumer Guide™ observed MPG			
5-speed OD manual		25.7	
3-speed automatic	23.8		
4-speed OD automatic			23.4

Built in USA.

RETAIL PRICES

	GOOD	AVERAGE	POOR
1995 Cavalier	$5,600-6,700	$4,800-5,900	$2,800-3,600
1995 Cavalier Z24	7,300-8,200	6,400-7,300	4,000-4,800
1995 LS Convertible	8,700-10,000	7,800-9,000	5,000-6,000
1996 Cavalier	7,000-8,000	6,200-7,200	4,000-4,800
1996 Cavalier Z24	8,700-9,700	7,900-8,800	5,300-6,200
1996 LS Convertible	10,000-12,000	9,000-11,000	6,200-7,800
1997 Cavalier	8,300-9,300	7,400-8,300	5,000-5,800
1997 Cavalier Z24	10,500-11,500	9,500-10,500	6,600-7,500
1997 LS Convertible	12,000-14,500	11,000-13,200	8,000-9,800
1998 Cavalier	10,000-11,500	9,000-10,500	6,500-7,700
1998 Cavalier Z24	12,500-13,700	11,500-12,500	8,500-9,400
1998 Z24 Convertible	16,000-18,000	14,500-16,500	11,000-12,500

AVERAGE REPLACEMENT COSTS

A/C Compressor $555
Alternator 270
Radiator 347
Timing Chain or Belt 315
Automatic Transmission or
    Transaxle........................895

Clutch, Pressure Plate,
    Bearing............................550
Constant Velocity Joints.....480
Brakes.................................210
Shocks and/or Struts 640
Exhaust System 320

TROUBLE SPOTS

• **Traction control indicator light** The Enhanced Traction Control (ETC) warning light "ETC OFF" may glow and the cruise control stops working, but there is no problem with the system. If the computer failure memory is cleared, everything returns to normal. No current fix. (1996)

• **Brake wear** The front brakes wear out prematurely because of the friction compound. GM and several aftermarket companies have brakes with lining that will last longer. The GM part number is 12510050. This is not considered a warranty item. (1995)

RECALL HISTORY

1995 Missing welds in lower front suspension control arms assemblies can result in separation of front bushing sleeve subassembly from control arm, resulting in loss of vehicle control. **1995-96** Front and/or rear hazard warning lamps might not work. **1996** Interior lamps might come on unexpectedly while vehicle is being driven. **1996** Accelerator cable in a few cars could be kinked, causing high pedal effort, or sticking or broken cable. **1996-97** Air bag could deploy inadvertently during low-speed crash, or when an object strikes the floor pan. **1997** Driver's wiper blades on a few cars are 17 inches long instead of the required 22 inches. **1997** Spare tire on small number of cars may have incorrect rim.

1990-96 CHEVROLET CORSICA

1991 Chevrolet Corsica LT 4-door sedan

FOR Driver-side air bag (1991-96) • Anti-lock brakes (1992-96) • Acceleration (V-6) • Price

AGAINST Control layout • Engine noise (4-cylinder) • Rear seat room • Acceleration (early 4-cylinder)

EVALUATION Four-cylinder engines are noisy and anemic, even with the increased power for 1992 and again for '94, delivering barely adequate acceleration. That makes the V-6 a much wiser choice. Fuel economy suffers a bit with the V-6, but you benefit from much better performance.

Although the LTZ offered the ultimate Corsica setup for power and handling, it suffered a noticeable loss in ride comfort. The combination of base suspension and tires discourages even moderately aggressive driving. Some cars have an optional sport suspension that gives more sporting handling with no penalty in ride harshness.

Space is ample up front, but rear leg room is marginal for tall passengers. Trunk space is adequate. The early 5-door body style offered fine cargo carrying versatility, but optional fold-down rear seatbacks help extend the usefulness of the sedan's trunk. The dashboard layout, as revised for 1991, is quite serviceable, but rotary headlamp and wiper dials cannot be operated without taking your hands off the steering wheel.

Neither assembly quality nor refined driving quality can match Japanese compact rivals. Even though a capable Corsica doesn't quite stand out, though, it's a sensible buy secondhand, just as it was when new.

NHTSA CRASH TEST RESULTS
1994 Chevrolet Corsica   4-DOOR SEDAN

Driver   ☆☆☆

4-DOOR SEDAN

Passenger ☆☆

(The National Highway Traffic Safety Administration tests a vehicle's crashworthiness in front and side collisions. Their ratings suggest the chance of serious injury: ☆☆☆☆☆—10% or less; ☆☆☆☆—10-20% or less; ☆☆☆—20-30% or less; ☆☆—35-45% or less; ☆—More than 45%.)

SPECIFICATIONS	4-door sedan	4-door hatchback
Wheelbase, in.	103.4	103.4
Overall length, in.	183.4	183.4
Overall width, in.	68.2	68.2
Overall height, in.	56.2	56.2
Curb weight, lbs.	2638	2706
Cargo volume, cu. ft.	13.5	39.1
Fuel capacity, gals.	15.6	15.6
Seating capacity	5	5
Front head room, in.	38.1	38.1
Max. front leg room, in.	43.4	43.4
Rear head room, in.	37.4	37.4
Min. rear leg room, in.	35.0	35.0

Powertrain layout: transverse front-engine/front-wheel drive

ENGINES	ohv I-4	ohv V-6
Size, liters/cu. in.	2.2/133	3.1/191
Horsepower	95-120	135-160
Torque (lbs./ft.)	120-130	185
EPA city/highway mpg		
5-speed OD manual	25/34	19/28
3-speed automatic	24/31	20/28
4-speed OD automatic		21/29
Consumer Guide™ observed MPG		
3-speed automatic		22.7
4-speed OD automatic		23.4

Built in USA.

RETAIL PRICES	GOOD	AVERAGE	POOR
1990 Corsica	$1,900-2,800	$1,400-2,200	$600-1,000
1991 Corsica	2,400-3,200	1,800-2,600	900-1,300
1992 Corsica	2,800-3,600	2,200-3,000	1,200-1,600
1993 Corsica	3,400-4,200	2,700-3,500	1,500-2,000
1994 Corsica	4,200-5,000	3,500-4,300	2,000-2,700
1995 Corsica	5,200-6,000	4,500-5,300	2,800-3,400
1996 Corsica	6,400-7,500	5,700-6,700	3,700-4,500

AVERAGE REPLACEMENT COSTS

A/C Compressor $545	Clutch, Pressure Plate,
Alternator 230	Bearing 620
Radiator 450	Constant Velocity Joints.....535
Timing Chain or Belt 265	Brakes.................................225
Automatic Transmission or	Shocks and/or Struts 450
Transaxle.....................1,020	Exhaust System 320

TROUBLE SPOTS

• **Engine noise** Ticking noise from the engine shortly after cold starts on V-6 models may be due to loose piston wrist pins requiring replacement of all six pistons and pins. (1994-95)

• **Engine noise** A rattling noise that seems to come from the engine on cold startups could be due to oil pump starvation and cavitation in the automatic transmission, which GM claims will not harm the transmission or cause drivability problems. (1994-95)

• **Transmission leak** A revised transmission oil seal (green in color) was created to correct a leak at the right front (drive) axle. (1992-94)

• **Water leak** Water leaks onto the right front floor are caused by a gap between the air inlet screen at the bottom of the windshield. (1991-94)

• **Brakes** Original equipment front brake pads do not last as long as most motorists believe they should so GM offers a revised pad with a longer life lining. (1992-95)

RECALL HISTORY

1991 Steering wheel nut may not have been properly tightened, allowing steering wheel to separate from column, causing loss of control and potential for crash without warning.

1991-96 CHEVROLET CORVETTE

FOR Acceleration • Dual air bags (1994-96) • Anti-lock brakes • Steering/handling

AGAINST Ride • Fuel economy • Noise • Entry/exit • Price

EVALUATION Since the beginning, Corvettes have been cars for those who enjoy life in the fast lane—and are willing to sacrifice some comfort for the privilege. Improved assembly has greatly reduced the number of squeaks and rattles. The '90s suspension no longer jars your teeth while passing over bumps, but it's still quite firm. Corvettes offer great grip and ultra-quick reflexes, though bumpy roads upset the composure of the stiff suspension. On the positive side, wide tires, a firm suspension, and a low center of gravity allow Corvettes

1994 Chevrolet Corvette coupe

to handle like a race car as long as the pavement is reasonably smooth.

Getting in and out of the deep bucket seats in the pitlike cabin tends to be a challenge. Luggage space and interior room are at a premium, and visibility could be better. Noise levels are high. A husky exhaust note is prominent at all times, accompanied by abundant tire noise at highway speeds.

Acceleration is sheer magnificence: lusty and bold, whether from the standard LT1 engine in 1992-96 models, the prior L98, or the super-powered ZR-1. Each engine delivers a seamless rush of power from virtually any speed, causing the car to vault ahead under moderate to hard throttle. An LT1 pushes you back in your seat all the way to its 5500-rpm redline and feels discernably smoother than its predecessor. Fuel economy is nothing to boast about. There's an undeniable performance advantage in the ZR-1 package, but not enough to justify the huge prices that model commands.

Acceleration Slip Regulation in 1992-96 models squelches the wheel spin that nearly incapacitated earlier Corvettes when accelerating on slippery surfaces.

Rivals such as a Nissan 300ZX Turbo and Toyota Supra are more refined, but simply cannot match a Corvette's all-American macho flavor. To those who love them, there's nothing like a Corvette.

SPECIFICATIONS

	2-door coupe	2-door conv.
Wheelbase, in.	96.2	96.2
Overall length, in.	178.5	178.5
Overall width, in.	70.7	73.1
Overall height, in.	46.3	47.3
Curb weight, lbs.	3298	3360
Cargo volume, cu. ft.	12.6	6.6
Fuel capacity, gals.	20.0	20.0
Seating capacity	2	2
Front head room, in.	36.5	37.0

CHEVROLET

	2-door coupe	2-door conv.
Max. front leg room, in.	42.0	42.0
Rear head room, in.	—	—
Min. rear leg room, in.	—	—

Powertrain layout: longitudinal front-engine/rear-wheel drive

ENGINES

	ohv V-8	ohv V-8	dohc V-8
Size, liters/cu. in.	5.7/350	5.7/350	5.7/350
Horsepower	245	300-330	375-405
Torque (lbs./ft.)	340	330-340	370-385

EPA city/highway mpg

6-speed OD manual	16/25	16/27	17/25
4-speed OD automatic	16/24	17/25	

Consumer Guide™ observed MPG

4-speed OD automatic	16.6

Built in USA.

RETAIL PRICES

	GOOD	AVERAGE	POOR
1991 Corvette	$13,200-14,500	$12,200-13,300	$9,500-10,500
1991 Convertible	15,500-17,000	14,000-15,500	11,000-12,500
1991 Corvette ZR-1	23,000-25,000	21,000-23,000	17,000-18,500
1992 Corvette	14,700-16,500	13,200-15,000	10,500-12,000
1992 Convertible	17,500-19,500	16,000-18,000	13,000-14,500
1992 Corvette ZR-1	26,000-28,500	24,000-26,000	20,000-22,500
1993 Corvette	16,000-18,000	14,500-16,500	11,500-13,500
1993 Convertible	19,500-21,500	18,000-20,000	15,000-16,500
1993 Corvette ZR-1	30,000-33,000	27,500-30,000	23,000-25,500
1994 Corvette	17,800-20,000	16,000-18,000	13,000-15,000
1994 Convertible	21,500-23,500	19,500-21,500	16,500-18,500
1994 Corvette ZR-1	35,000-37,500	32,500-35,000	27,500-30,000
1995 Corvette	20,000-22,000	18,500-20,500	15,000-17,000
1995 Convertible	23,700-26,000	21,500-23,500	18,000-20,000
1995 Corvette ZR-1	39,000-42,500	36,000-39,000	31,000-33,500
1996 Corvette	22,500-25,000	21,000-23,000	17,500-19,000
1996 Convertible	26,500-29,500	24,500-27,000	21,000-23,000

AVERAGE REPLACEMENT COSTS

A/C Compressor $820	Clutch, Pressure Plate,
Alternator 280	Bearing 785
Radiator 495	Universal Joints 305
Timing Chain or Belt 990	Brakes...............................365
Automatic Transmission or	Shocks and/or Struts 730
Transaxle........................890	Exhaust System.................995

TROUBLE SPOTS

• **Transmission slippage** Unless the shift detent ball roller has been replaced, it may be hard to shift the manual 6-speed into reverse because transmission oil gets trapped behind the shift lever detent. (1995)

• **Climate control** The CD player may skip when driving on rough roads unless foam tape was applied to the top and bottom of the radio to keep it from shaking. (1991-94)

• **Engine misfire** To keep the distributor vacuum vent wiring harness from rubbing on the power steering pulley, there was a campaign to tie-strap the harness to the throttle body coolant hose. (1995)

• **Engine misfire** If the cars with a manual 6-speed transmission surge, sag, or chuggle at engine speeds below 2500 rpm, there is a revised PROM to correct it. (1995)

• **Transmission leak** Fluid may leak from the pump body on 4L60-E transmissions due to the pump bushing walking out of the valve body. (1995-96)

RECALL HISTORY

1992-93 w/LT1 engine Power steering gear inlet hose can fracture, causing flammable fluid to spray into engine compartment.

1990-94 CHEVROLET LUMINA

✓ BEST BUY

1990 Chevrolet Lumina 4-door

FOR Acceleration (3.4- and 3.8-liter V-6) • Handling (Euro, Z34) • Passenger and cargo room • Anti-lock brakes (later models)

AGAINST No air bags • Climate controls • Ride • Steering feel • Acceleration (4-cylinder)

CHEVROLET

EVALUATION Lumina's base 2.5-liter 4-cylinder engine delivers only so-so action. The 2.2-liter of 1993 isn't sufficient, either. The 3.1-liter V-6 is snappier, especially with 4-speed automatic transmission. However, the automatic's aversion to downshifts makes the car feel sluggish. Acceleration off-the-line is quick, but once underway, a heavy throttle foot is needed to overcome the transmission's reluctance. Highway cruising is quiet and relaxed, however.

The twin-cam 3.4-liter engine, available from 1991 onward delivers outstanding acceleration, but most of its power is concentrated at high engine speeds.

Body lean in turns is well controlled. While the suspension absorbs most bumps without much disturbance, freeway dips set the body to jouncing. Steering feel is imprecise and heavy, contributing to the car's ponderous feel in urban driving. All-disc brakes have good stopping power, but the pedal is too firm and hard to modulate.

Non-Euros lag a bit in performance and handling, though both versions deliver a solid feel on the road. For competent handling, the Euro's sport suspension and bigger tires are a necessity. Even so, Euros have proved to be disappointing. Their suspensions fail to filter out the bumps well, and still allow too much bounce over wavy surfaces. With its sport suspension, the Z34 is quick but rides rougher than its more sedate mates.

Gauges are not easy to read at a glance, and some controls are hard to reach. Climate controls are large and simple. Luminas are roomy inside for adults, front and rear, with plenty of cargo space on a flat trunk floor. Rear seat cushions are too short for long distance comfort. Every door has a map pocket, and the center storage console is handy, but the glovebox is tiny.

Though quiet and capable cruisers, Luminas don't quite match Taurus in overall style, features, or performance. On the other hand, a reasonable secondhand price can overcome at least a few of those objections.

NHTSA CRASH TEST RESULTS
1994 Chevrolet Lumina   4-DOOR SEDAN

Driver	☆☆☆☆☆
Passenger	☆☆☆☆

(The National Highway Traffic Safety Administration tests a vehicle's crashworthiness in front and side collisions. Their ratings suggest the chance of serious injury: ☆☆☆☆☆—10% or less; ☆☆☆☆—10-20% or less; ☆☆☆—20-30% or less; ☆☆—35-45% or less; ☆—More than 45%.)

SPECIFICATIONS

	2-door coupe	4-door sedan
Wheelbase, in.	107.5	107.5

	2-door coupe	4-door sedan
Overall length, in.	198.3	198.3
Overall width, in.	71.7	71.0
Overall height, in.	53.3	53.6
Curb weight, lbs.	3269	3333
Cargo volume, cu. ft.	15.7	15.7
Fuel capacity, gals.	16.5	16.5
Seating capacity	6	6
Front head room, in.	37.5	38.7
Max. front leg room, in.	42.4	42.4
Rear head room, in.	37.1	38.0
Min. rear leg room, in.	34.8	36.9

Powertrain layout: transverse front-engine/front-wheel drive

ENGINES

	ohv I-4	ohv I-4	ohv V-6	dohc V-6
Size, liters/cu. in.	2.2/133	2.5/151	3.1/191	3.4/207
Horsepower	110	105-110	135-140	200-210
Torque (lbs./ft.)	130	135	180-185	215
EPA city/highway mpg				
5-speed OD manual				17/27
3-speed automatic	21/29	21/28	19/27	
4-speed OD automatic			19/29	17/26
Consumer Guide™ observed MPG				
4-speed OD automatic			20.1	17.6

Built in Canada.

AVERAGE REPLACEMENT COSTS

A/C Compressor	$550	Clutch, Pressure Plate, Bearing 670
Alternator	200	Constant Velocity Joints.....485
Radiator	310	Brakes..........................189
Timing Chain or Belt	325	Shocks and/or Struts 865
Automatic Transmission or Transaxle......1,150		Exhaust System.................360

RETAIL PRICES	GOOD	AVERAGE	POOR
1990 Lumina	$1,700-2,700	$1,100-2,000	$500-1,000
1991 Lumina	2,400-3,600	1,700-2,900	900-1,500
1991 Lumina Z34	4,600-5,500	3,900-4,800	1,900-2,900
1992 Lumina	3,100-4,700	2,400-4,000	1,200-2,200
1992 Lumina Z34	5,500-6,500	4,700-5,700	2,600-3,600
1993 Lumina	4,000-5,800	3,200-5,000	1,700-3,000
1993 Lumina Z34	6,500-7,500	5,700-6,700	3,400-4,200
1994 Lumina	5,300-7,000	4,500-6,200	2,500-4,000

CHEVROLET

	GOOD	AVERAGE	POOR
1994 Lumina Z34	7,700-8,800	6,800-7,800	4,300-5,000

TROUBLE SPOTS

• **Engine noise** A tick or rattle when the engine is started cold may be due to too much wrist-pin-to-piston clearance. New piston and pin sets will be replaced under warranty if the customer complains of the noise. (1993-95)

• **Engine noise** What sounds like a rattling noise from the engine that lasts less than a minute when the car is started after sitting overnight is often caused by automatic transmission pump starvation or cavitation, or a sticking pressure regulator valve. According to GM, no damage occurs and it does not have a fix for the problem. (1991-94)

• **Transaxle leak** The right front axle seal at the automatic transaxle is prone to leak and GM issued a revised seal to correct the problem and it is supposed to be installed whenever a car is in for transmission or axle shaft service of any sort. (1992-94)

• **Steering noise** The upper bearing mount in the steering column can get loose and cause a snapping or clicking that can be both heard and felt requiring a new bearing spring and turn signal cancel cam, which the manufacturer will warranty. (1994)

• **Oil leak** The plastic valve covers on the 3.1L engine were prone to leaks and should be replaced with redesigned aluminum valve covers. (GM no longer stocks the plastic ones.) (1995)

• **Transmission slippage** The 4T60E transmission may drop out of drive (neutral condition) while cruising, shift erratically, have no third or fourth gear, or no second and third gear because of a bad ground connection for the shift solenoids. Poor grounds also allow wrong gear starts. Many transmissions have been mistakenly rebuilt, which does not correct the problem. (1991-94)

• **Transmission slippage** Any car with a model TH-125 or 440-T4 automatic transmission may shift late or not upshift at all. The problem is a stuck throttle valve inside the transmission. It may be overlooked during rebuilding since the valve appears fine because it is hydraulic pressure, not a physical binding, that makes it stick. The problem is fixed by enlarging the hydraulic fluid balance hole by 0.010 inch. (1991-93)

RECALL HISTORY

1990 Front seatbelt may not properly restrain passenger in an accident. **1990** Front shoulder safety belt webbing may separate at upper guide loops on either side of front seat. **1990** Brake lights may not illuminate or, in some cases, will not stay illuminated all the time when brakes are applied, due to faulty stoplight switch. **1990** Cracks may develop in mounting surface of certain Kelsey-Hayes steel wheels; wheel will separate from vehicle. **1990-91** Due to corrosion at front sub-frame, steering shaft could separate from steering gear, resulting in crash. **1991** Front door shoulder belt guide loops may be cracked and not in compliance with federal standard; occupant faces increased risk of injury in a sudden stop or accident. **1992** Reverse servo apply pin of 4-speed automatic transmission may bind, which could cause loss or slipping of reverse, poor performance, or transmission to remain in "Reverse" while the indicator shows "Neutral" position. **1993** Some front seatbacks may recline without prior warning.

1995-98 CHEVROLET LUMINA/ MONTE CARLO

1995 Chevrolet Lumina LS

FOR Air bags, dual • Anti-lock brakes • Passenger and cargo room • Ride • Automatic transmission performance

AGAINST Steering feel • Fuel economy (3.4-liter) • Engine noise (3.4-liter) • Rear visibility (Monte Carlo) • Rear seat entry/exit (Monte Carlo)

EVALUATION Performance is adequate from the 3.1-liter engine, though it feels a little slow initially. The 4-speed automatic transmission changes gears smoothly and downshifts promptly when passing power is needed. We've averaged 20.1 mpg in a Lumina with the base engine, with about half of the driving on expressways.

Expect about 3 mpg less with the stronger 3.4-liter engine. That one has more potent passing punch, but gets louder during hard acceleration. The smooth 3.8-liter on some '98 models is

CHEVROLET

even more powerful—especially around town.

An absorbent suspension on the Lumina soaks up bumpy pavement without harshness or excessive bouncing. Steering in the Lumina is light and has little road feel.

As many as six people can fit in a Lumina—though everyone will be squeezed somewhat. There's ample room for four in the Monte Carlo, but a fifth might feel unwelcome.

The Monte Carlo requires plenty of room to fully open its wide doors, and climbing into the back seat demands some bending. Thick rear pillars hurt over-the-shoulder visibility in the Monte Carlo, whereas relatively narrow pillars and deep side windows in the Lumina help give a good view to all directions.

Dashboards have a clean, contemporary design. Simple controls are easy to see and reach while driving. Trunks in both models are roomy, with a flat floor that reaches well forward.

The Lumina is a pleasant, competent family sedan, which deserves consideration if you're shopping in the mid-size field.

NHTSA CRASH TEST RESULTS
1995 Chevrolet Lumina/Monte Carlo 4-DOOR SEDAN

Driver	☆☆☆☆☆
Passenger	☆☆☆☆

(The National Highway Traffic Safety Administration tests a vehicle's crashworthiness in front and side collisions. Their ratings suggest the chance of serious injury: ☆☆☆☆☆—10% or less; ☆☆☆☆—10-20% or less; ☆☆☆—20-30% or less; ☆☆—35-45% or less; ☆—More than 45%.)

SPECIFICATIONS

	2-door coupe	4-door sedan
Wheelbase, in.	107.5	107.5
Overall length, in.	200.7	200.9
Overall width, in.	72.5	72.5
Overall height, in.	55.2	53.8
Curb weight, lbs.	3306	3330
Cargo volume, cu. ft.	15.7	15.7
Fuel capacity, gals.	17.1	17.1
Seating capacity	6	6
Front head room, in.	38.4	37.9
Max. front leg room, in.	42.4	42.4
Rear head room, in.	37.4	36.9
Min. rear leg room, in.	36.6	34.9

Powertrain layout: transverse front-engine/front-wheel drive

ENGINES

	ohv V-6	dohc V-6	ohv V-6
Size, liters/cu. in.	3.1/191	3.4/207	3.8/231
Horsepower	160	210-215	200
Torque (lbs./ft.)	185	215-220	225

EPA city/highway mpg
4-speed OD automatic 20/29   17/26   19/30

Consumer Guide™ observed MPG
4-speed OD automatic 20.1   19.1

Built in Canada.

RETAIL PRICES	GOOD	AVERAGE	POOR
1995 Lumina	$6,900-8,000	$6,100-7,200	$4,000-5,000
1995 Monte Carlo	8,800-10,500	8,000-9,600	5,500-6,500
1996 Lumina	8,200-9,500	7,300-8,500	5,000-5,900
1996 Monte Carlo	10,200-12,000	9,200-11,000	6,000-7,500
1997 Lumina	10,000-12,000	9,000-11,000	6,500-7,700
1997 Monte Carlo	11,500-13,500	10,500-12,200	7,500-8,800
1998 Lumina	12,000-14,500	11,000-13,200	8,000-9,300
1998 Monte Carlo	13,500-16,000	12,200-14,500	9,000-10,800

AVERAGE REPLACEMENT COSTS

A/C Compressor $525
Alternator 200
Radiator 430
Timing Chain or Belt 450
Automatic Transmission or
    Transaxle......................1,180

Clutch, Pressure Plate,
    Bearing.............................NA
Constant Velocity Joints.....915
Brakes.................................270
Shocks and/or Struts 665
Exhaust System.................385

TROUBLE SPOTS

• **Fuel pump** Excess material used to manufacture the plastic fuel tank can collect on the fuel pickup filter, restrict fuel flow, and cause reduced performance. (1995-96)

• **Suspension noise** A popping or scrunching noise from the front end is caused by a problem with the struts which can be corrected with an additional jounce bumper. (1995-96)

• **Engine temperature** The engine may overheat due to a problem with the heater hoses which swell, then loosen from the heater core pipes and leak. (1996)

• **Oil leak** Some cars have high oil consumption which is corrected by replacing the PCV harness as well as the valve cover, spark plugs and wires and oil fill cap. (1995)

• **Hard starting** There is a new Flash PROM available to correct hard starting and stalling under high-load, slow-speed operation such as parking. (1996)

RECALL HISTORY

1995 Lumina Steering-column bracket bolts on some cars may not be tightened. **1995** Right lower control arm ball-joint mounting hole

CHEVROLET

was incorrectly positioned. **1995** Seatbelt anchor can fracture in crash. **1995** Wiper/washer operation may be intermittent or nonexistent. **1995** Strained or separated windshield wiper/washer switch wire can cause intermittent or nonexistent wash/wipe operation. **1996** Brake booster tab is improperly located; if stopping distance is short, crash could occur. **1996 Lumina** Left front brake line can contact transaxle bracket or bolt and wear through.

1990-96 CHEVROLET LUMINA APV/MINIVAN

1995 Chevrolet Lumina APV

FOR Air bag, driver (later models) • Acceleration (3.8-liter V-6) • Noise • Passenger and cargo room • Ride

AGAINST Acceleration (3.1-liter) • Visibility

EVALUATION The long sloping snout with steep windshield cuts into interior space and looks oddly daunting from the driver's seat—almost like you're steering from the back seat. Most people quickly get used to that, but it's still difficult to see the front end while maneuvering. Even after the snout was shortened for 1994, forward visibility could be a problem.

Don't be dissuaded by appearances, as the APV has several notable virtues. This minivan drives much like a passenger car, cornering with commendable control and absorbing most bumps without harshness or wallowing. Smooth and quiet on the road, the minivan leans modestly in turns and offers good rain/snow traction, but steering feels much too light.

Lack of power is a major drawback in early models, especially at passing speeds when fully loaded. The 3.1-liter V-6 simply runs out of breath in a hurry. So, give yourself plenty of time and room to merge into traffic or overtake other vehicles. Once at highway speed, on the other hand, the minivan settles in for fine cruising. An optional 165-horsepower "3800" V-6 with 4-speed automatic, offered since '92, moves more quickly and gives the Lumina performance to match or exceed its rivals from Ford and Chrysler. The 3.4-liter V-6 installed in final Minivans feels stronger than the 3.1, but less lively than the 3.8-liter.

Undersized climate controls are the only serious flaw on the dashboard. Storage bins are everywhere, and there's no engine hump to hinder passage to the rear. Versatile interiors seat up to seven, using modular seats that weigh just 34 pounds each and remove in seconds. With all seats installed, there's little room for cargo, but each rear seatback folds down to create a 4x6-foot load space. The optional power sliding door is convenient.

If you need cargo space but demand the smooth ride and handling of a car, and don't like boxy vans, look no further. Dodge and Plymouth have long been the class leaders, but Luminas tend to be cheaper.

SPECIFICATIONS

	4-door van
Wheelbase, in.	109.8
Overall length, in.	191.5
Overall width, in.	73.9
Overall height, in.	65.7
Curb weight, lbs.	3686
Cargo volume, cu. ft.	112.6
Fuel capacity, gals.	20.0
Seating capacity	7
Front head room, in.	39.2
Max. front leg room, in.	40.0
Rear head room, in.	39.0
Min. rear leg room, in.	36.1

Powertrain layout: transverse front-engine/front-wheel drive

ENGINES

	ohv V-6	ohv V-6	ohv V-6
Size, liters/cu. in.	3.1/191	3.4/207	3.8/231
Horsepower	120	180	165-170
Torque (lbs./ft.)	170-175	205	220-225
EPA city/highway mpg			
3-speed automatic	19/23		
4-speed OD automatic		19/26	17/25
Consumer Guide™ observed MPG			
3-speed automatic	17.4		
4-speed OD automatic		17.5	16.5

Built in USA.

CHEVROLET

RETAIL PRICES

	GOOD	AVERAGE	POOR
1990 Lumina APV	$2,800-3,800	$2,200-3,100	$900-1,500
1991 Lumina APV	3,600-4,800	2,900-4,000	1,400-2,200
1992 Lumina APV	4,400-5,600	3,700-4,800	1,900-2,800
1993 Lumina APV	5,200-6,500	4,400-5,600	2,500-3,500
1994 Lumina Minivan	6,600-7,900	5,800-7,000	3,600-4,500
1995 Lumina Minivan	8,200-10,000	7,200-9,000	4,700-6,200
1996 Lumina Minivan	10,500-12,500	9,300-11,000	6,500-8,000

AVERAGE REPLACEMENT COSTS

A/C Compressor $565
Alternator 280
Radiator 430
Timing Chain or Belt 310
Automatic Transmission or
    Transaxle.....................1,095

Constant Velocity Joints.....505
Brakes.................................230
Shocks and/or Struts 430
Exhaust System.................310

TROUBLE SPOTS

• **Oil consumption** Models with the 3800 (3.8L) engine are prone to excessive oil consumption often accompanied by spark knock (pinging) during normal driving conditions due to failure of the valve stem seals. (1993-95)

• **Engine knock** Bearing knock was common on many 3300 and 3800 (3.3L and 3.8L) engines due to too much clearance on the number one main bearing requiring it to be replaced with a 0.001-inch undersize bearing. (1992-94)

• **Transaxle leak** The right front axle seal at the automatic transaxle is prone to leak and GM issued a revised seal to correct the problem and it is supposed to be installed whenever a car is in for transmission or axle shaft service of any sort. (1992-94)

• **Engine noise** What sounds like a rattling noise from the engine that lasts less than a minute when the car is started after sitting overnight is often caused by automatic transmission pump starvation or cavitation, or a sticking pressure regulator valve. According to GM, no damage occurs and it does not have a fix for the problem. (1992-95)

• **Transmission slippage** Any van with a model TH-125 automatic transmission may shift late or not upshift at all. The problem is a stuck throttle valve inside the transmission. It may be overlooked during rebuilding since the valve appears fine because it is hydraulic pressure, not a physical binding, that makes it stick. The problem is fixed by enlarging the hydraulic fluid balance hole by 0.010 inch. (1990-94)

• **Steering noise** The upper bearing mount in the steering column can get loose and cause a snapping or clicking that can be both heard and felt, requiring a new bearing spring and turn signal cancel cam, which the manufacturer will warranty. (1994-96)

• **Transmission slippage** The 4T60E transmission may drop out of drive (neutral condition) while cruising, shift erratically, have no third or fourth gear, or no second and third gear because of a bad ground connection for the shift solenoids. Poor grounds also allow wrong gear starts. Many transmissions have been mistakenly rebuilt, which does not correct the problem. (1992-94)

RECALL HISTORY

1990 Rear modular seat frame hold-down hooks on some vans may not meet the required pull force at rear seat anchorage. **1990-91** Due to corrosion, steering shaft could separate from steering gear. **1992-93** Seatbelt for left third-row seat of six-passenger van, or center second-row seat of seven-passenger van, may lock up. **1992-95** Transmission cooler line in cars with certain powertrains, sold in specified states, can separate at low temperature. **1993-94 with optional power sliding door** Second-row, right-hand shoulder belt can become pinched, unable to retract properly. **1994** Pawl spring may be missing from retractors for rear center lap belts. **1994** Third-row seatbelt retractors may lock up when van is on a slope. **1995** On some vehicles, brake pedal arm can fracture during braking. **1995 with 3.1-liter engine** Throttle cable support brackets could contact throttle-lever system and inhibit throttle return; engine speed would then decrease more slowly than anticipated.

1990-94 CHEVROLET S10 BLAZER

1993 Chevrolet S10 Blazer LT 4-door

FOR Anti-lock brakes • Acceleration • 4WD traction • Passenger and cargo room • Ride (5-door)

CHEVROLET

AGAINST   Rear seat comfort • Fuel economy • Noise • Ride (3-door models)

EVALUATION   The 4.3-liter engine develops considerable torque at low engine speeds, yielding strong acceleration around town, plus plenty of towing power. It's also noisy.

Suspensions are among the least compliant in their class, but the 4-door's longer wheelbase improves ride quality. With a 2-door you can expect to bounce and bang over bumpy roads.

Body lean in turns isn't bad, but Blazers don't match the smaller Jeep Cherokee in urban nimbleness. Interior room is good, but not as spacious as an Explorer or Grand Cherokee. Dashboard layout also is pleasing on the whole, but some controls are a long reach, and radio buttons are small. Interior noise gets bothersome on the highway.

Back seats are hard to get at in 2-doors. Four-door models, with their extra 6.5 inches of wheelbase, boast vastly improved access. Rear leg room is identical in each body style, but the 5-door's longer wheelbase allowed the back seat to be fitted ahead of rear wheelwells, for 15 inches more hip room than the 2-door.

Shift-on-the-fly 4WD and 4-wheel ABS are particularly appealing features. By 1993, when Jeep launched its Grand Cherokee with a driver-side air bag and available V-8, the Blazer was showing its age. Grand Chreokee and Explorers beat the Blazer in refinement, but the S10 Blazer still is a good choice in a smaller sport-utility.

SPECIFICATIONS

	2-door wagon	4-door wagon
Wheelbase, in.	100.5	107.0
Overall length, in.	170.3	176.8
Overall width, in.	65.4	65.4
Overall height, in.	64.1	64.3
Curb weight, lbs.	3536	3776
Cargo volume, cu. ft.	67.3	74.3
Fuel capacity, gals.	20.0	20.0
Seating capacity	4	6
Front head room, in.	39.1	39.1
Max. front leg room, in.	42.5	42.5
Rear head room, in.	38.7	38.8
Min. rear leg room, in.	35.5	36.5

Powertrain layout: longitudinal front-engine/rear- or 4-wheel drive

ENGINES

	ohv V-6	ohv V-6
Size, liters/cu. in.	4.3/262	4.3/262
Horsepower	160-165	200
Torque (lbs./ft.)	230-235	260

EPA city/highway mpg

5-speed OD manual	16/21	
4-speed OD automatic	17/22	16/22

Consumer Guide™ observed MPG

4-speed OD automatic	16.2	15.3

Built in USA.

RETAIL PRICES

	GOOD	AVERAGE	POOR
1990 S10 Blazer	$3,300-5,000	$2,600-4,300	$1,300-2,500
1991 S10 Blazer	4,500-6,700	3,700-5,900	2,000-3,700
1992 S10 Blazer	5,600-8,200	4,800-7,400	2,800-5,000
1993 S10 Blazer	6,700-9,700	5,900-8,800	3,700-6,000
1994 S10 Blazer	8,400-11,500	7,600-10,500	5,200-7,500

AVERAGE REPLACEMENT COSTS

A/C Compressor	$365
Alternator	195
Radiator	415
Timing Chain or Belt	205
Automatic Transmission or Transaxle	735
Clutch, Pressure Plate, Bearing	390
Universal Joints	160
Brakes	210
Shocks and/or Struts	275
Exhaust System	405

TROUBLE SPOTS

• **Engine knock** Engine knock when the engine (4.3L, 5.7L, or 7.4L) is started is usually eliminated by using an oil filter with a check valve (such as Fram PH3980), but if this does not fix it, GM has revised PROMs for the computers and will even replace the main bearings if all else fails. (1990-95)

• **Transmission slippage** Any truck with a model TH-700-R4 automatic transmission may shift late or not upshift at all. The problem is a stuck throttle valve inside the transmission. It may be overlooked during rebuilding since the valve appears fine because it is hydraulic pressure, not a physical binding, that makes it stick. The problem is fixed by enlarging the hydraulic fluid balance hole by 0.010 inch. (1990 94)

RECALL HISTORY

1990-91 Fuel tank sender seal may be out of position, which could result in fuel leakage. **1990-92 with 2.5-liter engine and no air conditioning** Fan blades could break off while engine is running. **1991** Rear seatbelt buckle release button can stick in unlatched position, under certain conditions. **1993** Rear seatbelts may not meet government requirements. **1994 with VR4 weight-distribution trailer hitch option** Trailer hitch attaching bolts were not tightened adequately.

1990-93 CHEVROLET S10 PICKUP

1991 Chevrolet S10 Extended Cab

FOR   Acceleration (V-6) • Payload

AGAINST   Acceleration (4-cylinder) • Control layout

EVALUATION   We prefer V-6 engines, because automatic transmissions rob too much performance from the 4-cylinder. If you definitely must have a 4-cylinder, stick with manual shift. The 2.8-liter V-6 is adequate for most 2-wheel-drive requirements, but the brawny 4.3-liter engine sends these trucks to the head of their class for acceleration and towing prowess. A basic long-bed 2WD with the 4.3-liter V-6 and automatic averaged about 21.5 mpg. A short-bed with the same powertrain but with a Baja 4x4 package averaged just 16 mpg. Rear-wheel ABS improves control in stops but otherwise braking power is nothing special.

Extended-cab models have 18.3 cubic feet of storage space behind the front seats (13.7 cubic feet if equipped with optional jump seats, which are large enough only for children). Even when equipped with extra-cost interior trim packages, these pickups tend to feel crude inside, with too many sharp plastic edges and a cheap feel to most controls.

The optional front stabilizer bar improves steering response and reduces body lean in turns. Heavy-duty shock absorbers also are a good idea, cutting down on bouncing and pitching. Analog gauges were standard, and are easier to read than the optional electronic cluster.

Popular for both work and play, S10 pickups score well against their natural rival: the Ford Ranger, and the availability of the 4.3-liter V-6 engine placed the S10 a step ahead of its competition.

SPECIFICATIONS

	reg. cab short bed	reg. cab long bed	ext. cab
Wheelbase, in.	108.3	117.9	122.9
Overall length, in.	178.2	194.2	192.8
Overall width, in.	64.7	64.7	64.7
Overall height, in.	61.3	61.3	61.3
Curb weight, lbs.	2635	2773	3024
Max. payload lbs.	1886	1902	1869
Fuel capacity, gals.	20.0	20.0	20.0
Seating capacity	3	3	5
Front head room, in.	39.1	39.1	39.1
Max. front leg room, in.	42.5	42.5	42.5
Rear head room, in.	NA	NA	NA
Min. rear leg room, in.	NA	NA	NA

Powertrain layout: longitudinal front-engine/rear- or 4-wheel drive

ENGINES

	ohv I-4	ohv V-6	ohv V-6
Size, liters/cu. in.	2.5/151	2.8/173	4.3/262
Horsepower	94-105	125	160-165
Torque (lbs./ft.)	130-135	150	230-235
EPA city/highway mpg			
5-speed OD manual	23/27	19/25	18/23
4-speed OD automatic	20/26		18/24
Consumer Guide™ observed MPG			
5-speed OD manual	22.9		
4-speed OD automatic			16.2

Built in USA.

RETAIL PRICES

	GOOD	AVERAGE	POOR
1990 S10	$1,300-3,700	$800-3,000	$300-1,700
1991 S10	1,800-5,500	1,200-4,700	500-2,800
1992 S10	2,800-6,800	2,200-6,000	900-3,700
1993 S10	3,600-7,800	2,900-7,000	1,300-4,500

AVERAGE REPLACEMENT COSTS

A/C Compressor	$365
Alternator	195
Radiator	325
Timing Chain or Belt	205
Automatic Transmission or Transaxle	735
Clutch, Pressure Plate, Bearing	415
Universal Joints	190
Brakes	207
Shocks and/or Struts	370
Exhaust System	335

TROUBLE SPOTS

• **Transmission slippage** Any truck with a model 700-R4 automatic transmission may shift late or not upshift at all. The problem is a stuck throttle valve inside the transmission. It may be overlooked during rebuilding since the valve appears fine because it is hydraulic pressure, not a physical binding, that makes it stick. The problem is fixed by enlarging the hydraulic fluid balance hole by 0.010 inch. (1990-93)

RECALL HISTORY

1990-92 without air conditioning Fan blades on 2.5-liter engine can break as a result of fatigue. **1991** Fuel tank sender seal may be out of position. **1993 S10/T10 with folding rear seats** Outboard rear seatbelt assembly will not release webbing from retracted position. **1996-97 with 4.3-liter V-6 engine** Front brake line can contact oil pan, causing wear that may result in fluid loss.

1994-98 CHEVROLET S-SERIES PICKUP

1994 Chevrolet S10 SS

FOR Air bag, driver (1995-later) • Passenger room • Acceleration (V-6) • Control layout • Ride (2WD models) • Optional third door (1996-later) • Handling

AGAINST Fuel economy • Ride (4WD models) • No passenger-side air bag • Rear seat room (extended cab)

EVALUATION In their latest form, these compact pickups rank among the best in overall performance, ergonomics, and refinement. Pleasant to drive, the S-Series is a solid-feeling truck. Cabins feel roomier than before, with more rearward seat travel and storage space. Extra glass area gives great visibility and an airy feel. Wind noise is reduced.

Acceleration is good with the V-6. Automatic-transmission gearchanges are smooth, though downshifts might be delayed for low-speed passing. An extended-cab V-6 LS averaged 17.2 mpg in a long-term trial. When cold, however, that engine ran somewhat roughly, and its fan was intrusively loud. If you prefer a 4-cylinder pickup, your best bet is manual shift.

An extended-cab 2WD LS delivered ride quality as smooth as many cars. These pickups easily absorb most bumps, and take dips with minimal bouncing, but some optional tire/suspension setups are rougher. When the cargo bed is empty, the tail tends to hop over sharp bumps and ridges. Body lean is evident in turns, but the truck feels balanced and poised in directional changes. Standard anti-lock brakes prevent lock-up during simulated panic stops, but brake-pedal feel on early models is disturbingly spongy.

A Dodge Dakota has heftier hauling ability and an available V-8 engine, but most buyers will be pleased with the Chevrolet. It outsells the Dakota and is a worthy contender to the sales-leading Ford Ranger.

NHTSA CRASH TEST RESULTS
1997 Chevrolet S-Series

REG. CAB SHORT BED

Driver	☆☆☆
Passenger	☆☆

(The National Highway Traffic Safety Administration tests a vehicle's crashworthiness in front and side collisions. Their ratings suggest the chance of serious injury: ☆☆☆☆☆—10% or less; ☆☆☆☆—10-20% or less; ☆☆☆—20-30% or less; ☆☆—35-45% or less; ☆—More than 45%.)

SPECIFICATIONS

	reg. cab short bed	reg. cab long bed	ext. cab
Wheelbase, in.	108.3	117.9	122.9
Overall length, in.	188.6	204.6	203.3
Overall width, in.	67.9	67.9	67.9
Overall height, in.	62.1	62.1	62.2
Curb weight, lbs.	2822	2874	3081
Max. payload, lbs.	1654	1715	1460
Fuel capacity, gals.	19.0	19.0	19.0
Seating capacity	3	3	5
Front head room, in.	39.5	39.5	39.5
Max. front leg room, in.	43.2	43.2	43.2
Rear head room, in.	NA	NA	NA
Min. rear leg room, in.	NA	NA	NA

Powertrain layout: longitudinal front-engine/rear- or 4-wheel drive

ENGINES

	ohc I-4	ohv V-6	ohv V-6
Size, liters/cu. in.	2.2/134	4.3/262	4.3/262
Horsepower	118-120	155-170	180-195
Torque (lbs./ft.)	130	235	245-260
EPA city/highway mpg			
5-speed OD manual	23/30	18/25	18/25
4-speed OD automatic	20/27	20/24	20/24

CHEVROLET

Consumer Guide™ observed MPG
5-speed OD manual 22.3
4-speed OD automatic 18.4   18.0
Built in USA.

RETAIL PRICES	GOOD	AVERAGE	POOR
1994 S10	$5,000-9,800	$4,200-8,800	$2,100-6,300
1995 S-Series	6,200-11,500	5,400-10,500	3,200-7,500
1996 S-Series	7,300-12,800	6,400-11,800	4,000-8,800
1997 S-Series	8,500-15,000	7,500-14,000	5,000-10,500
1998 S-Series	10,500-17,000	9,300-15,500	6,500-12,000

AVERAGE REPLACEMENT COSTS

A/C Compressor $550
Alternator 255
Radiator 410
Timing Chain or Belt 420
Automatic Transmission or
   Transaxle........................750

Clutch, Pressure Plate,
   Bearing............................545
Universal Joints 190
Brakes................................210
Shocks and/or Struts 345
Exhaust System.................460

TROUBLE SPOTS

• **Engine knock** Engine knock when the engine (4.3L, 5.7L, or 7.4L) is started is usually eliminated by using an oil filter with a check valve (such as Fram PH3980), but if this does not fix it, GM has revised PROMs for the computers and will even replace the main bearings if all else fails. (1990-95)

RECALL HISTORY

1994 w/2.2-liter engine Vacuum hose can detach from power brake booster check valve, as a result of engine backfire. **1995 w/air conditioning and V-6 engine** Rivet can break and allow fan blade to separate from hub. **1996** Top coat of paint on a few trucks peels severely. **1996 2WD manual-shift w/2.2-liter engine** Drive wheels could seize and lock while truck is moving. **1994-95 Postal Vehicle** Loose/worn steering shaft can result in separation from steering gear. **1994-97** Seatbelt webbing on certain models can separate during frontal impact. **1996-97 w/V-6 engine** Front brake line can contact oil pan, causing wear that may result in fluid loss. **1998** Fatigue fracture of rear-axle brake pipe can occur, causing slow fluid leak and resulting in soft brake pedal; if pipe breaks, driver would face sudden loss of rear-brake performance. **1998** Wiring-harness clip can melt and drip onto exhaust manifold, possibly resulting in fire.

1995-98 CHRYSLER CIRRUS

1996 Chrysler Cirrus LXi

FOR Air bags, dual • Anti-lock brakes • Acceleration (V-6) • Ride • Steering/handling • Passenger and cargo room • Instruments/controls

AGAINST Road noise • Rear visibility

See the 1995-98 Dodge Stratus report for an evaluation of the 1995-98 Chrysler Cirrus.

NHTSA CRASH TEST RESULTS
1996 Chrysler Cirrus 4-DOOR SEDAN

Driver	☆☆☆
Passenger	NA

(The National Highway Traffic Safety Administration tests a vehicle's crashworthiness in front and side collisions. Their ratings suggest the chance of serious injury: ☆☆☆☆☆—10% or less; ☆☆☆☆—10-20% or less; ☆☆☆—20-30% or less; ☆☆—35-45% or less; ☆—More than 45%.)

SPECIFICATIONS

	4-door sedan
Wheelbase, in.	108.0
Overall length, in.	186.0
Overall width, in.	71.0
Overall height, in.	54.1
Curb weight, lbs.	3150
Cargo volume, cu. ft.	15.7
Fuel capacity, gals.	16.0
Seating capacity	5
Front head room, in.	38.1
Max. front leg room, in.	42.3
Rear head room, in.	36.8
Min. rear leg room, in.	37.8

Powertrain layout: transverse front-engine/front-wheel drive

ENGINES

	dohc I-4	ohc V-6
Size, liters/cu. in.	2.4/148	2.5/152
Horsepower	150	168
Torque (lbs./ft.)	165-167	170

EPA city/highway mpg

4-speed OD automatic....................................	20/29	20/28

Consumer Guide™ observed MPG

4-speed OD automatic....................................	21.0

Built in USA.

RETAIL PRICES

	GOOD	AVERAGE	POOR
1995 Cirrus	$8,000-9,500	$7,000-8,500	$4,500-6,000
1996 Cirrus	9,500-11,500	8,500-10,500	6,000-7,500
1997 Cirrus	11,000-13,200	10,000-12,000	7,500-9,000
1998 Cirrus	13,500-16,500	12,300-15,000	9,300-12,000

AVERAGE REPLACEMENT COSTS

A/C Compressor $450	Clutch, Pressure Plate, Bearing 560
Alternator 315	Constant Velocity Joints.....375
Radiator 440	Brakes.................................320
Timing Chain or Belt 255	Shocks and/or Struts 375
Automatic Transmission or Transaxle......................1,015	Exhaust System.................380

TROUBLE SPOTS

• **Headlights** Poor illumination from headlights corrected by replacing both headlamp modules. (1996-97)

• **Air conditioner** Air conditioning compressor fails on cars with 2.5L engine, especially If car is driven mostly in heavy traffic in hot weather. (1995-96)

• **Air conditioner** Air conditioning may be intermittent or stop completely due to failed pressure transducer. (1995)

• **Transmission slippage** Transmission may shudder when accelerating from a stop, thump when coasting down to a stop, or slip when shifting. (1995)

• **Tail/brake lights** Moisture builds up in tail lamps. (1995)

• **Water leak** Water leaks in between the door and interior door trim panel or from the cowl/plenum/floor/A-pillar seams. (1995-96)

RECALL HISTORY

1995 Rear seatbelt anchors will not withstand loading required by Federal standard. **1995-96** Brake master cylinder can leak fluid, due to damaged seal; warning light will signal impairment prior to partial brake-system loss. **1995-96** Corrosion of ABS hydraulic control unit can cause solenoid valves to stick open, so car tends to pull from a straight stop when brakes are applied. **1995-96 w/2.4-liter** Oil leakage could cause engine-compartment fire. **1995-97** Lower ball joint can separate due to loss of lubrication; could cause loss of control. **1996-97** Secondary hood latch spring can disengage if hood is slammed.

1993-97 CHRYSLER CONCORDE/NEW YORKER/LHS

1993 Chrysler Concorde

FOR Air bags • Anti-lock brakes • Acceleration (3.5-liter) • Passenger and cargo room • Steering/handling • Ride

AGAINST Climate controls • Acceleration (3.3-liter) • Fuel economy • Rear visibility (LHS/New Yorker)

EVALUATION The unusually long wheelbase translates to ample leg room front and rear, while the sleek "cab-forward" profile pushes wheels out to the corners for exceptional backseat width. Three large adults can ride in the rear without crowding, and cargo space is ample. A low waistline and large windows add to the impression of spaciousness. Wide door openings ease entry/exit. New Yorker/LHS sedans offer all the space in the Concorde, and more yet for rear occupants.

With the Touring Package, the all-independent suspension delivers crisp, assured handling and a comfortable, controlled ride. The base '93 suspension isn't bad, but permits more body and wheel motion over large humps and dips.

Performance ranks only as adequate with the smaller engine. The bigger 24-valve V-6 is a bit gruff under load, but offers more pulling power. Acceleration is definitely quick, but won't slam anyone into the seat. Reaching 60 mph took just 8.2 seconds with the 3.5-liter engine. The 3.3-liter takes about two seconds longer. Either way, the automatic transmissions shifts smoothly. Fuel economy is about right for this league, even if it won't win any awards with either engine.

A well-arranged dashboard contains clear gauges and logical controls, though some interior trim is on the plasticky side. Climate controls, mounted low and in the center, are difficult to adjust while driving. Interior noise levels are low, but road noise can be noticeable in all LH sedans. Visibility to the rear is restricted by a narrow back window in the LHS/New Yorker.

Chrysler introduced the LH sedans to great fanfare and each version is well worth a test drive, including the New Yorker and LHS with their even more abundant backseats.

NHTSA CRASH TEST RESULTS
1994 Concorde/New Yorker/LHS   4-DOOR SEDAN

Driver	☆☆☆☆
Passenger	☆☆☆☆

(The National Highway Traffic Safety Administration tests a vehicle's crashworthiness in front and side collisions. Their ratings suggest the chance of serious injury: ☆☆☆☆☆—10% or less; ☆☆☆☆—10-20% or less; ☆☆☆—20-30% or less; ☆☆—35-45% or less; ☆—More than 45%.)

SPECIFICATIONS

	4-door sedan	4-door sedan
Wheelbase, in.	113.0	113.0
Overall length, in.	201.5	207.4
Overall width, in.	74.4	74.5
Overall height, in.	56.3	55.9
Curb weight, lbs.	3492	3587
Cargo volume, cu. ft.	16.6	17.9
Fuel capacity, gals.	18.0	18.0
Seating capacity	6	6
Front head room, in.	38.4	38.9
Max. front leg room, in.	42.3	42.3
Rear head room, in.	37.3	37.8
Min. rear leg room, in.	38.7	41.7

Powertrain layout: longitudinal front-engine/front-wheel drive

ENGINES

	ohv V-6	ohc V-6
Size, liters/cu. in.	3.3/201	3.5/215
Horsepower	153-161	214
Torque (lbs./ft.)	181	221

EPA city/highway mpg

4-speed OD automatic	19/27	18/26

Consumer Guide™ observed MPG
4-speed OD automatic 19.1

Built in Canada.

RETAIL PRICES	GOOD	AVERAGE	POOR
1993 Concorde	$6,300-7,400	$5,500-6,600	$3,500-4,500
1994 Concorde	7,500-8,600	6,700-7,800	4,500-5,500
1994 New Yorker	7,900-8,900	7,000-8,000	4,600-5,600
1994 LHS	9,200-10,200	8,200-9,200	5,800-6,900
1995 Concorde	8,900-10,200	8,000-9,200	5,500-6,500
1995 New Yorker	9,900-11,000	8,900-10,000	6,200-7,200
1995 LHS	11,500-12,500	10,300-11,300	7,400-8,300
1996 Concorde	11,000-13,200	10,000-12,000	7,000-8,500
1996 New Yorker	12,000-13,000	10,800-11,800	7,500-8,300
1996 LHS	14,000-15,000	12,500-13,500	9,000-10,000
1997 Concorde	13,200-16,000	12,000-14,500	9,000-11,000
1997 LHS	15,500-17,000	14,000-15,500	10,500-11,800

AVERAGE REPLACEMENT COSTS

A/C Compressor	$365	Constant Velocity Joints	310
Alternator	190	Brakes	250
Timing Chain or Belt	340	Shocks and/or Struts	480
Radiator	230	Exhaust System	540
Automatic Transmission or Transaxle	1,089		

TROUBLE SPOTS

• **Transmission slippage** If the transmission shudders under light to moderate acceleration, the transmission front pump could be leaking due to a worn bushing, which requires replacement of the pump as well as the torque converter under the powertrain warranty. (1993-96)

• **Transmission slippage** Bad seals in the transmission lead to premature friction component wear, which causes shudder when starting from a stop, a bump when coasting to a stop, and slipping between gears. Chrysler will warranty the seals, clutches, and if necessary, the torque converter. (1993-95)

• **Transmission slippage** A defective throttle positions sensor, not a transmission problem, could be the cause of late, erratic, or harsh shifting on models with the 3.3L, 3.5L, or 3.8L engine. It is covered under the drivetrain warranty. (1994)

• **Engine noise** The motor mount on the left side of the engine tends to break, which causes a snap or click when accelerating. (1992-93)

• **Transmission slippage** Vehicles with 41TE or 42LE automatic transaxle could take several seconds to engage at startup because of a problem with the valve body. The company will replace defective ones and replace the filter and fluid under normal warranty. (1993-95)

• **Engine noise** Hard starting and a miss at idle can be traced to defective fuel rails, which are replaced under warranty. (1993-94)

RECALL HISTORY

1993 w/3.3-liter engine Deterioration of O-rings at fuel-injector tubes can cause fuel leakage, with potential for fire. **1994** Right steering tie rod can rub through automatic-transmission wiring harness, causing short circuit; may result in stalling, or allow engine to start when selector is not in "park" position.

1990-95 CHRYSLER LeBARON COUPE/CONVERTIBLE

1990 Chrysler LeBaron Convertible

FOR Air bags (later models) • Acceleration (V-6 and turbo) • Anti-lock brakes

AGAINST Rear seat room • Road noise • Cargo room • Engine noise • Automatic transmission performance

EVALUATION With a Mitsubishi V-6 beneath the hood, the shapely LeBarons gained refined power to match their sharp looks. Both the base 4-cylinder engine and its turbocharged counterparts are gruff and noisy, while the Mitsubishi-built V-6 provides smoother performance. Sure, it has less power and torque than either of the turbocharged fours, but it's much quieter and delivers its strength in a far more linear manner. If you simply must have a turbocharged engine, note that the 2.5-liter turbo is less raucous than the earlier 2.2, which disappeared after 1990. We averaged 22.9 mpg with a V-6 convertible, in city/highway driving. Regardless of engine, automatic transmissions shift sloppily.

Convertibles lag somewhat in solidity. Even minor bumps cause the body to twist and flex more than most open cars. For anything beyond merely competent handling and roadholding, look for a GTC with its performance suspension and tires. But be prepared for a choppy ride over rough pavement.

The new, modern interior installed for 1990 is a vast improvement over prior dashboards, positioning controls closer to the driver. Gauges are easy to see, controls easy to use. Climate and radio controls are readily accessible. Six-footers are likely to be comfortable in front. Backseats are bigger than in most coupes, but insufficient for adults on long drives. Trunks are small.

Though not devoid of flaws, they still look sharp and perform reasonably well—at least with the smooth V-6 engine.

SPECIFICATIONS

	2-door coupe	2-door conv.
Wheelbase, in.	100.5	100.6
Overall length, in.	184.8	184.8
Overall width, in.	69.2	69.2
Overall height, in.	53.3	52.4
Curb weight, lbs.	2863	3010
Cargo volume, cu. ft.	14.4	10.3
Fuel capacity, gals.	14.0	14.0
Seating capacity	5	4
Front head room, in.	37.6	38.3
Max. front leg room, in.	42.5	42.5
Rear head room, in.	36.3	37.0
Min. rear leg room, in.	33.0	33.0

Powertrain layout: transverse front-engine/front-wheel drive

ENGINES

	Turbocharged ohc I-4	ohc I-4	Turbocharged ohc I-4	ohc V-6
Size, liters/cu. in.	2.2/135	2.5/153	2.5/153	3.0/181
Horsepower	174	100	152	141
Torque (lbs./ft.)	210	135	210-211	171
EPA city/highway mpg				
5-speed OD manual	20/28	24/34	20/27	19/28
3-speed automatic		23/28	19/24	21/27
4-speed OD automatic				20/29
Consumer Guide™ observed MPG				
5-speed OD manual		25.1		
3-speed automatic		22.5		
4-speed OD automatic				22.9

Built in USA.

CHRYSLER

RETAIL PRICES

		GOOD	AVERAGE	POOR
1990	LeBaron Coupe	$2,200-3,000	$1,600-2,300	$600-900
1990	Convertible	2,800-3,800	2,200-3,100	1,000-1,600
1991	LeBaron Coupe	2,600-3,800	2,000-3,100	900-1,400
1991	Convertible	3,600-4,800	2,900-4,000	1,400-2,200
1992	LeBaron Coupe	3,200-4,500	2,600-3,800	1,300-1,900
1992	Convertible	4,500-5,700	3,800-4,900	2,000-2,900
1993	LeBaron Coupe	3,900-5,200	3,200-4,500	1,700-2,400
1993	Convertible	5,400-6,600	4,700-5,900	2,700-3,700
1994	Convertible	6,500-7,600	5,700-6,800	3,400-4,200
1995	Convertible	7,900-9,000	6,900-8,000	4,400-5,200

AVERAGE REPLACEMENT COSTS

A/C Compressor	$450	Clutch, Pressure Plate, Bearing	515
Alternator	315	Constant Velocity Joints	375
Radiator	315	Brakes	240
Timing Chain or Belt	345	Shocks and/or Struts	340
Automatic Transmission or Transaxle	905	Exhaust System	325

TROUBLE SPOTS

• **Oil consumption** High oil consumption and smoke from the exhaust at idle and deceleration on 3.0L V6 engines (Mitsubishi built) is caused by exhaust valve guides that slide out of the heads. If the guides are not too loose, they can be retained with snap rings. Otherwise, the heads have to be replaced. The repair will be handled under normal warranty coverage. (1990-93)

• **Alternator belt** Unless a shield is installed under the engine on the right side, deep snow could knock the serpentine belt off the pulleys of a 3.0L engine. Usually the first sign that this has happened is a low voltmeter reading or the battery light coming on. (1991-95)

• **Cold starting problems** A 2.2L or 2.5L engine may idle rough or stumble when first started below freezing temperatures unless a revised intake manifold (with an "X" cast into the number 1 runner) was installed (1992) or a revised computer (PCM) was installed (1992-93) or the computer was reprogrammed (1994).

• **Air conditioner** If the air conditioner gradually stops cooling and/or the airflow from the vents decreases, the computer (PCM) may not be sending a signal to the compressor clutch relay to cycle off, which causes the AC evaporator to freeze up. When the ice melts, after the car sits for awhile, the AC works again briefly. Many technicians overlook this as the source of trouble. (1991-95)

• **Transmission slippage** If the transmission shudders under light to moderate acceleration, the transmission front pump could be leaking due to a worn bushing, which requires replacement of the pump as well as the torque converter under the powertrain warranty. (1990-95)

• **Transmission slippage** Vehicles with 41TE or 42LE automatic transaxle could take several seconds to engage at startup because of a problem with the valve body. The company will replace defective ones and replace the filter and fluid under normal warranty. (1993-95)

• **Transmission slippage** Bad seals in the transmission lead to premature friction component wear, which causes shudder when starting from a stop, a bump when coasting to a stop, and slipping between gears. Chyrsler will warranty the seals, clutches, and if necessary, the torque converter. (1993-95)

• **Engine noise** The motor mount on the left side of the engine tends to break, which causes a snap or click when accelerating. (1992-93)

RECALL HISTORY

1990 Engine valve cover gasket may dislocate and allow oil leak, which could cause a fire. **1991** Front disc brake caliper guide pin bolts may not be adequately tightened and could loosen. **1991** On small number of cars, mismatched parking brake cable to rear wheels may reduce braking capability to one wheel, possibly allowing inadvertent roll-away. **1992** Zinc plating of some upper steering column shaft coupling bolts caused hydrogen embrittlement and breakage of the bolt. **1992** Hood latch assembly may not have been properly installed and secondary latch may be prevented from engaging when hood is closed.

1995-98 CHRYSLER SEBRING

1997 Chrysler Sebring LX coupe

FOR Air bags, dual • Passenger and cargo room • Acceleration (V-6) • Steering/handling • Anti-lock brakes (optional on some)

AGAINST Rear visibility • Radio controls • Noise • Acceleration (2.0-liter automatics)

See the 1995-98 Dodge Avenger report for an evaluation of the 1995-98 Chrysler Sebring.

NHTSA CRASH TEST RESULTS
1997 Chrysler Sebring convertible   2-DOOR CONV.

Driver	☆☆☆☆
Passenger	☆☆☆☆

(The National Highway Traffic Safety Administration tests a vehicle's crashworthiness in front and side collisions. Their ratings suggest the chance of serious injury: ☆☆☆☆☆—10% or less; ☆☆☆☆—10-20% or less; ☆☆☆—20-30% or less; ☆☆—35-45% or less; ☆—More than 45%.)

SPECIFICATIONS

	2-door coupe	2-door conv.
Wheelbase, in.	103.7	106.0
Overall length, in.	187.4	193.0
Overall width, in.	69.7	69.2
Overall height, in.	53.0	54.2
Curb weight, lbs.	2908	3350
Cargo volume, cu. ft.	13.1	11.3
Fuel capacity, gals.	16.0	16.0
Seating capacity	5	4
Front head room, in.	39.1	38.7
Max. front leg room, in.	43.3	42.4
Rear head room, in.	36.5	37.0
Min. rear leg room, in.	35.0	35.2

Powertrain layout: transverse front-engine/front-wheel drive

ENGINES

	dohc I-4	dohc I-4	ohc V-6
Size, liters/cu. in.	2.0/122	2.4/148	2.5/152
Horsepower	140	150	155-168
Torque (lbs./ft.)	130	167	170
EPA city/highway mpg			
5-speed OD manual	22/31		
4-speed OD automatic	21/30	20/29	20/27
Consumer Guide™ observed MPG			
4-speed OD automatic			25.6

Built in USA and Mexico.

RETAIL PRICES

	GOOD	AVERAGE	POOR
1995 Sebring coupe	$9,700-11,500	$8,700-10,500	$6,500-8,000
1996 Sebring coupe	11,500-13,500	10,500-12,500	8,000-9,500
1996 Convertible	13,300-16,500	12,000-15,000	9,000-11,500
1997 Sebring coupe	13,800-15,500	12,000-14,000	9,000-11,000

	GOOD	AVERAGE	POOR
1997 Convertible	15,200-18,500	13,900-17,000	10,500-13,500
1998 Sebring coupe	15,200-18,000	13,800-16,500	10,800-13,200
1998 Convertible	18,000-23,000	16,500-21,500	13,500-17,500

AVERAGE REPLACEMENT COSTS

A/C Compressor $730

Alternator 230

Radiator 570

Timing Chain or Belt 220

Automatic Transmission or
   Transaxle..........................905

Constant Velocity Joints.....375

Clutch, Pressure Plate,
   Bearing............................575

Brakes..................................255

Shocks and/or Struts 490

Exhaust System.................285

TROUBLE SPOTS

• **Hard starting** A corroded connector behind the left headlight may cause hard starting, intermittently flashing "Check Engine" light, and radiator/condenser fan that will not run. (1995)

• **Sunroof/moonroof** The pivot pin in the power sunroof may come out, or the plastic tabs on the control unit may cause interference, preventing the sunroof from closing completely. (1995) Or, the sunroof may open by itself if water wicks along the drive cable into the control unit. (1995-96)

• **Transmission slippage** Transmission tends to default to the "limp-in" mode, which is second gear only, for no apparent reason requiring the transmission control computer to be reprogrammed. (1996)

• **Engine misfire** Engine idles rough, hesitates, stalls, hard to restart, during cold weather until the engine warms up may require a new engine control computer. (1995)

• **Transmission slippage** Transmission may shudder when accelerating from a stop, thump when coasting down to a stop or slip when shifting. (1995)

• **Alarm system** The theft alarm may go off randomly, most often in high winds, and is often due to a misaligned hood. (1995-96)

• **Hard starting** Intermittent no-starts may be due to a damaged wire near the transaxle shift lever. (1995)

RECALL HISTORY

1995-97 Lower ball joint can separate due to loss of lubrication; could cause loss of control. **1996 JX w/2.5-liter engine** Disconnected vacuum hose may cause increase in engine idle speed and loss of braking power assist. **1996 convertible** Electrical contacts of power mirror switch can accumulate road salt, which may result in fire. **1997 coupe** On small number of cars, improperly-welded head restraint support bracket on passenger side can break.

1996-98 CHRYSLER TOWN & COUNTRY

1996 Chrysler Town & Country LXi

FOR Air bags, dual • Anti-lock brakes • Acceleration (3.8-liter) • Ride • Passenger and cargo room

AGAINST Fuel economy • Wind noise

EVALUATION The latest Town & Country is more spacious and practical. Door sills were lowered by 1.4 inches, to improve entry and exit, which is easy all around—especially with the available driver's side sliding door. Step-in height is actually among the lowest in the minivan class. The dashboard is lower and side windows deeper, so visibility is improved. Choosing a long-wheelbase minivan means everyone has plenty of room. You get ample cargo space at the rear in long wheelbase models, and adequate space in the standard-size version. Cupholders and storage bins are sprinkled throughout the interior, with plenty of space for stashing small items.

Steering is precise, and hard cornering produces only modest body lean. The ride is supple, yet well controlled at highway speeds. Acceleration is adequate with the 3.3-liter V-6, even in the heavier long-wheelbase models, but the bigger engine has enough extra muscle to make a noticeable difference when merging onto the expressway and running uphill. Fuel economy is gloomy with either engine: expect an average of 15-17 mpg in urban driving, or into the low 20s on the highway. Tire noise is low, but wind noise grows prominent at highway speeds. All seats are comfortable for long treks.

Chrysler's minivans feel like big cars on the road. Ford's Windstar and the latest GM minivans also are tempting, but Chrysler deserves to hang on to its title of best all-around buy. All of the Town & Country's extras are appealing, but of course a Dodge Caravan or Plymouth Voyager offers most of the same features, for fewer dollars.

NHTSA CRASH TEST RESULTS
1997 Chrysler Town & Country

4-DOOR VAN

Driver	☆☆☆
Passenger	☆☆☆☆

(The National Highway Traffic Safety Administration tests a vehicle's crashworthiness in front and side collisions. Their ratings suggest the chance of serious injury: ☆☆☆☆☆—10% or less; ☆☆☆☆—10-20% or less; ☆☆☆—20-30% or less; ☆☆—35-45% or less; ☆—More than 45%.)

SPECIFICATIONS

	4-door van	4-door van
Wheelbase, in.	113.3	119.3
Overall length, in.	186.3	199.6
Overall width, in.	75.6	75.6
Overall height, in.	68.5	68.5
Curb weight, lbs.	3863	3951
Cargo volume, cu. ft.	141.9	167.0
Fuel capacity, gals.	20.0	20.0
Seating capacity	7	7
Front head room, in.	39.8	39.8
Max. front leg room, in.	41.2	41.2
Rear head room, in.	40.1	39.6
Min. rear leg room, in.	35.2	37.3

Powertrain layout: transverse front-engine/front- or all-wheel drive

ENGINES

	ohv V-6	ohv V-6
Size, liters/cu. in.	3.3/201	3.8/230
Horsepower	158	166-180
Torque (lbs./ft.)	203	277
EPA city/highway mpg 4-speed OD automatic	17/24	17/24
Consumer Guide™ observed MPG 4-speed OD automatic	17.4	15.1

Built in USA.

RETAIL PRICES	GOOD	AVERAGE	POOR
1996 Town & Country	$16,500-21,500	$15,000-20,000	$11,500-16,000
1997 Town & Country	19,500-24,500	18,000-22,500	14,500-18,500
1998 Town & Country	23,000-29,500	21,000-27,500	17,000-23,000

AVERAGE REPLACEMENT COSTS

A/C Compressor $490	Clutch, Pressure Plate,
Alternator 310	Bearing 605
Radiator 480	Constant Velocity Joints.....385
Timing Chain or Belt 230	Brakes.................................390
Automatic Transmission or	Shocks and/or Struts 330
Transaxle.....................1,040	Exhaust System.................330

TROUBLE SPOTS

• **Brakes** The anti-lock brakes may activate at speeds under 10 mph due to one or more faulty wheel speed sensors. (1996)

• **Transmission slippage** Transmission may shudder when accelerating from a stop, thump when coasting down to a stop or slip when shifting. (1996)

• **Vehicle noise** A thud or thump (sometimes described as a sounding like a bowling ball) when accelerating or stopping which comes from the rear is caused by fuel sloshing in the tank. A foam pad and strap kit does not always fix the problem. (1996-97)

• **Dashboard lights** The instrument cluster, mini-trip computer and/or compass may show incorrect information or go completely blank due to a bad relay for the heated backlight (window). (1997)

• **Windshield wipers** Windshield wipers come on by themselves or fail to stop when the switch or key is turned off due to a problem with the multifunciton switch on the column. (1996)

• **Blower motor** Blower motors make a whine in low and second speed. (1996)

• **Doors** Sliding door and/or liftgate power locks fail to lock or unlock both manually or electrically. (1996)

• **Radiator** The radiator fan may run after the key is turned off, or may not run leading to overheating because the fan relay attaching screws break and the relay overheats. (1996-97)

RECALL HISTORY

1996 Fuel tank rollover valve can allow fuel to enter vapor canister, creating potential for leakage and fire. **1996** Static charge could cause spark as tank is filled; vapors could ignite. **1996** On a few minivans, bolts holding integrated child seat modules to seat frame can break. **1997** Certain master cylinder seals will not seal adequately, allowing hydraulic fluid to be drawn into power-assist vacuum reservoir; brake warning lamp will then illuminate. **1998 w/integrated child seats** Shoulder harness webbing was incorrectly routed around reinforcement bar; can fail to restrain child properly.

1995-98 DODGE AVENGER

1995 Dodge Avenger ES

FOR Air bags, dual • Passenger and cargo room • Acceleration (V-6) • Steering/handling • Anti-lock brakes (std. or opt.)

AGAINST Acceleration (4-cylinder, auto.) • Radio controls • Road noise • Rear visibility

EVALUATION Front bucket seats offer plenty of head and leg space for two adults. Rear seats are equally pleasing, with space for two adults. However, large people may not want to spend long periods in back, and getting in and out can be a chore. Avenger's trunk has a wide, flat floor, and split-folding rear seatbacks. Although you sit relatively low, visibility is generally good in all directions. However, a narrow back window, tall parcel shelf, and wide roof pillars make it a difficult to see what's directly behind the car. Instruments are easy to read, though auxiliary gauges are small. Most controls are easy to reach while driving. However, the radio is mounted too low and has too many small buttons.

Both engines provide adequate acceleration from a stop, but the 4-cylinder is noisy and slowed by the automatic transmission. Four-cylinder pickup is acceptable with manual shift. The V-6 is smooth and more powerful, and fairly lively, but it doesn't produce much torque at low speeds. Step on the gas, and there might be a rather long pause before the automatic transmission downshifts.

Each model handles adeptly, zipping around corners and through curves with good grip and only moderate body lean. Roadholding is good overall, and the car responds well to steering inputs. Ride quality from the firm suspension is on the choppy side, and when encountering certain pavement separators.

DODGE

Road, engine, and wind noise might all become intrusive at high speeds.

Attractively styled and capable on the road, the Avenger has a lot going for it: proven mechanical elements, reasonable prices, and wholly adequate room for four.

NHTSA CRASH TEST RESULTS
1995 Dodge Avenger

2-DOOR COUPE

Driver	☆☆☆☆☆
Passenger	☆☆☆☆☆

(The National Highway Traffic Safety Administration tests a vehicle's crashworthiness in front and side collisions. Their ratings suggest the chance of serious injury: ☆☆☆☆☆—10% or less; ☆☆☆☆—10-20% or less; ☆☆☆—20-30% or less; ☆☆—35-45% or less; ☆—More than 45%.)

SPECIFICATIONS

	2-door coupe
Wheelbase, in.	103.7
Overall length, in.	187.2
Overall width, in.	68.5
Overall height, in.	53.0
Curb weight, lbs.	2879
Cargo volume, cu. ft.	13.1
Fuel capacity, gals.	16.0
Seating capacity	5
Front head room, in.	39.1
Max. front leg room, in.	43.3
Rear head room, in.	36.5
Min. rear leg room, in.	35.0

Powertrain layout: transverse front-engine/front-wheel drive

ENGINES

	dohc I-4	ohc V-6
Size, liters/cu. in.	2.0/122	2.5/152
Horsepower	140	155-163
Torque (lbs./ft.)	130	160-170

EPA city/highway mpg

5-speed OD manual	22/31	
4-speed OD automatic	21/30	20/27

Consumer Guide™ observed MPG

4-speed OD automatic	23.6

Built in USA.

RETAIL PRICES

	GOOD	AVERAGE	POOR
1995 Avenger	$8,300-9,500	$7,500-8,500	$5,000-5,800
1995 Avenger ES	9,500-10,700	8,500-9,700	5,800-6,500
1996 Avenger	9,800-11,200	8,800-10,200	6,000-6,800
1996 Avenger ES	10,500-12,000	9,500-11,000	6,500-7,500

DODGE

	GOOD	AVERAGE	POOR
1997 Avenger	11,500-13,000	10,500-12,000	7,500-8,800
1997 Avenger ES	12,500-14,000	11,300-13,800	8,200-10,000
1998 Avenger	13,500-15,000	12,500-14,000	9,000-10,000
1998 Avenger ES	15,000-16,500	13,800-15,200	10,000-11,000

AVERAGE REPLACEMENT COSTS

A/C Compressor $400
Alternator 315
Radiator 530
Timing Chain or Belt 190
Automatic Transmission or
   Transaxle........................905
Clutch, Pressure Plate,
   Bearing............................560
Constant Velocity Joints.....370
Brakes.................................265
Shocks and/or Struts 375
Exhaust System.................320

TROUBLE SPOTS

• **Hard starting** A corroded connector behind the left headlight may cause hard starting, intermittently flashing "Check Engine" light, and radiator/condenser fan that will not run. (1995)

• **Transmission slippage** Transmission tends to default to the "limp-in" mode, which is second gear only, for no apparent reason requiring the transmission control computer to be reprogrammed. (1996)

• **Engine misfire** Engine idles rough, hesitates, stalls, hard to restart, during cold weather until the engine warms up may require a new engine control computer. (1995)

• **Sunroof/moonroof** The pivot pin in the power sunroof may come out, or the plastic tabs on the control unit may cause interference, preventing the sunroof from closing completely. (1995) Or, the sunroof may open by itself if water wicks along the drive cable into the control unit. (1995-96)

• **Transmission slippage** Transmission may shudder when accelerating from a stop, thump when coasting down to a stop, or slip when shifting. (1995)

• **Alarm system** The theft alarm may go off randomly, most often in high winds, and is often due to a misaligned hood. (1995-96)

• **Hard starting** Intermittent no-starts may be due to a damaged wire near the transaxle shift lever. (1995)

RECALL HISTORY

1997 On a small number of cars, improperly-welded head restraint support bracket on passenger side can break.

1991-95 DODGE CARAVAN

1994 Dodge Grand Caravan ES

FOR Passenger and cargo room • Ride

AGAINST Fuel economy • Acceleration (4-cylinder) • Reliability

EVALUATION With the Caravan, avoid the weak 4-cylinder engine and balky 5-speed manual transmission. They are more trouble than the initial savings you make in a lower purchase price. The 3.0- and 3.3-liter V-6 engines provide adequate accleration, but the 3.8-liter V-6 delivers the best action in all situations. It's also the quietest. With any of the V-6 engines, don't expect to get more than 20 mpg.

The standard front-wheel drive provides sufficient traction for most situations; however, the effective AWD system is a boon in the snow belt. But beware: AWD makes the ride rougher, hurts acceleration, and lessens fuel economy. The Caravan's ride is carlike and secure, but there's too much body lean and not enough traction for these vehicles to score as anything other than minivans when it comes to handling.

Though the regular-length versions can seat seven people, it gets crowded if everyone is an adult. In addition, cargo room is only adequate with all the seats in place. Grand Caravans have more space for everyone and ample cargo room. Though the middle and rear seats can be removed, they are quite heavy. The dashboard has a convenient design, and climate and radio controls are easy to use. However, front seat occupants might find themselves craving more leg room.

The design has been around for over a decade, and most of the bugs were worked out in the first generation. With so much versatility, these vans are an exceptional secondhand value. If you're shopping for a minivan, Caravan and its twins should be first on your list.

NHTSA CRASH TEST RESULTS
1995 Dodge Caravan

3-DOOR VAN

Driver	☆☆☆☆
Passenger	☆☆☆☆

(The National Highway Traffic Safety Administration tests a vehicle's crashworthiness in front and side collisions. Their ratings suggest the chance of serious injury: ☆☆☆☆☆—10% or less; ☆☆☆☆—10-20% or less; ☆☆☆—20-30% or less; ☆☆—35-45% or less; ☆—More than 45%.)

SPECIFICATIONS

	3-door van	3-door van
Wheelbase, in.	112.3	119.3
Overall length, in.	178.1	192.8
Overall width, in.	72.0	72.0
Overall height, in.	66.0	66.7
Curb weight, lbs.	3305	3573
Cargo volume, cu. ft.	117.0	141.3
Fuel capacity, gals.	20.0	20.0
Seating capacity	7	7
Front head room, in.	39.1	39.1
Max. front leg room, in.	38.3	38.3
Rear head room, in.	38.5	38.4
Min. rear leg room, in.	37.6	37.7

Powertrain layout: transverse front-engine/front- or all-wheel drive

ENGINES

	ohc I-4	ohc V-6	ohv V-6	ohv V-6
Size, liters/cu. in.	2.5/153	3.0/181	3.3/202	3.8/230
Horsepower	100	141-142	150-162	162
Torque (lbs./ft.)	135	173	194	213
EPA city/highway mpg				
5-speed OD manual	19/25			
3-speed automatic	20/30	19/24		
4-speed OD automatic		19/25	18/23	17/23
Consumer Guide™ observed MPG				
5-speed OD manual	21.6			
3-speed automatic	19.9	18.2		
4-speed OD automatic		19.7	18.5	18.5

Built in USA and Canada.

RETAIL PRICES

	GOOD	AVERAGE	POOR
1991 Caravan	$2,800-6,000	$2,200-5,300	$1,000-3,300
1991 Grand Caravan	4,000-6,800	3,300-6,000	1,700-3,800
1992 Caravan	3,500-6,900	2,800-6,200	1,400-4,000

DODGE

	GOOD	AVERAGE	POOR
1992 Grand Caravan	4,600-7,900	3,800-7,000	2,100-4,800
1993 Caravan	4,500-8,200	3,700-7,300	2,000-5,000
1993 Grand Caravan	5,800-9,300	5,000-8,400	2,900-5,800
1994 Caravan	5,700-9,900	4,900-9,000	2,800-6,200
1994 Grand Caravan	7,000-11,000	6,200-10,000	4,000-7,000
1995 Caravan	7,000-11,500	6,200-10,500	3,900-7,500
1995 Grand Caravan	8,500-13,000	7,500-11,800	5,000-8,500

AVERAGE REPLACEMENT COSTS

A/C Compressor $455	Constant Velocity Joints.....385
Alternator 310	Brakes.................................275
Radiator 325	Shocks and/or Struts 230
Timing Chain or Belt 265	Exhaust System.................400
Automatic Transmission or Transaxle....................1,040	

TROUBLE SPOTS

• **Oil consumption** High oil consumption and smoke from the exhaust at idle and deceleration on 3.0L V-6 engines (Mitsubishi built) is caused by exhaust valve guides that slide out of the heads. If the guides are not too loose, they can be retained with snap rings. Otherwise, the heads have to be replaced. The repair will be handled under normal warranty coverage. (1990-93)

• **Alternator belt** Unless a shield is installed under the engine on the right side, deep snow could knock the serpentine belt off the pulleys of a 3.0L engine. Usually the first sign that this has happened is a low voltmeter reading or the battery light coming on. (1991-95)

• **Engine noise** The motor mount on the left side of the engine tends to break, which causes a snap or click when accelerating. (1992-93)

• **Cold starting problems** A 2.2L or 2.5L engine may idle rough or stumble when first started below freezing temperatures unless a revised intake manifold (with an "X" cast into the number 1 runner) was installed (1992) or a revised computer (PCM) was installed (1992-93) or the computer was reprogrammed (1994).

• **Air conditioner** If the air conditioner gradually stops cooling and/or the airflow from the vents decreases, the computer (PCM) may not be sending a signal to the compressor clutch relay to cycle off, which causes the AC evaporator to freeze up. When the ice melts, after the car sits for awhile, the AC works again briefly. Many technicians overlook this as the source of trouble. (1991-95)

• **Transmission slippage** Any minivan with the 3.3L or 3.5L engine may have late, harsh, or erratic automatic transmission shifts that are not transmission related, but caused by a defective throttle position sensor. (1994)

- **Transmission slippage** If the transmission shudders under light to moderate acceleration, the transmission front pump could be leaking due to a worn bushing, which requires replacement of the pump as well as the torque converter under the powertrain warranty. (1990-95)

- **Transmission slippage** Vehicles with 41TE or 42LE automatic transaxle could take several seconds to engage at startup because of a problem with the valve body. The company will replace defective ones and replace the filter and fluid under normal warranty. (1993-95)

- **Transmission slippage** Bad seals in the transmission lead to premature friction component wear, which causes shudder when starting from a stop, a bump when coasting to a stop, and slipping between gears. Chyrsler will warranty the seals, clutches, and if necessary, the torque converter. (1993-95)

RECALL HISTORY

1991 with ABS High-pressure hose in anti-lock braking system may leak or detach, which increases likelihood of brake lockup. **1991 with ABS** High-pressure pump of anti-lock braking system may be porous, resulting in increased stopping distances. **1991-92** Steering wheel mounting armature can develop cracks and separate from the center hub attachment to the steering column. This can result in loss of vehicle control. **1991-93** Seatbelt release button can stick inside cover, so buckle is only partly latched; also, center rear belt anchor clip can disconnect. **1991-93 with ABS** Piston seal in control unit can wear excessively; ABS could fail, and power assist might be reduced. **1992** Zinc plating of some upper steering column shaft coupling bolts caused hydrogen embrittlement and breakage. **1992** Bolts that attach gas strut to rear liftgate can accumulate fatigue damage, if loose; liftgate could fall suddenly. **1992** Brake pedal pad attachment to pedal arm may not have adequate strength. **1992** Fuel tank may drop or lines may rupture near fuel tank, leading to possible fire. **1992** Brake pedal pad attachment arm on small number of vehicles could break. **1993-94** Lug nuts on optional 15-inch stamped steel wheels may have been improperly installed, which could lead to wheel separation.

1996-98 DODGE CARAVAN

FOR Air bags, dual • Anti-lock brakes • Acceleration (3.8-liter) • Ride • Passenger and cargo room

AGAINST Fuel economy • Wind noise

EVALUATION These highly impressive second-generation Caravans are a clear step ahead of the hugely popular 1984-95 minivans. Among other bonuses, you get more space in all seating posi-

DODGE

1996 Dodge Grand Caravan ES

tions. Design features include a lower dashboard and larger windows for improved visibility, and a 1.4-inch lower step-in height for easier entry and exit. A driver's side sliding door also helps on that latter score. The new dashboard has a more user-friendly layout, putting most controls within easy reach of the driver. Illuminated markers for the power window switches and other controls make them easier to find in the dark.

The innovative removable seats are handy, but each seat weighs about 90 pounds, so it might take two people to lift one in and out. You also get an assortment of storage bins, nooks, and crannies for stashing miscellaneous items. Performance with the 3.3-liter engine is adequate in daily driving, but the 3.8-liter is better yet, giving the Caravan enough power to pass and merge easily. Gas mileage should run 15-17 mpg in the city, and just above 20 on the highway. The 4-cylinder engine has nearly as much power as the 3.0-liter V-6, but both are taxed by a full load of passengers.

Quieter and even more carlike than before, these minivans handle more like large sedans than vans, rolling along with a stable, comfortable attitude. Caravans hold the road well and lean moderately in tight turns. Road and wind noise grow obtrusive at higher speeds, but otherwise these minivans are great for long-distance cruising.

Caravans and their Chrysler-Plymouth cousins rank at the head of their class, just as their predecessors did.

NHTSA CRASH TEST RESULTS
1997 Dodge Caravan

3-DOOR VAN

Driver	☆☆☆☆☆
Passenger	☆☆☆☆☆

(The National Highway Traffic Safety Administration tests a vehicle's crashworthiness in front and side collisions. Their ratings suggest the chance of serious injury: ☆☆☆☆☆—10% or less; ☆☆☆☆—10-20% or less; ☆☆☆—20-30% or less; ☆☆—35-45% or less; ☆—More than 45%.)

SPECIFICATIONS

	3-door van	3-door van
Wheelbase, in.	113.3	119.3
Overall length, in.	186.3	199.6
Overall width, in.	75.6	75.6
Overall height, in.	68.5	68.5
Curb weight, lbs.	3528	3680
Cargo volume, cu. ft.	146.2	172.3
Fuel capacity, gals.	20.0	20.0
Seating capacity	7	7
Front head room, in.	39.8	39.8
Max. front leg room, in.	41.2	41.2
Rear head room, in.	40.1	40.0
Min. rear leg room, in.	36.6	39.6

Powertrain layout: transverse front-engine/front- or all-wheel drive

ENGINES

	dohc I-4	ohc V-6	ohv V-6	ohv V-6
Size, liters/cu. in.	2.4/148	3.0/181	3.3/201	3.8/230
Horsepower	150	150	158	166-180
Torque (lbs./ft.)	167	176	203	227-240

EPA city/highway mpg

3-speed automatic	20/26	19/25		
4-speed OD automatic		18/26	18/24	17/24

Consumer Guide™ observed MPG

4-speed OD automatic			19.2	17.7

Built in USA and Canada.

RETAIL PRICES

	GOOD	AVERAGE	POOR
1996 Caravan	$10,500-15,000	$9,300-13,700	$7,000-10,500
1996 Grand Caravan	11,700-17,000	10,500-15,500	8,000-12,000
1997 Caravan	12,500-17,200	11,000-15,500	8,500-12,000
1997 Grand Caravan	14,500-20,000	13,000-18,500	10,000-14,500
1998 Caravan	14,500-19,500	13,000-18,000	10,000-14,000
1998 Grand Caravan	17,000-23,500	15,500-22,000	12,000-17,500

AVERAGE REPLACEMENT COSTS

A/C Compressor	$490
Alternator	310
Radiator	480
Timing Chain or Belt	230
Automatic Transmission or Transaxle	1,040
Clutch, Pressure Plate, Bearing	605
Constant Velocity Joints	385
Brakes	390
Shocks and/or Struts	330
Exhaust System	330

TROUBLE SPOTS

• **Vehicle noise** A thud or thump, which comes from the rear (sometimes described as a sounding like a bowling ball) when accelerating or stopping, is caused by fuel sloshing in the tank. A foam pad and strap kit does not always fix the problem. (1996-97)

• **Brakes** The anti-lock brakes may activate at speeds under ten mph due to one or more faulty wheel speed sensors. (1996)

• **Doors** Sliding door and/or liftgate power locks fail to lock or unlock both manually or electrically. (1996)

• **Windshield wipers** Windshield wipers come on by themselves or fail to stop when the switch or key is turned off due to a problem with the multifunction switch on the column. (1996)

• **Transmission slippage** Transmission may shudder when accelerating from a stop, thump when coasting down to a stop, or slip when shifting. (1996)

• **Radiator** The radiator fan may run after the key is turned off, or may not run, leading to overheating because the fan relay attaching screws break and the relay overheats. (1996-97)

• **Dashboard lights** The instrument cluster, mini-trip computer and/or compass may show incorrect information or go completely blank due to a bad relay for the heated backlight (window). (1997)

• **Blower motor** Blower motors make a whine in low and second speed. (1996)

RECALL HISTORY

1996 Fuel tank rollover valve can allow fuel to pass into vapor canister, resulting in potential for leakage and fire. **1996** Static charge could cause spark as tank is being filled; vapors could ignite. **1996** On a few minivans, bolts holding integrated child seat modules to seat frame can break. **1996 with bench seats, built at Windsor plant ("R" in 11th position of VIN)** Rear-seat bolts can fracture; in an accident, seat could break away. **1997** Certain master cylinder seals will not seal adequately, allowing hydraulic fluid to be drawn into power-assist vacuum reservoir; brake warning lamp will then illuminate. **1997** Wheels on small number of minivans were damaged by equipment used for mounting. **1997 w/P215/65R15 Goodyear Conquest tires on steel wheels** Tires were damaged, and may lose pressure suddenly. **1998 w/integrated child seats** Shoulder harness webbing was incorrectly routed around reinforcement bar; can fail to restrain child properly.

1990-96 DODGE DAKOTA ✓ BEST BUY

FOR Passenger room • Acceleration (V-6, V-8)

AGAINST Interior storage space • Acceleration (4-cylinder)

EVALUATION Regular cabs have ample space for three

1994 Dodge Dakota Sport 4x2

adults, but neither the bench seat nor the available buckets are particularly comfortable (1993 and later buckets are better). Not much storage space is available behind the seat, unless you opt for the Club Cab. But it's hard to get into the rear seat, which isn't sufficient for three and has limited knee room. The floor-mounted 4WD lever is low and sits well forward, so you have to reach under the dash to shift from 2WD to 4WD High. Other controls are easy to reach.

The base 4-cylinder engine is adequate, but not a wise choice unless you rarely carry cargo. Relaxed at highway speeds, the husky early V-6 develops enough low-speed torque to haul heavy loads, but it's still no fireball when pushing hard. The "Magnum" V-6 introduced for 1992 yields better acceleration (Dodge claimed 0-60 mph time of 8.3 seconds), but engine and exhaust noise are more noticeable under hard throttle. Acceleration is more robust yet with the V-8, which is the choice for towing. Dakotas handle competently and ride well considering their size, though the ride gets bouncy when the cargo box is empty. Despite ABS, rear wheels tend to lock prematurely in hard stops. We'd prefer a later model with the optional 4-wheel anti-lock braking. Solid and robust, a Dakota makes a good practical choice. A long-wheelbase version with the 8-foot bed might serve nearly as well as a full-size pickup.

NHTSA CRASH TEST RESULTS
1994 Dodge Dakota

REG. CAB LONG BED

Driver	☆☆☆☆☆
Passenger	☆☆☆☆

(The National Highway Traffic Safety Administration tests a vehicle's crashworthiness in front and side collisions. Their ratings suggest the chance of serious injury: ☆☆☆☆☆—10% or less; ☆☆☆☆—10-20% or less; ☆☆☆—20-30% or less; ☆☆—35-45% or less; ☆—More than 45%.)

SPECIFICATIONS

	reg. cab short bed	reg. cab long bed	ext. cab
Wheelbase, in.	111.9	123.9	130.9
Overall length, in.	189.0	207.5	208.0
Overall width, in.	69.4	69.4	69.4
Overall height, in.	65.0	65.0	65.6
Curb weight, lbs.	3042	3124	3528
Cargo volume, cu. ft.	NA	NA	NA
Fuel capacity, gals.	15.0	15.0	15.0
Seating capacity	3	3	6
Front head room, in.	39.5	39.5	39.5
Max. front leg room, in.	41.8	41.8	41.8
Rear head room, in.	NA	NA	37.9
Min. rear leg room, in.	NA	NA	24.8

Powertrain layout: longitudinal front-engine/rear- or 4-wheel drive

ENGINES

	ohc I-4	ohc V-6	ohv V-8
Size, liters/cu. in.	2.5/153	3.9/239	5.2/318
Horsepower	99-120	125-180	165-230
Torque (lbs./ft.)	132-145	195-225	250-295

EPA city/highway mpg

5-speed OD manual	21/25	16/22	14/20
4-speed OD automatic		16/20	14/18

Consumer Guide™ observed MPG

5-speed OD manual	20.2		15.4
4-speed OD automatic			13.9

Built in USA.

RETAIL PRICES

	GOOD	AVERAGE	POOR
1990 Dakota	$2,200-4,800	$1,600-4,100	$700-2,400
1991 Dakota	2,900-7,000	2,200-6,300	1,000-4,000
1992 Dakota	3,500-8,000	2,800-7,200	1,400-4,800
1993 Dakota	4,200-9,500	3,500-8,700	1,800-5,800
1994 Dakota	5,000-11,000	4,200-10,000	2,300-7,000
1995 Dakota	6,100-12,500	5,300-11,500	3,000-8,300
1996 Dakota	7,200-15,000	6,400-14,000	3,900-10,300

AVERAGE REPLACEMENT COSTS

A/C Compressor $415	Clutch, Pressure Plate, Bearing.............................525
Alternator 295	Universal Joints 130
Radiator 405	Brakes.................................315
Timing Chain or Belt 190	Shocks and/or Struts 190
Automatic Transmission or Transaxle.........................790	Exhaust System.................310

TROUBLE SPOTS

• **Oil leak** The rear main seals on 2.5L and 4.0L engines are prone to leakage if the vehicle is operated in dirty conditions. Dirt acts as an abrasive when it collects on the seal. To prevent future failures Chrysler has a rubber plug available that goes in a hole above the starter that protects the rear main seal. Beware of vehicles that have been regularly driven on dirt roads or off-road. (1996)

• **Oil leak** A chronic oil leak at the filter on 3.9L, 5.2L, and 5.9L engines is likely due to a warped adapter plate, not the filter itself. Under warranty, the adapter and its gasket will be replaced. (1995)

• **Exhaust backfire** Exhaust backfire and/or a popping noise in the exhaust may be caused by a defective Powertrain Control Module (computer), which may be replaced under the emission control warranty. (1994-95)

• **Water leak** The roof seams leak water that travels to the front and seeps down behind the dashboard onto the floor. This difficult to locate leak may be covered under a goodwill warranty if pursued aggressively. (1993-95)

• **Oil pump** Oil pump gear wear results in bucking and surging when the engine is warm and lack of lubrication when the engine is cold. Beware of additional internal wear if the vehicle has high mileage and the pump has not been replaced. (1992-93)

• **Air conditioner** If the air conditioner gradually stops cooling and/or the airflow from the vents decreases, the computer (PCM) may not be sending a signal to the compressor clutch relay to cycle off, which causes the AC evaporator to freeze up. When the ice melts, the AC works again briefly. Many technicians overlook this as the source of trouble. (1991-95)

• **Engine fan noise** In warm weather, the fan makes a roaring sound, which gives some drivers the impression that the automatic transmission is slipping (it is not), but Dodge will replace the fan, the fan clutch, and, on max cooling systems, the radiator cap. (all)

• **Transmission slippage** If the transmission won't upshift for about the first quarter mile in cool weather, it is probably due to defective cast iron seal rings in the governor drive. This repair is covered under the standard warranty. (1992-94)

RECALL HISTORY

1990 Valve cover gasket may allow oil leakage. **1990 light-duty 4x2 and club-cab with V-8** Frame can crack at steering gear attachment and/or mounting bolts can fracture, allowing steering gear to separate. **1991 with 4-speed automatic** Fuel hose may contact wiring harness, resulting in leakage. **1991** Premium steering wheel could crack and separate from hub. **1991 2WD** Right front brake hose may rub against tire during full-left turn. **1993 ABS** could become inoperative when hard pedal effort is applied. **1996 with 2.5-liter engine** Power brake vacuum hose in some trucks could be improperly installed; disconnected hose can cause increase in idle speed and loss of power assist.

1993-97 DODGE INTREPID

1994 Dodge Intrepid ES

FOR Air bags • Anti-lock brakes • Acceleration (3.5-liter) • Passenger and cargo room • Steering/handling • Ride (base suspension)

AGAINST Road noise • Ride (Performance Handling Group) • Climate controls • Acceleration (3.3-liter) • Rear Visibility

EVALUATION Acceleration is adequate with that 3.3-liter V-6, but it's not too snappy for quick passing. For that reason, an early ES is the better choice with the larger V-6 engine and touring suspension employing 16-inch tires. This combination offers fine overall performance, including precise handling and cornering. But watch out for an ES with the optional Performance Handling Group, which yields a stiff ride.

By 1994, all Intrepids had the touring suspension as standard, delivering a satisfying level of handling precision without much loss in comfort. Even base Intrepids with that suspension handle as well as some smaller sports sedans, zipping through tight turns with little body lean and commendable grip. The ride is firm, but not harsh. Gas mileage with an ES sedan averaged 22 mpg in a long-term trial, including considerable highway mileage—not quite a miser, but better than some all-out full-size automobiles. Even stop-and-go commuting usually resulted in 16-18 mpg economy.

Three adults fit in back without crowding.Head room is good in front and adequate in back. Ergonomics are great.

Instruments and controls are logically arranged and convenient, except for climate controls that are mounted too low for easy access. Lightweight plastic on the dashboard and door panels does not feel too durable. Cargo space is fine and the trunk opens at bumper level for easier loading of luggage. Road noise is prominent at highway speeds, even with the sound insulation added for 1996. Wind noise is low.

Workmanship is generally tight and solid, but some cars have suffered minor creaks, rattles, or assembly flaws—even when new. Intrepid is an impressive and worthy family sedan with flair, offering good value for the money.

NHTSA CRASH TEST RESULTS
1996 Dodge Intrepid 4-DOOR SEDAN

Driver	☆☆☆☆
Passenger	☆☆☆☆

(The National Highway Traffic Safety Administration tests a vehicle's crashworthiness in front and side collisions. Their ratings suggest the chance of serious injury: ☆☆☆☆☆—10% or less; ☆☆☆☆—10-20% or less; ☆☆☆—20-30% or less; ☆☆—35-45% or less; ☆—More than 45%.)

SPECIFICATIONS

	4-door sedan
Wheelbase, in.	113.0
Overall length, in.	201.7
Overall width, in.	74.4
Overall height, in.	56.3
Curb weight, lbs.	3318
Cargo volume, cu. ft.	16.7
Fuel capacity, gals.	18.0
Seating capacity	6
Front head room, in.	38.4
Max. front leg room, in.	42.4
Rear head room, in.	37.5
Min. rear leg room, in.	38.8

Powertrain layout: longitudinal front-engine/front-wheel drive

ENGINES

	ohv V-6	ohc V-6
Size, liters/cu. in.	3.3/201	3.5/215
Horsepower	153-161	214
Torque (lbs./ft.)	177-181	221
EPA city/highway mpg		
4-speed OD automatic	19/27	18/26
Consumer Guide™ observed MPG		
4-speed OD automatic	21.9	22.0

Built in Canada.

DODGE

RETAIL PRICES	GOOD	AVERAGE	POOR
1993 Intrepid	$5,400-6,900	$4,700-6,200	$2,700-3,900
1994 Intrepid	6,300-7,900	5,500-7,100	3,400-4,500
1995 Intrepid	7,700-9,600	6,900-8,700	4,400-5,700
1996 Intrepid	9,400-11,200	8,500-10,200	5,800-7,000
1997 Intrepid	11,500-14,000	10,300-12,500	7,200-9,000

AVERAGE REPLACEMENT COSTS

A/C Compressor $365
Alternator 190
Radiator 350
Timing Chain or Belt 230
Automatic Transmission or
   Transaxle.....................1,089

Constant Velocity Joints.....310
Brakes................................250
Shocks and/or Struts 480
Exhaust System.................418

TROUBLE SPOTS

• **Transmission slippage** If the transmission shudders under light to moderate acceleration, the transmission front pump could be leaking due to a worn bushing, which requires replacement of the pump as well as the torque converter under the powertrain warranty. (1993-96)

• **Transmission slippage** A defective throttle positions sensor, not a transmission problem, could be the cause of late, erratic, or harsh shifting on models with the 3.3L, 3.5L, or 3.8L engine. It is covered under the powertrain warranty. (1994)

• **Transmission slippage** Bad seals in the transmission lead to premature friction component wear, which causes a shudder when starting from a stop, a bump when coasting to a stop, and slipping between gears. Chyrsler will repair the seals, clutches, and if necessary, the torque converter. (1993-95)

• **Engine noise** The motor mount on the left side of the engine tends to break, which causes a snap or click when accelerating. (1992-93)

• **Transmission slippage** Vehicles with 41TE or 42LE automatic transaxle could take several seconds to engage at startup because of a problem with the valve body. The company will replace defective ones and replace the filter and fluid under normal warranty. (1993-95)

• **Air conditioner** The air conditioner lines are prone to leak at the compressor because of nicks and sharp edges on the A/C line grooves for the O-rings, making it necessary to replace the lines. (1993-94)

• **Air conditioner** If the air conditioner is intermittent or quits altogether, but the refrigerant charge is OK, the pressure transducer is probably malfunctioning and Chrysler has a "certified" replacement available. (all)

• **Cold starting problems** Hard starting and a miss at idle can be traced to defective fuel rails, which are replaced under warranty. (1993-94)

RECALL HISTORY

1993 Lower control arm washers in front suspension of some cars can crack and fall off due to hydrogen embrittlement; will cause clunking sound during braking and eventually result in loss of steering control. **1993 w/3.3-liter engine** O-rings used to seal interface of fuel-injector tubes are insufficiently durable; deterioration can cause fuel leakage, with potential for fire. **1994** Right steering tie rod can rub through automatic-transmission wiring harness, causing short circuit; may result in stalling, or allow engine to start when selector is not in "Park" position.

1995-98 DODGE NEON

✓ BEST BUY

1995 Dodge Neon 2-door

FOR Air bags, dual • Anti-lock brakes (optional) • Passenger and cargo room • Steering/handling • Ride • Fuel economy • Instruments/controls

AGAINST Engine noise • Automatic transmission performance

EVALUATION The base engine is quick off the line with either transmission, but it growls loudly under hard throttle. Even so, it transmits little vibration to the car's interior and cruises quietly. The automatic transmission shifts abruptly during brisk acceleration, and tends to be oversensitive to the throttle. It also downshifts unexpectedly. Although the available dual-cam four is live-

DODGE

lier than the base engine, the difference isn't big enough to make it a priority, and it's no quieter, either.

Fuel economy is commendable. We averaged 31 mpg with a 5-speed base engine model in a mix of city and highway driving. A Sport Neon with the base engine and automatic averaged 24.2 mpg, with most driving in and around urban areas.

Neons feel solid and well-planted on the road. The firm suspension soaks up bumps with little harshness, and neither floats nor bottoms out, though bad pavement can deliver a few jolts. Handling is sporty, even with the base model. Steering is firm, feels natural, and centers quickly, producing agile response on winding roads. Brakes have strong stopping power, too.

Passenger space is impressive for such a small vehicle. There's enough head and leg room to seat four 6-footers without squeezing, though rear doors are too small to allow easy entry and exit. The modern dashboard layout offers simple, convenient controls. The Neon's trunk opens at bumper level to a wide, flat cargo floor that reaches well forward to yield good luggage space.

In all Neon offers a solid domestic alternative to the imports. Whether to pick a Dodge or Plymouth is a matter of individual choice; except for the insignia on the body, they're exactly the same car.

NHTSA CRASH TEST RESULTS
1996 Dodge Neon   4-DOOR SEDAN

Driver	☆☆☆☆
Passenger	☆☆☆☆

(The National Highway Traffic Safety Administration tests a vehicle's crashworthiness in front and side collisions. Their ratings suggest the chance of serious injury: ☆☆☆☆☆—10% or less; ☆☆☆☆—10-20% or less; ☆☆☆—20-30% or less; ☆☆—35-45% or less; ☆—More than 45%.)

SPECIFICATIONS

	2-door coupe	4-door sedan
Wheelbase, in.	104.0	104.0
Overall length, in.	171.8	171.8
Overall width, in.	67.5	67.5
Overall height, in.	53.0	52.8
Curb weight, lbs.	2385	2416
Cargo volume, cu. ft.	11.8	11.8
Fuel capacity, gals.	11.2	11.2
Seating capacity	5	5
Front head room, in.	39.6	39.6
Max. front leg room, in.	42.5	42.5
Rear head room, in.	36.5	36.5
Min. rear leg room, in.	35.1	35.1

Powertrain layout: transverse front-engine/front-wheel drive

ENGINES

	ohc I-4	dohc I-4
Size, liters/cu. in.	2.0/122	2.0/122
Horsepower	132	150
Torque (lbs./ft.)	129	130-133

EPA city/highway mpg

5-speed OD manual	28/38	28/38
3-speed automatic	25/33	25/33

Consumer Guide™ observed MPG

5-speed OD manual	31.0	25.4
3-speed automatic	23.6	

Built in USA and Mexico.

RETAIL PRICES

	GOOD	AVERAGE	POOR
1995 Neon	$5,000-6,000	$4,400-5,300	$2,600-3,300
1995 Neon Sport	5,800-6,500	5,200-5,800	3,200-3,800
1996 Neon	6,000-7,200	5,300-6,500	3,300-4,300
1996 Neon Sport	7,000-8,000	6,300-7,200	4,000-4,800
1997 Neon	7,200-8,500	6,400-7,600	4,300-5,200
1998 Neon	8,700-10,500	8,000-9,500	5,800-7,000

AVERAGE REPLACEMENT COSTS

A/C Compressor	$400	Clutch, Pressure Plate, Bearing	535
Alternator	300	Constant Velocity Joints	345
Radiator	375	Brakes	295
Timing Chain or Belt	190	Shocks and/or Struts	450
Automatic Transmission or Transaxle	555	Exhaust System	290

TROUBLE SPOTS

• **Air conditioner** A lack of cooling caused by the A/C evaporator freezing up because the compressor does not cycle off causing. (1995)

• **Brakes** If the ABS (anti-lock brakes) warning light comes on, which disables the ABS, the ABS controller will be replaced under normal warranty provisions. (1995)

• **Climate control** In cold weather, ice may form in the blower motor housing, which prevents the blower from moving and blows the fuse. Under warranty, the drain tube will be rerouted, the blower motor replaced and a new fuse installed. (1995-97)

• **Brakes** The front brakes wear abnormally fast (and make noise) on cars with four wheel studs, so heavy duty linings should be used to replace them.

DODGE

• **Battery** Batteries that go dead may be the result of one or more of the following: a glove box without a raised pad that closes the light switch, misaligned doors, a faulty trunk lid switch and lamp assembly, or a missing door-ajar bumper pad. (1995)

RECALL HISTORY

1995 Fuel and rear-brake tubes can experience accelerated corrosion between metallic tubes and rubber isolator; may lead to brake fluid or fuel leakage. **1995** Steering column coupler can become disconnected when vehicle sustains underbody impact. **1995-96 w/ACR competition package** Brake master cylinder can leak fluid due to damaged seal; warning light will signal impairment prior to partial brake-system loss. **1996 built in Toluca, Mexico** Engine wiring harness can short-circuit due to contact with exhaust gas recirculation tube; can cause various malfunctions, including engine stalling. **1996** Wiring harness in Mexican-built cars could short circuit; can cause various malfunctions, including stalling. **1997** Air bag could deploy inadvertently when ignition is shut off.

1990-93 DODGE RAM PICKUP

1990 Dodge Ram D150 Club Cab

FOR   Passenger and cargo room • Trailer towing capability • Acceleration (V-8)

AGAINST Acceleration (V-6) • Fuel economy

EVALUATION   The Ram's standard V-6 lacks vigor for other than light-duty chores, though later versions are a bit stronger. Each V-8 delivers plenty of torque for moving heavy loads, without using too much more gas than a V-6 engine. For serious heavy-duty hauling, the brawny Cummins Turbodiesel is your best bet, delivering monumental torque output below 2000 rpm.

That translates to a towing capacity as high as 11,900 pounds.

Long-wheelbase 250- and 350-series Ram pickups are the best choices for handling challenging loads, with payloads comparable to Ford and GM full-size trucks. All cargo beds are 70 inches wide between walls, and 51 inches between rear wheels, giving room for cargo that's 4 feet wide, flat on the floor. If you need a truck for hard work, look for a Ram. But if leisure activities are your prime consideration, or you prefer a dual-usage vehicle, consider Ford and GM pickups first.

SPECIFICATIONS

	reg. cab short bed	reg. cab long bed	ext. cab short bed	ext. cab long bed
Wheelbase, in.	115.0	131.0	133.0	149.0
Overall length, in.	199.9	219.9	211.8	237.9
Overall width, in.	79.5	79.5	79.5	79.5
Overall height, in.	70.1	69.0	68.9	69.8
Curb weight, lbs.	3732	3831	4220	4229
Max. payload, lbs.	2251	5400	1835	4363
Fuel capacity, gals.	22.0	22.0	30.0	30.0
Seating capacity	3	3	5	5
Front head room, in.	40.5	40.5	40.5	40.5
Max. front leg room, in.	39.4	39.4	39.4	39.4
Rear head room, in.	—	—	40.4	40.4
Min. rear leg room, in.	—	—	NA	NA

Powertrain layout: longitudinal front-engine/rear- or 4-wheel drive

ENGINES

	ohv V-6	ohv V-8	ohv V-8	Turbodiesel ohv I-6
Size, liters/cu. in.	3.9/239	5.2/318	5.9/360	5.9/360
Horsepower	125-180	170-230	190-230	160
Torque (lbs./ft.)	195-220	260-280	292-325	400

EPA city/highway mpg

5-speed OD manual	15/19	13/17	11/15	NA
3-speed automatic	15/17	13/16		
4-speed OD automatic	15/20	13/17	12/16	

Consumer Guide™ observed MPG

4-speed OD automatic		14.7	13.2	

Built in USA and Mexico.

RETAIL PRICES

	GOOD	AVERAGE	POOR
1990 Ram 150	$2,500-5,000	$1,900-4,300	$900-2,400
1990 Ram 250/350	3,100-5,300	2,500-4,600	1,300-2,800
1991 Ram 150	3,200-6,800	2,600-6,100	1,400-4,000
1991 Ram 250/350	4,000-7,300	3,400-6,500	2,000-4,000
1992 Ram 150	4,100-7,800	3,400-7,000	1,800-4,700
1992 Ram 250/350	5,000-10,000	4,200-9,000	2,400-6,000

DODGE

	GOOD	AVERAGE	POOR
1993 Ram 150	5,100-9,200	4,200-8,200	2,400-5,500
1993 Ram 250/350	6,500-12,500	5,500-11,500	3,400-8,500

AVERAGE REPLACEMENT COSTS

A/C Compressor $495	Clutch, Pressure Plate,
Alternator 300	Bearing............................720
Radiator 685	Brakes.................................320
Timing Chain or Belt 190	Shocks and/or Struts 305
Automatic Transmission or	Exhaust System.................265
Transaxle........................795	

TROUBLE SPOTS

• **Air conditioner** The A/C evaporator freezes up because the compressor does not cycle off causing a lack of cooling. (1991-93)

• **Engine misfire** Intermittent power loss, delayed start, no-start and stalling when starting from a stop may be due to inadequate fuel pressure requiring a pump module with larger filter. (1991-93)

• **Engine noise** A lifter (tappet) noise, that seems to come from varying locations on 3.9L engines, is corrected by replacing the timing chain and sprockets with a double-roller chain. (1992-93)

• **Fuel gauge** The fuel gauge reads lower than actual fuel level giving the illusion of too much reserve or the wrong size tank. The in-tank module must be replaced. (1991-93)

• **Engine misfire** A faulty idle air control motor causes erratic idle, stalling after hot soak or during low speed deceleration. (1992-93)

• **Transmission leak** Transmission fluid leaks from the O-ring on the speed sensor. (1993)

RECALL HISTORY

1990 with 6-foot box, EFI, and no rear bumper In rear-end collision, crossmember could contact fuel line. **1991** Premium steering wheel can crack and separate from hub. **1992** On some vehicles, parking brake might not fully engage. **1993** Anti-lock braking might be inoperative when hard pedal effort is applied.

1994-98 DODGE RAM PICKUP

FOR Air bag, driver • Acceleration (V-8, V-10) • Interior room • Cargo and towing ability • Optional 4-wheel anti-lock brakes

AGAINST Acceleration (V-6) • Ride • Noise • Fuel economy

EVALUATION All told, the impressive Ram is as accommodating and refined as any Ford or General Motors rival.

1996 Dodge Ram Club Cab 1500 4WD

Acceleration is more than adequate with the 5.2-liter V-8, which delivered average fuel economy of 14.4 mpg. We don't recommend a V-6 for heavy-duty work. A burly Cummins turbodiesel also is available, but not too many folks really need that much pull. You don't get neck-snapping pickup with the V-10, but it does propel the Ram with more authority than any V-8, and generates less noise than expected. Gas mileage is dismal, however: just 10 mpg in mostly city travel. A turbodiesel delivered 14.6 mpg, but is slower in standing-start acceleration than a gas engine, and idles as roughly as a big rig.

Even with a base suspension, a Ram 1500 can get bouncy over dips and bumps when the bed is empty. Turns may be taken with good grip and balance, and gusty crosswinds have little effect on directional stability. Ride quality in a 2500-series is undeniably stiff. Four wheel anti-lock braking brings this pickup to a halt with fine control. Engine and road noise are modest for a truck, but wind roar around front roof pillars is a problem.

Space is ample for three-across seating. The cab has plenty of space behind the seat, making it possible to recline seatbacks—a rarity in full-size pickups. The seatback center folds into an armrest that doubles as a compartmented console. Opening the large padded lid to gain access to the compartments, however, is not so easy while driving. Three can sit abreast in the back of a Club Cab, but the seat cushion is too short to offer real thigh support, and rear leg room is no better than in a compact car.

Gauges are plainly marked; controls near at hand and logical. Three simple knobs operate the climate control. Most controls are lit at night. A slide-out holder is big enough to carry two 16-ounce beverage containers, but it obstructs the radio controls when in use. Even if you're leaning toward

DODGE

another brand, it's a good idea to test-drive a Ram before buying any full-size pickup.

NHTSA CRASH TEST RESULTS
1994 Dodge Ram 1500

REG. CAB LONG BED

Driver	☆☆☆☆☆
Passenger	NA

(The National Highway Traffic Safety Administration tests a vehicle's crashworthiness in front and side collisions. Their ratings suggest the chance of serious injury: ☆☆☆☆☆—10% or less; ☆☆☆☆—10-20% or less; ☆☆☆—20-30% or less; ☆☆—35-45% or less; ☆—More than 45%.)

SPECIFICATIONS

	reg. cab short bed	reg. cab long bed	ext. cab short bed	ext. cab long bed
Wheelbase, in.	118.7	134.7	138.7	154.7
Overall length, in.	204.1	224.1	224.0	244.0
Overall width, in.	79.4	79.4	79.4	79.4
Overall height, in.	71.9	71.8	71.6	71.5
Curb weight, lbs.	4009	4180	4529	4649
Max. payload, lbs.............	2372	5340	3915	5151
Fuel capacity, gals.	26.0	35.0	26.0	35.0
Seating capacity	3	3	6	6
Front head room, in.	40.2	40.2	40.2	40.2
Max. front leg room, in. ...	41.0	41.0	41.0	41.0
Rear head room, in.	NA	NA	39.4	39.4
Min. rear leg room, in.	NA	NA	31.6	31.6

Powertrain layout: longitudinal front-engine/rear- or 4-wheel drive

ENGINES

	ohv V-6	ohv V-8	ohv V-8	Turbodiesel ohv I-6	ohv V-10
Size, liters/cu. in.	3.9/239	5.2/318	5.9/360	5.9/360	8.0/488
Horsepower	170-175	220	230-235	160-215	300
Torque (lbs./ft.)	230	300	330	420-440	440-450

EPA city/highway mpg

5-speed OD man.	16/20	14/19	12/16	NA	NA
4-speed OD auto.	14/18	13/17	12/17	NA	NA

Consumer Guide™ observed MPG

4-speed OD auto.		14.4		14.6	10.0

Built in USA and Mexico.

RETAIL PRICES

	GOOD	AVERAGE	POOR
1994 Ram pickup	$7,700-14,000	$7,000-13,000	$4,800-10,000
1995 Ram pickup	9,100-17,000	8,300-16,000	5,800-12,500
1996 Ram pickup	10,500-20,000	9,200-18,500	6,500-15,000
1997 Ram pickup	12,000-22,000	10,500-20,500	7,500-16,500
1998 Ram pickup	13,500-24,500	12,000-23,000	8,800-18,500

AVERAGE REPLACEMENT COSTS

A/C Compressor $380	Clutch, Pressure Plate,
Alternator 295	Bearing 610
Radiator 325	Universal Joints 225
Timing Chain or Belt 235	Brakes................................295
Automatic Transmission or	Shocks and/or Struts 230
Transaxle........................795	Exhaust System.................260

TROUBLE SPOTS

• **Air conditioner** If the air conditioner gradually stops cooling and/or the airflow from the vents decreases, the computer (PCM) may not be sending a signal to the compressor clutch relay to cycle off, which causes the AC evaporator to freeze up. When the ice melts, the AC works again briefly. Many technicians overlook this as the source of trouble. (1994-95)

• **Transmission leak** Automatic transmission fluid leaks from the speed sensor in the transmission, which Chyrsler will replace under its powertrain warranty. (1994)

• **Transmission slippage** If the transmission will not engage (from 2 to 8 seconds) when first started, chances are the torque converter is draining down. Chrysler will correct the problem by installing a check valve in the fluid line leading to the transmission cooler as long as the vehicle is still under warranty. (1993) If the transmission won't upshift for about the first quarter mile in cool weather, it is probably due to defective cast iron seal rings in the governor drive. This repair is covered under the normal warranty. (1993-94)

• **Suspension noise** A rattle or clunk from the front can often be traced to the sway bar links where they attach to the sway bar. Chyrsler will replace both the bar and the links with new ones having tapered holes and studs under normal warranty. (1994-95)

RECALL HISTORY

1994 Component within passenger-side seatbelt buckle assembly shatters, causing belt to release. **1994 BR1500/2500 with no rear bumpers** Does not meet rear-impact test requirements, with increased risk of fuel spill. **1994** Seatback release latch lever might remain in released position. **1994 4WD** Front suspension attachment to axle may not be adequately tightened; can cause axle vibration. **1994-95** While making a turn, extra keys in keyring can lodge in holes in back of steering wheel. **1994-95** Secondary hood latch rod can bind and prevent engagement. **1994-95** Lower steering shaft can separate from upper shaft if the retaining plastic pins and metal clip break; can result in loss of vehicle control. **1994-96 w/gasoline engine** Valve on fuel tank can allow fuel to leak onto ground; could

DODGE

result in fire. **1994-97** Under certain high-load conditions, fluid line could separate from transmission; fluid may then spray onto exhaust manifold. **1995-96 with diesel engine** Vacuum hose may deteriorate and partially collapse, possibly reducing power-brake assist. **1996 w/6800- or 9000-pound GVW rating** Tire/wheel specification information on certification label indicates smaller tire than is required. **1997 w/diesel engine** Exhaust pipe may contact, or be too near, dash panel silencer pad, causing smoldering and igniting of adjacent materials. **1998** Brake rotor material strength on some trucks is not sufficient, causing hub fatigue fracture that can result in crack propagation and, ultimately, in wheel separation.

1990-94 DODGE SHADOW

1994 Dodge Shadow ES Coupe 2-door

FOR Air bag, driver • Acceleration (V-6, Turbo) • Cargo room • Anti-lock brakes • Ride/handling

AGAINST Rear-seat room • Entry/exit

EVALUATION Performance is listless with the basic 2.2-liter engine, which is on the noisy side. Action is somewhat better—and smoother—with the 2.5-liter four, which doesn't consume much more fuel, either. It's a better choice with automatic, in particular, but by no means devoid of noise. Either turbo engine delivers swift acceleration, but it's accompanied by plenty of raucous behavior beneath the hood. The V-6 engine is smooth and flexible, making a Shadow downright frisky when coupled to manual shift. Lacking an overdrive gear, the 3-speed automatic isn't the best choice for highway gas mileage and quiet cruising.

The standard suspension is firm for a domestic car. Handling beats most small cars, even in base form, and Shadows produce a stable highway ride. An ES version is tauter, but not harsh over

154 CONSUMER GUIDE

most pavement surfaces. Quick-ratio power steering has good feel and centers well.

Interiors are nicely packaged, with reclining front bucket seats, tachometer, and gauges. Rear-seat room could be better but folding the seatbacks creates a generous cargo hold.

Convertibles displayed some cowl shake and body flex even when new, but not to a troubling degree. Assembly quality doesn't match that of Japanese competitors, and Shadows aren't the most refined small cars around. Some might call even them mechanically crude. Still, Dodge's subcompact is a solid vehicle that looks good, performs well, and costs considerably less.

SPECIFICATIONS

	2-door hatchback	4-door hatchback	2-door conv.
Wheelbase, in.	97.2	97.2	97.0
Overall length, in.	171.9	171.9	171.7
Overall width, in.	67.3	67.3	67.3
Overall height, in.	52.7	52.7	52.6
Curb weight, lbs.	2613	2884	2916
Cargo volume, cu. ft.	33.3	33.3	13.2
Fuel capacity, gals.	14.0	14.0	14.0
Seating capacity	5	5	4
Front head room, in.	38.3	38.3	38.3
Max. front leg room, in.	42.0	42.0	42.0
Rear head room, in.	37.4	37.4	37.4
Min. rear leg room, in.	33.7	33.7	33.7

Powertrain layout: transverse front-engine/front-wheel drive

ENGINES	ohc I-4	Turbocharged ohc I-4	ohc I-4	Turbocharged ohc I-4	ohc V-6
Size, liters/cu. in.	2.2/135	2.2/135	2.5/153	2.5/153	3.0/181
Horsepower	93	174	100	150-152	141
Torque (lbs./ft.)	122	210	135	180	171
EPA city/highway mpg					
5-speed OD man.	26/33	20/28	24/29	20/26	19/28
3-speed auto.	23/30		22/27	19/23	
4-speed OD auto.					19/24
Consumer Guide™ observed MPG					
5-speed OD man.		25.2	19.8		
4-speed OD auto.				21.7	

Built in USA.

RETAIL PRICES	GOOD	AVERAGE	POOR
1990 Shadow	$1,600-2,500	$1,000-1,900	$300-800
1991 Shadow	2,000-3,000	1,400-2,400	600-1,100
1991 Shadow Convertible	2,800-3,700	2,200-3,000	1,000-1,500
1992 Shadow	2,400-3,600	1,800-3,000	900-1,400

DODGE

	GOOD	AVERAGE	POOR
1992 Shadow Convertible	3,600-4,500	3,000-3,800	1,400-2,100
1993 Shadow	3,000-4,200	2,400-3,500	1,200-1,700
1993 Shadow Convertible	4,300-5,300	3,600-4,600	1,800-2,500
1994 Shadow	3,700-5,000	3,000-4,300	1,500-2,100

AVERAGE REPLACEMENT COSTS

A/C Compressor $450
Alternator 280
Radiator 325
Timing Chain or Belt 150
Automatic Transmission or
   Transaxle.........................675

Clutch, Pressure Plate,
   Bearing............................625
Constant Velocity Joints.....445
Brakes..................................250
Shocks and/or Struts 330
Exhaust System 260

TROUBLE SPOTS

• **Oil consumption** High oil consumption and smoke from the exhaust at idle and deceleration on 3.0L V-6 engines (Mitsubishi built) is caused by exhaust valve guides that slide out of the heads. If the guides are not too loose, they can be retained with snap rings. Otherwise, the heads have to be replaced. The repair will be handled under normal warranty coverage. (1992-93)

• **Alternator belt** Unless a shield is installed under the engine on the right side, deep snow could knock the serpentine belt off the pulleys of a 3.0L engine. Usually the first sign that this has happened is a low voltmeter reading or the battery light coming on. (1991-94)

• **Engine noise** The motor mount on the left side of the engine tends to break, which causes a snap or click when accelerating. (1992-93)

• **Cold starting problems** A 2.2L or 2.5L engine may idle rough or stumble when first started below freezing temperatures unless a revised intake manifold (with an "X" cast into the number 1 runner) was installed (1992) or a revised computer (PCM) was installed (1992-93) or the computer was reprogrammed (1994).

• **Air conditioner** If the air conditioner gradually stops cooling and/or the airflow from the vents decreases, the computer (PCM) may not be sending a signal to the compressor clutch relay to cycle off, which causes the AC evaporator to freeze up. When the ice melts, the AC works again briefly. Many technicians overlook this as the source of trouble. (1991-94)

• **Transmission slippage** If the transmission shudders under light to moderate acceleration, the transmission front pump could be leaking due to a worn bushing, which requires replacement of the pump as well as the torque converter under the powertrain warranty. (1990-94)

• **Transmission slippage** Vehicles with 41TE or 42LE automatic transaxle could take several seconds to engage at startup because of a problem with the valve body. The company will replace defective ones, and replace the filter and fluid under normal warranty. (1993-95)

• **Transmission slippage** Bad seals in the transmission lead to premature friction component wear, which causes shudder when starting from a stop, a bump when coasting to a stop and slipping between gears. Chrysler will warranty the seals, clutches, and if necessary, the torque converter. (1993-95)

RECALL HISTORY

1991 Front disc brake caliper guide pin bolts may not be adequately tightened and could loosen, which could cause reduced braking effectiveness that might result in an accident. **1991** Both air bag system front impact sensors may not be secured to mounting brackets, so air bag would not deploy. **1992** Zinc plating of some upper steering column shaft coupling bolts caused hydrogen embrittlement and breakage of the bolt. **1991-92** Steering wheel mounting armature can develop cracks and separate from the center hub attachment to the steering column; can result in loss of vehicle control. **1991-92** Lower driver's seatback attaching bolt can fail and separate.

1990-95 DODGE SPIRIT

1991 Dodge Spirit ES

FOR Air bag, driver (later models) • Anti-lock brakes (optional later models) • Passenger and cargo room • Acceleration (V-6, Turbo)

AGAINST Engine noise • Road noise • Wind noise • Ride • Rear-seat room

EVALUATION Acceleration with the base four is barely adequate and particularly meager when passing/merging. But gas mileage is impressive—a 4-cylinder Spirit averaged 22.3 mpg in

DODGE

mixed expressway/highway driving. The V-6 is smooth and responsive, but its 4-speed automatic transmission shifts too quickly into higher gears, and also holds backs on downshifts when trying to pass. A 3-speed automatic is less frugal, but operates more dependably. Some turbos suffer lag that detracts from initial acceleration, but they're strong and swift after that opening period. Revisions for 1991 improved low-speed response, but the engine is noisy and coarse. Takeoffs are smooth and vigorous with the Spirit R/T, which suffers minimal turbo lag and offers balanced performance.

Roomy interiors for a car this size offer top-notch visibility. Getting in and out is a snap, and the big trunk with a flat floor is easy to load. Gauges are readable on a dashboard that's nicely laid out. Front seats feel fine, and rear head/knee room is adequate; but rear cushions are too low and short for comfort.

Solid, spacious, and competent, a Spirit might fail to stimulate anyone's spirit—unless it happens to be the wheel-twisting R/T, that is. Even in tamer form, Dodge's practical domestic sedan is worth a look.

NHTSA CRASH TEST RESULTS
1995 Dodge Spirit

4-DOOR SEDAN

Driver	☆☆☆☆
Passenger	☆☆☆

(The National Highway Traffic Safety Administration tests a vehicle's crashworthiness in front and side collisions. Their ratings suggest the chance of serious injury: ☆☆☆☆☆—10% or less; ☆☆☆☆—10-20% or less; ☆☆☆—20-30% or less; ☆☆—35-45% or less; ☆—More than 45%.)

SPECIFICATIONS

	4-door sedan
Wheelbase, in.	103.3
Overall length, in.	181.2
Overall width, in.	68.1
Overall height, in.	53.5
Curb weight, lbs.	2863
Cargo volume, cu. ft.	14.4
Fuel capacity, gals.	16.0
Seating capacity	6
Front head room, in.	38.4
Max. front leg room, in.	41.9
Rear head room, in.	37.9
Min. rear leg room, in.	38.3

Powertrain layout: transverse front-engine/front-wheel drive

ENGINES	Turbocharged ohc I-4	ohc I-4	Turbocharged ohc I-4	ohc V-6
Size, liters/cu. in.	2.2/135	2.5/153	2.5/153	3.0/181

	Turbocharged ohc I-4	ohc I-4	Turbocharged ohc I-4	ohc V-6
Horsepower	224	100-101	150-152	141-142
Torque (lbs./ft.)	217	135-140	210	171
EPA city/highway mpg				
5-speed OD manual	24/34	24/29	19/27	21/26
3-speed automatic	23/27	22/28		
4-speed OD automatic.....				19/24
Consumer Guide™ observed MPG				
5-speed OD manual		21.2		
3-speed automatic		22.3		

Built in USA and Mexico.

RETAIL PRICES	GOOD	AVERAGE	POOR
1990 Spirit	$1,700-2,500	$1,100-1,900	$400-800
1991 Spirit	2,100-3,000	1,500-2,400	700-1,100
1991 Spirit R/T	2,900-3,700	2,300-3,000	1,100-1,500
1992 Spirit	2,700-3,900	2,100-3,200	1,000-1,500
1992 Spirit R/T	3,700-4,400	3,000-3,700	1,500-1,900
1993 Spirit	3,500-4,800	2,800-4,100	1,300-2,000
1994 Spirit	4,400-5,300	3,700-4,600	1,800-2,400
1995 Spirit	5,300-6,200	4,600-5,400	2,400-2,900

AVERAGE REPLACEMENT COSTS

A/C Compressor $415		Constant Velocity Joints.....660
Alternator 315		Brakes..................................250
Radiator 335		Shocks and/or Struts 340
Timing Chain or Belt 290		Exhaust System..................320
Automatic Transmission or Transaxle.........................905		

TROUBLE SPOTS

• **Oil consumption and exhaust smoke** High oil consumption and smoke from the exhaust at idle and deceleration on 3.0L V-6 engines (Mitsubishi built) is caused by exhaust valve guides that slide out of the heads. If the guides are not too loose, they can be retained with snap rings. Otherwise, the heads have to be replaced. The repair will be handled under normal warranty coverage. (1990-93)

• **Cold starting problems** A 2.2L or 2.5L engine may idle rough or stumble when first started below freezing temperatures unless a revised intake manifold (with an "X" cast into the number 1 runner) was installed (1992) or a revised computer (PCM) was installed (1992-93) or the computer was reprogrammed. (1994)

• **Engine noise** The motor mount on the left side of the engine tends

DODGE

to break, which causes a snap or click when accelerating. (1992-93)

• **Alternator belt** Unless a shield is installed under the engine on the right side, deep snow could knock the serpentine belt off the pulleys of the 3.0L engine. Usually the first sign that this has happened is a low voltmeter reading or the battery light coming on. (1991-95)

• **Air conditioner** If the air conditioner gradually stops cooling and/or the airflow from the vents decreases, the computer (PCM) may not be sending a signal to the compressor clutch relay to cycle off, which causes the AC evaporator to freeze up. When the ice melts, the AC works again briefly. Many technicians overlook this as the source of trouble. (1991-95)

• **Transmission slippage** Vehicles with 41TE or 42LE automatic transaxle could take several seconds to engage at startup because of a problem with the valve body. The company will replace defective ones and replace the filter and fluid under normal warranty. (1993-95)

• **Transmission slippage** If the transmission shudders under light to moderate acceleration, the transmission front pump could be leaking due to a worn bushing, which requires replacement of the pump as well as the torque converter under the powertrain warranty. (1990-95)

• **Transmission slippage** Bad seals in the transmission lead to premature friction component wear, which causes shudder when starting from a stop, a bump when coasting to a stop, and slipping between gears. Chrysler will warranty the seals, clutches, and if necessary, the torque converter. (1993-95)

RECALL HISTORY

1991 Front disc brake caliper guide pin bolts may not be adequately tightened and could loosen. **1991** Both air bag system front impact sensors may not be secured to mounting brackets, so air bag would not deploy. **1992** Zinc plating of some upper steering column shaft coupling bolts caused hydrogen embrittlement and breakage of the bolt. **1994** Seatbelt assembly on small number of cars may fail in accident, increasing risk of injury.

1995-98 DODGE STRATUS

FOR Air bags, dual • Anti-lock brakes (ES) • Acceleration • Ride • Steering/handling • Passenger and cargo room

AGAINST Noise • Rear visibility

EVALUATION Although Stratus has the exterior dimensions of a compact car, it offers the interior room of a mid-size model. In fact, there's plenty of leg space fore and aft, and sufficient

1995 Dodge Stratus ES

rear-seat width for three medium-size adults to travel without feeling like sardines.

Visibility is great to all angles except the rear. The high rear parcel shelf makes it hard to see out the back window. A large trunk with a flat floor and low liftover gives the Stratus good cargo-carrying ability. The driving position is comfortable, and the dashboard layout logical. The sedan's abundant, airy interior is well designed; however, some trim pieces on the dashboard and door panels look and feel cheap.

Of the three engine choices, we recommend the 2.5-liter V-6 for its smoother running and livelier acceleration. It's not the quietest engine around, but takeoffs from a standstill are spirited. However, you're likely to experience a long pause, before the automatic transmission downshifts for passing. Despite being shy two cylinders, the 2.4-liter 4-cylinder offers nearly as much punch as the V-6, though at the expense of some refinement. The 2.0-liter four is noisier and a trifle slower, but gets great mileage with the 5-speed manual.

Stratus rides and handles more like a sports sedan than a typical American car. That means more interior noise and road vibrations than people may be used to. You benefit from agile handling with little body lean and good grip, making it easy to thread along twisting roads. An ES, in particular, takes corners and curves adeptly. Ride comfort is generally good on both models, despite the firmer suspension on the ES, and the Stratus does feel smoother than a Ford Contour.

Overall, the large, comfortable interior, moderate price, and attractive styling make the well-equipped Stratus a good buy. Our only reservation might be Chrysler's past reputation for poor build quality.

NHTSA CRASH TEST RESULTS
1995 Dodge Stratus

4-DOOR SEDAN

Driver	☆☆☆
Passenger	NA

(The National Highway Traffic Safety Administration tests a vehicle's crashworthiness in front and side collisions. Their ratings suggest the chance of serious injury: ☆☆☆☆☆—10% or less; ☆☆☆☆—10-20% or less; ☆☆☆—20-30% or less; ☆☆—35-45% or less; ☆—More than 45%.)

SPECIFICATIONS

	4-door sedan
Wheelbase, in.	108.0
Overall length, in.	186.0
Overall width, in.	71.7
Overall height, in.	54.1
Curb weight, lbs.	2899
Cargo volume, cu. ft.	15.7
Fuel capacity, gals.	16.0
Seating capacity	5
Front head room, in.	38.1
Max. front leg room, in.	42.3
Rear head room, in.	36.8
Min. rear leg room, in.	37.8

Powertrain layout: transverse front-engine/front-wheel drive

ENGINES

	ohc I-4	dohc I-4	ohc V-6
Size, liters/cu. in.	2.0/122	2.4/148	2.5/152
Horsepower	132	150	164-168
Torque (lbs./ft.)	129	165-167	161-170

EPA city/highway mpg

5-speed OD manual	25/36		
4-speed OD automatic		20/29	20/28

Consumer Guide™ observed MPG

5-speed OD manual	24.7	
4-speed OD automatic		20.3

Built in USA.

RETAIL PRICES

	GOOD	AVERAGE	POOR
1995 Stratus	$7,100-8,000	$6,400-7,200	$4,000-4,700
1995 Stratus ES	7,700-8,700	7,000-8,000	4,500-5,400
1996 Stratus	8,200-9,200	7,400-8,400	5,000-5,800
1996 Stratus ES	9,200-10,500	8,300-9,600	5,800-6,900
1997 Stratus	9,500-10,800	8,500-9,800	6,000-7,000
1997 Stratus ES	10,500-12,000	9,500-11,000	7,000-8,000
1998 Stratus	11,500-12,800	10,500-11,800	7,800-9,000
1998 Stratus ES	12,500-13,500	11,500-12,500	8,800-9,800

AVERAGE REPLACEMENT COSTS

A/C Compressor $425	Clutch, Pressure Plate,
Alternator 300	Bearing 545
Radiator 440	Constant Velocity Joints.....345
Timing Chain or Belt 190	Brakes.................................325
Automatic Transmission or	Shocks and/or Struts 375
Transaxle 1,115	Exhaust System.................290

TROUBLE SPOTS

• **Headlights** Poor illumination from headlights corrected by replacing both headlamp modules. (1996-97)

• **Air conditioner** Air conditioning compressor fails on cars with 2.5L engine, especially if car is driven mostly in heavy traffic in hot weather. (1995-96)

• **Air conditioner** Air conditioning may be intermittent or stop completely due to failed pressure transducer. (1995)

• **Transmission slippage** Transmission may shudder when accelerating from a stop, thump when coasting down to a stop, or slip when shifting. (1995)

• **Water leak** Water leaks in between the door and interior door trim panel or from the cowl/plenum/floor/A-pillar seams. (1995-96)

RECALL HISTORY

1995-96 w/ABS Corrosion of ABS hydraulic control unit can cause solenoid valves to stick open, so car tends to pull from a straight stop when brakes are applied. **1995-96** Brake master cylinder can leak fluid, due to damaged seal; warning light will signal impairment prior to partial brake-system loss. **1995-96 w/2.4-liter** Oil leakage could cause engine-compartment fire. **1995** Rear seatbelt anchors will not withstand loading required by Federal standard. **1995-97** Lower ball joint can separate due to loss of lubrication; could cause loss of control. **1996-97** Secondary hood latch spring can disengage if hood is slammed.

1993-96 EAGLE SUMMIT

FOR   Fuel economy • Maneuverability • Anti-lock brakes (optional) • Dual air bags (later models)

AGAINST Rear-seat room • Acceleration (automatic) • Engine and road noise

EVALUATION You get a supple ride for a subcompact, but for handling proficiency you need a model with 14-inch wheels and tires (which were standard on the ES 4-door, and optional on

1993 Eagle Summit 4-door

other models). Interior space is about on par for the subcompact class. That means roomy enough up front, but fairly cramped in the backseat.

These notchbacks are less noisy and feel more solid. However, cargo space was better with the old hatchback. Also, the lightweight construction filters out little road and engine noise.

Acceleration with the base 1.5-liter engine is modest, even with manual shift. Passing power with an automatic transmission is meager. The 1.8-liter 4-doors are quicker with either transmission, and their wider tires deliver better control. Later coupes might also have that bigger engine, and are worth looking for.

The addition of air bags in 1994 and '95 was considered an important safety advance, but anti-lock braking was available only on top sedans. Summits and their Colt/Mirage mates can match the refinement of a Honda Civic or Geo Prizm, but they cost markedly less as secondhand automobiles. For that reason alone, they're worth a look.

SPECIFICATIONS

	2-door coupe	4-door sedan
Wheelbase, in.	96.1	98.4
Overall length, in.	171.1	174.0
Overall width, in.	66.1	66.1
Overall height, in.	51.4	51.4
Curb weight, lbs.	2085	2195
Cargo volume, cu. ft.	10.5	10.5
Fuel capacity, gals.	13.2	13.2
Seating capacity	5	5
Front head room, in.	38.6	38.4
Max. front leg room, in.	42.9	42.9
Rear head room, in.	36.4	36.2
Min. rear leg room, in.	31.1	33.5

Powertrain layout: transverse front-engine/front-wheel drive

ENGINES

	ohc I-4	ohc I-4
Size, liters/cu. in.	1.5/90	1.8/112
Horsepower	92	113
Torque (lbs./ft.)	93	166

EPA city/highway mpg

5-speed OD manual	32/39	26/33
3-speed automatic	28/32	
4-speed OD automatic		26/33

Consumer Guide™ observed MPG

5-speed OD manual		28.5
3-speed automatic	27.1	

Built in Japan.

RETAIL PRICES	GOOD	AVERAGE	POOR
1993 Summit	$2,500-4,000	$1,900-3,400	$900-1,700
1994 Summit	3,300-5,000	2,700-4,300	1,400-2,400
1995 Summit	4,100-6,300	3,400-5,600	1,900-3,300
1996 Summit	5,000-7,200	4,200-6,300	2,500-3,900

AVERAGE REPLACEMENT COSTS

A/C Compressor $835	Clutch, Pressure Plate, Bearing 475
Alternator 685	Constant Velocity Joints.....750
Radiator 415	Brakes.................................260
Timing Chain or Belt 250	Shocks and/or Struts 745
Automatic Transmission or Transaxle........................960	Exhaust System.................390

TROUBLE SPOTS

• **Transmission leak** The transmission cooler hoses are prone to leaking, which can result in transmission failure. (1993)

• **Engine misfire** Intermittent rough idle and stalling upon acceleration due to a bad ground connection for the engine control computer. (1993)

• **Transmission slippage** Hard shifting and gear clash can be eliminated by installing revised synchronizer components. (1991)

• **Transmission slippage** The pulse generator often gets installed backwards after a transmission rebuild resulting in third-gear starts and/or "limp in," third gear only. (1994)

• **Transmission slippage** An accelerator switch that is out of adjustment causes harsh coast-down downshifts. (1994)

• **Transmission slippage** No second gear (transmission skips from first to third) and/or a loud tapping noise when shifted into or out of any forward range. (1993-94)

RECALL HISTORY

1993 Excess lubrication can cause rubber door latch switch cover to deform and switch to malfunction; shoulder-belt anchorage may remain at A-pillar when car door is closed. **1993** Over time, abrading force on the lower edges of the chamber for the moving cable that controls driver's shoulder belt may be sufficient to allow cable to drop; could cause shoulder-belt anchorage to become stuck.

1990-94 EAGLE TALON

1992 Eagle Talon

FOR Acceleration (except 1.8-liter) • Handling/roadholding • AWD traction (TSi AWD) • Anti-lock brakes (optional)

AGAINST Rear-seat room • Visibility • Cargo room • Engine noise • Road noise

See the **1990-94 Mitsubishi Eclipse** for an evaluation of the **1990-94 Eagle Talon.**

SPECIFICATIONS

	2-door hatchback
Wheelbase, in.	97.2
Overall length, in.	172.4
Overall width, in.	66.7
Overall height, in.	51.4
Curb weight, lbs.	2549
Cargo volume, cu. ft.	25.7
Fuel capacity, gals.	15.8
Seating capacity	4
Front head room, in.	37.9

	2-door hatchback
Max. front leg room, in.	43.9
Rear head room, in.	34.1
Min. rear leg room, in.	28.5

Powertrain layout: transverse front-engine/front- or all-wheel drive

ENGINES

	ohc I-4	dohc I-4	Turbocharged dohc I-4
Size, liters/cu. in.	1.8/107	2.0/122	2.0/122
Horsepower	92	135	180-195
Torque (lbs./ft.)	105	125	203

EPA city/highway mpg

5-speed OD manual	23/32	22/29	21/28
4-speed OD automatic	23/30	22/27	19/23

Consumer Guide™ observed MPG

5-speed OD manual			20.4
4-speed OD automatic		22.6	

Built in USA.

RETAIL PRICES

	GOOD	AVERAGE	POOR
1990 Talon	$2,500-3,200	$1,900-2,600	$800-1,200
1990 Talon TSi	2,900-3,800	2,200-3,100	1,000-1,400
1991 Talon	3,100-3,800	2,500-3,200	1,200-1,500
1991 Talon TSi	3,600-4,800	2,900-4,100	1,400-2,000
1992 Talon	3,800-4,500	3,100-3,800	1,500-1,800
1992 Talon TSi	4,500-5,600	3,800-4,800	1,900-2,400
1993 Talon	4,100-5,000	3,400-4,300	1,800-2,200
1993 Talon TSi	5,700-7,000	4,900-6,200	2,700-3,400
1994 Talon	5,100-6,300	4,300-5,500	2,300-3,000
1994 Talon TSi	7,000-8,300	6,200-7,500	3,700-4,500

AVERAGE REPLACEMENT COSTS

A/C Compressor $635	Clutch, Pressure Plate, Bearing 480
Alternator 695	Constant Velocity Joints..1,040
Radiator 395	Brakes...................................240
Timing Chain or Belt 235	Shocks and/or Struts 480
Automatic Transmission or Transaxle.........................885	Exhaust System.................680

TROUBLE SPOTS

• **Vehicle shake** If the car shakes and vibrates as though the wheels are out of balance, but they check out OK, Chrysler will replace the engine and transmission mounts with ones that do not transmit vibrations as much as the originals under normal warranty provisions. (1990-94)

EAGLE

- **Hard starting** Technicians reportedly have trouble tracking down the cause of hard or no starting, and possibly no fan on cars built before May 1995. It may be caused by corrosion of a splice in the wiring harness near the left headlight caused by water getting into the wiring. (1990-94)

- **Brake noise** The rear disc brakes are prone to squealing or squeaking so Chrysler has released a shim kit to quiet them down. The kits will be installed free on cars still under warranty, but are available for field service on older models. (1992-94)

RECALL HISTORY

1990 Operation of factory-installed sunroof in "non-standard" manner may cause hinge disengagement. **1990** Diluted primer may have been used on windshield opening flanges of a few cars, which would not provide required retention of glass. **1990-91** Front seatbelt release button can break and pieces can fall inside.

1995-98 EAGLE TALON

1995 Eagle Talon ESi

FOR Air bags, dual • Acceleration (TSi, TSi AWD) • Steering/ handling • AWD traction (AWD models) • Anti-lock brakes (optional)

AGAINST Acceleration (base/ESi auto.) • Rear-seat room • Noise

See the 1995-98 Mitsubishi Eclipse report for an evaluation of the Eagle Talon.

NHTSA CRASH TEST RESULTS
1997 Eagle Talon

2-DOOR HATCHBACK

Driver	☆☆☆☆
Passenger	☆☆☆☆

(The National Highway Traffic Safety Administration tests a vehicle's crashworthiness in front and side collisions. Their ratings suggest the chance of serious injury: ☆☆☆☆☆—10% or less; ☆☆☆☆—10-20% or less; ☆☆☆—20-30% or less; ☆☆—35-45% or less; ☆—More than 45%.)

SPECIFICATIONS

	2-door hatchback
Wheelbase, in.	98.8
Overall length, in.	172.2
Overall width, in.	68.3
Overall height, in.	51.0
Curb weight, lbs.	2789
Cargo volume, cu. ft.	16.6
Fuel capacity, gals.	15.9
Seating capacity	4
Front head room, in.	37.9
Max. front leg room, in.	43.3
Rear head room, in.	34.1
Min. rear leg room, in.	28.4

Powertrain layout: transverse front-engine/front- or all-wheel drive

ENGINES	dohc I-4	Turbocharged dohc I-4
Size, liters/cu. in.	2.0/122	2.0/122
Horsepower	140	205-210
Torque (lbs./ft.)	130	214
EPA city/highway mpg		
5-speed OD manual	22/32	20/27
4-speed OD automatic	20/30	23/31
Consumer Guide™ observed MPG		
5-speed OD manual	23.6	

Built in USA.

RETAIL PRICES	GOOD	AVERAGE	POOR
1995 Talon ESi	$8,200-9,200	$7,500-8,500	$5,000-6,000
1995 Talon TSi	9,500-11,000	8,500-10,000	5,800-7,000
1996 Talon/ESi	9,500-10,500	8,700-9,600	6,200-7,000
1996 Talon TSi	11,000-13,000	10,000-12,000	7,000-8,500
1997 Talon/ESi	11,000-12,200	10,000-11,200	7,500-8,500
1997 Talon TSi	13,000-15,000	11,800-13,500	8,500-10,000
1998 Talon/ESi	13,000-14,500	11,800-13,000	9,000-10,000
1998 Talon TSi	15,500-18,500	14,000-17,000	10,500-13,000

AVERAGE REPLACEMENT COSTS

A/C Compressor	$710
Alternator	225
Radiator	430
Timing Chain or Belt	255
Automatic Transmission or Transaxle	995
Clutch, Pressure Plate, Bearing	555
Constant Velocity Joints	680
Brakes	225
Shocks and/or Struts	565
Exhaust System	655

TROUBLE SPOTS

• **Headlights** A corroded connector behind the left headlight may cause hard starting, intermittently flashing "Check Engine" light, and radiator/condenser fan that will not run. (1995)

• **Engine misfire** Engine may idle rough, hesitate, stall, be hard to restart, during cold weather until the engine warms up requiring a new engine control computer. (1995)

• **Transmission slippage** Transmission tends to default to the "limp-in" mode, which is second gear only, for no apparent reason requiring the transmission control computer to be reprogrammed. (1996)

• **Transmission slippage** Transmission may shudder when accelerating from a stop, thump when coasting down to a stop, or slip when shifting. (1995)

• **Sunroof/moonroof** The pivot pin in the power sunroof may come out, or the plastic tabs on the control unit may cause interference, preventing the sunroof from closing completely. (1995) Or, the sunroof may open by itself if water wicks along the drive cable into the control unit. (1995-96)

• **Alarm system** The theft alarm may go off randomly, most often in high winds, and is often due to a misaligned hood. (1995)

RECALL HISTORY

1995-96 Tank gaskets for fuel pump and/or gauge unit could have been incorrectly installed, allowing fuel or fumes to escape. **1997** On small number of cars, improperly-welded head restraint support bracket on passenger side can break.

1993-97 EAGLE VISION

FOR Air bags • Steering/handling • Acceleration (3.5-liter) • Passenger and cargo room • Anti-lock brakes (optional)

AGAINST Climate and radio controls • Acceleration (3.3-liter) • Rear visibility

See the 1993-97 Dodge Intrepid report for an evaluation of the Eagle Vision.

NHTSA CRASH TEST RESULTS
1996 Eagle Vision

	4-DOOR SEDAN
Driver	☆☆☆☆
Passenger	☆☆☆☆

(The National Highway Traffic Safety Administration tests a vehicle's crashworthiness in front and side collisions. Their ratings suggest the chance of serious injury: ☆☆☆☆☆—10% or less; ☆☆☆☆—10-20% or less; ☆☆☆—20-30% or less; ☆☆—35-45% or less; ☆—More than 45%.)

1993 Eagle Vision ESi

SPECIFICATIONS

	4-door sedan
Wheelbase, in.	113.0
Overall length, in.	201.6
Overall width, in.	74.4
Overall height, in.	56.3
Curb weight, lbs.	3371
Cargo volume, cu. ft.	16.6
Fuel capacity, gals.	18.0
Seating capacity	5
Front head room, in.	38.4
Max. front leg room, in.	42.4
Rear head room, in.	37.5
Min. rear leg room, in.	38.8

Powertrain layout: longitudinal front-engine/front-wheel drive

ENGINES

	ohv V-6	dohc V-6
Size, liters/cu. in.	3.3/201	3.5/215
Horsepower	153-161	214
Torque (lbs./ft.)	177-181	221

EPA city/highway mpg

4-speed OD automatic	19/27	18/26

Consumer Guide™ observed MPG

4-speed OD automatic		18.9

Built in Canada.

AVERAGE REPLACEMENT COSTS

A/C Compressor	$365
Alternator	190
Radiator	340
Timing Chain or Belt	230
Automatic Transmission or Transaxle	1,089

Clutch, Pressure Plate, Bearing Constant Velocity Joints	310
Universal Joints	300
Brakes	250
Shocks and/or Struts	480
Exhaust System	418

RETAIL PRICES	GOOD	AVERAGE	POOR
1993 Vision ESi	$5,500-6,300	$4,800-5,600	$2,800-3,500
1993 Vision TSi	6,600-7,400	5,800-6,600	3,600-4,200
1994 Vision ESi	6,700-7,500	6,000-6,800	3,600-4,200
1994 Vision TSi	7,700-8,700	6,900-7,900	4,300-5,000
1995 Vision ESi	7,500-8,500	6,800-7,800	4,300-4,900
1995 Vision TSi	9,200-10,200	8,400-9,400	5,600-6,200
1996 Vision ESi	9,600-10,700	8,800-9,800	5,800-6,600
1996 Vision TSi	11,400-12,500	10,500-11,500	7,500-8,400
1997 Vision ESi	10,700-12,000	9,700-11,000	6,700-7,700
1997 Vision TSi	13,000-14,300	11,800-12,800	8,500-9,300

TROUBLE SPOTS

• **Transmission slippage** Bad seals in the transmission lead to premature friction component wear, which causes shudder when starting from a stop, a bump when coasting to a stop, and slipping between gears. Chyrsler will warranty the seals, clutches, and if necessary, the torque converter. (1993-95)

• **Transmission slippage** Vehicles with 41TE or 42LE automatic transaxle could take several seconds to engage at startup because of a problem with the valve body. The company will replace defective ones, and replace the filter and fluid under normal warranty. (1993-95)

• **Air conditioner** The air conditioner belt rolls over in the pulleys and replacement belts do the same. The fix is to replace the A/C pulley and idler pulley, which is covered under the normal warranty. (1993-94)

RECALL HISTORY

1993 Lower control arm washers in front suspension of some cars can crack and fall off; will cause clunking sound during braking, and eventually result in loss of steering control. **1993 w/3.3-liter engine** O-rings used to seal interface of fuel-injector tubes are insufficiently durable; deterioration can cause fuel leakage, with potential for fire. **1994** Right tie rod can rub through automatic-transmission wiring harness, causing short circuit; may result in stalling, or allow engine to start when selector is not in "Park" position.

1990-97 FORD AEROSTAR

FOR Air bag (later models) • Trailer towing capability • Optional AWD traction • Passenger and cargo room

AGAINST Fuel economy • Entry/exit • Ride

EVALUATION The 3.0-liter engine produces adequate muscle, but the extra grunt of a 4.0-liter V-6 is welcome, helping to

1991 Ford Aerostar XL

haul around the hardware of the available 4-wheel-drive system. Don't expect great gas mileage with either engine: around 15 mpg in city/suburban driving, or low 20s on the highway.

Poor traction can be a problem in rain or snow, with the rear-drive Aerostar. Ride quality is another drawback, even with the Aerostar's long wheelbase. Suspensions are not very compliant, producing a rather harsh experience over bumps, though an Aerostar is stable and well-controlled.

Cabins are roomy. Seven people can sit without squeezing, and the XLT and Eddie Bauer models contain plush and comfortable interior furnishings. Getting into the front seats requires a high step up. Cargo space is unimpressive in standard-size models, when all seats are in place.

Aerostar and the Chevrolet Astro/GMC Safari are better suited to heavy-duty work, such as hauling hefty payloads or towing trailers (up to 4800 pounds), than the league-leading front-drive Chrysler minivans.

NHTSA CRASH TEST RESULTS
1994 Ford Aerostar

3-DOOR VAN

Driver	☆☆☆☆
Passenger	☆☆☆

(The National Highway Traffic Safety Administration tests a vehicle's crashworthiness in front and side collisions. Their ratings suggest the chance of serious injury: ☆☆☆☆☆—10% or less; ☆☆☆☆—10-20% or less; ☆☆☆—20-30% or less; ☆☆—35-45% or less; ☆—More than 45%.)

SPECIFICATIONS	3-door van	3-door van
Wheelbase, in.	118.9	118.9
Overall length, in.	174.9	190.3
Overall width, in.	71.7	72.0
Overall height, in.	72.2	72.3

FORD

	3-door van	3-door van
Curb weight, lbs.	3374	3478
Cargo volume, cu. ft.	141.4	170.0
Fuel capacity, gals.	21.0	21.0
Seating capacity	7	7
Front head room, in.	39.5	39.5
Max. front leg room, in.	41.4	41.4
Rear head room, in.	38.8	38.3
Min. rear leg room, in.	39.5	40.5

Powertrain layout: longitudinal front-engine/rear- or all-wheel drive

ENGINES

	ohv V-6	ohv V-6
Size, liters/cu. in.	3.0/182	4.0/244
Horsepower	135-145	152-155
Torque (lbs./ft.)	160-165	215-230
EPA city/highway mpg		
4-speed OD automatic	17/23	17/23
5-speed OD automatic		16/22
Consumer Guide™ observed MPG		
4-speed OD automatic	13.5	14.6

Built in USA.

RETAIL PRICES

	GOOD	AVERAGE	POOR
1990 Aerostar	$2,800-4,200	$2,200-3,500	$1,000-1,600
1991 Aerostar	3,300-5,500	2,700-4,800	1,400-2,700
1992 Aerostar	3,900-6,400	3,200-5,600	1,800-3,400
1993 Aerostar	4,800-7,400	4,000-6,500	2,400-4,000
1994 Aerostar	6,000-9,000	5,200-8,000	3,200-5,500
1995 Aerostar	7,600-10,500	6,700-9,500	4,500-6,700
1996 Aerostar	9,600-13,000	8,500-11,800	6,000-8,500
1997 Aerostar	11,500-15,000	10,200-13,500	7,500-10,000

AVERAGE REPLACEMENT COSTS

A/C Compressor	$410
Alternator	315
Radiator	360
Timing Chain or Belt	400
Automatic Transmission or Transaxle	775
Clutch, Pressure Plate, Bearing	450
Universal Joints	160
Brakes	305
Shocks and/or Struts	255
Exhaust System	445

TROUBLE SPOTS

• **Engine noise** A hammering noise accompanied by an erratic temperature gauge reading is caused by a weak water pump and a revised pump is available. (1994-97)

• **Steering noise** When the steering wheel is turned, there may be a clanging noise that comes from the power steering cooler and a replacement will eliminate the noise. (1990-96)

• **Radio** Whining noises in the radio speakers is caused by the fuel pump in the gas tank. An electronic noise filter must be installed on the fuel pump. (1990-96)

• **Air conditioner** Air conditioner compressors are prone to failure if there is not enough A/C oil in the system. (1994-97)

• **Engine noise** The dash panel rattles or buzzes on some vans due to interference between the trim on the front pillar (A-pillar) and the side quarter glass. (1992-96)

RECALL HISTORY

1990 With quad captain's chairs, tilt-forward latch of right-hand seat in second row may release under severe frontal impact. **1990** Inability to maintain pressure in master cylinder could increase brake-pedal travel. **1990-91** Ignition switch could short-circuit, causing smoke and possible fire. **1990-91** When automatic transmission is in "Park" position, pawl does not always engage park gear. **1992-97 w/all-wheel drive** Structural failure of transmission and/or transfer case can occur, resulting in fluid expulsion, driveshaft separation, or loss of drive. **1995** Underbody spare tire can contact brake lines, resulting in fracture of line. **1996** When in secondary latched position, driver's door may not sustain specified load. **1996** Certification label shows incorrect rear tire inflation pressure.

1995-98 FORD CONTOUR

1995 Ford Contour

FOR   Air bags, dual • Acceleration (V-6) • Steering/handling

FORD

• Automatic transmission performance • Optional anti-lock brakes and traction control

AGAINST Engine noise (4-cylinder) • Rear seat room • Instruments/controls

EVALUATION Smooth, responsive, and lively in acceleration, the 170-horsepower V-6 is more than adequate for all ordinary driving situations. During testing, a V-6 Contour accelerated to 60 mph in 9.3 seconds. The 190-horsepower SVT engine is even more powerful, but you really have to work the transmission to get the extra power. By contrast, the 4-cylinder engine feels sluggish when going uphill and requires a heavy throttle foot for brisk acceleration. A V-6 Contour with automatic averaged 21.7 miles per gallon. Under similar conditions, the 4-cylinder with automatic did only a little better: 23 mpg, to be exact. Road noise has been prominent on all models.

Precise steering, sporty handling, and a firm ride make a Contour feel more German than American. Most road-testers praised the sporty SE, in particular, for its fun-to-drive qualities, though a few were less enthusiastic about its ride quality.

Front leg room is ample, but back-seat space for adults is barely adequate in 1995 Contours. That shortage of space was slightly improved in '96 models, but remains a drawback. Head room is generous in front and adequate in back.

The modern, attractive dashboard is well designed, but the stereo has too many small buttons that are difficult to decipher. Large gauges are easy to read. The climate system is controlled by three rotary dials that are clearly labeled and easy to use.

Ford took a huge step forward in performance, refinement, and overall execution with its compact sedan. All told, Contour is a formidable rival to Japanese compacts and to the Chrysler Cirrus and Dodge Stratus.

NHTSA CRASH TEST RESULTS
1995 Ford Contour

4-DOOR SEDAN

Driver	☆☆☆☆☆
Passenger	☆☆☆☆

(The National Highway Traffic Safety Administration tests a vehicle's crashworthiness in front and side collisions. Their ratings suggest the chance of serious injury: ☆☆☆☆☆—10% or less; ☆☆☆☆—10-20% or less; ☆☆☆—20-30% or less; ☆☆—35-45% or less; ☆—More than 45%.)

SPECIFICATIONS

	4-door sedan
Wheelbase, in.	106.5
Overall length, in.	183.9

	4-door sedan
Overall width, in.	69.1
Overall height, in.	54.5
Curb weight, lbs.	2769
Cargo volume, cu. ft.	13.9
Fuel capacity, gals.	14.5
Seating capacity	5
Front head room, in.	39.0
Max. front leg room, in.	42.4
Rear head room, in.	36.7
Min. rear leg room, in.	34.3

Powertrain layout: transverse front-engine/front-wheel drive

ENGINES

	dohc I-4	dohc V-6	dohc V-6
Size, liters/cu. in.	2.0/121	2.5/155	2.5/155
Horsepower	125	170	195
Torque (lbs./ft.)	130	165	165
EPA city/highway mpg			
5-speed OD manual	24/34		20/29
4-speed OD automatic	23/32		
Consumer Guide™ observed MPG			
5-speed OD manual			24.3
4-speed OD automatic	23.0	21.7	

Built in USA and Mexico.

RETAIL PRICES	GOOD	AVERAGE	POOR
1995 Contour	$6,500-7,600	$5,800-6,800	$3,800-4,700
1995 Contour SE	7,600-8,400	6,800-7,600	4,700-5,400
1996 Contour	7,500-8,700	6,800-7,900	4,700-5,600
1996 Contour SE	8,700-9,600	7,800-8,600	5,600-6,300
1997 Contour	8,700-10,500	8,000-9,700	5,600-7,000
1997 Contour SE	10,500-11,500	9,500-10,500	7,000-8,000
1998 Contour	10,800-12,500	9,800-11,500	7,000-8,500
1998 Contour SE	12,000-13,500	11,000-12,500	8,300-9,500

AVERAGE REPLACEMENT COSTS

A/C Compressor $360	Clutch, Pressure Plate,
Alternator 455	Bearing............................750
Radiator 345	Constant Velocity Joints.....465
Timing Chain or Belt 175	Brakes..................................290
Automatic Transmission or	Shocks and/or Struts 700
Transaxle.........................800	Shocks and/or Struts 345

FORD

TROUBLE SPOTS

• **Engine misfire** Lack of acceleration or power in freezing weather (below 32°F) on the 2.5-L engine is often due to ice on the throttle plate. A revised engine computer prevents the problem. (1995)

• **Transmission slippage** The transmission may go into limp-in mode (second gear only) due to a faulty manual lever position sensor. (1995)

• **Transmission noise** If there is gear clash going into third on the manual transmission, under warranty the input gear shaft will be rebuilt and a new shift fork installed. (1995-97)

• **Dashboard lights** A slipping drive belt causes a lack of power steering and the charge warning light to glow. Under warranty, the belt, idler pulley, and a splash kit will be installed. (1995-97)

• **Steering problems** If the steering wheel vibrates while idling with the transmission engaged and the A/C running, the steering mass damper, air bag module, and radiator mounts will be replaced under warranty. (1995-97)

• **Brakes** Ice in the parking brake cables will not allow the parking brake to release or release fully, and both cables will be replaced under normal warranty provisions. (1995-97)

RECALL HISTORY

1995 If right rear door window breaks, glass fragments will exceed allowable size. **1995** Metal shield on plastic fuel filler pipe can develop static charge during refueling; could serve as ignition source. **1995** Fuel tank filler reinforcement can leak. **1995** Passenger air bag's inflator body is cracked and may not inflate properly. **1995** Front seatbelt anchor tabs may be cracked. **1995-96 w/traction control** Throttle cables were damaged during assembly, leading to fraying or separation; could prevent engine from returning to idle. **1996-97 w/bi-fuel engine** If natural-gas fuel line is damaged in a collison, gas leakage could occur. **1998** Text and/or graphics for headlamp aiming instructions, provided in owner guides, are not sufficiently clear.

1992-98 FORD CROWN VICTORIA

FOR Air bags (later models) • Acceleration • Passenger and cargo room • Trailer towing capability • Optional anti-lock brakes

AGAINST Fuel economy • Steering feel • Radio controls (early models)

EVALUATION The Crown Vic's extra-smooth V-8 sets the

1992 Ford Crown Victoria

heavy sedan into motion swiftly enough, and past highway traffic without delay. Mid-range response is more sluggish, however, worsened by the fact that the transmission seems reluctant to downshift. Gas mileage is nothing to boast about. One early test LX Crown Victoria averaged an impressive 19.9 mpg. Later, an LX yielded only 15.3 mpg.

Handling and stability are fine for a big sedan. The base suspension absorbs bumps nicely, yet doesn't wallow or float past pavement swells. The handling/performance option delivers a jittery ride, aggravated by too-light, numb power steering that easily turns twitchy. Traction can be a problem in the snowbelt.

You're likely to hear virtually no road, wind, or engine noise. Expansive seating for six is marred only by a lack of lateral support in the driver's seat. Controls are grouped logically and work smoothly though tiny horn buttons are an annoyance. Visibility is fine and the trunk ranks as close to cavernous, but a large well in the center of the floor could induce a little back strain when loading heavy objects.

Vastly more impressive than the prior generation, this Crown Vic mixes traditional values with contemporary virtues—a good choice if you like rear-drive in a body-on-frame vehicle.

NHTSA CRASH TEST RESULTS
1995 Ford Crown Victoria   4-DOOR SEDAN

Driver	☆☆☆☆
Passenger	☆☆☆☆☆

(The National Highway Traffic Safety Administration tests a vehicle's crashworthiness in front and side collisions. Their ratings suggest the chance of serious injury: ☆☆☆☆☆—10% or less; ☆☆☆☆—10-20% or less; ☆☆☆—20-30% or less; ☆☆—35-45% or less; ☆—More than 45%.)

SPECIFICATIONS

	4-door sedan
Wheelbase, in.	114.4

FORD

	4-door sedan
Overall length, in.	212.0
Overall width, in.	77.8
Overall height, in.	56.8
Curb weight, lbs.	3780
Cargo volume, cu. ft.	20.6
Fuel capacity, gals.	20.0
Seating capacity	6
Front head room, in.	39.4
Max. front leg room, in.	42.5
Rear head room, in.	38.0
Min. rear leg room, in.	39.6

Powertrain layout: longitudinal front-engine/rear-wheel drive

ENGINES

	ohv V-8
Size, liters/cu. in.	4.6/281
Horsepower	190-215
Torque (lbs./ft.)	260-270

EPA city/highway mpg
4-speed OD automatic	17/25

Consumer Guide™ observed MPG
4-speed OD automatic	15.3

Built in Canada.

RETAIL PRICES

	GOOD	AVERAGE	POOR
1992 Crown Victoria	$3,400-5,700	$2,700-5,000	$1,000-2,800
1993 Crown Victoria	4,400-6,400	3,700-5,700	1,800-3,400
1994 Crown Victoria	6,200-8,000	5,400-7,200	3,200-4,500
1995 Crown Victoria	8,000-10,200	7,200-9,300	4,600-6,000
1996 Crown Victoria	10,500-12,500	9,500-11,500	6,500-8,000
1997 Crown Victoria	13,000-15,300	11,800-14,000	8,500-10,000
1998 Crown Victoria	15,500-19,000	14,000-17,500	10,000-13,000

AVERAGE REPLACEMENT COSTS

A/C Compressor	$380	Universal Joints	125
Alternator	375	Brakes	275
Radiator	380	Shocks and/or Struts	505
Timing Chain or Belt	330	Exhaust System	353
Automatic Transmission or Transaxle	870		

TROUBLE SPOTS

• **Vehicle noise** A broken gusset or weld separation at the frame crossmember causes a rattle from the rear of the car. Ford will weld new gussets into place under the bumper-to-bumper warranty (1992) or basic warranty on prior models. (1990-92)

• **Hard starting** The connector at the starter solenoid tends to corrode resulting in a "no crank" condition. Under warranty, the automaker will replace the connector and slather the terminal with dielectric grease to prevent it from happening again. (1992-94)

• **Oil leak** The oil filter balloons and leaks because the oil pump relief valve sticks. Higher than recommended viscosity oils cause wear to the valve bore. Under normal warranty provisions, the pump will be replaced with one less sensitive to this problem, but Ford warns that owners should only use the type of oil spelled out in the owners manual. (1992-94)

• **Transmission slippage** The transmission may slip (lack of torque) and the engine may flare when the transmission shifts into fourth gear, which can often be traced to a bad TR/MLP sensor that will be replaced along with a speed sensor on AODE automatic transmissions under the normal warranty provisions. (1992-95)

• **Transmission slippage** The automatic transmission in cars with more than 20,000 miles is notorious for shuddering or vibrating under light acceleration or when shifting between third and fourth gear above 35 mph. It requires that the transmission fluid (including fluid in the torque converter) be changed and that only Mercon® fluid be used. It usually takes at least 100 miles of driving after the fluid change for the shudder to go away. (1992-94)

• **Vehicle noise** A chattering noise that can be felt, and sometimes heard, coming from the rear during tight turns after highway driving is caused by a lack of friction modifier or over-shimming of the clutch packs in the Traction-Lok (limited-slip) differential. A replacement clutch pack and friction modifier will be installed under the company's warranty programs. (1992-96)

• **Air springs** Air springs are prone to leaks caused by the bag rubbing against the axle or control arm. Often, the car will be sitting low on one corner after being parked for any length of time. Leaking air springs will be replaced as a warranty item. (when equipped)

• **Hard starting** If the engine does not start or cranks for a long time then stalls, the idle air control valve may be sticking and Ford will replace it under warranty. (1996)

• **Engine noise** The drive belt tensioner pulley or idler pulley bearings are apt to make a squealing noise when the engine is started in cold weather. Under the bumper-to-bumper warranty, the pulley(s) will be replaced. (1993-96)

RECALL HISTORY

1992 "anti-lock" brake warning lights in small number of cars will not actuate. **1993-94 with police option** Upper control arm bolts can loosen and fracture, causing substantial negative camber and steering pull; fracture at both holes could result in loss of control. **1994** Nuts and bolts that attach rear brake adapter to axle flange can loosen and eventually separate. **1995** On some cars, passenger air bag's inflator body is cracked and may not inflate properly; also, igniter end cap can separate. **1995** Seal material between fuel filler pipe and tank may not have been fully cured, which could allow fuel to leak. **1995** In the event of short-circuit or overload, both headlamps can go out without warning. **1995** Rivet heads holding rear outboard seatbelt D-rings may fracture under load, reducing belt's restraining capability. **1995-96 fleet cars only** Corrosion of inadequately-lubricated Pitman arms can cause abnormal wear of joint, resulting in separation. **1996** Driver's door, when closed only to secondary latched position, may not sustain specified load.

1991-96 FORD ESCORT

1992 Ford Escort 4-door

FOR   Air bags (later models) • Fuel economy • Ride • Acceleration (GT, LX-E) • Anti-lock brakes (optional)

AGAINST   Engine noise • Road noise • Rear-seat room

EVALUATION   In hard acceleration, either engine causes the automatic transmission to jolt between gears. With automatic, there's just not enough low-end power for quick getaways. Acceleration to 60 mph took a leisurely 12.5 seconds. Though more powerful, the GT's engine gets lazy below 3500 rpm; but it runs smoother than the 1.9-liter. Both engines vibrate at idle, and are noisy while cruising. Gas mileage is great. An early automatic LX averaged 25.9 mpg. A later edition did better yet, averaging 26.8 mpg even while commuting.

Stable and well controlled at highway speeds, the Escort's suspension is surprisingly absorbent on harsher pavement. A GT handles crisply, courtesy of its sport suspension and 15-inch tires. The same cannot be said of Pony and LX hatchbacks, whose 13-inch rubber easily loses grip in brisk cornering. Standard 4-wheel disc brakes on the GT bring the Escort to a swift, sure stop. Wind and road noise are noticeable, especially at highway speeds.

Visibility is good from the Escort's airy cabin. Head room isn't bad for a subcompact, unless it has the optional sunroof. Leg room is adequate, but three in back is a rear squeeze. The cargo area of hatchbacks and wagons is quite narrow between wheelwells, but wider at the rear. Controls are logically positioned, simply marked, operating with smooth precision that belies the car's modest roots.

With Escort you get plenty of practical value. Though the Escort can't match a Honda Civic or Toyota Corolla for refinement, it does give the impression of true quality in the subcompact field.

NHTSA CRASH TEST RESULTS
1995 Ford Escort

4-DOOR SEDAN

Driver	☆☆☆☆
Passenger	☆☆☆☆

(The National Highway Traffic Safety Administration tests a vehicle's crashworthiness in front and side collisions. Their ratings suggest the chance of serious injury: ☆☆☆☆☆—10% or less; ☆☆☆☆—10-20% or less; ☆☆☆—20-30% or less; ☆☆—35-45% or less; ☆—More than 45%.)

SPECIFICATIONS	2-door hatchback	4-door sedan	4-door hatchback	4-door wagon
Wheelbase, in.	98.4	98.4	98.4	98.4
Overall length, in.	170.0	170.9	170.0	171.3
Overall width, in.	66.7	66.7	66.7	66.7
Overall height, in.	52.5	52.7	52.5	53.6
Curb weight, lbs.	2355	2404	2385	2451
Cargo volume, cu. ft.	35.2	12.1	36.0	66.9
Fuel capacity, gals.	11.9	11.9	11.9	11.9
Seating capacity	5	5	5	5
Front head room, in.	38.4	38.4	38.4	38.4
Max. front leg room, in.	41.7	41.7	41.7	41.7
Rear head room, in.	37.6	37.4	37.6	38.5
Min. rear leg room, in.	34.6	34.5	34.6	34.6

Powertrain layout: transverse front-engine/front-wheel drive

ENGINES

	ohc I-4	dohc I-4
Size, liters/cu. in.	1.9/114	1.8/109
Horsepower	88	127
Torque (lbs./ft.)	108	114
EPA city/highway mpg		
5-speed OD manual	31/38	25/31

FORD

	ohc I-4	dohc I-4
4-speed OD automatic..	26/34	23/29
Consumer Guide™ observed MPG		
5-speed OD manual..		21.6
4-speed OD automatic.....................................	25.9	

Built in USA and Mexico.

RETAIL PRICES

	GOOD	AVERAGE	POOR
1991 Escort	$1,500-2,300	$1,000-1,700	$300-700
1991 Escort GT	2,100-2,700	1,500-2,100	700-1,000
1992 Escort	1,900-3,100	1,300-2,500	500-1,000
1992 Escort GT	2,900-3,500	2,200-2,800	1,000-1,400
1993 Escort	2,500-3,900	1,800-3,200	800-1,300
1993 Escort GT	3,700-4,400	3,000-3,700	1,400-1,900
1994 Escort	3,200-4,500	2,500-3,800	1,100-1,600
1994 Escort GT	4,500-5,200	3,800-4,500	1,800-2,400
1995 Escort	4,100-5,500	3,400-4,800	1,600-2,300
1995 Escort GT	5,600-6,300	4,800-5,500	2,400-2,900
1996 Escort	5,200-6,600	4,400-5,800	2,400-3,000
1996 Escort GT	6,900-7,600	6,000-6,700	3,300-3,800

AVERAGE REPLACEMENT COSTS

A/C Compressor	$470	Clutch, Pressure Plate,	
Alternator	370	Bearing	275
Radiator	382	Constant Velocity Joints	585
Timing Chain or Belt	145	Brakes	260
Automatic Transmission or		Shocks and/or Struts	620
Transaxle	1,160	Exhaust System	375

TROUBLE SPOTS

• **Fuel pump** Under general campaign number 94B55, Ford will install a fused jumper harness in the fuel pump electrical circuit to prevent erratic fuel gauge readings, stalling, or wiring damage, which could be caused by an electrical short. Refunds will be made to anyone who paid for this service. (1991-94)

• **Horn** Sometimes the horn will not work due to a poor ground circuit in the steering column. Under the bumper to-bumper warranty, a redundant ground will be installed so the horn works in all steering wheel positions. (1995-96)

• **Brake noise** Wear spots and ridges on the front brake caliper sleeves cause a knocking noise when gently applying the brakes. There is a new sleeve available, made from a harder material that resists wear, and may be eligible for replacement under the basic or bumper-to-bumper warranty. (1991-96)

• **Engine knock** Carbon build-up on the pistons causes a knocking noise that is most evident after a cold start. If the noise does not go away after cleaning the carbon from the pistons using carburetor cleaner ingested through the intake manifold, the pistons must be replaced with redesigned ones under the basic bumper-to-bumper warranty. (1991-93)

• **Hard starting** If the engine does not start or cranks for a long time then stalls, the idle air control valve may be sticking and Ford will replace it under warranty. (1995-96)

• **Blower motor** Squeaking or chirping blower motors are the result of defective brush holders, so Ford has issued a redesigned motor and will replace those that are under normal warranty. (1993-94)

• **Transmission noise** If a whine comes from the transmission during coast-down, it is probably because the idler gear teeth were not machined properly. A new gear will be installed under warranty. (1995-96)

• **Vehicle noise** A grinding noise while turning is most likely due to dirt accumulating in the top strut mount bushing. Ford has released a redesigned bushing to help keep the dirt out. (1991-92)

• **Brake wear** Although there is no warranty coverage, there is a redesigned brake master cylinder and brake booster available that provides better pedal feel and travel. (1993-95)

RECALL HISTORY

1991 Interference may occur between bolt that secures fuel line shield to lower dash and gas pedal, causing pedal to stick wide open. **1991** Pins securing ignition lock can separate or move out of position; cylinder may disengage, causing steering column to lock up. **1991-92** On some cars, fatigue crack can develop in solder joint between fuel return tube and fuel pump sending unit; fuel vapor could escape when tank is full, and small amount may leak. **1991-93** On small number of front suspension units made by Dana Corp., the offset toe adjusting pin may fracture under certain conditions, resulting in loss of control. **1993** Driver's seat in some cars may not engage fully in its track in positions near midpoint; could move in event of crash. **1994-95** On a few cars, driver-side air bag may deploy improperly and expel hot gases. **1995** Two bolts that attach passenger-side air bag may be missing; in frontal impact, the air bag could fail to restrain the passenger. **1995 cars in certain states** Cracks can develop in plastic fuel tank, resulting in leakage.

1991-98 FORD EXPLORER

1996 Ford Explorer V-8 4-door

FOR Air bags (later models) • Acceleration (V-8) • Passenger and cargo room • 4WD traction • Anti-lock brakes (optional later models) • Visibility

AGAINST Fuel economy • Engine noise • Entry/exit (2-door) • Wind noise

EVALUATION Explorers are easy to enter and depart from, due to a relatively low step-in height. Head room is generous all around. Rear leg space is adequate. There's plenty of space for three abreast in the back of a 4-door. Split front seat backs fold flat to create a long load floor that suffers little intrusion from the rear wheels. There's no spare tire in the way of cargo, either. Controls are simple, analog gauges clearly legible, visibility fine.

Acceleration is adequate from the ohv V-6 engine, but it is sluggish and rough when first stomping the pedal and averaged a low 15.9 mpg. Eight-cylinder engines provide outstanding acceleration, and equally depressing fuel economy. The new ohc V-6 is probably the best option. It offers ample acceleration and averaged 20.4 mpg. The automatic transmission responds neatly, and shifts nearly flawlessly—quick and unobtrusive.

The relatively long, wide stance gives either Explorer reasonable stability in turns, though you get a choppy ride from the shorter-wheelbase 3-door. Steering precisely, cornering confidently, an Explorer suffers less body lean than Chevrolet's Blazer.

Not cheap, an Explorer offers the utility of a minivan and the hauling power of a truck. If you're a likely prospect for a smaller sport-utility, best not to buy until you've test-driven Ford's compact. But try a Chevy Blazer and Jeep Grand Cherokee too.

NHTSA CRASH TEST RESULTS
1996 Ford Explorer

4-DOOR SEDAN

Driver   ☆☆☆☆

Passenger   ☆☆☆☆

(The National Highway Traffic Safety Administration tests a vehicle's crashworthiness in front and side collisions. Their ratings suggest the chance of serious injury: ☆☆☆☆☆—10% or less; ☆☆☆☆—10-20% or less; ☆☆☆—20-30% or less; ☆☆—35-45% or less; ☆—More than 45%.)

SPECIFICATIONS

	2-door wagon	4-door wagon
Wheelbase, in.	101.7	111.5
Overall length, in.	178.6	188.5
Overall width, in.	68.2	70.2
Overall height, in.	67.5	67.3
Curb weight, lbs.	3690	3915
Cargo volume, cu. ft.	69.4	81.6
Fuel capacity, gals.	17.5	21.0
Seating capacity	4	6
Front head room, in.	39.8	39.8
Max. front leg room, in.	42.4	42.4
Rear head room, in.	39.1	39.3
Min. rear leg room, in.	36.6	37.7

Powertrain layout: longitudinal front-engine/rear- or 4-wheel drive

ENGINES

	ohv V-6	ohc V-6	ohv V-8
Size, liters/cu. in.	4.0/245	4.0/245	5.0/302
Horsepower	145-160	205	210-215
Torque (lbs./ft.)	220-225	250	280-288

EPA city/highway mpg

5-speed OD manual	16/20		
4-speed OD automatic	15/20		14/18
5-speed OD automatic		15/20	

Consumer Guide™ observed MPG

5-speed OD manual	16.1		
4-speed OD automatic	15.9		12.4
5-speed OD automatic		20.4	

Built in USA.

RETAIL PRICES	GOOD	AVERAGE	POOR
1991 Explorer	$4,200-6,800	$3,500-6,000	$1,700-3,700
1992 Explorer	5,200-8,200	4,500-7,400	2,500-4,700
1993 Explorer	6,300-10,300	5,500-9,500	3,400-6,500
1994 Explorer	8,500-12,500	7,500-11,500	5,000-8,000
1995 Explorer	11,300-16,000	10,000-14,500	7,000-10,500

FORD

	GOOD	AVERAGE	POOR
1996 Explorer	13,500-19,000	12,000-17,500	8,600-13,300
1997 Explorer	15,000-22,000	13,500-20,500	10,000-16,000
1998 Explorer	17,500-24,000	16,000-22,500	12,000-18,000

AVERAGE REPLACEMENT COSTS

A/C Compressor $505
Alternator 280
Radiator 440
Timing Chain or Belt 400
Automatic Transmission or
    Transaxle........................840

Clutch, Pressure Plate,
    Bearing 435
Universal Joints 105
Brakes.................................265
Shocks and/or Struts 175
Exhaust System.................295

TROUBLE SPOTS

• **Vehicle noise** A chattering noise that can be felt, and sometimes heard, coming from the rear during tight turns after highway driving is caused by a lack of friction modifier or over-shimming of the clutch packs in the Traction-Lok (limited-slip) differential. A replacement clutch pack and friction modifier will be installed under the company's warranty programs. (1991-96)

• **Hard starting** If the engine does not want to start or cranks for a long time then stalls, the idle air control valve may be sticking and Ford will replace it under warranty. (1996)

• **Air conditioner** Water may drip onto the floor when the air conditioner is operated because the evaporator strip seals were not properly positioned at the factory. They will be repositioned under normal warranty provisions. (1995-96)

• **Radiator** The radiator may leak in cold weather because of a bad seal between the tank and core. Ford will replace the radiator under warranty. (1995-96)

• **Vehicle noise** Synthetic rubber radius arm bushings separate internally, causing noise and degraded steering control. Some aftermarket parts are available with metal inserts for extended life. (all)

• **Vehicle noise** For vehicles under warranty, Ford will replace any loose frame rivets with bolts (welding is not approved). (1991-96)

RECALL HISTORY

1991 Seatbelts may be defective, resulting in insufficiently latched or unlatched belt. **1991** Front heat shield may contact plastic fuel tank, causing damage to the extent of penetration. **1991** Hot weld that attaches vapor vent valve carrier to plastic fuel tank may partially fracture, allowing escape of fuel vapor. **1991 w/A4LD automatic transmission** Vehicle may appear to be in "park" position, when gear is not truly engaged. **1991-93 w/factory sunroof** Sunroof glass panel assembly can separate while vehicle is moving. **1991-94** On cars sold or registered in specified southern California counties, studs that attach master cylinder to power brake booster assembly can develop stress corrosion cracking after extended period; fractures could cause separation of master cylinder when brakes are applied. **1992-93** Bracket welds for liftgate's hydraulic lift cylinders can fracture. **1992-94** Short circuit can occur in remote power mirror switch's circuit board; overheated board and other plastic and elastomeric components can result in smoke or fire. **1993-94 with manual shift** Parking brake self-adjust pawl does not line up properly and can slip. **1995** Passenger-side air bag's inflator body may be cracked and not inflate properly; also, igniter end cap can separate, causing hot gases to be released. **1995** Inner tie rod assemblies can fracture, resulting in shaking or shimmy at low speeds. **1995 2-door** Brake tubes in some models were misrouted, resulting in excessive stopping distance. **1996** Driver's door, when closed only to secondary latched position, may not sustain specified load. **1996** Gas cylinder bracket may not properly support rear liftgate. **1996** Certification label shows incorrect rear tire inflation pressure. **1996-97 in 15 northern states** After operation at highway speeds, at below -20 degrees (F), engine may not return to idle. **1997-98 w/SOHC 4.0-liter engine** Fuel lines can be damaged and fire could result if vehicle is jump started and ground cable is attached to fuel line bracket near battery. **1998 Eddie Bauer and Limited** Key-in-ignition/door-open warning chime may not function properly.

1991-96 FORD F-SERIES PICKUP

1990 Ford F-150

FOR Acceleration (V-8) • Passenger and cargo room • Trailer-towing capability

AGAINST Fuel economy • Noise • Handling • Interior storage space

EVALUATION Even though the 6-cylinder engine nearly matches torque output of a 5.0-liter V-8, we prefer gasoline V-8 models on the basis of their impressive acceleration and passing ability. That was our appraisal of an F-150 XLT with the 5.0 and 4-speed automatic. The 5.0 was just about as responsive as a 5.8-liter, in fact, but both returned horrid gas mileage: around 12.5 mpg in a city/highway mix. Some 4-speed automatics have demonstrated slurred, lurching gear changes, plus sluggish downshifting for passing.

Tall and square, Ford trucks can be blown around in heavy crosswinds, but otherwise hold the road well—even with an empty cargo box. Steering feels looser than in a GM or Dodge pickup, and requires a bit more correction on the highway. An unloaded short-wheelbase 4x4 rides harshly over city streets, but longer-wheelbase models cope much better with bumps. Engine noise and tire rumble can annoy, though wind noise is modest.

Regular-cab models easily hold three adults, though the center rider straddles the transmission tunnel. Dashboards are better after 1991, with an easy-to-use climate system and audio controls grouped near the driver. All trucks have plenty of head room. The steering wheel sits near the driver's chest, and pedals are close to the chair-height seat cushion. SuperCab rear seats are a convenience, but have minimal knee and foot space.

If you're in the market for a pickup in this league, also look at the Chevrolet C/K and Dodge Ram. But we put the F-Series at the top of our list in terms of room, power, payload, and trailer-towing ability.

NHTSA CRASH TEST RESULTS
1995 Ford F-150

EXT. CAB LONG BED

Driver	☆☆☆☆☆
Passenger	☆☆☆☆☆

(The National Highway Traffic Safety Administration tests a vehicle's crashworthiness in front and side collisions. Their ratings suggest the chance of serious injury: ☆☆☆☆☆—10% or less; ☆☆☆☆—10-20% or less; ☆☆☆—20-30% or less; ☆☆—35-45% or less; ☆—More than 45%.)

SPECIFICATIONS	reg. cab short bed	reg. cab long bed	ext. cab short bed	ext. cab long bed
Wheelbase, in.	116.8	133.0	138.8	155.0
Overall length, in.	197.1	213.3	219.1	235.3
Overall width, in.	79.0	79.0	79.0	79.0
Overall height, in.	71.0	71.0	71.9	74.0

	reg. cab short bed	reg. cab long bed	ext. cab short bed	ext. cab long bed
Curb weight, lbs.	3886	3982	4186	4316
Max. payload, lbs.............	2310	5100	3855	4655
Fuel capacity, gals.	34.7	37.2	34.7	37.1
Seating capacity	3	3	6	6
Front head room, in.	40.3	40.3	39.9	39.9
Max. front leg room, in. ...	41.1	41.1	41.0	41.0
Rear head room, in.	—	—	37.6	37.6
Min. rear leg room, in.	—	—	28.8	28.8

Powertrain layout: longitudinal front-engine/rear- or 4-wheel drive

ENGINES	ohv I-6	ohv V-8	ohv V-8	ohv V-8	Diesel ohv V-8
Size, liters/cu. in.	4.9/300	5.0/302	5.8/351	7.5/460	7.3/444
Horsepower	145	185-205	200-210	245-250	185-210
Torque (lbs./ft.)	265	270-275	300-325	400-410	360-425

EPA city/highway mpg

4-speed manual		15/16			
5-speed OD manual	15/19	15/19	NA	NA	NA
3-speed automatic	NA		NA	NA	NA
4-speed OD auto.	14/18	14/19	12/17	NA	NA

Consumer Guide™ observed MPG

4-speed OD auto.	15.2		12.9

Built in USA, Mexico, and Canada.

AVERAGE REPLACEMENT COSTS

A/C Compressor $395		Clutch, Pressure Plate, Bearing 515
Alternator 290		Universal Joints 175
Radiator 425		Brakes.................................295
Timing Chain or Belt 200		Shocks and/or Struts 160
Automatic Transmission or Transaxle.........................560		Exhaust System 375

RETAIL PRICES	GOOD	AVERAGE	POOR
1990 F-150	$2,600-5,700	$2,000-5,000	$700-3,000
1990 F-250	4,200-6,000	3,500-5,300	1,500-3,200
1991 F-150	3,300-7,500	2,600-6,800	1,000-4,000
1991 F-250	5,300-8,000	4,500-7,200	2,200-4,400
1992 F-150	4,000-9,000	3,300-8,200	1,400-5,000
1992 F-250	6,200-9,500	5,400-8,700	2,900-5,500
1993 F-150	4,800-10,000	4,000-9,100	1,800-5,800
1993 F-250	7,300-10,800	6,500-9,800	3,700-6,400
1994 F-150	5,700-11,500	4,900-10,500	2,400-7,000

FORD

	GOOD	AVERAGE	POOR
1994 F-250	9,000-12,500	8,200-11,500	5,000-7,800
1995 F-150	7,400-13,500	6,500-12,500	3,800-8,500
1995 F-250	10,500-14,500	9,500-13,300	6,000-9,300
1996 F-150	8,600-16,000	7,700-15,000	4,700-10,500
1996 F-250	12,000-16,500	10,800-15,300	7,000-11,000

TROUBLE SPOTS

• **Hard starting** Hesitation, miss, stumble, no-start, or stalling could be due to a short in the wiring harness for the powertrain control module (PCM). Since the computer and its circuits are emission controls, they will be covered by the emissions warranty if not the regular warranty. (1993-95)

• **Vehicle noise** A chattering noise that can be felt, and sometimes heard, coming from the rear during tight turns after highway driving is caused by a lack of friction modifier or over-shimming of the clutch packs in the Traction-Lok (limited-slip) differential. A replacement clutch pack and friction modifier will be installed under the company's warranty programs. (1990-96)

• **Transmission slippage** The transmission may slip (lack of torque) and the engine may flare when the transmission shifts into fourth gear, which can often be traced to a bad TR/MLP sensor that will be replaced along with a speed sensor on AODE automatic transmissions under the normal warranty provisions. (1994-95)

• **Transmission slippage** If the transmission does not shift from second to third, the valve body separator plate may be distorted which will be replaced under normal warranty provisions. (1990-94)

• **Manual transmission** On trucks with a diesel engine, the clutch may not release even though the pedal is pushed all the way to the floor, due to a leaking slave cylinder, which will be replaced with a more robust cylinder under warranty. (1993-95)

• **Suspension problems** The front leaf springs are prone to sag over time and must be replaced in order to restore proper ride height and so that the alignment (camber) can be adjusted. (1991-94)

• **Ball joints** If water gets into the ball joints, they will wear out early and have to be replaced. Ford has new joints available with a better seal, which should be used for service replacement. (1990-96)

• **Alternator belt** If the accessory drive belt on 4.9L engines chirps, the pulley for the power steering may be misaligned on the pump or the A/C compressor may have to be repositioned. If the belt squeals, the automatic tensioner must be replaced under normal warranty conditions. (1990-94)

• **Hard starting** If the engine does not start or cranks for a long time then stalls, the idle air control valve may be sticking and Ford will replace it under warranty. (1995-96)

• **Suspension problems** Front tire cupping is common with Twin Axle suspension. Often new springs will help, but sometimes other suspension parts must also be replaced. Regular alignment is crucial. (all)

• **Vehicle noise** For vehicles under warranty, Ford will replace any loose frame rivets with bolts (welding is not approved). (1990-96)

• **Doors** The passive restraint belts may work intermittently or fail (blown fuse), the key buzzer and dome light may stay on because the wiring for the passive restraints gets chaffed under the back seat and short out. (1992-93)

• **Spark plugs** The spark plugs tend to break during removal, especially the first time, because the threads were not coated with anti-seize compound. (1990-93)

RECALL HISTORY

1990 "Fasten seatbelts" and other warning lights on some cars may not work. **1990-91** Front seatbelt release button can break and pieces can fall inside, causing improper operation. **1990 4x2 with one-piece driveshaft and E40D transmission** Under certain conditions, snap ring may fracture and park gear would not engage. **1990 w/dual fuel tanks** Supply and return fuel lines may be crossed on some trucks. **1990-91 F-250/350 with 7.3/.5 liter engine, and 4x4 with 5.8-liter** Brake fluid may overheat, diminishing braking effectiveness. **1990-91** Ignition switch could short-circuit and overheat, causing smoke and possible fire. **1990-93 w/dual fuel tanks** Portion of unused fuel from one tank may be returned to the second, causing spillage. **1992 F-250/350 diesel** Sound insulation can contact exhaust manifold. **1992** Door latch may malfunction in below-freezing temperatures. **1992-94 w/manual shift** Parking brake pawl can slip; brake might not hold. **1993 F-150 w/Touch Drive** Transfer case can slip out of 4x4 high gear during coasting or with power applied in reverse. **1994 F-150/250** Air bag and its warning light might not function; or, air bag might deploy when passenger door is slammed while key is turned to start position. **1994-95 Super Cab with 40/20/40 power driver's seat** Wiring harness for power lumbar support could overheat, leading to melting, smoke, or possible ignition of surrounding materials. **1996 Super/F-250/F-350** Fuel tank strap could loosen or disconnect. **1996 F-250/F-350/Super Duty** Undersized fasteners on a few trucks can separate, causing fuel-tank strap to become disconnected. **1996-97 F-250** Certification label shows incorrect rear tire inflation pressure.

1990-93 FORD MUSTANG

✓ BEST BUY

1992 Ford Mustang GT convertible

FOR Air bag, driver • Handling/roadholding • Acceleration (V-8 models)

AGAINST Fuel economy (V-8) • Rear-seat room • Noise • Ride • Acceleration (4-cylinder)

EVALUATION Best to skip the weak, noisy 4-cylinder engine, with its poor repair record. For reliable and strong performance choose the V-8, but watch out for its notorious poor wet-weather traction and dismal fuel economy, especially in town. Four-cylinder models average in the low twenties.

Ride quality is well controlled on base models. In the GT, you can definitely expect to jiggle and jounce over harsh pavement, courtesy of an admittedly stiff suspension. However, it is that suspension the makes the GT model handle so well, while the base model leans over heavily even in modest turns. Brakes are one of the bigger bugaboos. Front-disc/rear-drum brakes are simply not up to par for a car of this caliber.

Passenger space is fine up front but tight in back. Hatchbacks offer plenty of cargo space with the rear seatback folded down. Convertibles are fun, of course, but bodies are likely to be loose and rattly. Controls are small and some awkwardly placed, but overall better than a Chevy Camaro.

To be frank, few other cars offer as much bang for the buck. Only the Chevrolet Camaro and Pontiac Firebird rank as true rivals. Despite high insurance rates and poor gas mileage, Mustangs still deliver good overall value, new or used.

SPECIFICATIONS	2-door coupe	2-door hatchback	2-door conv.
Wheelbase, in.	100.5	100.5	100.5

	2-door coupe	2-door hatchback	2-door conv.
Overall length, in.	179.6	179.6	179.6
Overall width, in.	68.3	68.3	68.3
Overall height, in.	52.1	52.1	52.1
Curb weight, lbs.	2775	2834	2996
Cargo volume, cu. ft.	10.0	30.0	6.4
Fuel capacity, gals.	15.4	15.4	15.4
Seating capacity	4	4	4
Front head room, in.	37.0	37.0	37.6
Max. front leg room, in.	41.7	41.7	41.7
Rear head room, in.	35.9	35.7	37.0
Min. rear leg room, in.	30.7	30.7	30.7

Powertrain layout: longitudinal front-engine/rear-wheel drive

ENGINES

	ohc I-4	ohc I-4	ohv V-8	ohv V-8
Size, liters/cu. in.	2.3/140	2.3/140	5.0/302	5.0/302
Horsepower	88	105	205-225	245
Torque (lbs./ft.)	132	135	275-300	320
EPA city/highway mpg				
5-speed OD manual	23/29	22/30	17/24	NA
4-speed OD automatic		22/29	17/24	
Consumer Guide™ observed MPG				
5-speed OD manual			15.3	
4-speed OD automatic		19.8		

Built in USA.

RETAIL PRICES	GOOD	AVERAGE	POOR
1990 Mustang LX	$2,300-3,400	$1,800-2,800	$700-1,100
1990 Mustang GT	4,000-4,800	3,400-4,100	1,500-2,000
1990 LX Convertible	3,600-4,800	2,900-4,000	1,200-1,900
1990 GT Convertible	5,700-6,400	5,000-5,600	2,500-3,100
1991 Mustang LX	2,700-3,900	2,100-3,200	900-1,400
1991 Mustang GT	4,800-5,600	4,100-4,800	2,000-2,600
1991 LX Convertible	4,400-5,600	3,700-4,800	1,800-2,500
1991 GT Convertible	6,400-7,400	5,600-6,600	3,000-3,800
1992 Mustang LX	3,200-4,600	2,600-3,900	1,200-1,800
1992 Mustang GT	5,500-6,300	4,700-5,500	2,500-3,100
1992 LX Convertible	5,200-6,200	4,400-5,400	2,400-3,000
1992 GT Convertible	7,200-8,200	6,400-7,400	3,600-3,400
1993 Mustang LX	3,800-5,700	3,100-5,000	1,500-2,600
1993 Mustang GT	6,500-8,000	5,700-7,200	3,300-4,300
1993 LX Convertible	6,000-7,000	5,200-6,200	3,000-3,600
1993 GT Convertible	8,000-9,200	7,200-8,200	4,200-5,000

AVERAGE REPLACEMENT COSTS

A/C Compressor $410	Clutch, Pressure Plate,
Alternator 535	Bearing 480
Radiator 360	Universal Joints 95
Timing Chain or Belt 215	Brakes 245
Automatic Transmission or	Shocks and/or Struts 435
Transaxle........................675	Exhaust System.................565

TROUBLE SPOTS

• **Windshield wipers** Because water commonly seeps past the hood seal onto the wiper motor, the wipers may be erratic or quit working. Ford has a redesigned motor with a water shield that snaps over it to correct the problem, but not as a warranty. (1990-93)

• **Suspension problems** It may be impossible to align the front end and get the camber correct due to the dimensions of the crossmember across the spring seats, so Ford has issued a kit that provides up to two degrees of camber adjustment. (1990-93)

• **Vehicle noise** A chattering noise that can be felt, and sometimes heard, coming from the rear during tight turns after highway driving is caused by a lack of friction modifier or over-shimming of the clutch packs in the Traction-Lok (limited-slip) differential. A replacement clutch pack and friction modifier will be installed under the company's warranty programs. (1990-93)

• **Blower motor** Squeaking or chirping blower motors are the result of defective brush holders, so Ford has issued a redesigned motor and will replace those that are under normal warranty. (1993)

RECALL HISTORY

1990-93 Ignition switch could short-circuit and overheat, causing smoke and possible fire. **1991** Park rod assembly of automatic overdrive transmission may contain a cam with inadequate surface hardness, which could lead to disengagement or non-engagement when lever is placed in "Park" position; with parking brake off, vehicle could then roll away.

1994-98 FORD MUSTANG

FOR Air bags • Acceleration (V-8)
• Handling/roadholding • Anti-lock brakes (optional)

AGAINST Fuel economy (V-8) • Rear-seat room • Ride (GT)

EVALUATION All Mustangs take quick corners smartly, but because of a softened suspension, base cars ride with only mod-

1994 Ford Mustang GT 2-door

est jarring—considerably less shocking than in the past. A more stiffly-suspended GT, on the other hand, grows harsh, actually crashing and banging over broken surfaces. Cobras are stiffer-suspended yet, as expected, but their ride quality isn't noticeably worse.

Acceleration is agequate with the V-6 and either transmission, though automatic downshifts tend to be delayed when dashing uphill. Obviously, the V-8 is the choice for performance, though increased weight in this generation makes that engine seem a little less peppy than before. Fuel economy is good with a V-6, but not with V-8 power. The 4.6-liter V-8 in later models yields little acceleration improvement, but it's smoother and more refined. Thrilling is the operative word for a session behind the wheel of a Cobra, savoring the feel of the 5-speed gearbox and high-performance engine.

Wet-weather traction continues to be a problem on all Mustangs, especially V-8s. All-disc brakes are fine, but we'd look for a Mustang with the optional anti-locking.

Entry/exit is easy enough, courtesy of the Mustang's relatively upright stance (compared to Camaro, at any rate). Backseat space is truly tight, but the cockpit has an open, airy feel. Instruments are unobstructed, controls near at hand, and the dual air bags are a safety bonus. A major improvement, and more user friendly for everyday driving than Chevy's Camaro, the current Mustang is well worth a test drive.

NHTSA CRASH TEST RESULTS
1994 Ford Mustang   2-DOOR COUPE

Driver	☆☆☆☆
Passenger	☆☆☆☆

(The National Highway Traffic Safety Administration tests a vehicle's crashworthiness in front and side collisions. Their ratings suggest the chance of serious injury: ☆☆☆☆☆—10% or less; ☆☆☆☆—10-20% or less; ☆☆☆—20-30% or less; ☆☆—35-45% or less; ☆—More than 45%.)

FORD

SPECIFICATIONS

	2-door coupe	2-door conv.
Wheelbase, in.	101.3	101.3
Overall length, in.	181.5	181.5
Overall width, in.	71.8	71.8
Overall height, in.	52.9	52.8
Curb weight, lbs.	3077	3257
Cargo volume, cu. ft.	10.9	7.7
Fuel capacity, gals.	15.4	15.4
Seating capacity	4	4
Front head room, in.	38.1	37.9
Max. front leg room, in.	42.6	42.6
Rear head room, in.	35.9	35.8
Min. rear leg room, in.	30.3	30.3

Powertrain layout: longitudinal front-engine/rear-wheel drive

ENGINES

	ohv V-6	ohv V-8	ohc V-8	dohc V-8
Size, liters/cu. in.	3.8/232	5.0/302	4.6/281	4.6/281
Horsepower	145-150	215-240	215-225	305
Torque (lbs./ft.)	215	285	285	300

EPA city/highway mpg

5-speed OD manual	20/30	17/25	18/27	18/26
4-speed OD automatic	20/20	17/24	17/24	

Consumer Guide™ observed MPG

5-speed OD manual			17.5	
4-speed OD automatic		16.5	15.7	

Built in USA.

RETAIL PRICES

	GOOD	AVERAGE	POOR
1994 Mustang	$7,000-8,000	$6,200-7,200	$4,000-4,800
1994 Mustang GT	9,000-10,000	8,200-9,200	5,500-6,200
1994 Convertible	9,200-10,200	8,200-9,300	5,500-6,200
1994 GT Convertible	11,000-12,000	10,000-11,000	7,000-7,800
1995 Mustang	8,400-9,500	7,500-8,500	5,000-5,900
1995 Mustang GT	10,200-11,200	9,300-10,200	6,300-7,000
1995 Convertible	10,500-11,500	9,500-10,500	6,500-7,400
1995 GT Convertible	12,500-13,500	11,500-12,300	8,200-8,900
1996 Mustang	10,000-11,000	9,000-10,000	6,000-6,900
1996 Mustang GT	12,000-13,000	11,000-12,000	7,800-8,500
1996 Mustang Cobra	15,500-17,000	14,000-15,500	10,500-11,500
1996 Convertible	12,500-14,000	11,500-13,000	8,000-9,500
1996 GT Convertible	14,000-15,000	12,800-13,500	9,300-10,000
1996 Cobra Convertible	18,500-20,000	17,000-18,500	13,000-14,000
1997 Mustang	11,500-12,500	10,300-11,200	7,200-8,000
1997 Mustang GT	13,700-15,000	12,500-13,500	9,000-9,800

	GOOD	AVERAGE	POOR
1997 Mustang Cobra	18,500-20,000	17,000-18,500	13,000-14,000
1997 Convertible	14,000-15,500	12,800-14,000	9,300-10,200
1997 GT Convertible	16,500-18,000	15,000-16,500	11,000-12,000
1997 Cobra Convertible	21,500-23,000	20,000-21,500	15,500-16,500
1998 Mustang	13,500-15,000	12,000-13,500	8,800-10,000
1998 Mustang GT	16,000-17,500	14,500-16,000	10,500-11,700
1998 Mustang Cobra	21,500-23,000	20,000-21,500	16,000-17,000
1998 Convertible	16,500-18,000	15,000-16,500	11,000-12,200
1998 GT Convertible	19,000-21,000	17,500-19,500	13,500-15,000
1998 Cobra Convertible	24,500-26,500	22,500-24,500	17,500-19,000

AVERAGE REPLACEMENT COSTS

A/C Compressor $410	Clutch, Pressure Plate,
Alternator 535	Bearing 435
Radiator 480	Universal Joints 95
Timing Chain or Belt 215	Brakes................................245
Automatic Transmission or	Shocks and/or Struts 435
Transaxle.........................675	Exhaust System.................830

TROUBLE SPOTS

• **Vehicle noise** A chattering noise that can be felt, and sometimes heard, coming from the rear during tight turns after highway driving is caused by a lack of friction modifier or over-shimming of the clutch packs in the Traction-Lok (limited-slip) differential. A replacement clutch pack and friction modifier will be installed under the company's warranty programs. (1994-96)

• **Hard starting** If the engine does not want to start or cranks for a long time then stalls, the idle air control valve may be sticking and Ford will replace it under warranty. (1995-96)

• **Alternator belt** The drive belt tensioner pulley or idler pulley bearings are apt to make a squealing noise when the engine is started in cold weather. Under the bumper-to-bumper warranty, the pulley(s) will be replaced. (1994-96)

• **Transmission slippage** The automatic transmission in these cars over 20,000 miles is notorious for shuddering or vibrating under light acceleration or when shifting between third and fourth gear above 35 mph. It requires that the transmission fluid (including fluid in the torque converter) be changed and that only Mercon® fluid be used. It usually takes at least 100 miles of driving after the fluid change for the shudder to go away. (1994)

• **Transmission slippage** The transmission may slip (lack of torque) and the engine may flare when the transmission shifts into fourth gear, which can often be traced to a bad TR/MLP sensor that will be replaced along with a speed sensor on AODE automatic transmissions under the normal warranty provisions. (1994-95)

• **Blower motor** Squeaking or chirping blower motors are the result of defective brush holders, so Ford has issued a redesigned motor and will replace those that are under normal warranty. (1994)

RECALL HISTORY

1994 GT w/power lumbar adjustment Electrical short can result in overheating, melting, smoke, and ignition of surrounding materials. **1995** On some cars, passenger air bag's inflator body is cracked and may not inflate properly; also, igniter end cap can separate, causing hot gases to be released. **1995** Some outer tie rod ends can fracture within 50,000 miles; may result in shake or shimmy and cause wheel to tuck inward or outward. **1994-96** Tearing of bond between inner and outer hood panels during minor front-end collision can result in gap at leading edge of hood; could result in separation of outer panel. **1998 w/V-8 engine** Some cars have missing or inadequately brazed joints between fuel rail body and mounting brackets; separation can result in leakage.

1990-92 FORD PROBE

1990 Ford Probe GT

FOR Acceleration (GT and LX) • Handling/roadholding • Cargo room • Optional anti-lock brakes • Fuel economy (4-cylinder)

AGAINST Automatic transmission performance • Rear seat room • Torque steer (GT and LX) • Noise

EVALUATION Performance from the gruff base 2.2-liter 4-cylinder (12-valve) engine is passable but uninspiring, especially with automatic. So, availability of a V-6 was a welcome change—far more powerful than the basic 4-cylinder, but considerably more refined than the turbocharged GT. Hooked to automatic, the V-6 engine's low-speed and mid-range response give the Probe outstanding flexibility. Mated to the 5-speed, the V-6 adapts well to sporting, high-rpm driving.

The turbocharged GT is very quick, but it can be an unpredictable handful under hard throttle. The turbo's boost also kicks in too abruptly at low speeds. On the plus side, the GT's wide tires and sport-oriented suspension promise fine handling. All told, though, we've liked the well-rounded LX model best. When equipped with bigger (15-inch) tires, anti-lock braking, and analog instruments, the LX is the most appealing choice of them all. The Sport package, available in 1992, elevates the LX's already-capable road manners close to those of the GT, without losing much in ride comfort.

Cargo capacity is ample, even with the rear seatback up, but liftover is high. A low roof offers little headroom for anyone taller than 6 feet. Few adults will enjoy climbing into the back, which is fit only for children. Controls fall easily to hand, and analog instruments are clear.

Early models had reliability problems, but those seemed to be remedied by 1990. Best to steer clear of GT models, as the turbo four has a reputation for early failure.

SPECIFICATIONS

	2-door hatchback
Wheelbase, in.	99.0
Overall length, in.	177.0
Overall width, in.	67.9
Overall height, in.	51.8
Curb weight, lbs.	2730
Cargo volume, cu. ft.	41.9
Fuel capacity, gals.	15.1
Seating capacity	4
Front head room, in.	37.3
Max. front leg room, in.	42.5
Rear head room, in.	35.0
Min. rear leg room, in.	39.9

Powertrain layout: transverse front-engine/front-wheel drive

ENGINES	ohc I-4	Turbocharged ohc I-4	ohv V-6
Size, liters/cu. in.	2.2/133	2.2/133	3.0/182
Horsepower	110	145	140-145
Torque (lbs./ft.)	130	190	160-165
EPA city/highway mpg			
5-speed OD manual	24/31	21/27	19/26
4-speed OD automatic	21/28	19/25	18/24

FORD

Consumer Guide™ observed MPG
5-speed OD manual 25.3   22.5
4-speed OD automatic 21.0
Built in USA.

RETAIL PRICES

	GOOD	AVERAGE	POOR
1990 Probe GL/LX	$2,100-2,800	$1,500-2,200	$600-1,000
1990 Probe GT	2,600-3,200	2,000-2,500	900-1,200
1991 Probe GL/LX	2,700-3,400	2,100-2,700	900-1,400
1991 Probe GT	3,400-4,000	2,700-3,300	1,300-1,700
1992 Probe GL/LX	3,400-4,200	2,700-3,500	1,300-1,800
1992 Probe GT	4,200-4,800	3,400-4,000	1,800-2,300

AVERAGE REPLACEMENT COSTS

A/C Compressor $630
Alternator 605
Radiator 440
Timing Chain or Belt 170
Automatic Transmission or
   Transaxle........................980

Clutch, Pressure Plate,
   Bearing............................475
Constant Velocity Joints.....565
Brakes.................................235
Shocks and/or Struts 735
Exhaust System.................475

TROUBLE SPOTS

• **Hard starting** The air inlet ducts tend to crack or the clamps get loose causing hard starting, hesitation, and rough idle on cars with 2.2L engines. (1990-92)

• **Dashboard lights** The engine speed sensor harness may short the crankshaft pulley illuminating the check engine light. (1993)

• **Water leak** Water gets into the wiring harness connectors in front of the radiator, which can drain the battery causing a no-start, failure of the under hood light, problems with the head-lights and retractors, lack of air conditioning or blower. (1990-91)

• **Water leak** Water contaminates the fuel pump cut-off switch, which causes the passive restraint shoulder belt to remain in the engaged (all the way back) position. (1990)

• **Air conditioner** Condensation from the air conditioning leaks onto the front carpets because there is too much insulation around the evaporator. (1990-92)

• **Exhaust system** Loose heat shields over the muffler and cat-alytic converter cause a rattling or buzzing noise. (1990-93)

• **Radio** Whining noises in the radio speakers are caused by the fuel pump in the gas tank. An electronic noise filter must be installed on the fuel pump. (1989-92)

RECALL HISTORY

1990 Throttle levers on some cars may have been bent during assembly, so throttle could stick. **1990-92** Rail of automatic shoulder belt can wear, causing cable to jam and render belt inoperative. **1991 GL** Brackets that mount automatic shoulder belt retractor assembly may have a spot weld of inadequate strength; belt could fail in a collision.

1993-97 FORD PROBE

✓ BEST BUY

1993 Ford Probe GT

FOR   Air bags (later models) • Acceleration (V-6) • Steering/handling (GT) • Visibility • Anti-lock brakes (optional) • Cargo room

AGAINST   Rear-seat room • Automatic transmission performance • Ride (GT)

EVALUATION   Acceleration is excellent with the GT's V-6 and standard 5-speed gearbox. Action from the 4-cylinder engine is adequate, at least with manual shift. Performance lags with optional 4-speed automatic, which also is slow to downshift. The engine's low-end torque simply isn't sufficient to move the car off with any degree of real vigor. Even the V-6 engine feels somewhat sluggish with automatic.

Base-model handling is secure and sporty. Firm suspension tuning and low-profile tires give the GT sharp, agile handling and a secure grip. In exchange, you can expect to endure a harsher, more jittery ride. A Probe GT jiggles on roads that feel smooth in the MX-6 LS. That level of roughness can lead to fatigue on a long trip. Base Probes are softer suspended for a better ride, without losing much handling competence. Ford softened the GT's suspension for 1996, but tires are still stiff so the ride isn't a whole lot better.

FORD

Visibility is better than in most sport coupes, due to the low cowl and relatively slim roof pillars. Space is adequate up front. Space is scant in back for grownups. Cargo room ranks as generous, especially with the split rear seatback folded down, though the rear sill is quite tall. The modern dashboard is neatly laid out, though climate and radio controls don't fall too easily to hand.

Significantly improved over the first (1989-92) generation, the latest Probe delivers plenty of punch and prowess for its price.

NHTSA CRASH TEST RESULTS
1994 Ford Probe

2-DOOR HATCHBACK

Driver	☆☆☆☆☆
Passenger	☆☆☆☆

(The National Highway Traffic Safety Administration tests a vehicle's crashworthiness in front and side collisions. Their ratings suggest the chance of serious injury: ☆☆☆☆☆—10% or less; ☆☆☆☆—10-20% or less; ☆☆☆—20-30% or less; ☆☆—35-45% or less; ☆—More than 45%.)

SPECIFICATIONS

	2-door hatchback
Wheelbase, in.	102.8
Overall length, in.	178.7
Overall width, in.	69.8
Overall height, in.	51.6
Curb weight, lbs.	2690
Cargo volume, cu. ft.	18.0
Fuel capacity, gals.	15.5
Seating capacity	4
Front head room, in.	37.8
Max. front leg room, in.	43.1
Rear head room, in.	34.8
Min. rear leg room, in.	28.5

Powertrain layout: transverse front-engine/front-wheel drive

ENGINES

	dohc I-4	dohc V-6
Size, liters/cu. in.	2.0/122	2.5/153
Horsepower	115-118	164
Torque (lbs./ft.)	124-127	156-160
EPA city/highway mpg		
5-speed OD manual	26/33	21/27
4-speed OD automatic	23/31	20/26
Consumer Guide™ observed MPG		
4-speed OD automatic	22.2	

Built in USA.

RETAIL PRICES

	GOOD	AVERAGE	POOR
1993 Probe	$4,300-5,000	$3,600-4,300	$1,600-2,200

	GOOD	AVERAGE	POOR
1993 Probe GT	5,500-6,200	4,800-5,500	2,500-3,000
1994 Probe	5,300-6,100	4,600-5,300	2,400-3,000
1994 Probe GT	6,500-7,300	5,700-6,500	3,200-3,700
1995 Probe	6,900-7,700	6,200-6,900	3,700-4,200
1995 Probe GT	8,300-9,200	7,500-8,400	4,700-5,300
1996 Probe	8,400-9,300	7,500-8,400	4,700-5,300
1996 Probe GT	10,000-11,000	9,000-10,000	6,000-6,700
1997 Probe	9,800-11,000	8,800-10,000	5,800-6,500
1997 Probe GT	11,500-12,700	10,500-11,500	7,300-8,200

AVERAGE REPLACEMENT COSTS

A/C Compressor $875
Alternator 380
Radiator 430
Timing Chain or Belt 180
Automatic Transmission or
   Transaxle......................1,075
Clutch, Pressure Plate,
   Bearing 590
Constant Velocity Joints.....780
Brakes..................................275
Shocks and/or Struts 770
Exhaust System.................485

TROUBLE SPOTS

• **Engine stalling** If the engine stalls when the transmission is shifted into drive, the problem may be a cracked mass airflow snorkel tube. This is often misdiagnosed as a problem with the transmissions, specifically with the torque converter clutch. Actually, unmetered air is getting into the engine—making it stall. Not a warranty or campaign item. (1993-94)

• **Transmission leak** Automatic transmission fluid leaks from the vent and gives the appearance of a leak at the cooler lines or main control cover. Ford will replace the vent with a "remote" vent, which is less likely to leak, under its bumper-to-bumper warranty. (1994-96)

• **Fuel gauge** The fuel gauge may only read ¾ full when the tank is full because the fuel return line is bent and interferes with the sender in the tank. Ford will replace the fuel pump and sender under warranty. (1995-96)

RECALL HISTORY

1993 Lower pivot pin that joins liftgate gas strut to body can separate from mounting bracket due to undersized rivet head; liftgate could descend suddenly, resulting in potential injury. **1994** Passenger-side air bag on small number of cars can detach from, and deform, the mounting bracket if it deploys during an accident and no one is occupying that seating position. **1995** On some cars, passenger air bag may not inflate properly; also, igniter end cap can separate, causing hot gases to be released. **1996** Supplementary inflatable restraint caution label on driver's sunvisor does not contain proper warning that rearward-facing child safety seats should not be installed in front passenger seat position.

1990-92 FORD RANGER PICKUP

1992 Ford Ranger

FOR Acceleration (V-6) • Reliability • Ride

AGAINST Fuel economy (V-6) • Handling

EVALUATION Even the small V-6 is impressive, but the star performer is the 4.0-liter. Tossing out abundant torque, the 4.0 makes Ranger genuinely fun to drive. It's also a more practical hauler than the 2.9-liter V-6, though the 2.9 and 3.0 are fine for light-duty work. The 4.0-liter engine does get rather growly when worked hard. Even a 4-cylinder Ranger is acceptable if you're using it mainly as a second car, though we strongly advise the 5-speed manual transmission with that smaller engine. Fuel economy could be a lot better. A 4.0-liter/automatic model averaged a mediocre 18.2 mpg. A regular-cab STX 4x4 with the 2.9 V-6 and automatic did better: 19.5 mpg.

Bench and bucket seats are both comfortable. But, a SuperCab's back seats are best suited for children. Instruments are functional, controls well-placed, though optional power window/door lock controls are too low and far forward on door panels. Cabin storage in regular-cab models is sparse, and only the XLT and STX have door map pockets.

Wind noise and tire rumble (especially with the knobby 4x4 rubber) are apparent, but not obtrusive for a pickup. The ride is fairly comfortable, and road behavior typical of small trucks. Steering is a bit vague, the body leans readily in corners, and tires offer only moderate grip.

With a Ranger, we're talking quality and refinement in a pleasant vehicle that's easy to live with. We'd put it first on our shopping list, but also take a close look at Ranger's closest competitors: the Chevrolet S10 and similar GMC Sonoma.

SPECIFICATIONS

	reg. cab short bed	reg. cab long bed	ext. cab
Wheelbase, in.	107.9	113.9	125.0
Overall length, in.	176.5	188.5	193.7
Overall width, in.	66.8	66.8	66.8
Overall height, in.	63.8	63.6	64.3
Curb weight, lbs.	2820	2857	3128
Max. payload, lbs.	1600	1600	1300
Fuel capacity, gals.	16.3	16.3	19.6
Seating capacity	3	3	5
Front head room, in.	39.2	39.2	39.4
Max. front leg room, in.	42.4	42.4	43.9
Rear head room, in.	NA	NA	NA
Min. rear leg room, in.	NA	NA	NA

Powertrain layout: longitudinal front-engine/rear- or 4-wheel drive

ENGINES

	ohc I-4	ohv V-6	ohv V-6	ohv V-6
Size, liters/cu. in.	2.3/140	2.9/177	3.0/182	4.0/245
Horsepower	100	140	145	145-160
Torque (lbs./ft.)	133	170	165	220-225
EPA city/highway mpg				
5-speed OD manual	23/28	18/23	20/25	18/23
4-speed OD automatic	20/23	17/21	18/24	17/21
Consumer Guide™ observed MPG				
4-speed OD automatic		19.5		18.2

Built in USA.

RETAIL PRICES

	GOOD	AVERAGE	POOR
1990 Ranger	$1,500-3,800	$1,000-3,200	$300-1,700
1991 Ranger	1,900-5,500	1,300-4,800	500-2,700
1992 Ranger	2,400-6,500	1,800-5,700	800-3,300

AVERAGE REPLACEMENT COSTS

A/C Compressor	$425
Alternator	420
Radiator	295
Timing Chain or Belt	130
Automatic Transmission or Transaxle	760
Clutch, Pressure Plate, Bearing	420
Universal Joints	105
Brakes	215
Shocks and/or Struts	285
Exhaust System	270

TROUBLE SPOTS

• **Cold starting problems** Water gets into the EGR valve vacuum regulator on the 2.3L engine, which usually turns on the Check Engine light. If the water freezes in cold weather, the engine stumbles when started. Ford has a replacement regulator available that has a formed rubber hose that prevents the water from entering. (1991-92)

• **Engine knock** A knocking noise from the lower left side of the 2.3L engine is caused by pressure problems in the oil system. To repair it, Ford has a revised oil pump and a gallery plug with a pressure dampening rod. (1992-93)

• **Oil leak** The only way to fix the leak at the oil pan is to replace the gasket with the one designed for the 1993 model 2.3L engine. However, to remove the oil pan, the engine must be removed from the truck. Beware of this before purchasing due to the high labor cost. (1990-92)

• **Vehicle noise** A chattering noise that can be felt, and sometimes heard, coming from the rear during tight turns after highway driving is caused by a lack of friction modifier or over-shimming of the clutch packs in the Traction-Lok (limited-slip) differential. A replacement clutch pack and friction modifier will be installed under the company's warranty programs. (1990-92)

• **Air conditioner** Water may drip onto the floor when the air conditioner is operated because the evaporator strip seals were not properly positioned at the factory. They will be repositioned under normal warranty provisions. (1995-96)

• **Radiator** The radiator may leak in cold weather because of a bad seal between the tank and core. Ford will replace the radiator under warranty. (1995-96)

• **Coolant leak** Cracked heads (between the intake and exhaust valves) on 2.9L engines allow coolant into the oil. If not caught in time, severe engine damage could occur.

• **Vehicle noise** For vehicles still under warranty, Ford will replace loose frame rivets with bolts (welding is not approved). (1990-92)

RECALL HISTORY

1990 with 4.0-liter V-6 Throttle may remain open after release of gas pedal. **1990-91 with A4LD automatic** Vehicle may appear to be in "Park" position when gear is not engaged. **1991-92 sold or currently registered in specified southern California counties** Studs that attach master cylinder to power brake booster assembly can develop stress corrosion cracking after extended period; if one or both studs fractures, master cylinder could separate from booster when brakes are applied, preventing brakes from activating.

1993-97 FORD RANGER PICKUP

1993 Ford Ranger XL Sport

FOR Acceleration (V-6) • Reliability • Ride

AGAINST Fuel economy (V-6) • Handling

EVALUATION Acceleration is about the same as in the prior generation. Though adequate with a 5-speed, the 4-cylinder engine labors under a heavy load and generally feels lethargic with automatic. Ranger's 4.0-liter V-6 uses only slightly more fuel than the 3.0-liter, and delivers good low-speed punch; but the 4.0 is somewhat coarse and noisy. A 4.0 should perform most tasks with relative ease, and it works well with the automatic to furnish prompt passing power. We averaged 16.5 mpg in a 4WD Splash SuperCab with the 4.0-liter V-6.

Rangers ride nicely and handle well (for a truck, that is), The suspension absorbs most big bumps without jarring, and the truck is stable in turns. Steering feedback and response are top-notch, and the Ranger has a notably solid feel overall.

Gauges are unobstructed, and the climate controls and radio are grouped efficiently. However, some buttons on optional stereos are too small, and climate controls demand quite a reach around the steering wheel. A regular-cab interior lacks space behind the seat. Also, the steering wheel protrudes too far, leaving no surplus of space for larger drivers.

Ford sought a more carlike look and feel for its Ranger—and succeeded. Some rugged truck characteristics may be gone, but we view the changes as improvements. Ranger is still one of the best in its class, but we recommend that you shop all three domestic brands—including the Dodge Dakota and Chevrolet S-Series—before deciding.

FORD

NHTSA CRASH TEST RESULTS
1995 Ford Ranger

REG. CAB LONG BED

Driver	☆☆☆☆
Passenger	☆☆☆☆

(The National Highway Traffic Safety Administration tests a vehicle's crashworthiness in front and side collisions. Their ratings suggest the chance of serious injury: ☆☆☆☆☆—10% or less; ☆☆☆☆—10-20% or less; ☆☆☆—20-30% or less; ☆☆—35-45% or less; ☆—More than 45%.)

SPECIFICATIONS

	reg. cab short bed	reg. cab long bed	ext. cab
Wheelbase, in.	107.9	113.9	125.2
Overall length, in.	184.3	196.3	198.2
Overall width, in.	69.4	69.4	69.4
Overall height, in.	64.0	64.0	64.1
Curb weight, lbs.	2970	3010	3300
Max. payload, lbs.	1650	1650	1550
Fuel capacity, gals.	17.0	17.0	20.5
Seating capacity	3	3	5
Front head room, in.	39.1	39.1	39.3
Max. front leg room, in.	42.4	42.4	42.4
Rear head room, in.	NA	NA	35.6
Min. rear leg room, in.	NA	NA	41.2

Powertrain layout: longitudinal front-engine/rear- or 4-wheel drive

ENGINES

	ohc I-4	ohv V-6	ohv V-6
Size, liters/cu. in.	2.3/140	3.0/182	4.0/245[1]
Horsepower	98-112	140-147	160
Torque (lbs./ft.)	130-135	162-170	220
EPA city/highway mpg			
5-speed OD manual	22/27	19/25	18/23
4-speed OD automatic	20/25	18/24	17/23
5-speed OD automatic			16/22
Consumer Guide™ observed MPG			
5-speed OD manual		17.8	16.5
4-speed OD automatic			14.2

1. Rangers with the 4.0-liter V-6 switched from a 4-speed to a 5-speed automatic for '97.

Built in USA.

RETAIL PRICES

	GOOD	AVERAGE	POOR
1993 Ranger	$3,800-8,000	$3,100-7,300	$1,600-4,500
1994 Ranger	4,800-10,500	4,100-9,700	2,300-6,200
1995 Ranger	5,800-12,000	5,000-11,000	3,000-7,300
1996 Ranger	6,900-14,000	6,000-13,000	3,800-9,000
1997 Ranger	8,000-16,000	7,200-14,800	4,700-10,500

AVERAGE REPLACEMENT COSTS

A/C Compressor	$425	Clutch, Pressure Plate, Bearing	390
Alternator	280	Universal Joints	90
Radiator	340	Brakes	300
Timing Chain or Belt	395	Shocks and/or Struts	285
Automatic Transmission or Transaxle	745	Exhaust System	215

TROUBLE SPOTS

• **Vehicle noise** A chattering noise that can be felt, and sometimes heard, coming from the rear during tight turns after highway driving is caused by a lack of friction modifier or over-shimming of the clutch packs in the Traction-Lok (limited-slip) differential. A replacement clutch pack and friction modifier will be installed under the company's warranty programs. (1993-96)

• **Hard starting** If the engine does not want to start or cranks for a long time then stalls, the idle air control valve may be sticking and Ford will replace it under warranty. (1995-96)

• **Vehicle noise** For vehicles under warranty, Ford will replace any loose frame rivets with bolts (welding is not approved). (1993-96)

RECALL HISTORY

1993-94 w/manual shift Parking brake might not hold. **1993-94 sold or currently registered in specified southern California counties** Studs that attach master cylinder to power brake booster assembly can develop stress corrosion cracking after extended period; if one or both studs fractures, master cylinder could separate from booster when brakes are applied, preventing brakes from activating. **1993-94 w/2.3-liter engine, registered in AK, ME, MI (upper peninsula), MN, MT, ND, NH, NY, VT or WI** During extreme cold in northern winters, ice can form in throttle body, causing throttle plate to remain in highway cruising position after accelerator is released or speed control is deactivated. **1993-94 with V-6 engine** Flexible hose in front fuel line is susceptible to cracking. **1996** Certification label shows incorrect rear tire inflation pressure.

1990-95 FORD TAURUS

FOR Air bags (later models) • Ride • Passenger and cargo room • Acceleration (V-6) • Handling/roadholding • Anti-lock brakes (optional)

AGAINST Acceleration (4-cylinder) • Fuel economy (V-6) • Climate controls • Radio controls

FORD

1995 Ford Taurus SE 4-door

EVALUATION Taurus feels composed over bumps and in corners. Steering is precise, and suspension movements are well controlled. Taurus is surefooted and agile, with balanced handling in turns and minimal body lean. The firm, Euro-style ride is just right, even if you can expect a few bumps on rougher surfaces.

The weak, noisy 4-cylinder engine just isn't strong enough to power a Taurus. A 3.0-liter V-6 promises much brisker passing, and the optional 3.8-liter V-6 noticeably stronger acceleration from a standstill, plus better mid-range response. Harsh shifts from the automatic transmission do occur occasionally in low-speed driving. Neither V-6 is frugal. One Taurus averaged just 17.9 mpg in commuting and expressway driving. For excitement behind the wheel of a seemingly sedate midsize sedan, SHO is the way to go. Acceleration rivals that of the world's leading sports sedans.

Head room is ample all around, and sedans have a deep, wide trunk. Variable-assist power steering was modified in 1992, resulting in a less precise feel at highway speed. Also on the downside, Taurus tires thump loudly over bumps. We rank Taurus/Sable among the most impressive domestic cars: solid, roomy, great to look at, and a joy to drive.

NHTSA CRASH TEST RESULTS
1994 Ford Taurus

4-DOOR SEDAN

Driver	☆☆☆☆
Passenger	☆☆☆☆

(The National Highway Traffic Safety Administration tests a vehicle's crashworthiness in front and side collisions. Their ratings suggest the chance of serious injury: ☆☆☆☆☆—10% or less; ☆☆☆☆—10-20% or less; ☆☆☆—20-30% or less; ☆☆—35-45% or less; ☆—More than 45%.)

SPECIFICATIONS

	4-door sedan	4-door wagon
Wheelbase, in.	106.0	106.0
Overall length, in.	192.0	193.1
Overall width, in.	70.7	70.7
Overall height, in.	54.1	55.5
Curb weight, lbs.	3118	3285
Cargo volume, cu. ft.	18.0	83.1
Fuel capacity, gals.	16.0	16.0
Seating capacity	6	8
Front head room, in.	38.3	38.5
Max. front leg room, in.	41.7	41.7
Rear head room, in.	37.6	38.1
Min. rear leg room, in.	37.7	36.9

Powertrain layout: transverse front-engine/front-wheel drive

ENGINES	ohv I-4	ohv V-6	dohc V-6	dohc V-6	ohv V-6
Size, liters/cu. in.	2.5/153	3.0/182	3.0/182	3.2/195	3.8/232
Horsepower	90-105	140	220	220	140
Torque (lbs./ft.)	130-140	160-165	200	215	215

EPA city/highway mpg

5-speed OD man.				18/26	
3-speed auto.		21/27			
4-speed OD auto.		20/30		18/26	19/28

Consumer Guide™ observed MPG

4-speed OD auto.				17.9	

Built in USA.

AVERAGE REPLACEMENT COSTS

A/C Compressor	$455	Constant Velocity Joints	505
Alternator	440	Brakes	230
Radiator	525	Shocks and/or Struts	495
Timing Chain or Belt	210	Exhaust System	365
Automatic Transmission or Transaxle	930		

RETAIL PRICES	GOOD	AVERAGE	POOR
1990 Taurus	$1,500-3,000	$1,000-2,400	$300-900
1990 Taurus SHO	3,000-3,800	2,300-3,000	900-1,200
1991 Taurus	2,000-4,200	1,400-3,600	600-1,600
1991 Taurus SHO	4,000-5,000	3,300-4,200	1,500-2,100
1992 Taurus	2,800-5,300	2,200-4,600	1,000-2,500
1992 Taurus SHO	5,000-6,000	4,200-5,200	2,200-2,700
1993 Taurus	3,800-6,200	3,200-5,500	1,600-3,300

FORD

	GOOD	AVERAGE	POOR
1993 Taurus SHO	6,200-7,300	5,400-6,400	3,000-3,600
1994 Taurus	5,000-7,400	4,200-6,600	2,300-4,100
1994 Taurus SHO	7,800-9,000	7,000-8,000	4,200-4,800
1995 Taurus	6,700-9,500	5,800-8,500	3,600-5,800
1995 Taurus SHO	9,800-11,200	8,900-10,200	5,700-6,300

TROUBLE SPOTS

• **Engine noise** The motor mounts are prone to wear out prematurely causing a clunking noise when accelerating, decelerating, or putting the transmission in gear, so the carmaker has issued a voluntary recall (number 92M77) to replace the right front and right rear mounts. The coverage is 6 years or 60,000 miles. (1992-93)

• **Hard starting** If the engine does not start or cranks for a long time then stalls, the idle air control valve may be sticking and Ford will replace it under warranty. (1995-96)

• **Tire wear** Premature tire wear and cupping is caused by rear wheel misalignment. Kits are available to replace the inward bushing on the rear control arm to provide camber adjustment to correct the problem. (1990-95)

• **Blower motor** Squeaking or chirping blower motors are the result of defective brush holders, so Ford has issued a redesigned motor and will replace those that are under normal warranty. (1990-94)

• **Transmission slippage** Because of problems with the automatic transmission, warranty coverage for erratic operation has been extended to 6 years or 60,000 miles. The trans will be repaired or replaced and the dealer will provide a loaner car. Work already done is subject to a refund. (1991)

RECALL HISTORY

1990-91 Front brake rotors on cars sold in 14 northeastern and Great Lakes states may suffer severe corrosion, resulting in reduced braking effectiveness. **1992 wagon** Children can accidentally lock themselves in footwell area of rear-facing third seat or in storage compartment in wagons that lack optional third seat; self-latching assembly should be replaced with a unit that can be closed only with a key. **1992 wagon** Secondary liftgate latch mechanism on some cars may not function, possibly allowing liftgate to open while car is in motion. **1992-93** On cars sold in 14 Midwestern and Northeastern states, body mounts at rear subframe corners (which support engine/transmission) may detach due to corrosion, allowing subframe to drop; could result in clunking noise or altered steering-wheel alignment or, if both corners drop, could make steering very difficult. **1993** Controllers intended for rear-drive vehicles (instead of front-drive) may have been installed in a few cars with optional anti-lock braking. **1995** On some cars, retainer that holds master cylinder pushrod to brake pedal arm is missing or not fully installed; can result in loss of braking. **1991-95 with 3.8-liter engine, in 23 states** Water can accumulate within speed-control conduit; if cable has frozen, throttle can stick and not return to idle. **1992-95 with 3.0- or 3.8-liter engine, in AK, IA, MN, NE, ND, or SD** During high winds, heavy snow and low temperatures, engine fan may become blocked or frozen; can cause smoke/flame. **1993-94** Headlights can flash intermittently as a result of a circuit-breaker opening.

1996-98 FORD TAURUS

✓ BEST BUY

1997 Ford Taurus SHO

FOR Dual air bags • Optional anti-lock brakes • Acceleration (LX, SHO) • Steering/handling • Passenger and cargo room

AGAINST Transmission performance (G, GL) • Rear visibility • Ride (SHO)

EVALUATION An LX accelerates with greater authority than its less-potent G/GL siblings. That 200-horsepower engine is smooth, refined, and potent at higher engine speeds. Low-speed torque is lacking, however, so you must floor the throttle to achieve brisk passing. The LX transmission shifts smoothly.

Not only is the G/GL V-6 engine less powerful, but it's noisier, rougher, and slower. Its transmission often stumbles, shifts roughly, and is slow to downshift for passing. Low-speed power also is lacking in the SHO's V-8, though it's plenty potent at higher speeds. You simply have to wait until engine speed reaches 3000 rpm or so before much happens.

Steering is light and precise. Both models corner with good

FORD

grip and commendable composure. Ride quality has improved somewhat, but the suspension does not absorb bumps well and feels too stiff on rough roads. Beware: The SHO's ride is stiff at all times. Wind and road noise have been reduced, compared to previous Tauruses.

The modern-looking control panel for the climate and audio systems is easy to see and reach, but buttons are overly abundant and many look alike. With optional automatic air conditioning, that control pad gets packed full.

Interior space is better all around than before, especially in the rear, where leg room has grown substantially. Sitting three across, however, will crowd everyone—in both front and rear. The sedan trunk is roomy—wide, deep, and reaching well forward. The driver enjoys a clear view to the front and sides, but it's difficult to see the trunk of the sedan.

Though not perfect, Taurus is roomy, well-built, and enjoyable to drive. Prices went up for this generation, but Tauruses remain a good value and an excellent choice, new or used.

NHTSA CRASH TEST RESULTS
1996 Ford Taurus

	4-DOOR SEDAN
Driver	☆☆☆☆
Passenger	☆☆☆☆

(The National Highway Traffic Safety Administration tests a vehicle's crashworthiness in front and side collisions. Their ratings suggest the chance of serious injury: ☆☆☆☆☆—10% or less; ☆☆☆☆—10-20% or less; ☆☆☆—20-30% or less; ☆☆—35-45% or less; ☆—More than 45%.)

SPECIFICATIONS

	4-door sedan	4-door wagon
Wheelbase, in.	108.5	108.5
Overall length, in.	197.5	199.6
Overall width, in.	73.0	73.0
Overall height, in.	55.1	57.6
Curb weight, lbs.	3326	3480
Cargo volume, cu. ft.	15.8	81.3
Fuel capacity, gals.	16.0	16.0
Seating capacity	6[1]	8[2]
Front head room, in.	39.2	39.3
Max. front leg room, in.	42.6	42.6
Rear head room, in.	36.2	38.9
Min. rear leg room, in.	38.9	38.5

1. 5 with front bucket seats. 2. 6 without optional thrid row seat.

Powertrain layout: transverse front-engine/front-wheel drive

ENGINES

	ohv V-6	dohc V-6	dohc V-8
Size, liters/cu. in.	3.0/182	3.0/181	3.4/207

	ohv V-6	dohc V-6	dohc V-8
Horsepower	145	200	235
Torque (lbs./ft.)	170	200	230
EPA city/highway mpg			
4-speed OD automatic	20/28	19/28	17/26
Consumer Guide™ observed MPG			
4-speed OD automatic	18.3	17.1	16.5

Built in USA.

RETAIL PRICES	GOOD	AVERAGE	POOR
1996 Taurus	$9,500-12,800	$8,500-11,700	$6,200-8,500
1996 Taurus SHO	14,000-16,000	12,500-14,500	9,500-11,000
1997 Taurus	11,000-15,000	9,800-13,500	7,300-10,000
1997 Taurus SHO	17,000-19,000	15,500-17,300	12,500-14,000
1994 Taurus	14,000-17,500	12,500-16,000	9,500-12,500
1994 Taurus SHO	21,000-23,000	19,500-21,500	16,000-17,500

AVERAGE REPLACEMENT COSTS

A/C Compressor	$440	Constant Velocity Joints	605
Alternator	350	Brakes	280
Radiator	585	Shocks and/or Struts	600
Timing Chain or Belt	350	Exhaust System	415
Automatic Transmission or Transaxle	1,115		

TROUBLE SPOTS

• **Suspension noise** The sway bar links wear prematurely causing a clunking noise, especially when going over speed bumps. Revised parts are available. (1996-97)

• **Vehicle noise** Rattling and buzzing from under the car is common due to loose heat shields on the catalytic converter and/or muffler. (1996 97)

• **Dashboard lights** The check engine light comes on for a variety of reasons including bad gasoline, a wobbling accessory drive pulley, vibration damper of bad spark plug. (1996-97)

• **Steering problems** The power steering gets harder to turn when decelerating from about 50 miles per hour or when shifting form reverse to drive requiring replacement of the control module and/or transmission range sensors. (1996)

• **Water leak** Water leaks onto the front floor because of poor sealing of the cabin air filter cowl inlet. (1996-98)

• **Tire wear** Rear tires wear prematurely due to incorrect rear alignment (toe and camber). (1996-97)

FORD

- **Automatic transmission** Vehicles with the AX4S automatic transmission may shift harshly from first to second gear. (1996-97)

- **Air conditioner** The air conditioning may not cool properly because the lines tend to leak at the spring-lock couplings and larger O-rings are available as a service replacement. (1996-97)

RECALL HISTORY

1996 with AX4S automatic transaxle "Park" pawl shaft was improperly positioned; pawl may occasionally fail to engage when selector lever is placed in "park" position, allowing vehicle to roll if parking brake has not been applied. **1996** Automatic-transmission "park" pawl shaft may not be free to rotate; vehicle could then roll as if in neutral, with shift lever in "park" position. **1996** Vacuum diaphragm in fuel pressure regulator was damaged during manufacture; if it tears or ruptures, liquid fuel could be released from air cleaner assembly or exhaust system. **1996** Brake fluid indicator can malfunction. **1996-97** "Park" pawl abutment bracket has sharp edge, which can cause pawl to hang up and not engage gear; vehicle can then move, even though indicator shows "Park."

1990-97 FORD THUNDERBIRD

✓ BEST BUY

1990 Ford Thunderbird

FOR Air bags (later models) • Acceleration (SC and V-8) • Ride • Handling/roadholding • Anti-lock brakes (optional)

AGAINST Acceleration (V-6) • Fuel economy (SC and V-8) • Entry/exit

EVALUATION Substantially heavier than prior T-Birds, the stylish but portly '90s edition is roomier inside. Three can fit into the rear, but head room is limited and the center occupant straddles a wide driveline tunnel. Controls are clear and easy to reach, analog gauges easy to read on a cockpit-style dash. The optional electronic dashboard isn't so easy.

Though smooth-running and capable, the base V-6 sets no acceleration records. The Super Coupe, on the other hand, is one swift cruiser. Unfortunately, the 5-speed manual gearshift gets balky, making automatic the better choice for an SC.

A V-8 engine is the sensible choice for those who like performance, but don't need the all-out muscle of the Super Coupe. The V-8 delivers a smooth power flow, not neck-snapping take-offs. A V-8 Thunderbird reached 60 mph in 8.8 seconds. The 4.6-liter V-6 is quieter, smoother than the older 5.0-liter, but yields unimpressive throttle response in the 30-50-mph range. Fuel economy is tempting only on base (V-6) models. A late LX V-8 got 18.2 mpg (just 15 in urban commuting). An automatic-transmission SC averaged 15.2 mpg.

All Thunderbirds have competent road manners. Base and LX models handle well and ride comfortably, but do tend to float and bound over dips as speed rises. SCs hug the road tightly, but heavy weight keeps even that Thunderbird from feeling truly agile, and the Super Coupe suffers from an overly firm ride. Even in its softest mode, the SC's standard adjustable suspension is on the harsh side. The Sport model (available only briefly) gives you V-8 power and a tauter ride than the base car. Thunderbirds can suffer poor traction on wet/slick pavement even with traction control.

Standard Thunderbirds are pretty and pleasant compared to front-drive GM coupes, such as the Chevrolet Monte Carlo and Pontiac Grand Prix. You get a solid feel, quiet ride, and modern appearance.

NHTSA CRASH TEST RESULTS
1994 Ford Thunderbird

2-DOOR COUPE

Driver	☆☆☆☆☆
Passenger	☆☆☆☆☆

(The National Highway Traffic Safety Administration tests a vehicle's crashworthiness in front and side collisions. Their ratings suggest the chance of serious injury: ☆☆☆☆☆—10% or less; ☆☆☆☆—10-20% or less; ☆☆☆—20-30% or less; ☆☆—35-45% or less; ☆—More than 45%.)

SPECIFICATIONS

	2-door coupe
Wheelbase, in.	113.0
Overall length, in.	200.3
Overall width, in.	72.7
Overall height, in.	52.5
Curb weight, lbs.	3536
Cargo volume, cu. ft.	15.1

FORD

	2-door coupe
Fuel capacity, gals.	18.0
Seating capacity	5
Front head room, in.	38.1
Max. front leg room, in.	42.5
Rear head room, in.	37.5
Min. rear leg room, in.	35.8

Powertrain layout: longitudinal front-engine/rear-wheel drive

ENGINES

	ohv V-6	Supercharged ohv V-6	ohc V-8	ohv V-8
Size, liters/cu. in.	3.8/232	3.8/232	4.6/281	5.0/302
Horsepower	140-145	210-230	203-205	200
Torque (lbs./ft.)	215	315-330	265-280	275
EPA city/highway mpg				
5-speed OD manual		18/26	17/25	
4-speed OD automatic	19/26	18/24	17/24	17/24
Consumer Guide™ observed MPG				
5-speed OD manual		15.8	18.2	
4-speed OD automatic		15.2	15.1	15.1

Built in USA.

AVERAGE REPLACEMENT COSTS

A/C Compressor	$365	Universal Joints	265
Alternator	445	Brakes	235
Radiator	405	Shocks and/or Struts	285
Timing Chain or Belt	340	Exhaust System	275
Automatic Transmission or Transaxle	810		

RETAIL PRICES

	GOOD	AVERAGE	POOR
1990 Thunderbird	$2,600-3,300	$2,000-2,600	$900-1,200
1990 Super Coupe	3,800-4,500	3,100-3,800	1,500-2,000
1991 Thunderbird	3,200-4,000	2,500-3,300	1,200-1,500
1991 Super Coupe	4,800-5,500	4,100-4,800	2,200-2,700
1992 Thunderbird	3,900-5,000	3,200-4,300	1,600-2,200
1992 Super Coupe	5,800-6,500	5,000-5,700	2,800-3,400
1993 Thunderbird	5,000-6,000	4,200-5,200	2,400-3,000
1993 Super Coupe	6,800-7,800	6,000-7,000	3,500-4,100
1994 Thunderbird	6,300-7,300	5,500-6,500	3,400-4,000
1994 Super Coupe	8,200-9,200	7,300-8,300	4,600-5,300
1995 Thunderbird	7,800-8,800	7,000-8,000	4,400-5,000
1995 Super Coupe	10,000-11,500	9,000-10,500	6,000-7,000
1996 Thunderbird	9,500-10,500	8,300-9,300	5,400-6,000

	GOOD	AVERAGE	POOR
1997 Thunderbird	11,300-12,800	10,000-11,500	7,000-8,000

TROUBLE SPOTS

• **Vehicle noise** A chattering noise that can be felt, and sometimes heard, coming from the rear during tight turns after highway driving is caused by a lack of friction modifier or over-shimming of the clutch packs in the Traction-Lok (limited-slip) differential. A replacement clutch pack and friction modifier will be installed under the company's warranty programs. (1990-96)

• **Oil leak** The oil filter balloons and leaks because the oil pump relief valve sticks. Higher than recommended viscosity oils cause wear to the valve bore. Under normal warranty provisions, the pump will be replaced with one less sensitive to this problem, but Ford warns that owners should only use the type of oil spelled out in the owners manual. (1992-94)

• **Air conditioner** Water drips onto the floor when the air conditioner is operated and may be due to over a half-dozen potential leak sources including seals, bad seams in the evaporator case, the heater core cover seal, etc. The leak will be fixed under the bumper-to-bumper warranty for 1992-96 model years. (1990-96)

• **Alternator belt** The drive belt tensioner pulley or idler pulley bearings are apt to make a squealing noise when the engine is started in cold weather. Under the bumper-to-bumper warranty, the pulley(s) will be replaced. (1993-96)

• **Transmission slippage** The automatic transmission in these cars over 20,000 miles is notorious for shuddering or vibrating under light acceleration or when shifting between third and fourth gear above 35 mph. It requires that the transmission fluid (including fluid in the torque converter) be changed and that only Mercon® fluid be used. It usually takes at least 100 miles of driving after the fluid change for the shudder to go away. (1994)

• **Transmission slippage** The transmission may slip (lack of torque) and the engine may flare when the transmission shifts into fourth gear, which can often be traced to a bad TR/MLP sensor that will be replaced along with a speed sensor on AODE automatic transmissions under the normal warranty provisions. (1994-95)

• **Blower motor** Squeaking or chirping blower motors are the result of defective brush holders, so Ford has issued a redesigned motor and will replace those that are under normal warranty. (1993-94)

RECALL HISTORY

1990-91 Nuts that hold windshield wiper motor may loosen or come off. **1990-93** Ignition switch could suffer short circuit, which can cause overheating, smoke, and possibly fire in steering-column area. **1991** Park rod assembly of automatic overdrive transmission may contain a cam with inadequate surface hardness, which could lead to disengagement or non-engagement when lever is placed in "Park" position. **1992-93 cars in specified states** Movement of fuel lines can result in leakage. **1996** Driver's door, when closed only to secondary latched position, may not sustain the specified 1000-pound transverse load. **1996 w/semi-automatic temperature-control** Under certain conditions, blower does not operate as intended.

1995-98 FORD WINDSTAR

✓ BEST BUY

1995 Ford Windstar

FOR Air bags, dual • Anti-lock brakes • Passenger and cargo room • Ride/handling

AGAINST Fuel economy • Instruments/controls • Rear seat entry/exit • Steering feel

EVALUATION Start-up acceleration with the 3.8-liter engine is okay, but the relatively heavy Windstar fails to feel truly lively. The automatic transmission typically pauses before downshifting to pass, and often shifts roughly. The stronger 1996 version of the 3.8-liter doesn't improve performance dramatically, but its extra passing power is appreciated. The 3.0-liter V-6 has to struggle, and feels sluggish when passing. Gas mileage is not the greatest either way. We averaged 15.9 mpg with one Windstar and just 13.8 with another. A 3.0-liter Windstar averaged 16 mpg in urban driving and 20-21 mpg on the highway.

The absorbent suspension delivers a comfortable, stable ride at highway speeds and also on bumpy urban streets. Body lean is moderate, and tires grip well in spirited cornering. On the downside, steering feels loose and imprecise.

Getting in and out of the front seats is just about as easy as in most passenger cars. Climbing into the rear, requires ducking around a shoulder belt for the middle seat. The rear seat must be pushed all the way back on its 7-inch track to produce adequate leg space.

Major controls are backlit at night, and the dashboard is conveniently laid out. The stereo is easy to reach, but controls are small and hard to decipher. Round dials for the climate system are easy to use. With all seats in place, Windstar offers 16 cubic feet of cargo room—more than a Grand Caravan/Voyager.

Windstars haven't proven to be quite as successful as Ford had hoped, but Ford's front-drive model equals or beats Chrysler's minivans in key areas of performance and accommodations. Windstar is well worth a try.

NHTSA CRASH TEST RESULTS
1995 Ford Windstar

3-DOOR VAN

Driver	☆☆☆☆☆
Passenger	☆☆☆☆☆

(The National Highway Traffic Safety Administration tests a vehicle's crashworthiness in front and side collisions. Their ratings suggest the chance of serious injury: ☆☆☆☆☆—10% or less; ☆☆☆☆—10-20% or less; ☆☆☆—20-30% or less; ☆☆—35-45% or less; ☆—More than 45%.)

SPECIFICATIONS

	3-door van
Wheelbase, in.	120.7
Overall length, in.	201.2
Overall width, in.	75.4
Overall height, in.	68.0
Curb weight, lbs.	3800
Cargo volume, cu. ft.	144.0
Fuel capacity, gals.	20.0
Seating capacity	7
Front head room, in.	39.3
Max. front leg room, in.	40.7
Rear head room, in.	38.9
Min. rear leg room, in.	39.2

Powertrain layout: transverse front-engine/front-wheel drive

ENGINES

	ohv V-6	ohv V-6
Size, liters/cu. in.	3.0/182	3.8/232
Horsepower	150	155-200
Torque (lbs./ft.)	170	220-230
EPA city/highway mpg		
4-speed OD automatic	17/25	17/24

FORD

Consumer Guide™ observed MPG

| 4-speed OD automatic | 20.9 | 15.9 |

Built in Canada.

RETAIL PRICES	GOOD	AVERAGE	POOR
1995 Windstar	$10,000-12,500	$9,200-11,500	$7,000-8,800
1996 Windstar	12,000-15,000	10,800-13,500	8,300-10,500
1997 Windstar	13,000-17,500	11,700-16,000	9,000-12,800
1998 Windstar	15,500-21,000	14,000-19,500	11,000-16,000

AVERAGE REPLACEMENT COSTS

A/C Compressor	$380	Constant Velocity Joints	476
Alternator	430	Brakes	320
Radiator	425	Shocks and/or Struts	515
Timing Chain or Belt	520	Exhaust System	425

TROUBLE SPOTS

• **Poor transmission shift** Vehicles with the AX4S automatic transmission may shift harshly from first to second gear. (1996-97)

• **Brakes** The parking brake may fail to release because the release rod breaks and will be replaced under warranty. (1995-98)

• **Air conditioner** Moaning air conditioners are repaired by replacing the A/C compressor clutch and pulley. (1995-97)

• **Engine noise** A clunk heard and/or felt from the floor on acceleration, deceleration, or turns is caused by movement between the body and subframe, which is corrected by installing revised insulators. (1995-96)

• **Air bags** Diagnostic trouble codes for the air bag system flash intermittently requiring reprogramming. (1995)

• **Radio** Whining noises in the radio speakers are caused by the fuel pump in the gas tank. An electronic noise filter must be installed on the fuel pump. (1990-96)

RECALL HISTORY

1995 Wiring harness insulation can abrade on a brace between instrument panel and cowl, resulting in short-circuit and possible fire. **1995** Some passenger air bags may not inflate properly; also, igniter end cap can separate, releasing hot gases. **1995** Improperly tightened alternator output wire may result in overheating and possible fire. **1995-96** Tearing of bond between inner and outer hood panels during minor front-end collisions can result in gap at leading edge of hood; could lead to total separation of outer hood panel. **1996** Due to improperly torqued fasteners, driver's seat on a few minivans may not hold properly in an accident. **1996 w/AX4S automatic transmission** "Park" pawl shaft was improperly positioned; pawl may occasionally fail to engage when selector lever is placed in "park" position, allowing vehicle to roll if parking brake has not been applied. **1996** "Park" pawl abutment bracket has sharp edge, which can cause pawl to hang up and not engage gear; vehicle can move even though indicator shows "Park." **1997** Servo cover can separate, causing transmission fluid to leak and contact catalytic converter; could result in fire. **1998** Damaged bearings on a few minivans can increase steering effort.

RECALL HISTORY
None to date.

1990-92 GEO PRIZM

1992 Geo Prizm GSi 4-door

FOR Acceleration (GSi) • Refinement • Ride • Visibility • Fuel economy

AGAINST Passenger and cargo room • Acceleration (base) • Handling (base)

EVALUATION Base-engine models actually qualify as quick with that stick shift, and the 102-horsepower engine is smooth. Three-speed automatic isn't too sluggish either, though you'll have to push the gas pedal hard when passing. Engine noise is only really bothersome at high speeds. Gas mileage, on the other hand, is sure to satisfy. For more vigorous motion, look for a GSi. With the more powerful engine, it moves out quickly and returns nearly the same gas mileage.

Prizms are agile and responsive in normal driving, though steering can grow twitchy. Expect plenty of body lean and little tire grip around any fast corner on the base model. Fortunately, ride quality is amazingly good as the soft suspension absorbs most bumps with ease.

GEO

The GSi rounds corners with confidence, exerting little penalty on ride quality.

Space in the airy cabin is adequate, though not exactly generous. Front seats offer adequate room, but adults may balk at head/leg space in the backseat. Controls are sensibly laid out, and gauges legible, though lack of a tachometer option on first-year LSi versions is a drawback. Radios are mounted too low for easy operation. Trunk space in the 4-door is skimpy, but the 5-door has an ample cargo hold and a more convenient bumper-height opening.

A high comfort level for the subcompact league, in fact, puts Prizms just below Honda Civic for all-around appeal.

SPECIFICATIONS

	4-door sedan	4-door hatchback
Wheelbase, in.	95.7	95.7
Overall length, in.	170.7	170.7
Overall width, in.	65.2	65.2
Overall height, in.	52.4	52.3
Curb weight, lbs.	2435	2450
Cargo volume, cu. ft.	11.2	32.2
Fuel capacity, gals.	13.2	13.2
Seating capacity	5	5
Front head room, in.	38.3	38.3
Max. front leg room, in.	40.9	40.9
Rear head room, in.	36.1	35.5
Min. rear leg room, in.	31.6	31.6

ENGINES

	dohc I-4	dohc I-4
Size, liters/cu. in.	1.6/98	1.6/98
Horsepower	102	130
Torque (lbs./ft.)	101	105
EPA city/highway mpg		
5-speed OD manual	28/33	25/31
3-speed automatic	25/29	
4-speed OD automatic		23/30
Consumer Guide™ observed MPG		
3-speed automatic	25.1	

Built in USA.

AVERAGE REPLACEMENT COSTS

A/C Compressor	$410	Clutch, Pressure Plate, Bearing	590
Alternator	560	Constant Velocity Joints	660
Radiator	360	Brakes	243
Timing Chain or Belt	215	Shocks and/or Struts	855
Automatic Transmission or Transaxle	975	Exhaust System	445

RETAIL PRICES	GOOD	AVERAGE	POOR
1990 Prizm	$1,500-2,500	$900-1,900	$200-700
1991 Prizm	2,000-3,100	1,400-2,500	500-1,000
1992 Prizm	2,700-3,700	2,100-3,100	800-1,300

TROUBLE SPOTS

• **Cold starting problems** Cars equipped with the 1.6L engine may hesitate or stall on hard acceleration when cold because of a problem with the engine control computer, which will be replaced under the standard warranty or the emissions warranty. (1990-92)

• **Radio** The radio/cassette player may have been built with a capacitor installed wrong causing a key-off battery drain. Chevrolet has a campaign to replace the radios at no charge regardless of mileage, vehicle age, or ownership. (1990)

• **Engine misfire** GM will replace the manifold absolute pressure sensor (an emissions part) and its wiring harness on cars that surge or buck at speeds above 45 mph regardless of mileage or age. (1990)

RECALL HISTORY

1991 Wheel lug nuts on some cars may have been torqued to lower than recommended specification, so wheel could become loose and fall off, with potential for loss of control.

1993-97 GEO PRIZM

✔ BEST BUY

1994 Geo Prizm LSi

FOR   Air bags (later models) • Ride • Fuel economy • Acceleration (1.8-liter) • Quietness • Anti-lock brakes (optional)

AGAINST   Rear-seat room • Radio controls

EVALUATION Acceleration is capable enough with the small engine and either transmission; better yet with the 1.8-liter four—which turns out to be quite zippy. A 1.8-liter LSi with 5-speed averaged 29.7 mpg, with considerable highway driving included, and an inspiring 27.5 mpg in rush-hour commuting. Even with automatic and plenty of commuting time, a Prizm scored 27.1 miles per gallon.

Handling produces no surprises, and the body leans quite a bit in turns but grips securely overall. In the base model, the tires will complain at the slightest hint of high-speed cornering. Optional power steering feels imprecise, but grows firmer once you're into a turn. Ride comfort is impressive for a subcompact, but expect some jolts when the going gets rougher. Wind noise and road rumble are minimal.

Rear passenger space is bigger than before, but occupants might find their knees pushed into the seatbacks ahead. Prizm's trunk is roomy, with a flat floor and bumper-level opening. A split-folding rear seatback adds versatility to the LSi edition. Gauges are easy to view. Climate controls are easy to use, but stereo controls are too low and obstructed by the pull-out beverage holder. The optional CD-player stereo has too many small buttons.

Few small cars are more polished than a Prizm, or as well-constructed. We rank it right alongside the Corolla and Honda's Civic as top subcompacts.

NHTSA CRASH TEST RESULTS
1994 Geo Prizm
4-DOOR SEDAN

Driver	☆☆☆☆
Passenger	☆☆☆☆

(The National Highway Traffic Safety Administration tests a vehicle's crashworthiness in front and side collisions. Their ratings suggest the chance of serious injury: ☆☆☆☆☆—10% or less; ☆☆☆☆—10-20% or less; ☆☆☆—20-30% or less; ☆☆—35-45% or less; ☆—More than 45%.)

SPECIFICATIONS

	4-door sedan
Wheelbase, in.	97.0
Overall length, in.	173.0
Overall width, in.	66.3
Overall height, in.	53.3
Curb weight, lbs.	2359
Cargo volume, cu. ft.	12.7
Fuel capacity, gals.	13.2
Seating capacity	5
Front head room, in.	38.5
Max. front leg room, in.	41.7

	4-door sedan
Rear head room, in.	36.4
Min. rear leg room, in.	33.1

Powertrain layout: transverse front-engine/front-wheel drive

ENGINES

	dohc I-4	dohc I-4
Size, liters/cu. in.	1.6/97	1.8/110
Horsepower	100-108	105-115
Torque (lbs./ft.)	100-105	115-117

EPA city/highway mpg

5-speed OD manual	28/34	29/34
3-speed automatic	26/30	
4-speed OD automatic		27/34

Consumer Guide™ observed MPG

5-speed OD manual	29.7
4-speed OD automatic	27.1

Built in USA.

RETAIL PRICES	GOOD	AVERAGE	POOR
1993 Prizm	$3,800-4,700	$3,200-4,000	$1,800-2,300
1994 Prizm	4,500-5,500	3,800-4,800	2,300-2,800
1995 Prizm	5,600-6,700	4,900-6,000	3,000-3,800
1996 Prizm	6,700-8,000	6,000-7,200	3,800-4,700
1997 Prizm	8,000-9,500	7,300-8,700	4,800-5,800
1998 Prizm	10,500-13,000	9,500-12,000	6,800-9,000

AVERAGE REPLACEMENT COSTS

A/C Compressor $640	Clutch, Pressure Plate, Bearing 530
Alternator 600	Constant Velocity Joints.....570
Radiator 300	Brakes....................................215
Timing Chain or Belt 150	Shocks and/or Struts 910
Automatic Transmission or Transaxle.........................935	Exhaust System 505

TROUBLE SPOTS

• **Steering noise** A squeak or rubbing noise from the steering column is often the result of a loose pinch bolt on the universal joint on the column inside the car. Although annoying, it is fixed by simply loosening and retightening the bolt. (1993-95)

• **Mirrors** The left-hand rear-view mirror can't be adjusted if the plate to which the cables attach cracks, and GM had a campaign to replace the mirrors. This warranty may be extended to subsequent owners. (1993)

GEO

• **Dashboard lights** During assembly some gauge panels' printed circuits were damaged and the panel lights may flash or not work and the fuel gauge may not work. Before replacing a fuel gauge, ask the dealer to check out the panel. (1993)

• **Radio** Because it has a sensor that detects broken tapes, the cassette player may eject CD adapters used with it. There is not necessarily anything wrong with the tape player. (1993-94)

RECALL HISTORY

1993-95 If liquid is spilled in console box area, air bag warning light can illuminate during normal driving conditions and cause air bag to malfunction, deploying inadvertently. **1994** Anchor straps in certain seatbelt assemblies made by Quality Safety Systems were improperly heat treated and can break. **1995** Battery may have defective weld inside terminal, which can result in no-start condition or explosion.

1990-98 GEO/ CHEVROLET TRACKER

1993 Geo Tracker 2-door

FOR 4WD traction (4WD) • Fuel economy • Air bags (later models)

AGAINST Ride • Noise • Rear-seat room

EVALUATION The initial 80-horsepower engine has sufficient power for decent acceleration and passing on the 2-door model. With automatic, you have to push the pedal to the floor often to keep up with traffic. That's true even with the 95-horsepower engine. In addition, four-doors are so sluggish with automatic that passing maneuvers have to be planned with care. Gas mileage is fine. We've averaged 24 mpg in a 4-wheel-drive convertible and 28.6 mpg with 2-wheel drive.

Tall and narrow, a Tracker must be driven with care through turns due to a high center of gravity. Even if it's not quite as precarious as it may seem while cornering, the abundant body lean quickly grows frightening. The ride is undeniably choppy, and noise levels are high. Two-wheel-drive Trackers are softer suspended for easier going on rough pavement, but even they get choppy.

A Tracker's interior is roomy for two in front, but the backseat is best for children. The driver's seat lacks much rearward travel, and suffers minimal space past one's left shoulder. Cargo space behind rear seat is minuscule, but at least you can fold the seat forward if a load of parcels has to be transported. Controls operate smoothly; gauges are simple. Four-door wagons offer lots of head room, adequate rear leg space, and ample cargo area.

More modern and refined than that paramilitary Wrangler, Trackers are appealing in many ways. But, Trackers and Suzuki Sidekicks are just too rough and noisy for service as daily drivers.

NHTSA CRASH TEST RESULTS
1996 Geo Tracker
2-DOOR CONVERTIBLE

Driver	☆☆
Passenger	☆☆☆

(The National Highway Traffic Safety Administration tests a vehicle's crashworthiness in front and side collisions. Their ratings suggest the chance of serious injury: ☆☆☆☆☆—10% or less; ☆☆☆☆—10-20% or less; ☆☆☆—20-30% or less; ☆☆—35-45% or less; ☆—More than 45%.)

SPECIFICATIONS	2-door conv.	4-door wagon
Wheelbase, in.	86.6	97.6
Overall length, in.	143.7	158.7
Overall width, in.	64.2	64.4
Overall height, in.	64.3	65.7
Curb weight, lbs.	2246	2434
Cargo volume, cu. ft.	32.9	45.9
Fuel capacity, gals.	11.1	14.5
Seating capacity	4	4
Front head room, in.	39.5	40.5
Max. front leg room, in.	42.1	42.1
Rear head room, in.	39.0	40.0
Min. rear leg room, in.	31.6	32.7

GEO

Powertrain layout: longitudinal front-engine/rear- or 4-wheel drive

ENGINES

	ohc I-4
Size, liters/cu. in.	1.6/97
Horsepower	80-95
Torque (lbs./ft.)	94-98

EPA city/highway mpg

5-speed OD manual	24/26
3-speed automatic	23/24
4-speed OD automatic	22/25

Consumer Guide™ observed MPG

5-speed OD manual	24.8
4-speed OD automatic	24.0

Built in Japan or Canada.

RETAIL PRICES

	GOOD	AVERAGE	POOR
1990 Tracker	$1,700-2,400	$1,100-1,800	$300-800
1991 Tracker	2,100-3,700	1,500-3,100	500-1,500
1992 Tracker	2,500-4,400	1,900-3,700	800-2,000
1993 Tracker	3,000-5,200	2,400-4,500	1,100-2,600
1994 Tracker	3,800-6,200	3,100-5,500	1,500-3,300
1995 Tracker	4,700-7,200	4,000-6,500	2,100-4,100
1996 Tracker	5,900-9,000	5,200-8,200	2,900-5,300
1997 Tracker	7,500-10,800	6,700-9,800	4,000-6,500
1998 Tracker	9,500-13,000	8,500-12,000	5,500-8,500

AVERAGE REPLACEMENT COSTS

A/C Compressor	$980
Alternator	395
Radiator	665
Timing Chain or Belt	210
Automatic Transmission or Transaxle	740
Clutch, Pressure Plate, Bearing	600
Universal Joints	175
Brakes	370
Shocks and/or Struts	270
Exhaust System	475

TROUBLE SPOTS

• **Exhaust system** The two-piece muffler/tailpipe may rust out prematurely, especially where salt is used on the roads. If the tailpipe rusts through, heat can damage the rear floor and carpet so GM will install a heat shield over the exhaust system. As a recall, this will be performed at no charge. (1990-91)

• **Engine misfire** The PCV breather hose may freeze up while driving in cold weather causing a loss of oil and engine damage, so Chevy will replace the narrow hose with a larger one and may extend coverage to subsequent buyers. (1990)

• **Transmission slippage** An automatic transmission that chuggles or hunts, may be suffering from a torque converter clutch that applies and releases too rapidly, so a time delay relay will be installed in the electrical circuit to correct the problem under normal warranty provisions. (1990-95)

• **Keys** The original keys were made with a soft metal compound that causes them to break. It is a good idea to get new keys made and discard the originals before they break off in a lock. (1990)

• **Brake wear** Aftermarket kits with valves designed to use the hydraulic pressure of the brake system to apply the brakes as a parking brake are reportedly popular. Chevrolet does not condone their usage and will not cover any problems that they deem were related to the add-on system. (1990-91)

RECALL HISTORY

1990-91 Front seatbelt release button can break and pieces can fall inside, causing improper operation. **1995** Steering wheel hub to spoke weld on some vehicles can fracture, allowing steering wheel to separate. **1996 4-door** Fuel tank can puncture during rear-end collision.

1990-94 GMC JIMMY

1992 GMC Jimmy SLT 4-door

FOR Air bag (later models) • Acceleration • 4WD traction • Passenger and cargo room • Anti-lock rear brakes

AGAINST Fuel economy • Noise • Ride • Rear seat entry/exit (2-doors) • No air bags (early models)

See the 1990-94 Chevrolet Blazer report for an evaluation of the 1990-94 GMC Jimmy.

SPECIFICATIONS

	2-door wagon	4-door wagon
Wheelbase, in.	100.5	107.0
Overall length, in.	170.3	176.8
Overall width, in.	65.4	65.4
Overall height, in.	64.3	64.3
Curb weight, lbs.	3536	3776
Cargo volume, cu. ft.	67.3	74.3
Fuel capacity, gals.	20.0	20.0
Seating capacity	4	6
Front head room, in.	39.1	39.1
Max. front leg room, in.	42.5	42.5
Rear head room, in.	38.7	38.8
Min. rear leg room, in.	35.5	36.5

Powertrain layout: longitudinal front-engine/rear- or 4-wheel drive

ENGINES

	ohv V-6	ohv V-6	Turbocharged ohv V-6
Size, liters/cu. in.	4.3/262	4.3/262	4.3/262
Horsepower	160-165	200	280
Torque (lbs./ft.)	230-235	260	350
EPA city/highway mpg			
5-speed OD manual	16/21		
4-speed OD automatic	17/22	16/21	15/19

Built in USA.

RETAIL PRICES

	GOOD	AVERAGE	POOR
1990 Jimmy	$3,300-5,000	$2,600-4,300	$1,300-2,500
1991 Jimmy	4,500-6,700	3,700-5,900	2,000-3,700
1992 Jimmy	5,800-8,400	5,000-7,500	2,900-5,100
1992 Typhoon	11,500-13,000	10,500-12,000	7,500-8,700
1993 Jimmy	6,900-10,000	6,000-9,000	3,800-6,100
1993 Typhoon	13,500-15,000	12,000-13,500	8,800-10,000
1994 Jimmy	8,400-11,500	7,600-10,500	5,200-7,500

AVERAGE REPLACEMENT COSTS

A/C Compressor $365	Clutch, Pressure Plate,
Alternator 195	Bearing 390
Radiator 415	Universal Joints 160
Timing Chain or Belt 205	Brakes...............................210
Automatic Transmission or	Shocks and/or Struts 275
Transaxle.......................735	Exhaust System.................405

TROUBLE SPOTS

• **Engine knock** Continued engine knock on 4.3L V-6 engines during acceleration or climbing a grade has been addressed by at least 15 PROM revisions due to carbon buildup on the pistons. (1992)

• **Transmission leak** Automatic transmission pump may leak (model 4L60). A revised pump bushing is available. (1995-96)

• **Dashboard lights** The oil pressure gauge may read high, move erratically, or not work because the oil pressure sensor is defective. (1990-93)

• **Dashboard lights** ABS system problems include false codes, a warning light that stays on, or speed sensor malfunctions. (1990-91)

• **Engine knock** Engine knock when the engine (4.3L, 5.7L, or 7.4L) is started is usually eliminated by using an oil filter with a check valve (such as Fram PH3980), but if this does not fix it, GM has revised PROMs for the computers and will even replace the main bearings if all else fails. (1990-95)

• **Transmission slippage** Any truck with a model TH-700-R4 automatic transmission may shift late or not upshift at all. The problem is a stuck throttle valve inside the transmission. (1990-94)

RECALL HISTORY

1990-91 Fuel tank sender seal may be out of position; could result in fuel leakage. **1991** Rear seatbelt buckle release button can stick in unlatched position. **1993** Rear seatbelts may not meet government requirements. **1994 with VR4 weight-distribution trailer hitch option** Trailer hitch attaching bolts were not tightened adequately.

1995-98 GMC JIMMY/ENVOY

✓ BEST BUY

1995 GMC Jimmy 4-door

FOR Air bag, driver • Acceleration • Passenger and cargo room • Ride • 4WD traction • Anti-lock brakes

AGAINST Rear-seat comfort • Fuel economy • No passenger-

GMC

side air bag

See the 1995-98 Chevrolet Blazer report for an evaluation of the 1995-98 GMC Jimmy/Envoy.

NHTSA CRASH TEST RESULTS
1997 GMC Jimmy

4-DOOR WAGON

Driver	☆☆☆
Passenger	☆

(The National Highway Traffic Safety Administration tests a vehicle's crashworthiness in front and side collisions. Their ratings suggest the chance of serious injury: ☆☆☆☆☆—10% or less; ☆☆☆☆—10-20% or less; ☆☆☆—20-30% or less; ☆☆—35-45% or less; ☆—More than 45%.)

SPECIFICATIONS

	2-door wagon	4-door wagon
Wheelbase, in.	100.5	107.0
Overall length, in.	175.1	181.2
Overall width, in.	67.8	67.8
Overall height, in.	66.9	67.0
Curb weight, lbs.	3825	4007
Cargo volume, cu. ft.	66.9	74.1
Fuel capacity, gals.	20.0	19.0
Seating capacity	4	6
Front head room, in.	39.6	39.6
Max. front leg room, in.	42.5	42.5
Rear head room, in.	38.2	38.2
Min. rear leg room, in.	36.3	36.3

Powertrain layout: longitudinal front-engine/rear- or 4-wheel drive

ENGINES

	ohv V-6
Size, liters/cu. in.	4.3/262
Horsepower	190-195
Torque (lbs./ft.)	250-260

EPA city/highway mpg

5-speed OD manual	17/22
4-speed OD automatic	16/21

Consumer Guide™ observed MPG

4-speed OD automatic	16.4

Built in USA.

RETAIL PRICES

	GOOD	AVERAGE	POOR
1995 Jimmy 2WD	$10,300-12,100	$9,300-11,100	$6,800-8,500
1995 Jimmy 4WD	12,200-14,200	11,000-13,000	8,200-10,000
1996 Jimmy 2WD	12,700-14,700	11,700-13,300	8,600-15,200
1996 Jimmy 4WD	14,700-16,700	13,400-15,200	10,200-12,000
1997 Jimmy 2WD	15,200-17,200	13,900-15,700	10,500-12,200

	GOOD	AVERAGE	POOR
1997 Jimmy 4WD	17,200-19,200	15,700-17,700	12,000-13,500
1998 Jimmy 2WD	17,700-19,700	16,000-18,200	12,500-14,000
1998 Jimmy 4WD	19,500-22,200	18,000-20,200	14,000-15,500

AVERAGE REPLACEMENT COSTS

A/C Compressor	$520	Clutch, Pressure Plate,	
Alternator	225	Bearing	800
Radiator	450	Universal Joints	270
Timing Chain or Belt	230	Brakes	220
Automatic Transmission or		Shocks and/or Struts	410
Transaxle	850	Exhaust System	485

TROUBLE SPOTS

• **Dashboard lights** The oil pressure gauge may read high, move erratically, or not work because the oil pressure sensor is defective. (1990-93)

• **Engine noise** The exhaust valves may not get enough lubrication causing a variety of noises that sound like lifter tick, rod knock or a "whoop-whoop" noise like a helicopter. Usually, the same engine consumes excess oil because the valve guide seals on the exhaust valves are bad and have to be replaced. (1996)

• **Engine knock** Engine knock when the engine is first started is usually eliminated by using an oil filter with a check valve (such as Fram PH3980), but if this does not fix it, GM has revised PROMs for the computers and may even replace the main bearings if no other solution is found. (1995)

• **Engine misfire** A problem with the powertrain control module may cause a lack of power (especially when carrying heavy loads or under heavy acceleration), early upshifts, late shifting in the 4WD-Low range, and otherwise erratic performance. (1996-97)

• **Transmission leak** Fluid may leak from the pump body on 4L60-E transmissions due to the pump bushing walking out of the valve body. (1995-96)

RECALL HISTORY

1995 Brake pedal bolt on some vehicles might disengage, causing loss of braking. **1995 4WD** A few upper ball joint nuts were undertorqued; stud can loosen and fracture. **1995 w/air conditioning** Fan blade rivets can break and allow blade to separate from hub. **1995-96 AWD/4WD** During testing, prop shaft contacted fuel tank, rupturing the tank; fuel leakage was beyond permissible level. **1998** Fatigue fracture of rear-axle brake pipe can occur, causing slow fluid leak and resulting in soft brake pedal; if pipe breaks, driver would face sudden loss of rear-brake performance. **1998 w/4WD or AWD** On a few vehicles, one or both attaching bolts for lower control arm could separate from frame, resulting in loss of control.

1990-93 GMC S15/ SONOMA PICKUP

✓ BEST BUY

1991 GMC Sonoma

FOR Acceleration (V-6) • Payload • Interior storage space (ext. cab)

AGAINST Acceleration (4-cylinder) • Refinement • Seat comfort

See the 1990-93 Chevrolet S10 report for an evaluation of the 1990-93 GMC S15/Sonoma.

SPECIFICATIONS	reg. cab short bed	reg. cab short bed	ext. cab
Wheelbase, in.	108.3	117.9	122.9
Overall length, in.	178.2	194.2	192.8
Overall width, in.	64.7	64.7	64.7
Overall height, in.	61.3	61.3	61.3
Curb weight, lbs.	2635	2773	3024
Max. payload lbs.	1892	1901	1776
Fuel capacity, gals.	20.0	20.0	20.0
Seating capacity	3	3	5
Front head room, in.	39.1	39.1	39.1
Max. front leg room, in.	42.5	42.5	42.5
Rear head room, in.	—	—	NA
Min. rear leg room, in.	—	—	NA

Powertrain layout: longitudinal front-engine/rear- or 4-wheel drive

ENGINES

	ohv I-4	ohv V-6	ohv V-6	Turbocharged ohc V-6
Size, liters/cu. in.	2.5/151	2.8/173	4.3/262	4.3/262
Horsepower	94-105	125	160-195	280
Torque (lbs./ft.)	130-135	150	230-260	360

EPA city/highway mpg

5-speed OD manual	23/27	19/25	17/22	
4-speed OD automatic.....	20/26		17/22	NA

Consumer Guide™ observed MPG

4-speed OD automatic.....	17.2

Built in USA.

RETAIL PRICES

	GOOD	AVERAGE	POOR
1990 S15 2WD	$1,400-2,400	$900-1,800	$300-700
1990 S15 4WD	2,600-3,800	2,000-3,100	900-1,600
1991 Sonoma 2WD	1,900-3,900	1,300-3,300	500-1,800
1991 Sonoma 4WD	3,500-5,500	2,800-4,800	1,400-2,000
1991 Syclone 4WD	9,000-10,500	8,000-9,500	5,500-6,500
1992 Sonoma 2WD	3,000-6,000	2,400-5,300	1,000-3,200
1992 Sonoma 4WD	4,800-7,200	4,100-6,500	2,300-4,000
1992 Syclone 4WD	10,500-12,000	9,200-10,500	6,500-7,500
1993 Sonoma 2WD	3,800-6,000	3,100-5,300	1,400-3,100
1993 Sonoma 4WD	5,300-8,300	4,500-7,500	2,500-4,800

AVERAGE REPLACEMENT COSTS

A/C Compressor $365	Clutch, Pressure Plate, Bearing............................415
Alternator 195	Universal Joints 190
Radiator 325	Brakes..................................207
Timing Chain or Belt 205	Shocks and/or Struts 370
Automatic Transmission or Transaxle.........................735	Exhaust System.................335

TROUBLE SPOTS

• **Engine knock** Continued engine knock on 4.3L V-6 engines during acceleration or climbing a grade due to carbon buildup on the pistons. (1992)

• **Dashboard lights** The oil pressure gauge may read high, move erratically or not work because the oil pressure sensor is defective. (1990-93)

• **Climate control** The temperature control lever may spontaneously slide from hot to cold, usually when the blower is on high speed. (1992-93)

• **Engine misfire** The EGR valve may stick open due to carbon

GMC

deposits causing rough idle (1994)

• **Automatic transmission** Any truck with a model 700-R4 automatic transmission may shift late or not upshift at all because of a stuck throttle valve inside the transmission. (1990-93)

• **Hard starting** Engines with TBI may be hard to start after hot soak. (1990-93)

RECALL HISTORY

1990-92 without air conditioning Fan blades on 2.5-liter engine can break as a result of fatigue. **1991** Fuel tank sender seal may be out of position. **1991 S15/T15** Nut used to attach lower control arms, rear spring/shackle/shocks could "strip."

1990-98 GMC SAFARI

1996 GMC Safari

FOR Air bags (later models) • Anti-lock brakes • Optional all-wheel drive traction • Passenger and cargo room • Trailer towing capability

AGAINST Fuel economy • Entry/exit • Ride

See the 1990-98 Chevrolet Astro report for an evaluation of the 1990-98 GMC Safari.

NHTSA CRASH TEST RESULTS
1996 GMC Safari

3-DOOR VAN

Driver	☆☆☆
Passenger	☆☆☆

(The National Highway Traffic Safety Administration tests a vehicle's crashworthiness in front and side collisions. Their ratings suggest the chance of serious injury: ☆☆☆☆☆—10% or less; ☆☆☆☆—10-20% or less; ☆☆☆—20-30% or less; ☆☆—35-45% or less; ☆—More than 45%.)

SPECIFICATIONS

	3-door van	3-door van	3-door van
Wheelbase, in.	111.0	111.0	111.0
Overall length, in.	176.8	186.8	189.8
Overall width, in.	77.0	77.0	77.0
Overall height, in.	76.4	76.4	76.1
Curb weight, lbs.	3960	3960	4068
Cargo volume, cu. ft.	151.8	170.4	170.4
Fuel capacity, gals.	27.0	27.0	27.0
Seating capacity	8	8	8
Front head room, in.	39.2	39.2	39.2
Max. front leg room, in.	41.6	41.6	41.6
Rear head room, in.	37.9	37.9	37.9
Min. rear leg room, in.	36.5	36.5	36.5

Powertrain layout: longitudinal front-engine/rear- or all-wheel drive

ENGINES

	ohv V-6	ohv V-6
Size, liters/cu. in.	4.3/262	4.3/262
Horsepower	150-165	175-200
Torque (lbs./ft.)	230-235	230-260
EPA city/highway mpg		
4-speed OD automatic	16/21	16/20
Consumer Guide™ observed MPG		
4-speed OD automatic	14.5	18.3

Built in USA.

AVERAGE REPLACEMENT COSTS

A/C Compressor	$515	Clutch, Pressure Plate, Bearing	555
Alternator	245	Universal Joints	153
Radiator	420	Brakes	225
Timing Chain or Belt	255	Shocks and/or Struts	247
Automatic Transmission or Transaxle	770	Exhaust System	320

RETAIL PRICES

	GOOD	AVERAGE	POOR
1990 Safari	$3,300-5,000	$2,600-4,200	$1,200-2,200
1991 Safari	4,100-6,700	3,300-5,700	1,600-3,500
1992 Safari	5,000-7,500	4,200-6,500	2,300-4,300
1993 Safari	6,000-8,800	5,000-7,800	3,000-5,400
1994 Safari	7,000-9,900	6,000-8,900	4,000-6,700
1995 Safari	9,100-11,800	7,800-10,300	5,500-7,500
1996 Safari	11,500-14,500	10,000-13,000	7,400-9,900
1997 Safari	13,600-16,700	12,100-14,900	9,000-11,500
1998 Safari	16,500-19,200	14,500-17,200	11,500-13,500

TROUBLE SPOTS

• **Engine noise** A whooping noise (similar to a helicopter) coming from the engine may be caused by the exhaust valves sticking in their guides, and new valve guide seals should correct the problem if the guides are not worn. (1996)

• **Cold starting problems** New valve guide seals should eliminate the blue smoke from the tailpipe during cold starting. (1990-93)

• **Hard starting** The fuel injector wires tend to get pinched when the air filter is reinstalled. (1990-93)

• **Doors** The sliding door is hard to open or close, or does not glide smoothly because various parts are out of adjustment. (1990-93)

• **Engine noise** A knocking sound from deep in the engine after sitting overnight may require either an oil filter having a built-in check valve, a revised PROM or replacing the main bearings. (1990-95)

• **Transmission leak** The rear seal on the transmission may leak on vans with a one-piece drive shaft. (1990-94)

• **Engine misfire** The engine speed may flare during downshifts between third and second due to a faulty transmission control solenoid. (1996)

RECALL HISTORY

1990-91 Bucket seat's knob recliner mechanism may loosen and cause bolt failure, allowing seatback to recline suddenly. **1995 w/L35 engine** Fuel lines at tank were improperly tightened and could loosen. **1995** On a few vans, left lower control arm bolt could loosen, fatigue, and break. **1996-97** Outboard seatbelt webbing on right rear bucket seat can separate during crash.

1990-98 GMC SIERRA PICKUP

FOR Air bag (later models) • Anti-lock brakes (later models) • Acceleration (V-8) • Trailer towing capability • Visibility • Passenger and cargo room

AGAINST Fuel economy • Instruments/controls • Ride • Noise

See the 1990-98 Chevrolet C/K report for an evaluation of the 1990-98 GMC Sierra.

NHTSA CRASH TEST RESULTS
1995 GMC Sierra

REG. CAB

Driver ☆☆☆☆☆

1992 GMC Sierra

Passenger ☆☆☆☆☆

(The National Highway Traffic Safety Administration tests a vehicle's crashworthiness in front and side collisions. Their ratings suggest the chance of serious injury: ☆☆☆☆☆—10% or less; ☆☆☆☆—10-20% or less; ☆☆☆—20-30% or less; ☆☆—35-45% or less; ☆—More than 45%.)

SPECIFICATIONS	reg. cab short bed	reg. cab long bed	ext. cab short bed	ext. cab long bed
Wheelbase, in.	117.5	131.5	141.5	155.5
Overall length, in.	194.5	213.4	218.4	237.1
Overall width, in.	76.8	76.8	76.8	76.8
Overall height, in.	70.4	70.4	70.4	74.9
Curb weight, lbs.	3849	4001	4140	7387
Max. payload, lbs.	2410	5380	3260	5040
Fuel capacity, gals.	25.0	34.0	34.0	34.0
Seating capacity	3	3	6	6
Front head room, in.	40.0	40.0	40.0	40.0
Max. front leg room, in.	41.7	41.7	41.7	41.7
Rear head room, in.	—	—	37.5	37.5
Min. rear leg room, in.	—	—	34.8	34.8

Powertrain layout: longitudinal front-engine/rear- or 4-wheel drive

ENGINES	ohv V-6	ohv V-8	ohv V-8	ohv V-8
Size, liters/cu. in.	4.3/262	5.0/305	5.7/350	7.4/454
Horsepower	160-200	175-230	200-255	230-290
Torque (lbs./ft.)	235-255	270-285	300-335	285-410
EPA city/highway mpg				
4-speed manual	18/20		13/16	
5-speed OD manual	17/22	15/20	14/20	
4-speed OD automatic	17/22	15/19	15/19	10/12

GMC

Consumer Guide™ observed MPG
4-speed OD automatic.....   14.5   13.0

Built in USA and Canada.

ENGINES

	Diesel ohv V-8	Diesel ohv V-8	Turbodiesel ohv V-8
Size, liters/cu. in.	6.2/379	6.5/400	6.5/400
Horsepower	140	155	180-190
Torque (lbs./ft.)	255	255	360

EPA city/highway mpg

	Diesel ohv V-8	Diesel ohv V-8	Turbodiesel ohv V-8
4-speed manual	19/21		
5-speed OD manual		19/23	
4-speed OD automatic	18/24	17/22	16/21

RETAIL PRICES

	GOOD	AVERAGE	POOR
1990 Sierra 1500	$2,800-6,500	$2,200-5,700	$1,000-3,800
1990 Sierra 2500	4,400-7,000	3,700-6,200	1,700-4,000
1991 Sierra 1500	3,800-8,600	3,100-7,800	1,400-5,200
1991 Sierra 2500	5,600-9,000	4,700-8,000	2,500-5,300
1992 Sierra 1500	4,600-10,500	3,800-9,500	1,700-6,600
1992 Sierra 2500	6,700-10,700	5,800-9,700	3,500-6,600
1993 Sierra 1500	5,500-11,800	4,700-10,500	2,400-7,500
1993 Sierra 2500	8,500-12,300	7,500-11,000	4,800-7,700
1994 Sierra 1500	6,300-14,200	5,500-13,000	3,200-9,800
1994 Sierra 2500	10,100-14,300	9,100-13,300	6,000-10,000
1995 Sierra 1500	7,500-15,700	6,700-14,500	3,700-11,300
1995 Sierra 2500	11,500-16,200	10,500-15,100	7,500-11,500
1996 Sierra 1500	9,200-17,900	8,000-16,400	5,000-12,800
1996 Sierra 2500	13,800-19,000	12,300-17,500	8,500-13,300
1997 Sierra 1500	11,200-20,200	9,700-18,700	6,300-14,500
1997 Sierra 2500	15,500-21,000	14,000-19,500	10,000-15,300
1998 Sierra 1500	13,200-22,500	11,700-21,000	8,000-16,300
1998 Sierra 2500	16,700-23,500	15,200-21,500	11,500-16,500

AVERAGE REPLACEMENT COSTS

A/C Compressor $560	Clutch, Pressure Plate,
Alternator 378	Bearing 595
Radiator 350	Brakes....................................230
Timing Chain or Belt 210	Shocks and/or Struts 335
Automatic Transmission or	Exhaust System.................420
Transaxle.........................725	

TROUBLE SPOTS

• **Engine knock** Continued engine knock on 4.3L V-6 engines during acceleration or climbing a grade has been addressed by at least 15 PROM revisions due to carbon buildup on the pistons. (1992)

• **Dashboard lights** The oil pressure gauge may read high, move erratically, or not work because the oil pressure sensor is defective. (1990-93)

• **Climate control** The temperature control lever may slide from hot to cold, usually when the blower is on high speed. (1992-94)

• **Transmission leak** Fluid may leak from the pump body on 4L60-E transmissions due to the pump bushing walking out of the valve body. (1995-96)

• **Engine noise** Engine knock when the engine (4.3L, 5.7L, or 7.4L) is started is usually eliminated by using an oil filter with a check valve (such as Fram PH3980), but if this does not fix it, GM has revised PROMs for the computers and will even replace the main bearings if all else fails. (1990-95)

• **Engine noise** The exhaust valves on the 4.3L, 5.0L, or 5.7L engine may not get enough lubrication causing a variety of noises that sound like lifter tick, rod knock, or a "whoop-whoop" noise like a helicopter.

• **Oil consumption** Usually, the same engine consumes excess oil because the valve guide seals on the exhaust valves are bad and have to be replaced. (1996)

• **Cruise control** If the cruise control cuts out and won't reset unless the key is turned off then back on, the cruise control module is too sensitive to vibrations at the brake pedal that cause switch contact bounce. (1994-95)

• **Transmission slippage** Transmission (4L60) binds in reverse, upshifts harshly, fails to upshift at WOT when hot, or sticks in first gear. (1990-91)

• **Transmission slippage** Any truck with a model 700-R4 automatic transmission may shift late or not upshift at all. The problem is a stuck throttle valve inside the transmission. (1990-92)

RECALL HISTORY

1990 diesel Fuel lines can contact automatic transmission linkage shaft or propshaft. **1994** Some driver's seats could loosen. **1994** Brake pedal retainer may be missing or mispositioned. **1990, 92** Brake-pedal bolt could disengage. **1994-95** Extended C10/15 with high-back buckets or 60/40 bench: Seatback might recline suddenly. **1995** Steering-column nut could detach. **1995-96 w/gas engine** throttle cable may contact dash mat and bind. **1996 C-10/15 w/7.4-liter engine** Fuel may leak. **1996** Rear-axle U-bolts could loosen and eventually fall off. **1997 C-15/25** One or two of the front seat mounting bolts were not installed; seat will not protect occupant properly in the event of a crash. **1998 extended-cab and 4-door utility** Steering gear bolt can loosen and fall out, resulting in separation of shaft from gear. **1998** On some trucks, one or both front brake rotor/hubs may have out-of-spec gray iron that can fail during life of vehicle.

1994-98 GMC SONOMA PICKUP

1994 GMC Sonoma

FOR Air bag (later models) • Passenger room • Acceleration (V-6) • Instruments/controls • Optional third door (later models)

AGAINST Seat comfort (front passenger) • Handling • Ride • Rear seat room

See the 1994-98 Chevrolet S-Series report for an evaluation of the 1994-98 GMC Sonoma.

NHTSA CRASH TEST RESULTS
1997 GMC Sonoma   REG. CAB

Driver	☆☆☆
Passenger	☆☆

(The National Highway Traffic Safety Administration tests a vehicle's crashworthiness in front and side collisions. Their ratings suggest the chance of serious injury: ☆☆☆☆☆—10% or less; ☆☆☆☆—10-20% or less; ☆☆☆—20-30% or less; ☆☆—35-45% or less; ☆—More than 45%.)

SPECIFICATIONS	reg. cab short bed	reg. cab long bed	ext. cab
Wheelbase, in.	108.3	117.9	122.9
Overall length, in.	189.0	205.0	203.7
Overall width, in.	67.9	67.9	67.9
Overall height, in.	62.1	62.1	62.2
Curb weight, lbs.	2930	2983	3168
Max. payload, lbs.	1667	1727	1461

	reg. cab short bed	reg. cab long bed	ext. cab
Fuel capacity, gals.	20.0	20.0	20.0
Seating capacity	3	3	5
Front head room, in.	39.5	39.5	39.5
Max. front leg room, in.	43.2	43.2	43.2
Rear head room, in.	—	—	NA
Min. rear leg room, in.	—	—	NA

Powertrain layout: longitudinal front-engine/rear- or 4-wheel drive

ENGINES

	ohv I-4	ohv V-6	ohv V-6
Size, liters/cu. in.	2.2/134	4.3/262	4.3/262
Horsepower	118	155-180	180-195
Torque (lbs./ft.)	130	235	245-260

EPA city/highway mpg

5-speed OD manual	23/30	18/25	18/25
4-speed OD automatic	20/27	19/24	20/24

Consumer Guide™ observed MPG

5-speed OD manual	22.3		
4-speed OD automatic		18.4	18.0

Built in USA.

RETAIL PRICES	GOOD	AVERAGE	POOR
1994 Sonoma	$5,200-10,000	$4,400-9,000	$2,200-6,400
1995 Sonoma	6,400-11,700	5,600-10,700	3,300-7,600
1996 Sonoma	7,700-13,000	6,700-12,000	4,200-9,000
1997 Sonoma	8,900-15,500	7,800-14,500	5,200-10,800
1998 Sonoma	10,800-17,500	9,500-16,000	6,600-12,200

AVERAGE REPLACEMENT COSTS

A/C Compressor $550	Clutch, Pressure Plate, Bearing............................545
Alternator 255	Universal Joints 190
Radiator 410	Brakes..................................210
Timing Chain or Belt 420	Shocks and/or Struts 345
Automatic Transmission or Transaxle.........................750	Exhaust System.................450

TROUBLE SPOTS

• **Doors** The power door locks may not operate although the doors can be locked manually due to a rubber bumper falling off of the actuator arm. (1997)

• **Engine knock** Engine knock when the engine (4.3L, 5.7L, or 7.4L) is started is usually eliminated by using an oil filter with a check valve (such as Fram PH3980), but if this does not fix it, GM has revised PROMs for the computers and will even replace the main bearings if all else fails. (1990-95)

- **Engine temperature** Poor cooling or irregular gauge reading possible after water pump replacement. (1994-95)
- **Hard starting** Engines with TBI may be hard to start after hot soak. (1994)
- **Fuel pump** The fuel pump may run after the key is turned off. (1994-95)

RECALL HISTORY

1994 w/2.2-liter engine Vacuum hose can detach from power brake booster check valve as a result of backfire. **1996 2WD manual shift w/2.2-liter engine** Drive wheels could seize and lock while truck is moving. **1996** Top coat of paint on a few trucks peels severely. **1997 w/4.3-liter engine** Front brake line can contact oil pan, causing wear that may result in fluid loss. **1994-97** Seatbelt webbing on certain models can separate during frontal impact. **1995 w/air conditioning and 4.3-liter engine** Rivets can break and allow fan blade to separate from hub; if hood were open, a person could be struck by blade. **1996-97 w/4.3-liter engine** Front brake line can contact oil pan, causing wear that may result in fluid loss. **1998** Fatigue fracture of rear-axle brake pipe can occur, causing slow fluid leak and resulting in soft brake pedal; if pipe breaks, driver would face sudden loss of rear-brake performance. **1998** Wiring-harness clip can melt and drip onto exhaust manifold, possibly resulting in fire.

1992-98 GMC YUKON/DENALI

✓ BEST BUY

1992 GMC Yukon 2-door

FOR Air bags (later models) • Anti-lock brakes • Ride (4-door)

• Quietness • Passenger and cargo room • Trailer towing capability

AGAINST Fuel economy • Maneuverability • Ride (2-door) • Entry/Exit (2-door & 4WD)

See the 1992-98 Chevrolet Tahoe report for an evaluation of the 1992-98 GMC Yukon/Denali.

NHTSA CRASH TEST RESULTS
1997 GMC Yukon   4-DOOR WAGON

Driver	☆☆☆☆
Passenger	☆☆☆☆

(The National Highway Traffic Safety Administration tests a vehicle's crashworthiness in front and side collisions. Their ratings suggest the chance of serious injury: ☆☆☆☆☆—10% or less; ☆☆☆☆—10-20% or less; ☆☆☆—20-30% or less; ☆☆—35-45% or less; ☆—More than 45%.)

SPECIFICATIONS

	2-door wagon	4-door wagon
Wheelbase, in.	111.5	117.5
Overall length, in.	188.5	199.1
Overall width, in.	77.1	76.4
Overall height, in.	72.4	70.2
Curb weight, lbs.	4731	5134
Cargo volume, cu. ft.	99.4	122.9
Fuel capacity, gals.	30.5	30.5
Seating capacity	6	6
Front head room, in.	39.9	39.9
Max. front leg room, in.	41.9	41.7
Rear head room, in.	37.8	38.9
Min. rear leg room, in.	36.3	36.7

Powertrain layout: longitudinal front-engine/rear- or 4-wheel drive

ENGINES	ohv V-8	ohv V-8	Turbodiesel ohv V-8
Size, liters/cu. in.	5.7/350	5.7/350	6.5/400
Horsepower	200-210	250-255	180
Torque (lbs./ft.)	300	330-335	360
EPA city/highway mpg			
5-speed OD manual	12/16		
4-speed OD automatic	12/15	14/17	15/18
Consumer Guide™ observed MPG			
4-speed OD automatic	12.5	14.3	

Built in USA and Mexico.

RETAIL PRICES	GOOD	AVERAGE	POOR
1992 Yukon 4WD	$9,500-11,500	$8,500-10,500	$6,000-7,500

GMC

	GOOD	AVERAGE	POOR
1993 Yukon 4WD	11,000-13,000	10,000-12,000	7,300-9,000
1994 Yukon 4WD	13,000-15,000	11,800-13,500	9,000-10,500
1995 Yukon 2WD 4-door	14,000-16,000	12,700-14,500	9,500-11,000
1995 Yukon 4WD	15,500-20,000	14,000-18,500	10,800-15,000
1996 Yukon 2WD	17,000-20,700	15,500-19,200	12,000-15,200
1996 Yukon 4WD	18,700-23,700	17,200-22,200	13,500-18,000
1997 Yukon 2WD	19,000-24,000	17,700-22,500	14,500-18,500
1997 Yukon 4WD	21,500-26,500	19,500-24,500	15,800-20,300
1998 Yukon 2WD	22,500-27,000	21,000-25,500	17,000-21,000
1998 Yukon 4WD	25,000-29,000	23,000-27,000	19,000-22,000

AVERAGE REPLACEMENT COSTS

A/C Compressor $555
Alternator 220
Radiator 650
Timing Chain or Belt 415
Automatic Transmission or
  Transaxle........................750

Clutch, Pressure Plate,
  Bearing............................730
Universal Joints 225
Brakes.................................260
Shocks and/or Struts 340
Exhaust System.................380

TROUBLE SPOTS

• **Dashboard lights** The oil pressure gauge may read high, move erratically, or not work because of a defective oil pressure sensor. (1992-93)

• **Engine noise** The exhaust valves may not get enough lubrication causing a variety of noises that sound like lifter tick, rod knock, or a "whoop-whoop" noise like a helicopter. Usually, the same engine consumes excess oil because the valve guide seals on the exhaust valves are bad and have to be replaced. (1996)

• **Engine knock** Engine knock when the engine (4.3L, 5.7L, or 7.4L) is started is usually eliminated by using an oil filter with a check valve (such as Fram PH3980), but if this does not fix it, GM has revised PROMs for the computers, or engine may require main bearings. (1995)

• **Engine misfire** A problem with the powertrain control module may cause a lack of power (especially when carrying heavy loads or under heavy acceleration), early upshifts, late shifting in the 4WD-Low range, and otherwise erratic performance. (1996)

• **Climate control** The temperature control lever may slide from hot to cold, usually when the blower is on high speed. (1992-94)

• **Transmission slippage** Automatic transmissions may suffer harsh or shuddering shifts between first and second or may buzz or vibrate in park or neutral. (1992)

RECALL HISTORY

1992 Brake-pedal pivot bolt can disengage, resulting in loss of brake control. **1995 w/M30/MT1 automatic transmission** When shift lever is placed in "Park" position, indicator may not illuminate. **1995-96 w/gas engine** Throttle cable may contact dash mat and bind; engine speed might then not return to idle. **1998** On some vehicles, one or both front brake rotor/hubs may have out-of-spec gray iron that can fail during life of vehicle.

1990-93 HONDA ACCORD

✓ BEST BUY

1990 Honda Accord EX 2-door

FOR   Air bag, driver • Anti-lock brakes (later models) • Passenger and cargo room • Fuel economy • Handling • Ride

AGAINST   Automatic transmission performance • Rear-seat room • Road noise

EVALUATION   Four-cylinder engines are both smoother and quieter, but takeoffs and passing response are not brisk enough to match the V-6 engines offered by rivals. In addition, the automatic transmission can be jerky at times, and occasionally harsh. On the plus side, fuel economy should be exceptional with any model.

Despite its added length, there is only modest rear-seat room (for a midsize car), and below-average head room in both sedans and coupes. The wagon is also smaller when compared with the Taurus and Camry, providing the least cargo room of the three.

Still, pluses tend to out number minuses. The Accord generally makes up for perceived deficiencies with high levels of overall quality, refinement, and performance when compared with the competition. Blessed with outstanding ride quality, high reliability, and sensible controls nestled in an airy, low-cowl cabin that's

HONDA

become a Honda trademark, the Accord continues to impress.

SPECIFICATIONS	2-door coupe	4-door sedan	4-door wagon
Wheelbase, in.	107.1	107.1	107.1
Overall length, in.	184.8	185.2	186.8
Overall width, in.	53.9	67.1	67.5
Overall height, in.	54.1	54.7	55.1
Curb weight, lbs.	2738	2733	3139
Cargo volume, cu. ft.	14.4	14.4	64.6
Fuel capacity, gals.	17.0	17.0	17.0
Seating capacity	5	5	5
Front head room, in.	38.8	38.9	39.0
Max. front leg room, in.	42.9	42.6	42.7
Rear head room, in.	36.5	37.5	37.6
Min. rear leg room, in.	32.3	34.3	34.1

ENGINES	ohc I-4	ohc I-4	ohc I-4
Size, liters/cu. in.	2.2/132	2.2/132	2.2/132
Horsepower	125	130	140
Torque (lbs./ft.)	137	142	142

EPA city/highway mpg

5-speed OD manual	24/30		22/27
4-speed OD automatic	22/28	22/28	22/28

Consumer Guide™ observed MPG

4-speed OD automatic		21.5	21.2

Built in USA and Japan.

RETAIL PRICES	GOOD	AVERAGE	POOR
1990 Accord	$3,400-4,800	$2,800-4,200	$1,200-2,000
1991 Accord	4,100-6,200	3,500-5,500	1,700-3,200
1992 Accord	4,900-7,500	4,300-6,800	2,300-4,300
1993 Accord	6,000-9,500	5,300-8,700	3,200-5,900

AVERAGE REPLACEMENT COSTS

A/C Compressor	$530
Alternator	355
Radiator	485
Timing Chain or Belt	350
Automatic Transmission or Transaxle	1,055
Clutch, Pressure Plate, Bearing	550
Constant Velocity Joints	670
Brakes	250
Shocks and/or Struts	545
Exhaust System	465

TROUBLE SPOTS

• **Engine noise** A squealing noise from under the hood is likely to be caused by a worn alternator bearing, and it may have failed because the belt tension was too great. Under warranty, the bearing (or alternator if it is damaged) will be replaced. (1990-93)

• **Brakes** The parking brake may not fully release (handle won't go all the way down) causing the warning light to stay on and an ABS light to come on because a rivet on the brake rod is too tight. (1993)

• **Radio** If the CD changer in the trunk will not eject, the company will exchange the CD magazines with a redesigned one. To get the old one out, slide a slim jim or metal ruler between the lower side of the CD magazine and the changer, then push the eject lever toward the back of the unit while pulling on the magazine. (All)

• **Steering noise** If there is a squeak or squeal in the steering, especially when making a slow, tight turn, look for a label on the power steering reservoir that says PSF-V additive was added. If the noise is still there after additive was installed, the right side end seal on the steering rack will have to be replaced; more additive will damage other seals. (1990-93)

• **Tire wear** Cars equipped with Goodyear tires are (were) eligible for replacement tires with better wear characteristics on a pro rata basis as well as a wheel alignment. As with all vehicles, proper toe and caster settings are vital. For extended tire life, buyers may choose not to replace tires with exactly the same ones as original equipment. (1990-93)

• **Transmission slippage** Cars with high mileage may begin to shift more harshly, which may be corrected by adding a bottle of Lubeguard conditioner to the automatic transmission fluid. If this does not soften the shifts, it may be necessary to rebuild the transmission. (1990-93)

RECALL HISTORY

1990-91 Front seatbelt release button can break and pieces can fall inside. **1991 wagon** Improperly attached washer in cargo area light may have fallen inside during assembly; if tailgate is open and switch is in its middle position, washer can cause short circuit that causes switch to overheat, resulting in fire. **1991-93 wagon** Rear outside seatbelts may lock-up at angles other than those required by federal standard; could increase risk of injury in sudden stop or accident. **1992** Left seatbelt assemblies on a few cars were installed on the right side; belt cannot be pulled out of the retractor, making it unusable.

1994-97 HONDA ACCORD ✓ BEST BUY

FOR Air bags • Acceleration (V-6) • Passenger and cargo room • Ride • Steering/handling

AGAINST Acceleration (4-cylinder) • Road noise • Anti-lock brakes (limited availability)

EVALUATION The best Accord yet, the 1994 to '96 models

HONDA

1996 Honda Accord EX 4-door

feel much more substantial than their predecessor. Four-cylinder performance is adequate for most driving needs, but the V-6's added punch comes in quite handy in passing situations. The automatic transmission still lags behind the competition in shift quality, but it's now at least acceptable. Steering is firm and the car tracks effortlessly. There's also less wind noise than before.

The body, now three inches wider than before, significantly increases the interior's feeling of spaciousness. Leg room is good both front and rear, but head room is only average at best. The driver's seat provides a commanding view of the road, thanks to thin pillars and a low cowl. A wider trunk opening is also greatly appreciated. And while the rear seatback drops forward to allow the transport of large and bulky objects, it does not fold fully flat.

Overall, the Accord continues to be a fine, solid-feeling family car with a refined, sporty manner. The new V-6 is most welcome, but long overdue. There is much stronger competition among midsize family sedans today than ever before, with Honda's rivals making noticeable strides in the areas of styling, power-train sophistication, chassis dynamics, ergonomics, and creature comforts.

NHTSA CRASH TEST RESULTS
1996 Accord 4-door

4-DOOR SEDAN

Driver	☆☆☆☆
Passenger	☆☆☆

(The National Highway Traffic Safety Administration tests a vehicle's crashworthiness in front and side collisions. Their ratings suggest the chance of serious injury: ☆☆☆☆☆—10% or less; ☆☆☆☆—10-20% or less; ☆☆☆—20-30% or less; ☆☆—35-45% or less; ☆—More than 45%.)

SPECIFICATIONS

	2-door coupe	4-door sedan	4-door wagon
Wheelbase, in.	106.9	106.9	106.9

	2-door coupe	4-door sedan	4-door wagon
Overall length, in.	185.6	185.6	188.4
Overall width, in.	70.1	70.1	70.1
Overall height, in.	54.7	55.1	55.9
Curb weight, lbs.	2855	2855	3053
Cargo volume, cu. ft.	13.0	13.0	25.7
Fuel capacity, gals.	17.0	17.0	17.0
Seating capacity	5	5	5
Front head room, in.	39.4	39.4	39.8
Max. front leg room, in.	42.9	42.7	42.7
Rear head room, in.	36.4	37.6	39.0
Min. rear leg room, in.	31.3	34.3	34.1

Powertrain layout: transverse front-engine/front-wheel drive

ENGINES

	ohc I-4	ohc I-4	ohc V-6
Size, liters/cu. in.	2.2/132	2.2/132	2.7/163
Horsepower	130	145	170
Torque (lbs./ft.)	139	147	165
EPA city/highway mpg			
5-speed OD manual	25/32	25/31	
4-speed OD automatic	23/31	23/29	19/25
Consumer Guide™ observed MPG			
4-speed OD automatic		23.3	21.0

Built in USA and Japan.

RETAIL PRICES	GOOD	AVERAGE	POOR
1994 Accord	$7,500-10,800	$6,800-10,000	$4,500-7,000
1995 Accord	9,000-13,200	8,200-12,200	5,700-9,000
1996 Accord	10,500-15,500	9,500-14,500	6,700-11,000
1997 Accord	12,000-18,000	11,000-16,800	7,500-12,500

AVERAGE REPLACEMENT COSTS

A/C Compressor	$530	Clutch, Pressure Plate, Bearing	550
Alternator	380	Constant Velocity Joints	670
Radiator	485	Brakes	250
Timing Chain or Belt	350	Shocks and/or Struts	545
Automatic Transmission or Transaxle	1,055	Exhaust System	540

TROUBLE SPOTS

• **Fuel gauge** The fuel gauge may not read full even though the tank is filled due to excessive resistance in the sending unit in the tank, which will be replaced under normal warranty conditions. (1994-95)

• **Dashboard lights** The heater control panel lights do not glow when the switch is pressed because of breaks in the circuit board solder joints. A new circuit board will be replaced under warranty. (1994-95)

• **Transmission noise** If the transmission grinds when shifting into 5th gear, the fork, sleeve set, and mainshaft gear must be replaced. The fork was manufactured improperly. If the car is out of warranty, the zone office may issue an extended goodwill repair. (1994-95)

• **Brake wear** Two types of rear brake pads are available: low noise and long life. Original equipment pads were the low noise design and may wear out faster than the car owner desires. This is not a normal warranty item. (1994-95)

• **Brakes** The parking brake may not fully release (handle won't go all the way down) causing the warning light to stay on and an ABS light to come on because a rivet on the brake rod is too tight. (1994)

• **Engine noise** The gasket for the mid-exhaust pipe sticks, causing a buzzing noise. Under normal warranty provisions, or goodwill extended coverage, the gasket will be replaced. (1994-95)

• **Radio** If the CD changer in the trunk will not eject, the company will exchange the CD magazines with a redesigned one. To get the old one out, slide a slim jim or metal ruler between the lower side of the CD magazine and the changer, then push the eject lever toward the back of the unit while pulling on the magazine. (All)

• **Vehicle noise** A noise coming from the area of the passenger footwell is most likely due to the air conditioning high pressure line vibrating against the power steering fluid line. The A/C line has to be bent upward to provide about a ¾-inch gap. (1995)

• **Transmission slippage** Cars with high mileage may begin to shift more harshly, which may be corrected by adding a bottle of Lubeguard conditioner to the automatic transmission fluid. If this does not soften the shifts, it may be necessary to rebuild the transmission. (1994-96)

RECALL HISTORY

1994 Some tire valve stems were damaged during assembly, resulting in sudden loss of air pressure and/or loss of control. **1995** Some supplemental restraint system electronic control units can cause unexpected air bag deployment.

1992-95 HONDA CIVIC

FOR Air bags (later models) • Fuel economy • Acceleration (EX and Si) • Ride (4-door) • Handling/roadholding

AGAINST Acceleration (CX and VX) • Rear-seat room (hatchback) • Noise (hatchback) • Cargo room (hatchback)

1992 Honda Civic Si 2-door hatchback

EVALUATION All four engines are weak on low-end torque, lacking in zest. Although they pull smoothly enough in the middle gears, they fail to exhibit much overall gusto—especially with automatic transmissions. To climb hills and keep up with highway traffic you'll have to shift gears often and push hard on the gas pedal. Automatic transmissions shift neatly, lacking the harsh jolt of earlier models. Fuel economy is great. Over a long-term trial, a 5-speed EX sedan averaged 29.6 mpg. Wind and exhaust sounds are reduced, especially in sedans, though tire noise is a problem.

Civics ride smoothly for a subcompact, although sedans have a much better ride than coupe and hatchback models. Handling can best be described as modest, with the narrow tires and softer suspension leaning over in tight turns. The steering and brakes work well.

Interior room is surprisingly good for a subcompact. Four adults can stretch out in modest comfort. Interior controls are thoughtfully designed and easy to use. Cargo space is good as well, but the hatchbacks split-opening makes loading and unloading difficult.

You pay a hefty price for a nice Civic, but in this case the expenditure might well be worth it. Flaws are few in these refined, quietly impressive subcompacts, overwhelmed by some highly tempting virtues. Civics stand apart from the crowd because of their nimble handling, smooth running, enjoyable operation, and miserly gas mileage.

NHTSA CRASH TEST RESULTS
1994 Honda Civic

4-DOOR SEDAN

Driver	☆☆☆
Passenger	☆☆☆

(The National Highway Traffic Safety Administration tests a vehicle's crashworthiness in front and side collisions. Their ratings suggest the chance of serious injury: ☆☆☆☆☆—10% or less; ☆☆☆☆—10-20% or less; ☆☆☆—20-30% or less; ☆☆—35-45% or less; ☆—More than 45%.)

HONDA

SPECIFICATIONS

	2-door coupe	2-door hatchback	4-door sedan
Wheelbase, in.	103.2	101.3	103.2
Overall length, in.	172.8	160.2	173.0
Overall width, in.	66.9	66.9	66.9
Overall height, in.	50.9	50.7	51.7
Curb weight, lbs.	2231	2108	2213
Cargo volume, cu. ft.	11.8	13.3	12.4
Fuel capacity, gals.	11.9	11.9	11.9
Seating capacity	5	5	5
Front head room, in.	38.5	38.6	39.1
Max. front leg room, in.	42.5	42.5	42.5
Rear head room, in.	34.9	36.5	37.2
Min. rear leg room, in.	31.1	30.5	32.8

Powertrain layout: transverse front-engine/front-wheel drive

ENGINES

	ohc I-4	ohc I-4	ohc I-4	ohc I-4
Size, liters/cu. in.	1.5/91	1.5/91	1.5/91	1.6/97
Horsepower	70	92	102	125
Torque (lbs./ft.)	90	97	98	106
EPA city/highway mpg				
5-speed OD manual	42/46	47/56	34/40	29/35
3-speed automatic				
4-speed OD automatic			29/36	26/34
Consumer Guide™ observed MPG				
5-speed OD manual				29.6

Built in USA, Canada, and Japan.

RETAIL PRICES

	GOOD	AVERAGE	POOR
1992 Civic	$2,700-5,700	$2,100-5,000	$800-3,000
1993 Civic	3,400-6,700	2,700-6,000	1,200-3,800
1994 Civic	4,400-8,200	3,700-7,500	1,900-5,000
1995 Civic	5,600-9,900	4,900-9,200	2,800-6,500

AVERAGE REPLACEMENT COSTS

A/C Compressor $470	Clutch, Pressure Plate,
Alternator 310	Bearing 455
Radiator 360	Constant Velocity Joints.....550
Timing Chain or Belt 190	Brakes 180
Automatic Transmission or	Shocks and/or Struts 580
Transaxle........................750	Exhaust System.................428

TROUBLE SPOTS

• **Water leak** There may be water leaking into the passenger footwell because of insufficient sealer on the seam at the firewall. To seal it, it is necessary to remove the front bumper, inner fender, wiper arms, and cowl. Look for rust on the floor pan and run water over the right lower corner of the windshield to watch for water leaks before buying the car. (1992-95)

• **Air conditioner** If the air conditioner belt repeatedly comes off, the splash shield under the engine is probably knocking it off when the car goes over a parking curb, etc. To correct the problem, some of the support ribs that stiffen the shield must be removed with a grinder to make the shield more flexible, which will be done under normal warranty. (1992-95)

• **Trunk latch** There may not be sufficient clearance on the trunk latch making it hard to open with the key. Under the normal warranty, the dealer will install a new latch and, if necessary, put shims on the striker. (1992-95)

• **Radio** If the CD changer in the trunk will not eject, the company will exchange the CD magazines with a redesigned one. To get the old one out, slide a slim jim or metal ruler between the lower side of the CD magazine and the changer, then push the eject lever toward the back of the unit while pulling on the magazine. (All)

• **Transmission slippage** Cars with high mileage may begin to shift more harshly, which may be corrected by adding a bottle of Lubeguard conditioner to the automatic transmission fluid. If this does not soften the shifts, it may be necessary to rebuild the transmission. (1992-95)

RECALL HISTORY

1992-94 Retaining clip at automatic transmission can come off, so position of lever does not match actual transmission gear range. **1994** Passenger-side air bag module on small number of cars may contain incorrect inflator, therefore unable to provide adequate protection.

1996-98 HONDA CIVIC

FOR Air bags, dual • Anti-lock brakes • Fuel economy • Ride • Visibility

AGAINST Road noise • Rear seat entry/exit

EVALUATION Based on interior volume, the sedan now qualifies as a compact, whereas the coupe and hatchback rank as subcompacts. Rear space in any body style is adequate for most people to fit without squeezing. Hatchbacks gained the most interior space. Thinner roof pillars and a bigger back window improved visibility on all body styles. The driver faces a low steering wheel and easy-to-read gauges. Split-folding rear seat

1997 Honda Civic LX sedan

backs on all Civics expanded cargo capacity.

Acceleration is liveliest with the EX, but all Civics perform at least adequately. Gas mileage also is a bonus: An EX with automatic reached 36 mpg on the highway, averaging 29 mpg in suburban commuting. Engine noise has been quieted, but road noise is still prominent at highway speeds.

Except for some overreaction to wavy surfaces, ride comfort is pleasing—well above average for a small car, with few jolts and minimal bounciness. Easy to maneuver, stable and well controlled on the highway, the Civic delivers superior steering feedback and excellent response.

This generation continues Civic's long-standing tradition of reliability and durability. Largely for that reason—coupled with the high new-car prices of LX and EX models, in particular—their resale prices as used vehicles tend to stay high.

NHTSA CRASH TEST RESULTS
1996 Honda Civic

4-DOOR SEDAN

Driver	☆☆☆☆
Passenger	☆☆☆☆☆

(The National Highway Traffic Safety Administration tests a vehicle's crashworthiness in front and side collisions. Their ratings suggest the chance of serious injury: ☆☆☆☆☆—10% or less; ☆☆☆☆—10-20% or less; ☆☆☆—20-30% or less; ☆☆—35-45% or less; ☆—More than 45%.)

SPECIFICATIONS

	2-door coupe	2-door hatchback	4-door sedan
Wheelbase, in.	103.2	103.2	103.2
Overall length, in.	175.1	164.5	175.1
Overall width, in.	67.1	67.1	67.1
Overall height, in.	54.1	54.1	54.7
Curb weight, lbs.	2262	2222	2319
Cargo volume, cu. ft.	11.9	13.4	11.9
Fuel capacity, gals.	11.9	11.9	11.9

	2-door coupe	2-door hatchback	4-door sedan
Seating capacity	5	5	5
Front head room, in.	38.8	38.8	39.8
Max. front leg room, in.	42.7	42.7	42.7
Rear head room, in.	36.2	37.2	37.6
Min. rear leg room, in.	34.1	34.1	34.1

Powertrain layout: transverse front-engine/front-wheel drive

ENGINES

	ohc I-4	ohc I-4	ohc I-4
Size, liters/cu. in.	1.6/97	1.6/97	1.6/97
Horsepower	106	115	127
Torque (lbs./ft.)	103	104	107

EPA city/highway mpg

5-speed OD manual	33/38	39/45	30/36
4-speed OD automatic	29/36		28/35

Consumer Guide™ observed MPG

5-speed OD manual			33.8
4-speed OD automatic			31.4

Built in USA and Canada.

RETAIL PRICES

	GOOD	AVERAGE	POOR
1996 Civic	$7,100-10,500	$6,400-9,700	$4,200-6,700
1996 Civic EX	11,000-12,000	10,200-11,200	7,000-7,800
1997 Civic	8,400-12,000	7,600-11,200	5,100-7,800
1997 Civic EX	12,300-13,400	11,500-12,500	8,000-8,900
1998 Civic	9,800-13,900	9,000-13,000	6,100-9,400
1998 Civic EX	14,000-15,500	13,000-14,500	9,300-10,500

AVERAGE REPLACEMENT COSTS

A/C Compressor	$465	Clutch, Pressure Plate, Bearing	470
Alternator	310	Constant Velocity Joints	590
Radiator	515	Brakes	185
Timing Chain or Belt	185	Shocks and/or Struts	690
Automatic Transmission or Transaxle	800	Exhaust System	405

TROUBLE SPOTS

• **Water leak** Water leaks onto the front floor (either or both sides) due to insufficient sealer on body seams. (1996-97)

• **Radio** Installing an aftermarket radio can result in loss of dome lights and keyless entry. Those two systems are tied into the Honda radio. (1997)

• **Seatbelts/safety** Seatbelts may not retract or may retract slowly.

Also, the button that keeps the seatbelt tongue (male half of seat belt) from sliding down breaks. The belts should be serviced under the Honda Lifetime Seat Belt Limited Warranty. (1996-97)

• **Cupholders** The cupholder lid sticks closed or will not close due to missing latch and will be replaced under warranty. (1996-97)

RECALL HISTORY

1996 Soapy lubricant used to insert brake booster check valve into vacuum hose causes sticky valve and loss of power assist. **1997-98** Some passenger air bag modules were improperly assembled; could prevent proper deployment.

1995-98 HONDA ODYSSEY

1995 Honda Odyssey

FOR Ride • Steering/handling • Entry/exit • Anti-lock brakes

AGAINST Engine noise • Road noise • Acceleration (full load)

EVALUATION Odyssey departs from the minivan herd by virtue of its fully-independent suspension, versus beam-type rear axles for most of the competition. It corners with little body lean and has good stability. Ride quality also is commendable: steady and firm at highway speeds; smoothly absorbent and comfortable when traversing bumpy urban pavement. Braking is nearly faultless.

Power from either the 2.2- or 2.3-liter engines is adequate, but the engines are loud when flooring the throttle. Also, when passing or engaging in quick sprints onto expressways, the Odyssey can feel underpowered. Gas mileage is great, more than 21 mpg in city/expressway driving. As in the Accord, Odyssey's automatic transmission delivers prompt shifts that are usually smooth. Full-throttle downshifts, on the other hand, can induce an unwanted lunge forward.

Because the Odyssey minivan is three to five inches narrower than rivals, cargo space is somewhat limited. There's also little walk-through room. On the plus side, the rear seat easily folds flush, and it's an easy minivan to park. The interior features plenty of space for six, but an extra person in the center seat of the 7-passenger version could be squeezed. Rear entry/exit is somewhat hampered by doors that don't open as wide as they should. Driving position in the Odyssey is comfortable; visibility good all around. The dashboard is attractive and well-organized.

Well-built, well-equipped, and likely to be reliable, Odyssey is worth a look—provided that it's big enough to meet your needs. Lack of a V-6 and modest dimensions tend to limit its appeal, however, against the league-leading Chrysler minivans and Ford's Windstar.

NHTSA CRASH TEST RESULTS
1995 Honda Odyssey   4-DOOR WAGON

Driver	☆☆☆☆
Passenger	☆☆☆☆

(The National Highway Traffic Safety Administration tests a vehicle's crashworthiness in front and side collisions. Their ratings suggest the chance of serious injury: ☆☆☆☆☆—10% or less; ☆☆☆☆—10-20% or less; ☆☆☆—20-30% or less; ☆☆—35-45% or less; ☆—More than 45%.)

SPECIFICATIONS

	4-door van
Wheelbase, in.	111.4
Overall length, in.	187.2
Overall width, in.	70.6
Overall height, in.	64.6
Curb weight, lbs.	3450
Cargo volume, cu. ft.	102.5
Fuel capacity, gals.	17.2
Seating capacity	7
Front head room, in.	40.1
Max. front leg room, in.	40.7
Rear head room, in.	39.3
Min. rear leg room, in.	40.2

Powertrain layout: transverse front-engine/front-wheel drive

ENGINES

	ohc I-4	dohc I-4
Size, liters/cu. in.	2.2/132	2.3/140
Horsepower	140	150
Torque (lbs./ft.)	145	152
EPA city/highway mpg		
4-speed OD automatic	20/24	21/26

HONDA

Consumer Guide™ observed MPG
4-speed OD automatic 21.5 21.3

Built in Japan.

RETAIL PRICES	GOOD	AVERAGE	POOR
1995 Odyssey	$11,500-13,500	$10,500-12,500	$7,800-9,500
1996 Odyssey	13,500-15,500	12,000-14,000	9,000-10,500
1997 Odyssey	15,500-18,000	14,000-16,500	10,800-12,800
1998 Odyssey	18,000-21,500	16,500-20,000	13,000-16,000

AVERAGE REPLACEMENT COSTS

A/C Compressor $510	Clutch, Pressure Plate, Bearing 485
Alternator 280	Constant Velocity Joints.....620
Radiator 415	Brakes...................................220
Timing Chain or Belt 290	Shocks and/or Struts 550
Automatic Transmission or Transaxle........................965	Exhaust System 510

TROUBLE SPOTS

• **Seatbelts/safety** Seat belts may not retract or may retract slowly. Also, the button that keeps the seat belt tongue (male half of seat belt) from sliding down breaks. The belts should be serviced under the Honda Lifetime Seat Belt Limited Warranty. (1995-97)

• **Glove box** The glove box door pops off because the latch assembly falls apart. (1995)

• **Fuel gauge** The fuel gauge on some vehicles does not go all the way to "F" because the arm on the sending unit is too long. (1995)

• **Cupholders** The cigarette lighter and front cupholder can come loose. (1995-96)

• **Engine noise** A problem with the power brakes' vacuum booster check valve causes a buzzing noise when idling in gear. (1995)

RECALL HISTORY

None to date.

1994-97 HONDA PASSPORT

FOR 4WD traction (optional) • Optional anti-lock brakes • Passenger and cargo room

AGAINST Fuel economy • Noise • No shift-on-the-fly

See the 1994-97 Isuzu Rodeo report for an evaluation of the 1994-97 Honda Passport.

1995.5 Honda Passport EX

NHTSA CRASH TEST RESULTS
1996 Honda Passport 4WD

4-DOOR WAGON

Driver	☆☆☆☆
Passenger	☆☆☆

(The National Highway Traffic Safety Administration tests a vehicle's crashworthiness in front and side collisions. Their ratings suggest the chance of serious injury: ☆☆☆☆☆—10% or less; ☆☆☆☆—10-20% or less; ☆☆☆—20-30% or less; ☆☆—35-45% or less; ☆—More than 45%.)

SPECIFICATIONS

	4-door wagon
Wheelbase, in.	108.7
Overall length, in.	176.5
Overall width, in.	66.5
Overall height, in.	66.5
Curb weight, lbs.	3545
Cargo volume, cu. ft.	74.9
Fuel capacity, gals.	21.9
Seating capacity	6
Front head room, in.	38.0
Max. front leg room, in.	42.5
Rear head room, in.	38.0
Min. rear leg room, in.	36.0

Powertrain layout: longitudinal front-engine/rear- or 4-wheel drive

ENGINES

	ohc I-4	ohc V-6
Size, liters/cu. in.	2.6/156	3.2/193
Horsepower	120	175-190
Torque (lbs./ft.)	150	188
EPA city/highway mpg		
5-speed OD manual	18/22	16/19
4-speed OD automatic		15/18
Consumer Guide™ observed MPG		
4-speed OD automatic		14.6

Built in USA.

RETAIL PRICES

	GOOD	AVERAGE	POOR
1994 Passport 2WD	$8,000-10,000	$7,200-9,200	$4,800-6,500
1994 Passport 4WD	11,000-13,500	10,000-12,500	7,200-9,500
1995 Passport 2WD	9,500-13,000	8,500-12,000	6,000-9,000
1995 Passport 4WD	13,000-16,000	11,800-14,500	8,500-11,000
1996 Passport 2WD	11,500-16,500	10,200-15,000	7,500-11,500
1996 Passport 4WD	15,500-19,000	14,000-17,500	10,500-13,500
1997 Passport 2WD	15,000-19,000	13,500-17,500	9,500-13,200
1997 Passport 4WD	17,500-21,500	16,000-19,800	12,500-15,500
1998 Passport 2WD	18,000-23,000	16,000-21,000	12,000-16,500
1998 Passport 4WD	21,000-26,000	19,000-24,000	14,500-19,000

AVERAGE REPLACEMENT COSTS

A/C Compressor $750	Clutch, Pressure Plate,
Alternator 375	Bearing 605
Radiator 445	Constant Velocity Joints.....250
Timing Chain or Belt 250	Brakes.................................305
Automatic Transmission or	Shocks and/or Struts 220
Transaxle.....................1,715	Exhaust System.................270

TROUBLE SPOTS

• **Oil leak** Leaks at the spark plug tubes allow oil to leak onto spark plugs and may be covered as a goodwill warranty. (1994-96)

• **Hard starting** Engine may be hard to start after sitting for 30-90 minutes due to fuel injection leak-down requiring replacement of injectors and may be covered by goodwill warranty. (1994-95)

• **Dashboard lights** The speedometer gear (in the transmission) seizes and gets stripped. (1994-96)

• **Seatbelts/safety** Seatbelts may not retract or may retract slowly. Also, the button that keeps the seatbelt tongue (male half of seat belt) from sliding down breaks. The belts should be serviced under the Honda Lifetime Seat Belt Limited Warranty. (1994-97)

RECALL HISTORY

1994 Camshaft seal end plug can become dislodged from cylinder head, allowing oil to leak; can cause engine damage and fire. **1994** Latch in seatbelt buckle could engage only partially, causing tongue to come out during collision or hard braking.

1992-96 HONDA PRELUDE ✓ BEST BUY

FOR Air bags, dual • Anti-lock brakes (except S) • Acceleration • Steering/handling

1995 Honda Prelude SE

AGAINST Passenger and cargo room • Instruments/controls

EVALUATION Space up front is okay, but split-back rear seats really are tight—best left to toddlers—and the Prelude's skimpy trunk is tinier than before. Controls are conveniently placed and typically Honda-friendly, but Prelude instruments are annoyingly odd. Warning lights stretch all across the dashboard top, sitting too far to the right for easy checking while underway. Vacuum-fluorescent fuel and temperature gauges are near the center, difficult to read.

On the plus side, expect strong performance and good fuel economy. All engines are turbine-smooth. While a base-model Prelude's acceleration is only adequate, The Si feels snappy, and the VTEC is sports-car quick. The automatic transmission hurts performance only slightly, but it has poor shift quality and seems to wander haphazardly through the gears at highway speeds. Test stick-shift Si Preludes have yielded a reasonably frugal 23.1 mpg in daily driving.

Cornering is flat and grippy, handling poised and responsive. Stopping ability is commendable, but lack of anti-lock braking on the S model is unfortunate. We haven't found that 4-wheel steering helps much, yielding only a small gain in maneuvering ease. Not many are around, anyway.

Expensive? Sure it is; but for buyers who value fine workmanship, refinement, and a solid, reassuring feel, Prelude deserves a trial.

SPECIFICATIONS

	2-door coupe
Wheelbase, in.	100.4
Overall length, in.	174.8
Overall width, in.	69.5
Overall height, in.	50.8
Curb weight, lbs.	2809

HONDA

	2-door coupe
Cargo volume, cu. ft.	7.9
Fuel capacity, gals.	15.9
Seating capacity	4
Front head room, in.	38.0
Max. front leg room, in.	44.2
Rear head room, in.	35.1
Min. rear leg room, in.	28.1

Powertrain layout: transverse front-engine/front-wheel drive

ENGINES

	ohc I-4	dohc I-4	dohc I-4
Size, liters/cu. in.	2.2/132	2.3/138	2.2/132
Horsepower	135	160	190
Torque (lbs./ft.)	142	156	158

EPA city/highway mpg

	ohc I-4	dohc I-4	dohc I-4
5-speed OD manual	24/29	22/27	22/26
4-speed OD automatic	22/27	21/26	

Consumer Guide™ observed MPG

	ohc I-4	dohc I-4	dohc I-4
5-speed OD manual		23.1	21.9
4-speed OD automatic	24.6		

Built in Japan.

RETAIL PRICES

	GOOD	AVERAGE	POOR
1992 Prelude	$6,200-8,000	$5,500-7,200	$3,500-4,700
1993 Prelude	7,400-10,000	6,600-9,200	4,400-6,500
1994 Prelude	8,800-11,000	8,000-10,000	5,500-7,000
1994 Prelude 4WS/VTEC	11,200-12,200	10,000-11,000	7,000-7,900
1995 Prelude	11,000-13,000	10,000-12,000	7,000-8,500
1995 Prelude SE/VTEC	13,000-14,000	12,000-13,000	8,800-9,500
1996 Prelude	13,000-15,200	11,700-13,800	8,500-10,200
1996 Prelude VTEC	15,500-17,000	14,000-15,500	10,500-11,700

AVERAGE REPLACEMENT COSTS

A/C Compressor	$370
Alternator	410
Radiator	480
Timing Chain or Belt	250
Automatic Transmission or Transaxle	965
Clutch, Pressure Plate, Bearing	520
Constant Velocity Joints	675
Brakes	210
Shocks and/or Struts	845
Exhaust System	670

TROUBLE SPOTS

• **Transmission noise** The transmission grinds when shifting into fifth gear due to mis-manufactured shift fork and may be eligible for a goodwill warranty. (1992-95)

- **Brakes** The parking brake may not fully release (handle will not go all the way down) and the warning light stays on because a rivet was installed too snugly. (1993-94)

- **Steering problems** The car may drift to the right on flat roads due to a faulty spool valve in the power steering system. (1992-93)

- **Seatbelts/safety** Seatbelts may not retract or may retract slowly. Also, the button that keeps the seatbelt tongue (male half of seat belt) from sliding down breaks. The belts should be serviced under the Honda Lifetime Seat Belt Limited Warranty. (1992-96)

RECALL HISTORY
None to date.

1992-95 HYUNDAI ELANTRA

1992 Hyundai Elantra 4-door

FOR Visibility • Control layout • Passenger and cargo room

AGAINST Noise • Ride • Radio controls

THE BASICS Sensing a gap in both size and price between its low-budget subcompact Excel and the up-level compact Sonata, Hyundai launched the Elantra. This "high end" subcompact 4-door sedan aimed at the Geo Prizm, Honda Civic, Toyota Corolla, Nissan Sentra, Ford Escort, and Saturn sedan.

The front-drive Elantra came in base or fancier GLS trim, with a 113-horsepower, 1.6-liter twin-cam 4-cylinder engine and 5-speed manual shift. Ordering 4-speed automatic transmission cut output to 105 horsepower.

1993 A larger, more powerful engine became available in 1993, on the GLS and all automatic-transmission models. Base cars now wore a black-finished grille, versus a body-color unit for the GLS, which also adopted newly-designed wheel covers and a 3-spoke steering wheel. Manual-shift base models stuck with the original 113-horsepower engine, but others got a 1.8-liter 4-cylinder that made 124 horsepower.

1994 Elantras added a driver-side air bag for 1994, plus optional anti-lock braking with 4-wheel discs for the GLS. Styling got a freshening, including a reshaped grille, headlamps, front bumpers, and taillights, plus modified interior trim.

1995 Awaiting a redesign for 1996, the existing Elantra faced its final season without significant change.

EVALUATION Early Elantras with the smaller engine exhibit fairly spirited performance with manual shift. But with the automatic transmission, you must use a heavy foot to keep up with traffic. Performance is better with the 1.8-liter engine that debuted for 1993. Though relatively smooth, the 1.6-liter engine isn't truly quiet. The 1.8-liter engine is smoother but not much quieter. Gas mileage isn't as great as might be expected. An automatic GLS averaged only 22.5 mpg. Road and wind noise is excessive for a modern small car.

Elantras have a floaty ride. The suspension does not absorb bumps well, and the ride can get rough over broken pavement. Wavy surfaces yield a bouncy and disjointed sensation. Body lean is excessive in sharp directional changes, and the front tires tend to resist turning. Brakes are adequate, if a bit over-assisted. The addition of optional anti-lock braking for 1994 was a sensible move, though ABS was available only on the GLS.

Passenger space is generous for a car in this class. Six-footers can sit comfortably in back, though the seat is too narrow for three adults. Head room is adequate all around. Except for low-mounted radio gauges, controls are well laid out. Out back, the large trunk has a low, bumper-height liftover.

Overall, Elantra rates no higher than average, but came better equipped than most competitors. Workmanship cannot match that of most rivals, so be sure any Elantra is inspected carefully before you make a purchase.

NHTSA CRASH TEST RESULTS
1994 Hyundai Elantra

4-DOOR SEDAN

Driver	☆☆☆☆
Passenger	☆

(The National Highway Traffic Safety Administration tests a vehicle's crashworthiness in front and side collisions. Their ratings suggest the chance of serious injury: ☆☆☆☆☆—10% or less; ☆☆☆☆—10-20% or less; ☆☆☆—20-30% or less; ☆☆—35-45% or less; ☆—More than 45%.)

SPECIFICATIONS

	4-door sedan
Wheelbase, in.	98.4
Overall length, in.	172.8
Overall width, in.	66.1
Overall height, in.	52.0
Curb weight, lbs.	2500
Cargo volume, cu. ft.	11.8
Fuel capacity, gals.	13.7
Seating capacity	5
Front head room, in.	38.4
Max. front leg room, in.	42.6
Rear head room, in.	37.6
Min. rear leg room, in.	33.4

Powertrain layout: transverse front-engine/front-wheel drive

ENGINES

	dohc I-4	dohc I-4
Size, liters/cu. in.	1.6/97	1.8/110
Horsepower	105-113	124
Torque (lbs./ft.)	102	116

EPA city/highway mpg

5-speed OD manual	22/29	21/28
4-speed OD automatic	22/29	22/29

Consumer Guide™ observed MPG

4-speed OD automatic	22.5

Built in South Korea.

RETAIL PRICES	GOOD	AVERAGE	POOR
1992 Elantra	$1,600-2,400	$1,100-1,800	$400-900
1993 Elantra	2,200-3,100	1,600-2,500	700-1,200
1994 Elantra	3,000-4,200	2,400-3,600	1,200-1,900
1995 Elantra	4,000-5,200	3,400-4,500	1,600-2,400

AVERAGE REPLACEMENT COSTS

A/C Compressor	$565
Alternator	315
Radiator	390
Timing Chain or Belt	195
Automatic Transmission or Transaxle	810
Clutch, Pressure Plate, Bearing	310
Constant Velocity Joints	355
Brakes	190
Shocks and/or Struts	595
Exhaust System	295

TROUBLE SPOTS

• **Manual transmission** Manual transaxles may grind when attempting to shift into reverse due to a problem with the reverse idle gear bushing and reverse shift lever or reverse synchronizer or a weak wave spring. (1992-94)

HYUNDAI

- **Hard starting** Hard starting may be due to a cracked in-tank fuel line. (1992-95)

- **Transmission slippage** If the transmission slips or will not go into fourth gear, the end clutch needs to be replaced. (1992-95)

- **Poor transmission shift** The automatic transmission may shift poorly between first and second or develop harsh shifting after the car reaches 15,000-20,000 miles. It can be corrected by adjusting the kickdown servo. (1992-95)

- **Engine misfire** In cool weather (50-70°F), the engine may stall or run rough which may be fixed by a replacement computer. (1992)

- **Brakes** Brake pedal pulsation is often due to brake disc thickness variations. (1992-95)

- **Hard starting** Models with 1.6L engine that do not start in temperatures below 10°F get a cold-start repair kit. (1992-94)

RECALL HISTORY

1994-95 Driver-side air bag warning light could illuminate because of increased electrical resistance; might prevent air bag from activating during a crash.

1990-94 HYUNDAI SONATA

1990 Hyundai Sonata

FOR Acceleration (V-6) • Passenger and cargo room • Visibility • Anti-lock brakes (optional)

AGAINST Fuel economy • Acceleration (4-cylinder) • Road noise • Engine noise • Wind noise • No air bags

THE BASICS Early in 1989, the Hyundai introduced a larger front-drive 4-door sedan caslled the Sonata. Dimensionally it ranks as a large compact. The standard 2.4-liter 4-cylinder engine was built under Mitsubishi licensing, but with Hyundai's multi-point fuel injection. A 3.0-liter V-6 arrived for 1990, hooked to an electronically controlled automatic transmission with Normal and Power shift modes.

Sonatas came in standard and plusher GLS trim. All Sonatas were equipped with motorized front shoulder belts to meet the federal passive-restraint equipment.

1991 Interiors were redesigned this year. New items included seats, console, instrument panel fascia, dual cupholders, and a fade-out light.

1992 A Mitsubishi-built 2.0-liter, 16-valve four replaced the 2.4-liter for 1992, and anti-lock braking became available on the GLS with V-6 power. Styling changes included a fresh grille, revised taillights, and slight sheetmetal alterations.

1993 Except for a body-color front air intake and new wheel covers, this year's Sonata changed little.

1994 No change at all hit the 1994 models, as the Sonata was awaiting redesign as an early '95 model.

EVALUATION Acceleration is fairly impressive with the 2.4-liter four and a 5-speed, but only adequate with automatic. Picking a V-6 doesn't make a lot of difference, but does offer quieter running. The 2.0-liter 4-cylinder engine, introduced for 1992, feels no more peppy than the old 2.4. In city/highway driving, we averaged 20.5 mpg with a 4-cylinder automatic Sonata and a decidedly thirsty 16.6 mpg with the V-6. Though relatively quiet mechanically, Sonatas suffer noticeable wind noise on the highway, along with excessive road noise.

Handling and roadholding are very capable for this class, but hardly agile. Steering feels light and responsive. The well-controlled, comfortably pliant ride is another "plus," though you get a bit of floatiness at times. Simulated panic stops from 60 mph were marred by sudden, early rear-wheel lockup as well as long stopping distances.

Four adults have plenty of room in the tall interior. Head and leg space are generous. Entry/exit is easy, due to fairly wide doors. A bumper-height opening makes the sizable trunk easy to load.

Not the most refined or exciting car on the block, and noisier than many, Sonata is still a sensible, well-designed family sedan. What this sedan lacks in refinement and assembly quality compared to a Honda Accord or Toyota Camry, it manages to make up for in price and value.

SPECIFICATIONS

	4-door sedan
Wheelbase, in.	104.3

HYUNDAI

	4-door sedan
Overall length, in.	184.3
Overall width, in.	68.9
Overall height, in.	55.4
Curb weight, lbs.	2813
Cargo volume, cu. ft.	14.0
Fuel capacity, gals.	17.2
Seating capacity	5
Front head room, in.	38.5
Max. front leg room, in.	42.9
Rear head room, in.	37.4
Min. rear leg room, in.	37.3

Powertrain layout: transverse front-engine/front-wheel drive

ENGINES

	Turbocharged dohc I-4	ohc I-4	ohc V-6
Size, liters/cu. in.	2.0/122	2.4/143	3.0/181
Horsepower	128	116	142
Torque (lbs./ft.)	121	142	158
EPA city/highway mpg			
5-speed OD manual	20/27	21/28	
4-speed OD automatic	21/27	21/26	18/24
Consumer Guide™ observed MPG			
5-speed OD manual	25.7		
4-speed OD automatic	20.5		16.6

Built in Canada.

RETAIL PRICES	GOOD	AVERAGE	POOR
1990 Sonata	$1,200-2,000	$700-1,400	$200-500
1991 Sonata	1,600-2,700	1,100-2,100	400-800
1992 Sonata	2,200-3,200	1,600-2,600	600-1,000
1993 Sonata	2,900-4,000	2,300-3,300	900-1,300
1994 Sonata	3,800-5,300	3,100-4,600	1,300-2,300

AVERAGE REPLACEMENT COSTS

A/C Compressor	$505
Alternator	340
Radiator	325
Timing Chain or Belt	210
Automatic Transmission or Transaxle	840
Clutch, Pressure Plate, Bearing	360
Constant Velocity Joints	700
Brakes	205
Shocks and/or Struts	485
Exhaust System	260

TROUBLE SPOTS

• **Blower motor** If the blower motor is noisy or jams and blows the fuse (especially in the winter), or if the inside of the windshield fogs up, the dealer will repair the water leak at the plenum under the standard warranty. (1990-94)

• **Water leak** Water on the floor from what appears to be a leaking heater core is really a leaking heater valve that will be replaced under warranty. (1990-94)

• **Engine misfire** A bad ground for the throttle position sensor causes stalling at idle, no air conditioning, and a "check engine" light. The dealer will splice a ground wire into the original one leading to the computer. (1990-94)

• **Transmission noise** Gear clashes or grinding when shifting from 2nd to 3rd gear is corrected by installing beefier synchronizers for 3rd and 4th gears under the normal warranty. (1992-94)

• **Transmission slippage** Harsh shifts into 2nd or 4th gears on cars with automatic transmissions is probably due to a missing or defective air exhaust plug. If its retainer ring comes off, it can cause scoring in the transmission housing that must be replaced. The company has extended the warranty to 60,000 miles provided the fluid was regularly changed at 15K, 30K, and 45K. (all)

RECALL HISTORY

1990 Safety catch on secondary hood latch striker could bind, allowing hood to fly open while car is moving if primary latch is released or hood is not completely closed. **1990** Spring clamp tangs on coolant bypass hose of 2.4-liter engine may contact and possibly damage the fuel supply hose, which could result in fuel leakage into engine compartment and possible fire. **1990-94** Motorized shoulder belt can travel slowly or chatter in its track; may eventually become inoperative, increasing risk of injury in sudden stop or accident.

1995-98 HYUNDAI SONATA

FOR Air bags, dual • Optional anti-lock brakes • Passenger and cargo room • Acceleration (V-6) • Ride

AGAINST Automatic transmission performance • Wind noise

EVALUATION The V-6 engine furnishes more than adequate acceleration from a standing start, capable of reaching 60 mph in just over nine seconds and delivering welcome passing response. A 4-cylinder Sonata with automatic is sluggish, but gets excellent fuel economy—a credible 23.8 mpg, versus 20.5 mpg for a V-6 sedan. Wind noise is prominent around the side windows at highway speeds, making long drives more fatiguing.

HYUDAI

1995 Hyundai Sonata

Ride quality is impressive. The suspension is firm enough to provide a stable, comfortable highway ride and absorbent enough to soak up most bumps. On the other hand, the ride can get jumpy when rolling over bad roads. A Sonata is easy to drive, but handling ranks just about average—acceptable, that is, but nothing to boast about.

While the previous Sonata was spacious, this one is noticeably roomier. Partly due to its longer wheelbase, the Sonata's back seat looks huge compared to space inside some competitors. Expect plenty of head, leg, and elbow room up front, and also in the rear. Cargo space is generous. The new dashboard has a more convenient design than its predecessor, with easy-to-read gauges and an amply-sized glovebox. Panel fit isn't always top-notch, but Sonatas appear to be tight and well-built.

Anyone seeking a low-priced family car with plenty of interior space should look over a Sonata before deciding on a purchase. Just don't expect it to shine above the competition.

NHTSA CRASH TEST RESULTS
1995 Hyundai Sonata

4-DOOR SEDAN

Driver	☆☆☆
Passenger	☆☆☆☆

(The National Highway Traffic Safety Administration tests a vehicle's crashworthiness in front and side collisions. Their ratings suggest the chance of serious injury: ☆☆☆☆☆—10% or less; ☆☆☆☆—10-20% or less; ☆☆☆—20-30% or less; ☆☆—35-45% or less; ☆—More than 45%.)

SPECIFICATIONS

	4-door sedan
Wheelbase, in.	106.3
Overall length, in.	185.0
Overall width, in.	69.7
Overall height, in.	55.3

	4-door sedan
Curb weight, lbs.	3025
Cargo volume, cu. ft.	13.2
Fuel capacity, gals.	17.2
Seating capacity	5
Front head room, in.	38.5
Max. front leg room, in.	43.3
Rear head room, in.	37.7
Min. rear leg room, in.	36.6

Powertrain layout: transverse front-engine/front-wheel drive

ENGINES

	dohc I-4	ohc V-6
Size, liters/cu. in.	2.0/122	3.0/181
Horsepower	137	142
Torque (lbs./ft.)	129	168

EPA city/highway mpg

5-speed OD manual	22/28	
4-speed OD automatic	21/29	18/24

Consumer Guide™ observed MPG

4-speed OD automatic	23.8	20.5

Built in South Korea.

RETAIL PRICES

	GOOD	AVERAGE	POOR
1995 Sonata	$4,800-6,800	$4,200-6,000	$2,400-3,800
1996 Sonata	6,000-8,000	5,300-7,300	3,300-5,000
1997 Sonata	8,000-10,200	7,200-9,400	5,000-6,800
1998 Sonata	9,000-12,000	8,100-11,000	5,900-8,200

AVERAGE REPLACEMENT COSTS

A/C Compressor	$950
Alternator	365
Radiator	420
Timing Chain or Belt	285
Automatic Transmission or Transaxle	1,010
Clutch, Pressure Plate, Bearing	325
Constant Velocity Joints	650
Brakes	170
Shocks and/or Struts	760
Exhaust System	345

TROUBLE SPOTS

• **Brakes** The brakes may pulsate under light application which is fixed by replacing the brake pads with a revised set plus a hardware kit. (1995-97)

• **Engine misfire** Engine problems (rough idle, speed vacillations) and transmission problems (shock shifting from park, hard upshifts and downshifts) may result from misadjusted throttle position sensor and idle switch. (1995-97)

• **Manual transmission** Manual transaxles may grind when attempting to shift into reverse and the problem is corrected with a new reverse idle gear bushing and reverse shift lever (1995) or reverse synchronizer. (1995-96)

• **Poor transmission shift** Automatic transmissions may suffer shift shock or harsh shifting when accelerating from a stop due to a problem with the transmission control module. (1995-97)

• **Transmission slippage** If the transmission slips or will not go into fourth gear, the end clutch needs to be replaced. (1995-96)

RECALL HISTORY

1995 On 356 cars with gas-filled shock absorbers, one or both lower rear spring seats are not securely attached. **1996-97** Wipers may not operate, due to contamination in contacts.

1991-96 INFINITI G20

1996 Infiniti G20t

FOR   Acceleration (manual) • Steering/handling • Anti-lock brakes • Air bags (later models)

AGAINST   Acceleration (early automatic transmission) • Engine noise • Road noise • Ride (early models) • Control layout

EVALUATION   The 5-speed gearbox blends neatly with the fast-revving engine for a lively feel, whether off the line or meandering through tight, twisty roads. However, the automatic transmission cuts rather sharply into performance, shifting too often even on moderate uphill grades and impairing standing-start action. As for economy, we averaged 21.7 mpg with an automatic G20.

Though wind noise is low, road and engine noise can be a problem. However, the G20 suffers a stiff, jolting ride as soon as any big bumps appear. On the plus side, softer suspension bushings, introduced in mid-1993, deliver a ride that's still firm, but no longer too stiff on bumpy roads. In any year, body lean is minimal, power steering is quick and responsive, and brakes respond eagerly.

Space is more than adequate for four adults, and the handsome dashboard is well-organized. Gauges are clearly marked; controls handy, except for a low heat/vent panel. A low beltline and thin roof pillars contribute to a commanding driving position and good visibility. Firm front bucket seats offer good support. Six-footers can ride in back without feeling cramped. The ample trunk has a long, flat floor, and its lid opens from bumper height to more than 90 degrees.

Though capable and well-designed, the small Infiniti's lack in the engine department—neither as quiet nor as quick as expected, especially with automatic—and in the overly taut suspension. Even so, it's a spirited machine with a sensible design, thus worth a test-drive.

SPECIFICATIONS

	4-door sedan
Wheelbase, in.	100.4
Overall length, in.	174.8
Overall width, in.	66.7
Overall height, in.	54.7
Curb weight, lbs.	2977
Cargo volume, cu. ft.	14.2
Fuel capacity, gals.	15.9
Seating capacity	5
Front head room, in.	38.8
Max. front leg room, in.	42.0
Rear head room, in.	37.3
Min. rear leg room, in.	32.2

Powertrain layout: transverse front-engine/front-wheel drive

ENGINES

	dohc I-4
Size, liters/cu. in.	2.0/122
Horsepower	140
Torque (lbs./ft.)	132
EPA city/highway mpg	
5-speed OD manual	24/32

INFINITI

	dohc I-4
4-speed OD automatic	22/28

Consumer Guide™ observed MPG

4-speed OD automatic	21.7

Built in Japan.

RETAIL PRICES	GOOD	AVERAGE	POOR
1991 G20	$4,400-5,300	$3,700-4,600	$1,900-2,500
1992 G20	5,200-6,100	4,500-5,400	2,500-3,100
1993 G20	6,500-7,500	5,800-6,800	3,500-4,200
1994 G20	8,200-9,500	7,400-8,700	4,800-5,600
1995 G20	9,800-11,200	9,000-10,200	6,000-7,000
1996 G20	11,800-13,000	10,500-11,700	7,200-7,900

AVERAGE REPLACEMENT COSTS

A/C Compressor	$710	Clutch, Pressure Plate, Bearing	485
Alternator	790	Constant Velocity Joints	430
Radiator	480	Brakes	200
Timing Chain or Belt	615	Shocks and/or Struts	820
Automatic Transmission or Transaxle	940	Exhaust System	520

TROUBLE SPOTS

• **Fuel odors** Owners who complain of fuel odors on cold start (especially in cold weather) may receive a free repair that may include new fuel injectors, hoses, fuel rails, regulator, and wiring. (1991-92)

• **Engine stalling** If a cold engine stalls when coming to a stop and is hard to restart because of a lack of compression, replacing the hydraulic valve lash adjusters may restore performance. If the camshafts show wear, they also have to be replaced. (1991-92)

• **Transmission noise** If the automatic transmission chirps when shifting from second to third, a redesigned input shaft and high clutch assembly with an improved friction material should eliminate the problem. (1991)

• **Dashboard lights** If the malfunction indicator lamp (check engine) light comes on, but the technician can find no faulty components, there may be inductive interference on the wiring harness leading to the onboard computer. Separating and isolating the wires from one another cures the problem. (1994-95)

• **Transmission slippage** A campaign was conducted to improve automatic transmission life by installing an in-line filter and auxiliary oil cooler. The transmission warranty was extended to 7 years/100,000 miles. (1991)

• **Transmission slippage** The dropping resistor on the inner left fender can be damaged by rain or windshield washer fluid causing harsh, noisy, or jerky transmission shifts. A new resistor, with a protective cover, is required to fix the problem. (1994)

• **Transmission slippage** If the transmission won't upshift to third after downshifting into second or during normal acceleration, or won't upshift to fourth, or slips on acceleration, the high clutch assembly may be burnt and debris gets lodged in the valve body. The new pump housing, with a bigger oil feed hole will prevent the replacement clutches from burning up. (1991-93)

• **Trunk latch** The electric trunk release solenoid may stick in the open position, preventing the trunk from closing properly. Improved actuators have been developed. (1992-94)

RECALL HISTORY

1991-92 Rear seatbelt buckle may engage only partially. **1991-96** Fuel filler tube assembly can corrode, resulting in leakage. **1993-95** Harness connector protector near seatbelt pre-tensioner can ignite, due to proximity to combustion gas generated by pre-tensioner when device is triggered; fire can then occur in passenger compartment.

1996-98 INFINITI I30

✓ BEST BUY

1996 Infiniti I30t

FOR Air bags, dual • Anti-lock brakes • Acceleration • Steering/handling

AGAINST Rear seat comfort • Fuel economy • Rear visibility

See the 1995-98 Nissan Maxima report for an evaluation of the 1996-98 Infiniti I30.

NHTSA CRASH TEST RESULTS
1996 Infiniti I30   4-DOOR SEDAN

Driver	☆☆☆☆
Passenger	☆☆☆

(The National Highway Traffic Safety Administration tests a vehicle's crashworthiness in front and side collisions. Their ratings suggest the chance of serious injury: ☆☆☆☆☆—10% or less; ☆☆☆☆—10-20% or less; ☆☆☆—20-30% or less; ☆☆—35-45% or less; ☆—More than 45%.)

SPECIFICATIONS

	4-door sedan
Wheelbase, in.	106.3
Overall length, in.	189.6
Overall width, in.	69.7
Overall height, in.	55.7
Curb weight, lbs.	3001
Cargo volume, cu. ft.	14.1
Fuel capacity, gals.	18.5
Seating capacity	5
Front head room, in.	40.1
Max. front leg room, in.	43.9
Rear head room, in.	37.4
Min. rear leg room, in.	34.3

Powertrain layout: transverse front-engine/front-wheel drive

ENGINES

	dohc V-6
Size, liters/cu. in.	3.0/181
Horsepower	190
Torque (lbs./ft.)	205

EPA city/highway mpg

5-speed OD manual	21/26
4-speed automatic	21/28

Consumer Guide™ observed MPG

5-speed OD manual	22.3
4-speed automatic	17.3

Built in Japan.

AVERAGE REPLACEMENT COSTS

A/C Compressor	$800	Clutch, Pressure Plate, Bearing	650
Alternator	410	Constant Velocity Joints	1,150
Radiator	475	Brakes	210
Timing Chain or Belt	690	Shocks and/or Struts	1,140
Automatic Transmission or Transaxle	920	Exhaust System	445

RETAIL PRICES	GOOD	AVERAGE	POOR
1996 I30	$16,800-19,000	$15,500-17,500	$12,000-13,500

	GOOD	AVERAGE	POOR
1997 I30	19,500-22,000	18,000-20,000	14,000-16,000
1998 I30	22,500-25,500	21,000-23,500	17,000-19,000

TROUBLE SPOTS

• **Engine knock** Spark knock, or ping, may result from a defective onboard computer. (1996-97)

• **Engine fan noise** The mounting flange for the fan (on the water pump) can come loose after service if the fan pulley is not installed properly during repairs. (1996-97)

RECALL HISTORY

None to date.

1993-97 INFINITI J30

1993 Infiniti J30t

FOR   Acceleration • Anti-lock brakes • Air bags, dual • Steering/handling

AGAINST   Fuel economy • Passenger and cargo room • Automatic transmission performance

EVALUATION   With a 0-60 mph time under nine seconds, the J30 is competitive among luxury sedans in its price range. On the whole, you get smooth, quiet running, except for an automatic transmission that shifts gears too often at in-town speeds. In hard acceleration, though, the engine gets surprisingly loud. Gas mileage also is somewhat disappointing. We reached 24 mpg in highway driving, but dropped below 16 mpg when traveling through urban areas.

Unlike some Japanese luxury sedans, the J30's suspension is firm enough to give plenty of road feel and spirited cornering. Yet, it's supple enough so the ride is never harsh. Handling is a tad more balanced than most front-drive rivals, courtesy of the car's rear-drive layout.

The cozy cabin is practical only for four adults, in fact. The combination of transmission hump and narrow interior make the J30 too tight in back for a third adult. Otherwise, the cabin is richly appointed and ergonomics are first-rate. Negative points are few, led by the marginal adult-size head/leg room (especially in back) and a minimal-size trunk.

A fine car overall, blending luxury extras and a somewhat sporty personality, the J30 simply fails to stand out among luxury 4-doors. All told, it lacks the polish and refinement of such rivals as the front-drive Lexus ES 300.

NHTSA CRASH TEST RESULTS
1994 Infiniti J30

4-DOOR SEDAN

Driver	☆☆☆☆
Passenger	☆☆☆☆

(The National Highway Traffic Safety Administration tests a vehicle's crashworthiness in front and side collisions. Their ratings suggest the chance of serious injury: ☆☆☆☆☆—10% or less; ☆☆☆☆—10-20% or less; ☆☆☆—20-30% or less; ☆☆—35-45% or less; ☆—More than 45%.)

SPECIFICATIONS

	4-door sedan
Wheelbase, in.	108.7
Overall length, in.	191.3
Overall width, in.	69.7
Overall height, in.	54.7
Curb weight, lbs.	3527
Cargo volume, cu. ft.	10.1
Fuel capacity, gals.	19.0
Seating capacity	5
Front head room, in.	37.7
Max. front leg room, in.	41.3
Rear head room, in.	36.7
Min. rear leg room, in.	30.5

Powertrain layout: longitudinal front-engine/rear-wheel drive

ENGINES

	dohc V-6
Size, liters/cu. in.	3.0/181
Horsepower	210
Torque (lbs./ft.)	193

EPA city/highway mpg

4-speed OD automatic	18/23

Consumer Guide™ observed MPG

4-speed OD automatic	20.1

Built in Japan.

RETAIL PRICES

	GOOD	AVERAGE	POOR
1993 J30	$10,500-12,000	$9,500-11,000	$7,000-8,000
1994 J30	12,500-14,200	11,500-13,000	8,500-9,500
1995 J30	15,000-17,000	13,500-15,500	10,000-11,500
1996 J30	18,000-20,000	16,500-18,500	12,500-14,000
1997 J30	21,500-24,000	20,000-22,000	15,500-17,000

AVERAGE REPLACEMENT COSTS

A/C Compressor $775
Alternator 890
Radiator 540
Timing Chain or Belt 260
Automatic Transmission or
    Transaxle.....................1,005

Universal Joints 1,170
Brakes.................................235
Shocks and/or Struts 1,400
Exhaust System.................865

TROUBLE SPOTS

• **Climate control** The automatic climate control occasionally blows hot, humid air for no apparent reason and depending on the VIN, there are about five different fixes. (1993)

• **Radio** The Bose stereo amplifier causes interference on the cellular phone requiring a filter on the phone antenna cable. (1993)

RECALL HISTORY

1993-94 Harness connector protector near seatbelt pre-tensioner can ignite when device is triggered.

1990-94 ISUZU AMIGO

1990 Isuzu Amigo XS

FOR 4WD traction • Driver seating • Anti-lock brakes

AGAINST Acceleration • Fuel economy • No air bags

ISUZU

EVALUATION Essentially a shortened Isuzu pickup (topped by a button-down canvas roof), the Amigo feels huskier and more stable than some mini-4x4s. Unfortunately, it's too heavy for even the 2.6-liter engine, so both acceleration and fuel economy are mediocre.

Road manners are better than many rivals, much like those of a compact 4WD pickup. The ride is firm but comfortable, noise levels fairly reasonable, braking distances acceptable. Handling appears balanced and safely predictable, provided that you respect the Amigo's short wheelbase and high center of gravity. Engaging 4WD is something of a chore, as you must stop and get out to lock the manual hubs.

Passenger and cargo space beat most rivals, but the optional rear bench is narrow and hard, not for long-term adult travel. Reclining front seats slide forward to ease access to the back, but getting there still isn't easy. Wide side pillars impair over-the-shoulder visibility, while the tailgate-mounted spare tire tends to block the rearward view. The Amigo's dashboard and instruments are almost carlike, with the exception of a low-mounted radio. Though not easy to erect, the snap-on canvas top is less complex than some.

Neither the quickest nor the thriftiest small sport-utility on the market, Amigo has quite a few virtues. Like its competitors, though, an Amigo is not a good bet for everyday transportation.

SPECIFICATIONS

	2-door wagon
Wheelbase, in.	91.7
Overall length, in.	168.1
Overall width, in.	70.1
Overall height, in.	69.9
Curb weight, lbs.	3615
Cargo volume, cu. ft.	51.0
Fuel capacity, gals.	21.9
Seating capacity	4
Front head room, in.	38.0
Max. front leg room, in.	42.5
Rear head room, in.	32.0
Min. rear leg room, in.	19.5

Powertrain layout: longitudinal front-engine/rear- or 4-wheel drive

ENGINES

	ohc I-4	ohc I-4
Size, liters/cu. in.	2.3/138	2.6/156
Horsepower	120	120
Torque (lbs./ft.)	123	146-150
EPA city/highway mpg		
5-speed OD manual		18/21

	ohc I-4	ohc I-4
4-speed OD automatic..		16/20
Consumer Guide™ observed MPG 5-speed OD manual...		14.4

Built in Japan.

RETAIL PRICES	GOOD	AVERAGE	POOR
1990 Amigo	$2,700-4,400	$2,100-3,700	$900-1,900
1991 Amigo	3,400-5,700	2,700-5,000	1,200-2,800
1992 Amigo	4,200-6,800	3,500-6,000	1,600-3,500
1993 Amigo	4,900-7,800	4,200-7,000	2,200-4,400
1994 Amigo	6,400-9,500	5,700-8,700	3,400-5,800

AVERAGE REPLACEMENT COSTS

A/C Compressor $570	Clutch, Pressure Plate,
Alternator 305	Bearing 560
Radiator 710	Universal Joints 140
Timing Chain or Belt 100	Brakes..................................280
Automatic Transmission or	Shocks and/or Struts 280
Transaxle.........................845	Exhaust System.................430

TROUBLE SPOTS

• **Oil leak** Oil leak from the distributor shaft on 2.3-liter engine. (1990-93)

• **Keys** The ignition key can be hard to remove because the lens over the shift lever interferes with the shift cable. (1992)

• **Steering noise** A knocking noise when the steering wheel is turned requires a steering column repair kit. (1990-94) Lack of grease causes squawks in column. (1993-94)

• **Air conditioner** The air conditioner gradually becomes warmer due to ice forming on the evaporator due to a dislocated thermostat. (1993)

RECALL HISTORY

1994 Latch in seatbelt buckle could engage only partially, causing tongue to come out during collision or hard braking.

1991-97 ISUZU RODEO

FOR 4WD traction • Ride • Anti-lock brakes (4-wheel opt. after '96) • Passenger and cargo room • Air bags (later models)

AGAINST Entry/exit • No shift-on-the-fly (pre '96) • Road noise • Wind noise • Fuel economy

ISUZU

1992 Isuzu Rodeo

EVALUATION Acceleration is adequate but less than brisk with the early V-6 and automatic. The 3.2-liter V-6, made available in 1993, is an improvement in terms of smoothness and quietness. That V-6 works well with automatic, which changes gears smoothly and downshifts promptly for passing. Gas mileage is nothing to boast about. One test Rodeo averaged just 16.1 mpg.

Ride is firm yet surprisingly comfortable, as the absorbent suspension handily soaks up just about every flaw on paved roads. Braking distances are acceptable, though a 2WD Rodeo turned out to be prone to abrupt front-wheel lockup. Road noise is prominent at highway speeds.

Occupants are treated well in a Rodeo. Rear leg room is ample, even with the front seats all the way back. Head clearance is good all around, and the driving position is comfortable for most people. Back doors are quite narrow at sill level, and open only about 70 degrees, so larger folks might feel squeezed when getting in and out. The full-size spare tire mounted inside many models cuts considerably into cargo space. Except for too many confusing buttons controlling lights and wipers, and a low-mounted radio, the dashboard is fine.

The need to stop the vehicle to engage 4WD, then stop and back up to disengage it, is an inconvenience. Otherwise, the competent and tightly-constructed Rodeo deserves a serious look, as it just might be the best Isuzu model on the market.

NHTSA CRASH TEST RESULTS
1996 Isuzu Rodeo 4x4

4-DOOR WAGON

Driver	☆☆☆☆
Passenger	☆☆☆

(The National Highway Traffic Safety Administration tests a vehicle's crashworthiness in front and side collisions. Their ratings suggest the chance of serious injury: ☆☆☆☆☆—10% or less; ☆☆☆☆—10-20% or less; ☆☆☆—20-30% or less; ☆☆—35-45% or less; ☆—More than 45%.)

SPECIFICATIONS

	4-door wagon
Wheelbase, in.	108.7
Overall length, in.	176.5
Overall width, in.	66.5
Overall height, in.	65.4
Curb weight, lbs.	3545
Cargo volume, cu. ft.	74.9
Fuel capacity, gals.	21.9
Seating capacity	6
Front head room, in.	38.2
Max. front leg room, in.	42.5
Rear head room, in.	37.8
Min. rear leg room, in.	36.1

ENGINES

	ohc I-4	ohv V-6	ohc V-6
Size, liters/cu. in.	2.6/156	3.1/191	3.2/193
Horsepower	120	120	175-190
Torque (lbs./ft.)	146-150	165	188
EPA city/highway mpg			
5-speed OD manual	18/22	15/19	16/19
4-speed OD automatic		15/18	15.18
Consumer Guide™ observed MPG			
5-speed OD manual			18.2
4-speed OD automatic		17.9	16.1

Built in USA.

RETAIL PRICES

	GOOD	AVERAGE	POOR
1991 Rodeo	$4,300-7,800	$3,600-7,000	$1,800-4,800
1992 Rodeo	5,000-9,000	4,200-8,100	2,400-5,700
1993 Rodeo	6,400-11,000	5,500-10,000	3,500-7,200
1994 Rodeo	7,500-13,000	6,500-12,000	4,200-8,800
1995 Rodeo	9,800-16,500	8,800-15,200	6,000-11,500
1996 Rodeo	11,500-19,000	10,200-17,500	7,200-13,500
1997 Rodeo	13,000-20,500	11,500-19,000	8,200-14,800
1998 Rodeo	15,500-24,500	14,000-23,000	10,000-18,500

AVERAGE REPLACEMENT COSTS

A/C Compressor	$685	Clutch, Pressure Plate, Bearing	595
Alternator	295	Universal Joints	120
Radiator	660	Brakes	280
Timing Chain or Belt	100	Shocks and/or Struts	200
Automatic Transmission or Transaxle	1,375	Exhaust System	320

TROUBLE SPOTS

• **Cruise control** The cruise control may not let the transmission shift down out of overdrive on hills. (1991)

• **Transmission noise** Lack of lube on the clutch shift fork pivot ball causes noises and squeaks and a new ball stud with a lube fitting is available to fix it. (1991-94)

• **Air conditioner** The air conditioner gradually becomes warmer due to ice forming on the evaporator because the thermostat was located in the wrong place. (1993)

• **Keys** The ignition key can be hard to remove because the lens over the shift lever interferes with the shift cable. (1992)

• **Steering noise** A knocking noise when the steering wheel is turned requires a steering column repair kit. (1991-94) Lack of grease causes squeaks in column. (1994)

RECALL HISTORY

1991 w/V-6 Incorrect transmission-fluid dipstick may have been installed. **1993-94** Camshaft plug can become dislodged, allowing oil to leak; can cause engine damage and fire. **1994** Latch in seatbelt buckle could engage only partially, causing tongue to come out during collision or hard braking.

1992-98 ISUZU TROOPER

1995 Isuzu Trooper 4-door

FOR 4WD traction • Passenger and cargo room • Anti-lock brakes • Air bags (1995-97)

AGAINST Fuel economy • Entry/exit • Lack of shift-on-the-fly (pre-96) • No air bags (early models)

EVALUATION All three V-6 engines are silky and quiet, if not quite frisky. An early automatic LS wagon accelerated to 60 mph in a wholly adequate 11.7 seconds, but speed trails off fast on steep grades. Although the automatic transmission hunts busily between gears in urban driving, it's smooth and responsive. Gas mileage isn't great—we averaged just 15.8 mpg.

The 4-door has a stable, pleasantly supple ride, dealing with most bumps in a manner comparable to a large station wagon. It fails to soak up big bumps well, though, and feels somewhat harsh on rough pavement. A Trooper easily tackles tough off-road terrain. Quick highway cornering induces mild body lean, but little of the typical tall-4WD queasiness. Tire roar is low, but wind noise high. Braking is above average for the sport-utility class.

Troopers rank among the roomiest sport-utility vehicles. Head room is bountiful, and the back seats three adults comfortably. Visibility is great. The driver's area is attractive and convenient.

Rating high on our list of upscale 4x4s, early Troopers trail such rivals as the Ford Explorer and Jeep Grand Cherokee mainly in their omission of shift-on-the-fly 4WD (on 1992-95 models) and an air bag (1992-94 models).

NHTSA CRASH TEST RESULTS
1996 Isuzu Trooper 4WD

4-DOOR WAGON

Driver	☆☆☆
Passenger	☆☆☆

(The National Highway Traffic Safety Administration tests a vehicle's crashworthiness in front and side collisions. Their ratings suggest the chance of serious injury: ☆☆☆☆☆—10% or less; ☆☆☆☆—10-20% or less; ☆☆☆—20-30% or less; ☆☆—35-45% or less; ☆—More than 45%.)

SPECIFICATIONS

	2-door wagon	4-door wagon
Wheelbase, in.	91.7	108.7
Overall length, in.	166.5	183.5
Overall width, in.	68.7	68.7
Overall height, in.	72.8	72.8
Curb weight, lbs.	4060	4210
Cargo volume, cu. ft.	68.3	90.0
Fuel capacity, gals.	22.5	22.5
Seating capacity	5	5
Front head room, in.	39.8	39.8
Max. front leg room, in.	40.8	40.8
Rear head room, in.	39.8	39.8
Min. rear leg room, in.	32.2	39.1

Powertrain layout: longitudinal front-engine/rear- or 4-wheel drive

ENGINES

	ohc V-6	dohc V-6	dohc V-6
Size, liters/cu. in.	3.2/193	3.2/193	3.5/213

ISUZU

	ohc V-6	dohc V-6	dohc V-6
Horsepower	175-190	190	215
Torque (lbs./ft.)	188	195	230
EPA city/highway mpg			
5-speed OD manual	16/18	14/17	16/19
4-speed OD automatic	14/18	14/17	
Consumer Guide™ observed MPG			
4-speed OD automatic	14.9	15.8	16.4

Built in Japan.

RETAIL PRICES	GOOD	AVERAGE	POOR
1992 Trooper	$6,300-9,500	$5,600-8,700	$3,500-6,000
1993 Trooper	8,200-11,500	7,500-10,500	5,000-7,400
1994 Trooper	10,500-14,000	9,500-12,800	6,500-9,500
1995 Trooper	13,000-18,000	11,700-16,500	8,500-12,500
1996 Trooper	15,200-23,000	13,800-21,500	10,000-17,000
1997 Trooper	18,000-26,000	16,500-24,000	12,500-19,500
1998 Trooper	20,000-28,500	18,500-26,500	14,500-22,000

AVERAGE REPLACEMENT COSTS

A/C Compressor $1,260	Clutch, Pressure Plate,
Alternator 295	Bearing............................660
Radiator 740	Universal Joints 190
Timing Chain or Belt 100	Brakes................................340
Automatic Transmission or	Shocks and/or Struts 320
Transaxle.....................1,465	Exhaust System.................370

TROUBLE SPOTS

• **Suspension noise** The differential may chatter and vibrate on turns requiring the oil to be drained and refilled including a bottle of limited-slip additive. (1992-93)

• **Keys** The ignition key can be hard to remove because the lens over the shift lever interferes with the shift cable. (1992)

• **Cruise control** The cruise control may not let the transmission shift down out of overdrive on hills. (1991)

• **Windows** The fuse for the power windows, cruise control and instrument panel may blow due to an intermittent short in the 3-4 gear switch for the transmission. (1994)

RECALL HISTORY

1992-94 Camshaft plug can become dislodged from cylinder head, allowing oil to leak; can cause engine damage and fire. **1996** Certain vehicles have incorrect rear center seatbelt buckle; tongue cannot be inserted. **1996-97** Left front brake line can be damaged, resulting in fluid leakage, reduced brake effectiveness, and longer stopping distance.

1990-96 JEEP CHEROKEE

1991 Jeep Cherokee Sport 2-door

FOR   Air bag, driver (later models) • Wet weather traction (4WD) • Acceleration (6-cylinder) • Passenger and cargo room

AGAINST   Fuel economy • Acceleration (4-cylinder) • Noise

EVALUATION   The base 4-cylinder Cherokee's engine is adequate with manual shift, weak under a heavy load, and downright feeble and unresponsive if hooked to an automatic transmission. With either transmission, the robust 6-cylinder engine lets you sprint away from stoplights and quickly pass other vehicles. Expect about 17 mpg with a manual-shift six, or 15 mpg with automatic. All models have higher-than-average wind, road, and engine noise.

These vehicles are spacious inside for their modest exterior dimensions—though not quite comparable to the Grand Cherokee or a Ford Explorer. Four sit in comfort. Head room is generous all around, and with a little squeezing, backseats accommodate three adults. Folding that rear seatback produces great luggage space, with a long and flat floor, and volume is acceptable with the seatback up. The long steering column puts the wheel too close to the driver's chest.

Cherokees, in short, offer a lot of temptations—an excellent alternative for those who cannot afford a Grand Cherokee or Explorer. Next to something like the latest Chevrolet Blazer, though, they do seem a step behind in civility.

NHTSA CRASH TEST RESULTS
1995 Jeep Cherokee

4-DOOR WAGON

Driver	☆☆☆☆
Passenger	☆☆☆☆

(The National Highway Traffic Safety Administration tests a vehicle's crashworthiness in front and side collisions. Their ratings suggest the chance of serious injury: ☆☆☆☆☆—10% or less; ☆☆☆☆—10-20% or less; ☆☆☆—20-30% or less; ☆☆—35-45% or less; ☆—More than 45%.)

SPECIFICATIONS

	2-door wagon	4-door wagon
Wheelbase, in.	101.4	101.4
Overall length, in.	166.9	166.9
Overall width, in.	67.7	67.7
Overall height, in.	63.8	63.8
Curb weight, lbs.	2905	2955
Cargo volume, cu. ft.	71.8	71.8
Fuel capacity, gals.	20.2	20.2
Seating capacity	5	5
Front head room, in.	38.3	38.3
Max. front leg room, in.	41.4	41.4
Rear head room, in.	38.5	38.5
Min. rear leg room, in.	34.9	34.9

Powertrain layout: longitudinal front-engine/rear- or 4-wheel drive

ENGINES

	ohv I-4	ohv I-6
Size, liters/cu. in.	2.5/151	4.0/242
Horsepower	121-130	177-190
Torque (lbs./ft.)	141-150	224-225

EPA city/highway mpg

5-speed OD manual	19/22	17/22
4-speed OD automatic		15/19

Consumer Guide™ observed MPG

5-speed OD manual	17.0
4-speed OD automatic	15.0

Built in USA.

RETAIL PRICES

	GOOD	AVERAGE	POOR
1990 Cherokee	$3,500-6,500	$2,800-5,700	$1,100-3,500
1991 Cherokee	4,200-6,800	3,500-6,000	1,600-3,700
1992 Cherokee	4,800-9,800	4,100-9,000	2,000-6,300
1993 Cherokee	5,600-9,500	4,800-8,700	2,500-5,800
1994 Cherokee	6,400-11,000	5,600-10,000	3,000-7,000
1995 Cherokee	7,600-13,200	6,800-12,200	3,800-8,500
1996 Cherokee	9,200-15,000	8,200-13,800	5,000-10,000
1997 Cherokee	11,300-17,700	10,100-16,200	6,500-12,000

	GOOD	AVERAGE	POOR
1998 Cherokee	13,200-20,500	12,000-19,000	8,000-14,500

AVERAGE REPLACEMENT COSTS

A/C Compressor $390
Alternator 355
Radiator 380
Timing Chain or Belt 185
Automatic Transmission or
   Transaxle........................680

Clutch, Pressure Plate,
   Bearing............................495
Universal Joints 145
Brakes...................................265
Shocks and/or Struts 190
Exhaust System.................270

TROUBLE SPOTS

• **Oil leak** The rear main seals on 2.5L and 4.0L engines are prone to leakage if the vehicle is operated in dirty conditions. Dirt acts as an abrasive when it collects on the seal. To prevent future failures Chrysler has a rubber plug available that goes in a hole above the starter, which protects the rear main seal. Beware of vehicles that have been regularly driven on dirt roads or off-road. (1991-96)

• **Air conditioner** If the air conditioner gradually stops cooling and/or the airflow from the vents decreases, the computer (PCM) may not be sending a signal to the compressor clutch relay to cycle off, which causes the AC evaporator to freeze up. When the ice melts, after the car sits for awhile, the AC works again briefly. Many technicians overlook this as the source of trouble. (1991-95)

• **Poor transmission shift** If the transmission will not engage (from two to eight seconds) when first started, chances are the torque converter is draining down. Chrysler will correct the problem by installing a check valve in the fluid line leading to the transmission cooler as long as the vehicle is still under warranty. (1993) If the transmission won't upshift for about the first quarter mile in cool weather, it is probably due to defective cast iron seal rings in the governor drive. This repair is covered under the standard warranty. (1993-94)

• **Transmission leak** Automatic transmission fluid leaks from the speed sensor in the transmission, which Chrysler will replace under its powertrain warranty. (1993-94)

RECALL HISTORY

1990 w/ABS Hydraulic fluid may be contaminated. **1990 w/4.0-liter engine and automatic** Could have intermittent high idle speed. **1990-91 w/ABS** Hydraulic control unit for anti-lock braking system can experience excessive brake actuator piston seal wear, which could lead to loss of anti-lock function and reduced power assist. **1990-91 in 15 states and Washington D.C.** Front disc brake rotors can experience severe corrosion if operated for extensive period in "salt belt;" can eventually compromise structural integrity, allowing wear surface to separate from hub. **1990-91 w/ABS** Improper insertion/crimping of hose fittings can result in loss of ABS function. **1991 w/ABS** Brake fluid tube may contact steering shaft and result in leakage. **1991** Jounce bumper could contact and collapse left rear brake tube. **1993** Retainer clip that secures master cylinder rod to brake pedal was not installed properly. **1993-96** High steering loads can cause steering-gear bolts to break or frame to crack. **1994** Rear seatbelt bolts may not support passengers in sudden stop. **1995** Certain air bags might not deploy in an accident. **1995** Parking brake handle release button can separate, so parking brake may not hold and vehicle could roll inadvertently. **1996** Fasteners that secure alternator fuse could have improper clamp load; arcing could cause fire in engine compartment. **1997** Fuel-level sending unit degrades over time, causing gauge to show significantly more fuel in tank than is actually present. **1998** Front seatbelt shoulder anchors were not properly heat treated and hardened; in crash, front occupant may not be properly restrained. **1998** Power brake booster vacuum reservoir diaphragm can split or tear; may cause increase in engine idle speed and loss of power brake assist.

1993-97 JEEP GRAND CHEROKEE

1993 Jeep Grand Cherokee Laredo

FOR Air bags (later models) • Anti-lock brakes • Wet weather traction (4WD) • Passenger and cargo room

AGAINST Fuel economy • Engine noise • Reliability (early models)

EVALUATION Base-engine power is adequate for most drivers, but the 5.2-liter V-8 is much better, especially in low-speed acceleration. It delivers strong off-the-line pickup as well as brisk passing response. The 5.9-liter in the Limited model has even more power at low speeds. We averaged 16.5 mpg in a 6-cylinder Grand Cherokee, and a meager 13.3 mpg with a V-8. All three engines can get noisy, though they're much quieter when cruising.

Interior room is good though the spare tire takes up space. Head and leg room are generous all around, and three fit the rear seat. Entry/exit to the front requires only a slight step up. Rear doors are narrow at the bottom and don't open wide enough to allow large people to get in or out without bending a little. With the rear seatback up, luggage space isn't much greater than in a mid-size car. Even with the child seat that became available during 1994, rear seatbacks can be folded down to create a long cargo floor.

Early Grand Cherokees suffered some reliability problems, so a later model might be a better bet. We rate the Grand a step behind the Ford Explorer, but both lead the field in refinement, ability, and overall quality. An Explorer is more trucklike, a trait that some buyers like and others do not, but the Grand Cherokee offers impressive on- and off-road performance, plus a broad range of engine and 4WD choices.

NHTSA CRASH TEST RESULTS
1996 Jeep Grand Cherokee 4-DOOR WAGON

Driver	☆☆☆
Passenger	☆☆☆☆

(The National Highway Traffic Safety Administration tests a vehicle's crashworthiness in front and side collisions. Their ratings suggest the chance of serious injury: ☆☆☆☆☆—10% or less; ☆☆☆☆—10-20% or less; ☆☆☆—20-30% or less; ☆☆—35-45% or less; ☆—More than 45%.)

SPECIFICATIONS

	4-door wagon
Wheelbase, in.	105.9
Overall length, in.	179.0
Overall width, in.	70.9
Overall height, in.	64.7
Curb weight, lbs.	3614
Cargo volume, cu. ft.	79.3
Fuel capacity, gals.	23.0
Seating capacity	5
Front head room, in.	38.9
Max. front leg room, in.	40.9
Rear head room, in.	39.1
Min. rear leg room, in.	35.7

Powertrain layout: longitudinal front-engine/rear- or 4-wheel drive

ENGINES

	ohv I-6	ohv V-8	ohv V-8
Size, liters/cu. in.	4.0/242	5.2/318	5.9/360

JEEP

	ohv I-6	ohv V-8	ohv V-8
Horsepower	185-190	220	245
Torque (lbs./ft.)	200-225	285-300	345

EPA city/highway mpg

5-speed OD manual	16/20		
4-speed OD automatic	15/20	14/18	13/17

Consumer Guide™ observed MPG

4-speed OD automatic	16.5	13.3	14.6

Built in USA.

RETAIL PRICES	GOOD	AVERAGE	POOR
1993 Grand Cherokee	$8,000-13,000	$7,300-12,000	$5,000-8,800
1994 Grand Cherokee	9,300-15,500	8,500-14,300	6,000-11,000
1995 Grand Cherokee	11,500-18,000	10,300-16,500	7,500-13,000
1996 Grand Cherokee	14,000-20,500	12,500-19,000	9,300-15,200
1997 Grand Cherokee	16,500-24,000	15,000-22,500	11,500-18,500
1998 Grand Cherokee	19,500-28,500	18,000-27,000	14,500-23,000

AVERAGE REPLACEMENT COSTS

A/C Compressor	$390	Clutch, Pressure Plate,	
Alternator	360	Bearing	375
Radiator	380	Universal Joints	135
Timing Chain or Belt	195	Brakes	300
Automatic Transmission or		Shocks and/or Struts	155
Transaxle	700	Exhaust System	270

TROUBLE SPOTS

• **Oil leak** The rear main seals on 2.5L and 4.0L engines are prone to leakage if the vehicle is operated in dirty conditions. Dirt acts as an abrasive when it collects on the seal. To prevent future failures Chrysler has a rubber plug available that goes in a hole above the starter, which protects the rear main seal. Beware of vehicles that have been regularly driven on dirt roads or off-road. (1993-96)

• **Oil leak** A chronic oil leak at the filter on 5.2L engine is likely due to a warped adapter plate, not the filter itself. Under warranty, the adapter and its gasket will be replaced. (1995)

• **Engine misfire** Because of a problem with the idle air control motor, the engine idles rough, stalls at low speeds or when decelerating, especially in warm weather. The IAC motor will be replaced under warranty. (1993-94)

• **Oil consumption and engine knock** Oil pump gear wear results in bucking and surging when the engine is warm and lack of lubrication when the engine is cold. Beware of additional internal wear if the vehicle has high mileage and the pump is noisy but has not been replaced. (1993)

• **Air conditioner** If the air conditioner gradually stops cooling and/or the airflow from the vents decreases, the computer (PCM) may not be sending a signal to the compressor clutch relay to cycle off, which causes the AC evaporator to freeze up. When the ice melts, the AC works again briefly. Many technicians overlook this as the source of trouble. (1993-95)

• **Transmission slippage** If the transmission will not engage (from two to eight seconds) when first started, chances are the torque converter is draining down. Chrysler will correct the problem by installing a check valve in the fluid line leading to the transmission cooler as long as the vehicle is still under warranty. (1993)

• **Transmission leak** Automatic transmission fluid leaks from the speed sensor in the transmission, which Chrysler will replace under its powertrain warranty. (1993-94)

• **Transmission slippage** If the transmission won't upshift for about the first quarter mile in cool weather due to defective cast iron seal rings in the governor drive. The repair may be covered under the standard warranty. (1993-94)

RECALL HISTORY

1993 Molded plastic pin that connects upper and lower steering column shafts may be sheared; shafts could separate, causing total loss of steering control. **1993** Eccentric cam adjuster bolts in both front lower suspension arm-to-front axle bracket attachments may fail, causing vehicle to pull to one side. **1993 in 15 states and Washington D.C.** Front disc brake rotors can experience severe corrosion if operated for extensive period in "salt belt;" can eventually compromise structural integrity, allowing wear surface to separate from hub. **1993** Retainer clip that secures master cylinder input rod to brake pedal could work loose, allowing separation, which may cause loss of braking. **1995** Parking brake release button can separate, so brake may not hold and vehicle could roll inadvertently. **1996** Fasteners that secure alternator fuse could have improper clamp load; arcing could cause fire in engine compartment. **1996 w/Quadra-Trac, temporary spare tire, and 225/70R16 or 245/70R15 tires** When temporary spare tire is in use, front axle can overheat; can force fluid out of seals, increasing risk of fire. **1997** Air bag could deploy inadvertently when ignition is shut off. **1997** Fuel-level sending unit degrades over time, causing gauge to show significantly more fuel in tank than is actually present. **1998** Power brake booster vacuum reservoir diaphragm can split or tear; may cause increase in engine idle speed and loss of power brake assist.

1990-95 JEEP WRANGLER

1991 Jeep Wrangler S

FOR   Wet weather traction • Acceleration (6-cylinder) • Maneuverability • Visibility • Anti-lock brakes (optional with 6-cylinder)

AGAINST   Ride/handling • Fuel economy • Entry/exit • Cargo room • Instruments/controls • Engine noise • Wind noise • Road noise

EVALUATION   Acceleration and drivability are only adequate from the initial 6-cylinder engine; gas mileage mediocre. Meager is the word for acceleration from the 4-cylinder engine. Performance got a welcome boost from the fuel-injected six of 1991. Jeep claimed a 0-60 mph acceleration time of 9.7 seconds, versus 14.3 seconds for the old carbureted 6-cylinder engine.

Climbing aboard isn't so easy, as it's a tall step over the door sills. Once inside, you get a cramped rear seat and tiny cargo area (unless the rear seat is tilted out of the way). Tall people have ample head room all around to sit comfortably upright. Once aboard, you can expect to be assaulted by road noise and wind buffeting—whether the top is up or down.

Consider seriously how you would use the vehicle, and if the compromises in on-road ride, handling, and fuel economy are worth it in the end. Also look at an Isuzu Amigo, which lacks the Jeep's classic image but feels just about as tough, as well as the Geo Tracker/Suzuki Sidekick, with their friendlier ergonomics. But none of those rivals have a muscular 6-cylinder engine like Wrangler's. We don't recommend any mini 4x4 as a daily driver, but plenty of people love them.

NHTSA CRASH TEST RESULTS
1994 Jeep Wrangler   2-DOOR CONVERTIBLE

Driver   ☆☆
Passenger   ☆☆☆☆

(The National Highway Traffic Safety Administration tests a vehicle's crashworthiness in front and side collisions. Their ratings suggest the chance of serious injury: ☆☆☆☆☆—10% *or less;* ☆☆☆☆—10-20% *or less;* ☆☆☆—20-30% *or less;* ☆☆—35-45% *or less;* ☆—*More than 45%.)*

SPECIFICATIONS

	2-door conv.
Wheelbase, in.	93.4
Overall length, in.	153.0
Overall width, in.	66.0
Overall height, in.	69.6
Curb weight, lbs.	NA
Cargo volume, cu. ft.	43.2
Fuel capacity, gals.	15.0/20.0
Seating capacity	4
Front head room, in.	40.2
Max. front leg room, in.	39.4
Rear head room, in.	40.5
Min. rear leg room, in.	35.0

Powertrain layout: longitudinal front-engine/rear- or all-wheel drive

ENGINES

	ohv I-4	ohv I-6	ohv I-6
Size, liters/cu. in.	2.5/150	4.0/242	4.2/256
Horsepower	117-123	180	112
Torque (lbs./ft.)	138-139	200	210

EPA city/highway mpg

5-speed OD manual	19/20	15/18	16/20
3-speed automatic	17/18	15/17	15/16

Consumer Guide™ observed MPG

5-speed OD manual	18.1		12.9
3-speed automatic		14.6	

Built in Canada.

RETAIL PRICES

	GOOD	AVERAGE	POOR
1990 Wrangler	$3,700-5,000	$3,000-4,300	$1,300-2,000
1991 Wrangler	4,600-6,500	3,900-5,800	1,900-3,200
1992 Wrangler	5,500-7,500	4,700-6,700	2,500-3,800
1993 Wrangler	6,300-8,800	5,500-8,000	3,100-4,800
1994 Wrangler	7,200-11,000	6,300-10,000	3,700-6,300
1995 Wrangler	8,400-12,500	7,400-11,500	4,400-7,500

AVERAGE REPLACEMENT COSTS

A/C Compressor $375	Clutch, Pressure Plate,
Alternator 315	Bearing.............................690
Radiator 355	Universal Joints 130
Timing Chain or Belt 185	Brakes..................................275
Automatic Transmission or	Shocks and/or Struts 180
Transaxle.........................690	Exhaust System.................255

TROUBLE SPOTS

• **Oil leak** The rear main seals on 2.5L and 4.0L engines are prone to leakage if the vehicle is operated in dirty conditions. Dirt acts as an abrasive when it collects on the seal. To prevent future failures Chrysler has a rubber plug available that goes in a hole above the starter, which protects the rear main seal. Beware of vehicles that have been regularly driven on dirt roads or off-road. (1991-96)

• **Transmission slippage** If the transmission will not engage (from two to eight seconds) when first started, chances are the torque converter is draining down. Chrysler will correct the problem by installing a check valve in the fluid line leading to the transmission cooler as long as the vehicle is still under warranty. (1993) If the transmission won't upshift for about the first quarter mile in cool weather, it is probably due to defective cast iron seal rings in the governor drive. This repair is covered under the standard warranty. (1992-94)

• **Transmission leak** Automatic transmission fluid leaks from the speed sensor in the transmission that Chrysler will replace under its powertrain warranty. (1992-94)

RECALL HISTORY

1990-91 in 15 states and Washington D.C. Front disc brake rotors can experience severe corrosion if operated for extensive period in "salt belt;" can eventually compromise structural integrity, allowing wear surface to separate from hub. **1990-92** Front brake hoses can wear due to contact with splash shields. **1990-93** Plastic fuel tank's sending unit gasket can crack, resulting in fuel and vapor leaks. **1991-93 w/manual shift** Salt corrosion between starter solenoid wire and battery feed may short these connections.

1997-98 JEEP WRANGLER

FOR Optional anti-lock brakes • 4WD versatility • Maneuverability

AGAINST Fuel economy • Acceleration (4-cylinder) • Noise • Ride

EVALUATION Wranglers really are more carlike than be-

1997 Jeep Wrangler Sahara

fore—far better in ride quality and ergonomics. Occupant comfort is vastly improved, though few would call the Wrangler experience comfortable. The new suspension is a lot more absorbent, true, but it still reacts abruptly to dips and bumps. Unless the pavement really gets nasty, though, the ride isn't jarring.

A 4-cylinder Wrangler with manual shift has trouble merging or overtaking fast-moving freeway traffic. Performance in a 5-speed Wrangler with the 6-cylinder engine gets reasonably vigorous—though accompanied by considerable engine and gear noise. Fuel economy is tolerable, but no bonus. A 5-speed Sahara with the 6-cylinder engine averaged 19.3 mpg.

Wind noise is abundant where the roof meets the windshield frame. Doors seal poorly, too, with the canvas top in place. That canvas top also flutters, while the optional hardtop "drums" at highway speeds. Taking the top up and down is easier than before, but still a frustrating chore. Full instruments now are clustered in front of the driver, not spread out as in prior Wranglers. Two adults now fit in back without squeezing, but the cushion and backrest are hard and short. Interior storage is better than in earlier Wranglers. Space behind the back seat is modest.

True Wrangler fans don't care about its flaws, of course. For other potential owners, the great strides made in safety, ride quality, and refinement in this generation brings Wrangler closer than before to serving as an everyday vehicle.

NHTSA CRASH TEST RESULTS
1997 Jeep Wrangler 2-DOOR CONVERTIBLE

Driver	☆☆☆☆
Passenger	☆☆☆☆☆

JEEP

(The National Highway Traffic Safety Administration tests a vehicle's crashworthiness in front and side collisions. Their ratings suggest the chance of serious injury: ☆☆☆☆☆—10% or less; ☆☆☆☆—10-20% or less; ☆☆☆—20-30% or less; ☆☆—35-45% or less; ☆—More than 45%.)

SPECIFICATIONS

	2-door conv.
Wheelbase, in.	93.4
Overall length, in.	151.8
Overall width, in.	66.7
Overall height, in.	70.2
Curb weight, lbs.	3092
Cargo volume, cu. ft.	55.7
Fuel capacity, gals.	15.0
Seating capacity	4
Front head room, in.	42.3
Max. front leg room, in.	41.1
Rear head room, in.	40.6
Min. rear leg room, in.	34.9

ENGINES

	ohv I-4	ohv I-6
Size, liters/cu. in.	2.5/151	4.0/242
Horsepower	120	181
Torque (lbs./ft.)	140	222
EPA city/highway mpg		
5-speed OD manual	19/20	15/18
3-speed automatic	17/18	15/17
Consumer Guide™ observed MPG		
5-speed OD manual		19.3
3-speed automatic		15.2

Built in USA.

RETAIL PRICES

	GOOD	AVERAGE	POOR
1997 Wrangler	$13,000-17,000	$11,800-15,500	$8,800-12,000
1998 Wrangler	14,500-19,000	13,000-17,500	9,500-13,500

AVERAGE REPLACEMENT COSTS

A/C Compressor	$375	Clutch, Pressure Plate, Bearing	2,165
Alternator	315	Universal Joints	220
Radiator	300	Brakes	270
Timing Chain or Belt	200	Shocks and/or Struts	190
Automatic Transmission or Transaxle	930	Exhaust System	220

TROUBLE SPOTS

• **Fuel gauge** The gas gauge needle may not point to full, may show

⅛ to ¼ full when the tank is empty. (1997)

- **Fuel odors** The gas tank may fill slowly or the pump nozzle will keep shutting off due to a problem with the fuel tank venting system. (1997)

- **Water leak** Water may leak onto the passenger side, front floor due to leaks in the heater and air conditioner housing or from a problem with the evaporator drain tube. (1997)

- **Steering problems** Fluid leaks from the power steering reservoir. (1997)

- **Doors** The doors may not unlock with the key requiring replacement of the door latches. (1997)

RECALL HISTORY

1997 Air bag control module on some vehicles contains an error that can delay deployment in certain crash situations. **1997** Air bag could deploy inadvertently when ignition is shut off. **1997 w/manual steering** Driver's air bag wiring harness can break when steering wheel is turned to "full lock" position; in crash, air bag would not deploy. **1998** Power brake booster vacuum reservoir diaphragm can split or tear; may cause increase in engine idle speed and loss of power brake assist. **1998** Front seatbelt shoulder anchors were not properly heat treated and hardened; in a crash, occupant may not be properly restrained.

1990-96 LEXUS ES 250/300

✓ BEST BUY

1990 Lexus ES 250

FOR Acceleration • Air bags (later models) • Anti-lock brakes • Ride/handling • Passenger and cargo room

AGAINST Road noise • Automatic transmission performance

LEXUS

• Fuel economy • Visibility

EVALUATION The ES 250 has a comfortable ride, soaking up bumps with little notice. It also tends to display good control and stability at high speed, while the standard anti-lock brakes provide strong, safe stops with good control. The ES 250 also provides a bright, airy interior with tall windows, which give the driver excellent visibility. Leg room is generous both front and back, but head room is about average.

More distinctive styling and a 3.0-liter V-6 gave the rebadged ES 300 both the extra size and power it needed. The 300 provides outstanding responsiveness and handling. The same smooth and quiet ride that has become a Lexus hallmark is quite evident in the ES 300. However, body roll is noticeable and the steering is on the light side. While not quite up to full European standards in the suspension or steering departments, the ride and handling should not be an issue with most buyers. On the plus side, the ES 300 offers more passenger space thatnits compact external dimensions suggest. Leg room and head room are generous, even with the optional sunroof. Drivers enjoy a comfortably upright stance ahead of a tilt steering wheel and an attractive, well-arranged dashboard that mimics the panel design of the big LS 400. Some rear-seat space is sacrificed, however, for the sake of trunk room, which is more than adequate.

Much more than a glorified Camry, the ES 250/300 has helped Lexus maintain a solid image in the luxury car market.

SPECIFICATIONS

	4-door sedan	4-door sedan
Wheelbase, in.	102.4	103.1
Overall length, in.	183.1	187.8
Overall width, in.	66.9	70.0
Overall height, in.	53.1	53.9
Curb weight, lbs.	3164	3362
Cargo volume, cu. ft.	13.1	14.3
Fuel capacity, gals.	15.9	18.5
Seating capacity	5	5
Front head room, in.	37.8	37.8
Max. front leg room, in.	42.9	43.5
Rear head room, in.	36.6	36.6
Min. rear leg room, in.	32.3	33.1

Powertrain layout: transverse front-engine/front-wheel drive

ENGINES

	dohc V-6	dohc V-6	dohc V-6
Size, liters/cu. in.	2.5/153	3.0/181	3.0/181
Horsepower	156	185	188

	dohc V-6	dohc V-6	dohc V-6
Torque (lbs./ft.)	160	195	203

EPA city/highway mpg

5-speed OD manual	19/26	18/24	
4-speed OD automatic	19/25	18/23	18/24

Consumer Guide™ observed MPG

5-speed OD manual	22.7		
4-speed OD automatic		19.5	19.3

Built in Japan.

RETAIL PRICES	GOOD	AVERAGE	POOR
1990 ES 250	$4,900-5,700	$4,200-4,900	$2,300-2,800
1991 ES 250	6,200-7,500	5,400-6,700	3,200-4,000
1992 ES 300	10,000-11,500	9,000-10,500	6,200-7,200
1993 ES 300	12,400-14,000	11,200-12,700	8,000-9,000
1994 ES 300	15,000-16,800	13,500-15,300	10,000-11,200
1995 ES 300	17,500-19,500	16,000-18,000	12,000-13,500
1996 ES 300	21,000-23,200	19,000-21,200	14,500-16,000

AVERAGE REPLACEMENT COSTS

A/C Compressor	$905	Clutch, Pressure Plate, Bearing	670
Alternator	370	Constant Velocity Joints.....	700
Radiator	640	Brakes..................................	195
Timing Chain or Belt	190	Shocks and/or Struts	870
Automatic Transmission or Transaxle......................	1,410	Exhaust System 435 (ES 2,50)	

TROUBLE SPOTS

• **Transmission leak** Automatic transmission fluid may leak from a casting knock hole or a bolt hole on the A51E transmission and will be sealed using Loctite "Weld-Stik" under normal warranty provisions. (1994)

• **Engine noise** If a thumping noise from the engine during low speeds is not due to the air conditioning compressor, it is necessary to install a larger main bearing on the No. 1 journal of the crankshaft. (1991)

• **Water pump** The water pump seals may leak, in which case the pump will be replaced with one with redesigned seals for up to 6 years/70,000 miles. The cooling systems will also be flushed and refilled. (1994-95)

• **Keyless entry** Because the screw holding the cover to the door lock transmitter key kept coming loose, the company has released new screws with a thread locking compound on them and will war-

LEXUS

rant their replacement for 4 years/50,000 miles. (1990-94)

• **Fuel gauge** If the fuel gauge is inaccurate, a revised gauge will be installed to stabilize the indicator needle. (1990-92)

• **Vehicle noise** A new, self-lubricating stabilizer bar bushing will be installed if the original rear bushings squeak on all ES 300 models.

• **Brake noise** Because owners had complained of rear brake squeak, Toyota has released new brake linings that eliminate the noise. (1992)

• **Brake noise** Groaning front brakes will be replaced with pads having a new, quieter material, but only for 12 months or 12,500 miles from the date the vehicle was placed in service in New York due to its Lemon Laws. (1992-96)

• **Climate control** If the ambient temperature display shows -22°F and the climate control misbehaves, there is an intermittent open in the temperature sensor circuit and, even if repaired, the display will not change until the fuse for the air conditioning control unit is removed briefly. (1990-95)

RECALL HISTORY

1997 cars in specified states In extreme cold, accumulated moisture can temporarily freeze in brake vacuum hose.

1990-94 LEXUS LS 400

1994 Lexus LS 400

FOR   Acceleration • Anti-lock brakes • Air bags • Quietness • Ride • Reliability

AGAINST   Fuel economy • Rear-seat room • Repair costs

EVALUATION   With either the standard coil spring suspension or optional air suspension, the LS 400 rides with reassuring stability at high speed, yet is supple enough to absorb tar strips and minor pot holes with little or no reaction. The standard anti-lock brakes we tested are quite powerful, stopping the car in a straight line, with excellent control. The standard V-8 provides ample acceleration and passing power. It is among the smoothest and most quiet engines available today.

The interior is elegant, comfortable, and generally accommodating. An electronic gauge cluster pops out at you with a 3-D effect when you turn on the ignition and the driver's seat has generous rearward travel. Backseat passengers will discover they have ample leg room, but little if any space under the front seats for placing their feet. While there is ample interior room, and the car's width will easily accommodate three in back, the LS 400 is a rear-wheel-drive car, meaning the middle passenger must straddle the driveline tunnel.

Outside, the car is flawlessly built, with world-class workmanship and quality. Inside, high-quality materials are used to cover all surfaces, not just the seats and door panels. In addition, all controls fall easily to hand and operate with commendable smoothness. The LS 400 is softer and a little more luxurious than rivals from both Europe and Japan.

SPECIFICATIONS

	4-door sedan
Wheelbase, in.	110.8
Overall length, in.	196.7
Overall width, in.	71.7
Overall height, in.	55.3
Curb weight, lbs.	3759
Cargo volume, cu. ft.	14.4
Fuel capacity, gals.	22.5
Seating capacity	5
Front head room, in.	38.5
Max. front leg room, in.	43.8
Rear head room, in.	36.8
Min. rear leg room, in.	34.3

Powertrain layout: longitudinal front-engine/rear-wheel drive

ENGINES

	dohc V-8
Size, liters/cu. in.	4.0/245
Horsepower	250
Torque (lbs./ft.)	260

EPA city/highway mpg
4-speed OD automatic	18/23

Consumer Guide™ observed MPG
4-speed OD automatic	19.5

Built in Japan.

LEXUS

RETAIL PRICES

	GOOD	AVERAGE	POOR
1990 LS 400	$10,000-11,500	$9,000-10,300	$6,000-7,000
1991 LS 400	12,000-14,000	10,800-12,800	7,500-9,000
1992 LS 400	14,500-16,800	13,000-15,300	9,500-11,200
1993 LS 400	17,500-20,000	15,800-18,000	12,000-13,500
1994 LS 400	21,500-24,200	19,500-22,000	15,500-17,500

AVERAGE REPLACEMENT COSTS

A/C Compressor $1,430
Alternator 735
Radiator 675
Timing Chain or Belt 290
Automatic Transmission or

Transaxle 1,380
Universal Joints................1125
Brakes................................210
Shocks and/or Struts 500

TROUBLE SPOTS

• **Brakes** To improve brake feel, Toyota began installing a larger master cylinder, brake booster, dual-position calipers, and thicker rotors on 1992 cars. These parts can be retrofitted to the 1990 model only if all parts, including brake pads, are used. (1990)

• **Brakes** Because of complaints about front brake noise and premature wear, the company now has a revised brake pad kit plus new brake rotors that must be replaced as a set to solve the problem. (1990-91)

• **Steering problems** If the steering wheel is turned hard against its stops, the whole rack-and-pinion housing can shift and the steering wheel will end up off center, so the automaker has issued new grommets to hold the rack more firmly in place. (1990-91)

• **Vehicle noise** A production change was made in 1995 to the strut bar cushions to eliminate a squeak or groan from the front end when stopping and the revised parts can be retrofitted into earlier models. (1990-95)

• **Climate control** If the ambient temperature display shows -22°F and the climate control misbehaves, there is an intermittent open in the temperature sensor circuit and, even if repaired, the display will not change until the fuse for the air conditioning control unit is removed briefly. (1990-94)

• **Keyless entry** Because the screw holding the cover to the door lock transmitter key kept coming loose, the company has released new screws with a thread locking compound on them and will warrant their replacement for 4 years/50,000 miles. (1990-94)

RECALL HISTORY

1990 Housing of center high-mounted stoplamp could become distorted after prolonged illumination and bulb might move from its original position, affecting luminous intensity.

1995-98
LINCOLN CONTINENTAL

1996 Lincoln Continental

FOR Acceleration • Passenger and cargo room • Instruments/controls • Air bags, dual • Anti-lock brakes

AGAINST Fuel economy • Noise • Electronic steering and suspension

EVALUATION Helped by its new V-8 engine, this Continental is a lot quicker, a bit more agile—and loaded with electronic gadgetry. In acceleration, the newly-energetic Continental can match a Cadillac Seville SLS. At 16.3 mpg, gas mileage has not improved and premium fuel is recommended.

Despite its multiple adjustments, Lincoln's high-tech electronic suspension/steering fails to succeed fully. High mode makes the steering stiffer, without increasing feel; Low mode leaves the steering rather light and vague. The suspension also works best in Normal, as the other two modes have little effect on absorption of bumps.

Interior space is great. Occupants have plenty of leg space front and rear, while head room is adequate for 6-footers, even with the optional moonroof. Storage space is fine. The Continental's trunk is wide, deep, and long.

Reflecting off a mirror above the instrument cluster, the dramatic virtual image gauges are strikingly bright at night, but hard to read in bright sunlight. Controls are plentiful, and most are handy, but climate controls and seat heaters are recessed into the dashboard and hard to reach.

Lincoln evidently attempted to make the Continental both a sports sedan and a traditional luxury car. It's not quite either, but worth a look anyway. Because sales have been tepid, used-car prices may be appealing.

SPECIFICATIONS

	4-door sedan
Wheelbase, in.	109.0
Overall length, in.	206.3
Overall width, in.	73.3
Overall height, in.	55.9
Curb weight, lbs.	3911
Cargo volume, cu. ft.	18.1
Fuel capacity, gals.	18.0
Seating capacity	6
Front head room, in.	39.1
Max. front leg room, in.	41.8
Rear head room, in.	39.0
Min. rear leg room, in.	39.2

Powertrain layout: transverse front-engine/front-wheel drive

ENGINES

	dohc V-8
Size, liters/cu. in.	4.6/281
Horsepower	260
Torque (lbs./ft.)	265

EPA city/highway mpg

4-speed OD automatic	17/25

Consumer Guide™ observed MPG

4-speed OD automatic	16.3

Built in USA.

RETAIL PRICES	GOOD	AVERAGE	POOR
1995 Continental	$14,000-16,000	$12,700-14,500	$9,500-10,500
1996 Continental	17,000-19,500	15,500-18,000	12,000-13,000
1997 Continental	20,500-23,500	18,500-21,500	14,500-16,500
1998 Continental	25,000-29,000	23,000-26,500	18,500-21,500

AVERAGE REPLACEMENT COSTS

A/C Compressor	$435	Constant Velocity Joints	470
Alternator	510	Brakes	320
Radiator	290	Shocks and/or Struts	1,165
Timing Chain or Belt	795	Exhaust System	540
Automatic Transmission or Transaxle	870		

TROUBLE SPOTS

• **Hard starting** The engine may be hard to start or may stall after hot soak due to the idle air control valve sticking (1995-96) or a poor connection at the crank position sensor. (1995-97)

• **Steering noise** The steering grunts or groans after making right hand turns requiring replacement of the steering gear. (1995-97)

• **Air conditioner** Air conditioner output may be low or nonexistent because of a problem with the compressor clutch. (1995)

• **Suspension noise** Clunking from the front end may be due to premature wear of the sway bar links from under the floor due to loose subframe insulators. (1995-97)

RECALL HISTORY

1995-96 "Autolamp" control module may fail. **1996** Vehicle can move even though indicator shows "Park." **1998** Text and/or graphics for headlamp aiming instructions, provided in owner guides, are not sufficiently clear.

1990-92 LINCOLN MARK VII

1990 Lincoln Mark VII

FOR   Acceleration • Anti-lock brakes • Air bag, driver • Quietness • Handling

AGAINST   Fuel economy • Rear seat room • Rear seat entry/exit • Ride (except 1990 Bill Blass) • Cargo room

EVALUATION   The brawny V-8 engine and 4-speed automatic furnish strong acceleration during takeoffs, plus brisk passing response on the highway. On the other hand, you have to endure an unfortunate tendency toward tardy downshifts from the automatic transmission. Gas mileage is fine on the highway, but gets

LINCOLN

more dismal around town: in the 15-17 mpg neighborhood.

Lincoln's coupes loaf along quietly at cruising speeds. Road manners are modern and competent. With its handling suspension, the LSC coupe corners flatly and promises a stable highway ride. Unfortunately, when rolling over bumps, that suspension also transmits some impact harshness to the occupants. The soft suspension and smaller tires on a 1990 Bill Blass edition might suit some drivers better. Ordinary braking causes the front end to dip down noticeably, and the pedal tends to feel spongy.

Interiors are roomy enough. Front bucket seats are well shaped and supportive, with ample space for each occupant. Power seat controls consist of separate buttons, shaped like the seat cushion and backrest. Leg space in the rear is ample for adults, but head room is minimal. Trunk space is small for a car of this size.

All told, the Mark VII can be a good alternative to the front-drive Cadillac Eldorado, the Acura Legend Coupe, or the Lexus SC 300.

SPECIFICATIONS

	2-door coupe
Wheelbase, in.	108.5
Overall length, in.	202.8
Overall width, in.	70.9
Overall height, in.	54.2
Curb weight, lbs.	3782
Cargo volume, cu. ft.	14.2
Fuel capacity, gals.	21.0
Seating capacity	5
Front head room, in.	37.8
Max. front leg room, in.	42.0
Rear head room, in.	37.1
Min. rear leg room, in.	36.9

Powertrain layout: longitudinal front-engine/rear-wheel drive

ENGINES

	ohv V-8
Size, liters/cu. in.	5.0/302
Horsepower	225
Torque (lbs./ft.)	300

EPA city/highway mpg
4-speed OD automatic ... 17/24

Consumer Guide™ observed MPG
4-speed OD automatic ... 15.2

Built in USA.

RETAIL PRICES	GOOD	AVERAGE	POOR
1990 Mark VII	$4,100-5,000	$3,400-4,300	$1,700-2,400

	GOOD	AVERAGE	POOR
1991 Mark VII	5,500-6,500	4,700-5,600	2,700-3,300
1992 Mark VII	7,300-8,500	6,500-7,500	4,000-4,700

AVERAGE REPLACEMENT COSTS

A/C Compressor $325
Alternator 425
Radiator 290
Timing Chain or Belt 220
Automatic Transmission or
   Transaxle.........................880

Universal Joints 470
Brakes.................................300
Shocks and/or Struts 235
Exhaust System.................540

TROUBLE SPOTS

• **Radio** Whining noises in the radio speakers is caused by the fuel pump in the gas tank. An electronic noise filter must be installed on the fuel pump. (1986-92)

• **Hard starting** In cold weather, the accelerator pedal is hard to depress the first time after sitting because ice forms in the throttle valve cable to the transmission. (1992)

• **Engine temperature** Defective temperature senders causes the gauge to read low (not warning the driver of impending overheating) or be erratic. (1990-92)

• **Dashboard lights** The fuel "distance to empty" reading may be erratic or quit working due to a circuit board problem. (1990-92)

• **Paint** The clearcoat paint tends to crack and flake off, especially on horizontal surfaces such as the hood, roof, etc. (1990-92)

RECALL HISTORY

None to date.

1993-98 LINCOLN MARK VIII

FOR Acceleration • Steering/handling • Air bags • Anti-lock brakes

AGAINST Visibility • Fuel economy • Rear-seat room • Wet-weather traction

EVALUATION With its new 280-horsepower V-8 (290 with the LSC), the Mark VIII is quick off the line and once above 15 mph, really flies. The engine is silky smooth, has a sporty growl in hard acceleration and delivers outstanding passing power at highway speeds. However, we averaged just 17.9 mpg, with our highest reading being 20.1 mpg. When we tested this car on snow and

1996 Lincoln Mark VIII

ice we were disappointed with the performance of the optional traction control system. The rear wheels spun readily in snow, making takeoffs slow and laborious.

The rear-drive Mark VIII is as agile as the front-drive Cadillac Eldorado, but has a more supple suspension. Steering and braking are top notch.

As with many sport coupes, interior space is not one of the Mark's strong points. Tall passengers don't have much head room, even without the optional moonroof. Rear leg room is also limited. Taking a closer look at the interior, the gauges on the sweeping 2-tier dash are clearly marked and controls are intuitive.

Despite its excellent drivetrain and smooth suspension, Mark VIII fails to impress us when compared to the less-expensive Buick Riviera or more-refined Luxus SC 300/400.

SPECIFICATIONS

	2-door coupe
Wheelbase, in.	113.0
Overall length, in.	207.3
Overall width, in.	74.8
Overall height, in.	53.6
Curb weight, lbs.	3768
Cargo volume, cu. ft.	14.4
Fuel capacity, gals.	18.0
Seating capacity	5
Front head room, in.	38.1
Max. front leg room, in.	42.6
Rear head room, in.	37.5
Min. rear leg room, in.	32.5

Powertrain layout: longitudinal front-engine/rear-wheel drive

ENGINES

	dohc V-8	dohc V-8
Size, liters/cu. in.	4.6/281	4.6/281
Horsepower	280	290

	dohc V-8	dohc V-8
Torque (lbs./ft.)	285	290
EPA city/highway mpg 4-speed OD automatic......................................	18/26	18/26
Consumer Guide™ observed MPG 4-speed OD automatic......................................	17.9	

Built in USA.

RETAIL PRICES	GOOD	AVERAGE	POOR
1993 Mark VIII	$9,500-11,000	$8,500-10,000	$5,800-6,800
1994 Mark VIII	11,000-12,500	10,000-11,500	7,000-8,000
1995 Mark VIII	14,000-16,000	12,700-14,500	9,500-10,500
1996 Mark VIII	18,000-20,000	16,500-18,500	12,500-14,000
1997 Mark VIII	22,500-25,000	21,000-23,500	16,500-18,000
1998 Mark VIII	26,000-29,500	24,000-27,500	18,500-21,000

AVERAGE REPLACEMENT COSTS

A/C Compressor $400		Universal Joints 160	
Alternator 455		Brakes.................................305	
Radiator 465		Shocks and/or Struts 1,060	
Timing Chain or Belt 445		Exhaust System.................485	
Automatic Transmission or Transaxle........................720			

TROUBLE SPOTS

• **Odometer** Because of a software problem, the odometer may quit registering after 65,531 miles. Under campaign number 95B72, the company will replace the virtual image cluster. (1995)

• **Engine stalling** The in-tank fuel delivery module may cause low or no fuel pressure. The engine may lose power or stall and may not restart. The module will be replaced at no charge under campaign number 95B71 up to December 31, 1999. (1995)

• **Hard starting** If the engine does not want to start or cranks for a long time then stalls, the idle air control valve may be sticking and Ford will replace it under warranty. (1995-96)

• **Transmission slippage** The automatic transmission in these cars over 20,000 miles is notorious for shuddering or vibrating under light acceleration or when shifting between third and fourth gear above 35 mph. It requires that the transmission fluid (including fluid in the torque converter) be changed and that only Mercon® fluid be used. It usually takes at least 100 miles of driving after the fluid change for the shudder to go away. (1992-94)

LINCOLN

• **Transmission slippage** The transmission may slip (lack of torque) and the engine may flare when the transmission shifts into fourth gear, which can often be traced to a bad TR/MLP sensor that will be replaced along with a speed sensor on AODE automatic transmissions under the normal warranty provisions. (1993-95)

• **Alternator belt** The drive belt tensioner pulley or idler pulley bearings are apt to make a squealing noise when the engine is started in cold weather. Under the bumper to bumper warranty, the pulley(s) will be replaced. (1993-96)

• **Blower motor** Squeaking or chirping blower motors are the result of defective brush holders, so Ford has issued a redesigned motor and will replace those that are under normal warranty. (1993-94)

RECALL HISTORY

1993-94 Headlights can flash intermittently as a result of a circuit-breaker opening.

1990-97 LINCOLN TOWN CAR

1996 Lincoln Town Car

FOR   Air bags (later models) • Anti-lock brakes (optional) • Passenger and cargo room

AGAINST   Fuel economy • Maneuverability • Visibility

EVALUATION   Despite its new V-8 engine, Town Car can hardly be classified as a sprinter, given the fact it tips scales at over two tons, but once underway there's strong acceleration and passing power. One drawback to brisk acceleration seems to be the 4-speed automatic, which is slow to downshift at times.

New suspension and further upgrades designed to the improve the car's handling arrive in the form of a Ride Control Package, the car retains much of its penchant for excessive body roll and the kind of pillowy ride characteristics preferred by domestic luxury car buyers. If you're not particular about handling, and need a spacious car, you've come to the right place. The Town Car is wide enough to accommodate six adults comfortably, while the large doors make entry and exit maneuvers effortless. For long trips, you can count on the spacious 22.3-cubic foot trunk to hold nearly all your worldly goods. Most controls are mounted high on the dashboard where they're easy to see and reach while driving. Though the power window, door lock and mirror controls are grouped on the driver's door, they aren't backlit at night.

While cars like the Town Car and its main rival, the Cadillac Fleetwood are plush, quiet and comfortable, there are newer luxury models now available that offer comparable luxury, more agility and better overall economy.

NHTSA CRASH TEST RESULTS
1996 Town Car
4-DOOR SEDAN

Driver	☆☆☆☆
Passenger	☆☆☆☆☆

(The National Highway Traffic Safety Administration tests a vehicle's crashworthiness in front and side collisions. Their ratings suggest the chance of serious injury: ☆☆☆☆☆—10% or less; ☆☆☆☆—10-20% or less; ☆☆☆—20-30% or less; ☆☆—35-45% or less; ☆—More than 45%.)

SPECIFICATIONS

	4-door sedan
Wheelbase, in.	117.4
Overall length, in.	218.9
Overall width, in.	76.7
Overall height, in.	56.9
Curb weight, lbs.	4040
Cargo volume, cu. ft.	22.3
Fuel capacity, gals.	18.0/20.0
Seating capacity	6
Front head room, in.	39.1
Max. front leg room, in.	42.5
Rear head room, in.	38.0
Min. rear leg room, in.	41.1

Powertrain layout: longitudinal front-engine/rear-wheel drive

ENGINES

	ohv V-8	dohc V-8	dohc V-8
Size, liters/cu. in.	5.0/302	4.6/281	4.6/281
Horsepower	150	190	210
Torque (lbs./ft.)	270	260-265	270-275
EPA city/highway mpg			
4-speed OD automatic	17/24	17/25	17/25

LINCOLN

Consumer Guide™ observed MPG
4-speed OD automatic 16.6   17.0
Built in USA.

RETAIL PRICES

	GOOD	AVERAGE	POOR
1990 Town Car	$4,400-5,700	$3,700-5,000	$1,800-2,400
1991 Town Car	5,300-6,800	4,600-6,000	2,500-3,500
1992 Town Car	6,800-8,700	6,000-7,800	3,500-4,800
1993 Town Car	8,500-10,700	7,500-9,700	4,500-6,000
1994 Town Car	11,000-13,200	9,800-12,000	6,500-8,000
1995 Town Car	14,200-17,000	13,000-15,500	9,000-11,000
1996 Town Car	17,500-20,500	16,000-19,000	11,500-14,000
1997 Town Car	21,500-24,500	20,000-22,500	15,000-17,000

AVERAGE REPLACEMENT COSTS

A/C Compressor $390
Alternator 375
Automatic Transmission or
   Transaxle........................495
Timing Chain or Belt 330

Automatic Transmission or
   Transaxle.........................700
Constant Velocity Joints.....140
Brakes..................................265
Shocks and/or Struts 365
Exhaust System.................690

TROUBLE SPOTS

• **Vehicle noise** A chattering noise that can be felt, and sometimes heard, coming from the rear during tight turns after highway driving is caused by a lack of friction modifier or over-shimming of the clutch packs in the Traction-Lok (limited-slip) differential. A replacement clutch pack and friction modifier will be installed under the company's warranty programs. (1990-96)

• **Vehicle noise** A broken gusset or weld separation at the frame crossmember causes a rattle from the rear or the car. Ford will weld new gussets into place under the bumper-to-bumper warranty (1992) or basic warranty on prior models. (1990-92)

• **Oil leak** The oil filter balloons and leaks because the oil pump relief valve sticks. Higher than recommended viscosity oils cause wear to the oil pump relief valve bore. Under normal warranty provisions, the pump will be replaced with one less sensitive to this problem, but Ford warns that owners should only use the type of oil spelled out in the owners manual. (1991-94)

• **Transmission slippage** The automatic transmission in these cars over 20,000 miles is notorious for shuddering or vibrating under light acceleration or when shifting between third and fourth gear above 35 mph. It requires that the transmission fluid (including fluid in the torque converter) be changed and that only Mercon® fluid be used. It usually takes at least 100 miles of driving after the fluid change for the shudder to go away. (1992-94)

• **Transmission slippage** The transmission may slip (lack of torque) and the engine may flare when the transmission shifts into fourth gear, which can often be traced to a bad TR/MLP sensor that will be replaced along with a speed sensor on AODE automatic transmissions under the normal warranty provisions. (1992-95)

• **Hard starting** The connector at the starter solenoid tends to corrode resulting in a "no-crank"-condition. Under warranty, the automaker will replace the connector and slather the terminal with dielectric grease to prevent it from happening again. (1991-94)

• **Hard starting** If the engine does not want to start or cranks for a long time then stalls, the idle air control valve may be sticking and Ford will replace it under warranty. (1996)

• **Air springs** Air springs are prone to leaks caused by the bag rubbing against the axle or control arm. Often, the car will be sitting low on one corner after being parked for any length of time. Leaking air springs must be replaced. (Any so-equipped)

• **Alternator belt** The drive belt tensioner pulley or idler pulley bearings are apt to make a squealing noise when the engine is started in cold weather. Under the bumper-to-bumper warranty, the pulley(s) will be replaced. (1993-96)

RECALL HISTORY

1990-91 On cars in 25 states, corrosion of hood latch striker causes detachment, so hood can open unexpectedly. **1991** Distorted fuel lines may contact steering-column universal joint and be damaged. **1991-92** Secondary hood latch may not engage; if primary latch releases when car is moving, hood could fly up. **1994** Brake pedal push rod retainer may be missing or improperly installed, which can cause disengagement and loss of braking. **1994** Nuts and bolts that attach rear brake adapter to axle housing flange can loosen and separate, allowing damage to ABS sensor, hydraulic line, and parking brake cable. **1995** Some passenger-side air bags may not inflate properly; also, igniter cap can separate, releasing hot gases. **1995** Seal between fuel filler pipe and tank may not be fully cured, which could allow fuel to leak. **1995-96 fleet cars only** Corrosion of inadequately-lubricated Pitman arms can cause abnormal wear of joint, resulting in separation. **1996** Driver's door, when closed only to secondary latched position, may not sustain the specified 1000-pound transverse load. **1996** Wrong parts may have been used to service seatbelts with switchable retractor for child restraints. **1997** Driver's air bag module could stay in position during deployment, but leave the steering wheel cavity afterward.

1990-92 MAZDA 626

✔ BEST BUY

1991 Mazda 626 LE 4-door

FOR   Acceleration (GT) • Anti-lock brakes (optional) • Fuel economy

AGAINST   Acceleration (automatic transmission) • Automatic transmission performance • Torque steer (GT)

EVALUATION   The basic 110-horsepower engine provides fairly brisk acceleration and lively passing power. With 5-speed manual shift, even a base model will provide some excitement. Unfortunately, the automatic transmission shifts harshly in hard acceleration, and also balks at downshifting to a lower gear to furnish additional power. Mazda's Turbo four packs quite a wallop, delivering ferocious acceleration, but coupled with excessive "torque steer."

Though stiffer than typical family cars, the ride is soft and supple. Handling and roadholding are more than competent, even in DX trim, suffering only moderate body lean in turns. Road and engine noise are stronger than in some Japanese rivals. Wind and tire sounds can grow annoying, but gas mileage is good with either engine. An LX averaged nearly 25 mpg overall. Turbo models and recent LX/GT editions may have optional anti-lock brakes, which we recommend.

Interiors feel roomier than in the prior generation. A 626 holds four adults without serious cramping. Still, because the wheelbase of a 626 is shorter than that of a Honda Accord or Toyota Camry, you can expect less leg room. Split rear seatbacks fold down for more cargo capacity.

All in all, this is a refined rival to the Honda Accord or Toyota Camry. In addition to a selection of practical virtues, you get Mazda's reputation for above-average reliability.

SPECIFICATIONS

	4-door sedan	4-door hatchback
Wheelbase, in.	101.4	101.4
Overall length, in.	179.3	179.3
Overall width, in.	66.5	66.5
Overall height, in.	55.5	54.1
Curb weight, lbs.	2610	2710
Cargo volume, cu. ft.	15.9	22.4
Fuel capacity, gals.	15.9	15.9
Seating capacity	5	5
Front head room, in.	39.0	38.7
Max. front leg room, in.	43.7	43.6
Rear head room, in.	37.8	37.2
Min. rear leg room, in.	36.6	32.9

Powertrain layout: transverse front-engine/front-wheel drive

ENGINES

	ohc I-4	Turbocharged ohc I-4
Size, liters/cu. in.	2.2/133	2.2/133
Horsepower	110	145
Torque (lbs./ft.)	130	190

EPA city/highway mpg

5-speed OD manual	24/31	21/28
4-speed OD automatic	22/28	19/25

Consumer Guide™ observed MPG

4-speed OD automatic	23.7

Built in USA and Japan.

RETAIL PRICES

	GOOD	AVERAGE	POOR
1990 626 sedan	$2,200-2,900	$1,600-2,300	$800-1,100
1990 626 hatchback	3,100-3,600	2,400-2,900	1,200-1,500
1991 626 sedan	2,700-3,600	2,000-2,900	1,100-1,400
1991 626 hatchback	4,000-4,700	3,300-4,000	1,800-2,300
1992 626 sedan	3,200-4,200	2,500-3,500	1,400-1,800

AVERAGE REPLACEMENT COSTS

A/C Compressor	$550
Alternator	230
Radiator	520
Timing Chain or Belt	170
Automatic Transmission or Transaxle	1,005
Clutch, Pressure Plate, Bearing	610
Constant Velocity Joints	565
Brakes	235
Shocks and/or Struts	715
Exhaust System	915

TROUBLE SPOTS

• **Suspension noise** A knocking noise from the front suspension during sharp turns or driving over a bump (such as a speed bump) is likely due to a missing rubber spring seat that must be replaced along with thrust plates and mounting rubbers. (1990-92)

• **Water leak** Water may leak into the taillight/brake light housing and into the trunk because of a bad seal in the housing. (1990-92)

• **Air conditioner** The air conditioning refrigerant may leak out because the steel clamp holding the aluminum pipe for the receiver/drier creates galvanic corrosion resulting in pin-holes. After the pipe is replaced, the problem will recur unless vinyl tape is wrapped around the pipe before installing the clamp. (1990)

RECALL HISTORY

1990-91 Molded door-latch handles may fail, permitting rod to fall inside frame; lowering of window could then release latch, allowing door to inadvertently open.

1993-97 MAZDA 626

1990 Mazda 626

FOR   Air bags, dual • Acceleration (V-6) • Fuel economy • Steering/handling

AGAINST   Automatic transmission performance • Road noise

EVALUATION   A V-6 and 5-speed deliver willing, capable performance and spirited acceleration. Both engines are smooth, free-revving, and fairly quiet, but neither has enough low-speed torque for pleasant, vigorous running with automatic. Automatics also are slow to downshift for passing. Worse yet, they suffer jerky full-throttle downshifts, especially with 4-cylinder power.

A 4-cylinder automatic achieved nearly 24 mpg, and a stick-shift V-6 averaged 20.7 mpg.

Ride quality is good, with the suspension filtering out most pavement imperfections. The sedan also handles better than you might expect. Body lean is moderate in turns, but the car feels secure and composed in spirited driving. "Panic" braking is swift and stable.

Rear seating disappoints, and rear doors could be bigger. Head room is adequate for tall people, even with a power sunroof installed. Leg space is ample all around. Space also is adequate for rear passengers' feet under front seats. Split rear seatbacks fold down for additional cargo space. Wind noise is low on the highway, though the 4-cylinder gets a little loud at higher speeds. Outward visibility is good, and the driver faces clear, simple control panels.

All told, the solidly-built 626 sedan is a strong contender against the Honda Accord and Toyota Camry, though the latter are quieter and more luxurious.

NHTSA CRASH TEST RESULTS
1996 Mazda 626   4-DOOR SEDAN

Driver	☆☆☆☆
Passenger	☆☆☆☆☆

(The National Highway Traffic Safety Administration tests a vehicle's crashworthiness in front and side collisions. Their ratings suggest the chance of serious injury: ☆☆☆☆☆—10% or less; ☆☆☆☆—10-20% or less; ☆☆☆—20-30% or less; ☆☆—35-45% or less; ☆—More than 45%.)

SPECIFICATIONS

	4-door sedan
Wheelbase, in.	102.8
Overall length, in.	184.4
Overall width, in.	68.9
Overall height, in.	51.6
Curb weight, lbs.	2804
Cargo volume, cu. ft.	13.8
Fuel capacity, gals.	15.9
Seating capacity	5
Front head room, in.	39.2
Max. front leg room, in.	43.5
Rear head room, in.	37.8
Min. rear leg room, in.	35.8

Powertrain layout: transverse front-engine/front-wheel drive

ENGINES

	dohc I-4	dohc V-6
Size, liters/cu. in.	2.0/122	2.5/153
Horsepower	114-118	160-164
Torque (lbs./ft.)	124-127	156-160
EPA city/highway mpg		
5-speed OD manual	26/34	21/26

MAZDA

	dohc I-4	dohc V-6
4-speed OD automatic	23/31	20/26

Consumer Guide™ observed MPG

5-speed OD manual..	25.1	20.7
4-speed automatic	23.8	

Built in USA.

RETAIL PRICES

	GOOD	AVERAGE	POOR
1993 626 DX/LX	$4,600-5,700	$3,900-5,000	$1,900-2,700
1993 626 ES	6,500-7,300	5,700-6,500	3,300-4,000
1994 626 DX/LX	6,000-7,500	5,300-6,700	3,000-4,000
1994 626 ES	7,800-8,700	7,000-7,800	4,400-5,200
1995 626 DX/LX	7,500-9,500	6,600-8,600	4,100-5,500
1995 626 ES	9,800-10,800	8,900-9,800	5,900-6,700
1996 626 DX/LX	8,900-11,500	8,000-10,500	5,200-7,000
1996 626 ES	11,500-12,700	10,500-11,700	7,300-8,200
1997 626 DX/LX	10,500-13,200	9,500-12,000	6,500-8,500
1997 626 ES	13,300-14,500	12,000-13,200	8,500-9,200

AVERAGE REPLACEMENT COSTS

A/C Compressor $360	Clutch, Pressure Plate,
Alternator 245	Bearing 625
Radiator 410	Brakes 245
Timing Chain or Belt 160	Shocks and/or Struts 670
Automatic Transmission or	Exhaust System 495
Transaxle.....................1,075	

TROUBLE SPOTS

• **Door handles** The outer door handles may come loose and rattle so the company will warrant the fix by replacing the original retaining nuts with ones that won't come loose. (1993-95)

• **Engine stalling** If the engine stalls when the transmission is shifted into drive, the problem may be a cracked mass airflow snorkel tube. This is often misdiagnosed as a problem with the transmissions, specifically with the torque converter clutch. Actually, unmetered air is getting into the engine making it stall. Not a warranty or campaign item. (1993-94)

• **Transaxle leak** A damaged torque converter hub seal allows fluid to leak from the automatic transmission. A new seal will be installed under warranty. (1994-96)

• **Vehicle shake** Vibration, which is usually felt in the steering wheel, shift lever, and floor is probably caused by mispositioned radiator dampers that the company will replace under normal warranty provisions. (1993-95)

• **Engine knock** Cars with a V-6 engine built before March 1993 may have engine knock, especially when cold, due to carbon buildup in the combustion chamber. To eliminate the noise, the company will replace the pistons and cylinder heads. Dealers have a special hotline to call if a customer reports this problem. (1993-94)

• **Power seats** The insulation on the wires for the power seat can wear through causing a short circuit disabling the power seat. The wires will be repaired and rerouted as a warranty repair. (1993-94)

• **Windshield wipers** The welds holding the wiper arm support bracket break causing a creak or rattle when the wipers are running. Under normal warranty, the welds will be drilled out and bolts/nuts will be installed. (1993-95)

• **Air conditioner** Poor A/C performance caused by defective relay will not let compressor cycle off on 6-cylinder models. (1993-95)

• **Engine noise** A metallic tapping noise from the rear of the engine could be due to slippage between the exhaust camshaft driven gear and friction gear. Although newer engines have a better contact surface, the company will fix cars in service by replacing the friction gear spring with a stouter one. (1993-95)

• **Engine mounts** Broken motor mounts allow the engine to rock back and forth when accelerating, decelerating, or starting from a stop. The company has a redesigned mount to replace the original. (1993-94)

RECALL HISTORY

1995 Some passenger-side air bags may not inflate properly; also, igniter cap can separate, causing hot gases to be released.

1994-97 MAZDA B-SERIES

FOR Acceleration (4.0-liter V-6) • Anti-lock brakes • Payload capacity • Build quality

AGAINST Acceleration (4-cylinder) • Fuel economy • Passenger room (reg. cab)

EVALUATION The 4.0-liter engine is indeed the best choice, though most buyers will be satisfied with 3.0-liter V-6, especially when equipped with manual shift. Using only a little more fuel than the 3.0-liter engine, the 4.0-liter V-6 delivers good low-speed punch, though it can get coarse and noisy. A 4-cylinder engine provides acceptable power with the 5-speed manual gearbox, but is sluggish when driving an automatic transmission.

MAZDA

1995 Mazda B-Series

It's an unwise choice for towing or hauling heavy payloads.

All models ride rather nicely, and road manners are good. You won't be assaulted by undue tire, engine, or wind noise, either. Off-road setups make for a stiff ride on 4x4s, but suspensions on other models absorb most big bumps without jarring the occupants.

Interiors are well designed, though the rear jump seats are usable only by small children. Ranger and B-Series were the only compact pickups to offer a passenger-side air bag, added for 1996 as an option.

Choosing between a Ford Ranger and Mazda B-Series is mainly a matter of styling details and price. Both the B-Series and its Ranger counterpart rank among the best in their class, but look also at the Chevrolet S10 or GMC Sonoma.

NHTSA CRASH TEST RESULTS
1997 Mazda B-Series

	REG. CAB
Driver	☆☆☆☆
Passenger	☆☆☆☆

(The National Highway Traffic Safety Administration tests a vehicle's crashworthiness in front and side collisions. Their ratings suggest the chance of serious injury: ☆☆☆☆☆—10% or less; ☆☆☆☆—10-20% or less; ☆☆☆—20-30% or less; ☆☆—35-45% or less; ☆—More than 45%.)

SPECIFICATIONS

	reg. cab short bed	reg. cab long bed	ext. cab
Wheelbase, in.	107.9	113.9	125.2
Overall length, in.	184.5	197.5	202.7
Overall width, in.	69.4	69.4	69.4
Overall height, in.	64.0	64.0	64.1
Curb weight, lbs.	2927	2955	3197
Fuel capacity, gals.	17.0	17.0[1]	20.5

	reg. cab short bed	reg. cab long bed	ext. cab
Seating capacity	3	3	5
Front head room, in.	39.1	39.1	39.4
Max. front leg room, in.	42.4	42.4	42.4
Rear head room, in.	—	—	35.6
Min. rear leg room, in.	—	—	41.2

1. 20.0 gals. optional.

Powertrain layout: longitudinal front-engine/rear- or 4-wheel drive

ENGINES

	ohc I-4	ohv V-6	ohv V-6
Size, liters/cu. in.	2.3/140	3.0/182	4.0/245
Horsepower	98-112	140-147	160
Torque (lbs./ft.)	130-135	160-162	220-225

EPA city/highway mpg

5-speed OD manual	22/27	19/25	18/23
4-speed OD automatic	20/25	18/24	17/23
5-speed OD automatic			16/22

Consumer Guide™ observed MPG

5-speed OD manual	17.8
4-speed OD automatic	16.5

Built in USA.

AVERAGE REPLACEMENT COSTS

A/C Compressor	$330	Clutch, Pressure Plate, Bearing	440
Alternator	290	Universal Joints	630
Radiator	190	Brakes	270
Timing Chain or Belt	400	Shocks and/or Struts	200
Automatic Transmission or Transaxle	660	Exhaust System	265

RETAIL PRICES

	GOOD	AVERAGE	POOR
1994 B2300	$4,400-6,900	$3,700-6,200	$1,700-3,500
1994 B3000	5,400-8,700	4,700-7,900	2,400-4,900
1994 B4000	6,000-10,500	5,200-9,700	2,800-6,400
1995 B2300	5,500-9,200	4,800-8,400	2,400-5,200
1995 B3000	7,100-11,000	6,300-10,100	3,600-6,400
1995 B4000	8,800-12,500	8,000-11,500	5,000-7,500
1996 B2300	6,700-10,500	5,900-9,600	3,300-6,200
1996 B3000	9,500-12,500	8,600-11,500	5,500-7,500
1996 B4000	11,000-14,500	10,000-13,500	6,500-8,800
1997 B2300	7,800-12,000	6,800-11,000	4,000-7,500
1997 B4000	12,000-15,500	11,000-14,300	7,500-9,800
1998 B2300	9,000-14,000	8,000-12,800	4,900-9,000

	GOOD	AVERAGE	POOR
1998 B3000	13,000-16,500	12,000-15,000	8,000-10,500
1998 B4000	13,500-17,500	12,500-16,000	8,500-11,000

TROUBLE SPOTS

• **Suspension noise** A chattering noise that can be felt, and sometimes heard, coming from the rear during tight turns after highway driving due to a lack of friction modifier or over-shimming of the clutch packs in the limited-slip differential. (1994-96)

• **Hard starting** The engine may not want to start or cranks for a long time then stalls, due to a sticking idle air control valve. (1995-96)

• **Engine stalling** Carbon builds up on the EGR valve seat causing stalling. (1994-96)

• **Engine misfire** Rough idle or stalling after a cold start when using reformulated gasoline is corrected with a revised engine control computer. (1994)

RECALL HISTORY

1994 in Southern California Studs that attach master cylinder to power brake booster can develop stress cracking after extended period. **1994 w/manual shift** Parking brake might not hold. **1994 V-6** Flexible hose in front fuel line is susceptible to cracking.

1990-97 MAZDA MIATA

✓ BEST BUY

1996 Mazda Miata MX-5

FOR Acceleration (manual transmission) • Steering/handling • Air bags, dual (later models) • Anti-lock brakes (optional) • Fuel economy

AGAINST Cargo room • Road noise

EVALUATION The Miata is lively, agile, simple, and fun-to-drive. While off-the-line acceleration is not terrific (0-60 in about 8.3 seconds), it shows flashes of brilliance in 2nd and 3rd gear, and it gets great mileage, with 25-27 mpg possible on a regular basis. The Miata maneuvers beautifully, is easy to handle, and hugs the road snugly. The ride can be choppy at times, given the fact body flex is the bane of all convertibles. Extra bracing added for the '94 model year seems to improve the situation, however.

Though the prominent exhaust note isn't inappropriate given the Miata's mission, there are also above-average quantities of wind and road noise. The cozy cockpit has well-placed gauges and controls, plus enough space to give tall people adequate working room. Leg room is not a problem, but the head room is tight. One golf bag, or a couple of gym bags and the tonneau cover are about all that will fit in the small trunk, which also holds the mini-spare. There's also usable storage behind the seats (perhaps as much as afforded by the trunk). Though the Miata has been around for nine years now, it still looks and feels as good as it did when it arrived in 1989.

NHTSA CRASH TEST RESULTS
1996 Mazda Miata
2-DOOR CONVERTIBLE

Driver	☆☆☆☆
Passenger	☆☆☆

(The National Highway Traffic Safety Administration tests a vehicle's crashworthiness in front and side collisions. Their ratings suggest the chance of serious injury: ☆☆☆☆☆—10% or less; ☆☆☆☆—10-20% or less; ☆☆☆—20-30% or less; ☆☆—35-45% or less; ☆—More than 45%.)

SPECIFICATIONS

	2-door conv.
Wheelbase, in.	89.2
Overall length, in.	155.4
Overall width, in.	65.9
Overall height, in.	48.2
Curb weight, lbs.	2293
Cargo volume, cu. ft.	3.6
Fuel capacity, gals.	11.9-12.7
Seating capacity	2
Front head room, in.	37.1
Max. front leg room, in.	42.7
Rear head room, in.	—
Min. rear leg room, in.	—

Powertrain layout: longitudinal front-engine/rear-wheel drive

MAZDA

ENGINES

	dohc I-4	dohc I-4
Size, liters/cu. in.	1.6/97	1.8/112
Horsepower	105-116	128-133
Torque (lbs./ft.)	100	110-114

EPA city/highway mpg

5-speed OD manual...	24/30	23/29
4-speed OD automatic.......................................	24/28	22/28

Consumer Guide™ observed MPG

5-speed OD manual...	26.7	21.9

Built in Japan.

RETAIL PRICES	GOOD	AVERAGE	POOR
1990 Miata	$4,400-5,400	$3,700-4,700	$2,000-2,800
1991 Miata	5,200-6,400	4,500-5,600	2,700-3,500
1992 Miata	6,100-7,300	5,400-6,500	3,400-4,200
1993 Miata	7,200-8,500	6,400-7,700	4,200-5,100
1994 Miata	8,500-10,500	7,500-9,500	5,000-6,500
1995 Miata	10,000-12,500	9,000-11,500	6,200-8,000
1996 Miata	11,500-14,000	10,400-12,800	7,400-9,500
1997 Miata	13,000-16,000	11,700-14,500	8,700-11,000
1998 Miata	15,000-18,000	13,500-16,500	10,500-13,000

AVERAGE REPLACEMENT COSTS

A/C Compressor $435	Clutch, Pressure Plate,
Alternator 245	Bearing 455
Radiator 500	Universal Joints 380
Timing Chain or Belt 205	Brakes................................245
Automatic Transmission or	Shocks and/or Struts 645
Transaxle........................940	Exhaust System 290

TROUBLE SPOTS

• **Timing belt** There is a revised, more robust timing belt tensioner pulley to replace the original that often caused squealing when the engine is started in cold weather. It will be replaced under normal warranty provisions. (1990-94)

• **Engine noise** A ticking noise from the top of the engine is likely due to inadequate hydraulic lash adjusters for the valves and new ones will be installed under normal warranty provisions and are available for field service. (1990-93)

• **Oil leak** Early models often developed an oil leak at the plug in the drain pan unless the plug was tightened by hand with the gasket squarely in place before snugging with a wrench. (1990)

• **Radio** If tapes get stuck in the Panasonic radio/tape player, the unit must be removed and sent to a factory service center. Owners who try to remove tapes themselves usually do more damage to the unit. (1990)

• **Windows** The windows may not fully open because a cable comes loose blocking the window's travel. The cable will be repositioned under the normal warranty. (1992-94)

RECALL HISTORY

1990-91 Rear turn signal lamps may have insufficient amount of reflecting paint on inner surface. **1990-93 with optional hardtop** Plastic buckles on optional hoist accessory kit can break, causing hardtop to fall. **1991 with ABS** Return fluid line of front brake system on some cars is misconnected to return; when anti-lock comes into use, all fluid from front brakes goes to rear system, which may lead to increased stopping distance.

1990-98 MAZDA MPV

1991 Mazda MPV 4WD

FOR Air bags, dual (later models) • Anti-lock brakes (optional) • Wet weather traction (4WD)

AGAINST Acceleration • Fuel economy

EVALUATION Acceleration on the early models ranged from anemic with the 4-cylinder to adequate with the V-6. Over the years though, MPV gained weight without gaining horsepower or torque to compensate. The result is that rear-drive versions now

MAZDA

feel sluggish in hilly terrain while the 4WD version, while well suited to Northern climates, is down-right slow. The extra weight is also sure to have a negative impact on fuel economy, which probably won't reach 20, even in normal highway driving.

The suspension is stable on smooth roads, but stiff and choppy on rough surfaces. The steering seems too light at times, requiring frequent corrections to stay on course. However, the MPV has only moderate body lean and offers good grip, handling more like a car in most situation than a van. The removable rear bench seat added for 1996 marks a big improvement in convenience for the MPV.

While recent improvements are welcome, the MPV still lags well behind such class leaders in the field, like the new Chrysler minivans and the Ford Windstar in overall roominess, performance, and value.

NHTSA CRASH TEST RESULTS
1997 Mazda MPV   4-DOOR VAN

Driver	☆☆☆☆
Passenger	☆☆☆☆

(The National Highway Traffic Safety Administration tests a vehicle's crashworthiness in front and side collisions. Their ratings suggest the chance of serious injury: ☆☆☆☆☆—10% or less; ☆☆☆☆—10-20% or less; ☆☆☆—20-30% or less; ☆☆—35-45% or less; ☆—More than 45%.)

SPECIFICATIONS

	4-door wagon
Wheelbase, in.	110.4
Overall length, in.	183.5
Overall width, in.	71.9
Overall height, in.	68.1
Curb weight, lbs.	3970
Cargo volume, cu. ft.	37.5
Fuel capacity, gals.	19.6
Seating capacity	8
Front head room, in.	40.0
Max. front leg room, in.	40.4
Rear head room, in.	39.7
Min. rear leg room, in.	33.4

Powertrain layout: longitudinal front-engine/rear- or all-wheel drive

ENGINES

	ohc I-4	ohc V-6
Size, liters/cu. in.	2.6/159	3.0/180
Horsepower	121	150-155
Torque (lbs./ft.)	149	165-169

EPA city/highway mpg

5-speed OD manual		20/25

	ohc I-4	ohc V-6
4-speed OD automatic	18/24	16/22

Consumer Guide™ observed MPG

4-speed OD automatic	17.2

Built in Japan.

RETAIL PRICES

	GOOD	AVERAGE	POOR
1990 MPV	$3,200-5,200	$2,600-4,500	$1,100-2,500
1991 MPV	4,100-6,800	3,400-6,000	1,500-3,500
1992 MPV	5,200-7,400	4,500-6,600	2,300-4,100
1993 MPV	6,000-9,000	5,300-8,200	3,000-5,400
1994 MPV	7,100-10,500	6,200-9,500	3,800-6,500
1995 MPV	8,500-13,500	7,500-12,500	4,900-9,000
1996 MPV	11,000-16,000	10,000-14,700	7,000-10,700
1997 MPV	13,500-18,500	12,300-17,000	8,700-12,500
1998 MPV	17,000-22,500	15,500-20,500	11,500-15,500

AVERAGE REPLACEMENT COSTS

A/C Compressor $905	Clutch, Pressure Plate, Bearing 540
Alternator 230	Universal Joints 680
Radiator 590	Brakes................................280
Automatic Transmission or Transaxle........................870	Shocks and/or Struts 520
	Exhaust System.................510

TROUBLE SPOTS

• **Transmission slippage** If the van starts out in third gear or falls out of third gear, or if it does not upshift, the problem is likely due to the one special short bolt for the transmission oil pan not being installed in the correct hole. If a long one is installed in its place, it damages the inhibitor switch. (1990-94)

• **Air conditioner** Refrigerant leaks from the A/C at the condenser block are often difficult to find using a detector. Mazda revised the O-rings, which now seal better. (1990-93)

• **Cold starting problems** The engine may not restart after sitting 30 minutes in the winter when fuels are more volatile. There are two revised fuel pressure regulators that cure the problem. (1992-94)

• **Vehicle noise** A groaning, popping, grinding noise from the front end is caused by the mounting rubber on the upper spring seat, which is corrected by replacing it with a new one that is a bit smaller. (1990-92)

• **Rear wipers** The hinge on the rear wiper rusts and gets stiff decreasing the pressure of the blade against the glass. A new, non-

MAZDA

ferrous arm was released to replace it. (1990-92)

• **Door handles** The outer door handles may come loose and rattle so the company will warrant the fix by replacing the original retaining nuts with ones that won't come loose. (1990-94)

RECALL HISTORY

1990-91 Front seatbelt release button can break and pieces can fall inside. **1990-91** Rear brake linings can change over time, producing inconsistent performance.

1990-92 MAZDA MX-6

1992 Mazda MX-6

FOR Acceleration (GT) • Optional anti-lock brakes • Fuel economy (110 horsepower engine)

AGAINST Automatic transmission performance • Torque steer (GT)

EVALUATION Four-cylinder coupes produce reasonably brisk acceleration and enthusiastic passing power. Reluctant downshifting from the automatic transmission makes a manual-shift model the better choice, however. For a real kick in an MX-6, pick the GT with its turbocharged 4-cylinder engine, which delivers 145 horses. Gas mileage is a pleasant bonus with either transmission, though, as expected, an MX-6 is more frugal with stick shift.

These competent coupes feel roomier inside than before and deliver a soft, supple ride—if stiffer than a typical family car. Only the GT's ride might be considered harsh through rough surfaces. Handling and roadholding are capable enough, even in the DX version, suffering only moderate body lean in turns. Wind and tire noise can grow annoying. Engine noise also is stronger than in some Japanese-brand rivals.

Because the MX-6 coupe rides a shorter wheelbase than its 626 sedan sibling, rear leg room is a bit tighter. Nevertheless, you can expect more passenger room than in most compact sport coupes. Cargo space also is above average for the car's class.

All in all, this is a nicely refined rival to the 2-door Honda Accord or Toyota Camry, and also a better daily driver than a rear-drive Ford Mustang or Chevrolet Camaro.

SPECIFICATIONS

	2-door coupe
Wheelbase, in.	99.0
Overall length, in.	177.0
Overall width, in.	66.5
Overall height, in.	53.5
Curb weight, lbs.	2560
Cargo volume, cu. ft.	15.4
Fuel capacity, gals.	15.9
Seating capacity	4
Front head room, in.	38.4
Max. front leg room, in.	43.6
Rear head room, in.	37.8
Min. rear leg room, in.	31.8

Powertrain layout: transverse front-engine/front-wheel drive

ENGINES

	ohc I-4	Turbocharged ohc I-4
Size, liters/cu. in.	2.2/133	2.2/133
Horsepower	110	145
Torque (lbs./ft.)	130	190

EPA city/highway mpg

5-speed OD manual	24/31	21/28
4-speed OD automatic	22/28	19/25

Consumer Guide™ observed MPG

5-speed OD manual	26.5	20.9
4-speed OD automatic		20.2

Built in USA and Japan.

RETAIL PRICES	GOOD	AVERAGE	POOR
1990 MX-6 DX, LX	$2,300-3,100	$1,600-2,400	$700-1,100
1990 MX-6 GT	3,100-3,700	2,400-3,000	1,100-1,500
1991 MX-6 DX, LX	3,000-3,900	2,300-3,200	1,000-1,800
1991 MX-6 GT	3,900-4,500	3,100-3,700	1,500-2,000
1992 MX-6 DX, LX	4,000-4,900	3,300-4,200	1,600-2,100
1992 MX-6 GT	5,000-5,600	4,200-4,800	2,200-2,700

AVERAGE REPLACEMENT COSTS

A/C Compressor $545	Clutch, Pressure Plate,
Alternator 235	Bearing 600
Radiator 420	Brakes................................210
Timing Chain or Belt 180	Shocks and/or Struts 700
Automatic Transmission or	Exhaust System 535
Transaxle.....................1,435	

TROUBLE SPOTS

• **Oil consumption** A plugged drainback hole in the cylinder head causes high oil consumption. (1991)

• **Water leak** Water leaks into the trunk through the taillight assembly. (1990-92)

• **Suspension noise** A knocking noise from the front end when driving over speed bumps caused by defective spring seats. (1990-92)

• **Air conditioner** The A/C may gradually stop working because pinhole leaks develop at the receiver drier. (1990)

• **Engine misfire** High idle or surging when cold could be due to a bad coolant sensor. (1990-92)

RECALL HISTORY

None to date.

1993-97 MAZDA MX-6

✓ BEST BUY

1995 Mazda MX-6

FOR Air bags, dual • Acceleration (V-6) • Steering/handling • Refinement • Anti-lock brakes (optional)

AGAINST Rear-seat room • Ride (LS) • Automatic transmission performance

EVALUATION While we prefer the V-6, be aware that the 4-cylinder engine does have adequate performance and better fuel economy. Equipped with a V-6 and 5-speed, the coupe delivers willing performance and spirited acceleration. The engine has plenty of low-end torque and revs freely to redline. While the V-6 runs smoothly and quietly at all speeds, the automatic tends to stifle the car's performance, even becoming balky when asked to perform a full-throttle downshift. The 4-cylinder likewise delivers decent power with the manual, but as expected, turns sluggish when paired with the automatic.

Handling is crisp and responsive, with little body roll in tight corners. Ride quality on the LS suffers some from the standard performance tires, which are rated for speeds up to 149 mph. However, the ride is still better than that provided by the Ford Probe GT. You can also expect the stiff tires to offer poor traction in snow.

The MX-6 is a snug 2+2. Front head room and leg room are adequate for 6-footers, the rear seats are so tiny that even some small children may complain about the lack of space.

Ford's Probe has the same mechanical features but at a lower price. Both the MX-6 and Probe are the cream of the crop among sports coupes, in our view.

NHTSA CRASH TEST RESULTS
1996 Mazda MX-6   2-DOOR COUPE

Driver	☆ ☆ ☆ ☆ ☆
Passenger	☆ ☆ ☆ ☆

(The National Highway Traffic Safety Administration tests a vehicle's crashworthiness in front and side collisions. Their ratings suggest the chance of serious injury: ☆☆☆☆☆—10% or less; ☆☆☆☆—10-20% or less; ☆☆☆—20-30% or less; ☆☆—35-45% or less; ☆—More than 45%.)

SPECIFICATIONS

	2-door coupe
Wheelbase, in.	102.8
Overall length, in.	181.5
Overall width, in.	68.9
Overall height, in.	51.6
Curb weight, lbs.	2625
Cargo volume, cu. ft.	12.4
Fuel capacity, gals.	15.5
Seating capacity	4
Front head room, in.	38.1
Max. front leg room, in.	44.0
Rear head room, in.	34.7
Min. rear leg room, in.	27.7

MAZDA

Powertrain layout: transverse front-engine/front-wheel drive

ENGINES

	dohc I-4	dohc V-6
Size, liters/cu. in.	2.0/122	2.5/153
Horsepower	114-118	160-164
Torque (lbs./ft.)	124-127	156-160

EPA city/highway mpg

5-speed OD manual	26/34	21/26
4-speed OD automatic	23/31	20/26

Consumer Guide™ observed MPG

5-speed OD manual	23.0

Built in USA.

RETAIL PRICES	GOOD	AVERAGE	POOR
1993 MX-6	$5,500-7,500	$4,800-6,700	$2,500-4,000
1994 MX-6	6,700-9,000	5,900-8,200	3,400-5,200
1995 MX-6	8,400-11,000	7,500-10,000	4,800-6,800
1996 MX-6	11,000-13,500	10,000-12,500	7,000-9,000
1997 MX-6	12,500-15,500	11,300-14,200	8,300-10,500

AVERAGE REPLACEMENT COSTS

A/C Compressor	$360	Clutch, Pressure Plate, Bearing	590
Alternator	245	Constant Velocity Joints	780
Radiator	410	Brakes	275
Timing Chain or Belt	180	Shocks and/or Struts	770
Automatic Transmission or Transaxle	1,,075	Exhaust System	485

TROUBLE SPOTS

• **Vehicle shake** Vibration, which is usually felt in the steering wheel, shift lever, and floor is probably caused by mis-positioned radiator dampers that the company will replace under normal warranty provisions. (1993-95)

• **Engine knock** Cars with a V-6 engine built before March 1993 may have engine knock, especially when cold, due to carbon buildup in the combustion chamber. To eliminate the noise, the company will replace the pistons and cylinder heads. Dealers have a special hotline to call if a customer reports this problem. (1993-94)

• **Engine noise** A metallic tapping noise from the rear of the engine could be due to slippage between the exhaust camshaft driven gear and friction gear. Although newer engines have a better contact surface, the company will fix cars in service by replacing the friction gear spring with a stouter one. (1993-95)

• **Power seats** The insulation on the wires for the power seat can wear through causing a short circuit disabling the power seat. The wires will be repaired and rerouted as a warranty repair. (1993-94)

• **Engine mounts** Broken motor mounts allow the engine to rock back and forth when accelerating, decelerating, or starting from a stop. The company has a redesigned mount to replace the original. (1993-94)

• **Transmission leak** A damaged torque converter hub seal allows fluid to leak from the automatic transmission. A new seal will be installed under warranty. (1994-96)

• **Windshield wipers** The welds holding the wiper arm support bracket break, causing a creak or rattle when the wipers are running. Under normal warranty, the welds will be drilled out and bolts/nuts will be installed. (1993-95)

RECALL HISTORY

None to date.

1995-98 MAZDA PROTEGE

1995 Mazda Protege ES

FOR Air bags, dual • Optional anti-lock brakes (LX, ES) • Passenger room • Fuel economy • Ride

AGAINST Handling • Acceleration • Radio controls • Entry/exit

EVALUATION Mazda obviously tuned the Protege's suspension more toward ride comfort than handling finesse, though steering response is good and the car reacts well in urban driving. Bumps are easily absorbed, though they often produce a loud "thump." Hard cornering brings lots of body lean, and the narrow 13-inch tires on DX and LX models start squealing early. The 14-inch ES tires have noticeably better cornering grip.

MAZDA

Space inside is ample for four adults, with abundant front head and rear leg room. However, rear doors are narrow at the bottom, making it awkward to climb in and out. You get a good-sized trunk and an average sized glovebox.

The 1.5-liter engine in DX and LX models delivers adequate acceleration with either transmission. With a full load the 1.5-liter 4-cylinder might be short on strength. Surprisingly, the 1.8-liter engine in the ES doesn't seem that much stronger, despite its 30-horsepower advantage. Highway passing and merging are notably easier, however. Both engines should return above-average fuel economy. A manual-shift LX averaged 30.2 mpg.

The dashboard is well laid out, with clear gauges and stalk-mounted light and wiper controls. Until the 1997 model year, however, the radio sat too low. Small buttons require a long look away from the road to make any adjustments. The radio moved to the top of the dashboard in 1997. Visibility is fine in all directions.

Exceptionally easy to drive, Protege provides a rewarding mixture of maneuverability, economy, and quietness, coupled with solid assembly quality.

NHTSA CRASH TEST RESULTS
1995 Mazda Protege

4-DOOR SEDAN

Driver	☆☆☆
Passenger	NA

(The National Highway Traffic Safety Administration tests a vehicle's crashworthiness in front and side collisions. Their ratings suggest the chance of serious injury: ☆☆☆☆☆—10% or less; ☆☆☆☆—10-20% or less; ☆☆☆—20-30% or less; ☆☆—35-45% or less; ☆—More than 45%.)

SPECIFICATIONS

	4-door sedan
Wheelbase, in.	102.6
Overall length, in.	174.8
Overall width, in.	67.3
Overall height, in.	55.9
Curb weight, lbs.	2385
Cargo volume, cu. ft.	13.1
Fuel capacity, gals.	14.5
Seating capacity	5
Front head room, in.	39.2
Max. front leg room, in.	42.2
Rear head room, in.	37.4
Min. rear leg room, in.	35.6

Powertrain layout: transverse front-engine/front-wheel drive

ENGINES

	dohc I-4	dohc I-4
Size, liters/cu. in.	1.5/91	1.8/110

	dohc I-4	dohc I-4
Horsepower	92	122
Torque (lbs./ft.)	96	117
EPA city/highway mpg		
5-speed OD manual	32/39	26/33
4-speed OD automatic	27/35	23/30
Consumer Guide™ observed MPG		
5-speed OD manual	30.2	
4-speed OD automatic		24.8

Built in Japan.

RETAIL PRICES

	GOOD	AVERAGE	POOR
1995 Protege	$5,500-7,200	$4,800-6,400	$2,800-3,900
1996 Protege	6,700-8,500	5,900-7,700	3,600-4,800
1997 Protege	8,000-10,000	7,200-9,000	4,400-5,800
1998 Protege	9,200-11,500	8,300-10,500	5,300-7,000

AVERAGE REPLACEMENT COSTS

A/C Compressor	$420	Constant Velocity Joints	840
Alternator	350	Brakes	230
Radiator	500	Shocks and/or Struts	600
Timing Chain or Belt	190	Exhaust System	555
Automatic Transmission or Transaxle	1,460		

TROUBLE SPOTS

• **Steering problems** The steering wheel may be off center requiring adjustment of the alignment (tie rods). (1995)

• **Engine knock** If engine knock occurs in hot weather, there is a revised engine control computer to correct the problem. (1995-96)

• **Exhaust system** There is a new tailpipe tip available to eliminate a hooting noise (like a horn) from the exhaust. (1995-96)

RECALL HISTORY

1995 w/1.5-liter engine Valve springs can develop minute cracks and break; can cause engine chatter, piston damage, and stalling.

1990-93 MERCEDES-BENZ 190

FOR Handling/roadholding • Anti-lock brakes • Air bag, driver • Acceleration (6-cylinder) • Ride

AGAINST Rear seat room • Cargo room • Price

MERCEDES-BENZ

1991 Mercedes-Benz 190E 2.3

EVALUATION Price has been the biggest drawback of these compact sedans. Considering how much they've cost, both new and secondhand, you're getting quite a cramped rear seat and a rather small trunk. Two people fit comfortably up front, but two adults in the back seat aren't likely to be pleased.

On the other hand, you get a good-sized list of Mercedes-Benz virtues, leading off with rock-solid construction, desirable safety features, and thoughtful engineering. Performance brings no complaints, either. The 4-cylinder engine in a 190 2.3 performs well once you're underway, but acceleration is rather gentle from a standing start. The 6-cylinder engine in a 190E 2.6 feels more robust. The six returns only slightly less fuel economy than the 4-cylinder. With automatic transmissions, a 190E 2.6 averaged 19.2 mpg, compared to 20.1 mpg in a 190 2.3.

Handling and roadholding are extremely capable on both models. The taut Mercedes-Benz suspension, while allowing low-speed bumps to thump through to the seat, is quite absorbent in most situations. It also helps produce good high-speed control. Everything is aimed toward serious driving: brakes, steering, seating, outward visibility, control placement.

Except for interior space and high maintenance costs, you can hardly ask for more—though it's worth trying out a BMW 3-Series and Lexus ES 300 before buying.

SPECIFICATIONS

	4-door sedan
Wheelbase, in.	104.9
Overall length, in.	175.1
Overall width, in.	66.5
Overall height, in.	54.1
Curb weight, lbs.	2900
Cargo volume, cu. ft.	11.7
Fuel capacity, gals.	16.1

	4-door sedan
Seating capacity	5
Front head room, in.	36.9
Max. front leg room, in.	41.9
Rear head room, in.	36.3
Min. rear leg room, in.	31.1

Powertrain layout: longitudinal front-engine/rear-wheel drive

ENGINES

	ohc I-4	ohc I-6
Size, liters/cu. in.	2.3/140	2.6/156
Horsepower	130	158
Torque (lbs./ft.)	146	162

EPA city/highway mpg

	ohc I-4	ohc I-6
5-speed OD manual	20/28	19/27
4-speed OD automatic	20/26	20/25
4-speed OD automatic	20.1	19.2

Built in Germany.

RETAIL PRICES

	GOOD	AVERAGE	POOR
1990 190E 2.6	$8,000-9,000	$7,200-8,200	$4,500-5,300
1991 190E 2.3	7,900-9,000	7,100-8,100	4,400-5,200
1991 190E 2.6	9,400-10,500	8,600-9,600	5,600-6,300
1992 190E 2.3	9,300-10,300	8,500-9,400	5,500-6,200
1992 190E 2.6	11,000-12,500	10,000-11,500	6,800-7,800
1993 190E 2.3	11,000-12,200	10,000-11,200	6,700-7,500
1993 190E 2.6	13,000-14,500	12,000-13,500	8,500-9,500

AVERAGE REPLACEMENT COSTS

A/C Compressor $1,035	Clutch, Pressure Plate,
Alternator 440	Bearing 795
Radiator 450	Universal Joints 535
Timing Chain or Belt 265	Brakes................................190
Automatic Transmission or	Shocks and/or Struts 1,240
Transaxle......................1,070	Exhaust System.................575

TROUBLE SPOTS

• **Cruise control** May jerk when traveling on level roads or when coasting down hills with the cruise control engaged due to problem in fuel shutoff switch. (1990-91)

• **Transmission slippage** The transmission may slip or the shifts may be soft due to too much clearance in the modulator valve assembly. (1991)

• **Transmission slippage** Transmission shifts may be harsh or errat-

MERCEDES-BENZ

ic due to a defective vacuum modulator. (1990-93)

• **Engine misfire** The idle speed control motor may stick causing a high idle or surging idle. (1990-93)

RECALL HISTORY

1993 Air bag intended for European models was installed on small number of cars, instead of correct U.S. version.

1994-98 MERCEDES-BENZ C-CLASS

1995 Mercedes-Benz C-Class

FOR   Air bags, dual • Anti-lock brakes • Steering/handling • Acceleration (C280, C36)

AGAINST   Road noise • Rear seat room • Wet-weather traction

EVALUATION   Both the 4- and 6-cylinder engines are quiet and refined, even when pushed hard, but suffer rather leisurely acceleration from a standing start. However, they gather steam quickly and deliver strong passing power—especially the C280. A C280 sedan accelerated to 60 mph in a brief 8.3 seconds. The automatic transmission downshifts promptly to deliver passing power when it's needed, though upshifts can feel sloppy during hard acceleration.

Steering response is excellent, and handling is balanced with fine grip through turns. You'll feel most of the bumps in either of these cars, even though the firm suspension absorbs the worst of the impacts. Road noise intrudes on the pleasure, too—especially emanating from the rear tires.

Controls are laid out in a user-friendly manner, and you get a comfortable driving position. Though more spacious than its 190 predecessor, the C-Class isn't exactly roomy. Tall drivers might lack sufficient head or leg room, even with the seat position considerably rearward. Moving the driver's seat all the way back cuts drastically into rear leg space, which is only adequate even under the best conditions. Cargo space is good in a usefully square trunk, and an optional folding rear seatback provides extra space.

All told, we've been impressed with the C-Class. This sedan is well worth a look if you're shopping in the luxury end of the compact-car league.

NHTSA CRASH TEST RESULTS
1994 Mercedes-Benz C-Class 4-DOOR SEDAN

Driver	☆☆☆☆
Passenger	☆☆☆☆

(The National Highway Traffic Safety Administration tests a vehicle's crashworthiness in front and side collisions. Their ratings suggest the chance of serious injury: ☆☆☆☆☆—10% or less; ☆☆☆☆—10-20% or less; ☆☆☆—20-30% or less; ☆☆—35-45% or less; ☆—More than 45%.)

SPECIFICATIONS

	4-door sedan
Wheelbase, in.	105.9
Overall length, in.	177.4
Overall width, in.	67.7
Overall height, in.	56.1
Curb weight, lbs.	3173
Cargo volume, cu. ft.	13.7
Fuel capacity, gals.	16.4
Seating capacity	5
Front head room, in.	37.2
Max. front leg room, in.	41.5
Rear head room, in.	37.0
Min. rear leg room, in.	32.8

Powertrain layout: longitudinal front-engine/rear-wheel drive

ENGINES

	dohc I-4	dohc I-4	dohc I-6	dohc I-6
Size, liters/cu. in.	2.2/132	2.3/140	2.8/173	3.6/220
Horsepower	147	148	194	268-276
Torque (lbs./ft.)	155	162	199	284
EPA city/highway mpg				
4-speed OD automatic	23/29		19/26	18/22
5-speed OD automatic		23/30	20/27	18/24
Consumer Guide™ observed MPG				
4-speed OD automatic			19.2	19.7

Built in Germany.

MERCEDES-BENZ

RETAIL PRICES

	GOOD	AVERAGE	POOR
1994 C220	$16,500-17,500	$15,500-16,500	$12,500-13,500
1994 C280	19,000-20,500	17,700-19,000	14,000-15,000
1995 C220	18,300-19,500	17,300-18,300	14,000-15,000
1995 C280	21,500-23,000	20,000-21,500	16,000-17,000
1995 C36	31,500-33,000	29,500-31,000	25,000-26,000
1996 C220	21,500-23,000	20,000-21,500	16,000-17,200
1996 C280	26,000-27,500	24,500-26,000	20,000-21,000
1996 C36	35,000-37,500	32,500-35,000	27,500-29,000
1997 C230	24,500-26,000	23,000-24,500	18,500-19,500
1997 C280	28,500-30,500	26,500-28,500	22,000-23,500
1997 C36	39,000-42,500	36,000-39,500	30,000-33,000
1998 C230	27,500-29,500	25,500-27,500	21,000-22,500
1998 C280	31,500-34,000	29,500-32,000	24,500-26,500
1998 C43	44,000-47,500	41,000-44,500	35,000-38,000

AVERAGE REPLACEMENT COSTS

A/C Compressor $865	Universal Joints 545
Alternator 330	Brakes..................................200
Radiator 445	Shocks and/or Struts 1,200
Timing Chain or Belt 305	Exhaust System.................650
Automatic Transmission or	
Transaxle....................1,035	

TROUBLE SPOTS

• **Brake noise** Brake squeal at low speeds (under 10 mph) may activate the anti-lock brake system. (1990-93)

• **Dashboard lights** The "EC" warning light may come on indicating loss of A/C refrigerant caused by a faulty refrigerant pressure sensor. (1997)

• **Hard starting** The starter may corrode due to the windshield water draining onto it. (1994-96)

• **Fuel gauge** Erroneous fuel gauge readings are often due to a bad potentiometer on the fuel level sensor. (1994-96)

• **Clock** The clock on the C220 may reset itself when starting the engine due to a faulty instrument cluster voltage regulator. (1994)

RECALL HISTORY

1994 C220 Cruise control linkage may be inadequately lubricated, subject to binding, so throttle will not return to closed position when pedal is released. **1994-95 C220/C280, C36** In minor frontal impact, hood latch hook may not function properly as secondary safety catch. **1996 C280** Drive belt pulley of a few 6-cylinder engines can develop fatigue cracks and break; car would then lack engine cooling, battery charging, and/or power steering.

1990-97 MERCURY COUGAR

1991 Mercury Cougar XR7

FOR Air bags, dual (later models) • Acceleration (V-8) • Handling

AGAINST Acceleration (V-6) • Fuel economy • Visibility

See the 1990-97 Ford Thunderbird report for an evaluation of the 1990-97 Mercury Cougar.

NHTSA CRASH TEST RESULTS
1995 Mercury Cougar

2-DOOR COUPE

	2-DOOR COUPE
Driver	☆☆☆☆☆
Passenger	☆☆☆☆☆

(The National Highway Traffic Safety Administration tests a vehicle's crashworthiness in front and side collisions. Their ratings suggest the chance of serious injury: ☆☆☆☆☆—10% or less; ☆☆☆☆—10-20% or less; ☆☆☆—20-30% or less; ☆☆—35-45% or less; ☆—More than 45%.)

SPECIFICATIONS

	2-door coupe
Wheelbase, in.	113.0
Overall length, in.	200.3
Overall width, in.	72.7
Overall height, in.	52.5
Curb weight, lbs.	3575
Cargo volume, cu. ft.	15.1
Fuel capacity, gals.	18.0
Seating capacity	5
Front head room, in.	38.1
Max. front leg room, in.	42.5

	2-door coupe
Rear head room, in.	37.5
Min. rear leg room, in.	35.8

Powertrain layout: longitudinal front-engine/rear-wheel drive

ENGINES

	ohv V-6	Supercharged ohv V-6	ohv V-8	ohc V-8
Size, liters/cu. in.	3.8/232	3.8/232	5.0/302	4.5/281
Horsepower	140-145	210	200	205
Torque (lbs./ft.)	215	315	275	280

EPA city/highway mpg

	ohv V-6	Supercharged ohv V-6	ohv V-8	ohc V-8
5-speed OD manual		17/24		
4-speed OD automatic	19/27	17/23	17/24	17/25

Consumer Guide™ observed MPG

	ohv V-6	Supercharged ohv V-6	ohv V-8	ohc V-8
4-speed OD automatic			15.5	18.2

Built in USA.

RETAIL PRICES

	GOOD	AVERAGE	POOR
1990 Cougar	$2,800-3,700	$2,100-3,000	$900-1,300
1991 Cougar	3,400-4,200	2,700-3,500	1,300-1,600
1992 Cougar	4,200-5,500	3,500-4,700	1,800-2,400
1993 Cougar	5,400-6,500	4,600-5,700	2,600-3,200
1994 Cougar	6,700-7,800	5,900-7,000	3,600-4,300
1995 Cougar	8,200-9,200	7,300-8,300	4,500-5,200
1996 Cougar	9,900-11,000	8,800-9,800	5,600-6,300
1997 Cougar	11,600-13,200	10,500-12,000	7,200-8,000

AVERAGE REPLACEMENT COSTS

A/C Compressor	$375	Universal Joints	260
Alternator	445	Brakes	275
Radiator	405	Shocks and/or Struts	430
Timing Chain or Belt	340	Exhaust System	280
Automatic Transmission or Transaxle	810		

TROUBLE SPOTS

• **Vehicle noise** A chattering noise that can be felt, and sometimes heard, coming from the rear during tight turns after highway driving is caused by a lack of friction modifier or over-shimming of the clutch packs in the Traction-Lok (limited-slip) differential. A replacement clutch pack and friction modifier will be installed under the company's warranty programs. (1990-96)

• **Water leak** Water drips onto the floor when the air conditioner is operated and may be due to over a half-dozen potential leak sources including seals, bad seams in the evaporator case, the heater core cover seal, etc. The leak will be fixed under the bumper-to-bumper warranty for 1992-96 model years. (1990-96)

• **Transmission slippage** The automatic transmission in these cars over 20,000 miles is notorious for shuddering or vibrating under light acceleration or when shifting between third and fourth gear above 35 mph. It requires that the transmission fluid (including fluid in the torque converter) be changed and that only Mercon® fluid be used. It usually takes at least 100 miles of driving after the fluid change for the shudder to go away. (1994)

• **Transmission slippage** The transmission may slip (lack of torque) and the engine may flare when the transmission shifts into fourth gear, which can often be traced to a bad TR/MLP sensor that will be replaced along with a speed sensor on AODE automatic transmissions under the normal warranty provisions. (1994-95)

• **Oil leak** The oil filter balloons and leaks because the oil pump relief valve sticks. Higher than recommended viscosity oils cause wear to the valve bore. Under normal warranty provisions, the pump will be replaced with one less sensitive to this problem, but Ford warns that owners should only use the type of oil spelled out in the owners manual. (1992-94)

• **Blower motor** Squeaking or chirping blower motors are the result of defective brush holders, so Ford has issued a redesigned motor and will replace those that are under normal warranty. (1993-94)

RECALL HISTORY

1990 Battery-to-starter cables on small number of cars with 3.8-liter engine are too long and could contact engine damper pulley. **1990-91** Nuts that hold windshield wiper motor may loosen. **1990-93** Ignition switch could suffer short circuit, which can cause overheating, smoke, and possibly fire in steering-column area. **1992-93 cars in specified states** Movement of fuel lines can result in leakage. **1996** Driver's door, when closed only to secondary latched position, may not sustain the specified 1000-pound transverse load. **1996 with semi-automatic temperature-control** Under certain conditions, blower does not operate as intended.

1992-98 MERCURY GRAND MARQUIS

✓ BEST BUY

FOR Acceleration • Passenger and cargo room • Air bags, dual • Anti-lock brakes (optional)

1992 Mercury Grand Marquis

AGAINST Fuel economy • Steering feel • Climate controls • Radio controls (early models)

See the 1992-98 Ford Crown Victoria report for an evaluation of the 1992-98 Mercury Grand Marquis.

NHTSA CRASH TEST RESULTS
1997 Mercury Grand Marquis

4-DOOR SEDAN

Driver	☆☆☆☆☆
Passenger	☆☆☆☆☆

(The National Highway Traffic Safety Administration tests a vehicle's crashworthiness in front and side collisions. Their ratings suggest the chance of serious injury: ☆☆☆☆☆—10% or less; ☆☆☆☆—10-20% or less; ☆☆☆—20-30% or less; ☆☆—35-45% or less; ☆—More than 45%.)

SPECIFICATIONS

	4-door sedan
Wheelbase, in.	114.4
Overall length, in.	212.0
Overall width, in.	77.8
Overall height, in.	56.8
Curb weight, lbs.	3776
Cargo volume, cu. ft.	6
Fuel capacity, gals.	18.0
Seating capacity	20.6
Front head room, in.	39.4
Max. front leg room, in.	42.5
Rear head room, in.	38.1
Min. rear leg room, in.	38.8

Powertrain layout: longitudinal front-engine/rear-wheel drive

ENGINES

	ohc V-8
Size, liters/cu. in.	4.6/281
Horsepower	190-210
Torque (lbs./ft.)	265-275

EPA city/highway mpg
4-speed OD automatic.. 17/25

Consumer Guide™ observed MPG
4-speed OD automatic.. 16.0

Built in Canada.

RETAIL PRICES	GOOD	AVERAGE	POOR
1992 Grand Marquis	$4,800-5,800	$4,100-5,000	$2,300-2,900
1993 Grand Marquis	6,500-7,500	5,800-6,700	3,500-4,100
1994 Grand Marquis	7,800-9,000	7,000-8,200	4,400-5,200
1995 Grand Marquis	9,500-11,200	8,500-10,200	5,500-6,800
1996 Grand Marquis	12,000-13,700	10,800-12,500	7,500-8,700
1997 Grand Marquis	14,500-16,700	13,200-15,300	9,500-11,000
1998 Grand Marquis	17,000-19,500	15,500-18,000	11,500-13,500

AVERAGE REPLACEMENT COSTS

A/C Compressor $380
Alternator 375
Radiator 380
Timing Chain or Belt 365
Automatic Transmission or
   Transaxle........................490

Universal Joints 90
Brakes.................................285
Shocks and/or Struts 290
Exhaust System.................680

TROUBLE SPOTS

• **Vehicle noise** A chattering noise that can be felt and sometimes heard, coming from the rear during tight turns after highway driving is caused by a lack of friction modifier or over-shimming of the clutch packs in the Traction-Lok (limited-slip) differential. A replacement clutch pack and friction modifier will be installed under the company's warranty programs. (1992-96)

• **Vehicle noise** A broken gusset or weld separation at the frame crossmember causes a rattle from the rear or the car. Ford will weld new gussets into place under the bumper-to-bumper warranty (1992) or basic warranty on prior models. (1990-92)

• **Oil pump** The oil filter balloons and leaks because the oil pump relief valve sticks. Higher than recommended viscosity oils cause wear to the valve bore. Under normal warranty provisions, the pump will be replaced with one less sensitive to this problem, but Ford warns that owners should only use the type of oil spelled out in the owners manual. (1992-94)

• **Transmission noise** The automatic transmission in these cars over 20,000 miles is notorious for shuddering or vibrating under light acceleration or when shifting between third and fourth gear above 35 mph. It requires that the transmission fluid (including fluid in the torque converter) be changed and that only Mercon® fluid be used. It usually takes at least 100 miles of driving after the fluid change for the shudder to go away. (1992-94)

• **Transmission slippage** The transmission may slip (lack of torque) and the engine may flare when the transmission shifts into fourth gear, which can often be traced to a bad TR/MLP sensor that will be replaced along with a speed sensor on AODE automatic transmissions under the normal warranty provisions. (1992-95)

• **Hard starting** The connector at the starter solenoid tends to corrode resulting in a "no-crank" condition. Under warranty, the automaker will replace the connector and slather the terminal with dielectric grease to prevent it from happening again. (1992-94)

• **Hard starting** If the engine does not start or cranks for a long time then stalls, the idle air control valve may be sticking. Ford will replace it under warranty. (1996)

• **Air springs** Air springs are prone to leaks caused by the bag rubbing against the axle or control arm. Often, the car will be "sitting low" on one corner after being parked for any length of time. Leaking air springs must be replaced. (Any so-equipped)

• **Cold starting problems** The drive belt tensioner pulley or idler pulley bearings are apt to make a squealing noise when the engine is started in cold weather. Under the bumper-to-bumper warranty, the pulley(s) will be replaced. (1993-96)

RECALL HISTORY

1994 Nuts and bolts that attach rear brake adapter to axle housing flange can loosen, allowing damage to ABS sensor, hydraulic line, or parking brake cable. **1995** Seal between fuel filler pipe and fuel tank may not be fully cured, which could allow fuel to leak. **1995** Some passenger-side air bags may not inflate properly; also, igniter end cap can separate, causing hot gases to be released. **1995** Non-cycling power window circuit breaker and cycling-type headlamp breaker were interchanged; in the event of short or overload in circuit, both headlamps can go out without warning. **1995** Heads of rivets holding rear outboard seatbelt D-rings may fracture under load, reducing belt's restraining capability in an accident. **1996** Driver's door, when closed only to secondary latched position, may not sustain the specified 1000-pound transverse load.

1995-98 MERCURY MYSTIQUE

FOR Air bags, dual • Optional anti-lock brakes • Acceleration (V-6) • Steering/handling

AGAINST Road noise • Rear seat room • Stereo controls • Engine noise (4-cylinder)

1996 Mercury Mystique

See the 1995-98 Ford Contour report for an evaluation of the 1995-98 Mercury Mystique.

NHTSA CRASH TEST RESULTS
1995 Mercury Mystique

4-DOOR SEDAN

Driver	☆☆☆☆☆
Passenger	☆☆☆☆

(The National Highway Traffic Safety Administration tests a vehicle's crashworthiness in front and side collisions. Their ratings suggest the chance of serious injury: ☆☆☆☆☆—10% or less; ☆☆☆☆—10-20% or less; ☆☆☆—20-30% or less; ☆☆—35-45% or less; ☆—More than 45%.)

SPECIFICATIONS

	4-door sedan
Wheelbase, in.	106.5
Overall length, in.	183.5
Overall width, in.	69.1
Overall height, in.	54.5
Curb weight, lbs.	2831
Cargo volume, cu. ft.	13.9
Fuel capacity, gals.	14.5
Seating capacity	5
Front head room, in.	39.0
Max. front leg room, in.	42.4
Rear head room, in.	36.7
Min. rear leg room, in.	34.3

Powertrain layout: transverse front-engine/front-wheel drive

ENGINES

	dohc I-4	dohc V-6
Size, liters/cu. in.	2.0/121	2.5/155
Horsepower	125	170
Torque (lbs./ft.)	130	165

MERCURY

EPA city/highway mpg

5-speed OD manual..	24/34	21/31
4-speed OD automatic......................................	23/32	21/30

Consumer Guide™ observed MPG

5-speed OD manual..		19.9
4-speed OD automatic......................................	20.7	19.5

Built in USA and Mexico.

RETAIL PRICES	GOOD	AVERAGE	POOR
1995 Mystique	$6,700-7,900	$6,000-6,900	$3,800-4,800
1996 Mystique	7,700-9,200	7,000-8,300	4,800-5,800
1997 Mystique	8,800-10,700	8,100-9,900	5,600-7,100
1998 Mystique	11,000-12,500	10,000-11,500	7,000-8,500

AVERAGE REPLACEMENT COSTS

A/C Compressor $360	Clutch, Pressure Plate,
Alternator 455	Bearing 750
Radiator 345	Constant Velocity Joints.....465
Timing Chain or Belt 175	Brakes..................................290
Automatic Transmission or	Shocks and/or Struts 700
Transaxle........................800	Exhaust System.................345

TROUBLE SPOTS

• **Engine misfire** Lack of acceleration or power in freezing weather (below 32 degrees F) on the 2.5L engine is often due to ice on the throttle plate. A revised engine computer prevents the problem. (1995)

• **Manual transmission** If there is gear clash going into third on the manual transmission, under warranty the input gear shaft will be rebuilt and a new shift fork installed. (1995-97)

• **Steering problems** If the steering wheel vibrates while idling with the transmission engaged and the A/C running, the steering mass damper, air bag module and radiator mounts will be replaced under warranty. (1995-97)

• **Brakes** Ice in the parking brake cables will not allow the parking brake to release or release fully, and both cables will be replaced under normal warranty provisions. (1995-97)

• **Steering problems** A slipping drive belt causes a lack of power steering and the charge warning light to glow. Under warranty, the belt, idler pulley, and a splash kit will be installed. (1995-97)

RECALL HISTORY

1995 Some passenger-side air bags may not inflate properly; also, igniter end cap can separate, releasing hot gases. **1995** Metal shield on plastic fuel filler pipe can develop static charge during refueling; could serve as ignition source for fuel vapors. **1995** Fuel tank filler reinforcement can leak, resulting in fire. **1995** Front seatbelt outboard anchor tabs may be cracked. **1995-96 w/traction control** Throttle cables were damaged during assembly, leading to fraying or separation; could prevent engine from returning to idle. **1998** Text and/or graphics for headlamp aiming instructions, provided in owner guides, are not sufficiently clear.

1990-95 MERCURY SABLE

1992 Mercury Sable 4-door

FOR Acceleration (3.8-liter V-6) • Ride • Passenger and cargo room • Air bags, dual (later models) • Anti-lock brakes (optional)

AGAINST Fuel economy • Radio controls • Instruments/controls (electronic)

See the 1990-95 Ford Taurus report for an evaluation of the 1990-95 Mercury Sable.

NHTSA CRASH TEST RESULTS
1995 Mercury Sable

	4-DOOR SEDAN
Driver	☆☆☆☆
Passenger	☆☆☆☆

(The National Highway Traffic Safety Administration tests a vehicle's crashworthiness in front and side collisions. Their ratings suggest the chance of serious injury: ☆☆☆☆☆—10% or less; ☆☆☆☆—10-20% or less; ☆☆☆—20-30% or less; ☆☆—35-45% or less; ☆—More than 45%.)

SPECIFICATIONS

	4-door sedan	4-door wagon
Wheelbase, in.	106.0	106.0
Overall length, in.	192.2	193.3

MERCURY

	4-door sedan	4-door wagon
Overall width, in.	70.9	70.9
Overall height, in.	54.1	55.5
Curb weight, lbs.	3144	3292
Cargo volume, cu. ft.	18.0	83.1
Fuel capacity, gals.	16.0	16.0
Seating capacity	6	8
Front head room, in.	38.3	38.6
Max. front leg room, in.	41.7	41.7
Rear head room, in.	37.7	38.1
Min. rear leg room, in.	37.1	36.9

Powertrain layout: transverse front-engine/front-wheel drive

ENGINES

	ohv V-6	ohv V-6
Size, liters/cu. in.	3.0/182	3.8/232
Horsepower	140	140
Torque (lbs./ft.)	165	215

EPA city/highway mpg

4-speed OD automatic	20/30	19/28

Consumer Guide™ observed MPG

4-speed OD automatic		16.8

Built in USA.

RETAIL PRICES

	GOOD	AVERAGE	POOR
1990 Sable	$2,000-3,100	$1,400-2,500	$500-900
1991 Sable	2,600-4,500	2,000-3,800	800-1,700
1992 Sable	3,300-5,400	2,700-4,700	1,300-2,500
1993 Sable	4,200-6,400	3,500-5,600	1,700-3,300
1994 Sable	5,400-7,600	4,600-6,800	2,400-4,200
1995 Sable	7,000-9,500	6,200-8,600	3,800-5,800

AVERAGE REPLACEMENT COSTS

A/C Compressor $455	Constant Velocity Joints.....485
Alternator 415	Brakes..................................230
Radiator 525	Shocks and/or Struts 680
Automatic Transmission or Transaxle.........................940	Exhaust System 430

TROUBLE SPOTS

• **Engine noise** The motor mounts are prone to wear out prematurely causing a clunking noise when accelerating, decelerating, or putting the transmission in gear, so the carmaker has issued a voluntary recall (number 92M77) to replace the right front and right rear mounts. The coverage is 6 years or 60,000 miles. (1992-93)

• **Hard starting** If the engine does not start or cranks for a long time then stalls, the idle air control valve may be sticking. Ford will replace it under warranty. (1995-96)

• **Tire wear** Rapid rear tire wear is caused by poor rear-wheel alignment. Kits are available to provide camber adjustment to correct the problem. (1990-95)

• **Blower motor** Squeaking or chirping blower motors are the result of defective brush holders, so Ford has issued a redesigned motor and will replace those that are under normal warranty. (1990-94)

• **Transmission slippage** Because of problems with the automatic transmission, warranty coverage for erratic operation has been extended to 6 years or 60,000 miles. The trans will be repaired or replaced and the dealer will provide a loaner car. Work already done is subject to a refund. (1991)

RECALL HISTORY

1990-91 Front brake rotors on salt belt cars may suffer corrosion, resulting in reduced braking effectiveness, abnormal pedal effort, loud noise, and possible increase in stopping distance. **1991-95 with 3.8-liter engine, in 23 states** Speed-control cable could freeze, causing throttle to stick and not return to idle. **1992 wagon** Secondary portion of liftgate latch on some cars may not function, possibly allowing liftgate to open while car is in motion if latch is not in primary position. **1992-95 in AK, IA, MN, NE, ND, or SD** During high winds, heavy drifting snow and low temperatures, engine fan may become blocked or frozen and fail to rotate; can cause smoke/flame. **1993** Controllers intended for use in rear-wheel drive vehicles (instead of front drive) may have been installed on small number of cars with optional anti-lock braking, which could result in reduced braking ability. **1993-94** Headlights can flash intermittently as a result of a circuit-breaker opwning. **1995** On some cars, retainer clip that holds master-cylinder pushrod to brake pedal arm is missing or not fully installed; components can separate, resulting in loss of braking.

1996-98 MERCURY SABLE ✓

FOR   Air bags, dual • Optional anti-lock brakes • Acceleration (LS) • Steering/handling • Passenger and cargo room

AGAINST   Automatic transmission performance (GS) • Rear visibility

See the 1996-98 Ford Taurus report for an evaluation of the 1996-98 Mercury Sable.

MERCURY

1996 Mercury Sable sedan

NHTSA CRASH TEST RESULTS
1996 Mercury Sable

4-DOOR SEDAN

Driver	☆☆☆☆
Passenger	☆☆☆☆

(The National Highway Traffic Safety Administration tests a vehicle's crashworthiness in front and side collisions. Their ratings suggest the chance of serious injury: ☆☆☆☆☆—10% or less; ☆☆☆☆—10-20% or less; ☆☆☆—20-30% or less; ☆☆—35-45% or less; ☆—More than 45%.)

SPECIFICATIONS

	4-door sedan	4-door wagon
Wheelbase, in.	108.5	108.5
Overall length, in.	199.7	199.1
Overall width, in.	73.0	73.0
Overall height, in.	55.4	57.6
Curb weight, lbs.	3388	3536
Cargo volume, cu. ft.	16.0	81.3
Fuel capacity, gals.	16.0	16.0
Seating capacity	6n1	8
Front head room, in.	39.4	39.3
Max. front leg room, in.	42.6	42.6
Rear head room, in.	36.6	48.9
Min. rear leg room, in.	38.9	48.5

1. Five passengers with bucket seats.

Powertrain layout: transverse front-engine/front-wheel drive

ENGINES

	ohv V-6	dohc V-6
Size, liters/cu. in.	3.0/182	3.0/181
Horsepower	145	200
Torque (lbs./ft.)	170	200
EPA city/highway mpg		
4-speed OD automatic	20/29	20/29

Consumer Guide™ observed MPG
4-speed OD automatic 15.7   18.9

Built in USA.

RETAIL PRICES

	GOOD	AVERAGE	POOR
1996 Sable sedan	$9,000-10,800	$8,300-10,000	$5,500-6,800
1996 Sable wagon	10,200-11,500	9,200-10,500	6,200-7,200
1997 Sable sedan	10,500-12,500	9,500-11,300	6,400-7,500
1997 Sable wagon	12,000-13,500	10,800-12,000	7,500-8,500
1998 Sable sedan	12,800-14,500	11,500-13,000	8,000-9,000
1998 Sable wagon	14,500-16,500	13,000-15,000	9,000-10,000

AVERAGE REPLACEMENT COSTS

A/C Compressor $440
Alternator 350
Radiator 585
Timing Chain or Belt 350
Automatic Transmission or
    Transaxle 1,115

Constant Velocity Joints.....605
Brakes..................................280
Shocks and/or Struts 600
Exhaust System 415

TROUBLE SPOTS

• **Dashboard lights** The check engine light comes on for a variety of reasons including bad gasoline, a wobbling accessory drive pulley, or bad spark plug. (1996)

• **Suspension noise** Clunking from the front end may be due to premature wear of the sway bar links; from under the floor due to loose subframe insulators. (1995-97)

• **Steering problems** The power steering gets harder to turn when decelerating from about 50 miles per hour or when shifting from reverse to drive requiring replacement of the control module and/or transmission range sensors. (1996)

• **Water leak** Water leaks onto the front floor because of poor sealing of the cabin air filter cowl inlet. (1996-98)

• **Tire wear** Rear tires wear prematurely due to incorrect rear alignment (toe and camber). (1996-97)

• **Transmission slippage** Vehicles with the AX4S automatic transmission may shift harshly from first to second gear. (1996-97)

• **Air conditioner** The air conditioning lines tend to leak at the spring-lock couplings and larger O-rings are available as a service replacement. (1996-97)

RECALL HISTORY

1996 Brake fluid indicator can malfunction. **1996 w/AX4S automat-**

ic transaxle "Park" pawl shaft was improperly positioned during assembly; could result in park pawl occasionally not engaging when selector lever is placed in "Park" position, allowing vehicle to roll if parking brake has not been applied. **1996** Small number of cars were inadvertently equipped with 18-gallon fuel tank rather than 16-gallon as specified; displacement of tank's shipping plug could result in leakage. **1996** "Park" pawl shaft may not be free to rotate; vehicle could roll as if in neutral, with shift lever in "park" position. **1996-97** "Park" pawl abutment bracket has sharp edge, which can cause pawl to hang up and not engage gear; vehicle can move even though indicator shows "Park." **1997** Servo cover can separate, causing transmission fluid to leak and contact catalytic converter; could result in fire. **1997-98** Headlamp aiming instructions in owner's manuals are not sufficiently clear.

1991-96 MERCURY TRACER

1993 Mercury Tracer 4-door

FOR Fuel economy • Air bags, dual (later models) • Price

AGAINST Engine noise • Road noise • Rear-seat room

See the 1991-96 Ford Escort report for an evaluation of the 1991-96 Mercury Tracer.

NHTSA CRASH TEST RESULTS
1995 Mercury Tracer

4-DOOR SEDAN

Driver	☆☆☆☆
Passenger	☆☆☆☆

(The National Highway Traffic Safety Administration tests a vehicle's crashworthiness in front and side collisions. Their ratings suggest the chance of serious injury: ☆☆☆☆☆—10% or less; ☆☆☆☆—10-20% or less; ☆☆☆—20-30% or less; ☆☆—35-45% or less; ☆—More than 45%.)

SPECIFICATIONS

	4-door sedan	4-door wagon
Wheelbase, in.	98.4	98.4

	4-door sedan	4-door wagon
Overall length, in.	170.9	171.3
Overall width, in.	66.7	66.7
Overall height, in.	52.7	53.6
Curb weight, lbs.	2409	2485
Cargo volume, cu. ft.	12.1	66.9
Fuel capacity, gals.	11.9	11.9
Seating capacity	5	5
Front head room, in.	38.4	38.4
Max. front leg room, in.	41.7	41.7
Rear head room, in.	37.4	38.5
Min. rear leg room, in.	34.6	34.6

Powertrain layout: transverse front-engine/front-wheel drive

ENGINES

	ohv I-4	dohc I-4
Size, liters/cu. in.	1.9/114	1.8/109
Horsepower	88	127
Torque (lbs./ft.)	108	114

EPA city/highway mpg

5-speed OD manual	31/38	25/31
4-speed OD automatic	26/34	23/29
4-speed OD automatic	27.4	22.7

Built in USA and Mexico.

RETAIL PRICES

	GOOD	AVERAGE	POOR
1991 Tracer	$1,800-2,800	$1,200-2,200	$400-900
1992 Tracer	2,300-3,300	1,700-2,700	600-1,100
1993 Tracer	3,000-4,200	2,300-3,500	1,000-1,500
1994 Tracer	3,900-5,500	3,200-4,700	1,400-2,300
1995 Tracer	4,900-6,400	4,200-5,600	2,100-2,900
1996 Tracer	6,200-7,600	5,500-6,800	3,000-3,800

AVERAGE REPLACEMENT COSTS

A/C Compressor	$470	Clutch, Pressure Plate, Bearing	235
Alternator	370	Constant Velocity Joints	585
Radiator	382	Brakes	260
Timing Chain or Belt	145	Shocks and/or Struts	620
Automatic Transmission or Transaxle	1,160	Exhaust System	375

TROUBLE SPOTS

• **Fuel pump** Under its general campaign number 94B55, Ford will install a fused jumper harness in the fuel pump electrical circuit to prevent erratic fuel gauge readings, stalling, or wiring damage, which could be caused by an electrical short. Refunds will be made to anyone who paid for this service. (1991-94)

• **Horn** Sometimes the horn will not work due to a poor ground circuit in the steering column. Under the bumper-to-bumper warranty, a redundant ground will be installed so the horn works in all steering wheel positions. (1995-96)

• **Brake noise** Wear spots and ridges on the front brake caliper sleeves cause a knocking noise when gently applying the brakes. There is a new sleeve, made from a harder material that resists wear, and may be eligible for replacement under the basic or bumper-to-bumper warranty. (1991-96)

• **Engine knock** Carbon build-up on the pistons causes a knocking noise that is most evident after a cold start. If the noise does not go away after cleaning the carbon from the pistons using carburetor cleaner ingested through the intake manifold, the pistons must be replaced with redesigned ones under the basic or bumper-to-bumper warranty. (1991-93)

• **Hard starting** If the engine does not start or cranks for a long time then stalls, the idle air control valve may be sticking. Ford will replace it under warranty. (1995-96)

• **Blower motor** Squeaking or chirping blower motors are the result of defective brush holders, so Ford has issued a redesigned motor and will replace those that are under normal warranty. (1993-94)

• **Transmission noise** If a whine comes from the transmission during coast-down, it is probably because the idler gear teeth were not machined properly. A new gear will be installed under warranty. (1995-96)

• **Steering noise** A grinding noise while turning is most likely due to dirt accumulating in the top strut mount bushing. A new bushing with a groove to help keep the dirt out. (1991-92)

• **Brakes** Although there is no warranty coverage, there is a redesigned brake master cylinder and brake booster available that provides better pedal feel and travel. (1993-95)

RECALL HISTORY

1991 Interference may occur between bolt that secures fuel line shield to lower dash and gas pedal, causing pedal to stick wide open. **1991** On some cars, fatigue crack can develop in solder joint between fuel return tube and fuel pump sending unit. **1992** Pins securing ignition lock in steering column housing can separate or move out of position, causing steering column to lock up. **1992** Stoplamp switch could intermittently malfunction. **1993** Driver's seat in some cars may not engage fully in its track; could move in event of crash. **1994-95** A few driver-side air bags may have inadequately-welded inflator canister, causing improper deployment and expelling hot gases. **1995 cars in certain states** Cracks can develop in plastic fuel tank, resulting in leakage.

1993-98 MERCURY VILLAGER

1993 Mercury Villager Nautica

FOR Air bags, dual (later models) • Passenger and cargo room • Steering/handling

AGAINST Control layout • Wind noise • Engine noise

EVALUATION Although the 3.0-liter Nissan engine is adequate, it can't quite match the muscle provided by the larger V-6s in the front-drive minivans from Ford, GM, and Chrysler. While engine and road noise are within a reasonable range, when the Villager reaches highway speeds the wind noise can become quite pronounced. A wide turning circle makes the Villager harder to maneuver in tight spots than most cars, but in most other situations the Villager feels remarkably carlike. When compared with other minivans, body lean is quite modest. The suspension is firm enough to minimize bouncing on wavy roads, and it absorbs most bumps without breaking a sweat.

Front head room and leg room are both quite good, but only adequate for the middle- and rear-seat passengers. With all seats in their normal positions, the rear cargo area is quite small. Trying to improve the Villager's hauling capacity requires removing the truly cumbersome center seats.

Compared with other minivans, the Villager has less interior room. It also lacks many of the standard features found on its rivals. Nevertheless it's a good choice if you need more than a mid-size station wagon but don't require the interior space pro-

MERCURY

vided in one of the larger minivans.

NHTSA CRASH TEST RESULTS
1995 Mercury Villager   3-DOOR VAN

Driver   ☆☆☆☆☆
Passenger   ☆☆☆

(The National Highway Traffic Safety Administration tests a vehicle's crashworthiness in front and side collisions. Their ratings suggest the chance of serious injury: ☆☆☆☆☆—10% or less; ☆☆☆☆—10-20% or less; ☆☆☆—20-30% or less; ☆☆—35-45% or less; ☆—More than 45%.)

SPECIFICATIONS

	3-door van
Wheelbase, in.	112.2
Overall length, in.	189.9
Overall width, in.	73.4
Overall height, in.	66.0
Curb weight, lbs.	3815
Cargo volume, cu. ft.	126.4
Fuel capacity, gals.	20.0
Seating capacity	7
Front head room, in.	39.4
Max. front leg room, in.	39.9
Rear head room, in.	39.7
Min. rear leg room, in.	34.8

Powertrain layout: transverse front-engine/front-wheel drive

ENGINES

	ohc V-6
Size, liters/cu. in.	3.0/181
Horsepower	151
Torque (lbs./ft.)	174

EPA city/highway mpg
4-speed OD automatic ... 17/23

Consumer Guide™ observed MPG
4-speed OD automatic ... 19.7

Built in USA.

AVERAGE REPLACEMENT COSTS

A/C Compressor	$345	Constant Velocity Joints	615
Alternator	420	Brakes	270
Radiator	505	Shocks and/or Struts	544
Timing Chain or Belt	185	Exhaust System	265
Automatic Transmission or Transaxle	555		

RETAIL PRICES	GOOD	AVERAGE	POOR
1993 Villager	$7,000-9,000	$6,300-8,200	$4,000-5,400

	GOOD	AVERAGE	POOR
1994 Villager	8,100-10,800	7,300-10,000	4,900-6,800
1995 Villager	9,600-13,000	8,700-12,000	5,800-8,500
1996 Villager	12,000-15,500	10,800-14,000	7,500-10,000
1997 Villager	13,800-17,800	12,500-16,500	9,000-12,300
1998 Villager	16,000-21,000	14,500-19,500	10,500-14,500

TROUBLE SPOTS

• **Crankshaft** The crankshaft breaks behind the front pulley if the belts are overtightened. (1993-96)

• **Blower motor** Squeaking or chirping blower motors are the result of defective brush holders, so Ford has issued a redesigned motor and will replace those that are under normal warranty. (1993-94)

RECALL HISTORY

1993 Brake master cylinder on some vans was improperly assembled or could have been damaged during assembly, which can result in loss of braking at two wheels, causing increased pedal travel, higher pedal effort, and increased stopping distance. **1993** One or both bolts securing automatic seatbelt restraint system tracks to B-pillars were not adequately tightened on some vans, increasing risk of injury in the event of a collision or sudden maneuver. **1993** Fuel filler hoses may have been cut prior to installation by knife used to open shipping box; fuel leakage could result, leading to fire if exposed to ignition source. **1993** Leaves and other foreign matter can enter through cowl panel air intake during operation of front heater and/or air conditioner, resulting in build-up in the plenum that can lead to noise, odors, or even a vehicle fire. **1995 with sliding third-row bench seats** Cable that connects seat adjustment level to latch might be pinched in roller assembly, preventing latch on left side from fully engaging seat rail. **1995** Rear lamp will not illuminate if the metal socket moves or separates from the plastic socket housing.This can result in failure of the stop or rear running lamps. **1997** Fuel line hoses could crack or split, resulting in leakage. **1997-98 with battery supplied by GNB Technologies** Defective negative battery post can cause acid leakage and related corrosion damage; could lead to engine fire or battery explosion.

1990-94 MITSUBISHI ECLIPSE ✓ BEST BUY

FOR Acceleration (except GS) • Wet-weather traction (AWD) • Handling/roadholding • Anti-lock brakes (optional)

AGAINST Rear-seat room • Cargo room • Engine noise • Road noise

MITSUBISHI

1990 Mitsubishi Eclipse GS

EVALUATION   Neither the base unit nor the GS equipped with the 92-horsepower 1.8-liter have enough low-speed muscle to be satisfying with the automatic transmission. However, when paired with the manual, these are fine for budget-minded sports car lovers. The DOHC version is much quicker in traffic and more responsive to the throttle. Both the GS Turbo and GSX are faster still, but the front-drive GS Turbo suffers from very noticeable torque steer, which causes us to prefer the GSX, which spreads the abundant power evenly between all four wheels. The all-wheel-drive set-up gives the GSX outstanding grip, making it the best-handling sports car in its class. While we appreciate the anti-lock brakes provided on the GSX, we wish Mitsubishi could provide them as an option on all models.

Ride quality varies, depending on model, ranging from compliant but occasionally choppy on base and GS version to taut and slightly choppy on those with firmer suspensions and larger tires.

The low-slung fastback styling and compact dimensions provide only modest interior room. The tight cockpit up front and "for-pets-only" rear seat may not appeal to all tastes.

In our view, the Mitsubishi Eclipse ranks as one of the best values among small sports coupes. We rate the GS with the 135-horsepower DOHC 4-cylinder and the turbocharged all-wheel-drive GSX as the "picks of the litter."

SPECIFICATIONS

	2-door hatchback
Wheelbase, in.	97.2
Overall length, in.	172.8
Overall width, in.	66.7
Overall height, in.	51.5
Curb weight, lbs.	2542
Cargo volume, cu. ft.	10.2

	2-door hatchback
Fuel capacity, gals.	15.9
Seating capacity	4
Front head room, in.	37.9
Max. front leg room, in.	43.9
Rear head room, in.	34.1
Min. rear leg room, in.	28.5

Powertrain layout: transverse front-engine/front- or all-wheel drive

ENGINES	ohc I-4	dohc I-4	Turbocharged dohc I-4
Size, liters/cu. in.	1.8/107	2.0/122	2.0/122
Horsepower	92	135	180-195
Torque (lbs./ft.)	105	125	203
EPA city/highway mpg			
5-speed OD manual	23/32	22/29	21/28
4-speed OD automatic	23/30	22/27	19/23
Consumer Guide™ observed MPG			
5-speed OD manual		26.4	18.4

Built in USA.

RETAIL PRICES	GOOD	AVERAGE	POOR
1990 Eclipse	$2,100-3,200	$1,500-2,600	$600-1,100
1990 Eclipse GSX	3,300-4,000	2,600-3,300	1,000-1,500
1991 Eclipse	2,600-4,200	2,000-3,500	900-1,400
1991 Eclipse GSX	4,200-5,300	3,500-4,300	1,600-2,100
1992 Eclipse	3,300-5,200	2,600-4,500	1,300-2,400
1992 Eclipse GSX	5,500-6,500	4,700-5,700	2,400-3,000
1993 Eclipse	4,000-6,500	3,300-5,700	1,800-3,200
1993 Eclipse GSX	6,300-7,300	5,500-6,500	3,000-3,600
1994 Eclipse	4,800-7,500	4,000-6,700	2,300-4,000
1994 Eclipse GSX	7,800-9,000	6,800-8,000	3,900-4,800

AVERAGE REPLACEMENT COSTS

A/C Compressor $540	Clutch, Pressure Plate, Bearing 470
Alternator 320	Constant Velocity Joints.....705
Radiator 355	Brakes.................................215
Timing Chain or Belt 240	Shocks and/or Struts 465
Automatic Transmission or Transaxle........................770	Exhaust System 680

TROUBLE SPOTS

• **Exhaust system** Cars with turbo engines had an emissions recall to replace the oxygen sensor with one that could endure higher temperatures. There is no mileage limit. (1991-92)

• **Timing belt** A campaign was conducted to replace the timing belt since they were susceptible to breakage on higher mileage engines and could cause severe internal damage. (1990-91)

• **Transaxle leak** A campaign was issued to replace the transaxle end clutch oil seal, which could leak leading to a loss of overdrive (fourth gear). (1994)

• **Poor transmission shift** Manual transmissions in which the shifter does not move smoothly between gears need a bottle of friction modifier added to the oil, but it must be installed through the speedometer gear opening, not the normal filler hole. (1990-92)

• **Steering problems** Cars that drift or pull to the right may be cured by replacing the lower control arm with one having rear bushing with a built-in offset. (1994)

• **Brake noise** Noise suppression shims were released to cure a squeaking problem with rear disc brakes. (1990-91)

• **Vehicle shake** Drivetrain vibrations, most evident between 45-55 mph, may be eliminated by replacing the transmission mounting brackets. (1990-94)

• **Vehicle shake** Vibration at idle, especially on cars with automatic trans, is probably due to the upper radiator mounting posts not centered in the mounting brackets. (1990-94)

RECALL HISTORY

1990 Operation of factory-installed sunroof in "non-standard" manner may cause hinge disengagement. **1990** Diluted primer may have been used on windshield opening flanges of small number of cars, which would not provide required retention of glass. **1990** Headlamp wiring harness on some early models may break due to stress created by their pop-up devices. **1990-91** Front seatbelt release button can break and pieces can fall inside.

1995-98 MITSUBISHI ECLIPSE

FOR Air bags, dual • Optional anti-lock brakes • Acceleration GS-T, GSX) • Steering/handling • All-wheel drive (GSX)

AGAINST Acceleration (RS, GS w/automatic) • Rear seat room • Cargo room • Road noise

EVALUATION The base engine revs smoothly and quickly without excess noise, but it's no powerhouse. Therefore, acceleration with the automatic transmission is marginal for freeway on-ramps and in passing sprints. Progress is livelier with the

1995 Mitsubishi Eclipse GS-T

slick-shifting 5-speed manual gearbox. Turbos are decidedly faster. Unfortunately, Eclipse still suffers from some "turbo lag."

All Eclipse models offer nimble handling, good grip, and quick, accurate steering. On the downside, the ride turns choppy on freeways and rough roads, especially on turbocharged models. You also must endure plenty of road noise. All-wheel-drive models are capable of exhibiting race-car-like moves, of the sort matched only by big-buck coupes.

Front occupants have adequate head room but may still feel crowded. The tiny back seat is strictly for pre-teens. The dashboard is well laid out, except for a center-mounted stereo unit that's too low. Cargo space is adequate, but with a tall liftover for loading and unloading.

Spyder convertibles look sharp, and deliver fun-in-the-sun driving at a comparatively reasonable price. Unfortunately, several convertibles we've driven have suffered from serious shakiness, even when rolling down smooth roads.

Though still one of the best sports coupes, the competition has caught up with Eclipse. Other than the all-wheel-drive model, Eclipse offers nothing you can't get for less money somewhere else.

NHTSA CRASH TEST RESULTS
1995 Mitsubishi Eclipse

2-DOOR HATCHBACK

Driver	☆☆☆☆
Passenger	☆☆☆☆

(The National Highway Traffic Safety Administration tests a vehicle's crashworthiness in front and side collisions. Their ratings suggest the chance of serious injury: ☆☆☆☆☆—10% or less; ☆☆☆☆—10-20% or less; ☆☆☆—20-30% or less; ☆☆—35-45% or less; ☆—More than 45%.)

SPECIFICATIONS

	2-door hatchback	2-door conv.
Wheelbase, in.	98.8	98.8

MITSUBISHI

	2-door hatchback	2-door conv.
Overall length, in.	172.2	172.2
Overall width, in.	68.3	68.3
Overall height, in.	50.2	51.6
Curb weight, lbs.	2767	2888
Cargo volume, cu. ft.	16.6	5.1
Fuel capacity, gals.	16.9	16.9
Seating capacity	4	4
Front head room, in.	37.9	38.7
Max. front leg room, in.	43.3	43.3
Rear head room, in.	34.3	34.9
Min. rear leg room, in.	28.4	28.4

Powertrain layout: transverse front-engine/front- or all-wheel drive

ENGINES

	dohc I-4	Turbocharged dohc I-4	dohc I-4
Size, liters/cu. in.	2.0/122	2.0/122	2.4/143
Horsepower	140	205-210	141
Torque (lbs./ft.)	130	214	148

EPA city/highway mpg

5-speed OD manual	22/33	23/31	22/30
4-speed OD automatic	21/31	20/27	

Consumer Guide™ observed MPG

5-speed OD manual	27.5	22.7	21.5
4-speed OD automatic		18.4	

Built in USA.

AVERAGE REPLACEMENT COSTS

A/C Compressor	$600	Clutch, Pressure Plate, Bearing	415
Alternator	360	Constant Velocity Joints	770
Radiator	470	Brakes	310
Timing Chain or Belt	260	Shocks and/or Struts	520
Automatic Transmission or Transaxle	975	Exhaust System	350

RETAIL PRICES

	GOOD	AVERAGE	POOR
1995 Eclipse RS, GS	$7,500-9,000	$6,800-8,200	$4,300-5,200
1995 Eclipse GS-T, GSX	10,200-12,500	9,300-11,500	6,400-8,000
1996 Eclipse RS, GS	9,000-11,000	8,200-10,000	5,400-6,700
1996 Eclipse GS-T, GSX	12,000-14,000	10,800-12,800	7,500-8,700
1996 Spyder convertible	12,500-14,500	11,000-13,000	7,700-8,900
1997 Eclipse base, RS	10,000-11,800	9,000-10,800	6,100-7,200
1997 Eclipse GS, GS-T, GSX	12,500-16,000	11,300-14,500	8,000-10,200
1997 Spyder convertible	14,200-16,700	12,700-15,200	9,000-11,000
1998 Eclipse RS	14,000-12,000	12,800-11,000	8,800-7,500

	GOOD	AVERAGE	POOR
1998 Eclipse GS, GS-T, GSX	18,000-14,500	16,500-13,000	12,000-9,500
1998 Spyder convertible	19,000-16,500	17,500-15,000	13,000-11,000

TROUBLE SPOTS

• **Engine misfire** Misfiring is common due to carbon tracking on the spark plugs and is corrected by replacing the plugs and plug wires. (1995)

• **Fuel pump** The vehicle is sensitive to fuel starvation caused by a clogged in-tank filter. (1995-97)

• **Fuel pump** Noisy fuel pump may be result of a bad fuel pressure regulator. (1995)

RECALL HISTORY

1995-96 Incorrectly-installed gaskets for fuel pump and/or gauge unit could allow fuel or fumes to escape. **1997** On a few cars, improperly-welded passenger head restraint support bracket on passenger side can break. **1998** Dash panel pad can shift, interfering with throttle cable control.

1994-98 MITSUBISHI GALANT

1995 Mitsubishi Galant LS V-6

FOR Air bags, dual • Anti-lock brakes • Passenger and cargo room • Ride

AGAINST Visibility • Engine noise • Fuel economy

EVALUATION The Galant's 141-horsepower 4-cylinder has more than adequate acceleration and passing power with the automatic transmission. It shifts smoothly and downshifts without argument when it comes time to pass. The 160-horsepower unit found on 1994 GS models feels stronger still.

MITSUBISHI

Galant's suspension absorbs bumps easily, while providing a stable, competent ride at highway speeds. The car handles corners with ease and the precise steering feel gives drivers a sense of confidence.

Firm, supportive seats and a generous front cabin area are Galant strong points. However, rear-seat passengers have only adequate head room, an inch less leg room than the previous model. The dashboard has an attractive four-dial gauge cluster and climate controls are stacked atop the center stereo controls in the center console. In a welcome departure for Mitsubishi, the stereo is mounted high enough for easy operation, even when driving. The trunk provides ample space, plus a wide flat floor and low liftover.

Although the Galant has several good qualities, and we consider it a solid buy, it lacks a single distinguishing feature to help it stand out in the crowded field of mid-size domestic and imported sedans, particularly given the absence of a V-6 option.

NHTSA CRASH TEST RESULTS
1996 Mitsubishi Galant

4-DOOR SEDAN

Driver	☆☆☆☆
Passenger	☆☆☆☆

(The National Highway Traffic Safety Administration tests a vehicle's crashworthiness in front and side collisions. Their ratings suggest the chance of serious injury: ☆☆☆☆☆—10% or less; ☆☆☆☆—10-20% or less; ☆☆☆—20-30% or less; ☆☆—35-45% or less; ☆—More than 45%.)

SPECIFICATIONS

	4-door sedan
Wheelbase, in.	103.7
Overall length, in.	187.0
Overall width, in.	68.1
Overall height, in.	53.1
Curb weight, lbs.	2755
Cargo volume, cu. ft.	12.5
Fuel capacity, gals.	16.9
Seating capacity	5
Front head room, in.	39.4
Max. front leg room, in.	43.3
Rear head room, in.	37.5
Min. rear leg room, in.	35.0

Powertrain layout: transverse front-engine/front-wheel drive

ENGINES

	ohc I-4	dohc I-4
Size, liters/cu. in.	2.4/144	2.4/144
Horsepower	141-143	160
Torque (lbs./ft.)	148	160

EPA city/highway mpg

5-speed OD manual...	23/30	22/28
4-speed OD automatic..	22/28	20/26

Consumer Guide™ observed MPG

4-speed OD automatic..	20.2

Built in USA.

RETAIL PRICES	GOOD	AVERAGE	POOR
1994 Galant	$5,500-8,200	$4,800-7,400	$2,800-4,700
1995 Galant	6,600-8,800	5,800-8,000	3,500-5,200
1996 Galant	8,000-11,000	7,300-10,000	4,700-7,000
1997 Galant	9,500-12,500	8,500-11,500	5,600-8,200
1998 Galant	11,000-15,000	10,000-13,800	6,800-10,000

AVERAGE REPLACEMENT COSTS

A/C Compressor $610	Clutch, Pressure Plate,
Alternator 335	Bearing 560
Radiator 595	Constant Velocity Joints.....725
Timing Chain or Belt 290	Brakes................................220
Automatic Transmission or	Shocks and/or Struts 460
Transaxle.........................865	Exhaust System.................500

TROUBLE SPOTS

• **Transaxle leak** A campaign was issued to replace the transaxle end clutch oil seal that could leak leading to a loss of overdrive (fourth gear). (1994)

• **Steering problems** Cars that drift or pull to the right may be cured by replacing the lower control arm with one having rear bushing with a built-in offset. (1994-95)

• **Dashboard lights** The headlights and dash lights may dim during deceleration because the computer switches on the electric cooling fan. To correct the problem, Mitsubishi has a modulator kit that is installed between the computer and its original connector. (1994-95)

• **Vehicle shake** Vibration at idle, especially on cars with automatic trans, is probably due to the upper radiator mounting posts not centered in the mounting brackets. (1994)

• **Exhaust system** A revised Vehicle Emission Control Information (VECI) label was mailed to all owners who were to place it over the old one that contained incorrect information. Make sure it is there. (1994)

RECALL HISTORY

None to date.

1992-98 MITSUBISHI MONTERO

1992 Mitsubishi Montero LS

FOR 4WD traction • Passenger and cargo room • Acceleration (215-horsepower engine) • Quietness • Ride

AGAINST Fuel economy • Entry/exit • Acceleration (151-horsepower engine)

EVALUATION The 3.0-liter V-6 is smooth and quiet, but could use a bit more muscle. Acceleration with the base engine, even in 177-horsepower form, is adequate rather than spirited. Passing power also ranks as adequate. With automatic, steep grades cause noticeable slowing and a lot of busy shifting. Fuel economy is on the dismal side: 16.0 mpg. An SR with the 215-horsepower engine accelerated to 60 mph in a brisk 10.0 seconds. Economy sagged to a gloomy 13.8 mpg. Mitsubishi's Active-Trac 4WD system is convenient and easy to use.

Montero is still one of the better-riding 4x4s, even more stable in corners than earlier versions, thanks to a slightly wider stance. A Montero doesn't feel as agile as a Jeep Grand Cherokee, however, showing more body lean in turns and even a slight tipsy sensation. Wavy surfaces produce little bouncing, but the firm suspension does not absorb bumps well.

The dashboard made everything easy to see, reach, and use, but the Multi Meter is little more than a gimmick. Rear-seat room grew from ample to spacious, but climbing aboard isn't easy. Passenger and cargo space are abundant, but the Montero sits high off the ground, so it's difficult to get in and out. Montero has more than enough cargo space for several grocery bags. Stowing the jump seats against the sidewalls creates a long, wide cargo area.

Despite some appealing features, Montero has not been at the top of our sport-utility list, when compared with such domestic rivals as the Ford Explorer, Jeep Grand Cherokee, and Chevrolet Blazer/GMC Jimmy, which tend to be more car-like.

NHTSA CRASH TEST RESULTS
1997 Mitsubishi Montero

4-DOOR WAGON

Driver	☆☆☆
Passenger	☆☆☆

(The National Highway Traffic Safety Administration tests a vehicle's crashworthiness in front and side collisions. Their ratings suggest the chance of serious injury: ☆☆☆☆☆—10% or less; ☆☆☆☆—10-20% or less; ☆☆☆—20-30% or less; ☆☆—35-45% or less; ☆—More than 45%.)

SPECIFICATIONS

	4-door wagon
Wheelbase, in.	107.3
Overall length, in.	185.2
Overall width, in.	66.7
Overall height, in.	73.4
Curb weight, lbs.	4265
Cargo volume, cu. ft.	72.7
Fuel capacity, gals.	24.3
Seating capacity	7
Front head room, in.	40.9
Max. front leg room, in.	40.3
Rear head room, in.	40.0
Min. rear leg room, in.	37.6

Powertrain layout: longitudinal front-engine/4-wheel drive

ENGINES	ohc V-6	ohc V-6	ohc V-6	dohc V-6
Size, liters/cu. in.	3.0/181	3.0/181	3.5/213	3.5/213
Horsepower	151	177	200	215
Torque (lbs./ft.)	174	188	228	228
EPA city/highway mpg				
5-speed OD manual	15/18	15/18		
4-speed OD automatic	15/18	15/18	16/19	14/18
Consumer Guide™ observed MPG				
4-speed OD automatic	15.6	16.0	15.5	13.8

Built in Japan.

RETAIL PRICES	GOOD	AVERAGE	POOR
1992 Montero	$7,300-9,300	$6,500-8,400	$4,000-5,300
1993 Montero	8,800-11,500	8,000-10,500	5,000-6,800
1994 Montero	11,500-14,800	10,300-13,300	6,800-9,000

	GOOD	AVERAGE	POOR
1995 Montero	14,000-17,500	12,500-16,000	8,500-11,500
1996 Montero	16,000-20,500	14,500-19,000	10,000-14,000
1997 Montero	18,700-23,200	17,000-21,200	12,000-15,800
1998 Montero	22,500-27,000	20,500-25,000	15,000-18,500

AVERAGE REPLACEMENT COSTS

A/C Compressor $825
Alternator 410
Radiator 665
Timing Chain or Belt 405
Automatic Transmission or
   Transaxle.......................930

Clutch, Pressure Plate, Bearing
   645
Universal Joints 1,180
Brakes.................................330
Shocks and/or Struts 300
Exhaust System.................370

TROUBLE SPOTS

• **Manual transmission** Hard shifting, gear clash, may come from the manual transmission due to a failure of the first-second gear synchronizers, while screeching noises are due to failed second-third synchros. (1992-95)

• **Dashboard lights** The check engine light may come on when the vehicle is driven at wide-open throttle (about 5000 rpm). (1997)

• **Steering problems** Shudder while cornering may be minimized by adding Mitsubishi Limited Slip Differential Additive to the rear differential. (1997)

• **Paint** Paint on the roof rack fades and peels. (1992-93)

RECALL HISTORY

1992-93 During conditions of full-lock steering and full suspension travel, front brake hose can crack, resulting in leakage. **1992-94 sold in Puerto Rico** Front brake hose can crack during full-lock steering and full suspension travel, resulting in fluid leakage.

1995-98 NISSAN 200SX

FOR Air bags, dual • Optional anti-lock brakes • Acceleration (SE-R) • Steering/handling • Fuel economy

AGAINST Acceleration (base and SE automatic) • Rear visibility • Ride

EVALUATION Regardless of model, the 200SX offers better-than-average passenger room for a small coupe, especially in back, though this cabin isn't huge by absolute standards. Space is adequate up front, and adults have at least a fighting chance of fitting into the back seat. Cargo room ranks near the top of its

1995 Nissan 200SX SE-R

class. Instruments are well-positioned and clearly marked, in a functional, ergonomically-designed dashboard that puts most controls close at hand. Visibility is fine except dead-astern.

The SE-R has above-average grip and modest body lean, which produce safe, enjoyable travel on twisting roads. Steering is firm and centers well. Ride quality is rather jumpy over rippled freeways and harsh pavement.

In terms of performance, the 200SX comes in two distinct flavors. The base engine provides adequate acceleration with the 5-speed but slow pickup with automatic. Moving a big step up, the SE-R's 2.0-liter four has enough torque for swift passing and even for pulling the optional automatic transmission. Gas mileage also is appealing, with either engine.

Overall, there's much to like about the 200SX—especially the SE-R. It's a reasonable, moderately-priced alternative to such higher-cost coupes as the Probe and MX-6, thus definitely worth a test-drive.

NHTSA CRASH TEST RESULTS
1997 Nissan 200SX   2-DOOR COUPE

Driver	☆☆☆☆☆
Passenger	☆☆☆☆

(The National Highway Traffic Safety Administration tests a vehicle's crashworthiness in front and side collisions. Their ratings suggest the chance of serious injury: ☆☆☆☆☆—10% or less; ☆☆☆☆—10-20% or less; ☆☆☆—20-30% or less; ☆☆—35-45% or less; ☆—More than 45%.)

SPECIFICATIONS

	2-door coupe
Wheelbase, in.	99.8
Overall length, in.	170.1
Overall width, in.	66.6
Overall height, in.	54.2
Curb weight, lbs.	2330

	2-door coupe
Cargo volume, cu. ft.	10.4
Fuel capacity, gals.	13.2
Seating capacity	4
Front head room, in.	39.1
Max. front leg room, in.	42.3
Rear head room, in.	35.4
Min. rear leg room, in.	31.4

Powertrain layout: transverse front-engine/front-wheel drive

ENGINES

	dohc I-4	dohc I-4
Size, liters/cu. in.	1.6/97	2.0/121
Horsepower	115	140
Torque (lbs./ft.)	108	132

EPA city/highway mpg

	dohc I-4	dohc I-4
5-speed OD manual	30/40	23/31
4-speed OD automatic	28/37	23/30

Consumer Guide™ observed MPG

5-speed OD manual	28.0
4-speed OD automatic	26.2

Built in USA.

RETAIL PRICES

	GOOD	AVERAGE	POOR
1995 200SX	$5,900-7,000	$5,200-6,200	$3,100-3,800
1995 200SX SE-R	7,400-8,100	6,600-7,300	4,200-4,800
1996 200SX	7,000-8,000	6,200-7,200	3,900-4,600
1996 200SX SE-R	8,800-9,600	8,000-8,700	5,300-5,800
1997 200SX	8,200-9,400	7,400-8,500	4,800-5,500
1997 200SX SE-R	10,000-11,000	9,000-10,000	6,000-6,800
1998 200SX	9,800-11,200	8,900-10,200	6,000-7,000
1998 200SX SE-R	11,800-12,800	10,800-11,800	7,500-8,300

AVERAGE REPLACEMENT COSTS

A/C Compressor $610	Clutch, Pressure Plate, Bearing 430
Alternator 320	Constant Velocity Joints ..1,230
Radiator 325	Brakes...................................200
Timing Chain or Belt 770	Shocks and/or Struts 520
Automatic Transmission or Transaxle.........................740	Exhaust System.................175

TROUBLE SPOTS

• **Sunroof/moonroof** The sunroof may tilt up, but not slide back due to a problem with the lifter mechanism. (1995-96)

• **Doors** The power door locks may spontaneously lock or unlock, especially in hot or humid weather due to a problem with the master switch. (1995)

• **Fuel gauge** The gauge may not register full even though the gas tank is completely filled due to the pump wires interfering with the float arm. (1995)

• **Engine noise** The timing chain tensioner guide tends to break and the chain becomes very noisy. (1995)

• **Dashboard lights** The check engine light comes on due to a problem with the rear heated oxygen sensor. (1995-96)

RECALL HISTORY

1995 w/ABS Hydraulic actuator was not properly purged; bubbles can cause increased stopping distances.

1995-98 NISSAN 240SX

1995 Nissan 240SX SE

FOR   Air bags, dual • Steering/handling • Instruments/controls • Optional anti-lock brakes

AGAINST   Noise • Rear seat room • Ride (SE) • Cargo room

EVALUATION   Acceleration is nothing special for a sports coupe. A base-model 240SX with the automatic transmission took 10 seconds flat to reach 60 mph. Takeoffs are strong enough at first, but acceleration tapers off at higher speeds. The engine produces a sporty but loud snarl under hard acceleration. Road noise also is prominent. As for gas mileage, we averaged 20.8 mpg with automatic and 25.2 mpg with a 5-speed.

Sharp steering and agile reactions are the bonuses of this coupe's rear-drive chassis, but poor traction on slippery roads remains a sore spot. Ride comfort depends on the model. The firmer SE suspension rides more harshly than the base version, which does a better job of absorbing bumps and tar strips.

Despite the lengthened wheelbase and wider body, the 240SX still suffers from a snug interior. Space is considerably less than the car's outside dimensions suggest, and the wraparound cockpit gives a somewhat closed-in feeling. Head room is limited for tall drivers. Even children will lack space in the rear seat, especially in terms of leg room. Seats are nicely supportive. Visibility is good all around, except past somewhat thick windshield pillars.

We've not been overwhelmed by either the styling or the performance of the 240SX, before or after the '97 facelift.

NHTSA CRASH TEST RESULTS
1997 Nissan 240SX   2-DOOR COUPE

Driver	☆☆☆
Passenger	☆☆☆☆

(The National Highway Traffic Safety Administration tests a vehicle's crashworthiness in front and side collisions. Their ratings suggest the chance of serious injury: ☆☆☆☆☆—10% or less; ☆☆☆☆—10-20% or less; ☆☆☆—20-30% or less; ☆☆—35-45% or less; ☆—More than 45%.)

SPECIFICATIONS

	2-door coupe
Wheelbase, in.	99.4
Overall length, in.	177.2
Overall width, in.	68.1
Overall height, in.	51.0
Curb weight, lbs.	2753
Cargo volume, cu. ft.	8.6
Fuel capacity, gals.	17.2
Seating capacity	4
Front head room, in.	38.3
Max. front leg room, in.	42.6
Rear head room, in.	34.3
Min. rear leg room, in.	20.8

Powertrain layout: longitudinal front-engine/rear-wheel drive

ENGINES

	dohc I-4
Size, liters/cu. in.	2.4/146
Horsepower	155
Torque (lbs./ft.)	160

EPA city/highway mpg

5-speed OD manual	22/28
4-speed OD automatic	21/26

Consumer Guide™ observed MPG

5-speed OD manual	25.2

dohc I-4

4-speed OD automatic.. 20.8

Built in Japan.

RETAIL PRICES	GOOD	AVERAGE	POOR
1995 240SX	$8,200-9,500	$7,400-8,700	$5,000-6,000
1996 240SX	10,000-11,800	9,000-10,500	6,000-7,000
1997 240SX	12,000-14,500	10,800-13,000	7,500-8,700
1998 240SX	14,000-17,000	12,500-15,500	9,000-11,200

AVERAGE REPLACEMENT COSTS

A/C Compressor $695
Alternator 290
Radiator 380
Timing Chain or Belt 660
Automatic Transmission or
   Transaxle.........................810

Clutch, Pressure Plate,
   Bearing 335
Constant Velocity Joints.....430
Brakes...................................220
Shocks and/or Struts 460
Exhaust System 180

TROUBLE SPOTS

• **Brakes** Nissan issued a voluntary recall to replace a defective diode that will not turn on the "low brake fluid" warning light on most models if the fluid level drops. (1995)

• **Air conditioner** Poor air conditioner performance due to compressor joint seals that tend to leak. (1995-96)

• **Engine temperature** The engine tends to overheat if any air trapped in the cooling system is not properly bled. (1995)

• **Dashboard lights** The check engine light may come on and set an erroneous trouble code for the crankshaft position sensor if certain wires in the computerized engine control circuits are not kept separated from one another. (1995)

RECALL HISTORY

1995 Brake warning light will not illuminate when fluid level drops.

1993-97 NISSAN ALTIMA

FOR Air bags, dual • Anti-lock brakes (optional) • Steering/handling • Instruments/controls • Fuel economy

AGAINST Engine noise • Road noise • Wind noise • Automatic transmission performance

EVALUATION Performance and fuel economy from the standard 150-horsepower 2.4-liter 4-cylinder engine are more than adequate. Even with the automatic transmission, passing

1994 Nissan Altima GLE

response is fine. But when called upon to pass quickly or make a merging maneuver aggressive use of the accelerator is required to coax the automatic to make its one- or two-gear downshift.

Benefiting from its wide standard tires (205/60R-15s), the Altima is more athletic and nimble than all but the Accord. Ride quality is comfortable, if firm, and braking is strong and progressive. Also contributing to the car's handling prowess is its crisp steering response. The only potential drawback is a cabin that could use a bit more sound insulation.

The interior provides adequate head room for all passengers and enough space for two adults in the rear seat. The trunk has a wide, flat floor, giving the Altima good cargo room for its size.

Overall we rate Nissan's compact sedan highly and encourage buyers to give it a close look before buying.

NHTSA CRASH TEST RESULTS
1996 Nissan Altima   4-DOOR SEDAN

Driver	☆☆☆☆
Passenger	☆☆☆☆

(The National Highway Traffic Safety Administration tests a vehicle's crashworthiness in front and side collisions. Their ratings suggest the chance of serious injury: ☆☆☆☆☆—10% or less; ☆☆☆☆—10-20% or less; ☆☆☆—20-30% or less; ☆☆—35-45% or less; ☆—More than 45%.)

SPECIFICATIONS

	4-door sedan
Wheelbase, in.	103.1
Overall length, in.	180.5
Overall width, in.	67.1
Overall height, in.	55.9
Curb weight, lbs.	2853
Cargo volume, cu. ft.	14.0
Fuel capacity, gals.	15.9

	4-door sedan
Seating capacity	5
Front head room, in.	39.3
Max. front leg room, in.	42.6
Rear head room, in.	37.6
Min. rear leg room, in.	34.7

Powertrain layout: transverse front-engine/front-wheel drive

ENGINES

	dohc I-4
Size, liters/cu. in.	2.4/146
Horsepower	150
Torque (lbs./ft.)	154

EPA city/highway mpg

5-speed OD manual	24/30
4-speed OD automatic	21/29

Consumer Guide™ observed MPG

4-speed OD automatic	20.2

Built in USA.

RETAIL PRICES	GOOD	AVERAGE	POOR
1993 Altima	$4,800-7,000	$4,100-6,300	$2,100-3,800
1994 Altima	5,800-8,300	5,000-7,500	2,800-4,600
1995 Altima	6,900-10,000	6,100-9,200	3,600-6,200
1996 Altima	8,800-11,800	7,800-10,800	5,000-7,500
1997 Altima	9,900-13,500	8,900-12,500	5,900-9,000

AVERAGE REPLACEMENT COSTS

A/C Compressor	$510	Clutch, Pressure Plate, Bearing	440
Alternator	275	Constant Velocity Joints	385
Radiator	280	Brakes	200
Timing Chain or Belt	755	Shocks and/or Struts	540
Automatic Transmission or Transaxle	900	Exhaust System	475

TROUBLE SPOTS

• **Brakes** A voluntary recall was issued to inspect the right rear brake hose for chafing on the rear suspension, which could lead to a leak and brake failure. (1995)

• **Transmission slippage** If the malfunction indicator lamp comes on, the gauges quit working, a fuse is blown, and the transmission slips, shifts harshly, or gets stuck in third gear, then a wiring harness may be chafing on the top of the transmission under the battery tray; or the instrument wiring harness is chafing on the air bag harness support bracket. Repairs will be made under normal warranty provisions. (1995)

• **Oil leak** Oil leaking from the front of the engine could be caused by a bad O-ring between timing cover and the engine block. (1993-95)

• **Transmission slippage** The transmission may not go into reverse and, upon checking the fluid you notice that it is full but burnt. The rear control valve and low/reverse brake (plate, piston, and retainer) must be replaced under normal warranty provisions. (1993-94)

• **Air conditioner** Poor air conditioner performance may be caused by a refrigerant leak at the compressor joint connector (not the compressor itself) and is fixed by replacing the O-ring. (1993-95)

• **Transmission slippage** If the transmission does not shift properly until warmed up, make sure it is filled only with Nissanmatic "C" transmission fluid.

RECALL HISTORY

1993-94 Engine movement can cause throttle-cable housing to pull out of its guide; engine may then not return to idle when gas pedal is released. **1995 with automatic** Shift lever lock plate can be broken; movement of lever without driver's knowledge can result in unexpected vehicle movement. **1995** On a few cars, right rear brake hose may contact suspension component, causing abrasion and eventual leakage. **1997** Seatbelts might not restrain occupant during a collision.

1990-94 NISSAN MAXIMA

1994 Nissan Maxima GXE

FOR Air bags, dual (later models) • Anti-lock brakes (optional) • Acceleration • Handling/roadholding • Ride • Instruments/controls

AGAINST Rear-seat room • Head room (w/optional sunroof) • Fuel economy

EVALUATION With 190 horsepower on tap, the SE is a potent and sporty performer that matches up well when compared with higher-priced European models. Those preferring a touch of luxury will discover the GXE is also well worth considering. Maxima comes with a well-organized instrument panel and comfortable driving position. It provides the kind of poised front-drive handling and competent road manners that others have tried to emulate. With its softer suspension the GXE leans a bit more in the turns than the firmer SE, but both models respond to steering inputs quickly and precisely.

Especially worthy of praise is the twin-cam V-6 that powers the SE model. It's smoother, quieter, and feels stronger than engines offered by most of the Maxima's rivals. It propels the Maxima SE to 60 mph in under 9.0 seconds with the manual transmission, while the GXE equipped with the mannerly 4-speed automatic performs the task in about 10.5 seconds. The interior has ample head room in front and back, plus enough leg room for tall people to stretch out comfortably. Our only complaints focus on the slow addition of air bags—dual air bags didn't become standard until 1995.

In conclusion, the Maxima heads our must-drive list of nea-r luxury sedans.

SPECIFICATIONS

	4-door sedan
Wheelbase, in.	104.3
Overall length, in.	187.6
Overall width, in.	69.3
Overall height, in.	55.1
Curb weight, lbs.	3129
Cargo volume, cu. ft.	14.5
Fuel capacity, gals.	18.5
Seating capacity	5
Front head room, in.	39.5
Max. front leg room, in.	43.7
Rear head room, in.	36.9
Min. rear leg room, in.	33.2

Powertrain layout: transverse front-engine/front-wheel drive

ENGINES

	ohc V-8	dohc V-6
Size, liters/cu. in.	3.0/181	3.0/181
Horsepower	160	190
Torque (lbs./ft.)	192	190

NISSAN

EPA city/highway mpg
5-speed OD manual... 20/26   21/26
4-speed OD automatic.. 19/26   19/25

Consumer Guide™ observed MPG
5-speed OD manual... 20.4   21.9

Built in Japan.

RETAIL PRICES	GOOD	AVERAGE	POOR
1990 Maxima	$4,200-5,200	$3,500-4,500	$1,700-2,400
1991 Maxima	5,000-6,200	4,300-5,400	2,400-3,100
1992 Maxima	6,000-7,200	5,300-6,400	3,200-4,000
1993 Maxima	7,000-8,300	6,200-7,500	4,000-4,800
1994 Maxima	8,300-9,800	7,500-9,000	5,000-6,000

AVERAGE REPLACEMENT COSTS

A/C Compressor $655
Alternator 240
Radiator 500
Timing Chain or Belt 370
Automatic Transmission or
    Transaxle.......................935

Clutch, Pressure Plate,
    Bearing 545
Constant Velocity Joints.....475
Brakes.................................190
Shocks and/or Struts 1,385
Exhaust System.................315

TROUBLE SPOTS

• **Air bags** A voluntary recall was issued to replace an air bag sensor to reduce the possibility of the bag deploying when it is not needed and will be performed at no charge. (1992-93)

• **Wheels** Some aluminum wheels got too much clear coat, which could allow the lug nuts to loosen, so the clear coat will be removed at no charge and a recall label (no. 94V-194) will be near the emissions label in the engine compartment. (1993-94)

• **Coolant leak** Coolant may leak from the front of the cylinder head, which may appear to be a head gasket, but comes from a threaded plug in the front of the head that must be cleaned and Teflon tape applied to the threads to prevent future leaks. (1990-94)

• **Transmission slippage** The transmission may not go into reverse and, upon checking the fluid will be full but burnt. The rear control valve and low/reverse brake (plate, piston, and retainer) must be replaced. (1993-94)

• **Clutch** The clutch plate, pressure plate, and release fork will be replaced if there is clutch judder on cars with manual transmission. (1990-92)

• **Transmission slippage** If the manual transmission slips, the clutch disc will be replaced with a revised one. The flywheel and pressure plate will only be replaced if they have heat discoloration. (1995)

• **Transmission slippage** If the transmission does not shift properly until warmed up, make sure it is filled only with Nissanmatic "C" transmission fluid.

RECALL HISTORY

1990-94 registered in CT, DE, DC, IA, IL, IN, MA, MD, ME, MI, MN, NH, NJ, NY, OH, PA, RI, VT, WI, and WV Mixture of mud and salt could become trapped between fuel filler tube and wheel housing; corrosion could result in fuel leakage. **1992-93 with driver-side air bag** In some underbody impacts, sensor activates and causes air bag to inflate when not needed. **1993-94 GXE with aluminum wheels** Excessive clear-coating may position wheel nuts too far away from hub when tightened.

1995-98 NISSAN MAXIMA

1995 Nissan Maxima SE

FOR Air bags, dual • Optional anti-lock brakes • Acceleration • Steering/handling • Ride

AGAINST Rear seat comfort • Fuel economy

EVALUATION Performance leads off the car's strong points, ranking as little short of stunning. We timed a GXE with the automatic transmission at 7.9 seconds to 60 mph. Tromp the gas pedal to the floor, and a Maxima nearly leaps ahead. Only modest engine roar is heard on such occasions, as the Maxima is otherwise quiet-running. Passing power also is impressive, but the automatic unit is slow to downshift for passing at times, and occasionally shifts harshly. As for fuel economy, we averaged 24.1 mpg with one GXE and 21.4 mpg with another.

NISSAN

Maxima offers a comfortable and stable ride, precise steering, and crisp handling. Body lean is noticeable in high-speed lane changes and when cornering swiftly, but the Maxima maintains a tight grip on the road surface.

Maxima feels really big inside—more so than its outside appearance suggests. With a little more head room and rear leg room than its predecessor, the latest Maxima is more accommodating for tall passengers. The wide trunk has a flat floor that provides plenty of cargo space. Instruments and controls are well positioned, easy to see and use while driving. The low dashboard permits a great view of the road ahead. Stereo and climate controls are in a slanted panel that's easy to reach. Round analog gauges are large.

If you're searching for a mid-size sedan that reaches above the run-of-the-mill offerings, a Maxima of any 1995-97 vintage is definitely worth a trial run.

NHTSA CRASH TEST RESULTS
1995 Nissan Maxima   4-DOOR SEDAN

Driver	☆☆☆☆
Passenger	☆☆☆

(The National Highway Traffic Safety Administration tests a vehicle's crashworthiness in front and side collisions. Their ratings suggest the chance of serious injury: ☆☆☆☆☆—10% or less; ☆☆☆☆—10-20% or less; ☆☆☆—20-30% or less; ☆☆—35-45% or less; ☆—More than 45%.)

SPECIFICATIONS

	4-door sedan
Wheelbase, in.	106.3
Overall length, in.	187.7
Overall width, in.	6937
Overall height, in.	55.7
Curb weight, lbs.	3001
Cargo volume, cu. ft.	14.5
Fuel capacity, gals.	18.5
Seating capacity	5
Front head room, in.	40.1
Max. front leg room, in.	43.9
Rear head room, in.	37.4
Min. rear leg room, in.	34.3

Powertrain layout: transverse front-engine/front-wheel drive

ENGINES

	dohc V-6
Size, liters/cu. in.	3.0/181
Horsepower	190
Torque (lbs./ft.)	205

EPA city/highway mpg

5-speed OD manual	22/27

	dohc V-6
4-speed OD automatic	21/28

Consumer Guide™ observed MPG

5-speed OD manual	24.1
4-speed OD automatic	21.4

Built in Japan.

RETAIL PRICES	GOOD	AVERAGE	POOR
1995 Maxima	$11,200-13,700	$10,200-12,700	$7,200-9,300
1996 Maxima	13,200-16,000	12,000-14,500	8,500-10,500
1997 Maxima	15,000-18,000	13,500-16,500	9,800-12,200
1998 Maxima	17,500-20,500	16,000-19,000	11,500-14,000

AVERAGE REPLACEMENT COSTS

A/C Compressor	$625
Alternator	450
Radiator	445
Timing Chain or Belt	1,305
Automatic Transmission or Transaxle	1,080
Clutch, Pressure Plate, Bearing	515
Constant Velocity Joints	1,145
Brakes	210
Shocks and/or Struts	1,530
Exhaust System	375

TROUBLE SPOTS

• **Engine knock** Spark knock, or ping, may result from a defective onboard computer. (1995-97)

• **Hard starting** Hard starting, stalling, or stumbling under load could be caused by corrosion of the coolant sensor. (1995-96)

• **Brake noise** Rear brakes rattle on rough road. (1995)

• **Hard starting** If the engine does not start on the first attempt, the engine may crank very slowly on the second attempt because of a problem with the engine control computer. (1995)

• **Clutch** The clutch may slip when accelerating hard in 4th or 5th gear due to a problem with the friction material. (1995)

• **Engine noise** Noise from the front of the engine may be caused by excessive play in the timing chain for which a new tensioner and chain guide are required. (1995-96)

RECALL HISTORY

None to date.

1996-98 NISSAN PATHFINDER

FOR Air bags, dual • Anti-lock brakes • Ride • Passenger and cargo room

NISSAN

1996 Nissan Pathfinder SE

AGAINST Rear visibility • Engine noise • Rear seat entry/exit • Rear seat comfort

EVALUATION Acceleration has improved over its predecessors, but Nissan's engine cannot quite match domestic rivals for low-speed performance, even though it does respond well. Smoother than its predecessor, the 3.3-liter V-6 is too noisy at highway speeds. Fuel economy is on the meager side: an SE 4x4 with automatic averaged just 14.1 mpg.

Ride and handling are among the most carlike of any sport-utilities.

A tight suspension and linear steering contribute to a sense of control. Ride quality is notably softer than before—firm, yes, but devoid of harshness over bumps. Road and wind noise are low.

Not only is the dashboard more modern, but this Pathfinder offers more space for people and cargo. Head room is good all around, but rear leg room is marginal for anyone taller than 5-foot-10 or so. Also, there's little space for toes under the front seats. A relatively low ride height makes it easy to get in and out of front seats, though entering and exiting the rear is more of a challenge. Back doors do not open 90 degrees, and leave little room to swing your feet and legs through the narrow openings.

Unlike several domestic rivals, Nissan has no permanent 4WD system, and no push-button shifting between 2WD and 4WD High. Pathfinders cannot really match the domestics for overall performance, either—especially at low speeds.

NHTSA CRASH TEST RESULTS
1997 Nissan Pathfinder   4-DOOR WAGON

Driver	☆☆☆
Passenger	☆☆☆

(The National Highway Traffic Safety Administration tests a vehicle's crashworthiness in front and side collisions. Their ratings suggest the chance of serious injury: ☆☆☆☆☆—10% or less; ☆☆☆☆—10-20% or less; ☆☆☆—20-30% or less; ☆☆—35-45% or less; ☆—More than 45%.)

SPECIFICATIONS

	4-door wagon
Wheelbase, in.	106.3
Overall length, in.	178.3
Overall width, in.	68.7
Overall height, in.	67.1
Curb weight, lbs.	3675
Cargo volume, cu. ft.	85.0
Fuel capacity, gals.	20.8
Seating capacity	5
Front head room, in.	39.5
Max. front leg room, in.	41.7
Rear head room, in.	37.5
Min. rear leg room, in.	31.8

ENGINES

	ohc V-6
Size, liters/cu. in.	3.3/201
Horsepower	168
Torque (lbs./ft.)	196

EPA city/highway mpg

5-speed OD manual	16/18
4-speed OD automatic	15/19

Consumer Guide™ observed MPG

4-speed OD automatic	14.1

RETAIL PRICES	GOOD	AVERAGE	POOR
1996 Pathfinder	$14,000-20,000	$12,500-18,500	$9,300-14,500
1997 Pathfinder	16,500-22,500	15,000-21,000	11,200-16,500
1998 Pathfinder	19,000-26,000	17,500-24,000	13,000-19,000

AVERAGE REPLACEMENT COSTS

A/C Compressor	$605	Clutch, Pressure Plate, Bearing	500
Alternator	760	Universal Joints	170
Radiator	490	Brakes	380
Timing Chain or Belt	200	Shocks and/or Struts	850
Automatic Transmission or Transaxle	845	Exhaust System	625

TROUBLE SPOTS

• **Vehicle shake** Vibration at 30-40 mph is often the result of the front driveshaft being installed out of phase since the alignment paint marks tend to wear off. (1996-97)

• **Radio** The radio presets and clock time memory may be lost due to loose connections or voltage spikes when the engine is started or jump-started. (1996)

NISSAN

• **Suspension noise** The front suspension squeaks on rough road due to a problem between the strut rod and rubber bumper. (1996)

RECALL HISTORY

1996 Due to type of lubricant used on some vehicles, effort required to turn steering wheel at low ambient temperatures could increase; some drivers would have difficulty. **1996** Due to thickness of carpet padding on some vehicles, space between brake pedal and transmission tunnel could catch driver's right foot.

1993-98 NISSAN QUEST

1996 Nissan Quest XE

FOR Air bags, dual (later models) • Passenger and cargo room • Steering/handling • Anti-lock brakes (optional)

AGAINST Control layout • Wind noise • Acceleration (with load)

See the 1993-98 Mercury Villager report for an evaluation of the Nissan Quest.

NHTSA CRASH TEST RESULTS
1995 Nissan Quest
3-DOOR VAN

Driver	☆☆☆☆
Passenger	☆☆☆

(The National Highway Traffic Safety Administration tests a vehicle's crashworthiness in front and side collisions. Their ratings suggest the chance of serious injury: ☆☆☆☆☆—10% or less; ☆☆☆☆—10-20% or less; ☆☆☆—20-30% or less; ☆☆—35-45% or less; ☆—More than 45%.)

SPECIFICATIONS

	3-door wagon
Wheelbase, in.	112.2

	3-door wagon
Overall length, in.	189.9
Overall width, in.	73.4
Overall height, in.	66.0
Curb weight, lbs.	3815
Cargo volume, cu. ft.	126.4
Fuel capacity, gals.	20.0
Seating capacity	7
Front head room, in.	39.4
Max. front leg room, in.	39.9
Rear head room, in.	39.7
Min. rear leg room, in.	34.8

Powertrain layout: transverse front-engine/front-wheel drive

ENGINES

	ohc V-6
Size, liters/cu. in.	3.0/181
Horsepower	151
Torque (lbs./ft.)	174

EPA city/highway mpg
4-speed OD automatic ... 17/23

Consumer Guide™ observed MPG
4-speed OD automatic ... 19.7

Built in USA.

RETAIL PRICES	GOOD	AVERAGE	POOR
1993 Quest	$7,600-9,500	$6,900-8,700	$4,400-5,800
1994 Quest	9,000-11,500	8,200-10,700	5,500-7,200
1995 Quest	10,500-14,000	9,600-13,000	6,500-9,000
1996 Quest	12,700-16,000	11,500-14,700	8,000-10,500
1997 Quest	15,200-18,200	13,800-16,700	9,700-12,500
1998 Quest	17,700-21,500	16,200-20,000	12,000-15,000

AVERAGE REPLACEMENT COSTS

A/C Compressor $330	Constant Velocity Joints.....615
Alternator 300	Brakes...................................255
Radiator 505	Shocks and/or Struts 380
Timing Chain or Belt 190	Exhaust System..................250
Automatic Transmission or Transaxle.........................835	

TROUBLE SPOTS

• **Doors** A rattle in either of the front doors may be caused by the door guard beam spot welds breaking loose and a campaign was conducted to repair both beams free of charge. (1993-94)

NISSAN

• **Coolant leak** Coolant may leak from the front of the cylinder head, which may appear to be a head gasket, but comes from a threaded plug in the front of the head that must be cleaned and Teflon tape applied to the threads to prevent future leaks. (1993-95)

• **Transmission slippage** The transmission may not go into reverse and, upon checking the fluid will be full but burnt. The rear control valve and low/reverse brake (plate, piston, and retainer) must be replaced under normal warranty provisions. (1993-94)

• **Tail/brake lights** If the tail/brake lights work intermittently, the socket may be loose from the plastic connector, which will be repaired with super glue. (1993-95)

• **Suspension noise** A new stabilizer bar and bushings will be installed if there is a crunching or scraping noise from the front end when going over bumps (such as speed bumps) or on highway ramps. (1993-95)

• **Transmission slippage** If the transmission does not shift properly until warmed up, make sure it is filled only with Nissanmatic "C" transmission fluid.

RECALL HISTORY

1993 Master cylinder on some vans was improperly assembled or damaged during assembly, which can result in loss of braking at two wheels, causing increased pedal travel and effort and increased stopping distance. **1993** One or both bolts securing automatic seatbelt tracks to B-pillars were not adequately tightened on some vans, increasing risk of injury in collision or sudden maneuver. **1993** Fuel filler hoses may have been cut prior to installation by knife used to open shipping box; fuel leakage could result, leading to fire if exposed to ignition source. **1993** Leaves and other foreign matter can enter through cowl panel air intake during operation of front heater and/or air conditioner, resulting in build-up in the plenum that can lead to noise, odors, or even a vehicle fire. **1995 with sliding third-row bench seats** Cable that connects seat adjustment level to latch might be pinched in roller assembly, preventing latch on left side from fully engaging seat rail. **1995** Rear lamp socket may not illuminate, resulting in malfunction of stoplamp of rear running lamps.

1991-94½ NISSAN SENTRA ✓ BEST BUY

FOR Air bags, driver (later models) • Anti-lock brakes (optional) • Fuel economy • Acceleration (SE-R) • Roadholding (SE-R) • Instruments/controls

AGAINST Engine noise • Road noise • Wind noise • Automatic transmission performance • Rear-seat room

1991 Nissan Sentra GXE 4-door

EVALUATION This lineup of Sentras really shines when compared to the 1987-1990 version offered by Nissan. A couple of glowing examples of excellence can be seen in the available anti-lock brakes for certain models and the decision to take a risk and produce the impressive SE-R sports coupe, with its lively twin-cam 2.0-liter engine. But even with the 1.6-liter base engine, acceleration is much quicker than before (thanks to the extra 20 horsepower), without any real decrease in fuel economy. The engine seems much happier when paired with the manual gearbox, however. The automatic tends to drain too much power, causing the 1.6-liter to feel strained and overworked. Nail the throttle and the automatic does downshift—reluctantly—with a rude jolt.

Getting back to the SE-R, it comes equipped with the 140-horsepower engine, plus four-wheel disc brakes. There are even anti-lock brakes on the option list. Should you find an SE-R, you'll discover a spirited, yet smooth-handling little sports coupe with a sense of refinement and competence usually found only on European sports cars costing considerably more.

Overall, these models feel much more solid than before and are worth a test drive.

SPECIFICATIONS

	2-door coupe	4-door sedan
Wheelbase, in.	95.7	95.7
Overall length, in.	170.3	170.3
Overall width, in.	65.6	65.6
Overall height, in.	53.9	53.9
Curb weight, lbs.	2266	2288
Cargo volume, cu. ft.	11.7	11.7
Fuel capacity, gals.	13.2	13.2
Seating capacity	5	5
Front head room, in.	38.5	38.5

	2-door coupe	4-door sedan
Max. front leg room, in.	41.9	41.9
Rear head room, in.	36.6	36.6
Min. rear leg room, in.	30.9	30.9

Powertrain layout: transverse front-engine/front-wheel drive

ENGINES

	dohc I-4	dohc I-4
Size, liters/cu. in.	1.6/97	2.0/122
Horsepower	110	140
Torque (lbs./ft.)	108	132

EPA city/highway mpg

5-speed OD manual	29/29	24/32
3-speed automatic	27/37	
4-speed OD automatic	27/36	23/30

Consumer Guide™ observed MPG

5-speed OD manual		24.3
4-speed OD automatic	26.4	

Built in USA.

RETAIL PRICES

	GOOD	AVERAGE	POOR
1991 Sentra	$1,800-3,500	$1,200-2,800	$400-1,200
1992 Sentra	2,300-3,800	1,700-3,200	700-1,500
1993 Sentra	2,800-4,600	2,100-3,900	1,000-2,000
1994 Sentra	3,500-5,800	2,800-5,000	1,400-2,800

AVERAGE REPLACEMENT COSTS

A/C Compressor $530	Clutch, Pressure Plate, Bearing............................470
Alternator 275	Constant Velocity Joints.....400
Radiator 205	Brakes................................205
Timing Chain or Belt 230	Shocks and/or Struts 810
Automatic Transmission or Transaxle.........................830	Exhaust System.................410

TROUBLE SPOTS

• **Fuel pump** The brushes for the electric fuel pump may wear prematurely so a campaign (no. 93-U3005) was conducted to replace the fuel pump with a revised unit. (1991-92)

• **Engine noise** Valve noise was caused by worn cam lobes and the intake cam, exhaust cam, or both must be replaced. (1991)

• **Fuel gauge** If the fuel gauge does not read full, drops from full too quickly, or the low fuel light does not come on even when it runs out of gas, the fuel gauge sending unit must be replaced. (1991-93) The fuel pump wires may be interfering with the float arm and must be rerouted. (1995)

- **Transmission slippage** If the transmission behaves normally until it warms up then will not upshift to third or fourth gear or slips, the high clutch may be burned or the control valve is sticking and must be replaced. (1991-93)

- **Engine knock** Spark knock or ping is commonly due to carbon buildup on the pistons, which may be cleaned off, but if it occurs in high temperature, low humidity environments, the air flow meter may have to be replaced. (1991-94)

- **Transmission slippage** It the transmission does not shift properly until warmed up, make sure it is filled only with Nissanmatic "C" transmission fluid.

RECALL HISTORY

1991 Front seatbelt release button can break and pieces can fall inside. **1991 model B12** Improper belt-guide performance on cars equipped with two-point passive non-motorized front shoulder belts can cause fraying of belt near the retractor.

1995-98 NISSAN SENTRA

1995 Nissan Sentra GXE

FOR Air bags, dual • Fuel economy • Ride • Optional anti-lock brakes (GXE, GLE)

AGAINST Acceleration (automatic transmission) • Rear head room • Seat comfort • Rear seat entry/exit

EVALUATION In terms of quietness and solidity, the 1995 redesign moved Sentra from the middle to near the front of the sub-compact class. Even when driven over the roughest roads, Sentras act and feel far more substantial than most small cars, with a supple yet well-controlled ride and a notable absence of body drumming and road rumble. Although wind noise rises appreciably above 60 mph, the little engine doesn't thrash or boom at most speeds.

You'll need to work the 1.6-liter engine hard when mated to the automatic transmission. But, when mated to the slick-shifting 5-speed manual, the Sentra feels frisky. The 140-horsepower engine in the SE has good acceleration with automatic and feels even more lively with the 5-speed.

Despite a bigger interior than prior models, Sentra remains practical for only four adults. Three grownups simply cannot fit comfortably in the back seat for longer trips. A functional, attractive dashboard gives the Sentra driver a user-friendly environment, but seats are flat and hard. Cargo space isn't the greatest, but the trunk has a flat floor and low opening, at bumper level.

Solid and refined, Sentra looks like a good value in the small-car hunt. We'd even place it on a par with the Toyota Corolla—today's standard of comparison in the subcompact league.

NHTSA CRASH TEST RESULTS
1996 Nissan Sentra

4-DOOR SEDAN

Driver	☆☆☆☆
Passenger	☆☆☆☆

(The National Highway Traffic Safety Administration tests a vehicle's crashworthiness in front and side collisions. Their ratings suggest the chance of serious injury: ☆☆☆☆☆—10% or less; ☆☆☆☆—10-20% or less; ☆☆☆—20-30% or less; ☆☆—35-45% or less; ☆—More than 45%.)

SPECIFICATIONS

	4-door sedan
Wheelbase, in.	99.8
Overall length, in.	170.1
Overall width, in.	66.6
Overall height, in.	54.5
Curb weight, lbs.	2315
Cargo volume, cu. ft.	10.7
Fuel capacity, gals.	13.2
Seating capacity	5
Front head room, in.	39.1
Max. front leg room, in.	42.3
Rear head room, in.	39.5
Min. rear leg room, in.	32.4

Powertrain layout: transverse front-engine/front-wheel drive

ENGINES

	dohc I-4	dohc I-4
Size, liters/cu. in.	1.6/97	2.0/122
Horsepower	115	140
Torque (lbs./ft.)	108	132
EPA city/highway mpg		
5-speed OD manual	30/40	23/31

	dohc I-4	dohc I-4
4-speed OD automatic	28/37	23.30

Consumer Guide™ observed MPG

5-speed OD manual	31.7	25.4
4-speed OD automatic	24.9	

Built in USA.

RETAIL PRICES

	GOOD	AVERAGE	POOR
1995 Sentra	$4,700-7,000	$4,000-6,200	$2,000-3,500
1996 Sentra	5,800-8,000	5,100-7,200	2,900-4,200
1997 Sentra	6,800-9,500	6,000-8,700	3,600-5,600
1998 Sentra	7,800-11,500	7,000-10,500	4,400-7,200

AVERAGE REPLACEMENT COSTS

A/C Compressor $610	Constant Velocity Joints..1,120
Alternator 310	Brakes..................................290
Radiator 300	Shocks and/or Struts 460
Timing Chain or Belt 620	Exhaust System 320
Clutch, Pressure Plate, Bearing 390	

TROUBLE SPOTS

• **Sunroof/moonroof** The sunroof may tilt up, but not slide back due to a problem with the lifter mechanism. (1995-96)

• **Brake noise** The rear drum brakes may squeal, grind or groan due to being over adjusted. This can also damage the drum(s), springs and brake shoes. (1995)

• **Fuel gauge** The gauge may not register full even though the gas tank is completely filled due to the pump wires interfering with the float arm. (1995)

• **Air conditioner** Poor air conditioning may be due to refrigerant leaking from the service fitting valves. (1996)

• **Dashboard lights** The check engine light comes on due to a problem with the rear heated oxygen sensor. (1995-96)

RECALL HISTORY

1995 w/anti-lock brakes Hydraulic actuator was not properly purged of all air; bubbles can cause increased pedal travel and stopping distances. **1996-97** Stop/taillamps do not meet illumination requirements of Federal Motor Vehicle Safety Standard (FMVSS) No. 108.

1992-97 OLDSMOBILE ACHIEVA

1993 Oldsmobile Achieva 2-door

FOR   Air bag, dual (later models) • Acceleration • Visibility • Steering/handling • Anti-lock brakes (optional)

AGAINST   Ride • Entry/exit • Fuel economy (V-6)

EVALUATION   Ever since its introduction in 1992 Oldsmobile has been striving to provide a 4-cylinder engine that matches the refinement of its Japanese rivals. The early versions delivered brisk acceleration and strong off-the-line performance, but were noisy and generated annoying vibrations that could be felt through the steering column. So up until 1995 and 1996, the V-6 engines are a better choice, providing lots of torque at low speeds and delivering the best all-around performance.

The Computer Command Ride exhibits little noticeable difference between the soft and sport modes. In either setting, handling and stability were commendable, without any severe impact harshness.

Inside, gauges are grouped into four round pods in a concave "wraparound" instrument panel. A center panel holds the radio and climate-control switches, which are clearly marked and easy to reach. Overall, interior appointments are a cut above previous Oldsmobile compacts. Thick rear C-pillars and a smaller back window tend to restrict visibility rearward on the 4-doors, but interior comfort is generally good, with adequate head room and leg/room to go around. While the Achieva is much more competitive than the previous Calais, it has no "stand out" features that make it exceptional. On the plus side, fully-equipped Achievas cost hundreds, even thousands, less than comparable versions of Japanese rivals.

NHTSA CRASH TEST RESULTS
1995 Oldsmobile Achieva

2-DOOR COUPE

Driver	☆☆☆☆
Passenger	☆☆☆

(The National Highway Traffic Safety Administration tests a vehicle's crashworthiness in front and side collisions. Their ratings suggest the chance of serious injury: ☆☆☆☆☆—10% or less; ☆☆☆☆—10-20% or less; ☆☆☆—20-30% or less; ☆☆—35-45% or less; ☆—More than 45%.)

SPECIFICATIONS

	2-door coupe	4-door sedan
Wheelbase, in.	103.4	103.4
Overall length, in.	187.9	187.9
Overall width, in.	67.5	67.5
Overall height, in.	53.4	53.4
Curb weight, lbs.	2738	2799
Cargo volume, cu. ft.	14.0	14.0
Fuel capacity, gals.	15.2	15.2
Seating capacity	5	5
Front head room, in.	37.8	37.8
Max. front leg room, in.	43.3	43.3
Rear head room, in.	36.5	37.0
Min. rear leg room, in.	30.9	35.0

Powertrain layout: transverse front-engine/front-wheel drive

ENGINES

	ohc I-4	dohc I-4	dohc I-4	ohv V-6	ohv V-6
Size, liters/cu. in.	2.3/138	2.3/138	2.4/146	3.1/191	3.3/204
Horsepower	115-120	150-190	150	155-160	150
Torque (lbs./ft.)	140	145-160	150	185	185

EPA city/highway mpg

5-speed OD man.	23/35	21/30	23/33		
3-speed auto.	24/32	23/29			20/29
4-speed OD auto.	22/31	21/30	22/32	20/29	

Consumer Guide™ observed MPG

5-speed OD man.	25.1	
4-speed OD auto.		23.6

Built in USA.

RETAIL PRICES	GOOD	AVERAGE	POOR
1992 Achieva	$3,300-4,200	$2,600-3,400	$1,200-1,800
1993 Achieva	4,000-5,300	3,300-4,500	1,700-2,600
1994 Achieva	4,800-6,400	4,100-5,600	2,300-3,300
1995 Achieva	5,900-7,000	5,100-6,200	3,300-4,000
1996 Achieva	7,200-8,200	6,300-7,200	4,300-5,100
1997 Achieva	8,400-9,500	7,400-8,500	5,300-6,200

OLDSMOBILE

AVERAGE REPLACEMENT COSTS

A/C Compressor	$540	Constant Velocity Joints	565
Alternator	225	Brakes	240
Radiator	500	Shocks and/or Struts	540
Timing Chain or Belt	325	Exhaust System	380
Automatic Transmission or Transaxle	1,105		

TROUBLE SPOTS

• **Engine noise** A tick or rattle when the engine is started cold may be due to too much wrist pin-to-piston clearance. New piston and pin sets will be replaced under warranty if the customer complains of the noise. (1994-95)

• **Engine noise** Bearing knock was common on many 3300 and 3800 (3.3L and 3.8L) engines due to too much clearance on the number-one main bearing, requiring it to be replaced with a 0.001-inch undersize bearing. (1992-93)

• **Valve cover leaks** The plastic valve covers on the 3.1L engine were prone to leaks and should be replaced with redesigned aluminum valve covers. (GM no longer stocks the plastic ones.) (1994-95)

• **Transaxle leak** The right front axle seal at the automatic transaxle is prone to leak and GM issued a revised seal to correct the problem and it is supposed to be installed whenever a car is in for transmission or axle shaft service of any sort. (1992-94)

• **Brake wear** The front brakes wear out prematurely because of the friction compound. GM and several aftermarket companies have brakes with linings that will last longer. The GM part number is 12510050. This is not considered a warranty item. (1992-95)

• **Radiator** Some cars mysteriously lose coolant, but no leaks can be found. The common problem is a bad seal on the pressure cap on the surge tank that is connected to the radiator. (1992-94)

• **Engine noise** What sounds like a rattling noise from the engine that lasts less than a minute when the car is started after sitting overnight is often caused by automatic transmission pump starvation or cavitation, or a sticking pressure regulator valve. According to GM, no damage occurs and it does not have a fix for the problem. (1994-95)

• **Transmission slippage** The 4T60E transmission may drop out of drive (neutral condition) while cruising, shift erratically, have no third or fourth gear, or no second and third gear because of a bad ground connection for the shift solenoids. Poor grounds also allow wrong gear starts. Many transmissions have been mistakenly rebuilt, which does not correct the problem. (1994)

• **Transmission slippage** Any car with a model TH-125 automatic transmission may shift late or not upshift at all. The problem is a stuck throttle valve inside the transmission. It may be overlooked during rebuilding since the valve appears fine because it is hydraulic pressure, not a physical binding, that makes it stick. The problem is fixed by enlarging the hydraulic fluid balance hole by 0.010 inch. (1991-94)

• **Dashboard lights** The Enhanced Traction Control (ETC) warning light "ETC OFF" may glow and the cruise control stop working, but there is no problem with the system. If the computer failure memory is cleared, everything returns to normal. No current fix. (1996)

• **Ignition switch** The ignition switch may not return from the start to the run position and the accessories such as the radio, wipers, cruise control, power windows, rear defroster, or heater may not work because the screws that hold the switch in place were over-tightened. (1992-94)

RECALL HISTORY

1994 Welds in rear assembly of fuel tank may be insufficient to prevent leakage in certain rear-impact collisions, increasing risk of fire. **1996** Front and/or rear hazard warning lamps might not work. **1996** During deployment of the passenger air bag, the air bag can snag on a reinforcement inside the instrument panel.This might cause the air bag to not deploy properly. **1996** Interior lamps might come on unexpectedly while vehicle is being driven. **1997** Omitted fuse cover could result in short circuit and possible fire.

1995-98 OLDSMOBILE AURORA

FOR Air bags, dual • Anti-lock brakes • Acceleration • Steering/handling • Passenger room

AGAINST Fuel economy • Wind noise • Rear visibility (1995)

EVALUATION Although the engine will not snap anyone's head back at takeoff, it delivers brisk acceleration and ample passing power. A test Aurora accelerated to 60 mph in a swift 8.2 seconds. The transmission shifts so smoothly, you'll seldom notice anything happening. Gas mileage is slightly better than expected: We averaged 20.3 mpg, but premium gasoline is required.

Road noise is noticeable, but not excessive. However, wind noise has been prominent around the side windows on Auroras that have been tested. Ride control is commendable at high speeds. Optional V-rated tires make the ride noticeably stiffer,

OLDSMOBILE

1995 Oldsmobile Aurora

however. With either tires, an Aurora offers sporty handling, displaying only minimal body roll in turns and excellent grip.

The Aurora's roomy interior has ample space for four adults. Controls are easy to reach and clearly labeled, analog gauges large and easy to read, in a well-designed dashboard. Luggage space is ample, with a long, flat trunk floor, though the opening is too small to load bulky objects.

Carrying Oldsmobile a big step forward, Aurora is competitive with Japanese and European sedans that cost thousands more when new. We recommend that you give it a trial run if you're shopping in the luxury-sedan league.

NHTSA CRASH TEST RESULTS
1996 Oldsmobile Aurora
4-DOOR SEDAN

Driver	☆☆☆
Passenger	☆☆☆

(The National Highway Traffic Safety Administration tests a vehicle's crashworthiness in front and side collisions. Their ratings suggest the chance of serious injury: ☆☆☆☆☆—10% or less; ☆☆☆☆—10-20% or less; ☆☆☆—20-30% or less; ☆☆—35-45% or less; ☆—More than 45%.)

SPECIFICATIONS

	4-door sedan
Wheelbase, in.	113.8
Overall length, in.	205.4
Overall width, in.	74.4
Overall height, in.	55.4
Curb weight, lbs.	3967
Cargo volume, cu. ft.	16.1
Fuel capacity, gals.	20.0
Seating capacity	5
Front head room, in.	38.4
Max. front leg room, in.	42.6
Rear head room, in.	36.9

	4-door sedan
Min. rear leg room, in.	38.4

Powertrain layout: transverse front-engine/front-wheel drive

ENGINES

	dohc V-8
Size, liters/cu. in.	4.0/244
Horsepower	250
Torque (lbs./ft.)	260

EPA city/highway mpg

4-speed OD automatic	17/26

Consumer Guide™ observed MPG

4-speed OD automatic	20.3

Built in USA.

RETAIL PRICES	GOOD	AVERAGE	POOR
1995 Aurora	$13,000-14,500	$11,800-13,000	$8,800-9,800
1996 Aurora	16,000-18,000	14,500-16,500	11,000-12,500
1997 Aurora	20,000-22,500	18,500-21,000	14,000-16,000
1998 Aurora	23,000-26,000	21,000-24,000	16,500-18,500

AVERAGE REPLACEMENT COSTS

A/C Compressor	$500	Constant Velocity Joints	905
Alternator	380	Brakes	430
Radiator	385	Shocks and/or Struts	500
Timing Chain or Belt	505	Exhaust System	295
Automatic Transmission or Transaxle	1,070		

TROUBLE SPOTS

• **Brake noise** The brakes make noises (squeals, crunches, groans, grunts, etc.) due to a problem with the rotors for which there are replacements with larger "cheeks." (1997)

• **Keyless entry** The keyless remote has a rather short range and can be corrected with a new module. (1996-97) To prevent inadvertent trunk release, a new transmitter (with a detent for the button) is available. (1996-97)

• **Mirrors** A problem with the memory seat/mirror module, the automatic parking-assist outside mirrors may point too high. (1997)

• **Vehicle noise** A problem with the power brake booster check valve causes a noise that appears to come from the dashboard. (1995-97)

RECALL HISTORY

1996 Damaged capacitor may cause failure of "Key in the Ignition" and driver seatbelt-unbuckled warnings, and other functions.

1991-94 OLDSMOBILE BRAVADA

1991 Oldsmobile Bravada

FOR Acceleration • Wet-weather traction • Anti-lock brakes (optional) • Passenger and cargo room

AGAINST Fuel economy • Engine noise

See the 1990-94 Chevrolet Blazer report for an evaluation of the Oldsmobile Bravada.

SPECIFICATIONS

	4-door wagon
Wheelbase, in.	107.0
Overall length, in.	178.9
Overall width, in.	65.2
Overall height, in.	65.6
Curb weight, lbs.	3939
Cargo volume, cu. ft.	74.3
Fuel capacity, gals.	20.0
Seating capacity	5
Front head room, in.	39.1
Max. front leg room, in.	42.5
Rear head room, in.	38.8
Min. rear leg room, in.	36.5

Powertrain layout: longitudinal front-engine/rear- or all-wheel drive

ENGINES

	ohv V-6	ohv V-6
Size, liters/cu. in.	4.3/262	4.3/262
Horsepower	160	200
Torque (lbs./ft.)	230	260

EPA city/highway mpg
4-speed OD automatic.. 17/22   16/21

Consumer Guide™ observed MPG
4-speed OD automatic.. 18.2

Built in USA.

RETAIL PRICES	GOOD	AVERAGE	POOR
1991 Bravada	$6,200-7,500	$5,400-6,700	$3,300-4,100
1992 Bravada	7,600-8,900	6,900-8,000	4,500-5,300
1993 Bravada	9,300-10,700	8,300-9,700	5,700-6,600
1994 Bravada	11,400-12,900	10,200-11,500	7,200-8,300

AVERAGE REPLACEMENT COSTS

A/C Compressor $415
Alternator 215
Radiator 415
Timing Chain or Belt 310
Automatic Transmission or
  Transaxle.......................900

Universal Joints 130
Brakes..................................200
Shocks and/or Struts 555
Exhaust System.................290

TROUBLE SPOTS

• **Transmission slippage** Any truck with a model TH-700-R4 automatic transmission may shift late or not upshift at all. The problem is a stuck throttle valve inside the transmission. It may be overlooked during rebuilding since the valve appears fine because it is hydraulic pressure, not a physical binding, that makes it stick. The problem is fixed by enlarging the hydraulic fluid balance hole by 0.010 inch. (1991-93)

• **Engine knock** Engine knock when the engine (4.3L, 5.7L, or 7.4L) is started is usually eliminated by using an oil filter with a check valve (such as Fram PH3980), but if this does not fix it, GM has revised PROMs for the computers and will even replace the main bearings if all else fails. (1991-92)

• **Exhaust system** The exhaust valves on the 4.3L, 5.0L, or 5.7L engine may not get enough lubrication causing a variety of noises that sound like lifter tick, rod knock, or a "whoop-whoop" noise like a helicopter. Usually, the same engine consumes excess oil because the valve guide seals on the exhaust valves are bad and have to be replaced. (1996)

RECALL HISTORY

1991 Rear seatbelt buckle release button can stick in unlatched position under certain conditions.

1996-98 OLDSMOBILE BRAVADA

1996 Oldsmobile Bravada

FOR   Air bag, driver • Anti-lock brakes • Acceleration • Passenger and cargo room • Ride

AGAINST   Fuel economy • Rear seat comfort

See the 1995-98 Chevrolet Blazer report for an evaluation of the Oldsmobile Bravada.

NHTSA CRASH TEST RESULTS
1997 Oldsmobile Bravada

4-DOOR WAGON

Driver	☆☆☆
Passenger	☆

(The National Highway Traffic Safety Administration tests a vehicle's crashworthiness in front and side collisions. Their ratings suggest the chance of serious injury: ☆☆☆☆☆—10% or less; ☆☆☆☆—10-20% or less; ☆☆☆—20-30% or less; ☆☆—35-45% or less; ☆—More than 45%.)

SPECIFICATIONS

	4-door wagon
Wheelbase, in.	107.0
Overall length, in.	180.9
Overall width, in.	66.5
Overall height, in.	67.0
Curb weight, lbs.	4184
Cargo volume, cu. ft.	74.2
Fuel capacity, gals.	19.0
Seating capacity	5
Front head room, in.	39.7
Max. front leg room, in.	42.4
Rear head room, in.	38.6
Min. rear leg room, in.	36.1

Powertrain layout: longitudinal front-engine/rear- or 4-wheel drive

ENGINES

ohv V-6

Size, liters/cu. in.	4.3/262
Horsepower	190
Torque (lbs./ft.)	250

EPA city/highway mpg
4-speed OD automatic........................ 16/21

Consumer Guide™ observed MPG
4-speed OD automatic........................ 18.7

Built in USA.

RETAIL PRICES	GOOD	AVERAGE	POOR
1996 Bravada	$16,000-18,000	$15,000-16,500	$11,500-12,500
1997 Bravada	19,000-21,000	17,500-19,500	13,500-15,000
1998 Bravada	22,000-24,500	20,000-22,500	15,500-17,000

AVERAGE REPLACEMENT COSTS

A/C Compressor	$520	Clutch, Pressure Plate, Bearing	800
Alternator	225	Universal Joints	270
Radiator	450	Brakes	220
Timing Chain or Belt	230	Exhaust System	485
Automatic Transmission or Transaxle	850	Shocks and/or Struts	410

TROUBLE SPOTS

• **Transmission leak** Automatic transmission pump may leak (model 4L60). A revised pump bushing is available. (1995-96)

• **Engine noise** The exhaust valves may not get enough lubrication causing a variety of noises that sound like lifter tick, rod knock or a "whoop-whoop" noise like a helicopter. The same engine may consume excess oil because the valve guide seals on the exhaust valves are bad and have to be replaced. (1996)

• **Engine knock** Engine knock when the engine is first started is usually eliminated by using an oil filter with a check valve (such as Fram PH3980), but if this does not fix it, GM has revised PROMs for the computers and may even replace the main bearings if no other solution is found. (1995)

• **Engine misfire** A problem with the powertrain control module may cause a lack of power (especially when carrying heavy loads or under heavy acceleration), early upshifts, late shifting in the 4WD-Low range and otherwise erratic performance. (1996)

RECALL HISTORY

1996 w/AWD or 4WD During testing, prop shaft contacted fuel tank, rupturing the tank; fuel leakage was beyond permissible level. **1998** Fatigue fracture of rear-axle brake pipe can occur, causing slow fluid leak and resulting in soft brake pedal; if pipe breaks, driver would face sudden loss of rear-brake performance. **1998 AWD or 4WD** On a few vehicles, one or both attaching nuts for lower control arm were not properly torqued; can result in separation from frame and loss of control.

1990-96 OLDSMOBILE CUTLASS CIERA

1995 Oldsmobile Cutlass Ciera

FOR Acceleration (V-6 engine) • Passenger and cargo room • Quietness

AGAINST Acceleration (4-cylinder)

EVALUATION Much to the confusion of many, including product planners at Oldsmobile, the conservatively-styled Cutlass Ciera constantly outsold the sleek and aerodynamic Cutlass Supreme. The Ciera has prevailed, primarily because it still offers good utility as both a sedan and wagon, and can be reasonably equipped for as much as $4000 less than comparable mid-size domestic and import models.

It's best to avoid the 4-cylinder models if possible. While they provide good economy, they simply can't provide adequate power for a car of this size and weight. You may save some, but are always penalized with puny performance. The V-6 versions are much smoother and more satisfying, providing ample torque for both off-the-line acceleration highway passing.

When compared to the Supreme, or competitors like the Ford Taurus and Buick Regal, the Ciera's suspension is much softer. While some prefer this softer ride, it bounces over wavy roads and doesn't absorb rough pavement well. It also doesn't corner as well as the Toyota Camry or Honda Accord, which provide better grip and handle turns with much greater ease. On the positive side, the Ciera is a pleasant and quiet family car with plenty of interior and cargo room.

SPECIFICATIONS

	4-door sedan	4-door wagon
Wheelbase, in.	104.9	104.9
Overall length, in.	190.3	194.4
Overall width, in.	69.5	69.5
Overall height, in.	54.1	54.5
Curb weight, lbs.	2833	3086
Cargo volume, cu. ft.	15.8	74.4
Fuel capacity, gals.	16.6	16.5
Seating capacity	6	8
Front head room, in.	38.6	38.6
Max. front leg room, in.	42.1	42.1
Rear head room, in.	38.3	38.9
Min. rear leg room, in.	35.8	34.7

Powertrain layout: transverse front-engine/front-wheel drive

ENGINES

	ohv I-4	ohc I-4	ohv V-6	ohv V-6
Size, liters/cu. in.	2.2/133	2.5/151	3.1/191	3.3/204
Horsepower	120	110	160	160
Torque (lbs./ft.)	130	135	185	185
EPA city/highway mpg				
3-speed automatic	25/31	23/30		20/27
4-speed OD automatic			19/29	20/29
Consumer Guide™ observed MPG				
3-speed automatic		21.8		
4-speed OD automatic			20.1	

Built in USA.

RETAIL PRICES	GOOD	AVERAGE	POOR
1990 Cutlass Ciera	$2,100-3,600	$1,500-2,900	$600-1,400
1991 Cutlass Ciera	2,700-4,100	2,000-3,400	1,100-1,700
1992 Cutlass Ciera	3,400-4,800	2,700-4,000	1,600-2,200
1993 Cutlass Ciera	4,100-5,500	3,400-4,800	2,100-2,800
1994 Cutlass Ciera	5,100-6,200	4,300-5,400	2,600-3,300
1995 Cutlass Ciera	6,400-7,600	5,600-6,800	3,600-4,500
1996 Cutlass Ciera	7,700-9,300	6,900-8,400	4,600-5,700

OLDSMOBILE

AVERAGE REPLACEMENT COSTS

A/C Compressor	$550	Constant Velocity Joints	525
Alternator	225	Brakes	210
Radiator	475	Shocks and/or Struts	430
Timing Chain or Belt	350	Exhaust System	375
Automatic Transmission or Transaxle	1,095		

TROUBLE SPOTS

• **Cold starting problems** A tick or rattle when the engine is started cold may be due to too much wrist-pin-to-piston clearance. New piston and pin sets will be replaced under warranty if the customer complains of the noise. (1994-95)

• **Engine noise** Bearing knock was common on many 3300 and 3800 (3.3L and 3.8L) engines due to too much clearance on the number-one main bearing, requiring it to be replaced with a 0.001-inch undersize bearing. (1992-93)

• **Valve cover leaks** The plastic valve covers on the 3.1L engine were prone to leaks and should be replaced with redesigned aluminum covers. (GM no longer stocks the plastic ones.) (1994-95)

• **Engine noise** What sounds like a rattling noise from the engine that lasts less than a minute when the car is started after sitting overnight is often caused by automatic transmission pump starvation or cavitation, or a sticking pressure regulator valve. According to GM, no damage occurs and it does not have a fix for the problem. (1994-95)

• **Transaxle leak** The right front axle seal at the automatic transaxle is prone to leak and GM issued a revised seal to correct the problem and it is supposed to be installed whenever a car is in for transmission or axle shaft service of any sort. (1992-94)

• **Steering noise** The upper bearing mount in the steering column can get loose and cause a snapping or clicking that can be both heard and felt, requiring a new bearing spring and turn signal cancel cam that the manufacturer will warranty. (1994-96)

• **Transmission slippage** The 4T60E transmission may drop out of drive (neutral condition) while cruising, shift erratically, have no third or fourth gear, or no second and third gear because of a bad ground connection for the shift solenoids. Poor grounds also allow wrong gear starts. Many transmissions have been mistakenly rebuilt, which does not correct the problem. (1994)

• **Transmission slippage** Any car with a model TH-125 or 440-T4 automatic transmission may shift late or not upshift at all. The problem is a stuck throttle valve inside the transmission. It may be overlooked during rebuilding since the valve appears fine because it is hydraulic pressure, not a physical binding, that makes it stick. The problem is fixed by enlarging the hydraulic fluid balance hole by 0.010 inch. (1990-94)

RECALL HISTORY

1990 with Kelsey-Hayes steel wheels Cracks may develop in wheel mounting surface; if severe, wheel could separate from car. **1990-91 with six-way power seats or power recliner** Short circuit could set seats on fire. **1990-96** Rear outboard seatbelt anchorages may not withstand required load; in collision, metal may tear and allow anchor to separate from body. **1992 wagon** Remote entry module may have a fault that causes actuation of interior lamps, door locks, and/or release of tailgate. **1993** Right front brake hose on some cars is improperly manufactured. **1994 with 3.1-liter V-6** If primary accelerator control spring fails, backup spring will not return throttle to closed position. **1994** Improperly-tightened spindle nut can cause premature wheel bearing failure. **1994** Water can cause short circuit in power-lock assembly.

1990-97 OLDSMOBILE CUTLASS SUPREME

1994 Oldsmobile Cutlass Supreme SL 2-door

FOR Air bags, dual (later models) • Passenger and cargo room

AGAINST Rear-seat room • Engine noise (4-cylinder)

EVALUATION Many of the early Quad 4 engines—while eager—produced little power at low speeds. But when revved for optimum power, they became much noisier than either the 3.1-liter or 3.4-liter V-6. The 24-valve V-6 runs smoothly and quietly,

OLDSMOBILE

revving quickly to higher speeds—even with the automatic. And the 3.1-liter V-6 was gradually improved, with power rising from 135 horsepower in 1990 to 160 in 1994.

Cutlass Supreme has a firm sports-oriented base suspension. While it provides good handling and stability, its firmness generates noticeable harshness over rough roads. The FE3 suspension in the International Series models (1990-1994) is even stiffer. Braking with standard 4-wheel disc and anti-lock brakes is good. Improvement in build quality means that road noise and harshness are under control, and the car offers fairly good ride comfort.

Interior leg and head room are adequate, but the rear seat cushions are too low and soft on long-distance comfort. There's also a roomy trunk and a handy cargo net on later models. The dual air bag instrument panel on 1995 models is a big improvement, putting the Supreme on par with its competition.

Despite all the changes, the Cutlass Supreme has never quite been able to catch up with the competition, even within GM.

SPECIFICATIONS	2-door coupe	4-door sedan	2-door conv.
Wheelbase, in.	107.5	107.5	107.5
Overall length, in.	193.9	193.7	193.9
Overall width, in.	71.0	71.0	71.0
Overall height, in.	53.3	54.8	54.3
Curb weight, lbs.	3307	3405	3651
Cargo volume, cu. ft.	15.5	15.5	12.1
Fuel capacity, gals.	16.5	16.5	16.5
Seating capacity	6	6	5
Front head room, in.	37.8	38.5	38.7
Max. front leg room, in.	42.3	42.4	42.3
Rear head room, in.	37.0	38.3	38.9
Min. rear leg room, in.	35.8	36.2	34.8

Powertrain layout: transverse front-engine/front-wheel drive

ENGINES

	dohc I-4	dohc I-4	ohv V-6	dohc V-6
Size, liters/cu. in.	2.3/138	2.3/138	3.1/191	3.4/207
Horsepower	160	180	135-160	210-215
Torque (lbs./ft.)	155	160	180-185	215-220
EPA city/highway mpg				
5-speed OD manual		22/31		
3-speed automatic	22/29		19/27	
4-speed OD automatic			19/29	17/26
Consumer Guide™ observed MPG				
3-speed automatic	22.3			

	dohc I-4	dohc I-4	ohv V-6	dohc V-6
4-speed OD automatic.....			20.6	

Built in USA.

RETAIL PRICES

RETAIL PRICES	GOOD	AVERAGE	POOR
1990 Cutlass Supreme	$2,900-3,800	$2,200-3,100	$1,100-1,800
1990 Convertible	4,800-5,800	4,000-4,900	2,000-2,600
1991 Cutlass Supreme	3,600-4,400	2,900-3,700	1,600-2,300
1991 Convertible	6,000-7,200	5,200-6,200	3,000-3,800
1992 Cutlass Supreme	4,400-6,000	3,600-5,200	2,200-3,100
1992 Convertible	7,500-8,800	6,600-7,800	4,000-4,800
1993 Cutlass Supreme	5,400-7,600	4,600-6,700	2,900-4,500
1993 Convertible	9,000-10,500	8,000-9,500	5,000-6,000
1994 Cutlass Supreme	6,700-7,800	5,900-6,900	3,900-4,700
1994 Convertible	10,500-12,000	9,500-11,000	6,000-7,200
1995 Cutlass Supreme	8,200-9,500	7,300-8,500	5,000-5,900
1995 Convertible	12,500-14,000	11,300-12,500	7,500-8,500
1996 Cutlass Supreme	9,500-10,800	8,500-9,800	6,000-7,000
1997 Cutlass Supreme	11,000-12,500	9,800-11,200	7,000-8,000

AVERAGE REPLACEMENT COSTS

A/C Compressor $555	Constant Velocity Joints.....470
Alternator 215	Brakes..................................200
Radiator 340	Shocks and/or Struts 1,855
Timing Chain or Belt 170	Exhaust System..................470
Automatic Transmission or Transaxle.....................1,070	

TROUBLE SPOTS

• **Cold starting problems** A tick or rattle when the engine is started cold may be due to too much wrist-pin-to-piston clearance. New piston and pin sets will be replaced under warranty if the customer complains of the noise. (1993-95)

• **Engine noise** What sounds like a rattling noise from the engine that lasts less than a minute when the car is started after sitting overnight is often caused by automatic transmission pump starvation or cavitation, or a sticking pressure regulator valve. According to GM, no damage occurs and it does not have a fix for the problem. (1991-95)

• **Transaxle leak** The right front axle seal at the automatic transaxle is prone to leak and GM issued a revised seal to correct the problem and it is supposed to be installed whenever a car is in for transmission or axle shaft service of any sort. (1992-94)

OLDSMOBILE

• **Valve cover leaks** The plastic valve covers on the 3.1L engine were prone to leaks and should be replaced with redesigned aluminum covers. (GM no longer stocks the plastic ones.) (1993-95)

• **Steering noise** The upper bearing mount in the steering column can get loose and cause a snapping or clicking that can be both heard and felt, requiring a new bearing spring and turn signal cancel cam that the manufacturer will warranty. (1994-96)

• **Transmission slippage** The 4T60E transmission may drop out of drive (neutral condition) while cruising, shift erratically, have no third or fourth gear, or no second and third gear because of a bad ground connection for the shift solenoids. Poor grounds also allow wrong gear starts. Many transmissions have been mistakenly rebuilt, which does not correct the problem. (1991-94)

• **Transmission slippage** Any car with a model TH-125 or 440-T4 automatic transmission may shift late or not upshift at all. The problem is a stuck throttle valve inside the transmission. It may be overlooked during rebuilding since the valve appears fine because it is hydraulic pressure, not a physical binding, that makes it stick. The problem is fixed by enlarging the hydraulic fluid balance hole by 0.010 inch. (1990-94)

RECALL HISTORY

1990 Front shoulder belt guide loop fastener may pull through door-mounted anchor plate. **1990** Brake lights may not illuminate. **1990** Front shoulder belt webbing may separate at upper guide loops. **1990-91** Steering shaft could separate. **1991-92** Front safety belts may not meet standard. **1992** Reverse servo pin of automatic transmission may bind. **1993** Manual recliner mechanisms on some front seats will not latch under certain conditions, causing seatback to recline without prior warning. **1993-94** Brake lines can contact transmission bracket and wear through. **1994-95** Wiper/washer may not operate. **1995** Seatbelt anchor can fracture during crash.

1992-98 OLDSMOBILE EIGHT EIGHT

FOR Air bags, dual (later models) • Anti-lock brakes (optional) • Acceleration • Automatic transmission performance • Passenger and cargo room

AGAINST Steering feel • Fuel economy

EVALUATION The Eighty Eight's base engine has ample energy for strong takeoffs and sufficient power for safe passing.

1994 Oldsmobile Eighty Eight Royale

Expect to realize 0-60 times around 9.0 seconds, which is very quick for a full-size family car. Fuel economy in our tests has been about 17 to 21 mpg. The optional supercharged engine available on the LSS has even stronger acceleration, but is just as refined. Fuel economy is slightly lower, and premium unleaded is required.

We feel the power steering on the base and LS models is too light and fails to provide adequate feedback. Also, the standard softly-sprung suspension allows too much body roll, causing the Eighty Eight to lean excessively in turns. The LSS provides improved steering and a firmer, more controlled ride.

The 6-passenger Eighty Eight provides easy entry/exit to all seats and ample cargo space. The dashboard is modern, with simple and logical controls for the stereo and climate control, making for more convenient operation of vehicle systems and amenities.

So if you are searching for a big sedan, capable of holding lots of people and cargo, put the Eighty Eight at the top of your shopping list.

SPECIFICATIONS

	4-door sedan
Wheelbase, in.	110.8
Overall length, in.	201.6
Overall width, in.	74.7
Overall height, in.	55.7
Curb weight, lbs.	3455
Cargo volume, cu. ft.	17.5
Fuel capacity, gals.	18.0
Seating capacity	6
Front head room, in.	38.7
Max. front leg room, in.	42.5
Rear head room, in.	38.3

OLDSMOBILE

	4-door sedan
Min. rear leg room, in.	38.7

Powertrain layout: transverse front-engine/front-wheel drive

ENGINES

	ohv V-6	ohv V-6	Supercharged ohv V-6
Size, liters/cu. in.	3.8/231	3.8/231	3.8/231
Horsepower	170	205	225-240
Torque (lbs./ft.)	200-225	230	275-280

EPA city/highway mpg

4-speed OD automatic	18/28	19/29	17/27

Consumer Guide™ observed MPG

4-speed OD automatic	21.7	17.2	

Built in USA.

RETAIL PRICES

	GOOD	AVERAGE	POOR
1992 Eighty Eight	$5,000-6,300	$4,300-5,500	$2,500-3,400
1993 Eighty Eight	6,100-7,500	5,300-6,700	3,300-4,500
1994 Eighty Eight	7,500-9,500	6,700-8,700	4,500-6,200
1995 Eighty Eight	9,300-11,500	8,400-10,500	5,900-7,500
1996 Eighty Eight	11,500-13,200	10,500-12,200	7,500-8,700
1996 LSS	13,500-14,500	12,200-13,200	9,000-10,000
1997 Eighty Eight	13,500-15,500	12,000-14,000	9,000-10,000
1997 LSS	16,000-17,500	14,500-16,000	11,000-12,000
1998 Eighty Eight	16,000-18,500	14,500-17,000	11,000-12,500
1998 LSS	18,500-20,500	17,000-19,000	13,000-14,000

AVERAGE REPLACEMENT COSTS

A/C Compressor $500	Universal Joints 505
Alternator 280	Brakes...................................230
Radiator 360	Shocks and/or Struts 840
Timing Chain or Belt 260	Exhaust System..................515
Automatic Transmission or Transaxle.........................970	

TROUBLE SPOTS

• **Engine knock and oil leak** Models with the 3800 (3.8L) engine are prone to excessive oil consumption often accompanied by spark knock (pinging) during normal driving conditions due to failure of the valve stem seals. (1993-95)

• **Engine noise** Bearing knock was common on many 3300 and 3800 (3.3L and 3.8L) engines due to too much clearance on the number-one main bearing requiring it to be replaced with a 0.001-inch undersize bearing. (1992-94)

• **Transaxle leak** The right front axle seal at the automatic transaxle is prone to leak and GM issued a revised seal to correct the problem and it is supposed to be installed whenever a car is in for transmission or axle shaft service of any sort. (1992-94)

• **Engine noise** What sounds like a rattling noise from the engine that lasts less than a minute when the car is started after sitting overnight is often caused by automatic transmission pump starvation or cavitation, or a sticking pressure regulator valve. According to GM, no damage occurs and it does not have a fix for the problem. (1992-95)

• **Transmission slippage** If the cruise control doesn't stay engaged, or drops out of cruise, the brake switch can usually be adjusted, but if it cannot, it will be replaced under normal warranty. (1992-95)

• **Steering noise** The upper bearing mount in the steering column can get loose and cause a snapping or clicking that can be both heard and felt, requiring a new bearing spring and turn signal cancel cam that the manufacturer will warranty. (1994-96)

• **Transmission slippage** The 4T60E transmission may drop out of drive (neutral condition) while cruising, shift erratically, have no third or fourth gear, or no second and third gear because of a bad ground connection for the shift solenoids. Poor grounds also allow wrong gear starts. Many transmissions have been mistakenly rebuilt, which does not correct the problem. (1992-94)

• **Transmission slippage** Any car with a model TH-440-T4 automatic transmission may shift late or not upshift at all. The problem is a stuck throttle valve inside the transmission. It may be overlooked during rebuilding since the valve appears fine because it is hydraulic pressure, not a physical binding, that makes it stick. The problem is fixed by enlarging the hydraulic fluid balance hole by 0.010 inch. (1991)

RECALL HISTORY

1992-93 Transmission cooler line in cars with certain powertrains, sold in specified states, can separate at low temperature. **1994-95** On some cars, spring in headlight switch can fail and lights would not remain illuminated. **1996** Damaged capacitor may cause failure of "Key in the Ignition" warning chime and driver seatbelt unbuckled warning chime and indicator lamp; other functions also may be impaired. **1996 with 3.8-liter V-6** Backfire during engine starting can cause breakage of upper intake manifold, resulting in non-start condition and possible fire.

1991-97 OLDSMOBILE NINETY EIGHT

1991 Oldsmobile Ninety Eight

FOR Acceleration • Passenger and cargo room • Anti-lock brakes (optional) • Air bags, dual (later models) • Automatic transmission performance

AGAINST Fuel economy • Visibility

EVALUATION For those who still appreciate Oldsmobile's former conservative approach, the Ninety Eight provides everything you can ask for including dual air bags (after 1994), standard anti-lock brakes, acres of passenger room and excellent acceleration from GM's 3.8-liter V-6, whether you choose the normally aspirated or supercharged versions. The engines deliver brisk acceleration off the line and the automatic transmission downshifts quickly to make ample passing power available. Expect 16-18 mpg in urban driving, about 25 on the highway.

Head room and leg room are generous for all seating positions in the Ninety Eight, which has room for six adults, if everyone is willing to squeeze a little. Trunk space (over 20 cubic feet) is generous as well, with the flat, wide floor capable of holding several suitcases. The instrument panel has large, well-marked controls and gauges that are easy to read and convenient to use. While it's easy to see all four corners of the car for parking, thick rear pillars block the driver's over-the-shoulder view.

The Ninety Eight's conservative styling has clearly begun to limit its appeal, but it's a less-expensive alternative to V-8 luxury sedans such as the Cadillac Fleetwood and Lincoln Town Car.

SPECIFICATIONS

	4-door sedan
Wheelbase, in.	110.8

	4-door sedan
Overall length, in.	205.7
Overall width, in.	74.6
Overall height, in.	54.8
Curb weight, lbs.	3412
Cargo volume, cu. ft.	20.2
Fuel capacity, gals.	18.0
Seating capacity	6
Front head room, in.	38.7
Max. front leg room, in.	42.5
Rear head room, in.	37.7
Min. rear leg room, in.	40.7

Powertrain layout: transverse front-engine/front-wheel drive

ENGINES

	ohv V-6	ohv V-6	Supercharged ohv V-6	Supercharged ohv V-6
Size, liters/cu. in.	3.8/231	3.8/231	3.8/231	3.8/231
Horsepower	170	205	225	240
Torque (lbs./ft.)	220	230	275	280
EPA city/highway mpg				
4-speed OD automatic	18/27	19/30	17/27	18/27
Consumer Guide™ observed MPG				
4-speed OD automatic	20.6		16.5	

Built in USA.

RETAIL PRICES

	GOOD	AVERAGE	POOR
1991 Ninety Eight	$5,200-6,100	$4,500-5,300	$2,500-3,200
1992 Ninety Eight	6,000-8,000	5,200-7,200	3,000-3,800
1993 Ninety Eight	7,300-9,700	6,400-8,800	3,900-5,900
1994 Ninety Eight	9,500-11,000	8,500-10,000	5,500-6,800
1995 Ninety Eight	12,000-13,500	10,700-12,000	7,300-8,400
1996 Ninety Eight	15,000-16,500	13,500-15,000	9,300-10,500
1997 Regency	17,000-20,000	15,500-18,500	11,000-13,500
1998 Regency	20,000-23,000	18,200-21,000	13,500-15,500

AVERAGE REPLACEMENT COSTS

A/C Compressor	$500
Alternator	280
Radiator	360
Timing Chain or Belt	260
Automatic Transmission or Transaxle	970
Constant Velocity Joints	725
Brakes	230
Shocks and/or Struts	1,355
Exhaust System	530

TROUBLE SPOTS

- **Engine knock and oil leak** Models with the 3800 (3.8L) engine are prone to excessive oil consumption often accompanied by spark knock (pinging) during normal driving conditions due to failure of the valve stem seals. (1993-95)

- **Engine noise** Bearing knock was common on many 3300 and 3800 (3.3L and 3.8L) engines due to too much clearance on the number-one main bearing, requiring it to be replaced with a 0.001-inch undersize bearing. (1992-94)

- **Engine noise** What sounds like a rattling noise from the engine that lasts less than a minute when the car is started after sitting overnight is often caused by automatic transmission pump starvation or cavitation, or a sticking pressure regulator valve. According to GM, no damage occurs and it does not have a fix for the problem. (1991-95)

- **Transaxle leak** The right front axle seal at the automatic transaxle is prone to leak and GM issued a revised seal to correct the problem and it is supposed to be installed whenever a car is in for transmission or axle shaft service of any sort. (1992-94)

- **Cruise control** If the cruise control doesn't stay engaged, or drops out of cruise, the brake switch can usually be adjusted, but if it cannot, it will be replaced under normal warranty. (1991-95)

- **Steering noise** The upper bearing mount in the steering column can get loose and cause a snapping or clicking that can be both heard and felt, requiring a new bearing spring and turn signal cancel cam that the manufacturer will warranty. (1994-96)

- **Transmission slippage** The 4T60E transmission may drop out of drive (neutral condition) while cruising, shift erratically, have no third or fourth gear, or no second and third gear because of a bad ground connection for the shift solenoids. Poor grounds also allow wrong gear starts. Many transmissions have been mistakenly rebuilt, which does not correct the problem. (1991-94)

RECALL HISTORY

1991 Parking brake lever assembly may release when applied; parking brake may then not hold the vehicle. **1991** Console-mounted shift lever may disengage, causing loss of gearshift operation. **1992-93** Transmission cooler line in cars with certain powertrains, sold in specified states, can separate at low temperature. **1994-95** Headlight switch spring can fail and prevent latching of headlamp in "On" position. **1995 with Twilight Sentinel** Current leakage can cause loss of headlights and parking lights; or, lights may turn on while car is parked. **1996** Damaged capacitor may cause failure of "Key in the Ignition" warning chime and driver seatbelt unbuckled warning chime and indicator lamp; other functions also may be impaired. **1996 with 3.8-liter V-6** Backfire during engine starting can cause breakage of upper intake manifold, resulting in non-start condition and possible fire.

1990-96 OLDSMOBILE SILHOUETTE

1991 Oldsmobile Silhouette

FOR Air bag, driver (later models) • Anti-lock brakes (optional) • Passenger and cargo room • Acceleration (3.8-liter V-6)

AGAINST Visibility

See the 1990-96 Chevrolet Lumina/APV report for an evaluation of the 1990-96 Oldsmobile Silhouette.

SPECIFICATIONS

	3-door van
Wheelbase, in.	109.8
Overall length, in.	194.7
Overall width, in.	73.9
Overall height, in.	65.7
Curb weight, lbs.	3704
Cargo volume, cu. ft.	112.6
Fuel capacity, gals.	20.0
Seating capacity	7
Front head room, in.	39.2
Max. front leg room, in.	40.0
Rear head room, in.	39.0
Min. rear leg room, in.	36.1

Powertrain layout: transverse front-engine/front-wheel drive

ENGINES

	ohv V-6	ohv V-6	ohv V-6
Size, liters/cu. in.	3.1/191	3.4/207	3.8/231

OLDSMOBILE

	ohv V-6	ohv V-6	ohv V-6
Horsepower	120	180	165-170
Torque (lbs./ft.)	175	205	200-225
EPA city/highway mpg			
3-speed automatic	19/23		17/24
4-speed OD automatic		19/26	17/25
Consumer Guide™ observed MPG			
4-speed OD automatic		18.5	17.2

Built in USA.

RETAIL PRICES

	GOOD	AVERAGE	POOR
1990 Silhouette	$3,700-4,500	$3,000-3,800	$1,300-1,900
1991 Silhouette	4,300-5,200	3,600-4,400	1,600-2,300
1992 Silhouette	5,100-6,400	4,400-5,600	2,100-3,200
1993 Silhouette	6,400-7,500	5,600-6,600	3,200-4,000
1994 Silhouette	8,000-9,500	7,100-8,500	4,500-5,500
1995 Silhouette	10,000-11,500	8,900-10,300	5,900-7,000
1996 Silhouette	12,200-14,000	11,000-12,500	7,800-9,000

AVERAGE REPLACEMENT COSTS

A/C Compressor	$510	Constant Velocity Joints	505
Alternator	240	Brakes	230
Radiator	430	Shocks and/or Struts	430
Timing Chain or Belt	250	Exhaust System	415
Automatic Transmission or Transaxle	980		

TROUBLE SPOTS

• **Engine knock and oil leak** Models with the 3800 (3.8L) engine are prone to excessive oil consumption often accompanied by spark knock (pinging) during normal driving conditions due to failure of the valve stem seals. (1993-95)

• **Engine noise** Bearing knock was common on many 3300 and 3800 (3.3L and 3.8L) engines due to too much clearance on the number-one main bearing, requiring it to be replaced with a 0.001-inch undersize bearing. (1992-94)

• **Steering noise** The upper bearing mount in the steering column can get loose and cause a snapping or clicking that can be both heard and felt, requiring a new bearing spring and turn signal cancel cam that the manufacturer will warranty. (1994-96)

• **Transaxle leak** The right front axle seal at the automatic transaxle is prone to leak and GM issued a revised seal to correct the problem and it is supposed to be installed whenever a car is in for transmission or axle shaft service of any sort. (1992-94)

• **Engine noise** What sounds like a rattling noise from the engine that lasts less than a minute when the car is started after sitting overnight is often caused by automatic transmission pump starvation or cavitation, or a sticking pressure regulator valve. According to GM, no damage occurs and it does not have a fix for the problem. (1992-95)

• **Transmission slippage** The 4T60E transmission may drop out of drive (neutral condition) while cruising, shift erratically, have no third or fourth gear, or no second and third gear because of a bad ground connection for the shift solenoids. Poor grounds also allow wrong gear starts. Many transmissions have been mistakenly rebuilt, which does not correct the problem. (1992-94)

• **Transmission slippage** Any van with a model TH-125 automatic transmission may shift late or not upshift at all. The problem is a stuck throttle valve inside the transmission. It may be overlooked during rebuilding since the valve appears fine because it is hydraulic pressure, not a physical binding, that makes it stick. The problem is fixed by enlarging the hydraulic fluid balance hole by 0.010 inch. (1990-94)

RECALL HISTORY

1990 Rear modular seat frame hold-down hooks on some vans may not meet required pull force. **1990** Right seat/shoulder belt retractor may have been installed in second-row left seat position. **1990-91** Due to corrosion, shaft could separate from steering gear, resulting in crash. **1992-95** Transmission cooler line in cars with certain powertrains, sold in specified states, can separate at low temperature. **1993-94 with optional power sliding door** Second-row, right-hand shoulder belt can become pinched between seat and door frame pillar trim. **1994** Pawl spring may be missing from retractors for rear center lap belt. **1994** Third-row seatbelt retractors may lock up when van is on a slope. **1995** Brake pedal arm can fracture during braking, resulting in loss of brake operation.

1990-95 PLYMOUTH ACCLAIM ✓

FOR Acceleration (V-6) • Anti-lock brakes (optional) • Air bag, driver (later models)

AGAINST Passenger and cargo room

See the 1990-95 Dodge Spirit report for an evaluation of the 1990-95 Plymouth Acclaim.

PLYMOUTH

1990 Plymouth Acclaim

NHTSA CRASH TEST RESULTS
1995 Plymouth Acclaim

4-DOOR SEDAN

Driver ☆☆☆☆

Passenger ☆☆☆

(The National Highway Traffic Safety Administration tests a vehicle's crashworthiness in front and side collisions. Their ratings suggest the chance of serious injury: ☆☆☆☆☆—10% or less; ☆☆☆☆—10-20% or less; ☆☆☆—20-30% or less; ☆☆—35-45% or less; ☆—More than 45%.)

SPECIFICATIONS

	4-door sedan
Wheelbase, in.	103.5
Overall length, in.	181.2
Overall width, in.	68.1
Overall height, in.	55.5
Curb weight, lbs.	2784
Cargo volume, cu. ft.	14.4
Fuel capacity, gals.	16.0
Seating capacity	6
Front head room, in.	38.4
Max. front leg room, in.	41.9
Rear head room, in.	37.9
Min. rear leg room, in.	38.3

Powertrain layout: transverse front-engine/front-wheel drive

ENGINES

	ohc I-4	Turbocharged ohc I-4	ohc V-6
Size, liters/cu. in.	2.5/153	2.5/153	3.0/181
Horsepower	100	150	141-142
Torque (lbs./ft.)	135	180	171
EPA city/highway mpg			
5-speed OD manual	25/32	21/29	
3-speed automatic	23/27	19/23	20/27

| | Turbocharged | | |
	ohc I-4	ohc I-4	ohc V-6
4-speed automatic............................			21/29
Consumer Guide™ observed MPG			
5-speed OD manual	25.3		
3-speed automatic...........................	22.9		
4-speed automatic............................			23.7

Built in USA.

RETAIL PRICES	GOOD	AVERAGE	POOR
1990 Acclaim	$1,600-2,400	$1,000-1,800	$300-700
1991 Acclaim	2,000-2,900	1,400-2,300	600-1,000
1992 Acclaim	2,700-3,400	2,100-2,700	1,000-1,300
1993 Acclaim	3,400-4,200	2,700-3,500	1,300-1,700
1994 Acclaim	4,400-5,300	3,700-4,600	1,800-2,400
1995 Acclaim	5,300-6,100	4,600-5,300	2,400-2,800

AVERAGE REPLACEMENT COSTS

A/C Compressor $415	Constant Velocity Joints.....660
Alternator 315	Brakes..................................250
Radiator 335	Shocks and/or Struts 340
Timing Chain or Belt 290	Exhaust System 320
Automatic Transmission or Transaxle........................905	

TROUBLE SPOTS

• **Oil consumption and exhaust smoke** High oil consumption and smoke from the exhaust at idle and deceleration on 3.0L V-6 engines (Mitsubishi built) is caused by exhaust valve guides that slide out of the heads. If the guides are not too loose, they can be retained with snap rings. Otherwise, the heads have to be replaced. The repair will be handled under normal warranty coverage. (1990-93)

• **Alternator belt** Unless a shield is installed under the engine on the right side, deep snow could knock the serpentine belt off the pulleys of a 3.0L engine. Usually the first sign that this has happened is a low voltmeter reading or the battery light coming on. (1991-95)

• **Engine mounts** The motor mount on the left side of the engine tends to break, which causes a snap or click when accelerating. (1992-93)

• **Rough idle** A 2.2L or 2.5L engine may idle rough or stumble when first started below freezing temperatures unless a revised intake manifold (with an "X" cast into the number 1 runner) was installed (1992) or a revised computer (PCM) was installed (1992-93) or the computer was reprogrammed (1994).

• **Air conditioner** If the air conditioner gradually stops cooling and/or the airflow from the vents decreases, the computer (PCM) may not be sending a signal to the compressor clutch relay to cycle off, which causes the AC evaporator to freeze up. When the ice melts, after the car sits for awhile, the AC works again briefly. Many technicians overlook this as the source of trouble. (1991-95)

• **Transmission slippage** If the transmission shudders under light to moderate acceleration, the transmission front pump could be leaking due to a worn bushing, which requires replacement of the pump as well as the torque converter under the powertrain warranty. (1990-95)

• **Transaxle leak** Vehicles with 41TE or 42LE automatic transaxle could take several seconds to engage at startup because of a problem with the valve body. The company will replace defective ones, and replace the filter and fluid under normal warranty. (1993-95)

• **Transmission slippage** Bad seals in the transmission lead to premature friction component wear, which causes shudder when starting from a stop, a bump when coasting to a stop, and slipping between gears. Chrysler will warranty the seals, clutches, and, if necessary, the torque converter. (1993-95)

RECALL HISTORY

1990 Oil may leak from engine valve cover gasket. **1991** Front outboard seatbelt may become difficult to latch; latch may open in sudden stop or accident. **1991** Front disc brake caliper guide pin bolts may not be adequately tightened and could loosen. **1991** Both air bag system front impact sensors may not be secured to mounting brackets, so air bag would not deploy. **1992** Zinc plating of some upper steering column shaft coupling bolts caused hydrogen embrittlement and breakage of the bolt. **1994** Seatbelt assembly on small number of cars may fail in accident, increasing risk of injury.

1990-94 PLYMOUTH LASER ✓ BEST BUY

FOR Acceleration (RS and RS Turbo) • Handling/roadholding • Optional anti-lock brakes • All-wheel drive (AWD model)

AGAINST Rear seat room • Engine and road noise • Cargo room • Visibility • Acceleration (1.8-liter automatic)

See the 1990-94 Mitsubishi Eclipse report for an evaluation of the 1990-94 Plymouth Laser.

SPECIFICATIONS

	2-door hatchback
Wheelbase, in.	97.2

1991 Plymouth Laser RS

	2-door hatchback
Overall length, in.	172.8
Overall width, in.	66.7
Overall height, in.	51.4
Curb weight, lbs.	2531
Cargo volume, cu. ft.	10.2
Fuel capacity, gals.	15.8
Seating capacity	4
Front head room, in.	37.9
Max. front leg room, in.	43.9
Rear head room, in.	34.1
Min. rear leg room, in.	28.5

Powertrain layout: transverse front-engine/front- or all-wheel drive

ENGINES	ohc I-4	dohc I-4	Turbocharged dohc I-4
Size, liters/cu. in.	1.8/107	2.0/122	2.0/122
Horsepower	92	135	180-195
Torque (lbs./ft.)	105	125	203
EPA city/highway mpg			
5-speed OD manual	23/32	22/27	21/28
4-speed OD automatic	23/30	22/29	19/23
Consumer Guide™ observed MPG			
5-speed OD manual		22.6	18.4
4-speed OD automatic		26.4	

Built in USA.

RETAIL PRICES	GOOD	AVERAGE	POOR
1990 Laser	$2,200-2,800	$1,600-2,200	$600-900
1990 RS Turbo	2,500-3,100	1,900-2,500	800-1,100
1991 Laser	2,600-3,300	2,000-2,600	800-1,100
1991 RS Turbo	3,300-4,000	2,600-3,300	1,000-1,500

PLYMOUTH

	GOOD	AVERAGE	POOR
1992 Laser	3,200-4,000	2,500-3,300	1,000-1,500
1992 RS Turbo	4,100-4,900	3,400-4,100	1,600-2,100
1993 Laser	4,000-4,800	3,300-4,100	1,700-2,100
1993 RS Turbo	4,300-6,500	4,500-5,700	2,300-2,900
1994 Laser	5,100-6,300	4,300-5,300	2,300-3,000
1994 RS Turbo	6,800-8,000	6,000-7,200	3,500-4,200

AVERAGE REPLACEMENT COSTS

A/C Compressor $635	Clutch, Pressure Plate,
Alternator 695	Bearing 480
Radiator 395	Constant Velocity Joints..1,040
Timing Chain or Belt	Brakes 240
Automatic Transmission or	Shocks and/or Struts 480
Transaxle 885	Exhaust System 680

TROUBLE SPOTS

• **Vehicle shake** If the car shakes and vibrates as though the wheels are out of balance, but they check out OK, replacement of the engine and transmission mounts are required. (1990-94)

• **Hard starting** Technicians reportedly have trouble tracking down is the cause of hard or no starting, and possibly no fan on cars built before May, 1995. It may be caused by corrosion of a splice in the wiring harness near the left headlight caused by water getting into the wiring. (1990-94)

• **Brake noise** The rear disc brakes are prone to squealing or squeaking and a shim kit has been released to quiet them down. (1992-94)

RECALL HISTORY

1990 Operation of factory-installed sunroof in "non-standard" manner may cause hinge disengagement. **1990** Diluted primer may have been used on windshield opening flanges of a few cars, which would not provide required retention of glass. **1990** Headlamp wiring harness on some early models may break due to stress created by their pop-up devices. **1990-91** Front seatbelt release button can break and pieces can fall inside.

1995-98 PLYMOUTH NEON

FOR Air bags, dual • Optional anti-lock brakes • Ride • Passenger and cargo room • Fuel economy

AGAINST Noise • Automatic transmission performance

1995 Plymouth Neon coupe

See the 1995-98 Dodge Neon report for an evaluation of the 1995-98 Plymouth Neon.

NHTSA CRASH TEST RESULTS
1996 Plymouth Neon   4-DOOR SEDAN

Driver	☆☆☆☆
Passenger	☆☆☆☆

(The National Highway Traffic Safety Administration tests a vehicle's crashworthiness in front and side collisions. Their ratings suggest the chance of serious injury: ☆☆☆☆☆—10% or less; ☆☆☆☆—10-20% or less; ☆☆☆—20-30% or less; ☆☆—35-45% or less; ☆—More than 45%.)

SPECIFICATIONS

	2-door coupe	4-door sedan
Wheelbase, in.	104.0	104.0
Overall length, in.	171.8	171.8
Overall width, in.	67.5	67.5
Overall height, in.	52.8	54.8
Curb weight, lbs.	2384	2416
Cargo volume, cu. ft.	11.8	11.8
Fuel capacity, gals.	11.2	11.2
Seating capacity	5	5
Front head room, in.	39.6	39.6
Max. front leg room, in.	42.5	42.5
Rear head room, in.	36.5	36.5
Min. rear leg room, in.	35.1	35.1

Powertrain layout: transverse front-engine/front-wheel drive

ENGINES

	ohc I-4	dohc I-4
Size, liters/cu. in.	2.0/122	2.0/122
Horsepower	132	150
Torque (lbs./ft.)	129	131

PLYMOUTH

EPA city/highway mpg

5-speed OD manual..	28/38	28/38
3-speed automatic	25/33	25/33

Consumer Guide™ observed MPG

5-speed OD manual..	31.4	26.1

Built in USA and Mexico.

RETAIL PRICES	GOOD	AVERAGE	POOR
1995 Neon	$4,900-6,100	$4,300-5,400	$2,500-3,400
1996 Neon	6,000-7,500	5,300-6,700	3,300-4,400
1997 Neon	7,200-8,500	6,400-7,600	4,300-5,200
1998 Neon	8,700-10,500	8,000-9,500	5,800-7,000

AVERAGE REPLACEMENT COSTS

A/C Compressor $400	Clutch, Pressure Plate,	
Alternator 300	Bearing 535	
Radiator 375	Constant Velocity Joints.....345	
Timing Chain or Belt 190	Brakes.................................295	
Automatic Transmission or	Shocks and/or Struts 450	
Transaxle........................555	Exhaust System.................290	

TROUBLE SPOTS

• **Air conditioner** The A/C evaporator freezes up because the compressor does not cycle off causing a lack of cooling. (1995)

• **Dashboard lights** If the ABS (anti-lock brakes) warning light comes on the ABS may be disables. The ABS controller will be replaced under normal warranty provisions. (1995)

• **Blower motor** In cold weather, ice may form in the blower motor housing, which prevents the blower from moving, which blows the fuse. Under warranty, the drain tube will be rerouted, the blower motor replaced, and a new fuse installed. (1995-97)

• **Brakes** The front brakes wear abnormally fast (and make noise) on cars with four wheel studs, so heavy duty linings should be used to replace them. (1995-97)

• **Battery** Batteries that go dead may be the result of one or more of the following: a glovebox without a raised pad that closes the light switch, misaligned doors, a faulty trunk lid switch and lamp assembly, or a missing door ajar bumper pad. (1995)

RECALL HISTORY

1995 Corrosion at fuel and rear-brake tubes may lead to brake fluid or fuel leakage. **1995** Steering column coupler can become disconnected when vehicle sustains underbody impact. **1995-96 including**

"ACR competition" package Brake master cylinder can leak. **1996** Wiring harness in Mexican-built car could short-circuit; can cause various malfunctions, including stalling. **1997** Air bag could deploy inadvertently when ignition is shut off.

1991-95 PLYMOUTH VOYAGER

✓ **BEST BUY**

1991 Plymouth Voyager

FOR Passenger and cargo room • Ride • Wet-weather traction (AWD) • Air bags, dual (later models) • Anti-lock brakes (later models)

AGAINST Acceleration (4-cylinder) • Fuel economy • Road noise • Wind noise

EVALUATION The primary focus of their redesign was the interior, which shows marked improvements in important areas. First of all, key controls were moved so they no longer are blocked by the steering wheel. Headlamps and wiper/washer switches are now on two pods flanking the steering wheel. Among a variety of thoughtful touches, climate and radio controls were moved closer to the driver, a new center console now features pull-out cupholders, and a locking glovebox has been added to the passenger side. Visibility is better all around, but especially at the rear where the window dips further into the liftgate.

A recalibrated suspension shows up in reduced body roll in turns, making Voyager's road manners even more carlike. The Voyager steers precisely and has exceptional stability. On the road, Voyager is remarkably well mannered for a minivan. Any of the 6-cylinder engines are preferable to the anemic 100-horsepower 4-cylinder. Power from the trio of V-6s range from adequate with the 3.0-liter to impressive with the 3.8-liter. The 3.3-

liter seems particularly smooth and responsive.

With all the revisions, Chrysler has reasserted its minivan leadership against a growing number of serious competitors. They remain the best-in-class minivans because they are carlike to drive and offer a range of models and features that no rival yet matches.

RATINGS

1994 Plymouth Voyager LX 3.3-liter V-6

Performance	3	Room	5
Economy	2	Cargo Capacity	4
Ride	3	Insurance Costs	5
Noise	3	**Total**	**25**

NHTSA CRASH TEST RESULTS
1995 Plymouth Voyager

3-DOOR VAN

Driver	☆☆☆☆
Passenger	☆☆☆☆

(The National Highway Traffic Safety Administration tests a vehicle's crashworthiness in front and side collisions. Their ratings suggest the chance of serious injury: ☆☆☆☆☆—10% or less; ☆☆☆☆—10-20% or less; ☆☆☆—20-30% or less; ☆☆—35-45% or less; ☆—More than 45%.)

SPECIFICATIONS

	3-door van	3-door van
Wheelbase, in.	112.3	119.3
Overall length, in.	178.1	192.8
Overall width, in.	72.0	72.0
Overall height, in.	66.0	66.7
Curb weight, lbs.	3305	3531
Cargo volume, cu. ft.	117.0	141.3
Fuel capacity, gals.	20.0	20.0
Seating capacity	7	7
Front head room, in.	39.1	39.1
Max. front leg room, in.	38.3	38.3
Rear head room, in.	36.6	38.5
Min. rear leg room, in.	37.6	37.7

Powertrain layout: transverse front-engine/front- or all-wheel drive

ENGINES

	ohc I-4	ohc V-6	ohv V-6	ohv V-6
Size, liters/cu. in.	2.5/153	3.0/181	3.3/201	3.8/204
Horsepower	100	142	150	162
Torque (lbs./ft.)	135	173	185	213
EPA city/highway mpg				
5-speed OD manual	20/28			
3-speed automatic	21/25	20/24		
4-speed OD automatic		19/25	18/23	17/23
Consumer Guide™ observed MPG				
3-speed automatic		17.0		

	ohc I-4	ohc V-6	ohv V-6	ohv V-6
4-speed OD automatic.....			18.5	

Built in USA and Canada.

RETAIL PRICES

	GOOD	AVERAGE	POOR
1991 Voyager	$2,700-5,200	$2,100-4,300	$1,000-2,300
1991 Grand Voyager	4,100-6,800	3,400-6,000	1,700-3,800
1992 Voyager	3,500-6,000	2,800-5,300	1,400-3,100
1992 Grand Voyager	4,600-7,700	3,800-6,800	2,100-4,600
1993 Voyager	4,500-7,500	3,700-6,600	2,000-4,300
1993 Grand Voyager	5,800-9,200	5,000-8,300	2,900-5,700
1994 Voyager	5,700-9,500	4,900-8,600	2,800-5,800
1994 Grand Voyager	6,800-10,800	6,000-9,800	3,800-6,800
1995 Voyager	7,000-10,800	6,200-9,800	3,900-6,800
1995 Grand Voyager	8,500-12,900	7,500-11,700	5,000-8,400

AVERAGE REPLACEMENT COSTS

A/C Compressor $455		Constant Velocity Joints.....385
Alternator 310		Brakes.................................275
Radiator 325		Shocks and/or Struts 230
Timing Chain or Belt 265		Exhaust System.................400
Automatic Transmission or		
Transaxle.....................1,040		

TROUBLE SPOTS

• **Oil consumption and exhaust smoke** High oil consumption and smoke from the exhaust at idle and deceleration on 3.0L V-6 engines (Mitsubishi-built) is caused by exhaust valve guides that slide out of the heads. If the guides are not too loose, they can be retained with snap rings. Otherwise, the heads have to be replaced. The repair will be handled under normal warranty coverage. (1990-93)

• **Alternator belt** Unless a shield is installed under the engine on the right side, deep snow could knock the serpentine belt off the pulleys of a 3.0L engine. Usually the first sign that this has happened is a low voltmeter reading or the battery light coming on. (1991-95)

• **Rough idle** A 2.2L or 2.5L engine may idle rough or stumble when first started below freezing temperatures unless a revised intake manifold (with an "X" cast into the number 1 runner) was installed (1992) or a revised computer (PCM) was installed (1992-93) or the computer was reprogrammed. (1994)

• **Engine mounts** The motor mount on the left side of the engine tends to break, which causes a snap or click when accelerating. (1992-93)

• **Transmission slippage** Any minivan with the 3.3L or 3.5L engine

PLYMOUTH

may have late, harsh, or erratic automatic transmission shifts that are not transmission related, but caused by a defective throttle position sensor. (1994)

• **Air conditioner** If the air conditioner gradually stops cooling and/or the airflow from the vents decreases, the computer (PCM) may not be sending a signal to the compressor clutch relay to cycle off, which causes the AC evaporator to freeze up. When the ice melts, after the car sits for awhile, the AC works again briefly. Many technicians overlook this as the source of trouble. (1991-95)

• **Transmission slippage** If the transmission shudders under light to moderate acceleration, the transmission front pump could be leaking due to a worn bushing, which requires replacement of the pump as well as the torque converter under the powertrain warranty. (1990-95)

• **Transaxle leak** Vehicles with 41TE or 42LE automatic transaxle could take several seconds to engage at startup because of a problem with the valve body. The company will replace defective ones, and replace the filter and fluid under normal warranty. (1993-95)

• **Transmission slippage** Bad seals in the transmission lead to premature friction component wear, which causes shudder when starting from a stop, a bump when coasting to a stop and slipping between gears. Chrysler will warranty the seals, clutches, and, if necessary, the torque converter. (1993-95)

RECALL HISTORY

1991 w/ABS High-pressure hose in anti-lock braking system may leak or detach, which increases likelihood of brake lockup. **1991 w/ABS** High-pressure pump of anti-lock braking system may be porous, resulting in increased stopping distances. **1991-92** Steering wheel mounting armature can develop cracks and separate from the center hub attachment to the steering column; can result in loss of vehicle control. **1991-93 w/ABS** Piston seal in control unit can wear excessively; ABS could fail, and power assist might be reduced. **1991-93** Seatbelt release button can stick inside cover, so buckle is only partially latched; also, center rear belt anchor clip can disconnect. **1992** Zinc plating of some upper steering column shaft coupling bolts caused hydrogen embrittlement and breakage. **1992** Brake pedal pad attachment to pedal arm may not have adequate strength. **1992** Fuel tank may drop, or lines may rupture near fuel tank, leading to possible fire. **1992** Brake pedal pad attachment arm on small number of vehicles could break. **1992** Bolts that attach gas strut to rear liftgate can accumulate fatigue damage, if loose; liftgate could fall suddenly. **1993-94** Lug nuts on optional 15-inch stamped steel wheels may have been improperly installed, which could lead to wheel separation.

1996-98 PLYMOUTH VOYAGER

1996 Plymouth Voyager Rallye

FOR Air bags, dual • Anti-lock brakes • Ride • Passenger and cargo room • Acceleration (3.3-liter)

AGAINST Fuel economy • Wind noise

EVALUATION Quieter and even more carlike than before, these minivans handle more like large sedans than vans. Steering is light and precise, and the suspension provides stable cornering with only modest body lean. The suspension easily irons out most smaller rough spots, and the ride is comfortable overall.

Performance with the 3.3-liter engine is quite strong, even in the longer Grand Voyager—provided that it's not loaded down with people and cargo. Even then, passing power is sufficient, making that engine a wise all-around choice for those who carry heavy loads or a full complement of passengers. The 4-cylinder engine is too weak for a vehicle of this weight, though acceleration is adequate with the smallest (3.0-liter) V-6. Fuel economy is about average for a minivan.

Well-designed and roomy inside, Voyager got a new dashboard with larger gauges and revised controls—closer to the driver than before. Occupants ride on supportive chair-height seats, while bigger windows and a lower dashboard improved visibility. Front seat travel also has increased, as has middle-row head room. A wider body also gives extra shoulder and hip space. Entry/exit also is easier, thanks to door sills and are 1.4 inches lower.

Most families are likely to appreciate that extra sliding door, so it's worth looking for a Voyager that has that option. Basically, you can hardly beat a Voyager or its Dodge near-twin in the minivan league.

NHTSA CRASH TEST RESULTS
1997 Plymouth Voyager

4-DOOR WAGON

Driver	☆☆☆☆
Passenger	☆☆☆☆☆

(The National Highway Traffic Safety Administration tests a vehicle's crashworthiness in front and side collisions. Their ratings suggest the chance of serious injury: ☆☆☆☆☆—10% or less; ☆☆☆☆—10-20% or less; ☆☆☆—20-30% or less; ☆☆—35-45% or less; ☆—More than 45%.)

SPECIFICATIONS	3-door van	3-door van
Wheelbase, in.	113.3	119.3
Overall length, in.	186.3	199.6
Overall width, in.	75.6	75.6
Overall height, in.	68.5	68.4
Curb weight, lbs.	3528	3680
Cargo volume, cu. ft.	146.2	172.3
Fuel capacity, gals.	20.0	20.0
Seating capacity	7	7
Front head room, in.	39.8	39.8
Max. front leg room, in.	41.2	41.2
Rear head room, in.	41.0	40.1
Min. rear leg room, in.	42.3	36.6

Powertrain layout: transverse front-engine/front-wheel drive

ENGINES	dohc I-4	ohc V-6	ohv V-6
Size, liters/cu. in.	2.4/148	3.0/181	3.3/201
Horsepower	150	150	158
Torque (lbs./ft.)	167	176	203

EPA city/highway mpg

3-speed automatic		19/24	
4-speed OD automatic			18/24

Consumer Guide™ observed MPG

4-speed OD automatic			16.7

Built in USA and Canada.

RETAIL PRICES	GOOD	AVERAGE	POOR
1996 Voyager	$10,500-13,000	$9,300-11,500	$7,000-8,500
1996 Grand Voyager	11,700-14,500	10,500-13,000	8,000-9,500
1997 Voyager	12,500-14,500	11,000-13,000	8,500-9,500
1997 Grand Voyager	14,500-16,000	13,000-14,500	10,000-11,000
1998 Voyager	14,500-16,700	13,000-15,200	10,000-11,500
1998 Grand Voyager	17,000-19,000	15,500-17,500	12,000-13,500

AVERAGE REPLACEMENT COSTS

A/C Compressor $490	Clutch, Pressure Plate,
Alternator 310	Bearing 605
Radiator 480	Constant Velocity Joints.....385
Timing Chain or Belt 230	Brakes................................390
Automatic Transmission or	Shocks and/or Struts 330
Transaxle.....................1,040	Exhaust System.................330

TROUBLE SPOTS

• **Brakes** The anti-lock brakes may activate at speeds under 10 mph due to one or more faulty wheel speed sensors. (1996)

• **Windshield wipers** Windshield wipers come on by themselves or fail to stop when the switch or key is turned off due to a problem with the multifunction switch on the column. (1996)

• **Vehicle noise** A thud or thump (sometimes described as a sounding like a bowling ball) when accelerating or stopping that comes from the rear is caused by fuel sloshing in the tank. A foam pad and strap kit does not always fix the problem. (1996-97)

• **Transmission slippage** Transmission may shudder when accelerating from a stop, thump when coasting down to a stop, or slip when shifting. (1996)

• **Engine fan** The radiator fan may run after the key is turned off, or may not run leading to overheating because the fan relay attaching screws break and the relay overheats. (1996-97)

• **Blower motor** Blower motors make a whine in low and second speed. (1996)

• **Doors** Sliding door and/or liftgate power locks fail to lock or unlock both manually or electrically. (1996)

• **Dashboard lights** The instrument cluster, mini-trip computer and/or compass may show incorrect information or go completely blank due to a bad relay for the heated backlight (window). (1997)

RECALL HISTORY

1996 w/bench seats, from Windsor plant ("R" in 11th position of VIN) Rear-seat bolts can fracture; in accident, seat could break away. **1996** Tank rollover valve can allow fuel to enter vapor canister, resulting in potential leakage and fire. **1996** Static charge could cause spark as tank is being filled; vapors could ignite. **1996** On a few minivans, bolts holding integrated child seats can break. **1997** Certain master cylinder seals will not seal adequately, allowing fluid to be drawn into power-assist reservoir. **1997** A few wheels were damaged during mounting. **1997 w/P215/65R15 Goodyear**

Conquest tires on steel wheels Tires were damaged, and may lose pressure suddenly. **1998 w/integrated child seats** Shoulder harness webbing was incorrectly routed around reinforcement bar; can fail to restrain child properly.

1992-98 PONTIAC BONNEVILLE

1992 Pontiac Bonneville SE

FOR   Air bags, dual (later models) • Acceleration • Automatic transmission performance • Passenger and cargo room

AGAINST   Fuel economy • Ride (SSE, SSEi)

EVALUATION   Even with the base engine, which currently delivers 205 horsepower, acceleration and passing response are brisk and sure. The supercharged version has all the feel of a burly V-8, but requires the use of costlier premium unleaded. Expect real-world fuel economy of 17-18 in the city for the base engine, 25 on the highway. That drops to 15-16 city mileage for the supercharged version and 23-24 on the highway. Both engines team with an automatic that shifts promptly and smoothly. The CCR feature in the SSEi felt too loose and bouncy in Touring mode, while in Performance mode it failed to absorb bumps very well.

Bonneville has the same spacious interior and trunk as its more sedate siblings at Buick and Oldsmobile. There's ample room for both passengers and cargo. The trunk is wide, has a flat floor and extends well forward, providing 18 cubic feet of storage. Inside, the seating is comfortable and the instrument panel is well executed.

The Chrysler LH/LHS sedans are roomier and have more daring styling, but the Bonneville and its GM cousins are high-quality cars that can be tailored to suit a variety of tastes, from cushy luxury to sporty performance.

NHTSA CRASH TEST RESULTS
1996 Pontiac Bonneville

4-DOOR SEDAN

Driver ☆☆☆☆☆

Passenger ☆☆☆

(The National Highway Traffic Safety Administration tests a vehicle's crashworthiness in front and side collisions. Their ratings suggest the chance of serious injury: ☆☆☆☆☆—10% or less; ☆☆☆☆—10-20% or less; ☆☆☆—20-30% or less; ☆☆—35-45% or less; ☆—More than 45%.)

SPECIFICATIONS

	4-door sedan
Wheelbase, in.	110.8
Overall length, in.	200.6
Overall width, in.	74.5
Overall height, in.	55.7
Curb weight, lbs.	3446
Cargo volume, cu. ft.	18.0
Fuel capacity, gals.	18.0
Seating capacity	6
Front head room, in.	39.0
Max. front leg room, in.	43.0
Rear head room, in.	38.3
Min. rear leg room, in.	38.0

Powertrain layout: transverse front-engine/front-wheel drive

ENGINES	ohv V-6	ohv V-6	Supercharged ohv V-6
Size, liters/cu. in.	3.8/231	3.8/231	3.8/231
Horsepower	170	205	225-240
Torque (lbs./ft.)	200-225	230	275-280
EPA city/highway mpg 4-speed OD automatic	18/28	19/29	17/27
Consumer Guide™ observed MPG 4-speed OD automatic		17.0	16.5

Built in USA.

RETAIL PRICES	GOOD	AVERAGE	POOR
1992 Bonneville SE	$5,100-6,000	$4,400-5,200	$2,600-3,200
1992 SSE/SSEi	7,000-8,000	6,200-7,200	3,900-4,600
1993 Bonneville SE	6,400-7,400	5,600-6,600	3,500-4,300
1993 SSE/SSEi	8,500-9,700	7,500-8,700	5,000-5,800
1994 Bonneville SE	7,800-8,900	7,000-8,000	4,700-5,500
1994 SSE/SSEi	10,500-12,000	9,500-10,800	6,500-7,500
1995 Bonneville SE	9,500-10,500	8,500-9,500	6,000-6,800
1995 SSE/SSEi	12,500-14,000	11,200-12,500	8,000-9,000

PONTIAC

	GOOD	AVERAGE	POOR
1996 Bonneville SE	11,300-12,500	10,300-11,500	7,300-8,300
1996 SSE/SSEi	14,500-16,000	13,000-14,500	9,500-10,500
1997 Bonneville SE	13,000-14,200	12,000-13,000	8,800-9,500
1997 SSE/SSEi	16,500-18,000	15,000-16,500	11,000-12,000
1998 Bonneville SE	15,500-16,800	14,200-15,500	10,500-11,300
1998 SSE/SSEi	19,000-21,000	17,500-19,500	13,000-14,500

AVERAGE REPLACEMENT COSTS

A/C Compressor $460
Alternator 190
Radiator 360
Timing Chain or Belt 260
Automatic Transmission or
   Transaxle........................970

Constant Velocity Joints.....730
Brakes....................................230
Shocks and/or Struts 750
Exhaust System...................500

TROUBLE SPOTS

• **Oil consumption and engine knock** Models with the 3800 (3.8L) engine are prone to excessive oil consumption often accompanied by spark knock (pinging) during normal driving conditions due to failure of the valve stem seals. (1993-95)

• **Engine noise** Bearing knock was common on many 3300 and 3800 (3.3L and 3.8L) engines due to too much clearance on the number-one main bearing, requiring it to be replaced with a 0.001-inch undersize bearing. (1992-94)

• **Steering noise** The upper bearing mount in the steering column can get loose and cause a snapping or clicking that can be both heard and felt, requiring a new bearing spring and turn signal cancel cam that the manufacturer will warranty. (1994-96)

• **Transaxle leak** The right front axle seal at the automatic transaxle is prone to leak and GM issued a revised seal to correct the problem and it is supposed to be installed whenever a car is in for transmission or axle shaft service of any sort. (1992-94)

• **Engine noise** What sounds like a rattling noise from the engine that lasts less than a minute when the car is started after sitting overnight is often caused by automatic transmission pump starvation or cavitation, or a sticking pressure regulator valve. According to GM, no damage occurs and it does not have a fix for the problem. (1992-95)

• **Cruise control** If the cruise control doesn't stay engaged, or drops out of cruise, the brake switch can usually be adjusted, but if it cannot, it will be replaced under normal warranty. (1992-95)

• **Transmission slippage** The 4T60E transmission may drop out of drive (neutral condition) while cruising, shift erratically, have no third or fourth gear, or no second and third gear because of a bad ground connection for the shift solenoids. Poor grounds also allow wrong gear starts. Many transmissions have been mistakenly rebuilt, which does not correct the problem. (1992-94)

RECALL HISTORY

1992 Parking brake lever may release one or more teeth when applied. **1992 with console shift** Control cable on some cars may disengage from bracket and falsely indicate gear position. **1992-93** Transmission cooler line in cars with certain powertrains, sold in specified states, can separate at low temperature. **1995 with Twilight Sentinel** Excess current leakage can cause loss of headlights and parking lights. **1996** Damaged capacitor may cause failure of "Key in the Ignition" warning chime and driver seatbelt unbuckled warning chime and indicator lamp; other functions also may be impaired. **1996 with 3.8-liter V-6** Backfire during engine starting can cause breakage of upper intake manifold, resulting in non-start condition and possible fire. **1997** Seat cover trim on a few cars does not meet flammability requirements.

1990-92 PONTIAC FIREBIRD

1991 Pontiac Firebird Trans Am 2-door

FOR Acceleration (V-8) • Handling

AGAINST Fuel economy • Ride • Passenger and cargo room

See the 1990-92 Chevrolet Camaro report for an evaluation of the 1990-92 Pontiac Firebird.

SPECIFICATIONS	2-door hatchback	2-door conv.
Wheelbase, in.	101.0	101.0

PONTIAC

	2-door hatchback	2-door conv.
Overall length, in.	195.1	195.1
Overall width, in.	72.4	72.4
Overall height, in.	49.7	49.8
Curb weight, lbs.	3121	3280
Cargo volume, cu. ft.	31.0	12.4
Fuel capacity, gals.	15.5	15.5
Seating capacity	4	4
Front head room, in.	37.0	37.1
Max. front leg room, in.	43.0	42.9
Rear head room, in.	35.6	36.1
Min. rear leg room, in.	28.9	28.3

Powertrain layout: longitudinal front-engine/rear-wheel drive

ENGINES

	ohv V-6	ohv V-8	ohv V-8	ohv V-8
Size, liters/cu. in.	3.1/191	5.0/305	5.0/305	5.7/350
Horsepower	140	170	200-230	235-240
Torque (lbs./ft.)	180	255	285-300	340
EPA city/highway mpg				
5-speed OD manual	17/27	17/26	16/26	
4-speed OD automatic	18/27	17/26	17/25	17/25
Consumer Guide™ observed MPG				
5-speed OD manual			16.5	
4-speed OD automatic	18.2			

Built in USA.

RETAIL PRICES

	GOOD	AVERAGE	POOR
1990 Firebird	$2,800-4,000	$2,100-3,300	$900-1,700
1990 Trans Am	4,000-5,500	3,200-4,700	1,400-2,200
1991 Firebird	3,800-5,000	3,100-4,200	1,400-2,400
1991 Trans Am	5,100-6,900	4,300-6,000	2,000-3,100
1991 Convertible	5,500-7,500	4,700-6,600	2,800-4,300
1992 Firebird	4,900-6,200	4,100-5,300	2,100-3,100
1992 Trans Am	6,300-8,400	5,500-7,400	2,900-4,200
1992 Convertible	6,900-9,800	6,000-8,600	3,900-5,900

AVERAGE REPLACEMENT COSTS

A/C Compressor	$365
Alternator	200
Radiator	360
Timing Chain or Belt	285
Automatic Transmission or Transaxle	745
Clutch, Pressure Plate, Bearing	515
Universal Joints	150
Brakes	200
Shocks and/or Struts	360
Exhaust System	340

TROUBLE SPOTS

• **Transmission slippage** Any car with a model TH-700-R4 automatic transmission may shift late or not upshift at all. The problem is a stuck throttle valve inside the transmission. It may be overlooked during rebuilding since the valve appears fine because it is hydraulic pressure, not a physical binding, that makes it stick. The problem is fixed by enlarging the hydraulic fluid balance hole by 0.010 inch. (1990-92)

RECALL HISTORY

1990 Fuel return hoses on 5.0- or 5.7-liter V-8 engines may break at either crimped coupling. **1990** Plastic components of seatbelt buckle assemblies could be weakened by exposure to direct sunlight and high interior temperatures. **1991** Metal latchplates of seatbelts may not engage buckle assemblies. **1992** Fuel filler neck's solder joint can develop cracks or leaks. **1992** Automatic-transmission shift control cable can separate.

1993-98 PONTIAC FIREBIRD

1996 Pontiac Firebird Formula coupe

FOR Air bags, dual • Acceleration (V-8s) • Steering/handling • Anti-lock brakes

AGAINST Fuel economy (V-8s) • Ride • Noise • Rear seat room • Entry/exit • Rear visibility

See the 1993-98 Chevrolet Camaro report for an evaluation of the 1993-98 Pontiac Firebird.

NHTSA CRASH TEST RESULTS
1995 Pontiac Firebird   2-DOOR COUPE

Driver	☆☆☆☆☆
Passenger	☆☆☆☆☆

PONTIAC

SPECIFICATIONS

	2-door coupe	2-door conv.
Wheelbase, in.	101.1	101.1
Overall length, in.	195.6	195.6
Overall width, in.	74.5	74.5
Overall height, in.	52.0	52.7
Curb weight, lbs.	3311	3481
Cargo volume, cu. ft.	33.7	12.9
Fuel capacity, gals.	15.5	15.5
Seating capacity	4	4
Front head room, in.	37.2	37.2
Max. front leg room, in.	43.0	43.0
Rear head room, in.	35.3	35.3
Min. rear leg room, in.	28.9	38.9

Powertrain layout: longitudinal front-engine/rear-wheel drive

ENGINES

	ohv V-6	ohv V-6	ohv V-8	ohv V-8
Size, liters/cu. in.	3.4/207	3.8/231	5.7/350	5.7/346
Horsepower	160	200	275-305	305-320
Torque (lbs./ft.)	200	225	325	335-345
EPA city/highway mpg				
5-speed OD manual	19/28	19/30		
6-speed OD manual			16/26	17/26
4-speed OD automatic	19/28	19/29	17/25	18/24
Consumer Guide™ observed MPG				
6-speed OD manual			16.0	15.5
4-speed OD automatic	18.8	18.8		

Built in Canada.

RETAIL PRICES

	GOOD	AVERAGE	POOR
1993 Firebird	$6,100-7,000	$5,300-6,200	$3,200-4,000
1993 Formula/Trans Am	6,900-8,200	6,000-7,300	3,800-4,600
1994 Firebird Coupe	7,100-8,000	6,300-7,200	4,000-5,000
1994 Formula/Trans Am	8,800-10,500	7,800-9,500	5,300-6,700
1994 Convertible	9,700-13,500	8,700-12,200	6,000-8,300
1995 Firebird Coupe	8,700-9,700	7,800-8,700	5,300-6,000
1995 Formula/Trans Am	10,700-12,000	9,400-10,700	6,500-7,500
1995 Convertible	11,200-15,200	10,000-13,900	7,200-10,500
1996 Firebird Coupe	10,500-11,500	9,500-10,500	6,800-7,700
1996 Formula/Trans Am	12,800-14,500	11,500-13,000	8,700-9,900
1996 Convertible	13,300-17,500	12,000-16,000	9,000-12,000

	GOOD	AVERAGE	POOR
1997 Firebird Coupe	12,500-13,600	11,200-12,700	8,100-9,400
1997 Formula/Trans Am	14,200-16,800	12,700-15,300	9,700-11,800
1997 Convertible	15,000-19,800	13,500-18,000	10,500-13,500
1998 Firebird Coupe	14,800-16,000	13,300-14,500	10,000-11,500
1998 Formula/Trans Am	16,500-19,500	15,000-18,000	12,000-14,500
1998 Convertible	18,000-23,000	16,500-21,000	13,000-16,500

AVERAGE REPLACEMENT COSTS

A/C Compressor $535
Alternator 290
Radiator 410
Timing Chain or Belt 330
Automatic Transmission or
   Transaxle.........................775

Clutch, Pressure Plate,
   Bearing............................755
Universal Joints 200
Brakes.................................255
Shocks and/or Struts 595
Exhaust System 470

TROUBLE SPOTS

• **Vehicle shake** Cars with the 5.7L V-8 may vibrate at highway speeds, which can be corrected by replacing the driveshaft with a lighter, aluminum shaft (although this usually results in axle noise becoming more apparent). (1993-96)

• **Manual transmission** Manual transmissions (5-speed and 6-speed) tend to pop out of gear in cold weather until the interior warms up. (1993-94)

• **Brake noise** Rear brake squeal can be eliminated by replacing the brake pads with revised ones, but it is vital that the technician burnish them in properly after the brake job. (1993-94)

• **Doors** The power door locks may not operate although the doors can be locked manually due to a rubber bumper falling off of the actuator arm. (1994-95)

• **Starter** The starter may keep running after the engine starts or the key is turned off due to a short in the wiring. (1995)

• **Transmission leak** Fluid may leak from the pump body on 4L60-E transmissions due to the pump bushing walking out of the valve body. (1995-96)

RECALL HISTORY

1994 Misrouted V-8 fuel line may contact "air" check valve; heat could damage line. **1995** Lower coupling of steering intermediate shaft could loosen and rotate, resulting in loss of control. **1997** Seatbelt retractors on some cars can lock-up on slopes.

1992-98 PONTIAC GRAND AM

1992 Pontiac Grand Am 4-door

FOR Air bags, dual (later models) • Steering/handling • Acceleration (V-6) • Anti-lock brakes (optional)

AGAINST Ride (GT) • Engine noise • Road noise • Rear-seat entry/exit • Rear-seat room

EVALUATION Acceleration with the base 115/120-horsepower Quad OHC is only adequate, and the engine becomes rough and raucous above 3000 rpm. Later 4-cylinders and V-6s provide excellent acceleration and both V-6s are smooth. All engines are fairly fuel efficient, but still have a ways to go before the catch the Honda Accord or Toyota Camry.

The base suspension furnishes a fairly well-controlled ride, but allows lots of body lean in turns, and the base tires have only modest grip in the corners. The SE's optional handling suspension package and wider tires improve the Grand Am's road manners without adding undue ride harshness. The GT handles crisply during sudden changes in direction, but tends to jolt and thump more over bumps. The standard anti-lock brakes stop the Grand Am quickly and precisely.

Though interior dimensions change only fractionally, the rear seat feels more spacious, partly due to new thin-line front seatbacks, more toe room under the front cushions, and a rear seatback that's not as vertical as before. With the new instrument panel, all gauges are larger and provide unobstructed views. Also, radio and climate-control systems are closer to the driver. Access to the trunk benefits from a new lid that opens at a 90-degree angle.

Grand Am has been far more successful than its cousins at Buick and Oldsmobile because Pontiac provides the right blend of image and price.

NHTSA CRASH TEST RESULTS
1996 Pontiac Grand Am

2-DOOR COUPE

Driver	☆☆☆☆
Passenger	☆☆☆☆☆

(The National Highway Traffic Safety Administration tests a vehicle's crashworthiness in front and side collisions. Their ratings suggest the chance of serious injury: ☆☆☆☆☆—10% or less; ☆☆☆☆—10-20% or less; ☆☆☆—20-30% or less; ☆☆—35-45% or less; ☆—More than 45%.)

SPECIFICATIONS	2-door coupe	4-door sedan
Wheelbase, in.	103.4	103.4
Overall length, in.	186.9	186.9
Overall width, in.	68.7	68.7
Overall height, in.	53.2	53.2
Curb weight, lbs.	2881	2954
Cargo volume, cu. ft.	13.2	13.2
Fuel capacity, gals.	15.2	15.2
Seating capacity	5	5
Front head room, in.	37.8	37.8
Max. front leg room, in.	43.3	43.3
Rear head room, in.	36.5	37.0
Min. rear leg room, in.	33.9	34.9

ENGINES	ohc I-4	dohc I-4	dohc I-4	ohv V-6	ohv V-6
Size, liters/cu. in.	2.3/138	2.3/138	2.4/146	3.1/191	3.3/204
Horsepower	115-120	155-180	150	155	160
Torque (lbs./ft.)	140	150-160	160	185	185

EPA city/highway mpg

5-speed OD man.		24/33	21/31	23/33	
3-speed auto.	24/31				19/29
4-speed OD auto.			22/32	21/29	

Consumer Guide™ observed MPG

5-speed OD man.			21.7		
4-speed OD auto.			20.8	21.9	

Built in USA.

RETAIL PRICES	GOOD	AVERAGE	POOR
1992 Grand Am	$3,600-5,000	$2,900-4,200	$1,400-2,500
1993 Grand Am	4,500-6,500	3,800-5,700	2,000-3,500
1994 Grand Am	5,400-7,500	4,600-6,700	2,800-4,500
1995 Grand Am	6,800-9,000	6,000-8,100	3,800-5,500
1996 Grand Am	8,000-10,400	7,100-9,400	4,900-6,500
1997 Grand Am	9,500-12,000	8,600-11,000	6,000-7,800
1998 Grand Am	11,500-14,000	10,400-12,800	7,400-9,300

PONTIAC

AVERAGE REPLACEMENT COSTS

A/C Compressor $540	Clutch, Pressure Plate,
Alternator 225	Bearing 555
Timing Chain or Belt 325	Constant Velocity Joints.....565
Automatic Transmission or	Brakes................................240
Transaxle.....................1,105	Shocks and/or Struts 540
	Exhaust System.................380

TROUBLE SPOTS

• **Engine noise** A tick or rattle when the engine is started cold may be due to too much wrist-pin-to-piston clearance. New piston and pin sets will be replaced under warranty if the customer complains of the noise. (1994-95)

• **Engine noise** Bearing knock was common on many 3300 and 3800 (3.3L and 3.8L) engines due to too much clearance on the number-one main bearing, requiring it to be replaced with a 0.001-inch undersize bearing. (1992-93)

• **Transaxle leak** The right front axle seal at the automatic transaxle is prone to leak and GM issued a revised seal to correct the problem and it is supposed to be installed whenever a car is in for transmission or axle shaft service of any sort. (1992-94)

• **Valve cover leaks** The plastic valve covers on the 3.1L engine were prone to leaks and should be replaced with redesigned aluminum covers. (GM no longer stocks the plastic ones.) (1994-95)

• **Radiator** Some cars mysteriously lose coolant, but no leaks can be found. The common problem is a bad seal on the pressure cap on the surge tank that is connected to the radiator. (1992-94)

• **Brake wear** The front brakes wear out prematurely because of the friction compound. GM and several aftermarket companies have brakes with linings that will last longer. The GM part number is 12510050. This is not considered a warranty item. (1992-95)

• **Engine noise** What sounds like a rattling noise from the engine that lasts less than a minute when the car is started after sitting overnight is often caused by automatic transmission pump starvation or cavitation, or a sticking pressure regulator valve. According to GM, no damage occurs and it does not have a fix for the problem. (1994-95)

• **Transmission slippage** The 4T60E transmission may drop out of drive (neutral condition) while cruising, shift erratically, have no third or fourth gear, or no second and third gear because of a bad ground connection for the shift solenoids. Poor grounds also allow wrong gear starts. Many transmissions have been mistakenly rebuilt, which does not correct the problem. (1994)

• **Transmission slippage** Any car with a model TH-125 automatic transmission may shift late or not upshift at all. The problem is a stuck throttle valve inside the transmission. It may be overlooked during rebuilding since the valve appears fine because it is hydraulic pressure, not a physical binding, that makes it stick. The problem is fixed by enlarging the hydraulic fluid balance hole by 0.010 inch. (1992-94)

• **Traction control indicator light** The Enhanced Traction Control (ETC) warning light "ETC OFF" may glow and the cruise control stops working, but there is no problem with the system. If the computer failure memory is cleared, everything returns to normal. No current fix. (1996)

• **Ignition switch** The ignition switch may not return from the start to the run position and the accessories such as the radio, wipers, cruise control, power windows, rear defroster, or heater may not work because the screws that hold the switch in place were over-tightened. (1992-94)

RECALL HISTORY

1992 Bolts and nuts that attach bearing-hub assembly to rear axle are insufficiently tightened on some cars. **1992** Small number of cars have incorrect upper spring seat at right rear. **1992 coupe** Passenger-side easy-entry seat adjuster on some cars may fail to fully lock into position after seatback has been tilted and seat slid forward. **1994** Welds in rear assembly of fuel tank may be insufficient to prevent leakage in certain rear-impact collisions, increasing risk of fire. **1996** Steering column lower pinch bolt was not properly tightened.This could cause loss of steering control. **1996** Front and/or rear hazard warning lamps might not work. **1996** Interior lamps might come on unexpectedly while vehicle is being driven. **1997** Omitted fuse cover could result in short circuit and possible fire.

1990-96 PONTIAC GRAND PRIX

FOR Air bags, dual (later models) • Handling • Anti-lock brakes (optional)

AGAINST Ride (STE, GT) • Engine noise • Road noise

EVALUATION It's best to avoid models with the noisy 4-cylinder engine, However, the 3.1-liter V-6 provides ample acceleration with much less noise and vibration. Turbo engines provide outstanding acceleration, but suffer from "turbo lag" and poor fuel economy. The best engine choice is the dohc 3.4-liter V-6 which provides the acceleration of the turbo engine without the lag and ruckus.

1993 Pontiac Grand Prix LE 4-door

Inside, the cabin of the 1990-1993 Grand Prix with its backlit red gauge cluster works hard to emulate the continental flair of the BMW. However, Pontiac is not quite able to capture the European maturity or purposefulness. Revisions to the cabin in 1994 bring long overdue improvements. The new controls are both simpler to use and easier to reach. Large rotary dials replace the climate system's fussy, undersized switches and sliders. Select either the coupe or sedan and you should find the cabin capable of transporting four adults in relative comfort.

Pontiac's suspension tuning gives the Grand Prix somewhat more composed road manners than the Lumina, Regal, and Cutlass Supreme, especially over bumps and dips. Cornering ability is especially impressive on cars equipped with the Y99 suspension package, but drivers must endure a harsher ride.

We rate the Taurus, Sable, and Honda Accord higher overall. But with the gradual improvements bestowed on the Grand Prix it is a good choice as well.

NHTSA CRASH TEST RESULTS
1995 Pontiac Grand Prix

2-DOOR COUPE

Driver ☆☆☆☆

Passenger ☆☆☆

(The National Highway Traffic Safety Administration tests a vehicle's crashworthiness in front and side collisions. Their ratings suggest the chance of serious injury: ☆☆☆☆☆—10% or less; ☆☆☆☆—10-20% or less; ☆☆☆—20-30% or less; ☆☆—35-45% or less; ☆—More than 45%.)

SPECIFICATIONS

	2-door coupe	4-door sedan
Wheelbase, in.	107.5	107.5
Overall length, in.	194.8	194.9
Overall width, in.	71.9	71.9
Overall height, in.	52.8	52.8

PONTIAC

	2-door coupe	4-door sedan
Curb weight, lbs.	3243	3318
Cargo volume, cu. ft.	14.9	15.5
Fuel capacity, gals.	16.5	16.5
Seating capacity	6	6
Front head room, in.	37.8	38.6
Max. front leg room, in.	42.3	42.4
Rear head room, in.	36.6	37.7
Min. rear leg room, in.	34.8	36.2

Powertrain layout: transverse front-engine/front-wheel drive

ENGINES

	dohc I-4	ohv V-6	Turbocharged ohv V-6	dohc V-6
Size, liters/cu. in.	2.3/138	3.1/191	3.1/191	3.4/207
Horsepower	160	140-160	205	210-215
Torque (lbs./ft.)	155	180-185	220	200-215

EPA city/highway mpg

	dohc I-4	ohv V-6	Turbocharged ohv V-6	dohc V-6
5-speed OD manual		19/28		17/27
3-speed automatic	21/29	19/27		
4-speed OD automatic		19/30	16/25	17/26

Consumer Guide™ observed MPG

		ohv V-6		dohc V-6
4-speed OD automatic		20.1		18.7

Built in USA.

RETAIL PRICES

	GOOD	AVERAGE	POOR
1990 Grand Prix	$2,600-3,300	$1,900-2,600	$1,000-1,400
1990 STE	3,500-4,200	2,800-3,500	1,400-1,800
1991 Grand Prix	3,300-4,100	2,600-3,400	1,300-2,000
1991 GT/STE	4,500-5,500	3,800-4,700	2,100-2,600
1992 Grand Prix	4,100-5,100	3,300-4,300	1,800-2,700
1992 GT/STE	5,500-6,600	4,700-5,800	2,700-3,400
1993 Grand Prix	5,000-6,200	4,200-5,300	2,500-3,300
1993 GT/STE	6,500-8,000	5,600-7,000	3,400-4,300
1994 Grand Prix	6,300-7,300	5,500-6,400	3,600-4,200
1995 Grand Prix	7,800-9,000	6,900-8,000	4,800-5,500
1996 Grand Prix	9,300-10,800	8,300-9,800	5,900-7,200

AVERAGE REPLACEMENT COSTS

A/C Compressor $555
Alternator 215
Radiator 340
Timing Chain or Belt 170
Automatic Transmission or Transaxle.....................1,070
Clutch, Pressure Plate, Bearing............................385
Constant Velocity Joints.....470
Brakes..................................200
Shocks and/or Struts 1,855
Exhaust System..................470

TROUBLE SPOTS

• **Engine noise** A tick or rattle when the engine is started cold may be due to too much wrist-pin-to-piston clearance. New piston and pin sets will be replaced under warranty if the customer complains of the noise. (1994-95)

• **Engine noise** What sounds like a rattling noise from the engine that lasts less than a minute when the car is started after sitting over night is often caused by automatic transmission pump starvation or a sticking pressure regulator valve. According to GM, no damage occurs and it does not have a fix for the problem. (1991-95)

• **Transaxle leak** The right front axle seal at the automatic transaxle is prone to leak and GM issued a revised seal to correct the problem and it is supposed to be installed whenever a car is in for transmission or axle shaft service of any sort. (1992-94)

• **Valve cover leaks** The plastic valve covers on the 3.1L engine were prone to leaks and should be replaced with redesigned aluminum covers. (GM no longer stocks the plastic ones.) (1994-95)

• **Steering noise** The upper bearing mount in the steering column can get loose and cause a snapping or clicking that can be both heard and felt, requiring a new bearing spring and turn signal cancel cam that the manufacturer will warranty. (1994-96)

• **Transmission slippage** The 4T60E transmission may drop out of drive (neutral condition) while cruising, shift erratically, have no third or fourth gear, or no second and third gear because of a bad ground connection for the shift solenoids. Poor grounds also allow wrong gear starts. Many transmissions have been mistakenly rebuilt, which does not correct the problem. (1991-94)

• **Transmission slippage** Any car with a model TH-125 or 440-T4 automatic transmission may shift late or not upshift at all. The problem is a stuck throttle valve inside the transmission. It may be overlooked during rebuilding since the valve appears fine because it is hydraulic pressure, not a physical binding, that makes it stick. The problem is fixed by enlarging the hydraulic fluid balance hole by 0.010 inch. (1990-94)

RECALL HISTORY

1990 Stoplamps may not illuminate. **1990 with Kelsey-Hayes steel wheels** Cracks may develop in wheel mounting surface. **1990-91** Steering shaft could separate from steering gear. **1991** Front door shoulder belt guide loops may be cracked. **1991 coupe** Fog lamps, low-beam headlamps and high-beam headlamp can be operated simultaneously on some cars, causing circuit breaker to overload and trip. **1992** Reverse servo pin of 4-speed automatic transmission may bind. **1993** Manual recliner mechanisms on some front seats will not latch under certain conditions, causing seatback to recline without prior warning. **1994-95** Wiper/washer may operate intermittently, or not at all. **1995** Seatbelt anchor can fracture in crash.

1990-94 PONTIAC SUNBIRD

1994 Pontiac Sunbird GT 2-door

FOR Acceleration (V-6) • Fuel economy (4-cylinder) • Handling/roadholding (SE, GT)

AGAINST Acceleration (4-cylinder) • Rear-seat room • Engine noise

See the 1990-94 Chevrolet Cavalier report for an evaluation of the 1990-94 Pontiac Sunbird.

SPECIFICATIONS	2-door coupe	4-door sedan	2-door conv.
Wheelbase, in.	101.3	101.3	101.3
Overall length, in.	180.7	180.7	180.7
Overall width, in.	66.2	66.2	66.2
Overall height, in.	52.2	53.9	52.4
Curb weight, lbs.	2484	2502	2661
Cargo volume, cu. ft.	12.6	15.2	10.4
Fuel capacity, gals.	13.6	13.6	13.6
Seating capacity	5	5	4
Front head room, in.	37.8	38.8	38.2
Max. front leg room, in.	42.1	42.1	42.1
Rear head room, in.	36.1	37.4	36.5
Min. rear leg room, in.	32.0	33.7	32.0

Powertrain layout: transverse front-engine/front-wheel drive

ENGINES	ohc I-4	Turbocharged ohc I-4	ohv V-6
Size, liters/cu. in.	2.0/121	2.0/121	3.1/191

PONTIAC

	ohc I-4	Turbocharged ohc I-4	ohv V-6
Horsepower	96-110	165	140
Torque (lbs./ft.)	118-124	175	180-185
EPA city/highway mpg			
5-speed OD manual	26/36	21/30	19/28
3-speed automatic	23/32	21/28	20/28
Consumer Guide™ observed MPG			
5-speed OD manual	25.7		
3-speed automatic	22.4		21.9

Built in USA.

RETAIL PRICES	GOOD	AVERAGE	POOR
1990 Sunbird	$1,800-3,100	$1,100-2,400	$600-1,200
1990 Convertible	2,700-3,400	2,000-2,700	900-1,200
1991 Sunbird	2,200-3,900	1,500-3,200	800-1,600
1991 Convertible	3,500-4,400	2,800-3,700	1,400-2,000
1992 Sunbird	2,800-4,600	2,100-3,900	1,200-2,100
1992 Convertible	4,500-5,500	3,700-4,700	1,900-2,500
1993 Sunbird	3,500-5,600	2,800-4,800	1,600-2,900
1993 Convertible	5,500-6,700	4,700-5,800	2,700-3,400
1994 Sunbird	4,300-6,700	3,500-5,900	2,000-3,800
1994 Convertible	6,600-7,800	5,700-6,900	3,600-4,400

AVERAGE REPLACEMENT COSTS

A/C Compressor $445	Clutch, Pressure Plate, Bearing 575
Alternator 190	Constant Velocity Joints 530
Radiator 410	Brakes 210
Timing Chain or Belt 155	Shocks and/or Struts 400
Automatic Transmission or Transaxle 865	Exhaust System 360

TROUBLE SPOTS

• **Transmission slippage** Any car with a model TH-125 automatic transmission may shift late or not upshift at all. The problem is a stuck throttle valve inside the transmission. It may be overlooked during rebuilding since the valve appears fine because it is hydraulic pressure, not a physical binding, that makes it stick. The problem is fixed by enlarging the hydraulic fluid balance hole by 0.010 inch. (1990-94)

• **Brake wear** The front brakes wear out prematurely because of the friction compound. GM and several aftermarket companies have brakes with linings that will last longer. The GM part number is 12510050. This is not considered a warranty item. (1992-94)

• **Transaxle leak** The right front axle seal at the automatic transaxle is prone to leak and GM issued a revised seal to correct the problem and it is supposed to be installed whenever a car is in for transmission or axle shaft service of any sort. (1992-94)

RECALL HISTORY

1991 Front door shoulder belt guide loops may be cracked. **1991** Front door interlock striker may fail. **1992** Accelerator cable may have been kinked during assembly; can cause high-effort operation, or sticking or broken cable. **1992** Secondary hood latch spring in some cars is improperly installed or missing. **1992-93** During cold weather, water entering throttle cable may freeze and cause cable to bind. **1993** Flawed rear brake hoses can cause reduced brake effectiveness. **1994** Drive-axle spindle nuts on a few cars may be overtorqued.

1995-98 PONTIAC SUNFIRE

1996 Pontiac Sunfire SE coupe

FOR Air bags, dual • Anti-lock brakes • Instruments/controls • Fuel economy

AGAINST Rear seat comfort • Noise • Rear visibility

TSee the 1995-98 Chevrolet Cavalier report for an evaluation of the 1995-98 Pontiac Sunfire.

NHTSA CRASH TEST RESULTS
1997 Pontiac Sunfire   2-DOOR COUPE

Driver	☆☆☆☆
Passenger	☆☆☆☆

(The National Highway Traffic Safety Administration tests a vehicle's crashworthiness in front and side collisions. Their ratings suggest the chance of serious injury: ☆☆☆☆☆—10% or less; ☆☆☆☆—10-20% or less; ☆☆☆—20-30% or less; ☆☆—35-45% or less; ☆—More than 45%.)

PONTIAC

SPECIFICATIONS

	2-door coupe	2-door conv.	4-door sedan
Wheelbase, in.	104.1	104.1	104.1
Overall length, in.	181.9	182.4	181.7
Overall width, in.	67.4	68.4	67.3
Overall height, in.	53.2	51.9	54.8
Curb weight, lbs.	2679	2835	2723
Cargo volume, cu. ft.	12.4	9.9	13.1
Fuel capacity, gals.	15.2	15.2	15.2
Seating capacity	5	4	5
Front head room, in.	37.6	38.8	38.9
Max. front leg room, in.	42.4	42.4	42.4
Rear head room, in.	36.6	38.5	37.2
Min. rear leg room, in.	32.0	32.7	34.4

Powertrain layout: transverse front-engine/front-wheel drive

ENGINES

	ohc I-4	dohc I-4	dohc I-4
Size, liters/cu. in.	2.2/133	2.3/138	2.4/146
Horsepower	120	150	150
Torque (lbs./ft.)	130	145	150
EPA city/highway mpg			
5-speed OD manual	25/37	22/32	22/33
3-speed automatic	24/31		
4-speed OD automatic	25/34	21/31	22/32
Consumer Guide™ observed MPG			
5-speed OD manual	25.2		
3-speed automatic	22.9		
4-speed OD automatic			21.0

Built in USA.

AVERAGE REPLACEMENT COSTS

A/C Compressor	$540	
Alternator	265	
Radiator	240	
Timing Chain or Belt	310	
Automatic Transmission or Transaxle	735	
Clutch, Pressure Plate, Bearing	350	
Constant Velocity Joints	875	
Brakes	310	
Shocks and/or Struts	550	
Exhaust System	300	

RETAIL PRICES

	GOOD	AVERAGE	POOR
1995 Sunfire	$6,500-7,700	$5,700-6,900	$3,300-4,200
1995 Convertible	9,500-10,500	8,500-9,500	5,500-6,400
1996 Sunfire	7,700-9,000	6,900-8,100	4,300-5,200
1996 Convertible	10,300-12,300	9,300-11,300	6,500-8,000
1997 Sunfire	8,900-11,000	8,000-10,000	5,400-6,800
1997 Convertible	11,000-14,200	10,000-13,000	7,000-9,500

	GOOD	AVERAGE	POOR
1998 Sunfire	10,500-12,500	9,500-11,500	6,800-8,000
1998 Convertible	13,000-15,500	11,800-14,000	8,500-10,000

TROUBLE SPOTS

• **Brake wear** Original equipment front brake pads do not last as long as most motorists believe they should, so GM offers a revised pad with a longer life lining. (1995)

• **Traction control indicator light** The traction control system may malfunction and when it does, the cruise control quits working. Although the "ETS OFF" light comes on, the check engine light does not. (1996)

• **Dashboard lights** The anti-lock brake system's hydraulic modulator is susceptible to failure and when it does, the ABS warning light will stay on. (1995)

• **Brake wear** Original equipment front brake linings wear prematurely and longer life pads are available, but they may make some noise during braking. (1995)

RECALL HISTORY

1995 Welds were omitted from lower control arms; excessive loads can result in separation. **1995** Automatic-transmission indicator may not reflect correct gear position. **1995-96** Front or rear hazard warning lamps (four-way flashers), or both, do not flash when switch is activated. **1996** Kinked accelerator cable in a few cars can result in unwanted acceleration. **1996** Interior lamps might come on unexpectedly while vehicle is being driven. **1996-97** Air bag could deploy inadvertently in a low-speed crash, or when an object strikes the floor pan. **1997** Spare tire on a few cars may have incorrect rim.

1990-96 PONTIAC TRANS SPORT

FOR Air bags, dual (later models) • Acceleration (3.8-liter V-6) • Passenger and cargo room

AGAINST Acceleration (3.1-liter V-6) • Visibility

EVALUATION Featuring a fiberglasslike composite shell bonded to a steel framework, rust isn't a problem, and the plasticlike bodies are good at absorbing parking lot dings. However, the long sloping nose of the Trans Sport has proven less than popular with the public. The view from the driver's seat is also disconcerting. A restyling job in 1994 added a driver-side air bag and shortened the front somewhat.

The Trans Sport's handling is much more carlike than truck

PONTIAC

1996 Pontiac Trans Sport

like. Acceleration is a bit below average the 3.1-liter V-6 and three-speed automatic. However, performance improves with the arrival of GM's "3800" 3.8-liter V-6 paired with a 4-speed automatic. Power is enhanced further in 1996 with the switch to the more fuel efficient 3.4-liter V-6 engine.

The interior is roomy, and the removable bucket seats weigh only 36 pounds. Pontiac also gained a convenient power function for its sliding door, which can be activated either by a button inside the vehicle or with the remote-entry key fob.

Overall, the Trans Sport is a capable and stylish minivan. It provides good interior room, the safety of an air bag and a power sliding door on newer models, plus less boxy styling. While the Trans Sport is no match overall for Chrysler's new minivans, it's reasonably priced and a good value in rust-belt areas that experience severe winters.

NHTSA CRASH TEST RESULTS
1995 Pontiac Trans Sport

	3-DOOR VAN
Driver	☆☆☆☆
Passenger	☆☆☆

(The National Highway Traffic Safety Administration tests a vehicle's crashworthiness in front and side collisions. Their ratings suggest the chance of serious injury: ☆☆☆☆☆—10% or less; ☆☆☆☆—10-20% or less; ☆☆☆—20-30% or less; ☆☆—35-45% or less; ☆—More than 45%.)

SPECIFICATIONS

	3-door van
Wheelbase, in.	109.8
Overall length, in.	194.5
Overall width, in.	74.6
Overall height, in.	65.7
Curb weight, lbs.	3598
Cargo volume, cu. ft.	112.6

462

	3-door van
Fuel capacity, gals.	20.0
Seating capacity	7
Front head room, in.	39.2
Max. front leg room, in.	40.1
Rear head room, in.	38.7
Min. rear leg room, in.	36.9

Powertrain layout: transverse front-engine/front-wheel drive

ENGINES

	ohv V-6	ohv V-6	ohv V-6
Size, liters/cu. in.	3.1/191	3.4/207	3.8/231
Horsepower	120	180	165-170
Torque (lbs./ft.)	175	205	220-225

EPA city/highway mpg

3-speed automatic	19/23		17/24
4-speed OD automatic		19/26	17/25

Consumer Guide™ observed MPG

4-speed OD automatic		17.1	17.2

Built in USA.

RETAIL PRICES	GOOD	AVERAGE	POOR
1990 Trans Sport	$3,300-4,200	$2,600-3,500	$1,200-1,800
1991 Trans Sport	4,100-5,400	3,400-4,600	1,700-2,700
1992 Trans Sport	5,000-6,600	4,300-5,800	2,400-3,600
1993 Trans Sport	6,000-7,500	5,200-6,600	3,100-4,300
1994 Trans Sport	7,500-9,000	6,700-8,000	4,200-5,400
1995 Trans Sport	9,500-11,200	8,500-10,200	5,500-7,000
1996 Trans Sport	11,500-13,700	10,300-12,300	7,200-8,800

AVERAGE REPLACEMENT COSTS

A/C Compressor $510	Constant Velocity Joints.....505
Alternator 240	Brakes.................................230
Radiator 430	Shocks and/or Struts 430
Timing Chain or Belt 250	Exhaust System.................415
Automatic Transmission or Transaxle.......................980	

TROUBLE SPOTS

• **Oil consumption and engine knock** Models with the 3800 (3.8L) engine are prone to excessive oil consumption often accompanied by spark knock (pinging) during normal driving conditions due to failure of the valve stem seals. (1993-95)

• **Engine noise** Bearing knock was common on many 3300 and

PONTIAC

3800 (3.3L and 3.8L) engines due to too much clearance on the number-one main bearing, requiring it to be replaced with a 0.001-inch undersize bearing. (1992-94)

• **Transaxle leak** The right front axle seal at the automatic transaxle is prone to leak and GM issued a revised seal to correct the problem and it is supposed to be installed whenever a car is in for transmission or axle shaft service of any sort. (1992-94)

• **Steering noise** The upper bearing mount in the steering column can get loose and cause a snapping or clicking that can be both heard and felt, requiring a new bearing spring and turn signal cancel cam that the manufacturer will warranty. (1994-96)

• **Engine noise** What sounds like a rattling noise from the engine that lasts less than a minute when the car is started after sitting overnight is often caused by automatic transmission pump starvation or cavitation, or a sticking pressure regulator valve. According to GM, no damage occurs and it does not have a fix for the problem. (1992-95)

• **Transmission slippage** The 4T60E transmission may drop out of drive (neutral condition) while cruising, shift erratically, have no third or fourth gear, or no second and third gear because of a bad ground connection for the shift solenoids. Poor grounds also allow wrong gear starts. Many transmissions have been mistakenly rebuilt, which does not correct the problem. (1992-94)

• **Transmission slippage** Any car with a model TH-125 automatic transmission may shift late or not upshift at all. The problem is a stuck throttle valve inside the transmission. It may be overlooked during rebuilding since the valve appears fine because it is hydraulic pressure, not a physical binding, that makes it stick. The problem is fixed by enlarging the hydraulic fluid balance hole by 0.010 inch. (1990-94)

RECALL HISTORY

1990 Rear modular seat frame hold-down hooks may not meet the required pull force. **1990** Right seat/shoulder belt retractor may have been installed in second-row left seat position. **1990-91** Steering shaft could separate from steering gear. **1992-95** Transmission cooler line in cars with certain powertrains, sold in specified states, can separate at low temperature. **1993-94 w/optional power sliding door** Shoulder belt can become pinched between seat and door frame pillar trim. **1994** Pawl spring may be missing from retractors for rear center lap belts. **1994** Third-row seatbelt retractors may lock up when van is on a slope. **1995** On some cars, brake pedal arm can fracture during braking. **1995 w/3.1-liter engine** Throttle cable support brackets could contact throttle-lever system and inhibit throttle return; engine speed would then decrease more slowly than anticipated.

1990-93 SAAB 900/TURBO

1991 Saab 900S convertible

FOR Acceleration (turbo) • Anti-lock brakes (optional) • Air bag, driver (later models) • Handling/roadholding • Passenger and cargo room

AGAINST Automatic transmission performance • Manual shift linkage • Ride (turbo) • Wind noise

EVALUATION Non-turbo versions are not able to match the acceleration of other cars in this price class. So the standard 5-speed manual is the transmission of choice for wringing what power there is out of both the 2.0-liter and 2.1-liter 4-cylinder engines. However, shift action can be notchy at times, as the lever balks going into gear.

Turbo models are much more spirited performers, but more costly as well. Their stiffer suspension delivers a rougher ride, and the performance tires produce noticeable thumping over rough pavement. We prefer the suspension on 900S models, which are wonderfully supple over bumps, yet firm at speed. Body lean is the rule in fast turns, but these cars stick to the pavement very well.

Saab 900's chair-like seating positions and spacious interiors provide ample room for four adults, though three-abreast seating in back is not recommended. Gauges are simple and controls close at hand. However, Saab retains a piece of its quirky heritage by being the only production car with the ignition switch located on the floor between the front seats. On hatchbacks and sedans, luggage space varies from ample with the rear seats up to cavernous with it folded down.

SAAB

All-in-all, the 900 is a bit too trouble-prone and quirky for our tastes, but it makes an interesting choice for someone looking for a luxury car that defies the norm.

SPECIFICATIONS	2-door hatchback	4-door sedan	2-door conv.
Wheelbase, in.	99.1	99.1	99.1
Overall length, in.	184.5	184.3	184.2
Overall width, in.	66.5	66.5	66.5
Overall height, in.	56.1	56.1	55.1
Curb weight, lbs.	2770	2810	2950
Cargo volume, cu. ft.	56.5	53.0	10.7
Fuel capacity, gals.	18.0	18.0	18.0
Seating capacity	5	5	4
Front head room, in.	36.8	36.8	36.8
Max. front leg room, in.	41.7	41.7	41.7
Rear head room, in.	37.4	37.4	NA
Min. rear leg room, in.	36.2	36.2	NA

Powertrain layout: transverse front-engine/front-wheel drive

ENGINES	dohc I-4	dohc I-4	Turbocharged dohc I-4	Turbocharged dohc I-4
Size, liters/cu. in.	2.0/121	2.1/129	2.0/121	2.0/121
Horsepower	128	140	160	175
Torque (lbs./ft.)	128	133	188	195
EPA city/highway mpg				
5-speed OD manual	22/28	20/26	22/29	21/28
3-speed automatic	19/22	18/21	19/23	
Consumer Guide™ observed MPG				
5-speed OD manual		20.1		

Built in Sweden.

RETAIL PRICES	GOOD	AVERAGE	POOR
1990 900	$3,200-4,600	$2,500-3,900	$1,100-1,700
1990 900Turbo	4,400-5,500	3,600-4,700	1,800-2,300
1990 Turbo Convertible	7,000-8,200	6,200-7,400	3,900-4,700
1991 900	4,500-6,000	3,800-5,200	2,000-2,800
1991 900Turbo	6,200-7,000	5,400-6,200	3,200-3,800
1991 Convertible	8,500-10,500	7,600-9,500	5,000-6,200
1992 900	5,700-7,400	5,000-6,600	2,800-4,000
1992 900Turbo	8,500-9,500	7,700-8,600	5,000-5,800
1992 Convertible	10,000-12,000	9,000-11,000	6,000-7,500
1993 900	7,500-8,800	6,700-8,000	3,900-5,000
1993 900Turbo	10,300-11,500	9,300-10,500	6,300-7,200
1993 Convertible	11,500-13,800	10,300-12,500	7,000-8,500

AVERAGE REPLACEMENT COSTS

A/C Compressor $605	Clutch, Pressure Plate,
Alternator 335	Bearing 385
Radiator 315	Constant Velocity Joints.....620
Timing Chain or Belt 715	Brakes..................................205
Automatic Transmission or	Shocks and/or Struts 480
Transaxle.....................1,245	Exhaust System 400

TROUBLE SPOTS

• **Tail/brake lights** The brake light switch tends to go out of adjustment and, coupled with a weak return spring, causes the brake lights to stay on and kill the battery. (1990-92)

• **Spark plugs** The owner's manual lists the wrong spark plugs. The correct plugs are NGK BCP5EV. (1992)

• **Engine fan** The battery may go dead because the cooling fan relay, which allows the fan to run 10 minutes after the engine is turned off, keeps the fan on. The time delay relay should be replaced with a standard relay. (1990+)

• **Power seat** The rheostat for the heated driver's seat on cars with velour upholstery gets damaged by static electricity discharges. After it is replaced, the heater element must be grounded to prevent future failures. (1991-92)

• **Hard starting** The turbo bypass valve is secured with plastic clamps that break, causing hard starting and poor drivability. They must be replaced with metal clamps, and dealers will do so whenever the car is in for service. No letters were sent to owners.

• **Poor drivability** Stumble, stalling, or hesitation during the first minutes after startup is corrected by replacing the engine control computer, which may be covered by the normal and/or emissions warranty. (1990-94)

RECALL HISTORY

1993 Front brakes are not adequately protected from road slush, salt, or water.

1994-98 SAAB 900

FOR Air bags, dual • Acceleration (V-6, turbo) • Steering/handling • Passenger and cargo room

AGAINST Ride • Wind noise • Road noise

EVALUATION This new Saab retains its upright stance and sticks to its hatchback design. As a result, it preserves such

SAAB

1996 Saab 900 SE Turbo convertible

virtues as generous head and leg room, plus enormous cargo space from what is basically a very compact car. However, mainstream buyers may find the key position is too disorienting and the cabin too narrow.

The dashboard is little changed, so most controls are close at hand. But the power-window buttons are mounted between the seats rather than on the door panels where they'd be more convenient to operate.

The V-6 feels strong and smooth, and works particularly well with the new 4-speed automatic. It shifts quickly and consistently with no hesitation. It downshifts smoothly, eagerly providing all the passing power you need. The 900's 2.3-liter 4-cylinder has adequate power with the manual, but feels underpowered when paired with the automatic.

Body lean is evident when taking turns at speed, but these cars have a generally sporty feel, with precise steering and excellent grip. The taut suspension provides excellent control, but combines with the modest wheelbase for a ride that's choppy enough over rough pavement to deter some buyers. Wind and road noise are disconcerting at highway speeds.

Mainstream shoppers interested in a near-luxury car still aren't likely to put the Saab 900 on their must-see list, but we credit Saab with making a better 900 for those who love and appreciate its quirky nature.

NHTSA CRASH TEST RESULTS
1996 Saab 900

4-DOOR HATCHBACK

Driver	☆☆☆☆
Passenger	☆☆☆☆

(The National Highway Traffic Safety Administration tests a vehicle's crashworthiness in front and side collisions. Their ratings suggest the chance of serious injury: ☆☆☆☆☆—10% or less; ☆☆☆☆—10-20% or less; ☆☆☆—20-30% or less; ☆☆—35-45% or less; ☆—More than 45%.)

SPECIFICATIONS

	2-door hatchback	4-door sedan	2-door conv.
Wheelbase, in.	102.4	102.4	102.4
Overall length, in.	182.6	182.5	182.6
Overall width, in.	67.4	67.4	67.4
Overall height, in.	56.5	56.5	56.5
Curb weight, lbs.	2940	2980	3130
Cargo volume, cu. ft.	49.8	49.8	28.3
Fuel capacity, gals.	18.0	18.0	18.0
Seating capacity	5	5	4
Front head room, in.	39.3	39.3	39.3
Max. front leg room, in.	42.3	43.3	43.3
Rear head room, in.	37.8	37.8	37.9
Min. rear leg room, in.	36.2	36.2	36.0

Powertrain layout: transverse front-engine/front-wheel drive

ENGINES

	dohc I-4	dohc I-4	Turbocharged dohc I-4	dohc V-6
Size, liters/cu. in.	2.1/129	2.3/140	2.0/129	2.5/152
Horsepower	140	150	160-185	170
Torque (lbs./ft.)	133	155	188-194	167
EPA city/highway mpg				
5-speed OD manual	20/26	20/29	21/28	18/25
3-speed automatic	18/21		19/23	
4-speed OD automatic		20/28		19/27
Consumer Guide™ observed MPG				
5-speed OD manual		24.4		19.3

Built in Sweden.

RETAIL PRICES

	GOOD	AVERAGE	POOR
1994 900	$9,500-12,300	$8,500-11,300	$6,000-8,000
1994 900Turbo	12,000-13,000	11,000-12,000	8,000-8,800
1994 900Convertible	13,500-16,500	12,000-15,000	9,000-11,500
1995 900	12,000-15,000	10,500-13,500	7,500-10,000
1995 900Turbo	14,200-15,500	13,000-14,000	9,500-10,300
1995 900Convertible	16,500-19,500	15,000-18,000	11,500-14,000
1996 900	14,500-17,500	13,000-16,000	9,500-12,000
1996 900Turbo	17,000-18,500	15,500-17,000	11,500-12,500
1996 900Convertible	19,500-23,000	18,000-21,500	14,000-17,000
1997 900	17,000-21,000	15,500-19,500	11,500-15,000
1997 900Turbo	21,000-23,000	19,500-21,200	15,000-16,000
1997 900Convertible	22,500-26,500	20,800-24,500	16,500-19,500

SAAB

	GOOD	AVERAGE	POOR
1998 900	20,000-24,000	18,500-22,500	14,000-17,500
1998 900Turbo	21,000-27,000	19,000-25,000	14,500-20,000
1998 900Convertible	27,000-33,000	25,000-31,000	20,000-26,000

AVERAGE REPLACEMENT COSTS

A/C Compressor	$665	Clutch, Pressure Plate, Bearing	655
Alternator	455	Constant Velocity Joints	485
Radiator	395	Brakes	265
Timing Chain or Belt	630	Shocks and/or Struts	990
Automatic Transmission or Transaxle	1,250	Exhaust System	640

TROUBLE SPOTS

• **Transmission leak** The gear selector shaft seal is prone to leak on manual transmissions and will be replaced under normal warranty provisions. (1994-96)

• **Radio** Scratches or microscopic cracks in the rear window heater grid cause interference ("static") in the radio when the rear defroster is turned on. (All)

• **Engine fan** The battery may go dead because the cooling fan relay, which allows the fan to run 10 minutes after the engine is turned off, keeps the fan on. The time delay relay should be replaced with a standard relay. (1990+)

• **Hard starting** The turbo bypass valve is secured with plastic clamps that break, causing hard starting and poor drivability. They must be replaced with metal clamps and dealers will do so whenever the car is in for service. No letters were sent to owners.

• **Poor drivability** Stumble, stalling, or hesitation during the first minute after startup is corrected by replacing the engine control computer, which may be covered by the normal and/or emissions warranty. (1994-95)

RECALL HISTORY

1994 On some manual front seats, trigger springs at fore/aft lever do not properly lock the seat rails. **1994 hatchback** Weld omitted from manual driver's seat rails. **1994** Weld points for side-protection beam in rear door may be out of position. **1994-95** Welds on recliner may be missing, allowing seatback to fall backward when under load. **1994-95 with manual shift** It is possible to move shift lever into reverse, remove key, and still be in neutral. **1994-98** Instructions for properly aiming headlights were omitted. **1995 w/Bosch "Motronic 2.10.3"** Upon startup, engine speed may fluctuate for up to 30 seconds. **1995 convertible** Steering-column shaft may be misaligned. **1996** Seatbelt anchorage on some cars may not properly secure the occupant in an accident. **1997-98** Air bag alert label on driver's sunvisor was omitted.

1991-96 SATURN COUPE

1995 Saturn SC2

FOR Air bags, dual (later models) • Anti-lock brakes (optional) • Fuel economy • Acceleration (SC2) • Instruments/controls

AGAINST Engine noise • Road noise • Acceleration (SC1) • Rear-seat room • Entry/exit

EVALUATION If possible, select a base model (1995-96) with the 100-horsepower base engine paired with the manual 5-speed. Acceleration is sluggish with the automatic. Also, the revised base engine performs better than the previous 85-horsepower unit. The more powerful twin-cam engine in the SC2 performs well with either transmission. We timed one with the automatic at 9.1 seconds to 60 mph. The same car averaged 25 mpg from mainly urban driving. The SC1 should prove even more economical. However, both engines are still too noisy at higher speeds.

Like most other sports coupes, these two suffer from limited rear-seat room, though there's plenty of space in front for tall people. The gauges are clearly marked and well lit at night, and the steering column stalks for both lights and wipers are at the driver's fingertips. The early climate controls are too low in the

SATURN

center of the dashboard and require a long look away from the road to find the right switch.

Saturn coupes are getting lots of competition from rivals, but a new used car certification program from Saturn dealerships could help ensure buyers will get a good deal on a used Saturn, plus the promise of higher-than-average customer service on repairs and warranty work after the purchase.

SPECIFICATIONS

	2-door coupe
Wheelbase, in.	99.2
Overall length, in.	173.2
Overall width, in.	67.5
Overall height, in.	50.6
Curb weight, lbs.	2284
Cargo volume, cu. ft.	10.9
Fuel capacity, gals.	12.8
Seating capacity	4
Front head room, in.	37.5
Max. front leg room, in.	42.6
Rear head room, in.	35.0
Min. rear leg room, in.	26.5

Powertrain layout: transverse front-engine/front-wheel drive

ENGINES

	ohc I-4	ohc I-4	dohc I-4
Size, liters/cu. in.	1.9/116	1.9/116	1.9/116
Horsepower	85	100	124
Torque (lbs./ft.)	110	114	122
EPA city/highway mpg			
5-speed OD manual	27/37	29/40	25/35
4-speed OD automatic	26/35	27/37	24/34
Consumer Guide™ observed MPG			
5-speed OD manual	24.0	31.9	25.8

Built in USA.

RETAIL PRICES

	GOOD	AVERAGE	POOR
1991 SC2	$3,600-4,300	$2,900-3,600	$1,400-1,900
1992 SC2	4,300-5,000	3,600-4,300	1,900-2,400
1993 SC1/SC2	4,800-5,800	4,100-5,000	2,300-2,800
1994 SC1/SC2	5,600-6,700	4,800-5,900	2,800-3,500
1995 SC1/SC2	7,000-8,500	6,200-7,700	4,000-4,900
1996 SC1/SC2	8,500-10,000	7,600-9,000	5,200-6,200

AVERAGE REPLACEMENT COSTS

A/C Compressor $390
Alternator 350
Radiator 350
Timing Chain or Belt 295
Automatic Transmission or
  Transaxle.........................905

Clutch, Pressure Plate,
  Bearing.............................530
Constant Velocity Joints.....380
Brakes..................................190
Shocks and/or Struts 485
Exhaust System 298

TROUBLE SPOTS

• **Cruise control** If the cruise control fluctuates at speeds over 64 mph, a new control module assembly will be installed. (1991-95)

• **Engine noise** Squealing from the front of the engine when the temperature is below 40°F will be fixed by replacing the drive belt idler pulley with one having a revised bearing. (1991-95)

• **Transmission slippage** If the automatic transmission shifts harshly, erratically, or sticks in gear or neutral (usually accompanied by a malfunction indicator light), iron sediment in the valve body may be the problem. (1993-94)

• **Tail/brake lights** A drop in fuel economy, brake noise, vehicle vibration and/or increased brake pedal travel could be caused by a mis-adjusted brake light switch that does not allow the pedal to return to full release. The switch must be adjusted or replaced. (1991-93)

• **Doors** If the doors will not open from the inside or the outside, the door latch assembly(s) will be replaced. (1991-93)

• **Engine stalling** During the first five minutes after starting, if the DOHC engine stalls, and does not restart, when coming to a stop, the oil may be the wrong viscosity. If the right oil is being used, the hydraulic lash adjusters are at fault and must be replaced. (1991-95)

• **Brake noise** Brakes that growl or grind during low speed stops are repaired by replacing the front pads and machining, or replacing, the rotors. (1991-95)

• **Trunk latch** If the trunk can be opened without the key, Saturn will fix the release mechanism with no limit to vehicle age or mileage. (1991-93)

• **Radio antenna** A whistling wind noise may be coming from the radio antenna and a revised one will correct the problem. (1991-95)

RECALL HISTORY

1991-93 Generator wiring harness could suffer excessive current flow. **1992** Automatic transaxle valve assemblies on some cars were improperly machined. **1993** Brake booster housing on some cars could separate. **1993 SC2** Battery cable terminal at solenoid may be formed incorrectly. **1995 with automatic** Improperly-adjusted cable makes it possible to shift from "Park" with key removed, or to remove key while lever is in position other than "Park." **1997** Belted front passenger could experience seat movement during frontal impact. **1997** Some ignition keys can be removed while in "run" position. **1997** Lock-up feature of seatbelt may not work properly.

1991-95 SATURN SEDAN/WAGON

1996 Saturn SL2 4-door

FOR Air bags, dual (later models) • Anti-lock brakes (optional) • Fuel economy • Acceleration (SL2, SW2)

AGAINST Engine noise • Road noise • Acceleration (base) • Rear-seat room

EVALUATION The single-cam engine in the SL1 and SW1 gives these cars adequate acceleration with the manual transmission, but with the automatic you often have to floor the throttle to keep up with traffic. The dual-cam engine provides lively acceleration and decent passing power with either transmission. Though some changes have been made over the years to decrease interior noise levels, engines still become loud and harsh at higher speeds.

Both the sedans and wagons have ample head room in front for 6-footers to sit comfortably, though the front buckets don't go back far enough for tall people to stretch out. Passengers in the back have just as much head room but less leg room. The wagon's firm rear seat has an upright backrest that some may find uncomfortable. Entry/exit is easy to the front, but tight through the narrow rear doors. The import-inspired dash is easy to use, and outward visibility is unobstructed. Trunk space is good for the class and the split rear seatbacks fold for more cargo room.

Responsive handling and adept roadhandling are high points, particularly on the SL2 and SW2 models. And the addition of a softer suspension and tires for '93 on these level "2" models provide a noticeable improvement in ride quality.

Saturn sedans aren't the best choice in a subcompact, but overall they rank only slightly below the class-leading Honda Civic and Toyota Corolla.

NHTSA CRASH TEST RESULTS
1996 Saturn Sedan/Wagon

4-DOOR SEDAN

Driver	☆☆☆☆
Passenger	☆☆☆☆

(The National Highway Traffic Safety Administration tests a vehicle's crashworthiness in front and side collisions. Their ratings suggest the chance of serious injury: ☆☆☆☆☆—10% or less; ☆☆☆☆—10-20% or less; ☆☆☆—20-30% or less; ☆☆—35-45% or less; ☆—More than 45%.)

SPECIFICATIONS

	4-door sedan	4-door wagon
Wheelbase, in.	102.4	102.4
Overall length, in.	176.3	176.3
Overall width, in.	67.6	67.6
Overall height, in.	55.5	53.7
Curb weight, lbs.	2325	2380
Cargo volume, cu. ft.	11.9	56.3
Fuel capacity, gals.	12.8	12.8
Seating capacity	5	5
Front head room, in.	38.5	38.8
Max. front leg room, in.	42.5	42.5
Rear head room, in.	36.3	37.4
Min. rear leg room, in.	32.6	32.6

Powertrain layout: transverse front-engine/front-wheel drive

ENGINES

	ohc I-4	ohc I-4	dohc I-4
Size, liters/cu. in.	1.9/116	1.9/116	1.9/116
Horsepower	85	100	124
Torque (lbs./ft.)	110	114	122
EPA city/highway mpg			
5-speed OD manual	27/37	29/40	25/35
4-speed OD automatic	26/35	27/37	24/34
Consumer Guide™ observed MPG			
5-speed OD manual		31.9	
4-speed OD automatic			22.3

Built in USA.

SATURN

RETAIL PRICES

	GOOD	AVERAGE	POOR
1991 SL1/SL2	$2,100-3,500	$1,500-2,800	$600-1,300
1992 SL/SL1/SL2	2,600-4,100	1,900-3,400	900-1,600
1993 SL/SL1/SL2/SW1/SW2	3,300-5,400	2,600-4,700	1,200-2,500
1994 SL/SL1/SL2/SW1/SW2	4,200-6,400	3,500-5,600	1,600-3,200
1995 SL/SL1/SL2/SW1/SW2	5,200-8,000	4,500-7,200	2,300-4,500

AVERAGE REPLACEMENT COSTS

A/C Compressor $390
Alternator 350
Radiator 295
Timing Chain or Belt 295
Automatic Transmission or
   Transaxle........................905

Clutch, Pressure Plate,
   Bearing............................530
Constant Velocity Joints.....355
Brakes................................190
Shocks and/or Struts 485
Exhaust System.................300

TROUBLE SPOTS

• **Cruise control** If the cruise control fluctuates at speeds over 64 mph, a new control module assembly will be installed. (1991-95)

• **Engine noise** Squealing from the front of the engine when the temperature is below 40°F may be fixed by replacing the drive belt idler pulley with one having a revised bearing. (1991-95)

• **Transmission slippage** If the automatic transmission shifts harshly, erratically, or sticks in gear or neutral (usually accompanied by a malfunction indicator light), iron sediment in the valve body may be the problem. (1993-94)

• **Tail/brake lights** A drop in fuel economy, brake noise, vehicle vibration, and/or increased brake pedal travel could be caused by a mis-adjusted brake light switch that does not allow the pedal to return to full release. The switch must be adjusted or replaced. (1991-93)

• **Doors** If the doors will not open from the inside or the outside, the door latch assembly(s) must be replaced. (1991-93)

• **Engine stalling** During the first five minutes after starting, if the DOHC engine stalls and does not restart when coming to a stop, the oil may be the wrong viscosity. If the right oil is being used, the hydraulic lash adjusters are at fault and must be replaced. (1991-95)

• **Brake noise** Brakes that growl or grind during low speed stops are repaired by replacing the front pads and machining, or replacing, the rotors. (1991-95)

• **Radio antenna** A whistling wind noise may be coming from the radio antenna and a revised one will correct the problem. (1991-95)

RECALL HISTORY

1991-93 Generator wiring harness could suffer excessive current flow. **1992** Automatic transaxle valve assemblies on some cars were improperly machined. **1993** Brake booster housing on some cars could separate. **1993 SL2/SW2** Battery cable terminal at starter solenoid may be formed incorrectly. **1995 SL with manual steering** Some pinion shafts could fracture, causing total loss of steering control. **1995 with automatic** Improperly-adjusted cable makes it possible to shift from "Park" with key removed, or to remove key while lever is in position other than "Park." **1996 station wagons** On some wagons, certain welds between roof and reinforcement panels do not meet specifications; flange sides could partially separate in a crash. **1996-97 SL with manual steering** Pinion bearing cage in steering gear can separate under high-load conditions, disengaging and causing loss of control. **1997** Ignition key on a few cars can be removed while in "run" position.

1993-98 SUBARU IMPREZA

1993 Subaru Impreza sedan

FOR Air bags, dual (later models) • Optional anti-lock brakes • All-wheel drive (AWD models) • Instruments/controls

AGAINST Acceleration (early AWD models) • Rear seat entry/exit • Rear seat room • Cargo room (exc. wagons)

EVALUATION With the 2.2-liter engine, acceleration of an AWD model is more than adequate with a manual transmission and adequate with automatic. Simply put, a 1.8-liter model lacks sufficient snap when you need to merge into expressway traffic, or pass other cars on the highway. The 2.5-liter on the RS is probably the best all-around engine, providing ample accelera-

SUBARU

tion and good passing power. All engines sound gruff and feel rough with manual shift. Our 1993 test wagon with AWD and a 5-speed felt sluggish from startup, while an AWD sedan with automatic was downright slow. We averaged 24.8 mpg overall with the early AWD wagon—very nice for an AWD car.

Interior space is comparable to that of a Honda Civic, Geo Prizm, or Toyota Corolla. That means sufficient space for four adults. But rear leg space is barely adequate, if the front seats are pushed back. Tall drivers might want more seat travel to get farther from the steering wheel and pedals. Visibility is good to all directions. Cargo space isn't so great, even in the wagon.

Dashboards are logically laid out, with controls grouped around the gauge cluster—easy to find and operate. On the down side, using the pull-out cup holder blocks access to the stereo controls.

With the exception of available AWD, the Impreza fails to stand apart. Later models might be more tempting—especially the Outback Sport wagon or the 2.5 RS coupe.

NHTSA CRASH TEST RESULTS
1996 Subaru Impreza

4-DOOR SEDAN

Driver	☆☆☆☆
Passenger	☆☆☆☆

(The National Highway Traffic Safety Administration tests a vehicle's crashworthiness in front and side collisions. Their ratings suggest the chance of serious injury: ☆☆☆☆☆—10% or less; ☆☆☆☆—10-20% or less; ☆☆☆—20-30% or less; ☆☆—35-45% or less; ☆—More than 45%.)

SPECIFICATIONS

	2-door coupe	4-door sedan	4-door wagon
Wheelbase, in.	99.2	99.2	99.2
Overall length, in.	172.2	172.2	172.2
Overall width, in.	67.1	67.1	67.1
Overall height, in.	55.5	55.5	55.5
Curb weight, lbs.	2400	2420	2750
Cargo volume, cu. ft.	11.1	11.1	62.1
Fuel capacity, gals.	13.2	13.2	13.2
Seating capacity	5	5	5
Front head room, in.	39.2	39.2	39.2
Max. front leg room, in.	43.1	43.1	43.1
Rear head room, in.	36.7	36.7	37.4
Min. rear leg room, in.	32.5	32.5	32.4

Powertrain layout: transverse front-engine/front- or all-wheel drive

ENGINES

	ohc F-4	ohc F-4	dohc F-4
Size, liters/cu. in.	1.8/109	2.2/135	2.5/150
Horsepower	110-115	135-137	165

478

	ohc F-4	ohc F-4	dohc F-4
Torque (lbs./ft.)	110-120	140-145	162
EPA city/highway mpg			
5-speed OD manual	25/31	22/29	22/28
4-speed automatic.............................			22/28
4-speed OD automatic	24/30	22/29	
Consumer Guide™ observed MPG			
5-speed OD manual	24.3		24.7
4-speed OD automatic		24.7	

Built in Japan.

RETAIL PRICES	GOOD	AVERAGE	POOR
1993 Impreza	$2,800-5,700	$2,100-5,000	$900-3,000
1993 Impreza AWD	4,600-6,200	3,800-5,400	1,800-3,000
1994 Impreza	3,500-6,000	2,800-5,200	1,300-3,200
1994 Impreza AWD	6,000-7,800	5,200-7,000	2,700-4,000
1995 Impreza	4,500-6,200	3,800-5,400	2,000-3,400
1995 Impreza AWD	6,000-9,400	5,100-8,400	2,600-5,000
1996 Impreza	6,700-10,500	5,800-9,500	3,300-6,000
1996 Impreza Outback	10,500-12,000	9,500-10,800	6,500-7,500
1997 Impreza	8,300-11,500	7,400-10,500	4,400-7,000
1997 Impreza Outback	12,000-13,500	11,000-12,000	7,500-8,400
1998 Impreza	10,500-15,500	9,300-14,000	6,000-10,000
1998 Impreza Outback	14,000-16,500	12,500-15,000	8,800-10,500

AVERAGE REPLACEMENT COSTS

A/C Compressor $725		Clutch, Pressure Plate,	
Alternator 410		Bearing 565	
Radiator 285		Constant Velocity Joints.....730	
Timing Chain or Belt 180		Brakes...................................350	
Automatic Transmission or		Shocks and/or Struts 470	
Transaxle........................850		Exhaust System.................260	

TROUBLE SPOTS

• **Engine misfire** Bucking and jerking at slow speeds when turning or decelerating is due to a defective transfer clutch on all-wheel-drive cars. (1993-97)

• **Hard starting** The engine may be hard to start after sitting overnight in cold weather because ice forms on the tips of the fuel injectors. (1993-96)

• **Dashboard lights** The hydraulic motor for the ABS system runs with the key turned off (due to a bad relay), which illuminates the ABS warning light on the dash and may discharge the battery. (1993-96)

SUBARU

• **Engine noise** The knock sensors in the cylinder heads may fail, which can cause pinging under load. They should be replaced under the emissions warranty. (1992-95)

RECALL HISTORY

1993 AWD Fuel filler system does not comply with federal leakage requirements.

1990-94 SUBARU LEGACY

1990 Subaru Legacy LSi Wagon

FOR Air bags, driver (later models) • Anti-lock brakes (optional) • Acceleration (turbo) • Wet-weather traction (4WD) • Handling/roadholding

AGAINST Fuel economy • Engine noise • Road noise • Wind noise • Manual transmission linkage

EVALUATION The Legacy's 2.2-liter solves our chief complaint lodged against previous Subarus. This new 4-cylinder is smooth and quiet, delivering spritely acceleration with either the 5-speed manual or 4-speed automatic. However, the 5-seed seemed a bit hesitant to engage during quick gear changes and was reluctant to go into reverse. The turbocharged engine is even more powerful, and virtually devoid of turbo lag. The downside is below-average fuel economy. We averaged only 17.4 mpg in our wagon in mostly urban driving.

Head room and leg room are adequate for adults both front and rear, but the back door opening is a bit narrow at the bottom, making it difficult to swing your feet in and out. A comfortable driving position is aided by the standard tilt steering wheel and, on LS and higher models, an adjustable-height driver's seat. All controls are well placed and easy to operate while driving. The spacious trunk is well trimmed, with a bumper-level opening and low liftover height.

While the Legacy is not an outstanding value, the Subaru AWD models have few competitors, unless you step up to a sport-utility vehicle and risk loosing your car-like amenities.

SPECIFICATIONS

	4-door sedan	4-door wagon
Wheelbase, in.	101.6	101.5
Overall length, in.	178.9	181.9
Overall width, in.	66.5	66.5
Overall height, in.	53.5	54.7
Curb weight, lbs.	2740	2860
Cargo volume, cu. ft.	14.3	71.0
Fuel capacity, gals.	15.9	15.9
Seating capacity	5	5
Front head room, in.	38.0	38.4
Max. front leg room, in.	43.1	43.1
Rear head room, in.	36.0	37.8
Min. rear leg room, in.	34.8	35.0

Powertrain layout: transverse front-engine/front- or all-wheel drive

ENGINES

	ohc F-4	Turbocharged ohc F-4
Size, liters/cu. in.	2.2/135	2.2/135
Horsepower	130	160
Torque (lbs./ft.)	137	181

EPA city/highway mpg

5-speed OD manual	23/31	19/25
4-speed OD automatic	22/29	18/23

Consumer Guide™ observed MPG

5-speed OD manual	24.1	17.4
4-speed OD automatic	22.7	19.0

Built in USA and Japan.

RETAIL PRICES

	GOOD	AVERAGE	POOR
1990 Legacy	$2,300-3,600	$1,700-2,900	$500-1,200
1991 Legacy	2,800-5,300	2,100-4,600	800-2,500
1992 Legacy	4,000-7,000	3,300-6,200	1,500-3,500
1993 Legacy	5,000-9,000	4,200-8,200	2,200-5,200
1994 Legacy	6,400-10,800	5,600-9,800	3,300-6,600

AVERAGE REPLACEMENT COSTS

A/C Compressor	$430	Clutch, Pressure Plate,	
Alternator	400	Bearing	480
Radiator	360	Constant Velocity Joints	460
Timing Chain or Belt	195	Brakes	245
Automatic Transmission or		Shocks and/or Struts	645
Transaxle	975	Exhaust System	340

TROUBLE SPOTS

• **Transmission slippage** If it is difficult to shift out of park, the transmission's parking pawl will be replaced under campaign number, WZP46 and, if the work was done, a label with this number will be found on the radiator support. (1990-91)

• **Heater core** To repair a clicking noise caused by the heater mode door actuator cycling over the electrical contacts causing it to continually reverse, a resistor will be installed in the wiring harness. (1992-94)

• **Seat** Misaligned side rails prevent the seat from locking in place when adjusting and shims must be added to the outer rail (usually) to correct the alignment. (1990-94)

• **Transmission slippage** If the transmission is slow to engage after being parked several hours, the torque converter is draining down and a new cooler line with a check valve will be installed. However, installing this kit on factory modified units can cause severe damage. (1990-91)

• **Hard starting** The engine will not start, and the technician often cannot find any obvious cause because silicone contaminated the ignition relay internally during assembly. Subaru will cover under normal warranty.

• **Automatic transmission** The automatic transmission dipstick may break requiring the broken bits to be removed with a magnet inserted in the dipstick tube or by draining the oil pan. (1990+)

RECALL HISTORY

1990 Lever pin of defroster shutter door may become dislocated and allow the shutter to close, preventing defroster from functioning and affecting visibility. **1990-91** Torque of latch screws on front doors may loosen over time, due to gap between latch base plate and inner door panel, so door could not be opened from inside the car. **1990-91** Under certain conditions on cars with 4EAT electronically controlled automatic transmission, park gear may not disengage immediately when lever is moved from "Park" to "Reverse," which could result in abrupt vehicle movement and possible loss of control. **1990-93 all-wheel drive** 5-speed manual gearbox may leak if driven continuously in extreme cold or high humidity; transmission could seize, bringing vehicle to sudden stop. **1992** Top of fuel tank may have been punctured during assembly, which could cause fuel leakage that results in fire if leak occurs near an ignition source.

1995-98 SUBARU LEGACY

1995 Subaru Legacy Brighton Wagon

FOR Air bags, dual • Anti-lock brakes (optional) • Wet-weather traction (traction control, 4WD) • Passenger and cargo room • Visibility

AGAINST Engine noise • Fuel economy (4WD)

EVALUATION Legacy's 2.2-liter engine is adequate for most circumstances, but it throbs and feels strained in hard acceleration and in hilly country. It's also more gruff-sounding than most 4-cylinders. The dual-overhead-cam 2.5-liter engine is quieter and smoother, with both excellent acceleration and passing power. But note that fuel economy is unimpressive on the AWD models.

Legacy's suspension strikes an admirable balance between ride and handling, with ride comfort taking precedence. Bumps are absorbed easily and all models feel stable. Body lean is noticeable in spirited cornering maneuvers, and the front end tends to plow when pushed hard—more so on front-drive versions than AWD models. A low dashboard and narrow roof pillars provide clear visibility in all directions. Front head and leg room are ample. In back, people under six feet tall should have adequate room, and both bodystyles provide outstanding cargo space.

With the addition of dual air bags, the new Legacy is a more competitive entry in the compact class. But its trump card remains its competent line of all-wheel-drive sedans and wagons, which Subaru is finally stressing in its advertising.

NHTSA CRASH TEST RESULTS
1995 Subaru Legacy

4-DOOR SEDAN

Driver	☆☆☆☆
Passenger	☆☆☆☆

(The National Highway Traffic Safety Administration tests a vehicle's crashworthiness in front and side collisions. Their ratings suggest the chance of serious injury: ☆☆☆☆☆—10% or less; ☆☆☆☆—10-20% or less; ☆☆☆—20-30% or less; ☆☆—35-45% or less; ☆—More than 45%.)

SPECIFICATIONS

	4-door sedan	4-door wagon
Wheelbase, in.	103.5	103.5
Overall length, in.	180.9	183.9
Overall width, in.	67.5	67.5
Overall height, in.	55.3	57.1
Curb weight, lbs.	2570	2685
Cargo volume, cu. ft.	13.0	73.0
Fuel capacity, gals.	15.9	15.9
Seating capacity	5	5
Front head room, in.	38.9	39.5
Max. front leg room, in.	43.3	43.3
Rear head room, in.	36.7	38.8
Min. rear leg room, in.	34.6	34.8

Powertrain layout: longitudinal front-engine/front- or all-wheel drive

ENGINES

	ohc F-4	ohc F-4
Size, liters/cu. in.	2.2/135	2.5/150
Horsepower	135-137	155-165
Torque (lbs./ft.)	140-145	155-162
EPA city/highway mpg		
5-speed OD manual	23/30	21/27
4-speed OD automatic	23/30	20/26
Consumer Guide™ observed MPG		
5-speed OD manual	23.6	22.9

Built in USA and Japan.

AVERAGE REPLACEMENT COSTS

A/C Compressor	$560	Clutch, Pressure Plate, Bearing	515
Alternator	345	Constant Velocity Joints	460
Radiator	360	Brakes	225
Timing Chain or Belt	195	Shocks and/or Struts	615
Automatic Transmission or Transaxle	940	Exhaust System	565

RETAIL PRICES

	GOOD	AVERAGE	POOR
1995 Legacy	$8,200-13,000	$7,500-12,200	$5,000-8,500

	GOOD	AVERAGE	POOR
1996 Legacy	9,700-15,000	8,800-14,000	5,800-10,000
1997 Legacy	11,500-16,800	10,500-15,500	7,000-11,500
1998 Legacy	13,500-18,800	12,000-17,300	8,200-13,000

TROUBLE SPOTS

• **Oil leak** An oil leak between the oil pump and block is repaired by drilling out the oil return hole to 6mm diameter. (1995)

• **Transmission slippage** Severely cracked secondary pulleys and pump drives that pull away from the impeller shaft cause the ECVT (constantly variable transmission) to slip. (1995)

• **Dashboard lights** If the check engine light mysteriously comes on in cold weather, but technicians can never find any trouble, it is likely due to ice forming in the vacuum line between the engine and transmission and a filter will be installed to keep the light from coming on. (1995)

• **Automatic transmission** The automatic transmission dipstick may break requiring the broken bits to be removed with a magnet inserted in the dipstick tube or draining the oil pan. (1990+)

RECALL HISTORY

1997 Hazard warning switch can stick in intermediate position, so turn signals become inoperable. **1997** Omitted bearing in throttle body assembly could eventually lead to incomplete return of throttle, resulting in fast idle. **1997-98 w/automatic transmission** Due to poor welds, ignition key can stick, shift lever/linkages can break, and improper movement of shift lever can occur. **1998** Purolator oil filter can fracture, causing vaporized oil spray and subsequent oil leak at hot exhaust system; could result in underhood fire.

1990-98 SUZUKI SIDEKICK

FOR 4WD traction • Maneuverability • Fuel economy

AGAINST Ride • Noise • No air bags • Acceleration (automatic) • Rear seat room

EVALUATION Acceleration with 80-horsepower engine is on the leisurely side, and the power boost in 1992 does not help much. The Sport model's larger engine finally offers acceptable performance. That 1.8-liter 4-cylinder works well with the 4-speed automatic transmission. A late-model wagon with manual shift averaged 25.3 mpg, though automatic dropped the figure to a so-so 21.4 mpg. However, even the latest Sidekick engines growl loudly under throttle. Wind and road noise are abundant at

SUZUKI

1992 Suzuki Sidekick 2-door

highway speeds, too.

Reasonably stable in corners and on the highway, Sidekick suffers a somewhat stiff and jiggly ride on rough surfaces. Four-door models endure less choppiness, credited to their longer wheelbase, but they're not that much more comfortable overall. Tall and narrow, Sidekicks must be driven with care through turns. Sidekick's 4-wheel-drive system is not for use on dry pavement.

Head room is plentiful up front, but the rear bench seat holds only two adults, for 4-passenger capacity. Worse yet, it's hard, with little leg space when the front seats are all the way aft—though space is adequate otherwise. In the Sidekick's narrow cabin, doors sit close to the seats, leaving little outside shoulder room. Cargo space is best in the 4-door, with its swing-open rear door and fold-down back seat.

Though better than the tiny old Samurai, this is still not a good choice for everyday driving, even in 4-door form.

NHTSA CRASH TEST RESULTS

1996 Suzuki Sidekick 2-DOOR CONVERTIBLE

Driver	☆☆
Passenger	☆☆☆

(The National Highway Traffic Safety Administration tests a vehicle's crashworthiness in front and side collisions. Their ratings suggest the chance of serious injury: ☆☆☆☆☆—10% or less; ☆☆☆☆—10-20% or less; ☆☆☆—20-30% or less; ☆☆—35-45% or less; ☆—More than 45%.)

SPECIFICATIONS	2-door conv.	4-door wagon	4-door wagon
Wheelbase, in.	86.6	97.6	97.6
Overall length, in.	143.7	158.7	162.4
Overall width, in.	64.2	64.4	66.7
Overall height, in.	64.3	65.7	66.3

	2-door conv.	4-door wagon	4-door wagon
Curb weight, lbs.	2339	2632	2917
Cargo volume, cu. ft.	32.9	45.0	45.0
Fuel capacity, gals.	11.1	14.5	18.5
Seating capacity	4	4	4
Front head room, in.	39.5	40.6	40.6
Max. front leg room, in.	42.1	42.1	42.1
Rear head room, in.	39.0	40.0	38.6
Min. rear leg room, in.	31.7	32.7	32.7

Powertrain layout: longitudinal front-engine/rear- or 4-wheel drive

ENGINES

	ohc I-4	dohc I-4	dohc I-4
Size, liters/cu. in.	1.6/97	1.6/97	1.8/112
Horsepower	80	95	120
Torque (lbs./ft.)	94	98	114
EPA city/highway mpg			
5-speed OD manual	25/27	23/26	23/25
3-speed automatic	23/24		
4-speed OD automatic		22/26	21/24
Consumer Guide™ observed MPG			
5-speed OD manual	25.3	24.8	
4-speed OD automatic		22.1	20.2

Built in Canada and Japan.

RETAIL PRICES	GOOD	AVERAGE	POOR
1990 Sidekick conv.	$1,700-2,700	$1,100-2,000	$300-800
1991 Sidekick conv.	2,400-3,500	1,700-2,800	600-1,200
1991 Sidekick 4-door	3,100-4,000	2,400-3,300	1,000-1,500
1992 Sidekick conv.	2,900-4,100	2,200-3,300	900-1,500
1992 Sidekick 4-door	4,100-5,000	3,400-4,300	1,600-2,100
1993 Sidekick conv.	3,400-4,800	2,700-4,000	1,200-2,000
1993 Sidekick 4-door	3,900-6,000	3,200-5,200	1,600-2,800
1994 Sidekick conv.	3,900-5,600	3,200-4,800	1,500-2,500
1994 Sidekick 4-door	4,400-6,700	3,700-5,900	1,900-3,300
1995 Sidekick conv.	4,600-6,300	3,800-5,500	1,900-3,000
1995 Sidekick 4-door	5,200-7,600	4,400-6,800	2,500-3,900
1996 Sidekick conv.	5,500-7,600	4,700-6,700	2,500-3,800
1996 Sidekick 4-door	6,200-10,000	5,400-9,100	3,000-5,700
1997 Sidekick conv.	6,800-9,000	5,900-8,000	3,400-4,800
1997 Sidekick 4-door	7,500-12,500	6,500-11,500	4,000-7,500
1998 Sidekick conv.	8,600-11,500	7,500-10,300	4,700-6,800
1998 Sidekick 4-door	9,300-14,500	8,300-13,000	5,300-9,000

AVERAGE REPLACEMENT COSTS

A/C Compressor	$385	Clutch, Pressure Plate,	
Alternator	420	Bearing	450
Radiator	295	Constant Velocity Joints	280
Timing Chain or Belt	230	Brakes	250
Automatic Transmission or		Shocks and/or Struts	650
Transaxle	515	Exhaust System	175

TROUBLE SPOTS

• **Hard starting** Hard starting or a no-start below freezing (32-degrees F), especially at high altitudes requires a Cold Start Harness Set attached to the computer. (1989-90)

• **Engine misfire** Using premium fuel can trigger trouble codes and cause poor starting and poor drivability in cold weather. (1996-97)

• **Transmission slippage** The transfer case binds and can be damaged if driven on dry roads in 4WD mode so the vehicle should be road tested in all ranges. (1990-97)

• **Automatic transmission** The automatic transmission may hunt or chuggle around 40-45 mph and a time delay module kit for the clutch is available to correct the condition. (1990-95)

• **Exhaust system** The exhaust system should have been replaced under a recall because a narrow section of pipe caused noise, poor power, and poor fuel economy. (1992-93)

RECALL HISTORY

1990-91 Front seatbelt button can break and pieces can fall inside.
1996 4-doors Fuel tank can puncture during rear-end collision.

1990-95 TOYOTA 4RUNNER

FOR Passenger and cargo room • Ride (later models) • Antilock brakes (optional) • Wet-weather traction (4WD) • Reliability

AGAINST Air bags (none) • Fuel economy • Acceleration • Entry/exit • Road noise • Engine noise • Wind noise • Handling

EVALUATION The 4Runner's chief attractions are tight, thorough assembly quality and a commendable reputation for quality. However, the 4Runner is much smaller inside than the top-selling Ford Explorer and Jeep Grand Cherokee, with barely adequate space for four adults. Exit/entry are hurt by a higher-than-usual stance—nearly two feet off the ground. Also, fuel economy is very mediocre. We averaged just 13.8 mpg with a V-6 model in our last test. Acceleration is nothing special either,

1995 Toyota 4Runner SR5

even with the V-6, which is hard-pressed to reach 60 mph in under 13 seconds. And you can forget the 4-cylinder, which is even slower.

Plus points include the convenient 4WDemand system and 4-wheel anti-lock brakes. Some Japanese rivals still have not adopted either shift-on-the-fly 4WD or 4-wheel ABS. Unfortunately ABS remains optional instead of standard. In addition, very high prices remain one of the 4Runner's biggest problems.

We prefer domestic rivals such as the Explorer, Grand Cherokee, Chevrolet Blazer, and GMC Jimmy, which have more room, a broader selection of features and models, plus better all-around performance for the money.

NHTSA CRASH TEST RESULTS
1995 Toyota 4Runner   4-DOOR WAGON

Driver	☆
Passenger	☆☆☆☆

(The National Highway Traffic Safety Administration tests a vehicle's crashworthiness in front and side collisions. Their ratings suggest the chance of serious injury: ☆☆☆☆☆—10% or less; ☆☆☆☆—10-20% or less; ☆☆☆—20-30% or less; ☆☆—35-45% or less; ☆—More than 45%.)

SPECIFICATIONS	2-door wagon	4-door wagon
Wheelbase, in.	103.3	103.3
Overall length, in.	176.0	176.0
Overall width, in.	66.5	66.5
Overall height, in.	66.1	66.1
Curb weight, lbs.	3720	3760
Cargo volume, cu. ft.	78.3	78.3
Fuel capacity, gals.	17.2	17.2
Seating capacity	5	5

TOYOTA

	2-door wagon	4-door wagon
Front head room, in.	38.7	38.7
Max. front leg room, in.	41.5	41.5
Rear head room, in.	38.3	38.3
Min. rear leg room, in.	31.6	31.6

Powertrain layout: longitudinal front-engine/rear- or 4-wheel drive

ENGINES

	ohc I-4	ohc V-6
Size, liters/cu. in.	2.4/144	3.0/180
Horsepower	116	150
Torque (lbs./ft.)	140	180

EPA city/highway mpg

5-speed OD manual	19/21	15/18
4-speed OD automatic		14/16

Consumer Guide™ observed MPG

4-speed OD automatic		13.8

Built in Japan.

RETAIL PRICES	GOOD	AVERAGE	POOR
1990 4Runner	$6,000-7,500	$5,300-6,700	$3,200-4,000
1991 4Runner	7,300-9,000	6,500-8,200	4,000-5,200
1992 4Runner	8,500-10,300	7,500-9,300	4,900-6,600
1993 4Runner	9,900-12,000	8,900-11,000	5,800-7,500
1994 4Runner	12,000-14,500	10,800-13,000	7,500-9,000
1995 4Runner	14,500-17,000	13,000-15,500	9,000-11,000

AVERAGE REPLACEMENT COSTS

A/C Compressor $1,155	Clutch, Pressure Plate,
Alternator 515	Bearing 500
Radiator 515	Constant Velocity Joints.....155
Timing Chain or Belt 615	Brakes..................................225
Automatic Transmission or	Shocks and/or Struts 190
Transaxle.....................1,280	Exhaust System.................261

TROUBLE SPOTS

• **Exhaust system** In compliance with emission control regulations, the oxygen sensor will be replaced free at the 80,000-mile scheduled maintenance. (1993-94)

• **Clutch** A leaking or damaged direct clutch in the transfer case causes a slip or chatter on acceleration when in the 2-wheel or 4-wheel high range. (1990-92)

• **Clutch** Because of clutch judder, the pressure plate and disc were enlarged (from 9.00-in to 9.5-in. diameter) for 4x4 models and can be retrofitted as a set. (1990-94)

• **Oil leak** Vehicles with the V-6 engine produced after April 1994 have redesigned head gaskets that are less prone to leaks. The gaskets will fit prior years. (1990-95)

RECALL HISTORY
None to date.

1996-98 TOYOTA 4RUNNER

✓ BEST BUY

1996 Toyota 4Runner SR5 V6

FOR Air bags, dual • Optional anti-lock brakes • Ride • Quietness • Passenger and cargo room

AGAINST Entry/exit • Fuel economy • Price

EVALUATION Because this version weighs less and also comes with stronger engines, they can charge up hills that would have overtaxed the old 4Runner. On-the-road performance is therefore more relaxed, especially when towing a trailer or hauling a full load of people and cargo. Acceleration with the smooth V-6 is indeed snappy in town, though highway passing is more ordinary. We recommend a V-6, because the 4-cylinder engine, despite being enlarged, still lacks the torque to propel such a heavy vehicle. Later models with the dealer-installed supercharger accelerate with authority—moving to the head of the midsize sport-utility class—aren't overly noisy, and don't consume much more fuel.

Solid-feeling on rough pavement, a 4Runner copes admirably when it encounters off-road terrain. Engine and tire noise are less noticeable than they used to be. The current suspension promises a comfortable ride on almost any surface. Steering is carlike and precise, delivering stable cornering.

TOYOTA

Running boards on the Limited are a virtual necessity when climbing aboard, due to the uncomfortably high step-in level. Once inside, space is ample for four adults, and not bad at all for a fifth. Cargo room is generous, even with the rear seat in use, helped by a spare tire that's mounted beneath the cargo floor. The 4Runner's power liftgate window is a convenience that's not offered by any other compact sport-utility.

Domestic rivals such as the Ford Explorer, Chevrolet Blazer, and Jeep Grand Cherokee might be better bargains, but a 4Runner includes Toyota's reputation for reliability.

NHTSA CRASH TEST RESULTS
1996 Toyota 4Runner

4-DOOR WAGON

Driver	☆☆☆
Passenger	NA

(The National Highway Traffic Safety Administration tests a vehicle's crashworthiness in front and side collisions. Their ratings suggest the chance of serious injury: ☆☆☆☆☆—10% or less; ☆☆☆☆—10-20% or less; ☆☆☆—20-30% or less; ☆☆—35-45% or less; ☆—More than 45%.)

SPECIFICATIONS

	4-door wagon
Wheelbase, in.	105.3
Overall length, in.	178.7
Overall width, in.	66.5
Overall height, in.	67.5
Curb weight, lbs.	3440
Cargo volume, cu. ft.	79.7
Fuel capacity, gals.	18.5
Seating capacity	5
Front head room, in.	39.2
Max. front leg room, in.	43.1
Rear head room, in.	38.7
Min. rear leg room, in.	34.9

Powertrain layout: longitudinal front-engine/rear- or 4-wheel drive

ENGINES

	dohc I-4	dohc V-6
Size, liters/cu. in.	2.7/164	3.4/207
Horsepower	150	183
Torque (lbs./ft.)	177	217
EPA city/highway mpg		
5-speed OD manual	16/21	16/19
4-speed OD automatic	18/22	16/19
Consumer Guide™ observed MPG		
5-speed OD manual		14.2
4-speed OD automatic		17.1

Built in Japan.

RETAIL PRICES

	GOOD	AVERAGE	POOR
1996 4Runner	$15,500-21,500	$14,200-20,000	$10,000-15,200
1996 4Runner Limited	23,000-25,000	21,500-23,000	16,500-17,500
1997 4Runner	17,000-23,000	15,500-21,500	11,000-16,500
1997 4Runner Limited	25,000-27,000	23,300-25,000	18,000-19,000
1998 4Runner	19,000-25,000	17,500-23,500	12,500-18,000
1998 4Runner Limited	27,000-30,000	25,000-28,000	19,500-22,000

AVERAGE REPLACEMENT COSTS

A/C Compressor $1,140
Alternator 485
Radiator 475
Timing Chain or Belt 610
Automatic Transmission or
    Transaxle.........................940

Automatic Transmission or
    Transaxle.........................940
Clutch, Pressure Plate,
    Bearing.............................400
Universal Joints 590
Brakes.................................220

TROUBLE SPOTS

• **Oil leak** Head gasket failures, particularly on higher mileage engines. In some cases the company has issued a service campaign or extended warranty. (1996)

RECALL HISTORY

1996 2WD Sticker alerting driver to "particular handling and maneuvering characteristics of utility vehicles" was not affixed to driver's sunvisor.

1995-98 TOYOTA AVALON

✓ BEST BUY

1995 Toyota Avalon XLS

FOR Air bags, dual • Optional anti-lock brakes • Passenger and

TOYOTA

cargo room • Quietness • Acceleration • Instruments/controls

AGAINST Fuel economy • Price

EVALUATION Except for more body lean and understeer on twisting roads, an Avalon drives much like the Toyota Camry. Although the Avalon's suspension is firmer, it still absorbs most bumps. Even on wavy roads, the sedan does not bounce or feel mushy. It also corners with good grip and moderate body lean.

Because there's a negligible weight difference between Avalon and the V-6 Camry, don't expect a discernible difference in acceleration or passing sprints. A test Avalon accelerated to 60 mph in 8.5 seconds—just about exactly as swift as a Camry. Toyota's V-6 engine is just as silky smooth in the Avalon as in the Camry, and nearly silent. Better yet, it's complemented by a smooth, responsive automatic transmission. As for gas mileage, an early model averaged 19.4 mpg, driving mostly in rush-hour commutes. The V-6 engine requires premium fuel.

Space is ample for four adults, and six can tolerate shorter trips in models with the front bench seat. Leg space is generous in the back seat, and rear doors open wide for easy entry/exit. The trunk is wide and deep, with a long, flat floor. Low liftover height makes it easier to load and unload, too.

Avalon's dashboard layout and materials are first-rate. Large round gauges are legible. Both the stereo and climate controls are high enough to easily see and reach while driving.

Roomy and competent, but markedly more costly than a Camry when new, Avalon might offer little excitement, but also suffers few faults. We've been impressed with the solid feel, good workmanship, and low noise levels.

NHTSA CRASH TEST RESULTS
1996 Toyota Avalon

Driver	☆☆☆☆
Passenger	☆☆☆☆☆

(The National Highway Traffic Safety Administration tests a vehicle's crashworthiness in front and side collisions. Their ratings suggest the chance of serious injury: ☆☆☆☆☆—10% or less; ☆☆☆☆—10-20% or less; ☆☆☆—20-30% or less; ☆☆—35-45% or less; ☆—More than 45%.)

SPECIFICATIONS

	4-door sedan
Wheelbase, in.	107.1
Overall length, in.	190.2
Overall width, in.	70.3
Overall height, in.	56.1
Curb weight, lbs.	3263

	4-door sedan
Cargo volume, cu. ft.	15.4
Fuel capacity, gals.	18.5
Seating capacity	5[1]
Front head room, in.	39.1
Max. front leg room, in.	44.1
Rear head room, in.	37.8
Min. rear leg room, in.	38.3

1. 6 passengers w/optional front bench seat.

Powertrain layout: transverse front-engine/front-wheel drive

ENGINES
dohc V-6

Size, liters/cu. in.	3.0/180
Horsepower	192-200
Torque (lbs./ft.)	210

EPA city/highway mpg
4-speed OD automatic 20/29

Consumer Guide™ observed MPG
4-speed OD automatic 21.1

Built in USA.

RETAIL PRICES	GOOD	AVERAGE	POOR
1995 Avalon	$14,000-16,000	$13,000-15,000	$10,000-11,300
1996 Avalon	15,800-18,000	14,500-16,500	11,000-12,500
1997 Avalon	17,800-20,000	16,500-18,500	12,500-14,000
1998 Avalon	20,000-23,000	18,500-21,500	14,000-16,000

AVERAGE REPLACEMENT COSTS

A/C Compressor	$880
Alternator	370
Radiator	465
Timing Chain or Belt	190
Automatic Transmission or Transaxle	710
Clutch, Pressure Plate, Bearing	NA
Constant Velocity Joints	1,100
Brakes	260
Shocks and/or Struts	850
Exhaust System	365

TROUBLE SPOTS

• **Brake noise** The front or rear (especially in reverse) disc brakes may make a moaning noise which can be corrected with revised brake pads. (1995-97)

• **Climate control** The ambient temperature occasionally gets stuck on 22 degrees and the climate control system may not work properly. (1995-96)

TOYOTA

- **Radio antenna** The radio may have poor reception or noise because of a poor ground on the glass-printed antenna. (1997)
- **Vehicle noise** There is a kit to eliminate wind noise from the A-pillars (between windshield and doors). (1995-96)

RECALL HISTORY

1997 in specified states In extreme cold, accumulated moisture can temporarily freeze in brake vacuum hose.

1992-96 TOYOTA CAMRY

1992 Toyota Camry SE 4-door

FOR Air bags, dual • Anti-lock brakes (optional) • Acceleration (V-6) • Ride • Quietness • Passenger and cargo room

AGAINST Fuel economy (V-6) • Rear-seat comfort

EVALUATION There's a lot of the Lexus ES 300 in the Camry, which we believe sets the standard for refinement among mid-size and compact family cars. It's smoother, quieter, and built with higher levels of quality than some luxury sedans costing thousands more.

The 4-cylinder engine is smooth and responsive, giving the Camry sedan adequate acceleration and passing power, even with the automatic transmission. We averaged 10.9 seconds to 60 mph in our test and nearly 23 mpg. The V-6 is much quicker, but uses more fuel (we averaged about 18 mpg in our test). However, the V-6 is perhaps the most polished engine in this class and works in concert with a highly refined automatic to deliver virtually vibration-free performance.

Camrys feature a soft, absorbent ride that soaks up most bumps and ruts quite easily. It also corners with good stability and has good traction on wet roads. While the Camry's 103.1-inch wheelbase put it in the compact class, it has more interior room than many mid-size models. Note, however, that the seatbacks tend to be stiff and too reclined, making them uncomfortable for some people.

New Camrys generally sold for more than its compact rivals, so expect pre-owned models to also be priced a bit more, given Toyota's generally high resale value and strong reputation for reliability.

NHTSA CRASH TEST RESULTS
1995 Toyota Camry

4-DOOR SEDAN

Driver	☆☆☆☆
Passenger	☆☆☆

(The National Highway Traffic Safety Administration tests a vehicle's crashworthiness in front and side collisions. Their ratings suggest the chance of serious injury: ☆☆☆☆☆—10% or less; ☆☆☆☆—10-20% or less; ☆☆☆—20-30% or less; ☆☆—35-45% or less; ☆—More than 45%.)

SPECIFICATIONS

	2-door coupe	4-door sedan	4-door wagon
Wheelbase, in.	103.1	103.1	103.1
Overall length, in.	187.8	187.8	189.4
Overall width, in.	69.7	69.7	69.7
Overall height, in.	54.9	55.1	56.3
Curb weight, lbs.	2910	2932	3263
Cargo volume, cu. ft.	14.9	14.9	74.8
Fuel capacity, gals.	18.5	18.5	18.5
Seating capacity	5	5	7
Front head room, in.	38.4	38.4	39.2
Max. front leg room, in.	43.5	43.5	43.5
Rear head room, in.	37.4	37.1	38.8
Min. rear leg room, in.	33.0	35.0	35.2

Powertrain layout: transverse front-engine/front-wheel drive

ENGINES

	dohc I-4	dohc I-4	dohc V-6	dohc V-6
Size, liters/cu. in.	2.2/132	2.2/132	3.0/180	3.0/180
Horsepower	130	125	185	188
Torque (lbs./ft.)	145	145	195	203
EPA city/highway mpg				
5-speed OD manual	22/30	23/31	18/24	
4-speed OD automatic	21/28	21/27	18/24	20/29
Consumer Guide™ observed MPG				
4-speed OD automatic	22.9		18.5	17.5

Built in USA and Japan.

TOYOTA

RETAIL PRICES	GOOD	AVERAGE	POOR
1992 Camry	$5,700-8,300	$5,000-7,500	$2,900-4,700
1993 Camry	6,600-9,700	5,800-8,900	3,500-6,000
1994 Camry	7,800-11,500	7,000-10,600	4,500-7,500
1995 Camry	9,400-14,000	8,500-13,000	5,500-9,500
1996 Camry	11,000-15,500	9,800-14,200	6,500-10,300

AVERAGE REPLACEMENT COSTS

A/C Compressor $865
Alternator 375
Radiator 580
Timing Chain or Belt 220
Automatic Transmission or
    Transaxle......................1,067

Clutch, Pressure Plate,
    Bearing...........................600
Constant Velocity Joints.....500
Brakes................................145
Shocks and/or Struts 800
Exhaust System.................550

TROUBLE SPOTS

• **Air conditioner** If the air conditioner gradually loses efficiency, the problem is likely caused by a problem with the expansion valve and there was a campaign to replace them. On vehicles out of warranty, the customer must pay for any additional repairs or recharging. (1992-93)

• **Transmission slippage** The A-40 series automatic transmissions may eventually shift harshly because rubber check balls (used in the valve bodies) become smaller, blow through the plate, and get dislodged. Replacement balls are less prone to wear. (1992+)

• **Suspension noise** To eliminate squeaks and groans, the front and rear sway bar bushings were redesigned using a self-lubricating material; as an alternative, they may be lubed with silicone (non-petroleum) grease. (1992-95)

• **Trunk latch** If the trunk won't stay open on sedans with a spoiler, the support torsion rod will be adjusted free under the normal warranty, but up to 24 months/18,000 miles in NY due to its lemon laws. (1992-96)

• **Water leak** Water leaks on the passenger side come from two sources, the SRS wiring harness grommet and the fresh air intake plenum. Both may be sealed using appropriate sealing chemicals. (1992-93)

• **Hard starting** Hard starting after cold soak due to ignition coil voltage leaking to an inappropriate ground path. (all)

• **Coolant leak** Head gasket failures on 3.0L engines allow coolant to get into the cylinders. Manufacturer has extended warranty to 8 years/100,000 miles on pre-1995 models if the gasket fails.

RECALL HISTORY

1996 Plastic material of bulb holders in taillight assembly of some cars lacks sufficient heat resistance; when the bulb is lit, its holder can deform.
1996 On some cars, when taillight bulb is lit, its holder can deform.

1990-93 TOYOTA CELICA

1990 Toyota Celica All-Trac hatchback

FOR   Air bag, driver • Acceleration (exc. ST) • Handling/road-holding • Fuel economy • Optional anti-lock brakes

AGAINST   Rear seat room • Rear visibility • Entry/exit • Cargo room • Engine noise • Acceleration (ST automatic)

EVALUATION   Handling and roadholding are decent with an ST and quite sporty with a GT or GT-S. Those two stick to the road tautly and respond well in changes of direction. Each model offers refined road manners and a solid "feel." The ST's suspension has the softest damping, therefore, ride quality is somewhat smoother. Other Celica models don't absorb bumps quite as well, but suffer minimal cornering lean and crisper steering response.

An All-Trac not only hugs the road tenaciously, but delivers a mighty blast of power. Refined road manners and an impressively solid bearing are particularly borne out by the convertible, which suffers only minimal body shake of the sort that's all too common in drop-tops.

Base-engine performance is adequate with a 5-speed, but automatic drains away its strength. Manual shift is also the best performance bet with the 2.2-liter engine, though acceleration and gas mileage are impressive with either transmission. Few cars in this category isolate their occupants better from engine and wind noise, but tire roar and exhaust sounds grow intrusive.

Low-set seats mix with a high-waisted profile to impair outward visibility. Space is okay up front, but tall drivers (and front passengers) might have to recline the front seatbacks to get adequate head room. The back seat is limited to youngsters, while cargo space is marginal in size and suffers from a high liftover.

Like most Toyotas, Celicas are well-built. They're also reliable, and serve as models of ergonomic intelligence.

SPECIFICATIONS

	2-door coupe	2-door hatchback	2-door conv.
Wheelbase, in.	99.4	99.4	99.4
Overall length, in.	176.0	173.6	176.0
Overall width, in.	67.1	67.1	67.1
Overall height, in.	50.6	50.6	50.6
Curb weight, lbs.	2447	2646	2844
Cargo volume, cu. ft.	12.6	24.7	12.6
Fuel capacity, gals.	15.9	15.9	15.9
Seating capacity	4	4	4
Front head room, in.	37.7	37.7	37.7
Max. front leg room, in.	42.9	42.9	42.9
Rear head room, in.	33.0	33.0	33.0
Min. rear leg room, in.	26.8	26.8	26.8

ENGINES

	dohc I-4	Turbocharged dohc I-4	dohc I-4
Size, liters/cu. in.	1.6/97	2.0/122	2.2/132
Horsepower	103	200	130-135
Torque (lbs./ft.)	102	200	140
EPA city/highway mpg			
5-speed OD manual	25/32	19/24	22/28
4-speed OD automatic	24/31		20/27
Consumer Guide™ observed MPG			
5-speed OD manual	22.3		
4-speed OD automatic			25.3

RETAIL PRICES

	GOOD	AVERAGE	POOR
1990 Celica	$3,200-4,500	$2,500-3,800	$900-1,700
1990 All-Trac	5,000-5,800	4,200-5,000	2,000-2,600
1991 Celica	4,000-5,900	3,300-5,100	1,300-2,700
1991 All-Trac	6,400-7,200	5,600-6,400	3,000-3,600
1991 Convertible	7,900-8,000	6,200-7,200	3,500-4,200
1992 Celica	4,900-6,900	4,100-6,000	1,900-3,400
1992 All-Trac	7,800-8,700	7,000-7,800	4,000-4,600

	GOOD	AVERAGE	POOR
1992 Convertible	8,500-9,800	7,500-8,800	4,500-5,400
1993 Celica	5,700-8,200	4,900-7,300	2,400-4,300
1993 All-Trac	9,200-10,300	8,200-9,300	5,000-5,800
1993 Convertible	10,000-11,500	9,000-10,500	5,500-6,500

AVERAGE REPLACEMENT COSTS

A/C Compressor $385	Clutch, Pressure Plate,
Alternator 520	Bearing 425
Radiator 465	Constant Velocity Joints.....950
Timing Chain or Belt 185	Brakes................................270
Automatic Transmission or	Shocks and/or Struts 1,040
Transaxle........................680	Exhaust System.................340

TROUBLE SPOTS

• **Doors** The fuel door may rattle requiring removal of the rear seat, quarter panel trim, etc. to tape it down. (1990-93)

• **Radio** Panasonic CD players may skip, fail to play, or show "ERR" (1992-93) while Fujitsu CD players may not load or eject. (1990-92)

• **Air conditioner** The air conditioning expansion valve fails and there was a service campaign to inject anti-corrosion lube into the system. If not done, repeated valve failure may occur. (1992-93)

• **Engine misfire** Poor engine performance under light throttle may be corrected with a new EGR vacuum modulator. (1990-93)

RECALL HISTORY

1990 Air bag inflator might be defective.

1994-98 TOYOTA CELICA

FOR Air bags, dual • Optional anti-lock brakes • Acceleration (GT) • Steering/handling • Instruments/controls • Fuel economy

AGAINST Engine noise • Rear seat room • Cargo room (exc. hatchback)

EVALUATION Handling is where Toyota's Celica excels: crisp, responsive, with fine grip in corners and minimal body lean. You get a surprisingly supple ride, too, even in a GT with the stiffly-sprung Sports Package option. Sure, it's stiffer and choppier than other Celicas, but you get a little extra cornering precision with that Sport option. Braking is good, too, though it would be better if more models had anti-locking.

The 1.8-liter dual-cam 4-cylinder engine in an ST is smooth

1995 Toyota Celica convertible

and lively with 5-speed manual shift, and economical, too. Optional 4-speed automatic saps its strength, because the engine lacks low-speed torque. The GT's 2.2-liter engine feels a lot stronger at all speeds, but makes plenty of noise doing it, roaring and throbbing in hard driving. As for economy, a GT hatchback with manual shift averaged 25.7 mpg. Tires aren't quiet, either—in any Celica.

This is a typical 2+2 layout, with little rear space for adults, and six-footers face marginal head clearance if a Celica coupe is sunroof-equipped. Controls and gauges are well laid out on a modern style, convenient dashboard. Trunk space is passable. The convertible's top is power-operated, but blocks the rear view substantially and robs rear-seat room and cargo space.

Even though the price may be high, if you want two-passenger fun and reliability, a Celica is worth the extra bucks.

SPECIFICATIONS

	2-door coupe	2-door hatchback	2-door conv.
Wheelbase, in.	99.9	99.9	99.9
Overall length, in.	177.0	174.0	177.0
Overall width, in.	68.9	68.9	68.9
Overall height, in.	51.0	50.8	51.6
Curb weight, lbs.	2395	2415	2755
Cargo volume, cu. ft.	10.6	16.2	6.8
Fuel capacity, gals.	15.9	15.9	15.9
Seating capacity	4	4	4
Front head room, in.	34.3	34.3	38.7
Max. front leg room, in.	44.2	44.2	44.2
Rear head room, in.	29.2	29.2	34.1
Min. rear leg room, in.	26.6	26.6	18.9

Powertrain layout: transverse front-engine/front-wheel drive

ENGINES

	dohc I-4	dohc I-4
Size, liters/cu. in.	1.8/208	2.2/132

	dohc I-4	dohc I-4
Horsepower	105-110	130-135
Torque (lbs./ft.)	115-117	145

EPA city/highway mpg

5-speed OD manual	29/34	22/29
4-speed OD automatic	27/34	22/29

Consumer Guide™ observed MPG

5-speed OD manual	25.7
4-speed OD automatic	17.6

Built in Japan.

RETAIL PRICES	GOOD	AVERAGE	POOR
1994 Celica	$7,800-9,800	$7,000-9,000	$4,700-6,000
1995 Celica	10,500-12,500	9,500-11,500	6,800-8,200
1995 Convertible	14,500-16,000	13,200-14,500	10,000-11,000
1996 Celica	12,500-14,700	11,500-13,500	8,500-10,000
1996 Convertible	17,000-19,000	15,500-17,500	12,000-13,200
1997 Celica	14,200-17,000	13,000-15,700	9,700-11,500
1997 Convertible	19,500-21,500	18,000-20,000	14,000-15,200
1998 Celica	16,500-19,500	15,000-18,000	11,000-13,500
1998 Convertible	22,500-24,500	21,000-23,000	16,500-18,000

AVERAGE REPLACEMENT COSTS

A/C Compressor	$880
Alternator	340
Radiator	520
Timing Chain or Belt	140
Automatic Transmission or Transaxle	710
Clutch, Pressure Plate, Bearing	425
Constant Velocity Joints	1,080
Brakes	210
Shocks and/or Struts	970
Exhaust System	250

TROUBLE SPOTS

• **Wheels** Proper wheel alignment may not be possible unless a special steering knuckle bolt is used to replace the original. (1994-96)

• **Radio** The Fujitsu 10-CD changer has a tendency to not accept or eject CDs. (1994-97)

• **Convertible top** The convertible top wears at the sail panel near the rear window from the balance rods rubbing. (1995-97)

• **Climate control** The rear defroster terminals tend to break on convertibles. (1995-97)

RECALL HISTORY

None to date.

1993-97 TOYOTA COROLLA

1995 Toyota Corolla 4-door

FOR   Air bags, dual • Anti-lock brakes (optional) • Fuel economy • Ride

AGAINST   Rear-seat room • Acceleration (automatic transmission)

EVALUATION   The 1.8-liter gives the Corolla DX and LE (pre-1996) models quicker acceleration and stronger passing power than the base sedan's 1.6-liter unit. We timed a Corolla with the 1.8-liter at 10.9 seconds to 60 mph, which is slower than a Honda Civic, but quicker than most other rivals. Though the automatic transmission generally works well with the 1.8-liter engine, it's slow to downshift for passing, unless you floor the throttle. The optional 3-speed automatic provided with the 1.6-liter engine is not only slow to downshift, it can be harsh at times. However, fuel economy is good with either engine—generally averaging about 30 mpg.

Corolla's suspension provides a stable highway ride and absorbs bumps better than some larger cars. Corolla is quieter than the similar Geo Prizm because Toyota includes more sound insulation in its cars. The car is roomier than most rivals, yet the rear seat is a tight fit for two adults, and more appropriate for children. Cargo space is adequate and can be expanded on DX models, thanks to the split folding rear seatback.

Corollas generally sold for more than comparable subcompact rivals, so expect pre-owned models to also be priced a bit more, given Toyota's generally high resale value and strong reputation for reliability.

NHTSA CRASH TEST RESULTS
1995 Toyota Corolla

4-DOOR SEDAN

Driver   ☆☆☆☆

Passenger   ☆☆☆☆

(The National Highway Traffic Safety Administration tests a vehicle's crashworthiness in front and side collisions. Their ratings suggest the chance of serious injury: ☆☆☆☆☆—10% or less; ☆☆☆☆—10-20% or less; ☆☆☆—20-30% or less; ☆☆—35-45% or less; ☆—More than 45%.)

SPECIFICATIONS

	4-door sedan	4-door wagon
Wheelbase, in.	97.0	97.0
Overall length, in.	172.0	172.0
Overall width, in.	66.3	66.3
Overall height, in.	54.3	56.1
Curb weight, lbs.	2315	2403
Cargo volume, cu. ft.	12.7	64.8
Fuel capacity, gals.	13.2	13.2
Seating capacity	5	5
Front head room, in.	38.8	38.8
Max. front leg room, in.	42.4	42.4
Rear head room, in.	37.1	39.7
Min. rear leg room, in.	33.0	33.0

Powertrain layout: transverse front-engine/front-wheel drive

ENGINES

	dohc I-4	dohc I-4	dohc I-4	dohc I-4
Size, liters/cu. in.	1.6/97	1.6/97	1.8/110	1.8/110
Horsepower	100	105	105	115
Torque (lbs./ft.)	105	105	117	115
EPA city/highway mpg				
5-speed OD manual	31/35	27/34	29/34	27/33
3-speed automatic	26/30	26/29		
4-speed OD automatic			27/34	26/33
Consumer Guide™ observed MPG				
3-speed automatic	26.4			
4-speed OD automatic			30.1	30.5

Built in USA, Canada, and Japan.

RETAIL PRICES	GOOD	AVERAGE	POOR
1993 Corolla	$4,000-5,800	$3,300-5,100	$1,600-3,100
1994 Corolla	5,000-7,000	4,300-6,200	2,400-3,900
1995 Corolla	6,600-8,800	5,800-8,000	3,500-5,200
1996 Corolla	8,000-10,500	7,200-9,600	4,500-6,500
1997 Corolla	9,200-11,500	8,300-10,500	5,400-7,200

AVERAGE REPLACEMENT COSTS

A/C Compressor $925	Clutch, Pressure Plate,
Alternator 415	Bearing 515
Radiator 440	Constant Velocity Joints.....805
Timing Chain or Belt 155	Brakes.................................200
Automatic Transmission or	Shocks and/or Struts 550
Transaxle.....................1,025	Exhaust System.................550

TROUBLE SPOTS

• **Transmission slippage** The A-40 series automatic transmissions may eventually shift harshly because rubber check balls (used in the valve bodies) become smaller, blow through the plate, and get dislodged. Replacement balls are less prone to wear. (1992+)

• **Water pump** Water pumps leak due to a defective seal. Pumps with a redesigned seal will be installed under warranty up to five years/60,000 miles. (1993-94)

• **Windshield washer** Windshield washer bottles frequently break, so new ones, made of more durable polypropylene, are available. (1993-95)

RECALL HISTORY

1993-94 Snow or water can penetrate carpet and result in short and possible fire. **1993-95** If liquid is spilled in console box area, air bag warning light can illuminate during normal driving conditions and cause air bag to malfunction, deploying inadvertently. **1994** Anchor straps in certain seatbelt assemblies were improperly heat-treated and can break. **1995** Battery may have defective weld inside positive or negative terminal, which can result in a no-start condition or explosion.

1990-97 TOYOTA LAND CRUISER

FOR 4WD traction • Passenger and cargo room • Anti-lock brakes (later models) • Air bags, dual (later models)

AGAINST Fuel economy • Acceleration (4.0-liter) • Ride • Entry/exit • Price

EVALUATION Steering was vague and over-assisted in the early version, and the ride gets choppy, even on roads that look smooth. The 1991-97 version has a slightly wider stance, so it's a little less tipsy in corners. Still, don't expect to rush through fast curves or tight low-speed turns without plenty of body lean.

Acceleration from early models is nothing to shout about,

1992 Toyota Land Cruiser

either: on the order of 15.4 seconds to reach 60 mph. The 4.5-liter engine gets its job done, bringing enough power and torque to move this big rig rather smartly. Heavy weight helps make fuel consumption horrid. An early Land Cruiser got only 10.5 mpg; another with the 4.0-liter engine managed just 13 mpg. The permanently-engaged 4-wheel-drive system installed in 1991 is a bonus, giving the driver the advantage of 4WD but no duties to perform.

Passenger space is ample all around. Seats are comfortable for long trips, and the cargo area is bountiful. A Land Cruiser stands tall, so step-up into the interior is high. Reaching the optional third seat is awkward because you have to clamber around the middle bench. It's kid-size, too, and leaves little cargo space at the rear. However, both the second and third seats pack up easily to expand cargo volume. Some controls in the pre-1991 model have a haphazard look, but full instrumentation was standard. The interior got a lot more modern in 1991, with instruments and controls handier and better organized. Overall, the interior has a sturdy, high-grade look, and body construction is tight and solid.

Expensive and sold in modest numbers, Land Cruisers continue to attract a modest but eager following. Still, most buyers find a Ford Explorer or Jeep Cherokee to be a better value.

SPECIFICATIONS	4-door wagon	4-door wagon
Wheelbase, in.	107.5[1]	112.2
Overall length, in.	184.0	189.8
Overall width, in.	70.9	76.0
Overall height, in.	68.9	73.2
Curb weight, lbs.	4480	4834
Cargo volume, cu. ft.	98.0	90.9

TOYOTA

	4-door wagon	4-door wagon
Fuel capacity, gals.	23.8	25.1
Seating capacity	5	8
Front head room, in.	40.0	40.3
Max. front leg room, in.	39.2	42.2
Rear head room, in.	40.4	40.0
Min. rear leg room, in.	34.6	33.6

1. 1990 model only.

ENGINES

	ohv I-6	dohc I-6
Size, liters/cu. in.	4.0/241	4.5/275
Horsepower	155	212
Torque (lbs./ft.)	220	275

EPA city/highway mpg

4-speed OD automatic	12/14	13/15

Consumer Guide™ observed MPG

4-speed OD automatic	13.0	12.6

Built in Japan.

RETAIL PRICES

	GOOD	AVERAGE	POOR
1990 Land Cruiser	$10,000-11,500	$9,000-10,500	$6,500-7,500
1991 Land Cruiser	12,000-13,500	11,000-12,200	8,000-9,000
1992 Land Cruiser	14,500-16,000	13,300-14,500	10,000-11,000
1993 Land Cruiser	18,000-20,000	16,500-18,500	13,000-14,500
1994 Land Cruiser	21,500-23,500	20,000-22,000	16,000-17,500
1995 Land Cruiser	26,000-28,500	24,000-26,500	19,500-21,500
1996 Land Cruiser	30,000-32,500	28,000-30,000	23,000-24,500
1997 Land Cruiser	34,000-37,000	32,000-34,500	26,000-28,000

AVERAGE REPLACEMENT COSTS

A/C Compressor	$1,055	Clutch, Pressure Plate, Bearing	520
Alternator	375	Universal Joints	520
Radiator	435	Brakes	230
Timing Chain or Belt	885	Shocks and/or Struts	510
Automatic Transmission or Transaxle	1,010	Exhaust System	330

TROUBLE SPOTS

• **Vehicle noise** The transfer case lever rattles and vibrates and is corrected by installing a new boot and hardware. (1990-94)

• **Radiator** The thermostat gasket had a tendency to leak in cold weather and a redesigned one is available. (1990-95)

- **Radiator** The thermostat gasket had a tendency to leak in cold weather and a redesigned one is available. (1990-95)

- **Radio** Static in the radio is caused by poor antenna ground, which usually requires a replacement antenna mast and cleaning of the contact area. (1990-96)

- **Automatic transmission** Automatic transmissions have delayed engagement in reverse. (1990-96)

RECALL HISTORY

1990 Heavy loads and high temperatures can create high pressure in fuel tank, resulting in cracks and leakage.

1992-97 TOYOTA PASEO

1992 Toyota Paseo

FOR Fuel economy • Maneuverability • Air bags, dual (later models)

AGAINST Noise • Rear seat room

EVALUATION Acceleration is more than adequate with manual shift, though the engine vibrates somewhat when worked hard. Takeoffs are less than brisk, but the engine revs eagerly to higher speeds. As expected, an automatic transmission saps some of the engine's pep, approaching the sluggish level. Exhaust resonance is noticeable and the engine gets loud, even during moderate acceleration. Gas mileage is a major bonus: With manual shift, we've averaged 34.3 mpg.

Ride quality is pleasantly supple and well-controlled with optional wider tires, despite light weight and short wheelbase.

TOYOTA

Most bumps register with a thump or a jolt, but the coupe feels reasonably solid. Modest size aids in handling, but the suspension and tires don't come close to furnishing true sports-car moves. A Paseo feels agile and competent in most maneuvers, though the body leans in tight turns, and front tires plow through corners. Road/tire noise gets annoying on coarse pavement.

Paseo is actually a 2+2 rather than a real 4-seater, so rear-seat space is for toddlers or groceries. Tall people might need more leg room in front, and there's no great abundance of head space. Well-bolstered bucket seats are comfortable. Controls are nicely laid out, though the steering wheel might be high for some drivers. The Paseo's over-the-shoulder view is impaired by thick rear pillars. Trunk space is better than average.

Paseos aren't the best or cheapest small sport coupes. Because convertibles were available for such a short time, they're sure to be rarities on the used-car market.

NHTSA CRASH TEST RESULTS
1997 Toyota Paseo

2-DOOR COUPE

Driver	☆☆☆☆
Passenger	☆☆☆☆

(The National Highway Traffic Safety Administration tests a vehicle's crashworthiness in front and side collisions. Their ratings suggest the chance of serious injury: ☆☆☆☆☆—10% or less; ☆☆☆☆—10-20% or less; ☆☆☆—20-30% or less; ☆☆—35-45% or less; ☆—More than 45%.)

SPECIFICATIONS

	2-door coupe	2-door conv.
Wheelbase, in.	93.7	93.7
Overall length, in.	163.6	163.6
Overall width, in.	65.4	65.4
Overall height, in.	51.0	51.0
Curb weight, lbs.	2025	2160
Cargo volume, cu. ft.	7.5	6.6
Fuel capacity, gals.	11.9	11.9
Seating capacity	4	4
Front head room, in.	37.8	NA
Max. front leg room, in.	41.1	NA
Rear head room, in.	32.0	NA
Min. rear leg room, in.	30.0	NA

Powertrain layout: transverse front-engine/front-wheel drive

ENGINES

	dohc I-4	dohc I-4
Size, liters/cu. in.	1.5/90	1.5/90
Horsepower	100	93
Torque (lbs./ft.)	91	100

EPA city/highway mpg
5-speed OD manual.............................. 28/34   30/35
4-speed OD automatic......................... 26/32   28/34

Consumer Guide™ observed MPG
5-speed OD manual.............................. 34.3   28.2
4-speed OD automatic......................... 25.9

Built in Japan.

RETAIL PRICES	GOOD	AVERAGE	POOR
1992 Paseo	$3,700-4,400	$3,000-3,700	$1,400-1,800
1993 Paseo	4,500-5,300	3,800-4,600	1,800-2,300
1994 Paseo	5,500-6,300	4,700-5,500	2,500-3,100
1995 Paseo	7,000-8,000	6,200-7,200	3,800-4,400
1996 Paseo	8,500-9,500	7,500-8,500	4,800-5,400
1997 Paseo coupe	10,000-11,000	9,000-10,000	6,000-6,700
1997 Convertible	12,500-14,000	11,500-12,800	8,300-9,300

AVERAGE REPLACEMENT COSTS

A/C Compressor $505
Alternator 350
Radiator 415
Timing Chain or Belt 155
Automatic Transmission or
    Transaxle.........................820

Clutch, Pressure Plate,
    Bearing 400
Constant Velocity Joints..1,150
Brakes.................................220
Shocks and/or Struts 900
Exhaust System.................380

TROUBLE SPOTS

• **Air conditioner** The air conditioner may randomly blow hot air
(compressor stops) and flash the air conditioning light due to a bad
wiring harness. (1992-94)

• **Climate control** Poor heater output can usually be corrected by
replacing the thermostat. (1995-96)

• **Wheels** Proper wheel alignment may be impossible without
installing new camber adjusting bolts. (1992-96)

RECALL HISTORY

None to date.

1990-94 TOYOTA PICKUP

FOR Acceleration (V-6) • Reliability

AGAINST Price • Engine noise

EVALUATION When behind the wheel, we discovered that

TOYOTA

1992 Toyota DLX 4WD

Toyota's 150-horsepower 3.0-liter V-6 is a little smoother than its Nissan counterpart, though neither has nearly the torque of the sixes in the domestics, such as the Ford Ranger or Chevy S-10. Nonetheless, performance from our 5-speed 4WD Xtracab SR5 V-6 was good: 13.1 seconds in the 0-60 sprint—not bad for the heaviest model in the line. Braking also was laudable, with short stopping distances and good resistance to rear-wheel locking.

Cab comfort, quietness, and driving ease all rate high. Even the ride is comfortable, especially for a tautly-sprung 4WD model. It provides stable cornering and feels confident and sure-footed. Toyota's 4WDemand system is easy to use and much more convenient than the other Toyota system. Less impressive is the tighter rear-seat room in Toyota's Xtracab, versus the Nissan King Cab or Isuzu's Spacecab.

While payload and towing capacities are better than the Japanese norm, they don't quite measure up to the domestics. When comparison shopping, Toyota may have an advantage in the fact they have perceptibly higher quality of workmanship, which might offset possible higher prices.

SPECIFICATIONS

	reg. cab	ext. cab
Wheelbase, in.	103.0	121.9
Overall length, in.	180.5	199.0
Overall width, in.	66.5	66.5
Overall height, in.	61.0	61.4
Curb weight, lbs.	2560	2740
Fuel capacity, gals.	15.1	15.1/18.0
Seating capacity	3	5
Front head room, in.	38.2	38.4
Max. front leg room, in.	41.7	42.8
Rear head room, in.	—	35.5
Min. rear leg room, in.	—	27.2

Powertrain layout: longitudinal front-engine/rear- or 4-wheel drive

ENGINES

	ohc I-4	ohc I-4	ohc V-6
Size, liters/cu. in.	2.4/144	2.4/144	3.0/181
Horsepower	102	116	150
Torque (lbs./ft.)	132	140	180

EPA city/highway mpg

4-speed manual..................................	19/23		
5-speed OD manual		22/26	18/23
4-speed OD automatic		22/23	18/23

Built in USA and Japan.

AVERAGE REPLACEMENT COSTS

A/C Compressor $1,315	Clutch, Pressure Plate,
Alternator 360	Bearing 915
Radiator 520	Universal Joints 200
Timing Chain or Belt 200	Brakes................................190
Automatic Transmission or	Shocks and/or Struts 210
Transaxle......................1,457	Exhaust System 242

RETAIL PRICES

	GOOD	AVERAGE	POOR
1990 Pickup	$2,800-5,800	$2,100-5,000	$900-2,800
1991 Pickup	3,500-7,500	2,800-6,700	1,300-4,000
1992 Pickup	4,200-8,800	3,400-8,000	1,600-5,000
1993 Pickup	4,800-10,500	4,000-9,600	2,000-6,500
1994 Pickup	5,600-12,000	4,700-11,000	2,600-7,700

TROUBLE SPOTS

• **Clutch** If the clutch-throwout bearing squeals, especially during the first five minutes after starting, it may be replaced with a redesigned one. (1990-91)

• **Automatic transmission** The column-mounted shift lever on trucks with automatic transmissions may bind requiring replacement of the shift cable, end rod holder, and return spring. (1990-91)

• **Engine temperature** Engine oil coolers became standard equipment beginning in 1991, but are available to retrofit previous models. (1990)

• **Transmission noise** A high-pitched whistling noise at speeds below 50 mph may be caused by the driveshaft, and a new, paper-lined shaft will eliminate the noise. (1990)

• **Exhaust system** In compliance with emission control regulations, the oxygen sensor will be replaced free at the 80,000-mile scheduled maintenance. (1993-95)

RECALL HISTORY
None to date.

1991-97 TOYOTA PREVIA

1992 Toyota Previa

FOR Air bags, dual • Anti-lock brakes (optional) • Passenger and cargo room

AGAINST Fuel economy • Control layout • Engine noise

EVALUATION Acceleration is decent, but when worked hard the engine gets noisy and sends an annoying vibration through the floor. It's responsive in everyday driving, however, thanks to an automatic transmission that shifts smoothly and promptly, and seldom hunts between third and fourth gears. We averaged 15 mpg in one test and 19 mpg in another. Though the 161-horsepower supercharged version doesn't move the Previa into the fast lane, it does make this minivan more responsive, particularly in passing situations.

While the Previa holds the road well and seems composed going around corners, neither its ride nor overall handling match that of the class champion Chrysler minivans.

The wild-looking W-shaped dashboard actually works rather well, putting most controls within easy reach, though the climate controls are poorly marked. Only the rear-seat headrests keep outward vision from being absolutely panoramic. Passenger space is ample, though the split third seat is too tight to accommodate three adults, and headroom beneath the sliding sunroof is only adequate for 6-footers. The center seat is removable and rear seat is split so that both halves can fold outward against the sides of the vehicle.

With its roomy, versatile nature and Toyota's reputation for reliability and durability, and the Previa qualifies as a good family vehicle.

NHTSA CRASH TEST RESULTS
1995 Toyota Previa

3-DOOR VAN

Driver ☆☆☆☆

Passenger ☆☆☆

(The National Highway Traffic Safety Administration tests a vehicle's crashworthiness in front and side collisions. Their ratings suggest the chance of serious injury: ☆☆☆☆☆—10% or less; ☆☆☆☆—10-20% or less; ☆☆☆—20-30% or less; ☆☆—35-45% or less; ☆—More than 45%.)

SPECIFICATIONS

	3-door van
Wheelbase, in.	112.8
Overall length, in.	187.2
Overall width, in.	70.8
Overall height, in.	68.7
Curb weight, lbs.	3755
Cargo volume, cu. ft.	152.3
Fuel capacity, gals.	19.8
Seating capacity	7
Front head room, in.	39.4
Max. front leg room, in.	40.1
Rear head room, in.	38.9
Min. rear leg room, in.	36.6

Powertrain layout: longitudinal mid-engine/rear- or all-wheel drive

ENGINES	dohc I-4	Supercharged dohc I-4
Size, liters/cu. in.	2.4/149	2.4/149
Horsepower	138	161
Torque (lbs./ft.)	154	201

EPA city/highway mpg

| 5-speed OD manual | 19/22 | |
| 4-speed OD automatic | 17/22 | 18/22 |

Consumer Guide™ observed MPG

| 4-speed OD automatic | 18.5 |

Built in Japan.

RETAIL PRICES	GOOD	AVERAGE	POOR
1991 Previa	$5,600-7,500	$4,800-6,700	$2,800-4,000
1992 Previa	6,800-9,500	6,000-8,600	3,600-5,500
1993 Previa	8,000-11,500	7,100-10,500	4,500-7,200
1994 Previa	10,000-13,500	9,000-12,300	6,000-8,800
1995 Previa	12,000-16,000	10,800-14,500	7,500-10,500
1996 Previa	14,500-18,500	13,000-17,000	9,500-13,000
1997 Previa	16,800-21,500	15,300-19,800	11,000-15,000

AVERAGE REPLACEMENT COSTS

A/C Compressor	$860	Clutch, Pressure Plate, Bearing	475
Alternator	390	Universal Joints	135
Radiator	555	Brakes	210
Timing Chain or Belt	890	Shocks and/or Struts	500
Automatic Transmission or Transaxle	830	Exhaust System	337

TROUBLE SPOTS

• **Coolant leak** Core plugs in the cylinder head may leak coolant and redesigned plugs and gaskets will be installed as a set under service campaign number L05. (1991)

• **Engine fan** The fan and fan shroud, and the radiator if it is damaged, are being replaced under service campaign L04. (1991)

• **Air conditioner** If the air conditioner gradually loses efficiency, the problem is likely caused by expansion valve and there was a campaign to replace them. On vehicles out of warranty, the customer must pay for any additional repairs or recharging. (1992-93)

• **Transmission slippage** The A-40 series automatic transmissions may eventually shift harshly because rubber check balls (used in the valve bodies) become smaller, blow through the plate, and get dislodged. Replacement balls are less prone to wear. (1992-94)

• **Exhaust system** In compliance with emission control regulations, the oxygen sensor will be replaced free at the 80,000-mile scheduled maintenance. (1993-95)

RECALL HISTORY

1991 Certain windshield wiper components are subject to premature failure. **1991** Failure of component in Fujitsu Ten radio causes short circuit that could result in fire. **1997** Oil leakage can occur at continuous speeds above 75 mph.

1993-98 TOYOTA T100

FOR Air bag, driver • Reliability

AGAINST Acceleration (4-cylinder, early V-6) • Price

THE BASICS The T100 looks like a full-size truck next to Toyota's compact, but actually slots in between the mid-size Dodge Dakota and the true full-size trucks. Toyota's 150-horsepower 3.0-liter V-6 was the only available powerplant. Limiting appeal of early models was the fact Initial T100s were only available in the regular-cab format.

1995 Toyota T100

Two trim levels are offered—Standard and SR5—both available in either 2WD or 4WD. Standard models come with a 60/40 split bench seat as does the SR5. T100s come with a small storage box behind the seats, and SR5s provide a built-in tool box. Power steering and rear anti-lock brakes are standard on all models.

1994 A driver-side air bag and the addition of a 4-cylinder as the new base engine are the major changes for the T100's second model year. A 150-horsepower, twin-cam 2.7-liter 4-cylinder bows in a new entry-level T100 model, available only in 2WD format. In addition to the driver-side air bag, all T100s gain the requisite side-door guard beams and a center high-mount stoplamp. Among the other changes, there's a new 2WD DX V-6 model, plus a One Ton model.

1995 Toyota finally adds an extended-cab model to its T100 lineup, and drops the previous V-6 for a new 190-horsepower V-6. The T100s new Xtracab is available in both DX and SR5 grades, and provides an extra 21.7 inches to the cab. They come equipped with a 60/40 split front bench seat, forward-facing 50/50 split jump seats for three, with accompanying safety belts. The new V-6 is available with either a 5-speed manual or 4-speed automatic, in 2- or 4-wheel drive.

1996 The T100 One Ton with its 2480-pound payload capacity is discontinued.

1997 Bucket seats and 16-inch-diameter wheels are new features available this year on Toyota's nearly full-size pickup.

1998 T100 sees no changes for '98. But an all-new model would be ready for '99.

EVALUATION   The 4-cylinder model delivers only modest performance and has been added to the line to serve primarily as a price leader. The 3.4-liter V-6 provides adequate acceleration in 2WD models, but in the heavier Xtracab 4WD versions, the manual transmission is necessary in order to maintain lively acceleration for passing and climbing hills. With the automatic, the V-6 gets off the line quickly and maintains strong acceleration if you keep the throttle wide open, but feels lethargic when a quick burst of power is needed in the 30-55 mph range.

The 2WD models absorb most bumps easily, but there's too much bouncing on wavy roads with an empty cargo bed. However, it tends to be more stable than a lot of big pickups. Steering and handling are better, too. The stiffer suspension of the 4WD models produces a choppier ride and the added ride height results in extra body lean when navigating turns. The T100's refinement is noticeable in the lack of cabin noise. The engines make themselves heard only during hard acceleration, and both wind and road noise are both moderate.

The big Toyota pickup earns high marks in most areas. It's wide enough for three adults to sit in front, but the middle passenger is required to rest their feet on the transmission tunnel and sit with knees only an inch or so from the stereo. The Xtracab's front passenger seat slides forward nicely, but it takes some twisting to climb into the rear seats. Once aboard, there's adequate leg and foot room for adults, and the slightly reclined backrest is a nice touch. But the rear-seat padding is quite thin and the lower cushion is uncomfortably flat. The T100's dashboard is modern and convenient, though when the dual cupholders near the top of the dash are being used, the climate controls are blocked.

The bottom line is this: If you want more than a compact pickup, don't need a V-8 engine, and think getting added refinement is worth paying a little extra to get, the T100 is a great way to go.

RATINGS

1996 Toyota T100 ext. cab 3.4-liter V-6

Performance	3	Room	4
Economy	2	Cargo Capacity	3
Ride	3	Insurance Costs	3
Noise	3	**Total**	**21**

NHTSA CRASH TEST RESULTS
1995 Toyota T100

REG. CAB LONG BED

Driver	☆☆☆☆
Passenger	☆☆☆☆

(The National Highway Traffic Safety Administration tests a vehicle's crashworthiness in front and side collisions. Their ratings suggest the chance of serious injury: ☆☆☆☆☆—10% or less; ☆☆☆☆—10-20% or less; ☆☆☆—20-30% or less; ☆☆—35-45% or less; ☆—More than 45%.)

SPECIFICATIONS

	reg. cab	ext. cab
Wheelbase, in.	121.8	121.8
Overall length, in.	209.1	209.1

	reg. cab	ext. cab
Overall width, in.	75.2	75.2
Overall height, in.	67.2	68.2
Curb weight, lbs.	3320	3550
Fuel capacity, gals.	24.0	24.0
Seating capacity	3	6
Front head room, in.	39.6	39.6
Max. front leg room, in.	42.9	42.9
Rear head room, in.	—	37.8
Min. rear leg room, in.	—	29.6

Powertrain layout: longitudinal front-engine/rear- or 4-wheel drive

ENGINES

	dohc I-4	ohc V-6	dohc V-6
Size, liters/cu. in.	2.7/163	3.0/181	3.4/181
Horsepower	150	150	190
Torque (lbs./ft.)	177	180	220

EPA city/highway mpg

	dohc I-4	ohc V-6	dohc V-6
5-speed OD manual	20/24	16/21	17/21
4-speed OD automatic	19/22	16/20	17/20

Consumer Guide™ observed MPG

5-speed OD manual	21.8		
4-speed OD automatic	18.7	15.7	

Built in Japan.

RETAIL PRICES

	GOOD	AVERAGE	POOR
1993 T100	$6,500-9,800	$5,700-9,000	$3,500-6,000
1994 T100	7,000-11,500	6,200-10,600	4,000-7,500
1995 T100	8,200-13,500	7,300-12,500	4,800-9,000
1996 T100	9,500-16,500	8,500-15,000	5,800-11,000
1997 T100	11,000-18,000	9,800-16,500	6,800-12,300
1998 T100	12,500-21,000	11,000-19,500	7,800-14,000

AVERAGE REPLACEMENT COSTS

A/C Compressor	$1,310	Clutch, Pressure Plate, Bearing	940
Alternator	360	Universal Joints	205
Radiator	575	Brakes	210
Timing Chain or Belt	170	Shocks and/or Struts	190
Automatic Transmission or Transaxle	1,400	Exhaust System	260

TROUBLE SPOTS

• **Transmission slippage** The A-40 series automatic transmissions may eventually shift harshly because rubber check balls (used in the valve bodies) become smaller, blow through the plate, and get dis-

TOYOTA

lodged. Replacement balls are less prone to wear. (1991+)

• **Water pump** The water pump seal was redesigned as a running production change and leaking prior units will be replaced under the 5-year/60,000 warranty. (1993-94)

• **Exhaust system** In compliance with emission control regulations, the oxygen sensor will be replaced free at the 80,000-mile scheduled maintenance. (1993-95)

RECALL HISTORY
None to date.

1995-98 TOYOTA TACOMA

1995 Toyota Tacoma SR5 V-6 4WD

FOR Acceleration (V-6) • Reliability

AGAINST Price • Engine noise • Ride

EVALUATION Acceleration with the base engine feels brisk, particularly with the manual transmission. The 2.7-liter 4-cylinder in 4WD models has marginally more horsepower and torque, but feels more taxed in all driving situations. Tacomas with the 3.4-liter V-6 have strong standing-start acceleration with either transmission. We averaged 16.1 mpg in our test.

Ride quality is poor. Tacoma pounds over bumps and bounds over dips in the pavement. Handling is nothing special either, but at least the brakes work well.

Inside, the Tacoma feels rather Spartan. There is enough room for two adults to stretch out in front, but the rear area, like in all compact pickups, is best left to cargo and not people. Controls are well arranged, but are a bit on the small side—especially radio controls. Visibility is excellent and noise levels are only marginally higher than in comparable Ford or Chevy compact trucks.

Tacoma's payload ratings are competitive with anything in this class, but even with the 3.4-liter V-6, towing limits fall short of the Ranger and S-Series by about 1000 pounds. Note also that Tacoma has only a single 6.2-foot cargo bed length; while nearly all competitors offer a regular-cab model with a cargo bed of 7 or 7.5 feet.

The only advantage a Tacoma might have over domestic compacts would be in reliability. This is one case where we would shop the competition despite Toyota's reputation.

NHTSA CRASH TEST RESULTS
1996 Toyota Pickup/Tacoma   REG. CAB LONG BED

| Driver | ☆☆ |
| Passenger | ☆☆☆ |

(The National Highway Traffic Safety Administration tests a vehicle's crashworthiness in front and side collisions. Their ratings suggest the chance of serious injury: ☆☆☆☆☆—10% or less; ☆☆☆☆—10-20% or less; ☆☆☆—20-30% or less; ☆☆—35-45% or less; ☆—More than 45%.)

SPECIFICATIONS

	reg. cab	ext. cab
Wheelbase, in.	103.3	121.9
Overall length, in.	184.5	203.1
Overall width, in.	66.5	66.5
Overall height, in.	61.8	62.0
Curb weight, lbs.	2560	2745
Fuel capacity, gals.	15.1	15.1
Seating capacity	3	5
Front head room, in.	38.2	38.4
Max. front leg room, in.	41.7	42.8
Rear head room, in.	—	35.5
Min. rear leg room, in.	—	27.2

Powertrain layout: longitudinal front-engine/rear- or 4-wheel drive

ENGINES

	dohc I-4	dohc I-6	dohc V-6
Size, liters/cu. in.	2.4/144	2.7/163	3.4/207
Horsepower	142	150	190
Torque (lbs./ft.)	160	177	220
EPA city/highway mpg			
5-speed OD manual	23/28	17/21	19/23
4-speed OD automatic	22/25	18/21	19/22
Consumer Guide™ observed MPG			
5-speed OD manual	20.1		19.2
4-speed OD automatic			16.1

Built in USA and Japan.

TOYOTA

RETAIL PRICES	GOOD	AVERAGE	POOR
1995 Tacoma	$15,500-19,000	$11,000-16,500	$8,200-12,000
1996 Tacoma	16,000-21,000	11,500-17,000	8,600-12,500
1997 Tacoma	16,250-22,500	12,500-17,650	8,900-13,000
1998 Tacoma	17,000-24,000	13,500-18,500	9,200-14,250

AVERAGE REPLACEMENT COSTS

A/C Compressor $1,315	Clutch, Pressure Plate,
Alternator 360	Bearing...........................915
Radiator 520	Universal Joints 200
Timing Chain or Belt 200	Brakes.................................190
Automatic Transmission or	Shocks and/or Struts 210
Transaxle......................1,457	Exhaust System.................242

TROUBLE SPOTS

• **Exhaust system** In compliance with emission control regulations, the oxygen sensor will be replaced free at the 80,000-mile scheduled maintenance. (1995)

RECALL HISTORY

1995 Battery may have defective weld inside positive or negative terminal, which can result in a no-start condition or explosion. **1995-96** Under certain conditions, front suspension support can crack.

1991-94 TOYOTA TERCEL

1991 Toyota Tercel 4-door

FOR Anti-lock brakes (optional) • Fuel economy • Maneuverability

AGAINST Engine noise • Road noise • Wind noise • Rear-seat room

EVALUATION The tiny engine produces adequate acceleration, but is noisy and feels stressed at freeway speeds. Also the automatic transmissions are rather slow to downshift when asked to deliver extra passing power. Good fuel economy is a strong point, however. We averaged 26.3 mpg with a DX/automatic model.

Once underway, we noticed the suspension allows lots of bouncing on wavy roads and the ride becomes choppy on rough surfaces. In addition, there is an above-average amount of annoying road noise. Also, the car's handling ability is hampered by the Tercel's tiny wheels and tires (155/80SR13s), which run out of grip early when asked to corner.

Adults have ample room in front, but the rear seat is tight for anyone over 5-foot-10. On the plus side, the dashboard is simple, functional, and conveniently laid out.

Unfortunately for the Tercel, Toyota has dictated that be the low-price leader in the automaker's very full model lineup and it shows. The car is simply outclassed by the plusher, more substantial subcompacts against which it must compete.

NHTSA CRASH TEST RESULTS
1995 Toyota Tercel   4-DOOR SEDAN

Driver ☆☆☆
Passenger ☆☆☆☆

(The National Highway Traffic Safety Administration tests a vehicle's crashworthiness in front and side collisions. Their ratings suggest the chance of serious injury: ☆☆☆☆☆—10% or less; ☆☆☆☆—10-20% or less; ☆☆☆—20-30% or less; ☆☆—35-45% or less; ☆—More than 45%.)

SPECIFICATIONS

	2-door coupe	4-door sedan
Wheelbase, in.	93.7	93.7
Overall length, in.	161.8	161.9
Overall width, in.	64.8	64.8
Overall height, in.	53.2	53.2
Curb weight, lbs.	1950	2005
Cargo volume, cu. ft.	10.7	10.7
Fuel capacity, gals.	11.9	11.9
Seating capacity	5	5
Front head room, in.	38.7	38.7
Max. front leg room, in.	41.2	41.2
Rear head room, in.	36.7	36.1
Min. rear leg room, in.	31.9	31.9

ENGINES

	ohc I-4
Size, liters/cu. in.	1.5/89
Horsepower	82
Torque (lbs./ft.)	90

EPA city/highway mpg
5-speed OD manual	29/35
3-speed automatic	26/29

Consumer Guide™ observed MPG
3-speed automatic	26.3

TOYOTA

Built in Japan.

RETAIL PRICES	GOOD	AVERAGE	POOR
1991 Tercel	$1,600-2,800	$1,000-2,200	$200-700
1992 Tercel	2,200-3,600	1,500-2,900	500-1,000
1993 Tercel	2,700-4,300	2,000-3,600	800-1,400
1994 Tercel	3,400-5,000	2,700-4,200	1,100-1,800

AVERAGE REPLACEMENT COSTS

A/C Compressor $1,368	Clutch, Pressure Plate,
Alternator 355	Bearing 460
Radiator 470	Constant Velocity Joints.....680
Timing Chain or Belt 210	Brakes.................................190
Automatic Transmission or	Shocks and/or Struts 635
Transaxle.....................1,010	Exhaust System.................395

TROUBLE SPOTS

• **Air conditioner** If the air conditioner does not cool, or the compressor runs intermittently and the A/C light flashes, the wiring harness must be rerouted and protected with a sleeve. (1991-94)

• **Oil consumption** Oil consumption due to worn valve stem seals may be eliminated by installing improved seals on both the intake and exhaust valves. (1991)

• **Windshield washer** New windshield washer buttons were made available for servicing problems with the system. (1991-92)

RECALL HISTORY

None to date.

1995-98 TOYOTA TERCEL

FOR Air bags, dual • Fuel economy • Maneuverability

AGAINST Noise • Rear seat room

EVALUATION The latest engine is noisy, but its greater power shows up in quicker acceleration. Nevertheless, performance is still far from lively, even with a manual transmission. Automatic transmissions are rather slow to downshift to deliver suitable highway passing power. Fuel economy is exceptional: We averaged 30 mpg in a DX model with automatic.

Though refreshingly frugal, long rides in a Tercel aren't all pleasure, by any means. The suspension allows a lot of bouncing on wavy roads, and the ride becomes choppy on rough surfaces. In addition, there's still plenty of road noise. Handling ability is ham-

1997 Toyota Tercel sedan

pered by narrow tires, which run out of grip early in hard cornering.

Inside, the dashboard is simple, functional, and conveniently laid out, but the rear seat remains tight for anyone over 5-foot-10. Adults have ample room up front, but trunk space is on the skimpy side.

Far from exciting in concept or reality, Tercel's mission has been to be the least-expensive Toyota, and it shows against the plusher, more substantial Corolla and other subcompact leaders. On the other hand, Toyota's reputation for reliability makes the Tercel worth considering if you need basic transportation but are on a tight budget.

NHTSA CRASH TEST RESULTS
1997 Toyota Tercel

	2-DOOR COUPE
Driver	☆☆☆☆
	2-DOOR COUPE
Passenger	☆☆☆☆

(The National Highway Traffic Safety Administration tests a vehicle's crashworthiness in front and side collisions. Their ratings suggest the chance of serious injury: ☆☆☆☆☆—10% or less; ☆☆☆☆—10-20% or less; ☆☆☆—20-30% or less; ☆☆—35-45% or less; ☆—More than 45%.)

SPECIFICATIONS

	2-door coupe	4-door sedan
Wheelbase, in.	93.7	93.7
Overall length, in.	161.8	161.8
Overall width, in.	64.8	64.8
Overall height, in.	53.2	53.2
Curb weight, lbs.	1950	2005
Cargo volume, cu. ft.	9.3	9.3
Fuel capacity, gals.	11.9	11.9
Seating capacity	5	5
Front head room, in.	38.6	38.6
Max. front leg room, in.	41.2	41.2

TOYOTA

	2-door coupe	4-door sedan
Rear head room, in.	36.5	36.5
Min. rear leg room, in.	31.9	31.9

Powertrain layout: transverse front-engine/front-wheel drive

ENGINES

	dohc I-4
Size, liters/cu. in.	1.5/89
Horsepower	93
Torque (lbs./ft.)	100

EPA city/highway mpg

5-speed OD manual	34/39[1]
3-speed automatic	31/35
4-speed OD automatic	30/39

Consumer Guide™ observed MPG

5-speed OD manual	32.5
4-speed OD automatic	30.0

1. 34/40 mpg with 4-speed manual.

Built in Japan.

AVERAGE REPLACEMENT COSTS

A/C Compressor	$1,350	Clutch, Pressure Plate, Bearing	370
Alternator	330	Constant Velocity Joints	1,045
Radiator	305	Brakes	220
Timing Chain or Belt	190	Shocks and/or Struts	1,100
Automatic Transmission or Transaxle	680	Exhaust System	355

RETAIL PRICES

	GOOD	AVERAGE	POOR
1995 Tercel	$4,600-6,000	$3,900-5,300	$2,000-2,800
1996 Tercel	5,800-7,400	5,100-6,600	2,800-3,800
1997 Tercel	7,500-9,000	6,700-8,200	3,900-5,000
1998 Tercel	9,000-10,800	8,000-9,500	5,000-6,000

TROUBLE SPOTS

• **Dashboard lights** The check engine light may come on when the car is driven at altitudes above 5900 feet which may require a new computer. (1995-96)

• **Climate control** Poor heater performance may be due to a defective thermostat. (1995-96)

• **Dashboard lights** Cars driven above 5900 feet may set false check engine lights for which there is a replacement computer. (1995-96)

• **Radio** A poor antenna ground causes static on the AM band of the radio. (1995-96)

• **Windows** The front windows may be hard to operate. (1995-96)

RECALL HISTORY

None to date.

1995-98 VOLKSWAGEN CABRIO

1995 Volkswagen Cabrio

FOR Air bags, dual • Anti-lock brakes • Steering/handling • Ride • Fuel economy

AGAINST Cargo room • Visibility

EVALUATION With either transmission, get-up-and-go is adequate from a stop, and passing power is decent on the highway. The engine produces a hearty growl under acceleration and cruises quietly. Gas mileage is a definite plus: Expect to average about 25 mpg. Road noise is moderate and top-up wind noise surprisingly low. The body feels more solid than most convertibles, and those Cabrios that we've driven when nearly new have been devoid of squeaks.

A Cabrio is stable at highway speeds and its ride is firm, but absorbent enough to soak up most bumps. You enjoy sprightly handling and firm, precise steering, as well as good grip on wet roads. Front power-window switches are on armrests, while rear-window switches are mounted oddly, at the dashboard center. Otherwise, the dashboard is conveniently laid out, with the climate controls and stereo mounted high enough to make them easy to see and operate.

Space is ample for adults in front, and the rear seat holds two adequately. Front seats are firm and supportive, but not wide enough to be comfortable for stout people. A Cabrio's top folds flatter than the old Cabriolet's, so it interferes less with rear visibility. With the top raised, rear side glass and a large rear window provide generally good visibility for a convertible. No glovebox is included, and trunk capacity is meager—a mere 7.8 cubic feet.

If a sharp-looking, crisp-handling convertible is on your shopping list, Volkswagen might be the place to look.

SPECIFICATIONS

	2-door conv.
Wheelbase, in.	97.2
Overall length, in.	160.4
Overall width, in.	66.7
Overall height, in.	56.0
Curb weight, lbs.	2701
Cargo volume, cu. ft.	7.8
Fuel capacity, gals.	14.5
Seating capacity	4
Front head room, in.	38.7
Max. front leg room, in.	42.3
Rear head room, in.	36.6
Min. rear leg room, in.	31.1

Powertrain layout: transverse front-engine/front-wheel drive

ENGINES

	ohc I-4
Size, liters/cu. in.	2.0/121
Horsepower	115
Torque (lbs./ft.)	122
EPA city/highway mpg	
5-speed OD manual	23/30
4-speed OD automatic	22/28
Consumer Guide™ observed MPG	
5-speed OD manual	27.5
4-speed OD automatic	25.1

Built in Germany and Mexico.

AVERAGE REPLACEMENT COSTS

A/C Compressor	$520	Automatic Transmission or Transaxle	675
Alternator	375	Constant Velocity Joints	1,430
Radiator	380	Brakes	270
Clutch, Pressure Plate, Bearing	370	Shocks and/or Struts	760
		Exhaust System	380

RETAIL PRICES	GOOD	AVERAGE	POOR
1995 Cabrio	$11,500-13,000	$10,500-12,000	$7,500-8,600

	GOOD	AVERAGE	POOR
1996 Cabrio	13,000-14,500	12,000-13,300	8,600-9,900
1997 Cabrio	14,500-16,000	13,200-14,500	9,800-10,800
1998 Cabrio	16,000-18,500	14,500-17,000	11,000-13,000

TROUBLE SPOTS

• **Dashboard lights** The "low coolant level" light may come on if either the concentration of antifreeze and water is wrong or if there is a bad coolant sensor. (1995-96)

• **Transmission noise** The final drive ring-and-pinion gears get damaged from a chipped reverse gear in transmissions built before build date 01047 (1997 model year) when a strainer was added during production. (1995-97)

• **Air bags** A magazine article reported that 1995-96 models could be retrofitted with an imported glove box from VW. (1995-96)

• **Doors** The door locks tend to freeze in cold weather and new locks, with drains began being installed in 1997 models. (1995-96)

• **Transmission slippage** The transmission may shift late, may not upshift, or may downshift unnecessarily due to a bad transmission fluid temperature sensor. (1997)

RECALL HISTORY

None to date.

1990-92 VOLKSWAGEN GOLF/JETTA

1991 Volkswagen Jetta Carat 4-door

FOR Steering/handling • Maneuverability • Cargo room

AGAINST Automatic transmission performance • Engine

VOLKSWAGEN

noise • Road noise • Wind noise

EVALUATION These cars impress us with their competent well-balanced road manners—even the base models. Even more impressive are the Jetta GLI and Golf GTI equipped with the 16-valve 2.0-liter 4-cylinder. Both provide excellent performance with brisk acceleration. Models with the 1.8-liter engine and automatic transmission also accelerate well, but tend to bog down once they shift into third gear. To get the automatic to downshift into second for extra passing power requires a heavy foot on the throttle. A real diamond-in-the-rough is the Jetta GL equipped with the ECOdiesel engine. Not only does it pollute less, it provides real-world fuel economy that approaches or exceeds 40 mpg.

All Golfs and Jettas are roomy inside, despite their subcompact dimensions, with adequate space in back for two adults. These utilitarian models both provide generous room for your cargo. The Jetta has a huge trunk, while the rear seats in the Golf fold forward, providing nearly 40 cubic feet of hauling capacity.

The tires grip tenaciously and the firm steering is very responsive. There's some body lean in tight turns, but overall the suspension provides better road handling ability than is generally found in a subcompact. The bucket seats are highly chair-like, providing outstanding back support. Radio and climate controls are mounted high in the center of the dash where they are easy to see and reach.

Neither the Golf or Jetta are likely to win any beauty contests. However, they are very roomy, economical cars that deliver European performance at a reasonable price.

SPECIFICATIONS	2-door hatchback	4-door hatchback	2-door coupe	4-door sedan
Wheelbase, in.	97.3	97.3	97.3	97.3
Overall length, in.	158.0	158.0	171.7	171.7
Overall width, in.	65.5	65.5	65.5	65.5
Overall height, in.	55.7	55.7	55.7	55.7
Curb weight, lbs.	2200	2270	2275	2330
Cargo volume, cu. ft.	39.6	39.6	16.6	16.6
Fuel capacity, gals.	14.5	14.5	14.5	14.5
Seating capacity	5	5	5	5
Front head room, in.	38.1	38.1	38.1	38.1
Max. front leg room, in.	39.5	39.5	39.5	39.5
Rear head room, in.	37.5	37.5	37.1	37.1
Min. rear leg room, in.	34.4	34.4	35.1	35.1

Powertrain layout: transverse front-engine/front-wheel drive

ENGINES

	ohc I-4	ohc I-4	dohc I-4	Diesel ohc I-4	Turbodiesel ohc I-4
Size, liters/cu. in.	1.8/109	1.8/109	2.0/121	1.6/97	1.6/97
Horsepower	100	105	134	52	59
Torque (lbs./ft.)	107	110	133	71	81

EPA city/highway mpg

5-speed OD man.	25/32	25/32	21/28	37/43	37/40
3-speed auto.	23/28	23/28			

EPA city/highway mpg (CGTM observed)

5-speed OD manual		28.3	25.5	22.6
3-speed automatic		24.2		

Built in Mexico and Germany.

RETAIL PRICES

	GOOD	AVERAGE	POOR
1990 Golf	$2,000-3,200	$1,300-2,500	$,500-1,000
1990 Jetta	2,100-3,700	1,400-3,000	,500-1,300
1990 Cabriolet	4,000-5,000	3,300-4,200	1,500-2,000
1991 Golf	2,500-4,200	1,800-3,500	,700-1,500
1991 Jetta	2,800-4,800	2,100-4,000	,900-1,800
1991 Cabriolet	5,000-6,300	4,200-5,500	2,100-2,900
1992 Golf	3,300-5,200	2,600-4,400	1,100-2,200
1992 Jetta	3,500-6,000	2,800-5,200	1,500-2,700
1992 Cabriolet	6,000-7,500	5,200-6,600	3,000-3,900

AVERAGE REPLACEMENT COSTS

A/C Compressor	$560	Clutch, Pressure Plate, Bearing	515
Alternator	295	Constant Velocity Joints.	1,,048
Radiator	200	Brakes	180
Timing Chain or Belt	220	Shocks and/or Struts	400
Automatic Transmission or Transaxle	670	Exhaust System	500

TROUBLE SPOTS

• **Poor drivability** Magnetic interference can cause drivability problems if the shielding for the oxygen sensor wiring is damaged and the wiring harness may have to be replaced. (1990-92)

• **Starter** A running change was made the starter drive in October 1991, but previous models may not engage properly, and the starter as well as the ring gear, may be damaged. (1990-91)

• **Hard starting** If the starter does not work when the engine is hot, a relay may have to be installed between the battery and starter solenoid. (1990-92)

• **Tire wear** Cupping or feather edging of the rear tires may be caused by too much positive rear toe, which is corrected by replacing the rear axle stub shafts. (1990-92)

• **Engine stalling** If the engine occasionally looses power, stalls, or stumbles, the problem may be vibration of the mass airflow sensor, and to correct the problem a converter will be installed in the MAF circuit. (1990-92)

RECALL HISTORY

1990 Brake fluid may exceed allowable operating temperature. **1990 Jetta** Power steering pump bracket on some cars could break. **1990** End cap connecting heat exchanger's core to engine cooling system could rupture and allow hot coolant to escape into passenger compartment. **1990-91** Engine preheating tube may not be supported, and may chafe against right front brake line. **1990-92 GLI/GTI with 16-valve engine and California emission control system** Throttle plate may not return to full idle position. **1991 Jetta** Some front brake hoses are too short and could stretch and develop cracks, which could result in fluid leakage and loss of braking ability. **1991 California Jettas with cruise control** Lock nut rod may not have been properly torqued, so adjustment could change. **1992 Jetta** On a few 4-door sedans with electric windows, rear-door panel openings have sharp edges that can damage insulation of wiring harness, resulting in short circuit and potential for fire.

1994-98 VOLKSWAGEN GOLF/JETTA

1996 Volkswagen Jetta GL

FOR Air bags, dual (all but early '94) • Anti-lock brakes (optional) • Acceleration • Passenger and cargo room • Steering/handling • Maneuverability

AGAINST Engine noise • Road noise

EVALUATION The 4-cylinder models have adequate acceleration from a standing start and lively passing power with either transmission. The 4-speed automatic downshifts promptly, providing adequate power for passing, but lacks smoothness. Naturally, acceleration is a bit friskier and fuel economy is better with the standard 5-speed manual. We averaged 23.8 mpg with the automatic and 26.5 mpg with the 5-speed. The GTI VR6 and GLX Jetta models with their 2.8-liter V-6 deliver very impressive acceleration, but be prepared to pay extra.

Unlike their predecessors, the current models don't suffer the constant thumping from the suspension and tires. Road noise is still prominent at highway speeds and the exhaust is too loud when cruising at 60-65 mph. Like the previous models, these third-generation Golf and Jetta models have sporty handling for family cars. The steering is firm and precise and the tires grip well when taking turns at speeds.

The dashboard has a functional layout, with all controls mounted high for easy operation while driving. Since they ride on the same 97.4-inch wheelbase as the preceding models, interior space is about the same. All body styles have ample cargo space and the Jetta's trunk is huge when compared to the car's compact size.

Our only reservation with these delightful subcompacts is Volkswagen reliability and high prices. Otherwise they are an excellent choice that is a little out of the norm.

NHTSA CRASH TEST RESULTS
1995 Volkswagen Golf/Jetta   4-DOOR HATCHBACK

Driver	☆☆☆
Passenger	☆☆☆

(The National Highway Traffic Safety Administration tests a vehicle's crashworthiness in front and side collisions. Their ratings suggest the chance of serious injury: ☆☆☆☆☆—10% or less; ☆☆☆☆—10-20% or less; ☆☆☆—20-30% or less; ☆☆—35-45% or less; ☆—More than 45%.)

SPECIFICATIONS	2-door hatchback	4-door hatchback	4-door sedan
Wheelbase, in.	97.4	97.4	97.4
Overall length, in.	160.5	160.5	173.4
Overall width, in.	66.7	66.7	66.7
Overall height, in.	56.2	56.2	56.1
Curb weight, lbs.	2511	2577	2647
Cargo volume, cu. ft.	17.5	16.9	15.0
Fuel capacity, gals.	14.5	14.5	14.5

VOLKSWAGEN

	2-door hatchback	4-door hatchback	4-door sedan
Seating capacity	5	5	5
Front head room, in.	39.2	39.2	39.2
Max. front leg room, in.	42.3	42.3	42.3
Rear head room, in.	37.4	37.3	37.4
Min. rear leg room, in.	31.5	31.5	31.5

Powertrain layout: transverse front-engine/front-wheel drive

ENGINES

	ohc I-4	ohc V-6	Turbodiesel ohc I-4
Size, liters/cu. in.	2.0/121	2.8/170	1.9/116
Horsepower	115	172	90
Torque (lbs./ft.)	122	173	149

EPA city/highway mpg
5-speed OD manual	23/30	19/26	40/49
4-speed OD automatic	22/28	18/24	

Consumer Guide™ observed MPG
5-speed OD manual	26.5	21.4	
4-speed OD automatic	23.8	20.3	

Built in Mexico.

RETAIL PRICES

	GOOD	AVERAGE	POOR
1994 Golf	$5,400-6,800	$4,700-6,000	$2,700-3,700
1994 Jetta	6,500-9,500	5,700-8,600	3,400-5,000
1995 Golf	6,800-9,500	6,000-8,600	3,500-5,600
1995 Jetta	7,900-11,800	7,000-10,800	4,500-7,000
1996 Golf	8,500-11,500	7,500-10,500	4,500-7,000
1996 Jetta	9,800-14,000	8,800-13,000	5,800-9,500
1997 Golf	10,000-14,000	9,000-13,000	5,800-9,500
1997 Jetta	11,300-15,500	10,000-14,000	6,800-10,500
1998 Golf	11,500-16,500	10,200-15,000	6,800-11,000
1998 Jetta	12,500-17,500	11,000-16,000	7,500-11,800

AVERAGE REPLACEMENT COSTS

A/C Compressor	$640
Alternator	660
Radiator	585
Timing Chain or Belt	110
Automatic Transmission or Transaxle	720
Clutch, Pressure Plate, Bearing	530
Constant Velocity Joints	845
Brakes	210
Shocks and/or Struts	410
Exhaust System	485

TROUBLE SPOTS

• **Water leak** Leaks at the bulkhead that allow water to enter the interior while driving (but not when parked) should have been corrected during pre-delivery inspection and will have a yellow sticker on the firewall if the job was done. (1993-94)

• **Poor drivability** Oil accumulating in the intake air system can eventually damage the airflow sensor causing drivability problems. The airflow sensor may be replaced under warranty, but the air intake systems must be inspected and cleaned periodically. (1993-95)

• **Poor drivability** Magnetic interference can cause drivability problems if the shielding for the oxygen sensor wiring is damaged, and the wiring harness may have to be replaced. (1993+)

• **Engine stalling** If the engine occasionally looses power, stalls, or stumbles, the problem may be vibration of the mass airflow sensor, and to correct the problem a converter will be installed in the MAF circuit. (1993)

• **Tire wear** Cupping or feather edging of the rear tires may be caused by too much positive rear toe, which is corrected by replacing the rear axle stub shafts. (1993-96)

• **Suspension noise** A dull clunking noise from the front end when driving over small bumps or dips may be due to too much free play in the upper MacPherson strut bearings requiring a new bearing cap and special grease. (1993-95)

RECALL HISTORY

1993-95 Jack could collapse during use. **1994-95 with V-6 engine** Improper material was used in manufacturing radiator fan motor shaft for VR6 engine, causing shaft to wear and become noisy; shaft could seize, rendering fan motor inoperative and eventually causing engine to overheat and stall.

1990-94 VOLKSWAGEN PASSAT

FOR Optional anti-lock brakes • Acceleration (V-6) • Passenger and cargo room • Handling/roadholding • Traction control (V-6)

AGAINST No air bags • Noise • Ride (GLX) • Automatic transmission performance (4-cylinder)

EVALUATION Early automatic transmissions are downright ill-mannered, shifting with unpleasant harshness and responding sluggishly. Too bad, because with the 4-cylinder engine, a Passat accelerates with some briskness, even with automatic. A GLX with the V-6 is faster still. Smooth and responsive, the V-6 does produce a lot of low-end torque for good acceleration from low speeds. More important, with the V-6 engine, the Passat's

1990 Volkswagen Passat GL sedan

automatic transmission operates much more smoothly. Fuel economy with the 4-cylinder engine is exceptional, and average for the V-6.

A taut suspension delivers a stable feel and nimble handling, though the ride grows nasty on rough spots. It's a little softer in 1994 models, but we also noticed some floatiness over high-speed dips. All Passats handle capably, but the GLX corners like a sport sedan. Though power steering demands rather high effort at parking speeds, it's quick and precise at higher velocities. One major negative: Road and wind noise are troublesome.

Four passengers have plenty of room, but the back seat isn't wide enough for three large folks. Leg space is ample front and rear, and 6-footers enjoy good head room. Not merely ample, the sedan's trunk borders on cavernous in size. Folding down one or both rear seatbacks creates even more space. Controls are well laid out and easy to reach. Visibility is good. Optional anti-lock braking provides strong stopping power and excellent control.

Roomy and competent, the 1990-94 Passat can be a good choice in a well-equipped compact sedan or wagon, if you can live with the ride harshness and tire noise.

SPECIFICATIONS	4-door sedan	4-door wagon
Wheelbase, in.	103.3	103.3
Overall length, in.	180.0	179.9
Overall width, in.	67.1	67.1
Overall height, in.	56.2	58.7
Curb weight, lbs.	3152	3197
Cargo volume, cu. ft.	14.4	68.9
Fuel capacity, gals.	18.5	18.5
Seating capacity	5	5

	4-door sedan	4-door wagon
Front head room, in.	37.6	38.0
Max. front leg room, in.	43.6	43.6
Rear head room, in.	37.4	39.0
Min. rear leg room, in.	35.3	35.3

Powertrain layout: transverse front-engine/front-wheel drive

ENGINES

	dohc I-4	ohc V-6
Size, liters/cu. in.	2.0/121	2.8/170
Horsepower	134	172
Torque (lbs./ft.)	133	177
EPA city/highway mpg		
5-speed OD manual	21/30	19/27
4-speed OD automatic	20/29	17/24
Consumer Guide™ observed MPG		
5-speed OD manual		23.1
4-speed OD automatic	22.2	20.8

Built in Germany.

AVERAGE REPLACEMENT COSTS

A/C Compressor	$620	Clutch, Pressure Plate, Bearing	585
Alternator	400	Constant Velocity Joints	1,320
Radiator	370	Brakes	450
Timing Chain or Belt	360	Shocks and/or Struts	610
Automatic Transmission or Transaxle	795	Exhaust System	410

RETAIL PRICES

	GOOD	AVERAGE	POOR
1990 Passat	$2,800-3,500	$2,100-2,800	$900-1,300
1991 Passat	3,600-4,300	2,900-3,600	1,200-1,600
1992 Passat	4,400-5,500	3,700-4,700	1,700-2,300
1993 Passat	5,800-7,800	5,000-7,000	2,600-4,200
1994 Passat	8,800-10,000	7,800-9,000	4,800-5,500

TROUBLE SPOTS

• **Tire wear** Uneven tire wear such as cupping and feathering may be due to improper alignment specifications (too much toe-in). A replacement rear stub axle is available. (1990-93)

• **Air conditioner** Models equipped with a variable displacement A/C compressor may not cool properly due to restrictions in the system. (1993-94)

• **Hard starting** No-starts or stalling may be traced to a faulty power relay to the engine control computer. (1994)

• **Battery** A broken wire between the alternator and warning light causes intermittent charging and often a dead battery. (1992)

• **Coolant leak** A low coolant level malfunction can be the result of the wrong concentration of antifreeze and water or a bad coolant sensor. (1990-94)

RECALL HISTORY

1990 If engine operates continuously in overheated condition, hot coolant might escape. **1990-92 w/16-valve engine and California emission controls** Tube in throttle valve housing can loosen and fall, preventing throttle plate from returning to full idle; results in unwanted engine speed when car goes into gear. **1993** Lock nuts may break and allow front axles to separate from struts, which can cause vehicle to pull to side and may result in loss of control. **1993-94 w/VR6 engine** Radiator fan motor shaft could wear, get noisy and seize, making fan inoperative and eventually causing engine to overheat and stall.

1993-97 VOLVO 850

1994 Volvo 850 Turbo Wagon

FOR Air bags, dual • Air bag, side (later models) • Passenger and cargo room

AGAINST Acceleration (base) • Automatic transmission performance

EVALUATION These 850s drive much like Volvo's larger 960 models, but their trimmer size and superior suspension give them truly athletic cornering ability. The suspension is firm enough to provide a stable highway ride with little bouncing and absorbent enough to soak most bumps without braking stride.

The standard engine lacks sufficient torque to provide good acceleration. But the turbocharged engine is an entirely different story. The 850 Turbo wagon can sprint from stop to 60 mph in an impressive 7.1 seconds. We do have a couple of disappointments to report, however. Turbocharged engines come only with a 4-speed automatic, which is often slow to downshift when climbing steep hills.

Speaking of jolts, on the Turbo versions the ride is often a bit too stiff, with excessive tire thump on route pavement.

As you'd expect from Volvo, there's plenty of head and leg room for four adults, but the interior isn't quite wide enough for comfortable three-across seating in back. The sedan's spacious trunk has a low bumper-height opening, and the wagon has a long, flat cargo area when the rear seat is folded down.

Though we're not overwhelmed by the 850, it's also a good job of breathing new life into what had become a now outdated product line. With the side air bags and turbo engines, it also has more going for it than some of rivals in the near-luxury market.

NHTSA CRASH TEST RESULTS
1995 Volvo 850

4-DOOR SEDAN

Driver	☆☆☆☆☆
Passenger	☆☆☆☆

(The National Highway Traffic Safety Administration tests a vehicle's crashworthiness in front and side collisions. Their ratings suggest the chance of serious injury: ☆☆☆☆☆—10% or less; ☆☆☆☆—10-20% or less; ☆☆☆—20-30% or less; ☆☆—35-45% or less; ☆—More than 45%.)

SPECIFICATIONS

	4-door sedan	4-door wagon
Wheelbase, in.	104.9	104.9
Overall length, in.	183.5	185.4
Overall width, in.	59.3	69.3
Overall height, in.	55.7	56.9
Curb weight, lbs.	3232	3342
Cargo volume, cu. ft.	14.7	67.0
Fuel capacity, gals.	19.3	19.3
Seating capacity	5	5
Front head room, in.	39.1	39.1
Max. front leg room, in.	41.4	41.4
Rear head room, in.	37.8	37.8
Min. rear leg room, in.	32.3	35.2

Powertrain layout: transverse front-engine/front-wheel drive

ENGINES

	dohc I-5[1]	Turbocharged dohc I-5
Size, liters/cu. in.	2.4/149	2.3/141
Horsepower	168-190	222-240
Torque (lbs./ft.)	162-191	221

EPA city/highway mpg

5-speed OD manual	20/29	
4-speed OD automatic	20/29[1]	19/26

Consumer Guide™ observed MPG

4-speed OD automatic	21.8	22.5

1. 1997 GLT models add a turbocharger to the 2.4-liter engine, which boosts the engine up to 190 horsepower. A slightly lower EPA highway rating of 27 mpg is the result.

Built in Sweden.

RETAIL PRICES	GOOD	AVERAGE	POOR
1993 850	$12,000-13,200	$11,000-12,000	$8,000-8,900
1994 850	14,000-16,000	12,800-14,500	9,500-10,800
1995 850	16,000-19,500	14,500-18,000	11,000-14,000
1996 850	18,000-23,500	16,500-22,000	12,500-17,500
1997 850	20,000-26,000	18,500-24,000	14,000-19,000

AVERAGE REPLACEMENT COSTS

A/C Compressor	$940	Clutch, Pressure Plate, Bearing	755
Alternator	425	Constant Velocity Joints	135
A/C Compressor	395	Brakes	170
Timing Chain or Belt	200	Shocks and/or Struts	470
Automatic Transmission or Transaxle	1,,305	Exhaust System	330

TROUBLE SPOTS

• **Transmission slippage** If the transmission is sometimes difficult to shift out of park, it is due to improper contact of the lockout microswitch. A campaign was issued to replace the microswitch and wiring. (1994-96)

• **Cruise control** If the cruise control will not engage, the plastic vacuum supply line may be damaged in the area of the left headlight for which there is a replacement hose kit. (1993-96)

• **Engine noise** Noise from the front of the engine at the drive belts may be caused by a defective belt tensioner and/or idler pulley. (1993-96)

• **Windshield washer** If the windshield washer does not work well, the jet can be replaced with a larger one that went into production cars in 1994. (1993-94)

• **Windshield washer** Washer leaks at the rear window can be prevented by installing a pressure valve in the line near the upper hinge of the window. (1993-95)

RECALL HISTORY

1994 Ice can form on throttle linkage, resulting in uneven throttle return or loss of low-speed engine control. **1995 with power seats** Threaded insert that attaches safety belt catch was incorrectly manufactured and can reduce restraining capability. **1995** Some jacks do not have the necessary load capacity. **1996-97** Screws that attach throttle plate to the throttle shaft can loosen, possibly preventing throttle from returning to idle position.

1991-98 VOLVO 940/960/S90/V90

1996 Volvo 960 4-door

FOR Acceleration (turbo) • Anti-lock brakes • Air bags, dual (later models) • Ride/handling • Passenger and cargo room

AGAINST Acceleration (base) • Fuel economy • Road noise • Wind noise

EVALUATION The base 940 and 960 models are decent values, but dropping the dual overhead-cam engine from the powertrain lineup in '92 for the underpowered 114-horsepower engine used by the entry-level 240 dooms the base 940 to lackluster performance. Selecting the 940 Turbo is one alternative, but then you suffer with "turbo lag" waiting for the power to arrive. We prefer the smoother 6-cylinder. It gives the 960 brisk takeoffs and ensures spirited passing ability. The 6-cylinder produces sporty, aggressive tone in hard acceleration and cruises comfortably. We timed a 1995 sedan at a brisk 8.7 seconds, despite a reduction of 20 horsepower that year. Fuel economy is about average. We recorded 17.8 mpg with a 960 in mostly city and suburban commuting.

On all cars, there is an excessive amount of wind noise at

speed, and stiffer tires added in '95 produce additional unwanted noise and vibration over rough pavement. Suspension changes improve cornering for this large, boxy sedan, but the harsher ride makes the wagons more preferable.

These premium Volvo sedans also provide very good passenger and cargo room, decent ride comfort, braking, and workmanship. But both the 940 and 960 have trouble competing now against such refined benchmarks as the front-wheel-drive Lexus ES 300 and Acura Legend.

SPECIFICATIONS

	4-door sedan	4-door wagon
Wheelbase, in.	109.1	109.1
Overall length, in.	191.7	189.3
Overall width, in.	69.3	69.3
Overall height, in.	55.5	56.5
Curb weight, lbs.	3205	3280
Cargo volume, cu. ft.	16.8	74.9
Fuel capacity, gals.	19.8	19.8
Seating capacity	5	5
Front head room, in.	38.6	38.6
Max. front leg room, in.	41.0	41.0
Rear head room, in.	37.1	37.6
Min. rear leg room, in.	34.7	34.7

Powertrain layout: longitudinal front-engine/rear-wheel drive

ENGINES

	ohc I-4	dohc I-4	Turbocharged ohc I-4	dohc I-6
Size, liters/cu. in.	2.3/141	2.3/141	2.3/141	2.9/178
Horsepower	114	153	162	181-201
Torque (lbs./ft.)	136	150	195	199-197
EPA city/highway mpg				
4-speed OD automatic	20/28	18/23	19/22	17/26
Consumer Guide™ observed MPG				
4-speed OD automatic			17.6	17.8

Built in Sweden, Belgium, and Canada

AVERAGE REPLACEMENT COSTS

A/C Compressor	$535
Alternator	410
Radiator	380
Timing Chain or Belt	145
Automatic Transmission or Transaxle	1,370
Constant Velocity Joints	165
Brakes	150
Shocks and/or Struts	1,075
Exhaust System	340

RETAIL PRICES	GOOD	AVERAGE	POOR
1991 940	$7,500-10,000	$6,600-9,000	$4,200-6,000
1992 940	8,500-10,500	7,500-9,500	5,000-6,400
1992 960	9,400-10,500	8,400-9,500	5,600-6,400
1993 940	10,500-13,000	9,500-11,800	6,500-8,200
1993 960	11,500-13,000	10,300-11,800	7,200-8,200
1994 940	11,800-14,300	10,500-13,000	7,300-9,000
1994 960	13,900-16,000	12,500-14,500	8,800-10,000
1995 940	13,800-16,500	12,400-15,000	8,700-10,200
1995 960	16,000-17,700	14,500-16,200	10,500-11,700
1996 960	19,000-20,800	17,500-19,000	13,000-14,000
1997 960	22,000-24,000	20,000-22,000	15,000-16,500
1998 S90/V90	26,000-29,000	24,000-27,000	18,000-20,000

TROUBLE SPOTS

• **Transmission slippage** If the transmission is sometimes difficult to shift out of park, it is due to improper contact of the lockout microswitch. A campaign was issued to replace the microswitch and wiring. (1994-96)

• **Brake noise** Cars equipped with ABS tend to have noisy, squealing brakes that can be corrected by installing anti-noise shims between the brake pads and calipers. (1991-96)

• **Steering noise** A springing sound from the steering wheel may be due to the retaining springs for the air bag, and replacing the four retaining bolts usually cures the problem. (1992-94)

• **Air conditioner** If the idle speed drops when the A/C engages, a capacitor kit may be installed in the circuit for the fuel injection control module along with the module itself. (1992-94)

• **Radio** Whining or crackling from the radio may be caused by a bolt on the side of the equalizer touching the cigar lighter socket. (1991) Generator whine while playing a tape is caused by interference from the cable harness under the dash, and rerouting the harness or installing a suppressor may cure the problem. (1991-94)

RECALL HISTORY

All w/Accessory Child Car Seat Pre-dynamic test buckle release force is lower than required by federal standard and may not retain child in seat in event of a crash. **1991 944/945** Chafed cable to seat heater, power seat, or seatbelt warning can develop low-resistance short circuit that could result in fire. **1991** On cars with 80-liter fuel tank, seepage could occur from top of tank. **1991-93** If car has been subjected to flood conditions, attempting to start the engine could

VOLVO

cause air bag deployment. **1992-93** Seatbelt webbing guide can break under heavy loads. **1993 944/945 Turbo** Plastic hood insulation clip(s) on some cars could interfere with throttle operation. **1995** Driver-side air bag may not deploy properly in a collision. **1996-97** Screws that attach throttle plate to the throttle shaft can loosen, possibly preventing throttle from returning to idle position.